Handbook of Biblical Chronology

Handbook of Biblical Chronology

Principles of Time Reckoning in the Ancient World and Problems of Chronology in the Bible

REVISED EDITION

Jack Finegan

HENDRICKSON
PUBLISHERS

P. O. Box 3473
Peabody, Massachusetts 01961-3473

Printed in the United States of America

First printing — April 1998

Library of Congress Cataloging-in-Publication Data

Finegan, Jack, 1908–
Handbook of biblical chronology: principles of time reckoning in the ancient world and problems of chronology in the Bible / by Jack Finegan. — Rev. ed.
Includes bibliographical references and index.
ISBN 1-56563-143-9
1. Bible—Chronology—Handbooks, manuals, etc. I. Title
BS637.2.F5 1995
220.9—dc20 95–30873
CIP

CONTENTS

PART TWO
PROBLEMS OF CHRONOLOGY IN THE BIBLE

PREFACE TO THE SECOND REVISED AND EXPANDED EDITION

I am appreciative of the reception and wide usage of this book in its original edition (1964), and of the many comments and inquiries about it which came to me, to many of which, under the pressure of other necessary concerns, I was unable to make proper acknowledgment or answer. Also, I am appreciative of the many notices and reviews of this book, including those in

Book Review Digest 60 (1964): 400.
Christian Century 81 (June 11, 1964): 806.
America 111 (Dec 5, 1964): 745.
Catholic Biblical Quarterly 27 (Jan 1965): 59–61, by Robert North.
Journal of Biblical Literature 84 (Mar 1965): 76–80, by Simon J. DeVries.
Christianity Today (May 21, 1965): 34, by J. M. Bald.
Scientific American 213 (July 1965): 123.
Bibliotheca orientalis 22 (May–July 1965): 184–185, by E. J. Bickerman.
Palestine Exploration Quarterly 97 (July-Oct 1965): 173–174, by P. R. Ackroyd.
American Historical Review 71 (Oct 1965): 126, by W. F. Albright.
Journal of Bible and Religion 33 (Oct 1965): 344–345, by H. Neil Richardson.
Virginia Quarterly Review 71 (Winter 1965): 26.
Interpretation 20 (Jan 1966), by R. H. Boyd.
Revue biblique 73 (Jan 1966): 146–147, by R. de Vaux.
Journal of Theological Studies 17 (Apr 1966): 113–115, by G. R. Driver.
Journal of Semitic Studies 11 (Spring 1966): 117–118, by P. Wernberg-Møller.
Review and Expositor 63 (Summer 1966): 338–339, by P. H. Kelley.

Likewise, I express appreciation of attention to my work in other articles and books, and among many I may mention especially the *Auseinandersetzung* with my book in the notes to chapter 11, pp. 372–433, "A Chronology of Jesus'

Life," in *A Marginal Jew: Rethinking the Historical Jesus,* vol. 1, *The Roots of the Problem and the Person* (ABRL; New York: Doubleday, 1991), by John P. Meier, Professor of New Testament at the Catholic University of America in Washington, D.C.[1] In all of the above I have benefited from the discussion, presentation of supplementary information, correction, and criticism, and my own notes in the present book make not infrequent acknowledgment of the same as well as indication of indebtedness in changes of my own opinions. Among many I will mention especially Ernest L. Martin and Paul Keresztes. I also try to give fair recognition to a number of opinions different from my own.

Finally, I thank Hendrickson Publishers for the invitation in August 1992 to prepare this "revised and expanded" edition, and for their patience with the time it took me to accomplish the task.

---

[1] Cf. John P. Meier, "Why Search for the Historical Jesus?" *BR* 9 (3, June 1993): 30ff.

PREFACE TO THE FIRST EDITION

i. In Gal 4:4 Paul refers to Jesus and says that God sent forth his Son "when the fulness of the time (τὸ πλήρωμα τοῦ χρόνου) was come." In various other passages Paul uses another Greek word for time, καιρός, *kairos,* which means a definite or fixed time, and hence can signify an opportune time, as in Gal 6:10, or even the eschatological end time as in 1 Cor 4:5. In view of this meaning of *kairos,* one might have expected that Paul would use it in speaking of what was assuredly the particular and proper time when God sent forth his Son. But instead, in Gal 4:4, he chooses to use for "time" the Greek word χρόνος, *chronos.* Over against *kairos,* which is a particular and appropriate time, *chronos* is time which is seen in its extent or duration. As *chronos,* time flows ceaselessly past us, a stream which cannot be stopped but which can be measured. It was in the fulness of this stream of *chronos* that the event of Jesus Christ took place. Therefore in Christian faith and in biblical study we are directed to the long sweep of time in which God has been working out his purpose, to time as *chronos,* and accordingly to the measurement of time, which is *chronometry,* the writing about and recording of time, which is *chronography,* and the science or doctrine of time, which is *chronology.*

ii. The chronological references in the biblical records are numerous but not always easy to understand correctly. Bible time extends through thousands of years and Bible history touches many different lands of the Near Eastern and Mediterranean world. In the periods and places involved, many different systems of time reckoning were employed, at least some of which may be presupposed in the biblical references. The work of early chronographers and commentators who occupied themselves with the biblical data is also important, and this extends the range of necessary inquiry even further. In this extremely complex and almost esoteric field much is, of course, not yet even known; what is known to the specialists in the areas involved is often quite inaccessible to the ordinary student and, if accessible, incomprehensible. A major part of our undertaking, therefore, is to give a clear description of the various matters involved and to provide, within the compass of one handbook, the necessary lists and tables with which to work, as well as to indicate sources and further literature.

iii. Then, on the basis of the best understanding we can obtain of the ancient methods of time reckoning—many of which, it may be added, are of a surprising degree of accuracy and sophistication—a further large part of the task is to try to work out against that background the correct significance of the biblical data themselves. Here it is not the attempt of the present handbook to deal with all the data or solve all the problems, but rather to indicate ways of taking up the problems in selected and representative areas. It may be hoped that some of the problems have been solved correctly. It may also be hoped that with the background materials of the first part of this handbook, and the sample engagements with particular problems in the second part, others may go on with those unfinished tasks in these areas, which will doubtless long continue to challenge students of ancient history and biblical record.

iv. My own involvement with such matters has come about in connection with the endeavor to write in the area of an archaeological approach to biblical history. In revising my *Light from the Ancient Past,* there has been a tendency to introduce, particularly in footnotes and appendix, an increasing amount of chronological material. Since the archaeological materials increase steadily too, limits are reached. Also notes and appendix may be obscure places in which to have to search. Therefore, with the permission of Princeton University Press, some of the chronological sections have been taken out of that book and incorporated in the present handbook, where they are set in a wider context of specifically chronological considerations and made more readily available for those interested.

v. Here, then, is a handbook prepared with the hope that it will be useful to those who concern themselves with that framework in time in which the events of Bible history are set. In his famous *Chronicle* Eusebius, who occupied himself with many of the same problems as we, quoted the saying that "it is not for you to know times or seasons (χρόνους ἢ καιρούς)" (Acts 1:7) as applying not only to the determination of the time of the end of the world but also to the attempted solution of other chronological problems. By the quotation he inculcates a proper humility in the approach to chronological questions; at the same time, by his own example in the vast labor of writing the *Chronicle,* he encourages us to believe that concern with the chronological data is one of the indispensable and unavoidable tasks in the study of the Bible. The materials in the present handbook are intended to assist such study.

LIST OF TABLES

ANCIENT SOURCES

LITERATURE: *DCB*; LSJ, xvi–xli; Simon **Hornblower** and Antony **Spawforth**, eds., *The Oxford Classical Dictionary* (3d ed.; Oxford: Oxford University Press, 1996); Johannes **Quasten**, *Patrology* (4 vols.; Westminster, Md.: Newman, 1950–1986); BAG, pp. xxx–xxxiii; Berthold **Altaner**, *Patrology* (8th ed.; Freiburg: Herder, 1978).

Africanus, Sextus Julius. Christian writer. A.D. c. 170–c. 240.
Aristotle. Greek philosopher. 384–322 B.C.
Artapanus. Hellenistic-Jewish historian. C. 100 B.C.
Avadyah. Jewish rabbi. B. A.D. c. 1325.
Barnabas, Epistle of. A.D. c. 100.
Biruni, al-. Muslim author. A.D. 973–1048.
Cassiodorus, Flavius Magnus Aurelius, Senator. Roman monk and historian. A.D. c. 490–c. 585.
Censorinus. Roman writer. Third century of the Christian era.
Chrysostom, John. Greek church father and preacher. A.D. c. 345–407.
Clement of Alexandria (Titus Flavius Clemens). Christian scholar. D. before A.D. 215.
Clement of Rome. Bishop of Rome. A.D. c. 92–c. 101.
Cyril of Alexandria. Christian theologian. D. A.D. 444.
Demetrius. Alexandrian-Jewish chronographer. Before 200 B.C.
Dio Cassius (Cassius Dio Cocceianus). Greek historian. B. between A.D. 155 and 164, d. A.D. c. 235.
Diodorus of Sicily (Diodorus Siculus). Greek historian. First century B.C.
Dionysius Exiguus. Roman monk. Fl. A.D. c. 525.
Dionysius of Halicarnassus (Dionysius Halicarnassensis). Greek historian. C. 54–c. 7 B.C.
Epiphanius. Bishop of Constantia (Salamis) on Cyprus. A.D. c. 315–403.
Eratosthenes of Alexandria. Greek astronomer. C. 276–c. 194 B.C.
Eupolemus. Palestinian-Jewish chronographer. C. 158 B.C.
Eusebius of Caesarea (Eusebius Caesariensis, Eusebius Pamphili). Church historian. A.D. 263–339.

Gamaliel I the Elder. Jewish rabbi, grandson of Hillel. Second third of the first century of the Christian era.
Gamaliel II, Gamaliel of Jabneh (Jamnia). Jewish rabbi, grandson of Gamaliel I. Fl. A.D. c. 80–116.
Gellius, Aulus. Latin writer. A.D. c. 123–c. 169.
Hanina. Jewish rabbi. Third century of the Christian era.
Herodotus. Greek historian. C. 484–425 B.C.
Hillel. Jewish teacher. C. 60 B.C.–A.D. c. 10.
Hipparchus. Greek astronomer. Fl. c. 146–c. 126 B.C.
Hippolytus of Rome. Presbyter and writer. A.D. c. 170–236.
Hippolytus of Thebes. Possibly identical with the foregoing.
Irenaeus. Greek bishop of Lyons. A.D. c. 130–c. 202.
Jerome. Latin church scholar. B. A.D. c. 347, d. A.D. 419 or 420.
John Malalas. Byzantine monk and chronicler. A.D. c. 491–c. 578.
Josephus. Jewish historian. A.D. c. 37–after 100.
Justin. Roman historian. Second century of the Christian era.
Justin Martyr. Christian apologist from Palestine. A.D. c. 114–165.
Lactantius Firmianus. Latin church father in Africa. Fl. A.D. c. 310.
Livy. Roman historian. 59 B.C.–A.D. 17.
Macarius Magnes. Bishop of Magnesia. Fl. A.D. c. 400.
Maimonides. Jewish philosopher. A.D. 1135–1204.
Ma Tuan-Lin. Chinese historian. Fl. A.D. 1240–1280.
Memnon of Heraclea Pontica. Hellenistic chronicler. First century of the Christian era.
Menander of Ephesus. Author of Greek history of the Phoenician kings. Cited by Josephus.
Origen. Christian scholar and theologian in Alexandria and Caesarea. A.D. c. 185–c. 253.
Orosius. Spanish historian and theologian. Fl. A.D. c. 415.
Pan Chao. Chinese historian. B. A.D. 45–51, d. 114–120.
Pan Ku. Chinese historian. A.D. 32–92.
Pan Piao. Chinese historian. A.D. 3–54.
Photius. Patriarch of Constantinople. A.D. c. 820–891.
Pliny the elder. Roman naturalist. A.D. 23–79.
Plutarch (Plutarchus). Greek biographer. A.D. c. 46–c. 120.
Polybius. Greek historian. C. 200–c. 118 B.C.
Polyhistor, Cornelius Alexander. Hellenistic-Roman author. Middle of the first century B.C.
Pompeius Trogus. Latin writer on history and natural science. Of the time of Augustus (44 B.C.–A.D. 14).
Porphyry of Tyre. Neoplatonist philosopher. A.D. 233–c. 304.
Pseudo-Eupolemus. Anonymous Samaritan writer. First half of the second century B.C.
Ptolemy (Claudius Ptolemaeus). Greco-Egyptian geographer. Second century of the Christian era.
Simeon II ben Gamaliel I. Jewish rabbi, son of Gamaliel I. Fl. A.D. c. 50–70.
Socrates. Church historian. B. A.D. c. 380, d. after A.D. 439.
Ssu-ma Ch'ien. Chinese historian. C. 140–c. 80 B.C.
Strabo. Greek geographer. C. 63 B.C.–after A.D. 21.

Suetonius. Roman historian. Fl. A.D. c. 100.
Syncellus (George the Monk). Attendant of the Patriarch of Constantinople. A.D. c. 800.
Tacitus. Roman historian. A.D. c. 55–c. 117.
Tatian. Syrian Christian apologist. Fl. A.D. c. 172.
Tertullian. Latin Christian writer at Carthage. B. A.D. c. 160, d. after A.D. 220.
Theodoret. Bishop of Cyrus. A.D. c. 393–453.
Theon. Alexandrian astronomer. Fourth century of the Christian era.
Thucydides. Athenian historian. C. 471–c. 400 B.C.
Tibullus. Latin poet. C. 54–19 B.C.
Timaeus of Sicily. Greek historian. C. 352–c. 256 B.C.
Varro. Roman historian. 116–27 B.C.
Virgil (Vergil). Roman poet. 70–19 B.C.
Warraq, al-, Abu 'Isa. Muslim author. Ninth century of the Christian era.
Yose ben Halafta. Jewish rabbi. D. A.D. c. 160.

LISTS OF ABBREVIATIONS

1. Books and Periodicals

ABC	*The Abingdon Bible Commentary,* ed. Frederick Carl Eiselen, Edwin Lewis, and David G. Downey (New York/Nashville: Abingdon-Cokesbury, 1929)
ABRL	Anchor Bible Reference Library
AJP	*American Journal of Philology*
AJSL	*American Journal of Semitic Languages and Literatures*
AKGWG	*Abhandlungen der Königlichen Gesellschaft der Wissenschaften zu Göttingen*
ANEA	James B. Pritchard, ed., *The Ancient Near East: An Anthology of Texts and Pictures* (Princeton: Princeton University Press, 1958)
ANEP	James B. Pritchard, ed., *The Ancient Near East in Pictures* (2d ed.; Princeton: Princeton University Press, 1969)
ANET	James B. Pritchard, ed., *Ancient Near Eastern Texts Relating to the Old Testament* (2d ed.; Princeton: Princeton University Press, 1955)
ANF	Alexander Roberts and James Donaldson, eds., rev. by A. Cleveland Coxe, *The Ante-Nicene Fathers: Translations of the Writings of the Fathers down to A.D. 325* (10 vols., 1885–87; repr. Peabody, Mass.: Hendrickson, 1994)
APOT	R. H. Charles, ed., *The Apocrypha and Pseudepigrapha of the Old Testament in English with Introductions and Critical and Explanatory Notes to the Several Books* (2 vols.; Oxford: Clarendon, 1913)

AS	Assyriological Studies (Oriental Institute)
ASAE	*Annales du Service des Antiquités de l'Egypt* (Cairo)
AUSS	*Andrews University Seminary Studies*
Ayer, *Source Book*	Joseph C. Ayer, *A Source Book for Ancient Church History* (New York: C. Scribner's Sons, 1913)
BA	*Biblical Archaeologist*
BAG	William F. Arndt, F. Wilbur Gingrich, and Frederick W. Danker, eds., *A Greek-English Lexicon of the New Testament and Other Early Christian Literature,* a translation and adaptation of Walter Bauer's *Griechisch-deutsches Wörterbuch zu den Schriften des Neuen Testaments und der übrigen urchristlichen Literatur* (2d ed.; Chicago: University of Chicago Press, 1958)
BASOR	*Bulletin of the American Schools of Oriental Research*
BIBOR	*Bibliotheca orientalis*
BJRL	*Bulletin of the John Rylands University Library*
BO	*Bibbia e oriente*
BR	*Bible Review*
Breasted, *Ancient Records*	James H. Breasted, *Ancient Records of Egypt* (5 vols.; Chicago: University of Chicago Press, 1906–1907)
Brownlee, *Manual of Discipline*	William H. Brownlee, *The Dead Sea Manual of Discipline* (BASOR Supplementary Studies 10–12; New Haven: American Schools of Oriental Research, 1951)
Burrows, *DSS*	Millar Burrows, *The Dead Sea Scrolls* (New York: Viking Press, 1955)
CAH	J. Bury, S. A. Cook, F. E. Adcock, M. P. Charlesworth, and N. H. Baynes, eds., *The Cambridge Ancient History* (12 vols. and 5 vols. of plates; Cambridge: Cambridge University Press, 1923–1939)
CH	*Churchman* (London)
CIL	*Corpus inscriptionum latinarum*
CKC	Jerry Vardaman and Edwin M. Yamauchi, eds., *Chronos, Kairos, Christos: Nativity and Chronological Studies Presented to Jack Finegan* (Winona Lake: Eisenbrauns, 1989)
CTQ	*Concordia Theological Quarterly*
DACL	*Dictionnaire d'archéologie chrétienne et de liturgie* (Paris: Letouzey et Ané, 1920–1953)
Danby	Herbert Danby, *The Mishnah Translated from the Hebrew with Introduction and Brief Explanatory Notes* (Oxford: Oxford University Press, 1933)
DCB	William Smith and Henry Wace, *A Dictionary of Christian Biography* (4 vols.; London: J. Murray, 1877–1887)

DJD	*Discoveries in the Judaean Desert,* vol. 1, *Qumran Cave I* (ed. D. Barthélemy and J. T. Milik; Oxford: Clarendon, 1955); vol. 2, *Les Grottes de Murabba'ât* (ed. P. Benoit, J. T. Milik, and R. de Vaux, 1961); vol. 3, *Les "petites grottes" de Qumrân* (ed. M. Baillet, J. T. Milik, and R. de Vaux, 1962)
EAE	*Encyclopedia of Archaeological Excavations in the Holy Land* (Jerusalem: Masada Press, 1975–1978)
EB	*The Encyclopaedia Britannica* (14th ed.; 24 vols.; New York: Encyclopedia Britannica, Inc., 1929); *The New Encyclopaedia Britannica* (15th ed.; 32 vols.; Chicago: Encyclopaedia Britannica, Inc., 1987)
Epstein, *BT*	I. Epstein, ed., *The Babylonian Talmud* (35 vols.; London: Soncino Press, 1935–1952)
EvQ	*The Evangelical Quarterly*
FC	The Fathers of the Church
Finegan, *Archaeological History*	Jack Finegan, *Archaeological History of the Ancient Middle East* (Boulder: Westview; Folkstone, England: Dawson, 1979)
Finegan, *Archeology NT* 1	Jack Finegan, *The Archeology of the New Testament: The Life of Jesus and the Beginning of the Early Church* (rev. ed.; Princeton: Princeton University Press, 1992)
Finegan, *Archeology NT* 2	Jack Finegan, *The Archeology of the New Testament: The Mediterranean World of the Early Christian Apostles* (Boulder: Westview; London: Croom Helm, 1981)
Finegan, *Let My People Go*	Jack Finegan, *Let My People Go: A Journey through Exodus* (New York: Harper & Row, 1963).
Finegan, *Light from the Ancient Past*	Jack Finegan, *Light from the Ancient Past: The Archeological Background of Judaism and Christianity* (2d. ed.; Princeton: Princeton University Press, 1959)
Finegan, *Myth and Mystery*	Jack Finegan, *Myth and Mystery: An Introduction to the Pagan Religions of the Biblical World* (Grand Rapids: Baker Book House, 1989)
GCS	Die griechischen christlichen Schriftsteller der ersten drei Jahrhunderte
Gaster, *DSS*	Theodor H. Gaster, *The Dead Sea Scriptures in English Translation* (Garden City, N.Y.: Doubleday, 1956)
Goldschmidt, *BT*	Lazarus Goldschmidt, *Der babylonische Talmud* (9 vols.; various publishers, 1897–1935)
Hastings, *DAC*	James Hastings, ed., *Dictionary of the Apostolic Church* (2 vols.; New York: Charles Scribner's Sons, 1922)

Hastings, *ERE*	James Hastings, ed., *Encyclopaedia of Religion and Ethics* (12 vols.; New York: C. Scribner's Sons, 1910–1922)
HDB	James Hastings, ed., *A Dictionary of the Bible* (4 vols.; New York: Scribner's 1898–1902)
Helm	Rudolf Helm, ed., *Die Chronik des Hieronymus,* vol. 7 of *Eusebius Werke* (GCS; 2d ed.; Berlin: Akademie, 1956).
HSNTA	Edgar Hennecke and Wilhelm Schneemelcher, *New Testament Apocrypha* (2 vols.; Philadelphia: Westminster, 1963–1965)
HUCA	*Hebrew Union College Annual*
HZNT	Handbuch zum Neuen Testament
IEJ	*Israel Exploration Journal*
JAOS	*Journal of the American Oriental Society*
JBL	*Journal of Biblical Literature*
JCS	*Journal of Cuneiform Studies*
JE	Isidore Singer, ed., *The Jewish Encyclopedia* (12 vols.; New York: Funk and Wagnalls, 1901–1905)
JEA	*Journal of Egyptian Archaeology*
JNES	*Journal of Near Eastern Studies*
JQR	*Jewish Quarterly Review*
JSOT	*Journal for the Study of the Old Testament*
JSS	*Journal of Semitic Studies*
JTS	*Journal of Theological Studies*
Karst	Josef Karst, ed., *Die Chronik aus dem Armenischen überbsetzt mit textkritischem Commentar*, vol. 5 of *Eusebius Werke* (GCS 20; Leipzig: Hinrichs, 1911).
KLT	Kleine Texte für theologische und philologische Vorlesungen und Übungen
LÄ	*Lexikon der Ägyptologie*
LCL	Loeb Classical Library
LSJ	*A Greek-English Lexicon,* compiled by Henry G. D. Liddell and Robert Scott, rev. by Henry S. Jones (new [9th] ed.; Oxford: Oxford University Press, 1940)
Luckenbill, *Ancient Records*	Daniel D. Luckenbill, *Ancient Records of Assyria and Babylonia* (2 vols.; Chicago, Ill.: University of Chicago Press, 1926–1927)
LXX	The Septuagint. Henry B. Swete, ed., *The Old Testament in Greek according to the Septuagint* (3 vols.; Cambridge: Cambridge University Press, 1925–1930); Alfred Rahlfs, ed., *Septuaginta, id est Vetus Testamentum Graece iuxta LXX interpretes* (2 vols. Stuttgart: Deutsche Bibelgesellschaft, 1935); *Septuaginta, Vetus Testamentum Graecum*

	auctoritate Societatis Litterarum Gottingensis editum (Göttingen : Vandenhoeck & Ruprecht, 1931ff.)
Manetho	*Manetho,* trans. W. G. Waddell (LCL, 1940).
MPG	Jacques Paul Migne, *Patrologiae cursus completus: Series graeca*
MPL	Jacques Paul Migne, *Patrologiae cursus completus: Series latina*
MVAG	*Mitteilungen der Vorderasiatisch-Aegyptischen Gesellschaft*
NAC	New American Commentary
NEAE	*The New Encyclopedia of Archaeological Excavations in the Holy Land* (4 vols.; Jerusalem: Israel Exploration Society and Carta; New York: Simon & Schuster, 1993)
NHMS	Nag Hammadi and Manichaean Studies
NovT	*Novum Testamentum*
NPNF[1, 2]	Philip Schaff and Henry Wace, eds., *A Select Library of Nicene and Post-Nicene Fathers of the Christian Church, First Series;* idem, *Second Series* (14 vols. in each series; repr. Peabody, Mass.: Hendrickson, 1994)
NSH	Samuel M. Jackson, ed., *The New Schaff-Herzog Encyclopedia of Religious Knowledge* (12 vols.; New York: Funk and Wagnalls, 1908–1912)
NTC	New Testament Commentary
NTS	*New Testament Studies*
OAB	Herbert G. May and Bruce M. Metzger, eds., *The Oxford Annotated Bible* (New York: Oxford University Press, 1962)
OxyP	*The Oxyrhynchus Papyri*
PCAE	Richard A. Parker, *The Calendars of Ancient Egypt* (SAOC 26; Chicago: University of Chicago Press, 1950)
PDBC	Richard A. Parker and Waldo H. Dubberstein, *Babylonian Chronology, 626 B.C.–A.D. 75.* (3d ed.; Providence: Brown University Press, 1956)
PEQ	*Palestine Exploration Quarterly*
PSBF	Publications of the Studium Biblicum Franciscanum (Jerusalem)
PSBFCMI	Publications of the Studium Biblicum Franciscanum, Collectio Minor
PW	Pauly-Wissowa, *Real-Encyclopädie der klassischen Altertumswissenschaft*
RA	Erich Ebeling and Bruno Meissner, eds., *Reallexikon der Assyriologie* (Berlin: W. de Gruyter, 1928ff.). Vols. 6ff. are titled

	Reallexikon der Assyriologie und vorderasiatischen Archäologie.
RAC	Theodor Klauser, ed., *Reallexikon für Antike und Christentum: Sachwörterbuch zur Auseinandersetzung des Christentums mit der antiken Welt* (Stuttgart: Hiersemann, 1950ff.)
RB	*Revue biblique*
RHR	*Revue de l'histoire des religions*
RQ	*Revue de Qumran*
SAOC	The Oriental Institute of the University of Chicago: Studies in Ancient Oriental Civilization
SBLSP	Society of Biblical Literature Seminar Papers
Schürer, *History*	Emil Schürer, *A History of the Jewish People in the Time of Jesus Christ* (5 vols.; New York: Scribner's, 1896); rev. ed., G. Vermes and F. Millar (3 vols. in 4; Edinburgh: T. & T. Clark, 1973–1987)
SPAW	Sitzungsberichte der Preussischen Akademie der Wissenschaften
Strack-Billerbeck	H. L. Strack and Paul Billerbeck, *Kommentar zum Neuen Testament aus Talmud und Midrasch* (6 vols. in 7; Munich: Beck, 1922–1961)
TB	*Tyndale Bulletin*
Thiele, *Chronology*	Edwin R. Thiele, *A Chronology of the Hebrew Kings* (Grand Rapids: Zondervan, 1977)
Thiele, *Mysterious Numbers*	Edwin R. Thiele, *The Mysterious Numbers of the Hebrew Kings* (1st ed.; Chicago: University of Chicago Press, 1951; 2d ed., Grand Rapids: Eerdmans, 1965; 3d ed., Grand Rapids: Zondervan, 1983)
TLZ	*Theologische Literaturzeitung*
Vermes/Millar, *History*	*See* Schürer, *History*
VT	*Vetus Testamentum*
VTSup	Vetus Testamentum Supplements
Wiseman, *Chronicles*	D. J. Wiseman, *Chronicles of Chaldaean Kings (626–556* B.C.*) in the British Museum* (London: Trustees of the British Museum, 1956)
WTJ	*Westminster Theological Journal*
WUNT	Wissenschaftliche Untersuchungen zum Neuen Testament
ZA	*Zeitschrift für Assyriologie*
ZÄS	*Zeitschrift für ägyptische Sprache*
ZAW	*Zeitschrift für die alttestamentliche Wissenschaft*
ZDPV	*Zeitschrift des Deutschen Palästina-Vereins*
ZNW	*Zeitschrift für die neutestamentliche Wissenschaft und die Kunde der älteren Kirche*
ZWT	*Zeitschrift für wissenschaftliche Theologie*

2. Biblical Books and Related Literature

(1) Old Testament

Gen	Genesis
Exod	Exodus
Lev	Leviticus
Num	Numbers
Deut	Deuteronomy
Josh	Joshua
Judg	Judges
Ruth	Ruth
1–2 Sam	1–2 Samuel
1–2 Kgs	1–2 Kings
1–2 Chron	1–2 Chronicles
Ezra	Ezra
Neh	Nehemiah
Esth	Esther
Job	Job
Psa/Pss	Psalms
Prov	Proverbs
Eccl	Ecclesiastes
Song Sol	Song of Solomon
Isa	Isaiah
Jer	Jeremiah
Lam	Lamentations
Ezek	Ezekiel
Dan	Daniel
Hos	Hosea
Joel	Joel
Amos	Amos
Obad	Obadiah
Jonah	Jonah
Mic	Micah
Nah	Nahum
Hab	Habakkuk
Zeph	Zephaniah
Hag	Haggai
Zech	Zechariah
Mal	Malachi

(2) New Testament

Matt	Matthew
Mark	Mark
Luke	Luke
John	John
Acts	Acts

Rom	Romans
1–2 Cor	1–2 Corinthians
Gal	Galatians
Eph	Ephesus
Phil	Philippians
Col	Colossians
1–2 Thess	1–2 Thessalonians
1–2 Tim	1–2 Timothy
Titus	Titus
Phlm	Philemon
Heb	Hebrews
Jas	James
1–2 Pet	1–2 Peter
1–2–3 John	1–2–3 John
Jude	Jude
Rev	Revelation

(3) Apocrypha

1 Esd	1 Esdras
Jth	Judith
2 Esd	2 Esdras
Ad Est	Additions to Esther
Tob	Tobit
Wisd	Wisdom of Solomon
Sir	Sirach
Sus	Susanna
Bel	Bel and the Dragon
Bar	Baruch
Pr Man	Prayer of Manasses
Ep Jer	Epistle of Jeremy
1 Macc	1 Maccabees
Thr Ch	Song of the Three Children
2 Macc	2 Maccabees

(4) Pseudepigrapha

Apoc. Bar.	*Apocalypse of Baruch*
Jub.	*Jubilees*
Asc. Isa.	*Ascension of Isaiah*
Pss. Sol.	*Psalms of Solomon*
As. Mos.	*Assumption of Moses*
Sib. Or.	*Sibylline Oracles*
T. 12 Patr.	*Testaments of the Twelve Patriarchs*

(5) The Dead Sea Scrolls and Related Literature

1QpHab	*Habakkuk Commentary,* i.e., the *pesher* or commentary on Habakkuk from Cave 1 at Qumran

1QJub	*Jubilees* fragments from Cave 1 at Qumran
1QS	*Manual of Discipline,* i.e., the *serek* or "order" of the community from Cave 1 at Qumran
1Q 17 and 18	Numbered fragments from Cave 1 at Qumran
CD	*Zadokite Document,* or *Cairo Document of the Damascus Covenanters*

3. Eras

A.Abr.	*anno Abraham* (in the year of Abraham)
A.A.C.	*anno ante Christum* (in the year before Christ)
A.Ad.	*anno Adam* or *Adami* (in the year of Adam)
A.C.	*ante Christum* (before Christ)
A.D.	*anno Domini* (in the year of the Lord)
A.Diocl.	*anno Diocletianii* (in the year of Diocletian)
A.M.	*anno mundi* (in the year of the world)
A.O.C.	*anno orbis conditi* (in the year of the foundation of the world)
A.S.	*anno Seleucidarum* (in the year of the Seleucids)
A.U.C.	*anno urbis conditae* (in the year of the foundation of the city) or *Ab urbe condita* (from the foundation of the city)
B.C.	before Christ
B.C.E.	before the common era
C.E.	common era
Ol.	Olympiad

4. Days

Sun	Sunday
Mon	Monday
Tue	Tuesday
Wed	Wednesday
Thu	Thursday
Fri	Friday
Sat	Saturday

5. Months

1. Jan	January
2. Feb	February
3. Mar	March
4. Apr	April
5. May	May
6. June	June
7. July	July
8. Aug	August

9.	Sept	September
10.	Oct	October
11.	Nov	November
12.	Dec	December

6. Miscellaneous

a.m.	*ante meridiem* (before noon)
b.	born
c.	*circa* (about, around)
cf.	*conferre* (compare)
d.	died
f., ff.	following
fl.	*floruit* (he flourished)
n.	note
p.	page
p.m.	*post meridiem* (after noon)
pp.	pages

CHRONOLOGICAL TABLES

1. Archaeological and Cultural Periods in the Holy Land

Palaeolithic (Old Stone Age)	Before 18,000 B.C.
Epipalaeolithic (Middle Stone Age)	18,000–8300
Neolithic (New Stone Age)	8300–4500
Chalcolithic (Copper-Stone Age)	4500–3300
Bronze Age (Canaanite Period)	
Early Bronze Age I	3300–3000
Early Bronze Age II	3000–2700
Early Bronze Age III	2700–2200
Middle Bronze Age I	2200–2000
Middle Bronze Age II	2000–1550
Late Bronze Age I	1550–1400
Late Bronze Age II	1400–1200
Iron Age (Israelite Period)	
Iron Age I	1200–1000
Iron Age II	1000–586
Babylonian and Persian Periods	586–332
Babylonian Period	586–538
Persian Period	538–332
Hellenistic Period	
Hellenistic I	332–167
Hellenistic II (Hasmonean)	167–37
Roman and Byzantine Periods	
Early Roman Period	37 B.C.–A.D. 132

Herodian Period	37 B.C.–A.D. 70
Late Roman Period	A.D. 132–324
Byzantine Period	324–638

Jewish Period

Period of the Soferim ("scribes") and Tannaim ("repeaters," i.e., teachers of the oral law), from the earlier half of the second century B.C. to the close of the second century A.D., whose teachings are preserved in the Tosephta and Mishna (from *shanah,* meaning "repeat" and so "to teach by repetition").[1]

Period of the Amoraim ("speakers," "interpreters"), who discussed the Mishnaic law, from its completion to around A.D. 500.

Period of the two Talmuds ("instruction," from a word meaning "to learn"), the Palestinian Talmud of the fourth century A.D. and the Babylonian Talmud of the fifth or sixth century A.D., each Talmud containing the same Mishna (text) but different Gemara ("completion" or commentary, the latter divided into Halakah which is purely legal, and Haggadah, which is explanatory matter on a wide range of subjects), the entire Talmud constituting the authoritative body of Jewish law and tradition.

Early Arab Period	638–1099
Crusader Period	1099–1291
Late Arab Period	1291–1516
(Fatimid and Mameluke)	
Ottoman Period	1516–1917[2]

2. Egyptian Dynasties with minimal and maximal dates at the present stand of research (asterisks for astronomically determined dates)

Dynasty	
1	3050/2960–2860/2780
2	2860/2780–2695/2640
3	2695/2640–2630/2575
4	2630/2575–2505/2460
5	2505/2460–2345/2310
6–8	2345/2310–2160/2134
9–10	2160/2134–2047/2033
11*	2134–1991
12*	1991–1785
13–14	1785–1660/1650

[1] Herbert Danby, *The Mishnah* (Oxford University Press; London: Humphrey Milford, 1933).

[2] *The New Encyclopedia of Archaeological Excavations in the Holy Land,* ed. Ephraim Stern (Jerusalem: Israel Exploration Society and Carta; New York: Simon & Schuster, 1993), 4:1529.

15–17	1660/1651–1560/1541
18*	1560/1551–1320/1306
19*	1320/1306–1200/1185
20	1200/1185–1085/1070
21	1085/1070–947/940
22–24	947/940–714/711
25	714/711–656/655
26*	664–525
27	525–404
28	404–398
29	399–380
30	380–342
31	342–332[3]

[3] Jürgen von Beckerath, "Chronologie," in *Lexikon der Ägyptologie,* ed. Wolfgang Helck and Eberhard Otto (Wiesbaden: O. Harrassowitz, 1972ff.), 1:967–971. Within the above parameters specific Egyptian dates in the present book are in agreement with the Chronology of the Dynasties in the *Histoire de l'Egypte ancienne* (Paris: Fayard, 1988), 541–560; and *A History of Ancient Egypt,* Eng. trans. by Ian Shaw (Oxford; Cambridge, Mass.: Blackwell, 1992), 389–395; by Nicolas-Christophe Grimal, professor in the University of Paris-Sorbonne and member of the Institut Français d'Archéologie Orientale, Cairo. For an explanation of the crucial date of Ramses II, see our §406.

PART ONE

Principles of Chronology in the Ancient World

Chapter 1

NUMERALS

1. A number is an amount or a quantity of units. It is also a character or symbol, such as a figure or word, which expresses such a magnitude. In the latter sense "number" is synonymous with "numeral." The statement of a number or numeral in the form of a word or words is a usage found regularly in the Bible. Examples are: in the Hebrew text of Gen 5:3, "thirty and a hundred years" (שלשים ומאת שנה), i.e., "one hundred and thirty years"; in the Greek text of Matt 4:2, "forty days and forty nights" (ἡμέρας τεσσεράκοντα καὶ τεσσεράκοντα νύκτας); and in the Latin text of Luke 3:1, "in the fifteenth year" *(anno quinto decimo).*

2. A number or numeral may also be expressed by a figure or symbol. In the development of such figures or symbols, several principles are recognizable. In an "acrophonic" system the initial letter of the word by which a number is called is used to represent the number itself. In an "alphabetic" system the sequential characters of the alphabet serve as numbers. In a system of what we may call "arbitrary" signs, accepted or conventional symbols are employed as figures. From very early times, as on the Palermo Stone (§148) for example, use was made simply of a straight mark or a succession of straight marks for at least the smaller numbers. Where individual symbols do not extend far enough to encompass all desired magnitudes, it is possible to make combinations of them to gain the desired result. In the combination the placement of the individual symbols may indicate the addition, or in some cases the subtraction, of the respective components.

3. In manuscripts and inscriptions where a numerical symbol, particularly an alphabetic character, might be relatively difficult to recognize as having this meaning, attention may be called to it as a numeral by leaving space around it or adding some mark of punctuation. In modern transcriptions it is often customary to use a mark above the line and following the letter like an acute accent, or also below the line and preceding the letter, to indicate numerals.

1. Hebrew Numerals

LITERATURE: Caspar **Levias**, "Numbers and Numerals," in *JE* 9:348–350.

4. The letters of the Hebrew alphabet are used for numerals as shown in Table 1.

TABLE 1. *Hebrew Numerals*

א	Aleph	1	י	Yodh	10	ק	Qoph	100
ב	Beth	2	כ	Kaph	20	ר	Resh	200
ג	Gimel	3	ל	Lamedh	30	ש	S(h)in	300
ד	Daleth	4	מ	Mem	40	ת	Taw	400
ה	He	5	נ	Nun	50			
ו	Waw	6	ס	Samekh	60			
ז	Zayin	7	ע	Ayin	70			
ח	Heth	8	פ	Pe	80			
ט	Teth	9	צ	Tsadhe	90			

To distinguish a character as a numeral an accent may be placed after it. Numbers which exceed the limits of the sequence of letters are formed by addition of characters. These composite groups are written thus, for example: ת״ק = 500, תת״ק = 900.

2. Greek Numerals

LITERATURE: Leonard **Whibley**, ed., *A Companion to Greek Studies* (4th ed.; Cambridge: Cambridge University Press, 1931), 698–699; A. G. **Woodhead**, *The Study of Greek Inscriptions* (Cambridge: Cambridge University Press, 1959), 107–111.

5. In early Greek, simple straight vertical marks were used for the numbers one to four. Beyond that point the initial letters of the names of the numerals were employed. Thus, for example, Γ (now written Π) = πέντε = 5, Δ = δέκα = 10, ΔΙ = 11, etc. This acrophonic system is attested from the fifth century to around 100 B.C.

6. From the first century B.C. to the end of the Roman empire and on into the Byzantine period, the less cumbersome alphabetic system was mainly used. The complete Ionic alphabet was employed including three signs now obsolete.

ϛ or Ϝ		Stigma or vau/digamma
ϙ or ϟ		Koppa
ϡ or Ͳ		Sampi

The numerical values of the letters of the alphabet are shown in Table 2.

TABLE 2. *Greek Numerals*

α	Alpha	1	ι	Iota	10	ρ	Rho	100
β	Beta	2	κ	Kappa	20	σ	Sigma	200
γ	Gamma	3	λ	Lambda	30	τ	Tau	300
δ	Delta	4	μ	Mu	40	υ	Upsilon	400
ϵ	Epsilon	5	ν	Nu	50	ϕ	Phi	500
ϝ	Vau	6	ξ	Xi	60	χ	Chi	600
ζ	Zeta	7	ο	Omicron	70	ψ	Psi	700
η	Eta	8	π	Pi	80	ω	Omega	800
θ	Theta	9	ϙ	Koppa	90	ϡ	Sampi	900

To indicate the numerical employment of the letters a mark like an acute accent is placed after the character or characters up through 999; a similar mark is used below the line and preceding the letter for 1000 and above. Thus, for example, ϕνϵ′ = 555, ͵ϵϕνϵ′ = 5555, etc. in the inscriptions and the papyri dates are given with the word ἔτος, "year," or ἔτους, "years," and this is often abbreviated to L.

3. Roman Numerals

LITERATURE: David E. **Smith**, "Roman Numerals," *EB* 16:612–613.

7. As in Greek, where in one system simple upright strokes were used for numbers one to four, so also in Latin the numerical system begins with I, II, III, IIII, and then goes on with other characters, V, X, L, C, and M, the derivation of which is at least in some cases recognizable as following the acrophonic principle, e.g., C = *centum* = 100, M = *mille* = 1,000. Similarly, too, addition and also subtraction of characters gives composite numbers, e.g., MC = 1,100, CM = 900, etc. Thousands are indicated by overlining. The elements of the system are shown in Table 3.

TABLE 3. *Roman Numerals*

I	1	XI	11	XXX	30
II	2	XII	12	XL	40
III	3	XIII	13	L	50
IIII or IV	4	XIIII or XIV	14	C	100
V	5	XV	15	D	500
VI	6	XVI	16	M	1,000
VII	7	XVII	17	$\overline{\text{II}}$	2,000
VIII	8	XVIII	18		
VIIII or IX	9	XVIIII or XIX	19		
X	10	XX	20		

Chapter 2

THE RECKONING OF TIME IN THE ANCIENT WORLD

A. UNITS OF TIME

LITERATURE: Cyrus **Adler**, "Calendar, History of," *JE* 3:498–501; Michael **Friedländer**, "Calendar," *JE* 3:501–508; F. H. **Colson**, *The Week: An Essay on the Origin & Development of the Seven-day Cycle* (Cambridge: Cambridge University Press, 1926; repr., Westport, Conn.: Greenwood, [1974]); C. W. C. **Barlow** and G. H. **Bryan**, *Elementary Mathematical Astronomy* (London: University Tutorial Press, 1933); Henry N. **Russell**, Raymond S. **Dugan**, and John Q. **Stewart**, *Astronomy: A Revision of Young's Manual of Astronomy,* vol. 1., *The Solar System* (rev. ed.; Boston: Ginn, 1945); *The American Ephemeris and Nautical Almanac* (Washington: U. S. Government Printing Office, 1855-1980); A. **Hermann**, F. **Schmidtke**, and L. **Koep,** *RAC* 3:30–60; Roland de **Vaux**, *Ancient Israel: Its Life and Institutions* (New York: McGraw-Hill, 1961), 178–194; Jerome **Wyckoff**, ed., *The Harper Encyclopedia of Science* (New York: Harper & Row, 1963); E. J. **Bickerman**, *Chronology of the Ancient World* (London: Thames & Hudson, 1968); Norriss S. **Hetherington**, *Ancient Astronomy and Civilization* (Tucson: Pachart, 1987).[1]

8. The chief units in the reckoning of time for calendrical purposes are the day, week, month, and year, while the year is also divided into seasons and the day into hours or other parts. Rev 9:15 mentions the units: hour, day, month, and year; and Gal 4:10 speaks of days, months, seasons, and years.

1. The Day

LITERATURE: Edouard **Mahler**, *Handbuch der jüdischen Chronologie* (Leipzig: Gustav Fock, 1916); Solomon **Zeitlin**, "The Beginning of the Jewish Day during the Second Commonwealth," *JQR* 36 (1945–46): 403–414.

---

[1] Initial reference to Barlow and Bryan and Wyckoff from Harold F. Weaver, Professor Emeritus of Astronomy, University of California, Berkeley.

9. In the Sumerian and Akkadian languages the word for "day" also means "wind." Likewise in Song Sol 2:17 and 4:6 it is said that "the day breathes" or literally that it blows, which can suggest that the daily land and sea breezes of the Mesopotamian and Palestinian coastlands were associated with the thought of the "day."[2]

10. Of all the recurrent phenomena of nature, however, the surely most impressive and universally observable, and therefore surely the most influential in the concept of the "day," is the rising and setting of the sun with the consequent alternation of a period of light and a period of darkness. Thus in Gen 1:3–5 the first of the works of creation was "light" in distinction from "darkness," and the light was called day, in Hebrew יוֹם *(yom),* the darkness night, לילה *(laylah).* Thus "day" can have the sense of daytime as distinct from nighttime, but the same word can also comprehend the complete cycle which includes both the daytime and the nighttime: "And there was evening and there was morning, one day" (Gen 1:5). In Greek the corresponding word ἡμέρα is used for the daytime as, for example, in Matt 4:2 where Jesus fasted for "forty days and forty nights." For the complete cycle of light and darkness there is a word, νυχθήμερον, which combines "night" (νύξ) and "day" (ἡμέρα) in one term. This is used in 2 Cor 11:25 where it is translated "a night and a day." Usually, however, the "day" which includes the nighttime and the daytime is simply designated with the word ἡμέρα and the context makes plain what is meant as, for example, in John 2:12 or Acts 9:19 where the several "days" are certainly several successive periods each comprising daytime and nighttime.[3]

11. A "day" in the sense of a complete period of light and darkness might be reckoned as beginning with the coming of the light or with the coming of the darkness, as well as of course theoretically at any other point. In ancient Egypt the day probably began at dawn,[4] in ancient Mesopotamia it began in the evening.[5] Among the Greeks the day was reckoned from sunset to sunset, while the Romans already began the day in the "modern" fashion at midnight.[6] Summing up the different reckonings among different people in his time Pliny wrote:

> The Babylonians count the period between two sunrises, the Athenians that between two sunsets, the Umbrians from midday to midday, the common people everywhere from dawn to dark, the Roman priests and the authorities who fixed the official day, and also the Egyptians and Hipparchus, the period from midnight to midnight.[7]

12. In the Old Testament the earlier practice seems to have been to consider that the day began in the morning. In Gen 19:34, for example, the

---

[2] Lewy, *HUCA* 17 (1942–43): 5–6.

[3] Mahler, *Handbuch,* 170–171.

[4] PCAE 10.

[5] PDBC 26.

[6] James Gow, *A Companion to School Classics* (3d ed.; London: Macmillan, 1893), 78, 147; Leonard Whibley, ed., *A Companion to Greek Studies* (3d ed.; Cambridge: Cambridge University Press, 1916), 589.

[7] *Natural History* 2.79.188.

"morrow" (ASV) or "next day" (RSV) clearly begins with the morning after the preceding night. The later practice was to count the day as beginning in the evening. In Lev 23:27 it is stated that the Day of Atonement is to be observed on the tenth day of the seventh month; in verse 32 it is said that the observance is to be "on the ninth day of the month beginning at evening, from evening to evening." These last words can hardly be intended to change the actual date of the fast; rather, they appear to be an addition which simply defines what the tenth day of the month was at a time when the day had come to be reckoned as beginning in the evening: the tenth day of the month is the day which begins on the evening of the ninth and continues until the following evening. In making the shift from a morning reckoning to an evening reckoning, the "day" was therefore in fact moved back so that it began a half day earlier than had been the case previously.[8]

13. In the New Testament in the Synoptic Gospels and Acts the day seems usually to be considered as beginning in the morning. Mark 11:11 states that Jesus entered Jerusalem, went into the temple, and when he had looked at everything, since it was "now eventide" (ASV) or "already late" (RSV), went out to Bethany with the twelve; verse 12 continues the narrative and tells that on the "morrow" (ASV) or the "following day" (RSV) they came back to the city. It is evident that the new day has begun with the morning following the preceding evening. Likewise Matt 28:1, Mark 16:1f., and Luke 23:56–24:1 all picture the first day of the week beginning with the dawn following the preceding Sabbath. And Acts 4:3, for an example in that book, tells how Peter and John were put in custody "until the morrow, for it was already evening," thus clearly indicating that the new day would begin the next morning. It has been suggested that this counting of the day as beginning with the morning is a continuation of the earlier Old Testament practice already described (§12), and that this usage was maintained in parts of Galilee and was followed by Jesus and the early disciples, which would account for its appearing so frequently in the Synoptic Gospels and Acts.[9] On the other hand, even though the common reckoning in the Synoptic Gospels is from the morning, in Mark 1:32 = Luke 4:40, the later Old Testament (§12) and Jewish usage of counting the one day as ending and the next as beginning at sunset is plainly reflected in the fact that the people of Capernaum were free to bring the sick to Jesus at sunset when the Sabbath came to an end. As for the Fourth Gospel, in John 20:1 Mary Magdalene comes to the tomb while it is still dark, yet it is already "on the first day of the week." This can be explained by supposing that the late Old Testament and Jewish usage is in view, according to which the new day had begun at the preceding sunset, or it can be explained equally well by supposing that John is giving the description in terms of the official Roman day which, as Pliny told us (§11), began at midnight. In either case, the new day had begun already before the sunrise.

14. The coming of light and the coming of darkness are, of course, gradual events, and it is therefore to periods of transition which are not

---

[8] Julian Morgenstern, *HUCA* 10 (1935): 15–28; 20 (1947): 34–38.
[9] Morgenstern, *Crozer Quarterly,* 26 (1949): 232–240.

necessarily sharply defined that the terms "morning" and "evening," as also "dawn" (e.g. Judg 19:25f.) and "twilight" (e.g. 1 Sam 30:17), refer. For a more precise line of demarcation between one day and the next the time of sunrise or sunset could be taken, and we have seen probable examples of such usage in Mark 16:2 and Mark 1:32, respectively. Or the determination could be made in terms of the intensity of the light or the completeness of the darkness. For example, it was held by the Jewish rabbis that Deut 6:4–7 required the recitation of the Shema in the evening and in the morning, and in the Talmud there is found an extended discussion of exactly what times are thereby intended. The recital could begin in the morning, it was declared, as soon as one could distinguish between blue and white (or between blue and green, as another rabbi taught), and it must be finished before sunrise.[10] As for the evening, Neh 4:21 was cited, where work went on "till the stars came out," and from that analogy it was shown that the appearance of the stars was the sign that the day had ended and the recital could begin.[11] Thus, in the morning it was either the dawning light or the following sunrise, and in the evening it was either the sunset or the ensuing nightfall, when the stars became visible, that provided the line of demarcation.[12]

15. Parts of the day were described at an early time in terms of the customary occupation then performed as, for example, the "time for animals to be gathered together" (Gen 29:7), or "the time when women go out to draw water" (Gen 24:11). The nighttime was divided into watches. Lam 2:19 speaks of "the beginning of the watches," Judg 7:19 mentions "the middle watch," and Exod 14:24 and I Sam 11:11 refer to "the morning watch." The rabbis debated whether there were three watches or four.[13] In the New Testament, as in Roman and Egyptian practice, we find four watches of the night: evening, midnight, cockcrow, and morning (Matt 14:25; Mark 13:35).[14] The daytime had recognizable periods such as "the heat of the day" (Gen 18:1) and "the cool of the day" (Gen 3:8), and was also divided broadly into morning, noon, and evening (Psa 55:17). A division of the daytime into three parts, and of the nighttime into three parts, is mentioned in *Jub.* 49:10,12.[15]

16. The word "hour" שעה *(sha'ah),* occurs several times in Daniel (3:6, etc.) in Aramaic, and is common in later Hebrew. In Daniel it still denotes simply a short period of time and the phrase "the same hour" (ASV) may properly be translated "immediately" (RSV). In Greek the corresponding word is ὥρα, and it too is used for an inexactly defined period of time, as for example in John 5:35, where πρὸς ὥραν is translated "for a while."

---

[10]*Berakot* 1:2; Danby 2.

[11]*Berakot* 2b; Epstein, *BT* 3.

[12]As the line between one day and the next, nightfall was later defined more precisely as the moment when three stars of the second magnitude became visible. Friedländer, *JE* 3: 501.

[13]*Berakot* 3a–b; Epstein, *BT* 5–8.

[14]R. de Vaux, *RB* 73 (1966): 146–147, review of FHBC.

[15]*APOT* 2:80.

17. In Mesopotamia the entire day was divided into twelve periods of what we would call two hours each.[16] Herodotus (2.109) refers to these "twelve divisions (μέρεα) of the day," and observes that the Greeks learned of them from the Babylonians. Among the Greeks themselves the day and the night were each divided into twelve hours.[17] These hours naturally varied in length depending upon the time of year and were known as ὧραι καιρικαί. For scientific purposes, an hour of standard length was used, the entire day (νυχθήμερον) being divided into twenty-four periods of equal length. The astronomer Hipparchus (c. 150 B.C.) speaks of these "equinoctial hours" (ὧραι ἰσημεριναί),[18] as he calls them, and Ptolemy[19] also distinguishes between ordinary and equinoctial hours. In order to measure the hours, there were available for the time when the sun was shining the sunclock (πόλος) and the sundial (γνώμων), which are mentioned by Herodotus in the passage cited just above with the statement that they came from Babylonia. The same principle of measurement by the shadow of the sun was, of course, also known in Egypt, where the obelisks were evidently used for astronomical measurements.[20] For the measurement of time during the darkness as well as the light, there was the water clock (κλεψύδρα), which is mentioned by Aristotle[21] and others.

18. The division of the day into twelve hours appears in John 11:9 where it is asked, "Are there not twelve hours in the day?" Likewise in Matt 20:1–12 the householder goes to hire laborers early in the morning, and again at the third, sixth, ninth and eleventh hours, and the last ones have only one hour of work before the end of the day. As we saw above (§11), Pliny tells us that the common people everywhere reckoned the day from dawn to dark, so the twelve hours were presumably counted within that period. If an average daytime lasting from six a.m. to six p.m. was taken as the basis, then the third hour was what we would call nine o'clock in the morning, and so on. In the Talmud[22] there is a discussion in connection with the testimony of witnesses of the extent of reasonable error in a man's estimate of what the hour is, and it is noted that "in the sixth hour the sun stands in the meridian."

19. In the Fourth Gospel, on the other hand, we saw (§13) that the day must have been reckoned from the preceding midnight, according to what Pliny (§11) tells us was official Roman usage. In this "modern" reckoning of the day from midnight, the first twelve hours would extend from midnight to midday, and another twelve hours would cover the time from midday to the next midnight. When various hourly notations are considered in the Gospel according to John, it is found that they do in fact work out well in terms of the Roman reckoning. For example, in John 1:39 a reckoning from the morning would make

---

[16] Georges Contenau, *Everyday Life in Babylon and Assyria* (London: E. Arnold, 1954), 11.
[17] Gow, *Companion,* 79.
[18] Hipparchus 2.4.5, ed. C. Manitius (Leipzig: Teubner, 1894), 184.
[19] *Tetrabiblos* 76, tr. F. E. Robbins (LCL, 1948), 165–167.
[20] Russell, Dugan, and Stewart, *Astronomy* 1:78.
[21] *Athenian Constitution* 67.2, tr. H. Rackham (LCL, 1952), 187; cf. Sontheimer, PW, Zweite Reihe 4.2, cols. 2017–2018.
[22] *Pesakhim* 11b–12b; Epstein, *BT* 51–56.

the "tenth hour" four o'clock in the afternoon, but a reckoning from midnight would make it ten o'clock in the morning, the later being more appropriate to the fact that the two disciples then stayed with Jesus "that day." In John 4:6 the "sixth hour" would be midday in the one case, but six o'clock in the evening in the other, and the latter would be a very likely time for the gathering at the well. In John 4:52 the "seventh hour" would be one p.m. or seven p.m., and the latter may be more likely for the arrival at Cana from Capernaum, a journey of twenty miles.[23]

20. Among the parts of the day, the "evening" was of special importance. We have already seen (§§12, 14) how the regularly used day in later Jewish times began in the evening rather than in the morning, and how either the sunset or the appearing of the stars was taken as the exact time of its beginning. The evening was also important because of the sacrifices which were made at that time, and in this connection there was a discussion of exactly what period of time was meant. According to Exod 12:6 the Passover lambs were to be killed "in the evening" of the fourteenth day of the first month, and Lev 23:5 gives the same date for "the Lord's Passover." In all three passages the Hebrew is literally "between the two evenings" (ASV margin), although in the first two cases the Septuagint translates simply πρός ἑσπέραν, "towards evening," and only in the Leviticus passage renders ἀνὰ μέσον τῶν ἑσπερινῶν, "between the evenings." The Mishna[24] states that the daily evening burnt offering was slaughtered at eight and a half hours, that is two-thirty o'clock, and offered at nine and a half hours, that is three-thirty o'clock. If it was the eve of Passover it was slaughtered at seven and a half hours, one-thirty o'clock, and offered at eight and a half hours, two-thirty o'clock, whether on a weekday or the Sabbath; if it was the eve of Passover and this fell on the eve of a Sabbath, that is on a Friday, it was slaughtered at six and a half hours, twelve-thirty o'clock, and offered at seven and a half hours, one-thirty o'clock; and then the Passover offering was slaughtered after that.

21. Explaining this procedure the accompanying Gemara[25] states that "between the evenings" means "from the time that the sun commences to decline in the west," and that the "two evenings " give "two and a half hours before and two and a half hours after and one hour for preparation" of the sacrifice. This means that "evening" begins as soon as the sun passes its midday zenith, and that the "two evenings" are from twelve to two-thirty o'clock, and from three-thirty until six o'clock respectively. Thus the daily evening burnt offering is ordinarily sacrificed in the hour between these two evenings, but when the Passover must also be sacrificed the same afternoon then the daily sacrifice is moved ahead. In another passage the Mishna[26] deals with the requirement of Exod 34:25 that the Passover sacrifice not be offered with leaven, and states that everything leavened must be burned at the beginning of the sixth hour, that is at twelve o'clock noon. As the accompanying discussion in the

---

[23] Norman Walker, *NovT* 4 (1960): 69–73.
[24] *Pesakhim* 5:1, Danby 141.
[25] *Pesakhim* 58a, Epstein, *BT* 287–288.
[26] *Pesakhim* 1:4, Danby 137.

Gemara[27] shows, this indicates that the sacrificing could begin immediately after noon. According to Josephus[28] the Passover sacrifices were conducted from the ninth to the eleventh hour, that is from three to five o'clock in the afternoon, and this was presumably the standard practice in the first century A.D.

22. According to the foregoing passages, the "evening" was substantially equivalent to the entire afternoon. In Deut 16:6, however, it is said that the Passover sacrifice is to be offered "in the evening at the going down of the sun." The Talmudic explanation of this was that the evening meant the afternoon and was the time when the Passover was to be slaughtered, and that the sunset was the time when it was to be eaten.[29] The Sadducees and the Samaritans, however, held that the slaughtering of the lamb itself was to take place between sunset and darkness.[30] *Jubilees* seems to agree with this when it says about the Passover lamb: "It is not permissible to slay it during the period bordering on the evening, and let them eat it at the time of the evening until the third part of the night" (49:12).[31] *Targum Onqelos* also rendered "between the two evenings" in Exod 12:6 as "between the two suns,"[32] and this was then explained as meaning the time between sunset and the coming out of the stars.[33]

23. In either case, however, whether it meant the afternoon time up until sunset, or the time from sunset until the stars became visible, the "evening" in the sense and in the regard just discussed evidently belonged to the closing part of the day, and it was only with the sunset or the appearing of the stars that the next day began.

2. The Week

LITERATURE: Hildegard and Julius **Lewy**, "The Origin of the Week and the Oldest West Asiatic Calendar," *HUCA* 17 (1942–43): 1–152c; Solomon **Gandz**, "The Origin of the Planetary Week or The Planetary Week in Hebrew Literature," *Proceedings of the American Academy for Jewish Research* 18 (1948/49): 213–254.

24. A sequence of seven days forms a week. Since the ancient Babylonians recognized seven winds, as may be seen in the Creation Epic where Marduk "sent forth the winds he had brought forth, the seven of them,"[34] one theory is that originally one day was dedicated to each of the winds and thus a week of seven days was formed.[35] In the time of Hammurabi, however, it does

---

[27] *Pesakhim* 5a, Epstein, *BT* 17.
[28] *War* 6.423.
[29] *Berakot* 9a, Epstein, *BT* 46–47.
[30] Emil G. Hirsch, *JE* 9:553.
[31] *APOT* 2:80.
[32] J. W. Etheridge, ed., *The Targums of Onkelos and Jonathan ben Uzziel on the Pentateuch: With the Fragments of the Jerusalem Targum from the Chaldee* (2 vols.; London : Longman, Green, Longman, and Roberts, 1862–1865), 1: 370.
[33] S. R. Driver, *The Book of Exodus* (The Cambridge Bible for Schools and Colleges; Cambridge: Cambridge University Press, 1911), 89 n.
[34] *ANET* 66.
[35] Lewy, *HUCA* 17 (1942–43): 6–25.

not appear that this concept of the week was clearly established[36] and the theory is improbable.[37] Much more likely is the influence of the widespread attention in the ancient world not only to the sun and moon but also to the five heavenly bodies which were observed to change their places in relation to the background of the so-called fixed stars, namely Mercury, Venus, Mars, Jupiter, and Saturn. In Egyptian they were called "the stars that know no rest," and in Greek their name was πλανητής, "a wanderer," "a planet." Together with the sun and moon, this made seven, and it was their number which most probably gave rise to the number of the days of the week, a supposition which is the more likely because of the names which were later quite universally given to the different days (§25).[38] A period of seven days a week was called שבוע *(shavua')* in Hebrew (Gen 29:27, etc.), from *sheva',* "seven"; and in Greek it was σάββατον (Luke 18:12, etc.). In the Bible the days of the week are simply numbered and the seventh day is also named the Sabbath (שבת, *shabbat;* σάββατον). In addition to this, the day before the Sabbath was called the day of Preparation,[39] and by the Christians the first day of the week was called the Lord's day (Rev 1:10).

25. The custom of naming the seven days of the week after the planets is attested in the first century B.C., when Tibullus (d. 19 B.C.) mentions the day of Saturn, and in the first century A.D. when Greek and Latin wall inscriptions at Pompeii (A.D. 79) list "the days of the gods," namely of Saturn, the sun, the moon, Mars, Mercury, Jupiter and Venus. This listing, with the later equivalents, is shown in Table 4.

TABLE 4. *The Planetary Names of the Days of the Week*

Θεων ημερας	*Dies*	*The Day of*	*English Name*
Κρονου	Saturni	Saturn	Saturday
Ηλιου	Solis	the sun	Sunday
Σεληνης	Lunae	the moon	Monday
Αρεως	Martis	Mars	Tuesday (Tiw's day)
Ερμου	(Mercurii)	Mercury	Wednesday (Woden's day)
Διος	Jovis	Jupiter	Thursday (Thor's day)
[Αφρο]δειτης	Veneris	Venus	Friday (Frigg's day)[40]

Dio Cassius (d. A.D. c. 235) says this custom of referring the days to the seven planets was instituted by the Egyptians and was in his own time found among all mankind.[41] Dio's remarks in this connection, that the Jews dedicate to their God "the day called the day of the Saturn," is of course correct as far as Jewish observance of Saturday or the Sabbath is concerned, but they would hardly have

[36] Mahler, *Handbuch,* 171.

[37] De Vaux, review of the first edition of this book, *RB* 73 (1966): 146–147.

[38] *EB* (1929) 4: 568.

[39] παρασκευή, Josephus, *Ant.* 16.163; Matt 27:62; Luke 23:54; John 19:31, 42; προσάββατον, Mark 15:42.

[40] Emil Schürer, *ZNW* 6 (1905): 25, 27.

[41] *Roman History* 37.17–19.

designated the day by the name which the pagan writer uses. In an apocryphal rabbinic work, however, the *Pirqe de Rabbi Eliezer,* the final edition of which probably dates in the ninth century A.D., the planets which rule the week are named. For each day a pair is given, the first being the ruler of the nighttime and the second the regent of the following daytime: "The planets serve . . . as the regents of the seven days of the week, to wit: On the first day, Mercury and the Sun; on the second, Jupiter and the Moon; on the third, Venus and Mars; on the fourth, Saturn and Mercury; on the fifth, the Sun and Jupiter; on the sixth, the Moon and Venus; on the seventh, Mars and Saturn."[42]

3. The Month

26. Like the Sumero-Akkadian word for day, which can at most suggest a measure of association of this time period with daily land and sea breezes (§19) rather than explain the origin of the idea of the "day," and the seven winds of the Babylonian epic of creation which, in spite of one theory, provide only an unlikely basis for the concept of the "week," which was probably not yet formalized in the time of Hammurabi (§24), so also the Gezer Calendar in which months and agricultural tasks are set side by side (§58), and the several Old Testament month names which describe their respective periods of time in terms of agricultural and climatic conditions (§59), have been seen in some views as pointing to the original basis of the "month." This, however, is also unlikely, for in the Gezer Calendar the primary reference is to the month and not to agriculture, and in fact the agricultural year is variable and therefore a poor basis for an exact calendar,[43] although the seasons are of sufficient regularity that a usable calendar needs to be kept in at least approximate harmony with them. Like the sun for the day and the planets for the week it is, therefore, another celestial object, namely, the moon, observation of which most probably led to the concept of the "month" and continued to determine the parameters of the month.

27. The etymological similarity of the words "month" and "moon" in many languages is the immediate indication of the connection between the time unit and the astronomical object. In Hebrew the word ירח *(yerakh)* means both "moon" and "month," as may be seen for example in Deut 33:14 where the alternative translations are, "the precious things of the growth of the moons" (ASV), and "the rich yield of the months" (RSV). Likewise the term חדש *(khodesh)*, which originally meant "the shining, glittering new moon," was later used as the designation of the festival of the day of the new moon, and also as the name of the entire month which is, as it were, the lifetime of the newly born moon. In Gen 29:14, for example, this word clearly means "month," in 1 Sam

---

[42] 6.13b. *Pirke de Rabbi Eliezer (The Chapters of Rabbi Eliezer the Great) according to the Text of the Manuscript Belonging to Abraham Epstein of Vienna,* ed. Gerald Friedländer (London, 1916), 32; Solomon Gandz in *Proceedings of the American Academy for Jewish Research* 18 (1948–49): 230.

[43] Simon J. de Vries, review of the first edition of the present book, *JBL* 84 (1965): 76–80.

20:5 and other passages it means the "new moon" day.[44] Likewise in Greek the word μήνη means "moon" and μήν means "month." In the Septuagint μήν is the translation of both ירח (Deut 33:14, etc.) and חדש (Gen 29:14). In the New Testament μήν regularly means "month" (Luke 1:24, etc.), but in one case (Gal 4:10) probably refers to the new moon festival.

28. Insofar as the month was related to the moon, the determination of its length depended upon observation of the phases of the moon. In Egypt, where the day probably began at dawn, it is thought that the month probably began with a lunar phenomenon which could be observed at that time of day. As the moon wanes, the old crescent is finally just visible in the eastern sky before sunrise one morning and on the next morning it is invisible. It may have been, therefore, on the morning when the old crescent could no longer be seen that the Egyptian lunar month began.[45] In Mesopotamia, on the other hand, the day began when the crescent of the new moon was first visible in the western sky at sunset.[46]

29. In modern astronomy the time from one new moon to the next, which is known as the synodic or ordinary month, is determined as 29.530588 days, or 29 days, 12 hours, 44 minutes, 2.8 seconds.[47] This means that on the average the new moon will be seen approximately every 29½ days, and that the full moon will come approximately 14¾ days after the appearing of the new moon, that is on the fourteenth day of the lunar month, with the day reckoned from evening to evening.[48] After the accumulation of data by observation, the month could have been calculated in advance. Likewise it could have been established as a standard unit, say of 30 days, rather than left variable as it must be to agree with the observed phases of the moon. A problem arises when the relation of the month to the year is brought into consideration. Twelve months of 29½ days each make a year of 354 days and 12 months of 30 days each make a year of 360 days, but the year measured by the sun is in round numbers 365 days in length; thus a lunar year of 360 days is 5 days short and a lunar year of 354 days is 11 days short. These two ways of counting the days of the month are found in the existing story of the flood in Gen 6:5–8:22. In Gen 7:11 the flood began in the second month, on the 17th day of the month; in Gen 8:3–4 the waters had abated at the end of 150 days and the ark came to rest upon the 17th day of the month; the intervening time was exactly 5 months or 150 days, i.e., the months were each 30 days in length. In Gen 8:13–15 the flood waters were dried from off the earth in the first month, the first day of the month, and in the second month, on the 27th day of the month, the earth was dry and Noah went forth from the ark. Since the flood began in the second month, on the 17th day of the month (Gen 7:11), this first day of the first month was the beginning of a new year and the 16th day of the ensuing second month was the last day of the first year of

---

[44] Solomon Gandz, *JQR* 39 (1948–49): 259–260.
[45] PCAE 9–23.
[46] PDBC 1.
[47] *The American Ephemeris and Nautical Almanac for the Year 1958* (1956), xvi.
[48] Julian Morgenstern, *HUCA* 10 (1953): 25.

the flood and the 17th day of that second month was the first day of the second year of the flood, whereby the 27th day of this same second month was the 11th day of the second year of the flood, i.e., the flood lasted for one year and 11 days, which makes exactly the 11-day difference between a lunar year of 354 days and the solar year of 365 days.[49] It is the same difference between the lunar year and the solar year that will be of much concern in respect to the Egyptian, Babylonian, and Jewish calendars.

4. The Year

30. The ordinary Hebrew word for "year" is שנה *(shanah)*. It is etymologically connected with the idea of "change" or "repeated action," and thus describes a "revolution of time." In the Septuagint it is translated both by ἐνιαυτός (Gen 1:14, etc.), properly a "cycle of time," and more frequently by ἔτος (Gen 5:3, etc.) and both Greek words are used for "year" in the New Testament (John 11:49, etc.; Luke 3:1, etc.).

31. Movement through the whole cycle of time was no doubt noticed from very early times because of changes in climate, in times of sowing and harvesting, and in lengths of days—all matters themselves of course dependent upon the sun—but more precise definition of a "year" waited upon more exact observation of the apparent movement of the sun. In Egypt the annual inundation of the Nile was an annually prominent reminder of the return of the cycle, and was regularly followed by the season of sowing. In Palestine the climate was marked by the "early rain" or "autumn rain" which came in Oct/Nov, and the "later rain" or "spring rain" which came in Mar/Apr (Deut 11:14; Jer 5:24),[50] as well as by the recurrence of summer and winter (Zech 14:8, etc.) and the agricultural seasons likewise returned regularly with the ripening of the olives in the fall (Sept/Oct–Oct/Nov), for example, and the shooting into ear of the barley in the spring (Mar/Apr).[51]

32. The autumn and spring seasons, to which attention was thus particularly drawn by climatic and agricultural events, were also marked by the equality in length of day and night which occurs everywhere when the sun crosses the equator in each season. Each such point is an equinox (equal night [and day] time) and by our reckoning the autumnal equinox falls about September 22, the vernal equinox about March 20. Likewise the summer and winter were marked respectively by the times when the sun seems to stand still in its northward movement and again in its southward movement. These points are the summer solstice and the winter solstice and come by our reckoning about June 21 and December 21. When these several points were recognized they provided definite markers in the course of the year, and it was no doubt possible to establish them even early with some precision by observation of the length of

---

[49] Mahler, *Handbuch,* 172 and n. 1.
[50] E. Hull, HDB 4: 195.
[51] W. F. Albright, *BASOR* 92 (Dec 1934): 22–23 n. 30 and n. 37.

day and night and by measurement of the shadow of the sun.[52] In more precise observations embodied in his famous star catalogue (completed in 129 B.C.), the Greek astronomer Hipparchus noticed that stars had shifted in a systematic way from earlier Babylonian (Chaldean) measures. He also discovered the precession of the equinoxes, i.e., their slow westward movement due to the slow gyration of the rotation axis of the earth.

33. When such a mark as the vernal equinox is established, the length of the year from that point through a "revolution of time" and back to the same point can be measured. In Egypt, as will be noted in discussing the Egyptian calendar below, the length of the year was probably recognized as early as the third millennium B.C. as being 365 days, and with more exact measurements it was later found to be about 365¼ days. Among the Jews, Mar Samuel (A.D. c. 165–c. 250), who directed a school at Nehardea in Babylonia and was said to be as familiar with the paths of heaven as with the streets of his own city,[53] reckoned the year at 365 days and 6 hours, while his contemporary, Rab Adda, made it 365 days, 5 hours, 55 minutes, 25 and a fraction seconds.[54] The Julian calendar (§144) accepted the standard figure of 365¼ days with which we are familiar, but was therewith about eleven minutes longer than the astronomical year. In modern astronomy the length of the ordinary, tropical (the year of the seasons, from *tropicus,* "belonging to a turn, turning"), or solar year, as it is called, is given as 365.24219879 days, or 365 days, 5 hours, 48 minutes, 45.975 seconds.[55]

34. When the four points of the vernal and autumnal equinoxes and the summer and winter solstices are taken, the year is readily divisible into four parts. Such a division of the solar year is found in the Talmud,[56] where the word תקופה *(tequfah)* is used as the name of each of the four periods. The word means "cycle" or "season," and a related form is found as "circuit" in the Manual of Discipline (§82).

35. In the course of the year the sun also seems to trace a path eastward against the background of the stars. This path is known as the zodiac. In a month the sun travels approximately one-twelfth of the way around this circle, and perhaps for this reason, the zodiac was divided into twelve positions.[57] Using the sexagesimal system of ancient Mesopotamia, the entire circle of the zodiac comprises 360 degrees, each of the twelve sections, 30 degrees. These divisions of the zodiac are designated according to the constellations of stars which they contain. Already in the Babylonian Creation Epic we read of the work of Marduk:

---

[52]Russell, Dugan, and Stewart, *Astronomy* 1:151; E. C. Krupp, ed., *In Search of Ancient Astronomies* (Garden City, N.Y.: Doubleday, 1978), 7.

[53]*Berakot* 58b; Epstein, *BT* 365.

[54]*JE* 3: 500.

[55]*American Ephemeris for Year 1958,* xvi.

[56]*Sanhedrin* 11b, Goldschmidt, *BT* 7: 36–37.

[57]F. Von Oefele, Hastings, *ERE* 12: 51.

He constructed stations for the great gods,
Fixing their astral likenesses as constellations.
He determined the year by designating the zones:
He set up three constellations for each of the twelve months.[58]

36. Later a single constellation was taken as the sign of each of the twelve parts of the zodiac. In the tractate *Berakot*[59] of the Talmud, the "Sovereign of the Universe" says: "Twelve constellations have I created in the firmament, and for each constellation I have created thirty hosts, and for each host I have created thirty legions, and for each legion I have created thirty cohorts, and for each cohort I have created thirty maniples,[60] and for each maniple I have created thirty camps, and to each camp I have attached three hundred sixty-five thousands of myriads of stars, corresponding to the days of the solar year." In the *Sefer Yesirah,* a Jewish work of unknown antiquity, the names of the constellations are given as follows:[61] Taleh, Shor, Te'omin, Sartan, Aryeh, Betulah, Moznayim, 'Aqrab, Qeshet, Gedi, Deli, and Dagim. The Greek names as found in Hipparchus, were as follows, the Latin forms and the meanings also being given: (1) ὁ Κριός, Aries, the Ram; (2) ὁ Ταῦρος, Taurus, the Bull; (3) οἱ Δίδυμοι, Gemini, the Twins; (4) ὁ καρκίνος, Cancer, the Crab; (5) ὁ Λέων, Leo, the Lion; (6) ἡ Παρθένος, Virgo, the Virgin; (7) αἱ Χηλαί, Libra, the Balance; (8) ὁ Σκορπίος, Scorpio, the Scorpion; (9) ὁ Τοξότης, Sagittarius, the Archer; (10) ὁ Ἀιγόκερως, Capricornus, the Goat; (11) ὁ Ὑδροξόος, Aquarius, the Water Carrier; (12) οἱ Ἰχθύες, Pisces, the Fishes. Since most of these were animals, from the word ζῴδιον, "a little animal," the entire zone was called ὁ ζῳδιακὸς κύκλος,[62] the zodiacal circle, or zodiac.

B. CALENDARS

1. The Egyptian Calendar

LITERATURE: Eduard **Meyer**, *Aegyptische Chronologie* (Berlin: Königlich Akademie der Wissenschaften, 1904), 1–212; *Nachträge zur ägyptischen Chronologie,* (Berlin: Königlich Akademie der Wissenschaften, 1907), 1–46; Eduard **Mahler**, *Etudes sur le calendrier Egyptien* (Annales du Musée Guimet: Bibliothèque d'études 24; Paris, E. Leroux, 1907), 1–135; Ludwig **Borchardt**, *Die Annalen und die zeitliche Festlegung des Alten Reiches der ägyptischen Geschichte.* (Berlin: Behrend, 1917); Ludwig **Borchardt**, *Die altägyptische Zeitmessung* (Berlin: Vereinigung Wissenschaftlicher Verlager, W. De Gruyter, 1920); O. **Neugebauer**, "The Origin of the Egyptian Calendar," in *JNES* 1 (1942): 396–403; Richard A. **Parker**, *The Calendars of Ancient Egypt* (= PCAE); Eugen **Strouhal**, *Life of the Ancient Egyptians* (trans. Deryck Viney; London: Opus Publishing; Norman: University of Oklahoma Press, 1992).

---

[58] *ANET* 67.
[59] 32b; Epstein, *BT* 201.
[60] Like the other terms, a subdivision of the Roman military organization.
[61] *JE* 12: 688.
[62] Hipparchus 1.6.4, ed. Manitius, 56.

37. In ancient Egypt the year was divided into three seasons, each about four lunar months in length. The first season was called *akhet* or "inundation," approximately July to October, and was the time when the Nile rose and overflowed the fields. The second was *peret* or "coming forth," approximately November to February, when the fields emerged again from the flood waters and seeding, tilling, and growth of crops took place. The third was *schemu* or "deficiency," approximately March to June, when harvest was followed by the time of low water before the next inundation.[63] The recognition of these seasons, based upon climatic and agricultural factors, was undoubtedly very old.

38. At least by the start of the Old Kingdom astronomical knowledge was well advanced, and astronomical factors related to the calendar were soon recognized. At an early time the year probably started with the lunar month which began after the Nile began to rise. The rise of the river normally began at Aswan in late May or early June, and was about ten days later at Memphis. Coming thus in the summer, the period of the great inundation included the time of the summer solstice (§32). At about the same time a celestial phenomenon took place which also attracted attention in Egypt at an early date, namely the heliacal rising of Sirius. Sirius is the brightest of all the fixed stars, and was known as Sothis in the Greek spelling of its Egyptian name (Sopdu), and also as Canicula, the Dog Star. After being hidden below the horizon for seventy days, Sirius reappeared in the east just before sunrise (heliacal rising), and this took place at about the beginning of the annual inundation of the Nile.[64] It may be added that the heliacal risings of thirty-six stars or constellations (Orion, etc.), which occurred approximately every ten days, were also noted and used, under the name of *decans,* to mark as many periods of the year.[65] Returning to Sirius, the length of the year from heliacal rising to heliacal rising of Sirius was very close to the length of the solar year (only twelve minutes shorter) which, as we have seen (§33), is now calculated as 365.24219879 days. In Table 5 the length of the Sirius-year is shown at several intervals.

TABLE 5. *The Length of the Sirius-Year*

Sirius-Year	*Length in Days*
4231 B.C.	365.2498352
3231	365.2500000
2231	365.2502291
1231	365.2505225
231	365.2508804
A.D. 770	365.2513026

[63] Henri Frankfort, *Kingship and the Gods* (Chicago: University of Chicago Press, 1948), 367 n. 3; PCAE 32.

[64] Finegan, *Myth and Mystery,* 41–42.

[65] Wilhelm Gundel, *Dekane und Dekansternbilder* (Studien der Bibliotek Warburg 19; Glückstadt and Hamburg: J. J. Augustin, 1936).

Thus, in 3231 B.C., the Sirius-year was 365¼ days in length, exactly the same as the value taken for the Julian year (§144), and it became longer only very slowly. In terms of the Julian calendar, the reappearance of Sirius at dawn in the latitude of Memphis fell on July 19 from the fifth millennium to the second half of the first millennium B.C.—i.e., throughout the whole course of ancient Egyptian history—and then gradually moved to July 20. In the same period of four thousand years, from 4231 to 231 B.C., in which the heliacal rising of Sirius moved later by one day in comparison with the Julian year, the summer solstice, on the other hand, moved thirty-one days earlier in the Julian year, namely from July 28 in the year 4231 to June 27 in the year 231 B.C. In accordance with these changes, the summer solstice took place in Memphis in the forty-third century (4300–4201) B.C., nine days after the heliacal rising of Sirius; in the thirty-first century (3100–3001) B.C., on the same day, i.e., on July 19; and in each century thereafter fell back another eighteen and two-thirds hours.[66] Thus, if the great summer inundation was originally taken as signaling the beginning of a new year in an agriculturally oriented reckoning, these two celestial events which fell within the same period, the summer solstice and the heliacal rising of Sirius which was at one time exactly coincident therewith, were available to provide a more precise point of beginning in an astronomically oriented reckoning. Since the reappearance of Sirius at sunrise was the more readily observable event, it is probable that this was what was first utilized. In fact, an inscription of the First Dynasty probably reads: "Sothis, the opener of the year; the inundation."[67] Since the event of the heliacal rising had the remarkable stability which we have noted, it provided a fixed point of reference for a very long time, as we shall see (§§41, 45–48).

(1) The Three Calendars

39. Since the year was composed of lunar months, the calendar whose probable origins have just been described may be called a lunar calendar; since the beginning of the year was fixed by reference to a star, it may be described more specifically as a lunistellar calendar. A year composed of twelve lunar months, ordinarily alternating between twenty-nine and thirty days in length, makes 354 days, which is approximately eleven days short of the solar year. To keep the calendar year beginning in the spring, in general, and at the time of the heliacal rising of Sothis in particular, it must have been necessary to insert an additional month every three years or so. It seems that when this occurred, the intercalary month was put at the head of the new lunar year. In our own calendar when an extra day is added to make a year of 366 rather than 365 days it is called a "leap" year (§144), and in any calendar in which there is intercalation of a day or a month the same term may be used. It is believed that this calendar, as just described, was the original lunar or "natural" calendar of Egypt and was in use before and in the early dynastic period and long thereafter.[68] Being controlled by the rising of Sirius to determine the new year, it was "fixed" and, as such was the calendar for religious affairs and everyday life.

---

[66] Meyer, *Aegyptische Chronologie,* 14–15, 23.
[67] PCAE 32, 34,74 n. 22.
[68] PCAE 30–50, 53.

40. Alongside the "natural" calendar of Egypt just described (§39), there was established for administrative, government, and business purposes a "public" or "civil" calendar.[69] Whether it was by averaging a series of the lunar years or by counting the days between the heliacal risings of Sirius at the time of the inundation, it became known that the true length of the year to the nearest number of days was 365. The disadvantages of a year composed now of twelve and again of thirteen lunar months must have been evident, and the knowledge of the year's length as 365 days made possible the new system. After the analogy of the lunar system the year was still divided into three seasons and twelve months, but for the sake of simplicity and regularity each month was made thirty days in length. This left a shortage of only five days and, after the example of the intercalated month at the beginning of the lunar year, five extra days (epagomenal days) were inserted before the new year. These were considered holidays in celebration of the "birthdays" of the gods Osiris, Seth, and Horus, and of the goddesses Isis and Nephthys. Since the months were no longer kept in relationship to the real moon but were fixed units in the solar year instead, this may be recognized as essentially a solar calendar, and since the units have an artificial regularity it may be called a "schematic" calendar. This system was introduced, there is reason to believe, between c. 2937 and c. 2821 B.C. and from then on served as the standard civil calendar of Egypt.[70]

41. The civil calendar of 365 days was still, however, not in exact agreement with the solar year since the latter is actually closer to 365¼ days in length. At the outset, it may be assumed, the first day of the civil year coincided with the heliacal rising of Sothis. After four years it would begin on the day before the rising of Sothis, after eight years, two days before, and so on, and was thus a "shifting" or "sliding" calendar. Only after 1,460 years would the beginning of the civil year have moved all the way around the cycle to coincide once again with the rising of Sothis. Since the original lunar calendar was periodically corrected to keep its beginning point in connection with the heliacal rising of Sothis, the civil calendar gradually diverged more and more from the lunar calendar. It is assumed that this divergence would have become apparent by, say, 2500 B.C., and that around that time a second lunar calendar was introduced which was thereafter maintained in substantial harmony with the civil year with such intercalation as was necessary, and, as before, was used to determine religious celebrations and duties.[71] Thus, from that time on, Egypt actually had no less than three calendars and three calendar years, and all of these continued in use throughout the remainder of ancient Egyptian history.[72] From here on we are chiefly concerned with the standard civil calendar.

---

[69] Hermann Kees, *Der Götterglaube im alten Ägypten* (Berlin: Akademie-Verlag, 1977), 259–260; Eugen Strouhal, *Life of the Ancient Egyptians*, 239–241.

[70] PCAE 53. This Egyptian calendar consisting of twelve months of thirty days each and five additional days at the end of each year has been called by O. Neugebauer (*The Exact Sciences in Antiquity* [Princeton, N.J.: Princeton University Press, 1952], 81) "the only intelligent calendar which ever existed in history."

[71] *EB* (1987), 15: 464.

[72] PCAE 54, 56.

(2) The Months

42. From early times the designation of the months of the Egyptian year was by number as, e.g., on the Palermo Stone, "Fourth month, thirteenth day;"[73] or by number within one of the three seasons as, e.g., on a stela of Thutmose III, "Second month of the second season, tenth day."[74]

43. The months were also given names, however, and in the Hellenistic and Roman periods these appear in Greek as shown in Table 6.

TABLE 6. *The Greek Names of the Egyptian Months*

1. Θώθ	Thoth	7. Φαμενώθ	Phamenoth
2. Φαῶφι	Phaophi	8. Φαρμοῦθι	Pharmuthi
3. Ἀθύρ	Hathyr	9. Παχών	Pachon
4. Χοίακ	Choiak	10. Παύνι	Pauni (or Payni)
5. Τῦβι	Tybi	11. Ἐπείφ	Epeiph
6. Μεχείρ	Mecheir	12. Μεσορή	Mesore
		ἐπαγόμεναι ἡμέραι	Epagomenal days

44. The preceding tabulation represents the year as beginning with the month Thoth, with Thoth 1 as New Year's day, which was the usual reckoning. There was also a reckoning from Mecheir 1. The latter is encountered in the papyri where it is indicated as ὡς αἱ πρόσοδοι. ἡ πρόσοδος means "a going to" and is used, mostly in the plural αἱ πρόσοδοι, for "the public revenues." Hence, ὡς αἱ πρόσοδοι means "according to the financial calendar." It was also possible to date from a given point in the king's reign and examples are found, varying from reign to reign, so the reference point probably represented the anniversary of the king's accession.[75] From here on we shall be chiefly concerned with the year beginning Thoth 1. The standard civil calendar beginning Thoth 1 is found, however, in two forms, the earlier form with a shifting year, the later form with a fixed year.

(3) The Standard Civil Calendar with a Shifting Year

45. In accordance with the nature of the standard civil calendar (§40), the months listed above had each thirty days, and the five days inserted before the beginning of the new year made a total year length of 365 days. Since the total was one-fourth day short of the solar year, in four years the calendar fell back one whole day (§41). This means that in each four years Thoth 1 fell one day earlier. The equivalents in Table 7, for example, have been established in the Ptolemaic period.

---

[73] Breasted, *Ancient Records* 1:93.

[74] *ANET* 234.

[75] C. Edgar Campbell, *Zenon Papyri in the University of Michigan Collection* (Ann Arbor: University of Michigan Press, 1931), 50.

TABLE 7. *Dates of Thoth 1 in the Ptolemaic Period*

Under Ptolemy I Soter	
305–302 B.C.	Thoth 1 = Nov 7
301–298	Thoth 1 = Nov 6
297–294	Thoth 1 = Nov 5
etc.	
Under Ptolemy II Philadelphus	
285–282	Thoth 1 = Nov 2
281–278	Thoth 1 = Nov 1
277–274	Thoth 1 = Oct 31
etc.	
Under Ptolemy III Euergetes	
245–242	Thoth 1 = Oct 23
241–238	Thoth 1 = Oct 22
237–234	Thoth 1 = Oct 21
etc.[76]	

Likewise, as already noted (§41), in 1,460 years as measured by the heliacal risings of Sirius, Thoth 1 would move back 365 days and, supposing it coincided in the first year of such a period with the annual heliacal rising of Sirius, it would only after those 1,460 years again so coincide. This period, which is called a Sothic cycle, would be measured, it is evident, in terms of Julian years as comprising 1,460 years, but in terms of the shorter Egyptian year as comprising 1,461 years.

46. The shifting or wandering year *(Wandeljahr)* just described and the long Sothic cycle through which it moved continued to be observed for a long time. A clear statement of how the Egyptian civil year *(annus civilis)* is not related to the moon, has 365 days, and moves to a fresh beginning in 1,461 years, is given by Censorinus, who also says that this Sothic period is called a "great year" *(annus magnus)* or "year pertaining to the Dog Star" *(annus canicularis* or κυνικός).[77] Writing in A.D. 238 he says[78] that in that year the Egyptian Thoth 1 fell on VII Kal Iul. = June 25 (for such dates see §141 below), and that one hundred years before when Antoninus Pius was consul for the second time along with Brutius Praesens, i.e., in A.D. 139 (for dating by consuls see below §§172ff.), it fell on XII Kal. Aug = July 21, a reference probably to be corrected to XIII Kal. Aug = July 20 which would agree with the date of the heliacal rising of Sirius in that period (§38). Thus the year beginning Thoth 1 = July 20, A.D. 139 was evidently the first year of a new Sothic cycle. Counting forward from 139/140 as the first year, the year 238/239 was in fact the one hundredth year, and in the one hundred years the beginning of the calendar year had moved twenty-five days from July 20 to June 25. Counting backward 1,460 years from

[76] A. Bouché-Leclercq, *Histoire des Lagides* (4 vols.; Paris: E. Leroux, 1903–1907), 3: 384–407.

[77] 18.10; *Censorini De die natali liber,* ed. F. Hultsch (Leipzig: Teubner, 1867), 38.

[78] 21.10, ed. Hultsch, 46.

139/140 A.D., the first year of the preceding Sothic cycle would have been the year from July 19, 1321, to July 18, 1320 B.C., and similar cyclic points prior to that would have been 2781/2780 and 4241/4240 B.C.[79] It is the date of 4241 B.C. which James Henry Breasted once called "the earliest fixed date in the history of the world."[80]

47. The Sothic cycle, whose first year was July 19, 1321, to July 18, 1320 B.C., is probably also attested by Theon, who wrote in the fourth century A.D. Expressly using the Egyptian shifting year, Theon reckons 1,605 years "from Menophres" (ἀπὸ Μενόφρεως) to the end of the era of Augustus. The era of Diocletian began on Aug 29, A.D. 284, and the last year of the Augustan era was accordingly 283/284. One thousand six hundred and five of the shorter shifting Egyptian years are equal to 1,604 Julian years less thirty-six days; and 1,604 years before A.D. 283/284 brings us back to 1321/1320 B.C. Thus reckoning "from Menophres" is probably the same as the reckoning from the Sothic period which began in 1321/1320 B.C. As for the name Menophres (Μενόφρης), it has been thought possible to recognize in it the praenomen of Ramses I, read as *Mn-ph-r*,[81] but the preferred date for the reign of Ramses I is now 1295–1294 B.C. (Table 117) so the connection with this king is no longer likely.

48. There is also reference to the Sothic cycle in Clement of Alexandria where he says that Moses went forth from Egypt three hundred and forty-five years before the Sothic period (πρὸ τῆς Σωθιακῆς περιόδου).[82] After this, dates are given out of Greek legendary history down to the first year of the first Olympiad, and if these figures were intact and complete it would again be possible to make a calculation relative to the Sothic date, but since they probably are not, this need not be considered further.[83]

(4) The Standard Civil Calendar with a Fixed Year

49. In contrast to this "wandering" year which existed for so long in the standard civil calendar of Egypt, we turn to what is known as the fixed Alexandrian year, which finally prevailed. In 22 B.C. Augustus introduced the Julian calendar (§§143f.) into Egypt and reformed the Egyptian calendar to bring it into harmony therewith. Every fourth year, in the year preceding the leap year of the Julian calendar—i.e., in A.D. 3/4, 7/8, etc.—a sixth epagomenal day was added in the Egyptian calendar. With this stabilization, the first day of Thoth was kept permanently on Aug 29 (where it fell at the time of the reform), except in the intercalary year when the addition of the sixth epagomenal day put Thoth 1 on Aug 30 and put each succeeding day through Phamenoth 4 = Feb 29 one

---

[79] Meyer, *Aegyptische Chronologie,* 23–29; Lászlo Kakósy, "Sothis," *LÄ* 5: 1110–1117; Ulrich Luft, "Sothisperiode," *LÄ* 5: 1117–1124.

[80] Breasted, *A History of Egypt from the Earliest Times to the Persian Conquest* (New York: Scribner, 1905), 26.

[81] Richard A. Parker, *JNES* 16 (1957): 39–43; M. B. Rowton, *JCS* 13 (1959): 8–9; *JNES* 19 (1960): 15–22; Jaroslav Verny, *JEA* 47 (1961): 150–152.

[82] *Stromata* 1.21, 136.

[83] Meyer, *Aegyptische Chronologie,* 30.

day later than in the common years. After the intercalary year the calendar returns to its normal relation, and always Phamenoth 5 = Mar 1.[84] Table 8 shows this fixed Egyptian calendar, with the number of days in the Egyptian months and the equivalent Julian dates for the months both in an Egyptian common year and in an Egyptian intercalary year. At the point of the transition from the portion of the calendar affected by the intercalary year to the part following, the presentation is amplified to show the details of the change. This is the calendar still observed by the Copts in Egypt.[85]

TABLE 8. *The Egyptian Civil Calendar with the Fixed Year*

MONTH	NUMBER OF DAYS		JULIAN CALENDAR	
	Common Year	*Intercalary Year*	*Common Year*	*Intercalary Year*
1. Thoth	30	30	Aug 29–Sept 27	Aug 30–Sept 28
2. Phaophi	30	30	Sept 28–Oct 27	Sept 29–Oct 28
3. Hathyr	30	30	Oct 28–Nov 26	Oct 29–Nov 27
4. Choiak	30	30	Nov 27–Dec 26	Nov 28–Dec 27
5. Tybi	30	30	Dec 27–Jan 25	Dec 28–Jan 26
6. Mecheir	30	30	Jan 26–Feb 24	Jan 27–Feb 25
7. Phamenoth	30	30	Feb 25–Mar 26	Feb 26–Mar 26
Phamenoth 1			Feb 25	Feb 26
Phamenoth 4			Feb 28	Feb 29
Phamenoth 5			Mar 1	Mar 1
Phamenoth 30			Mar 26	Mar 26
8. Pharmuthi	30	30	Mar 27–Apr 25	Mar 27–Apr 25
9. Pachon	30	30	Apr 26–May 25	Apr 26–May 25
10. Pauni	30	30	May 26–June 24	May 26–June 24
11. Epeiph	30	30	June 25–July 24	June 25–July 24
12. Mesore	30	30	July 25–Aug 23	July 25–Aug 23
Epagomenal days	5	6	Aug 24–Aug 28	Aug 24–Aug 29

2. The Babylonian Calendar

LITERATURE: Richard A. **Parker** and Waldo H. **Dubberstein**, *Babylonian Chronology, 626 B.C.–A.D. 75* (= PDBC).

50. In Mesopotamia also there was a lunar, or more strictly a lunisolar, calendar. The moon-god was very prominent in Mesopotamia,[86] and observa-

[84]George Milligan, *Selections from the Greek Papyri*, xviii; Bernard P. Grenfell and Arthur S. Hunt, *OxyP* 12: 291; cf. T. C. Skeat, *Mizraim* 8 (1937): 21, who says wrongly, I think, that Phamenoth 6 always equals Mar 1.

[85]Strouhal, *Life of the Ancient Egyptians*, 240.

[86]The moon-god was known as Nanna to the Sumerians (*ANET* 38), and as Sin to the Akkadians (*ANET* 88). Sin was the son of the air-god Enlil, the husband of the goddess Ningal, and they were the parents of the sun-god Shamash (*ANET* 164 n.10; 400 n.3). Sin was called "the lamp of heaven and earth" (*ANET* 390), and he was worshiped especially at the temple of Egishnugal in Ur (*ANET* 164). The crescent which is his symbol is familiar

tion of the moon no doubt began very early. The beginning of the month was based upon the sighting of the new moon, and already by the time of Hammurabi the months were alternately twenty-nine and thirty-days in length.[87] Sometimes months of the same length in days would come in sequence, and occasionally there seems even to have been a month of twenty-eight days, which is explained on the supposition that two months of twenty-nine days had come together but bad visibility had prevented the seeing of the crescent and the first month had been erroneously assigned thirty days. Whether the months were eventually determined by calculation instead of visual observation is not known.[88]

51. Twelve lunar months constituted the year, and the year began in the spring. The list in Table 9 gives the months in order together with their approximate equivalents in our calendar.[89]

TABLE 9. *The Babylonian Calendar*

Month		Month	
1. Nisanu	Mar/Apr	7. Tashritu	Sept/Oct
2. Aiaru	Apr/May	8. Arahsamnu	Oct/Nov
3. Simanu	May/June	9. Kislimu	Nov/Dec
4. Duzu	June/July	10. Tebetu	Dec/Jan
5. Abu	July/Aug	11. Shabatu	Jan/Feb
6. Ululu	Aug/Sept	12. Addaru	Feb/Mar

52. Twelve lunar months fell, of course, approximately eleven days short of the solar year. At first, the rectification of this discrepancy may have been made by simply taking the month which began nearest the vernal equinox as the first month of the new year. Later, the method of intercalating an additional month as necessary was employed. This system was developed by the Sumerians and Babylonians and was adopted by the Assyrians probably by the time of Tiglath-pileser I (c. 1114–c. 1076 B.C.).[90]

53. By the eighth century B.C. there is evidence that it was recognized in Babylonia that the insertion of seven additional lunar months within a nineteen-year period would closely approximate the additional time needed to stabilize the calendar. By the fourth century B.C. fixed points were established for these seven intercalations, and the nineteen-year cycle was fully standardized. The months added were a second Ululu, the sixth month, or a second Addaru, the twelfth month.[91]

---

in Mesopotamian art (*ANEP* Nos. 453, 518, etc.), and the god himself may be represented on the cylinder seal of an official of King Ur-Nammu of Ur (Hugo Gressman, *Altorientalische Bilder zum Alten Testament* [2d ed.; Berlin: W. de Gruyter, 1926], fig. 323).

[87] Mahler, *Handbuch,* 174, 180.

[88] PDBC 3.

[89] PDBC 26.

[90] Petrus van der Meer, *The Ancient Chronology of Western Asia and Egypt* (Leiden: Brill, 1947), 1–2.

[91] PDBC 1–2.

54. Since new-moon dates can be calculated astronomically for ancient Babylonia, and since the system of intercalation has been reconstructed on the basis of intercalary months actually mentioned in cuneiform texts, it is possible to construct tables which represent the Babylonian calendar with a high degree of probable accuracy.[92]

55. The achievement of the ancient Babylonian astronomers in devising the nineteen-year cycle with its seven intercalated months was indeed remarkable. It has been noted that one solar year equals 365.24219879 days while one lunar month equals 29.530588 days. Nineteen solar years, therefore, equals 6,939.601777 days. In nineteen 12-month years there are 228 months; adding seven more months equals 6,939.688180 days. Thus, the difference between 235 lunar months and 19 solar years is only 0.086403 day or 2 hours, 4 minutes, 25.22 seconds. This is how close the ancient Babylonian system came to solving the problem of the relationship between the lunar year and the solar year.[93]

56. How the system worked in actual practice may be seen in the accompanying tabulation (Table 10). This shows the first nineteen years of the reign of Nebuchadnezzar II (604–562 B.C.). The years are numbered and their equivalents in terms of B.C. are given. Leap years are indicated by an asterisk (*) by the year when first given. The month names are abbreviated; U II and A II mean a second Ululu and a second Addaru, respectively, where these are intercalated. From the source table,[94] which shows the first day of each month in terms of our Julian calendar, the number of days in each month is counted and it is this figure which is shown for each month. The total number of days for the nineteen years is 6,940; this is the nearest full number to the exact figure already noted above of 6,939.601777 days. Of the three columns headed "B.C.," the first shows the Julian year already in progress at the Babylonian new year in Nisanu (March–April); the second and third indicate the variable occurrence of the Julian new year with respect to the Babylonian month of Tebetu.

57. In Egypt, we saw that the complexity of the original lunar calendar led to the introduction of a simplified civil calendar with twelve months of thirty days each plus five additional days prior to the new year. In Mesopotamia, too, there was a second calendar of exactly this same sort which was used alongside the real lunar calendar. Since its twelve months of thirty days each, running on in regular sequence regardless of the real moon, were really standardized divisions of the solar year, this was a solar calendar or a "schematic calendar." In Babylonian documents many dates have been found which are evidently given in this schematic calendar, and, in some cases, it is not possible to prove whether it is the schematic calendar or the real lunar calendar which is intended. But

---

[92] PDBC 25, "a certain number of dates in our tables may be wrong by one day."

[93] Small as the difference is, it is precisely this discrepancy of 2 hour, 4 minutes, 25.22 seconds which provides the greatest complication in computing a perpetually fixed lunisolar calendar. Cf. Siegfried H. Horn, *JBL* 76 (1957): 169–170.

[94] PDBC 27–28.

TABLE 10. *The First Nineteen Years of Reign of Nebuchadnezzar II*

Year	*B.C.*	*Nis*	*Aia*	*Sim*	*Duz*	*Abu*	*Ulu*	*U II*	*Tas*	*Ara*	*Kis*	*B.C.*	*Teb*	*B.C.*	*Sha*	*Add*	*A II*	*Days in Year*
1	**(604)**	29	29	30	29	30	30		29	30	30		30	**603**	29	29		354
2	**(603)**	30	29	29	29	30	30	30	29	30	30	**602**	29		30	29		384
3	**(602)**	30	29	29	30	29	30		30	29	30	**601***	29		30	30		355
4	**(601)**	29	30	29	29	30	29		30	30	29		30	**600**	29	30		354
5	**(600)**	29	30	29	30	29	30	28	30	30	30	**599**	29		29	30		383
6	**(599)**	30	30	29	30	30	29		30	29	29		30	**598**	29	30		355
7	**(598)**	29	30	29	30	30	30	29	30	29	29	**597***	30		29	29		383
8	**(597)**	30	29	30	30	30	30		29	29	30	**596**	29		30	29		355
9	**(596)**	29	30	29	30	30	30	30	29	29	30	**595**	29		30	29		384
10	**(595)**	29	30	29	30	30	29		30	30	29	**594**	30		29	30		355
11	**(594)**	29	29	30	29	30	30		29	30	29	**593***	30		30	29	30	384
12	**(593)**	29	29	30	29	30	29		30	29	30	**592**	30		30	29		354
13	**(592)**	30	29	30	29	29	30		29	29	30	**591**	30		30	29		354
14	**(591)**	30	30	29	30	29	29		30	29	29		30	**590**	30	29	30	384
15	**(590)**	30	29	30	29	30	29		30	29	30	**589***	29		29	30		354
16	**(589)**	30	29	30	29	30	30		29	30	29	**588**	30		29	29		354
17	**(588)**	30	29	30	29	30	30		30	29	30		29	**587**	30	29	29	384
18	**(587)**	30	29	30	29	30	30		30	29	30	**586**	29		30	29		355
19	**(586)**	29	30	29	29	30	30		30	30	29	**585**	30		29	30		355
																	Total	6940

whereas the schematic calendar became the generally used civil calendar in Egypt, in Babylonia it seems to have been the lunar calendar which remained in most general usage, and Mesopotamia has been called "the classical country of the strictly lunar calendar";[95] while with the Babylonian system of intercalation to make adjustment to the solar year as well, it became the country of a truly remarkable lunisolar calendar.[96]

3. The Israelite Calendar

LITERATURE: Julian **Morgenstern**, "The Three Calendars of Ancient Israel," *HUCA* 1 (1924): 13–78; idem, "Supplementary Studies in the Calendars of Ancient Israel," *HUCA* 10 (1935): 1–148; idem, "The New Year for Kings," in *Occident and Orient: Gaster Anniversary Volume* (ed. Bruno Schindler; London, Taylor's Foreign Press, 1936), 439–456; idem, "The Chanukkah Festival and the Calendar of Ancient Israel," *HUCA* 20 (1947): 1–136; 21 (1948): 365–496; J. B. **Segal**, "Intercalation and the Hebrew Calendar," *VT* 7 (1957): 250–307.

58. The Gezer Calendar is a small limestone tablet, about four inches long and three inches wide, found at Tell Jezer in Palestine, the probable site of the Old Testament city of Gezer (Judg 1:29, etc.). On it is written, in good biblical Hebrew and perhaps simply as a schoolboy's exercise, a list of the months and the agricultural work done in them. The date of the text is probably around 925 B.C. It reads:

> His two months are (olive) harvest,
> His two months are planting (grain),
> His two months are late planting;
> His month is hoeing up of flax,
> His month is harvest of barley,
> His month is harvest and feasting.
> His two months are vine-tending,
> His month is summer fruit.[97]

The word used for "month" is ירח, and the months are obviously grouped and designated according to the type of agricultural work done in them. Since the agricultural seasons in Palestine are well known (§31), including the ripening of the olive crop in Sept/Oct–Oct/Nov, the shooting into ear of the barley in Mar/Apr, and the subsequent barley harvest in Apr/May,[98] it is possible to tabulate the sequence of months in the Gezer Calendar together with their equivalents in the outline of the year in Table 11.

---

[95]O. Neugebauer, *JNES* 1 (1942): 398–401.

[96]Ben Zion Wacholder and David B. Weinberg, "Visibility of the New Moon in Cuneiform and Rabbinic Sources," *HUCA* 42 (1972): 228.

[97]W. F. Albright, *ANET* 320 (*ANEA* 209f.); cf. *BASOR* 92 (Dec 1943): 16–20; Sabatino Moscati, *L'epigrafia ebraica antica, 1935–1950* (Rome: Pontifical Biblical Institute, 1951), 8–26.

[98]The harvest of barley begins in the Jordan Valley about the middle of April and in the highlands up to a month later. J. W. Paterson in HDB 1: 49.

TABLE 11. *The Months of the Gezer Calendar*

	Hebrew Months	*Agricultural Task*	*Julian Equivalent*
1	2 months	Olive harvest	Sept/Oct
2			Oct/Nov
3	2 months	Planting grain	Nov/Dec
4			Dec/Jan
5	2 months	Late planting	Jan/Feb
6			Feb/Mar
7	1 month	Hoeing flax	Mar/Apr
8	1 month	Harvest of barley	Apr/May
9	1 month	Harvest and festivity	May/June
10	2 months	Vine tending	June/July
11			July/Aug
12	1 month	Summer fruit	Aug/Sept

We see, therefore, that at this time in Palestine the year was reckoned as beginning in the fall, and that it contained twelve months which were related to agriculture.

59. Turning to the Hebrew Scriptures we find a group of month names which are connected with agriculture and climate. These are as follows: (1) the month Abib.[99] This word means a "fresh ear" of grain, as in Lev 2:14, and is used of barley when it is "in ear," as in Exod 9:31; hence used as a month name and with the article, "the Abib," it refers to the period when the barley shoots into ear. (2) The month Ziv.[100] This term signifies "splendor" and is used of the "beauty of flowers;" hence the month name refers to the time of flowers. (3) The month Etanim.[101] Coming from a word which means "permanent," this term is used in the plural and with the article as a month name which refers to "the permanent streams." (4) The month Bul.[102] The word probably refers to a period of "rain." (5) In a modern archaeological discovery, an ink inscription on a clay jar found at Arad, to be dated at the beginning of the sixth century B.C., mentions the third day of the month of Tsakh. This makes it possible to think that this month name occurs in Isa 18:4 where the phrase כחם צח, formerly translated "like clear heat" (RSV), may now be rendered, "like the heat of the month of Tsakh." Since the word is evidently connected with heat, Tsakh must be one of the summer months.[103] Of the foregoing words both Etanim and Bul have also been found as month names in North Semitic inscriptions,[104] hence these names, and probably others like them for other months, were no doubt common property among various Semitic peoples in this part of the world. We may call them the Canaanite month names.

---

[99] חדש האביב, Exod 13:4; 23:15; 34:18; Deut 16:1.
[100] חדש זו, 1 Kgs 6:1; ירח זו, 1 Kgs 6:37.
[101] ירח האתנים, 1 Kgs 8:2
[102] ירח בול, 1 Kgs 6:38.
[103] *PEQ* (Jan–June 1963): 3–4.
[104] Mark Lizbarski, *Handbuch der nordsemitischen Epigraphik nebst ausgewählten Inschriften* (Weimar: Felber, 1898), 1:231, 236, 412.

60. Since Abib is, by the etymology of the name, the month when the barley shoots into the ear, we know that it must have been approximately equivalent to Mar/Apr (§31), and it may therefore be equated with the seventh month in the list of the Gezer Calendar. According to Deut 16:1, Abib is the month of the Passover, and according to Exod 12:2f., the Passover is held in the first month. This manner of reference makes Abib the first month rather than the seventh, and must simply represent a time when the year was reckoned as beginning in the spring rather than the fall and when the months were numbered from the spring. Similarly Ziv, the month of flowers, must be a spring month, and in 1 Kgs 6:1 its name is followed by the explanation, "which is the second month." Likewise Bul, the month of rain, must be the month of "early rain" or Oct/Nov (§31), and it is called the eighth month in 1 Kgs 6:38. Etanim, too, is named as the seventh month in 1 Kgs 8:2. Showing, then, the months numbered both from the fall and from the spring, the Canaanite month names fit into the calendar as shown in Table 12.

TABLE 12. *The Canaanite Month Names*

Alternative Orderings		*Canaanite Month*	*Julian Equivalent*
1	7	Etanim	Sept/Oct
2	8	Bul	Oct/Nov
3	9		Nov/Dec
4	10		Dec/Jan
5	11		Jan/Feb
6	12		Feb/Mar
7	1	Abib	Mar/Apr
8	2	Ziv	Apr/May
9	3		May/June
10	4		June/July
11	5	Tsakh(?)	July/Aug
12	6		Aug/Sept

61. As far as the evidence goes, then, the early Israelite calendar, and the Canaanite calendar from which it borrowed, were of lunar character—the basic unit was the month and the name "month" was the name of the moon. Based on observation of the moon, the months tended to alternate between 29 and 30 days in length, thus averaging 29½ days and making a lunar year of 354 days or 50½ weeks ($29.5 \times 12 = 354$; $354 \div 7 = 50.571428$).[105] At the same time, it is probably not without significance that of the month names preserved in the Hebrew Scriptures Etanim and Bul are the first two months of the fall and Abib and Ziv are the first two of the spring. These are not only times of special importance in Palestinian agriculture but also the times of the two equinoxes when day and night are of equal length (presently reckoned at Mar 20 and Sept 22). Both the changing seasons of agriculture are, of course, broadly speaking, dependent upon the sun, and the changing lengths of day and night are, more exactly speaking, controlled by the sun. Therefore, it must have been at a

[105]Roger T. Beckwith, *RQ* 9 (1977): 85.

relatively early time that attention was called to the solar year as well as the lunar year, and it was necessarily to be observed that the lunar year of 354 days fell progressively out of line with the solar year and that rectification of some sort was called for. A way to maintain the months of a lunar year of approximately 354 days and make adjustment to the solar year of approximately 365 and a quarter days is to insert an additional month every two or three years. A study of the problem and the relevant evidence concludes that such intercalation—on the basis of agricultural and astronomical observation—was carried out in Israel in the early period of the monarchy and before the exile, and that, in addition to observation, computation of the requirements of intercalation was probably in use among the Jews in the second century B.C. and certainly in the first century A.D.[106]

62. The supposition is, therefore, that the Israelite calendar is originally lunar, with close relationship to agricultural and climatic factors, and that as it was harmonized more accurately with the movements of the celestial bodies it was primarily the relationship to the sun that was kept in view; thus the calendar became lunisolar.[107] In this period both Egyptian and Phoenician influences were strong in Israel, and both would be expected to have contributed to the solar emphasis. As far as Egypt is concerned, this was the great power which cast its shadow over Palestine until the defeat of Pharaoh Necho by Nebuchadnezzar in 605 B.C. In Egypt the sun was very prominent, as evidenced by the numerous sun deities in the pantheon, and by the occurrence of the schematic solar calendar (§40).

63. As far as Phoenicia is concerned, we know that Solomon, who reigned shortly before the time ascribed to the Gezer Calendar, entered into close relationships with Hiram, King of Tyre, particularly for help in the building of the temple at Jerusalem (1 Kgs 5, etc.). According to Josephus,[108] Hiram built new temples to Astarte and Herakles, which suggests interest in the celestial bodies, particularly including the sun, since Astarte was generally associated with the planet Venus or with the moon, and Herakles was connected with the sun especially in Phoenicia. According to Porphyry (A.D. 233–c. 304) who was born in Phoenicia, probably at Tyre, the Phoenicians gave the name of Herakles to the sun and considered the twelve labors of Herakles to represent the passage of the sun through the twelve signs of the zodiac.[109]

64. At Jerusalem, the temple which Hiram helped Solomon build may have been so constructed that the sun shone directly in through its eastern gate

[106]J. B. Segal, "Intercalation and the Hebrew Calendar," *VT* 7 (1957): 250–307, esp. 256–259, 284, 300–301.

[107]Mahler, *Handbuch,* 173; Bickerman, *Chronology of the Ancient World,* 24: "The pre-Babylonian time reckoning of the Hebrews is virtually unknown. It is certain that the calendar was lunisolar."

[108]*Ag. Apion* 1.18; *Ant.* 8.146.

[109]Quoted by Eusebius, *Praeparatio evangelica* 3.11.25, ed. Karl Mras, *Eusebius Werke* (GCS; Berlin: Akademie-Verlag, 1954), 8.1.139–140. Cf. Charles Anthon, *A Classical Dictionary* (New York: Harper, 1843), 599.

on the two equinoctial days of the year,[110] and we find later that Josiah "removed the horses that the kings of Judah had dedicated to the sun, at the entrance to the house of the Lord" and "burned the chariots of the sun with fire" (2 Kgs 23:11), and that again in Ezekiel's time men stood at the door of the temple, "with their backs to the temple of the Lord, and their faces toward the east, worshipping the sun toward the east" (Ezek 8:16). After the exile, however, it was the Babylonian calendar that was the most influential in Palestine.

4. The Babylonian Calendar in Palestine

LITERATURE: Solomon **Gandz**, "Studies in the Hebrew Calendar," *Proceedings of the American Academy for Jewish Research* 17 (1947–48): 9–17; idem, "Studies in the Hebrew Calendar," *JQR* 39 (1948–49): 259–280; 40 (1949–50): 157–172; 251–277; idem, "The Calendar of the *Seder Olam,*" in *JQR* 43 (1952–53): 177–192; 240–270; Elias **Auerbach**, "Die babylonische Datierung im Pentateuch und das Alter des Priester-Kodex," in *VT* 2 (1952): 334–342.

65. In the foregoing discussion of the Israelite calendar, it has been noted that the month names Abib, Ziv, Etanim, and Bul appear in the Old Testament, that these are probably the old Canaanite designations, and that in some instances the occurrences of the names is followed by an explanatory statement indicating, for example, that Ziv is the second month, Etanim is the seventh month, and so on. These numerical equivalents look as if they were added to the records at a time when the old names were no longer so commonly employed and when a different system had come into use, namely a designation of the months by number alone. Such a system is actually found elsewhere in Kings (1 Kgs 12:32, etc.), Jeremiah (1:3, etc.), Ezekiel (1:1, etc.), and many other books of the Old Testament, and all of the months from the first to the twelfth are so designated. Likewise, in the majority of the apocryphal and pseudepigraphical writings, the same system of indicating the months by number is followed.[111]

66. It has also been noted that in the earlier system the months were listed from the fall, but in the new system, where the months are designated by number, the numbering begins in the spring. In addition to evidence already cited, there is a plain example of the latter usage when Jer 36:9 mentions the ninth month and the following verse 22 indicates that it was in the winter: counting from the fall, the ninth month would be in summer; counting from the spring, the ninth month would be in winter.

67. The beginning of the year in the spring is in accordance with what we have seen was the usage in Mesopotamia, and it is therefore a reasonable surmise that the new calendrical system was derived from that source. The latest contemporary use of the old Canaanite names is probably in Deut 16:1.[112] The book of Deuteronomy is commonly supposed to have been edited in connection

---

[110] Julian Morgenstern, *HUCA* 6 (1929): 16–19.
[111] Morgenstern, *HUCA* 1 (1924): 19.
[112] Morgenstern, *HUCA* 1 (1924): 18.

with the reformation of Josiah and found in the temple in 621 B.C. (2 Kgs 22:8).[113] The new system no doubt came to Jerusalem after the Babylonian conquest of the city (586 B.C.) when the Jews began to reckon years by the regnal years of the Babylonian kings (e.g., 2 Kgs 24:12).[114]

68. That the new system of months numbered from a point of beginning in the spring was really the Babylonian system is shown by the fact that the Babylonian names for the months are also found later in the Old Testament. In a number of passages in Esther and Zechariah the month is cited first by number and then by name. The months which so appear are: "the first month, which is the month of Nisan" (Esth 3:7); "the third month, which is the month of Sivan" (Esth 8:9); "the ninth month, which is Chislev" (Zech 7:1); "the tenth month, which is the month of Tebeth" (Esth 2:16); "the eleventh month, which is the month of Shebat" (Zech 1:7); and "the twelfth month which is the month of Adar" (Esth 3:7, etc.). In Ezra and Nehemiah the month is sometimes referred by number (Ezra 7:8, etc.; Neh 7:73, etc.), but in the following cases is cited by name alone: Nisan (Neh 2:1), Elul (Neh 6:15), Chislev (Neh 1:1); Adar (Ezra 6:15). The sources just cited are generally considered to be among the latest books in the Old Testament, and thus the use of these month names must have begun relatively late, perhaps from the fourth century B.C. on.[115] The first work in which only the Babylonian names are employed is probably *Megillat Ta'anit,* the *Scroll of Feasting.* This is essentially a list of thirty-six Jewish festivals, written probably just after the beginning of the first century A.D. The book is divided into twelve chapters, corresponding to the twelve months. The first chapter treats the memorial days of the first month, Nisan, and so on to the twelfth chapter which deals with those of the twelfth month, Adar.[116]

69. The fact that the numbering of the months according to the Babylonian system came into use among the Jews before the actual month names were adopted may indicate a complex evolution,[117] but would seem to be explicable most simply on the grounds that the numbers did not carry the associations of pagan religions which some of the names did. Thus the month Tammuz (Babylonian Duzu) bore the name of the famous dying god of Mesopotamia, wept by the women of Jerusalem to the distress of Ezekiel (8:14); and the month Elul may have meant "shouting for joy" in the celebration of the restoration to life of the same deity.[118]

70. As a result of the development just sketched, then, the list of months in use among the Jews at the end of the Old Testament period was as shown in Table 13.[119]

---

[113]Robert H. Pfeiffer, *Introduction to the Old Testament* (5th ed.; New York: Harper, 1941), 181.

[114]Bickerman in BIBOR 22 (1965): 184.

[115]Morgenstern, *HUCA* 1 (1924): 20.

[116]Hans Lichtenstein, *HUCA* 8–9 (1931–32): 257–351; J. Z. Lauterbach, *JE* 8: 427–428.

[117]Morgenstern, *HUCA* 1 (1924): 21.

[118]I. Abrahams, HDB 4: 765.

[119]PDBC 24.

TABLE 13. *The Babylonian Calendar in Palestine*

Number	*Babylonian Name*	*Hebrew Name*		*Julian Equivalent*
1	Nisanu	ניסן	Nisan	Mar/Apr
2	Aiaru	איר	Iyyar	Apr/May
3	Simanu	סיון	Sivan	May/June
4	Duzu	תמוז	Tammuz	June/July
5	Abu	אב	Ab	July/Aug
6	Ululu	אלול	Elul	Aug/Sept
7	Tashritu	תשרי	Tishri	Sept/Oct
8	Arahsamnu	מרחשון	Marheshvan, or Heshvan	Oct/Nov
9	Kislimu	כסלו	Kislev	Nov/Dec
10	Tebetu	טבת	Tebet	Dec/Jan
11	Shabatu	שבט	Shevat	Jan/Feb
12	Addaru	אדר	Adar	Feb/Mar

71. The Babylonian calendar was, as we have seen (§§50ff.), essentially lunisolar. The months began with the first appearing of the crescent of the new moon in the evening sky, which made months for the most part of alternately twenty-nine and thirty days in length so that twelve of these lunar months made a year of 354 days, while the intercalation of seven months in nineteen years kept the year of lunar months in close approximation to the solar year (§52). The opinion has also been noted (§61) that intercalation was practiced in Israel from the early monarchy on, and the question which now arises is whether and to what extent, along with the Babylonian numbers and names of the months (§67), the full Babylonian system of intercalation was also adopted in Palestine, and when. On the one hand, it is held that the nineteen-year cycle of the Babylonian system (§53) was only introduced among the Jewish rabbis between the fourth and seventh centuries A.D.,[120] and caution is advised in the use of calendars and astronomy for chronological purposes.[121] On the other hand, there is much to make it look as if, in general, the Babylonian system came to prevail relatively early, but with some variations in Jewish practice from the Babylonian. Information (see immediately below) from the Mishna (second century B.C. to second century A.D.) reflects careful observation and not a little accurate knowledge of the relationships of sun and moon, texts from Qumran show attention to both lunisolar and solar calendars and their equivalences, and the rotation of the priestly courses also provided data for timekeeping. We may believe, therefore, that available materials, especially including the tables of Babylonian chronology (PDBC, see our §54), provide basis for high probabilities if not for complete assurance on many of the dates with which we are concerned. Further details about Jewish practice in the regulation of the calendar will appear in the sources which will be cited next.

72. In Palestine, it was the responsibility of the Sanhedrin in Jerusalem to determine matters connected with the calendar, and in practice this was done by a council of three men.

[120]Wacholder and Weinberg, *HUCA* 42 (1971): 227–242.

[121]Roger T. Beckwith, "Cautionary Notes on the Use of Calendars and Astronomy to Determine the Chronology of the Passion," *CKC* 183–205.

73. As in Babylonia, the month began when the new moon was first seen in the evening, but since the new moon was visible at Jerusalem thirty-seven minutes before it was visible at Babylon, it was possible that upon occasion the new month would begin a day earlier than in Babylonia.[122] The determination that the new moon had actually appeared and the declaration that the new month had thereby begun had to be made by the council just referred to, and the rules according to which this was done are presented and discussed in the Midrash in the tractate *Rosh Hashanah.*[123] The testimony of at least two witnesses was required to establish that the new moon had been seen. So important were the observations of these witnesses that, for the fixing of the new moons of Nisan and Tishri, the pivotal points of the year in the spring and fall, they might even exceed the travel limit of two thousand cubits on the Sabbath day to bring their report to Jerusalem.[124] In Jerusalem there was a special courtyard where the witnesses were examined and entertained. In earlier time, if they came on the Sabbath day, they could not leave this place the whole day because they had doubtless already used up their allowed travel distance, but Rabbi Gamaliel the Elder ruled that they could go two thousand cubits from it.[125] In the examination of the witnesses they were asked five questions, which were phrased so as to be understandable by ordinary observers, but which showed real astronomical knowledge on the part of the examiners: "Tell us how you saw the moon: facing the sun or turned away from it? to the north or to the south? how high was it? to which side was it leaning? and how broad was it?" The point of the second query, for example, lay in the fact that the new moon always appears due west; hence in the summer when the sun sets in the northwest the new moon is seen to the south of the sun, in the winter it is to the north of the sun.[126] More complex relationships of moon and sun are reflected in other queries. Rabbi Gamaliel II (about A.D. 80–116) had pictures of the various shapes of the moon on a tablet and on the wall of his upper chamber, and used these in the questioning of witnesses.[127] A study of *Rosh Hashanah* 2:6 and related sources concludes that, while witnesses were not required to be knowledgeable in astronomy, the examiners were able to deal with the main elements in a lunar theory, such as a solar longitude and declination, lunar longitude and elongation, latitude and declination, and parallax.[128]

74. When it was determined that the new moon had been seen, the beginning of the new month was proclaimed. On the scriptural warrant of Lev 23:44 where "Moses declared . . . the appointed feasts of the Lord," this was done by the solemn declaration of the head of the Sanhedrin that the new moon was "sanctified."[129] Also, a trumpet was sounded,[130] as it is said in Psa 81:3,

---

[122]PDBC 23–24.

[123]1:3–3:1; 18z–25b; Danby 188–191; Epstein, *BT* 73–115; cf. *Sanhedrin* 1:2; Danby 382.

[124]*Rosh Hashanah* 19b; Epstein, *BT* 81 n.4.

[125]*Rosh Hashanah* 2:5; 23b; Epstein, *BT* 101.

[126]*Rosh Hashanah* 2:6; 23b–24a; Epstein, *BT* 102f.

[127]*Rosh Hashanah* 2:8; 24a; Epstein, *BT* 105.

[128]Ernest Wiesenberg, "Elements of a Lunar Theory in the Mishnah, Rosh Hashanah 2:6, and the Talmudic Complements Thereto," *HUCA* 33 (1962): 153–196.

[129]*Rosh Hashanah* 2:7; 24a; Epstein, *BT* 104.

[130]*Rosh Hashanah* 3:3; 26a; Epstein, *BT* 115.

"Blow the trumpet at the new moon." At one time flares were lighted also to signal the new month, but when the Samaritans introduced confusion by lighting misleading flares, messengers were sent out instead.[131]

75. While it was considered "a religious duty to sanctify [the new moon] on the strength of actual observation,"[132] it was also recognized that conditions might be such that the actual visual sighting could not be made and, in this case, it was established that one month would have thirty days and the next twenty-nine. The month with twenty-nine days was considered "deficient" by half a day, the month with thirty days was "full," being half a day over the true lunar period. It was agreed that the year should not have less than five nor more than seven "full" months. At least in post-Talmudic times Nisan, Sivan, Ab, Tishri, Chislev, and Shevat had thirty days, and Iyyar, Tammuz, Elul, Heshvan, Tebeth, and Adar had twenty-nine. The science by which these determinations were made was known as the "fixing of the month" or as the "sanctification of the new moon."[133]

76. In his work entitled *Sanctification of the New Moon,* Maimonides (A.D. 1135–1204) gives in chapters 1–5 a description of the way in which the calendar was anciently regulated by the Sanhedrin, and in his description of the manner of determining the new moon, he shows that calculation as well as observation was employed. Maimonides writes:[134]

> Just as the astronomers who discern the positions and motions of the stars engage in calculation, so the Jewish court, too, used to study and investigate and perform mathematical operations, in order to find out whether or not it would be possible for the new crescent to be visible in its "proper time," which is the night of the 30th day. If the members of the court found that the new moon might be visible, they were obliged to be in attendance at the court house for the whole 30th day and be on the watch for the arrival of witnesses. If witnesses did arrive, they were duly examined and tested, and if their testimony appeared trustworthy, this day was sanctified as New Moon Day. If the new crescent did not appear and no witnesses arrived, this day was counted as the 30th day of the old month, which thus became an embolismic[135] month.

77. It was also necessary for the same council of the Sanhedrin to determine when an intercalary month should be added to the year. There is a discussion of "the intercalating of the year" in the tractate *Sanhedrin*.[136] Here, in addition to mention of the council of three, it is also stated that "A year cannot be intercalated unless the Nasi sanctions it."[137] The Nasi was the "prince" or chief

---

[131]*Rosh Hashanah* 2:2–4; 22b–23b; Epstein, *BT* 96–100.

[132]*Rosh Hashanah* 20a; Epstein, *BT* 81.

[133]*JE* 3: 499–500 (Cyrus Adler); 502–503 (M. Friedländer).

[134]*The Code of Maimonides,* Book Three, Treatise Eight, *Sanctification of the New Moon* (trans. by Solomon Gandz, with introduction by Julian Obermann, and astronomical commentary by Otto Neugebauer; Yale Judaica Series 11; New Haven, Yale University Press, 1956), 4–5 (1:6).

[135]That is, a month containing an added day.

[136]1:2; Danby 382; 10b–13b; Epstein, *BT* 42–61.

[137]11a; Epstein, *BT* 47.

of the Sanhedrin, and it would appear that he might or might not be a member of the council of three. An example is given where "Rabban Gamaliel was away obtaining permission from the Governor of Syria,"[138] and as his return was delayed, the year was intercalated subject to Rabban Gamaliel's later approval.[139]

78. The rabbis taught, it is stated, that "a year may be intercalated on three grounds: on account of the premature state of the corn crops; or that of the fruit trees; or on account of the lateness of the *tequfah*. Any two of these reasons can justify intercalation, but not one alone."[140] The minute calculations involved are referred to, and an example is given where the rabbis did not finish their calculation until the last day of the month preceding the month to be intercalated.[141] In Babylonia, as we saw, either a second Ululu or a second Addaru might be inserted in the year, but here it is stated flatly that "only an Adar can be intercalated."[142] When the intercalation took place the added month was called the Second Adar,[143] and the year with a Second Adar was a "leap" year (§39) in contrast with an ordinary year. The length of the added month was left to the judgment of the council, and it might be either twenty-nine or thirty days in length.[144] Leap years were frequent and fell, on average, rather more than once in three years.[145]

79. In the same tractate letters are quoted which were sent out by Rabbi Simeon ben Gamaliel and Rabban Gamaliel II. Simeon, son of Gamaliel I and head of the Sanhedrin in the two decades before the destruction of the temple, wrote as follows: "We beg to inform you that the doves are still tender and the lambs still young, and the grain has not yet ripened. I have considered the matter and thought it advisable to add thirty days to the year." The letter of Gamaliel II differs only in that he, more modestly as the Talmud observes, associates his "colleagues" with himself in the decision of intercalation.[146]

80. In agreement with the foregoing, Maimonides[147] also gives a lucid account of the process of intercalation as conducted under the Sanhedrin. Noting that the solar year exceeds the lunar year by approximately eleven days, he says that whenever this excess accumulates to about thirty days, or a little more or less, one month is added and the particular year is made to consist of thirteen months. The extra month is never anything other than an added Adar, and hence an intercalated year has a First Adar and a Second Adar. This added

---

[138]Probably to obtain confirmation of his appointment as Nasi rather than to secure permission for intercalating the year, since it seems unlikely that the latter would have been required.

[139]11a; Epstein, *BT* 47.

[140]11b; Epstein, *BT* 49.

[141]12b; Epstein, *BT* 57.

[142]12b; Epstein, *BT* 55.

[143]The book of Esther was specified to be read in the month Adar, and in *Megillah* 1:4 (Danby 202) it is discussed whether, if the book has already been read in the First Adar and the year is subsequently intercalated, it must be read again in the Second Adar.

[144]11a; Epstein, *BT* 48.

[145]Roger T. Beckwith, *RQ* 9 (1977): 83.

[146]11a–11b; Epstein, *BT* 47–49.

[147]*Sanctification of the New Moon,* 1:2; 4:1–17. ed. Gandz, 4, 16–22.

month may consist of either twenty-nine or thirty days. The decision is made by the Council of Intercalation, with a minimum membership of three; if the *nasi* or chief of the supreme court was not one of them, his assent was also necessary. Continuing with his own exposition of the mathematics involved, Maimonides states that each group of nineteen years contains seven intercalated years and twelve ordinary years.[148] Therefore, in spite of the fact that the Jewish system used only added Adars, the result was the same as in the Babylonian system and seven months were intercalated in nineteen years.

81. Both the tractate *Sanhedrin* and Maimonides[149] also show that the solar year was divided likewise into four seasons or *tequfot* and into twelve signs of the zodiac (§§34–36). On the basis of a year of 365¼ days, one *tequfah* was reckoned at 91 days, 7½ hours. The four *tequfot* were: the *tequfah* of Nisan, which began at the vernal equinox when the sun enters the constellation of Aries; the *tequfah* of Tammuz at the summer solstice when the sun enters Cancer; the *tequfah* of Tishri at the autumnal equinox when the sun enters Libra; and the *tequfah* of Tebet at the winter solstice when the sun enters Capricorn.

5. The Calendar at Qumran

LITERATURE: William H. **Brownlee**, *The Dead Sea Manual of Discipline* (BASOR Supplementary Studies 10–12; New Haven: American Schools of Oriental Research, 1951); S. **Talmon**, "Yom Hakkippurim in the Habakkuk Scroll," in *Biblica* 32 (1951): 549–563; H. H. **Rowley**, *The Zadokite Fragments and the Dead Sea Scrolls* (Oxford: Blackwell, 1952); A. **Jaubert**, "Le calendrier des Jubilés et de la secte de Qumrân, ses origines bibliques," in *VT* 3 (1953): 250–264; D. **Barthélemy** and J. T. **Milik**, eds., *Qumran Cave I* (Discoveries in the Judaean Desert 1; Oxford: Clarendon, 1955); Millar **Burrows**, *The Dead Sea Scrolls* (New York: Viking, 1955); Theodor H. **Gaster**, *The Dead Sea Scriptures in English Translation* (Garden City, N.Y.: Doubleday Anchor, 1956); J. T. **Milik**, *Ten Years of Discovery in the Wilderness of Judaea* (Studies in Biblical Theology 26; Naperville, Ill.; Alec R. Allenson, 1959), 107–110; Ernst E. **Ettisch**, "Die Gemeinderegel und der Qumrankalender," *RQ* 9 (1961): 125–133; Roger T. **Beckwith**, "The Modern Attempt to Reconcile the Qumran Calendar with the True Solar Year," *RQ* 7 (1970): 379–396.

82. In the Jewish community at Qumran, known through the now famous Dead Sea Scrolls and probably to be identified or connected with the Essenes described in Josephus,[150] Philo,[151] and Pliny,[152] there was a special interest in and emphasis upon times, seasons, and the calendar. The *Manual of Discipline* (1QS) describes the members of the covenant as desiring to walk before God "perfectly in all things that are revealed according to their appointed seasons" (I, 8–9; III, 10). They are also "not to advance their times, nor to lag

---

[148]*Sanctification of the New Moon,* 6:10 ed. Gandz, 29.

[149]*Sanhedrin* 11b; Epstein, *BT* 49 and n.5; Maimonides, *Sanctification of the New Moon,* 9:2–3, ed. Gandz, 36f.

[150]*Ant.* 18.18–22; *War* 2.119–161.

[151]*Every Good Man is Free* 75–91.

[152]*Nat. Hist.* 5.15.

behind any of their seasons" (I, 14–15). Likewise the duties of the council of fifteen include "the proper reckoning of the time" (VIII, 4),[153] while the wise man is admonished "to walk . . . according to the proper reckoning of every time," "to do God's will according to all that has been revealed for any time at that time, and to study all the wisdom found with reference to the times" (LX, 12–13).

83. Again in the latter part of our copy of the same *Manual* there is a long poem in which it is told how the devout worshiper blesses God at different times and seasons. The section with which we are concerned begins as follows (LX, 26–X, 1):

> With an offering of the lips he shall bless Him
> During the periods which Aleph ordained:
> At the beginning of the dominion of light with its circuit;
> And at its withdrawal to the habitation of its ordinance.

84. Aleph is the first letter of the Hebrew word for God (אלהים, *'Elohim*) and is probably used here as a somewhat mysterious abbreviation for God. The "beginning of the dominion of light" is evidently dawn. In this connection it may be noted that Josephus says it was the custom of the Essenes to offer certain traditional prayers "before the sun is up" and "as though entreating him to rise,"[154] and in another passage reports them as regarding the rays of the sun as "the rays of the deity" (τὰς αὐγὰς τοῦ θεοῦ).[155] The word "circuit" (תקופתו, *tequfato*) is the same that is used in Psa 19:6[156] for the circuit of the sun. The withdrawal of the light is likewise sunset, and the word (אסף, *'asaf*) is the same that is also used in the Old Testament for the setting of moon (Isa 60:20) and stars (Joel 2:10). Thus, sunrise and sunset were taken account of by the community as times of worship.

85. After this the poem mentions the time "when luminaries shine from the abode of holiness" (X, 2–3). The word "luminaries" (מאורות, *me'orot*) is the same as that translated "lights" in Gen 1:14, and the "abode of holiness" (זבול קודש, *zebul qodesh*) is the same as the "holy habitation" of God in Isa 63:15. According to Gen 2:14 the "lights" serve "for signs and for seasons and for days and years," and the Qumran community undoubtedly looked to the heavenly bodies for the marking out of periods of time.

86. Using the same word "seasons" (מועדים, *mo'adim*) as in Gen 1:14, the poem next speaks of "the coming together of seasons to the days of the new moon" (X, 3). This probably means in effect, "whenever the days and nights add up to a month,"[157] and indicates concern with this unit of time.

87. Following this the characters mem and nun are introduced into the poem (X, 4). As seemed probable in the case of the aleph above (X, 1), there

---

[153]Another translation, however, is simply, "in conduct appropriate to every occasion" (Gaster, *DSS* 55).

[154]*War* 2.128.

[155]*War* 2.148.

[156]Verse 7 in the Hebrew text.

[157]Brownlee, *Manual of Discipline,* 39 n. 13.

was doubtless also an esoteric meaning attaching to these letters. Mem, it may be noted, is the first letter of the word "luminaries" and also of the word "seasons." As it lends itself readily to doing, the letter nun is written in the manuscript in a form which looks like a simple key, and the text reads, "the sign Nun is for the unlocking of His eternal mercies, at the beginnings of seasons in every period that will be" (X, 4–5). Together aleph, mem and nun form the word "amen," and it seems probable that this acrostic is intended. A possible allusion contained in it would be to Isa 65:16 where it is said that "he who blesses himself in the land shall bless himself by the God of Amen,"[158] while the probable relationship to the calendar will be explained below (§111).

88. Having spoken of days and months, the poem refers also to times "at the beginnings of years at the completion of their terms" (X, 6). In this connection there is mention of how the seasons are joined to each other, namely "the season of reaping to the season of summer-fruit, the season of sowing to the season of green herbage" (X, 7), this manner of speech being reminiscent of the Gezer Calendar (§58). Then the poem speaks of the adding together of "seasons of years to their weeks, and the beginning of their weeks to a season of release" (X, 7–8). The week of years must refer to the provision found in Lev 25:1–7 according to which the children of Israel are to sow their fields for six years but in the seventh year to allow the land "a Sabbath of solemn rest;" and the season of release must be the "year of Jubilee" of Lev 25:8–55 when, after seven "weeks" of seven years, in the fiftieth year they are to proclaim liberty throughout the land and each return to his property and his family (§§224f.).

89. The *Zadokite Document* (CD) reveals a similar interest in times and seasons and shows that the covenant community believed that it was faithful to the divine laws in these regards, whereas all the rest of Israel had erred (III, 12–16 = 5:13): "But with them that held fast to the commandments of God who were left over of them, God established His covenant with Israel even until eternity, by revealing to them hidden things concerning which all Israel had gone astray. His holy Sabbaths and His glorious appointed times, His righteous testimonies and His true ways and the requirements of His desire, which man shall do and live thereby, these He laid open before them; and they digged a well for much water, and he that despises it shall not live."

90. Over against the failure of Israel otherwise, it was the undertaking of those who entered the covenant "to keep the Sabbath day according to its exact rules and the appointed days and the fast-day according to the finding of the members of the new covenant in the land of Damascus" (VI, 18–19 = 8:15). The "appointed days" must be those of the various religious festivals of the year. The "fast-day" (יום התענית, *yom hata'anit*), although only designated with the same general word for fasting which occurs in Ezra 9:5, is no doubt the most solemn fast of the year, the Day of Atonement (יום הכפרים, *yom hakippurim*), described in Lev 16 and 23:26–32, and in Acts 27:9 also called simply "the fast" (ἡ νηστεία).

---

[158]See the margin of the ASV, and cf. 2 Cor 1:20; Rev 3:14. Brownlee, *Manual of Discipline,* 38 n. 2.

91. Again, even as the *Manual of Discipline* referred to the "season of release" which must be the year of Jubilee, so the *Zadokite Fragment* says that "the exact statement of the epochs of Israel's blindness" can be learned "in the Book of the Divisions of Times into Their Jubilees and Weeks" (XVI, 2–4 = 20:1). This seems plainly enough to be a reference to the writing commonly called the *Book of the Jubilees,* the prologue of which begins: "This is the history of the division of the days of the law and of the testimony, of the events of the years, of their (year) weeks, of their Jubilees throughout all the years of the world."[159] Since two fragments of *Jubilees* were found in Cave 1 at Qumran (1WJub = 1Q17 and 18), it is evident that the work was used by this community.[160]

92. In the *Habakkuk Commentary* (1QpHab) there is reference to the observance by the community of the Day of Atonement *(yom hakippurim)*, and it is stated that "the wicked priest," an enemy for whom various identifications have been proposed, chose that very occasion to appear among them in order "to confound them and to make them stumble on the day of fasting, their Sabbath of rest" (XI, 6–8, commenting on Hab 2:15).[161] That the wicked priest could break in upon the community on this solemn occasion would suggest that they were celebrating the fast on a day other than that which he himself recognized, and thus again it is indicated that the Qumran group was separated from other Jews by its calendar of festivals and feasts.[162]

93. The foregoing references suggest, then, that the Qumran community had its own religious calendar and that this was similar to the calendar of *Jubilees*. This has been confirmed by the discovery, announced in 1956 by J. T. Milik, in Cave 4 at Qumran of an actual liturgical calendar. The fragments on which this is contained appear to belong, paleographically, to the first part of the first century A.D. The text is one of several which deal with the priestly courses (4Q Mishmarot, cf. §§237ff.), and the calendar gives the dates of service in rotation of the priestly families and the dates of the religious festivals. These dates are always stated in terms of days of the week and sometimes in days of the month. The liturgical days fall regularly on Wednesday, Friday, and Sunday. The Passover is celebrated on Tuesday evening. The offering of the sheaf of first fruits (Lev 23:11) falls on the twenty-sixth day of the first month, a Sunday. The New Year begins on the first day of the seventh month, a Wednesday. The Day of Atonement, the tenth day of the seventh month (Lev 16:29), comes on Friday. The Feast of Tabernacles, the fifteenth day of the seventh month (Lev 23:34), is on Wednesday. Occasionally, in the case of historical rather than liturgical dates, these are expressed in terms of Babylonian month names. This suggests that a calendar derived from Babylonia was in common use for everyday purposes, but that the other calendar, which was presumably more ancient, was adhered to for liturgical purposes.

---

[159]*APOT* 2:11.
[160]*DJD* 1:82–84.
[161]Burrows, *DSS* 370; cf. Gaster, *DSS* 255, 268f.
[162]See S. Talmon in *Biblica* 32 (1951): 549–563.

6. The Calendar of *Jubilees*

LITERATURE: R. H. **Charles**, *The Book of Jubilees or The Little Genesis* (London: Adam & Charles Black, 1902); idem, *APOT* 2:1–82; Julian **Morgenstern**, "The Calendar of the Book of Jubilees: Its Origin and Its Character," in *VT* 5 (1955): 34–76; A. **Jaubert**, "Le calendrier des Jubilés et les jours liturgiques de la semaine," *VT* 7 (1957): 35–61; E. R. **Leach**, "A Possible Method of Intercalation for the Calendar of the Book of Jubilees," *VT* 7 (1957): 392–397; Joseph M. **Baumgarten**, "The Beginning of the Day in the Calendar of Jubilees," *JBL* 77 (1958): 355–360; Klaus **Berger**, *Das Buch der Jubiläen* (part 3 of *Unterweisung in erzählender Form,* which is vol. 2 of the series Jüdische Schriften aus hellenistisch-römischer Zeit; Gütersloh: G. Mohn, 1961; for this series see below under LITERATURE for Early Jewish Chronographers, §253); J. C. **VanderKam**, *Textual and Historical Studies in the Book of Jubilees* (HSM 14; Missoula: Scholars Press, 1977); idem, *The Book of Jubilees* (CSCO 511; Scriptores aethiopici, tomus 88; Louvain: Peeters, 1989); idem, "Jubilees: How It Rewrote the Bible," BR 8, 6 (Dec 1992): 32–39, 60–62; Joseph M. **Baumgarten**, *Studies in Qumran Law* (Studies in Judaism in Late Antiquity 24; Leiden: Brill, 1977), 115–130.

94. In the foregoing discussion it has been established that the Qumran community was zealous in its observance of what it held to be correct times and seasons, that these were different from what other Jews adhered to, that in this connection the community cited and possessed the book of *Jubilees,* and that in fragments of an actual calendar found in Cave 4 at Qumran, historical dates are cited in Babylonian month names but liturgical dates are given in a system in which days of the week are fixed points as well as days of the month. The date of Passover, for example, is fixed by Old Testament law (Exod 12:6) as the evening of the fourteenth day of the first month of the year. It is evident that this date can readily be ascertained in terms of the Babylonian calendar, but that in this calendar the date will fall on different days of the week in different years. The Qumran liturgical calendar, however, also identifies the Passover date as the evening of Tuesday, hence this was a calendar in which the days of the week remained constant in relation to the days of the month. Since the clue is available that the community referred to *Jubilees* in the reckoning of time, it is necessary to ascertain if the calendar of *Jubilees* satisfies the condition just mentioned and to establish the nature of this calendar.

95. According to the evidence of the many available manuscripts and manuscript fragments, and quotations in ancient sources, *Jubilees* was written originally in Hebrew, translated from Hebrew into Greek and Syriac, and translated from Greek into Latin and Ethiopic.[163] The oldest complete manuscripts are the Ethiopic, and a critical edition of the Ethiopic, together with the evidence of the Syriac, Greek and Latin versions, provides the best knowledge of the original book.[164] That the original language of the book was Hebrew is confirmed by the fact that the Hebrew fragments from Qumran are the oldest witnesses to the text, and by the fact that the book itself calls Hebrew "the language of creation" (12:26).[165] On paleographic grounds the origin of the

---

[163] VanderKam, *Textual and Historical Studies.*
[164] VanderKam, *Book of Jubilees.*

Qumran fragments is put not later than 100 B.C., in more exact terms of historical relationships the composition of the original book was attributed by R. H. Charles to the period between 135 and 105 B.C.,[166] but is now more generally assigned to a time between 167 and 140 B.C. or more narrowly to the time between 145 and 140 B.C.[167] or to a time about 160–150 B.C.[168] Essentially, *Jubilees* is a rewriting of Genesis and Exodus, which books are regularly quoted or paraphrased in *Jubilees,* together with the insertion of additional material, with the provision of a precise chronological framework of years, weeks of years, and Jubilees, and with much emphasis upon the institution and proper observance of the festivals of the religious year. The whole is presented in the form of a communication from "the angel of the presence" to Moses on Mount Sinai when he went up to receive the stone tablets of the law and the commandments (Prologue and 1:27).

96. The passage in this book which tells most about the calendar is *Jub.* 6:23–32.

> And on the new moon of the first month, and on the new moon of the fourth month, and on the new moon of the seventh month, and on the new moon of the tenth month are the days of remembrance, and the days of the seasons in the four divisions of the year. These are written and ordained as a testimony for ever. And Noah ordained them for himself as feasts for the generations for ever, so that they have become thereby a memorial unto him. And on the new moon of the first month he was bidden to make for himself an ark, and on that (day) the earth became dry and he opened (the ark) and saw the earth. And on the new moon of the fourth month the mouths of the depths of the abyss beneath were closed. And on the new moon of the seventh month all the mouths of the abysses of the earth were opened, and the waters began to descend into them. And on the new moon of the tenth month the tops of the mountains were seen, and Noah was glad. And on this account he ordained them for himself as feasts for a memorial for ever, and thus are they ordained. And they placed them on the heavenly tablets, each had thirteen weeks; from one to another (passed) their memorial, from the third to the fourth. And all the days of the commandment will be two and fifty weeks of days, and (these will make) the entire year complete. Thus it is engraven and ordained on the heavenly tablets. And there is no neglecting (this commandment) for a single year or from year to year. And command thou the children of Israel that they observe the years according to this reckoning—three hundred and sixty-four days, and (these) will constitute a complete year, and they will not disturb its time from its days and from its feasts; for everything will fall out in them according to their testimony, and they will not leave out any day nor disturb any feasts.

---

[165]Berger, *Buch der Jubiläen,* 285–286.

[166]Charles, *Book of Jubilees*, xiii; *APOT* (1913), 2:1.

[167]Berger, *Buch der Jubiläen,* 300.

[168]VanderKam, *Textual and Historical Studies,* 207–288 (287: "almost certainly between 161 and 140 B.C. and probably between 161 and 152"); idem, *Book of Jubilees*, v ("between 161 and 152"); idem, *BR* 8, 6 (Dec 1992): 33 ("about 160–150").

From this we learn that the year was divided into four periods or seasons. The beginning of each of the four successive periods was marked by the "new moon," which probably means simply the "first day," of the first month, the fourth month, the seventh month, and the tenth month; in other words each period comprised three months. Each period also contained thirteen weeks. Since this equals 91 days, there must have been two months of 30 days each and one month of 31 days in each group of three months. The complete year was composed, therefore, as it is also explicitly stated, of 52 weeks or of 364 days.

97. The nature of the calendar just outlined will be discussed further in a moment, but first it is necessary to indicate that what seems to be the same system of reckoning is found in the book of *Enoch*. *Enoch*[169] is a large and composite work preserved in a number of Ethiopic manuscripts and Greek and Latin fragments. Of the 108 chapters into which it is customarily divided, chapters 72–82 are called the Book of the Heavenly Luminaries and constitute a treatise on the laws of the celestial bodies. This part, and at least much of the rest of the book, was probably written originally in Hebrew. This section must be referred to in *Jub.* 4:17 where it is said that Enoch "wrote down the signs of heaven according to the order of their months in a book, that men might know the seasons of the years according to the order of their separate months." This citation indicates a date earlier than *Jubilees* for the Book of the Heavenly Luminaries, sometime in the second century B.C., and also shows that the author of *Jubilees* held it in high regard and therefore presumably agreed with it as to calendar.

98. In the Book of the Heavenly Luminaries the motion of the sun is described (*1 Enoch* 72) in relation to twelve "portals" which must be equivalent to the signs of the zodiac. Beginning at what must be the vernal equinox, the sun rises, it is said, in the fourth of the six eastern portals. It comes forth through that portal thirty mornings in succession, during which time the day grows daily longer and the night nightly shorter. Moving into the fifth portal, the sun rises for thirty mornings; moving on into the sixth portal, it rises for thirty-one mornings. The relative lengths of the day and night continue to change, and by this time the day reaches its maximum duration and the night its minimum; in other words, it is the summer solstice. Then "the sun mounts up to make the day shorter and the night longer" (v. 15), and after thirty, thirty, and thirty-one mornings the day and night are of equal length; in other words, the autumnal equinox is reached. The corresponding sequence is followed on through the second half of the year until, at last, day and night are again of equal length and the cycle has been completed at the vernal equinox. So, it is concluded, "the year is exactly as to its days three hundred and sixty-four" (v. 32).

---

[169]Also known as *1 Enoch* or the *Ethiopic Enoch*. On the book see *APOT* 2:163–187; R. H. Charles in HDB 1: 705–708. For a date for all the principal sections of *1 Enoch* in the reign or shortly after the death of Antiochus Epiphanes see H. H. Rowley, *Jewish Apocalyptic and the Dead Sea Scrolls*, (London: University of London, Athlone Press, 1957), 8–9.

99. This certainly appears to be the same calendar as in *Jubilees,* and is of special importance because it answers a question on which specific information was not provided in *Jubilees,* namely, which month in each series of three months has the added day to make it thirty-one days in length. Here we learn that in each group of three months their respective lengths are thirty-days, thirty days, and thirty-one days.

100. We may, accordingly, outline a series of three months in the calendar of *Jubilees* and *1 Enoch* as shown in Table 14:[170]

TABLE 14. *The Months in the Calendar of* Jubilees

I. IV. VII. X.					II. V. VIII. XI.					III. VI. IX. XII.				
1	8	15	22	29		6	13	20	27		4	11	18	25
2	9	16	23	30		7	14	21	28		5	12	19	26
3	10	17	24		1	8	15	22	29		6	13	20	27
4	11	18	25		2	9	16	23	30		7	14	21	28
5	12	19	26		3	10	17	24		1	8	15	22	29
6	13	20	27		4	11	18	25		2	9	16	23	30
7	14	21	28		5	12	19	26		3	10	17	24	31

101. Since thirteen weeks are thus filled out exactly, it is evident that this same tabulation can represent not only the first three-month period of the year but also the second, third, and fourth groups of months as well. In other words, the first month is identical with the fourth, seventh, and tenth months; the second month is identical with the fifth, eighth, and eleventh months; and the third month is identical with the sixth, ninth and twelfth months. Thus the one tabulation suffices to represent the entire year.

102. From *1 Enoch* we also learn that the calendar year must have been considered as beginning at the vernal equinox, since the description there starts at the point where the days are first beginning to grow longer than the nights.

103. It is also necessary to ask on what day of the week the calendar begins. A clue is found in *The Chronology of Ancient Nations* by the Muslim author al-Biruni (A.D. 973–1048). As a source concerning Jewish sects, al-Biruni uses the Kitab al-Maqalat, a manual of history of religions written by Abu ‘Isa al-Warraq in the ninth century. In this work this author speaks, says al-Biruni,

> of a Jewish sect called the Maghribis, who maintain that the feasts are not legal unless the moon rises in Palestine as a full moon in the night of Wednesday, which follows after the day of Tuesday, at the time of sunset. Such is their New Year's Day. From this point the days and months are counted, and here begins the rotation of the annual festivals. For God created the two great lights on a Wednesday. Likewise they do not allow Passover to fall on any other day except

[170]A. Jaubert, *VT* 7 (1957): 35.

on Wednesday. And the obligations and rites prescribed for Passover they do not hold to be necessary, except for those who dwell in the country of the Israelites. All this stands in opposition to the custom of the majority of the Jews, and to the prescriptions of the Torah.[171]

104. The Maghribis were a "cave sect," and there is a reason to believe that they may have been the Qumran group or others connected with them.[172] Since it is stated that Wednesday is their New Year's Day, the calendar should probably begin with that day, and the days of the week should fall as shown in the tabulation below. The theological reason given for this beginning point is that on a Wednesday God created the two great lights. This is an obvious reference to Gen 1:14–19 where God made the sun, moon, and stars on the "fourth day," and ordained that these "lights in the firmament" should be "for signs and for seasons and for days and years." It is evident that though the year begins with Wednesday, as far as numbering the days of the week is concerned Wednesday is still the fourth day, Saturday or the Sabbath is the seventh, and so on. That the beginning of the year is also marked by the rise of the full moon can hardly be taken as anything other than an ideal statement, since even if in a given year Wednesday was full moon day, it would not be so regularly.

TABLE 15. *The Days of the Week in the Calendar of* Jubilees

MONTHS	DAYS						
	Sun	*Mon*	*Tue*	*Wed*	*Thu*	*Fri*	*Sat*
I. IV. VII. X				1	2	3	4
	5	6	7	8	9	10	11
	12	13	14	15	16	17	18
	19	20	21	22	23	24	25
	26	27	28	29	30		
II. V. VIII. XI						1	2
	3	4	5	6	7	8	9
	10	11	12	13	14	15	16
	17	18	19	20	21	22	23
	24	25	26	27	28	29	30
III. VI. IX. XII	1	2	3	4	5	6	7
	8	9	10	11	12	13	14
	15	16	17	18	19	20	21
	22	23	24	25	26	27	28
	29	30	31				

[171]*The Chronology of Ancient Nations* (ed. C. Edward Sachau; London: Allen, 1879), 278.

[172]R. de Vaux, *RB* 57 (1950): 422–423; Rowley, *The Zadokite Fragments and the Dead Sea Scrolls,* 23–24; cf. Ernst Bammel, *ZNW* 49 (1958): 77–88.

105. While in the calendar that is arranged as we have just indicated, the days of the week and the days of the month cannot possibly remain in a fixed relationship to the phases of the moon, it is plain that the days of the week do remain in a fixed relation with the days of the month. Therefore, it is possible to identify the position of festivals or other dates in terms of both the day of the month and the day of the week. Thus, if the Passover sacrifice is slain on the fourteenth day of the first month (Exod 12:6) and the fifteenth day is the first day of Passover,[173] it is Tuesday which is the eve of Passover and Wednesday which is the Passover day, and this is the case in every year. This agrees with the date of Passover as given in the calendar fragments from Qumran Cave 4, and the other festival dates as given there (§93) are also in exact agreement with what may be ascertained in our present tabulation, falling regularly on Wednesday, Friday, and Sunday.

106. The fixed relationship of the days of the month with the days of the week is, of course, precisely what is not found in a calendar of lunar months. As we have stated, in the Babylonian lunisolar calendar the fourteenth day of the first month falls upon different days of the week in different years. The point at issue here was evidently of much importance to those who used the calendar of *Jubilees*. By the observance of this calendar, it was said, as we have seen, "they will not disturb its time from its days and from its feasts . . . and they will not leave out any day nor disturb any feasts." Together with this positive affirmation concerning its own calendar, *Jubilees* speaks strongly of the harm that is done by the use of a different calendar (6:36–37):

> For there will be those who will assuredly make observations of the moon—how (it) disturbs the seasons and comes in from year to year ten days too soon. For this reason the years will come upon them when they will disturb (the order), and make an abominable (day) the day of testimony, and an unclean day a feast day, and they will confound all the days, the holy with the unclean, and the unclean day with the holy; for they will go wrong as to the months and sabbaths and feasts and jubilees.

107. That the calendar to which *Jubilees* objects is a lunar calendar is shown by the statement that it is based upon "observations of the moon," and also that it makes the year come in annually "ten days too soon." According to *Jubilees,* "364 days . . . constitute a complete year"; in the Babylonian calendar, 12 lunar months of alternately 29 and 30 days each make a year of 354 days.

108. If *Jubilees* objects to lunar reckoning, its own system is presumably essentially solar. That this is indeed its basis is made explicit by the mention of "the rule of the sun" in *Jub.* 4:21, and the fuller statement in *Jub.* 2:9: "And God appointed the sun to be a great sign on the earth for days and for sabbaths and for months and for feasts and for years and for sabbaths of years and for jubilees and for all seasons of the years." As a solar calendar, then, it evidently began the year with the vernal equinox, and it divided the year into 4 solar periods, 12 solar months, 52 weeks, and 364 days as has already been outlined.

---

[173] *JE* 3: 505.

109. While the calendar is thus based upon the solar year and actually corresponds with it quite closely and subdivides it quite symmetrically, its total of 364 days is still actually about one and one-quarter days short of the true solar year of about 365¼ days. With the passage of time this annual shortage would have accumulated into an obvious discrepancy with the seasons and would have required rectification. How the rectification was accomplished is not indicated in the sources with which we have just been dealing, but there is a possible clue in *Pirqe de Rabbi Eliezer* 6 where it is stated: "The great cycle of the sun is 28 years."[174] In twenty-eight years an annual shortage of one and one quarter days would amount to thirty-five days. Thus, if there were some system for intercalating five weeks in each 28-year cycle, the calendar would be kept in adjustment. Since a nineteen-year cycle of intercalation was derived from the Babylonian calendar, this 28-year cycle must have had some other origin, and it could have fitted with the calendar of *Jubilees.* Study of other evidence, however, leads to the conclusion that Qumran did not intercalate its calendar but simply allowed the discrepancy to accumulate. It would theoretically take about 290 years for a discrepancy of a full year to develop. Likewise it is calculated that, if the calendar was in use from, say, around 124 B.C., the discrepancy would have amounted to two months by the beginning of the Christian era and to seven or eight months by the time of the crucifixion of Jesus, and this in itself provides a difficulty for the theory that the Last Supper was observed in terms of the Qumran calendar (§609).[175]

110. The calendar of *Jubilees* seems, therefore, to have been the calendar of the Qumran community. The community was willing to use the Babylonian calendar for matters of everyday life, but for dating the all-important festivals of the religious year it adhered to this other calendar which did "not leave out any day nor disturb any feasts." The Babylonian calendar was no doubt in general and official use at this time, but the community of the covenant evidently did not feel that it did justice to the requirements of the religious year. The calendar to which the community adhered was presumably, therefore, an older one which was believed to be connected with the proper arrangement of the festivals from some authoritative antiquity.

111. In the poem on times and seasons in the *Manual of Discipline,* we found (§§84–87) the acrostic Aleph, Mem, Nun, forming the word Amen. The numerical values of these letters of the Hebrew alphabet are 1, 40, and 50, making a total of 91, exactly the number of days in each of the four divisions of the calendar. Thus, to the initiated ear, the liturgical response of the community in its prayers was a solemn affirmation of the divine wisdom so marvelously shown forth in the stately movement of the sun through the four 91–day seasons of the solar year, a movement which set the splendid pattern within which the divine Being was rightly to be worshiped.

---

[174]Ed. Friedländer, 34. This work, already cited above (§25), treats of the creation and at this point has reached the fourth day (6–8), therefore discusses the course of the planets, the sun, and the moon.

[175]Roger T. Beckwith, *RQ* 7 (1970): 379–396.

7. The Greek Calendar

LITERATURE: **Bischoff**, "Kalender (griechischer)," in PW 10.2, cols. 1568–1602; James **Gow**, "The Calendar," in *A Companion to Greek Studies* (ed. Leonard Whibley; 3d ed.; Cambridge: Cambridge University Press, 1916), 589–591; H. J. **Rose**, "Calendar, Greek," in *EB* 4: 578–579; Benjamin D. **Merritt**, *The Athenian Year,* (Berkeley: University of California Press, 1961); Alan E. **Samuel**, *Greek and Roman Chronology: Calendars and Years in Classical Antiquity* (Munich: Beck, 1972); Jon D. **Mikalson**, *The Sacred and Civil Calendar of the Athenian Year* (Princeton: Princeton University Press, 1975).

112. The Greek calendar is not of major concern in relation to biblical dates but will be considered briefly, principally because of its relationship to the Macedonian calendar (§§116ff.) and to the Greek era of the Olympiads (§185). At least in its later form the Greek year was lunisolar. The month began with the new moon and the lunar months varied between twenty-nine and thirty days. Within the month there was a division of three decades, and the days were counted within the decade. Extra months or days were intercalated from time to time, and in an early system an additional month was inserted every other year. From the Greek ἐμβάλλω, "to throw in," an inserted month was called μὴν ἐμβόλιμος, an "embolismic month," and this designation was abbreviated in inscriptions as EM or EMB. The names of the months were mostly based on the names of deities or of festivals with which the month was particularly connected, and the names differed from city to city. The year, too, began at different points in different states.

113. At Athens, chief city of Attica, the year began at the first new moon after the summer solstice. Between 432 and 263 B.C., it has been computed, the date of this event ranged from June 22 to August 9, but, in the majority of cases, fell in July.[176] For the purpose of the Table 16 we may take July 1 as the approximate beginning point of the year and list the months with approximate equivalents as shown. Here the intercalary month was usually a second sixth month, Posideion.

TABLE 16. *The Calendar at Athens*

1.	Ἑκατομβαιών	Hekatombaion	July
2.	Μεταγειτνιών	Metageitnion	Aug
3.	Βοηδρομιών	Boedromion	Sept
4.	Πυανοψιών	Pyanopsion	Oct
5.	Μαιμακτηριών	Maimakterion	Nov
6.	Ποσιδηιών	Posideion	Dec
7.	Γαμηλιών	Gamelion	Jan
8.	Ἀνθεστηριών	Anthesterion	Feb
9.	Ἐλαφηβολιών	Elaphebolion	Mar
10.	Μουνυχιών	Mounychion	Apr
11.	Θαργηλιών	Thargelion	May
12.	Σκιροφοριών	Skirophorion	June

[176]R. D. Hicks, *A Companion to Greek Studies,* 71.

114. At Delphi, in Phocis, the year began at about the same time as at Athens and the months, listed from the beginning of the new year on approximately July 1, are shown in Table 17. Here the intercalary month was usually a second sixth month, Poitropios.

TABLE 17. *The Calendar at Delphi*

1.	Ἀπελλαῖος	Apellaios	July
2.	Βουκάτιος	Boukatios	Aug
3.	Βοαθόος	Boathoos	Sept
4.	Ἡραῖος	Heraios	Oct
5.	Δαιδαφόριος	Daidaphorios	Nov
6.	Ποιτρόπιος	Poitropios	Dec
7.	Ἀμάλιος	Amalios	Jan
8.	Βύσιος	Bysios	Feb
9.	Θεοξένιος	Theoxenios	Mar
10.	Ἐνδυσποιτρόπιος	Endyspoitropios	Apr
11.	Ἡράκλειος	Herakleios	May
12.	Ἰλαῖος	Ilaios	June

115. The days of the month in the Greek calendar were divided into three groups. The first ten days were days of the "rising" month and were referred to thus, for example: "on the sixth day of the rising month of Metageitnion (Μεταγειτνιῶνος ἕκτῃ ἱσταμένου)." The next ten days were indicated as "plus ten." On the sixteenth day of Metageitnion, for example, was expressed as: "on the sixth day plus ten of Metageitnion (Μεταγειτνιῶνος ἕκτῃ ἐπὶ δέκα)." The last nine or ten days were days of the "waning" month, or days "after the twenties," and were counted backward from the end of the month. So, for the twenty-sixth day of Metageitnion, for example, we have: "on the fifth day of the waning month of Metageitnion (Μεταγειτνιῶνος πέμπτῃ φθίνοντος)"; or: "on the fifth day after the twenties of Metageitnion (Μεταγειτνιῶνος πέμπτῃ μετ' εἰκάδας)." As already noted (§11), the Greek day began at sundown.[177]

8. The Macedonian Calendar

LITERATURE: "Hémérologue ou Calendrier de différentes villes, comparé avec celui de Rome," in *Histoire de l'Académie Royale des Inscriptions et Belles-Lettres* 47 (Paris, 1809): 66–84; Ludwig **Ideler**, *Handbuch der mathematischen und technischen Chronologie* (2 vols.; Berlin, Rucker, 1825–1826); Campbell C. **Edgar**, *Zenon Papyri in the University of Michigan Collection,* (Ann Arbor: University of Michigan Press, 1931).

116. Since the Macedonians were related to the Greeks in origin, language, and culture, it is to be expected that their calendar would be similar to the Greek calendar. Like the Greek calendar, the Macedonian was lunisolar and made up of lunar months, but the year began in the fall. The beginning point was presumably at the new moon after the autumnal equinox, hence about the

177Samuel, *Greek and Roman Chronology,* 59–61.

end of September, and in Table 18, for a rough preliminary equivalent, we may show the first month of the year as approximately corresponding to October. More exact equivalents in different areas will be shown later.

TABLE 18. *The Macedonian Months*

1.	Δῖος	Dios	Oct
2.	Ἀπελλαῖος	Apellaios	Nov
3.	Αὐδυναῖος	Audynaios	Dec
4.	Περίτιος	Peritios	Jan
5.	Δύστρος	Dystros	Feb
6.	Ξανθικός, Ξανδικός	Xanthikos, or Xandikos	Mar
7.	Ἀρτεμίσιος	Artemisios	Apr
8.	Δαίσιος	Daisios	May
9.	Πάνεμος	Panemos	June
10.	Λῷος	Loos	July
11.	Γορπιαῖος	Gorpiaios	Aug
12.	Ὑπερβερεταῖος	Hyperberetaios	Sept

117. As lunar months, these most probably alternated between thirty and twenty-nine days in length. This is confirmed by Egyptian papyri which give Gorpiaios and Hyperberetaios together fifty-nine days, and Apellaios thirty days, and Audynaios twenty-nine days.[178]

118. There must also have been some system of intercalation. In his *Life of Alexander* (16), Plutarch states that the Macedonian kings were not accustomed to going into battle in the month of Daisios, and relates that Alexander, accordingly, on the eve of the battle of Granicus ordered the month to be called a second Artemisios. Whether this was the regular intercalary month in Macedonia is not certain. In Egypt a papyrus of the late second century of the Christian era[179] gives a date in terms of a day of

μη[νος] Αρτεμι[σι
ου εμβο[λ]ιμου

i.e., "of the intercalary month Artemisios," which supports the idea that, at least in that place and time, this month was so treated. On the other hand, there is evidence that under Ptolemy II Philadelphus, the month Peritios was repeated every second year.[180]

119. With the conquests of Alexander the Great, the Macedonian calendar became widely used throughout Asia. Interesting evidence of the dissemination is to be seen in the Ἡμερολόγιον μηνῶν διαφόρων πόλεων, a *hemerologium* or calendar of the months of different cities. This work, preserved in two manuscripts, one in Florence, one in Leiden, gives the Roman calendar beginning in January and, in comparison with it, the calendars of some sixteen other

[178]Edgar, *Zenon Papyri,* 51.
[179]*OxyP* No. 2082, fragment 3, lines 17–18.
[180]Edgar, *Zenon Papyri,* 51; *OxyP* 17 (1927): 93.

peoples and cities. In the manuscript at Florence are given the calendars of (1) the Alexandrians, (2) the Greeks (meaning the Syrian Greeks, especially the inhabitants of the chief city of the Seleucid empire and later of the Roman province of Syria, Antioch), and of the peoples of (3) Tyre, (4) Arabia, (5) Sidon, (6) Heliopolis (i.e., Baalbek), (7) Lycia, (8) Asia (i.e., the Roman province), (9) Crete, (10) Cyprus, (11) Ephesus, (12) Bithynia, and (13) Cappadocia. In the manuscript at Leiden, in place of Crete, Cyprus, and Ephesus are given the calendars of (14) Gaza, (15) Ascalon, and (16) Seleucia Pieria. In a tabulation of these calendars[181] one readily recognizes in the majority of them some or all of the Macedonian month names. For example, Xanthikos is found in the calendars of the Greeks and of Tyre, Arabia, Sidon, Lycia, Ephesus, Cappadocia, Gaza, Ascalon, and Seleucia Pieria; Artemisios is found in Asia; Hyperberetaios in Crete; Loos in Cyprus. The comparative tables show also the dates of the beginnings of the months and the number of days in them. Since the *Hemerologium* represents the Roman period, it will be cited at a relatively late point in each area dealt with in what follows.[182]

(1) In Syria and in Babylonia

LITERATURE: *The Excavations at Dura-Europos, Second Season,* ed. by P. V. C. **Baur** and M. L. **Rostovtzeff** (New Haven: Yale University Press, 1931); Jotham **Johnson**, *Dura Studies* (Ph.D. thesis, University of Pennsylvania, 1932); Robert H. **McDowell**, *Coins from Seleucia on the Tigris* (University of Michigan Studies: Humanistic Series 37; Ann Arbor: University of Michigan Press, 1935); *The Excavations at Dura-Europos: Preliminary Report of the Seventh and Eighth Seasons of Work,* ed. by M. I. **Rostovtzeff**, F. E. **Brown**, and C. B. **Welles** (New Haven, Yale University Press, 1939).

120. In Syria, as in Macedonia, the year began in the fall and, in connection with the Seleucid era, we will note (§193) how, when the Seleucid administration was centered in Syria, the Macedonian New Year (Dios 1) in the fall was made the beginning point of the era. In Syria many of the local month names were recognizably similar to the Babylonian and Jewish, and this will appear in column 2 of Table 19, where variant spellings, approximating the Syrian pronunciation, are shown.[183] It will be noted that, at the beginning of the year, there were two months Tishri, a first and a second, and also two months Kanun, a first and a second. According to the *Chronicle* of John Malalas,[184] it was Seleucus I Nicator (312–281 B.C.), founder of the Seleucid empire and builder of Antioch (in Syria), who commanded that the months of Syria be named according to the Macedonian names. The resultant equation of months was probably that shown in Table 19, a table which may be labeled (for reasons which will appear later) as giving the earlier correlation of the months.

---

[181]*Histoire de l'Académie Royale* 47 (1809): 66–84; Ideler, *Handbuch* 1:410ff.

[182]For the *hemerologia*, including an additional text in the Vatican, see Samuel, *Greek and Roman Chronology,* 171–178.

[183]Ideler, *Handbuch* 1:430 n. 1.

[184]*Chronicle of John Malalas* (trans. Matthew Spinka; Chicago: University of Chicago Press, 1940), 14.

TABLE 19. *The Macedonian Calendar in Syria (Earlier Correlation)*

Macedonian Months	*Syrian Months*	*Jewish Months*
1. Dios	The first Tishri or Teschrin	Tishri
2. Apellaios	The second Tishri or Teschrin	Marheshvan
3. Audynaios	The first Kanun or Conun	Chislev
4. Peritios	The second Kanun or Conun	Tebeth
5. Dystros	Shebat or Schvot	Shebat
6. Xanthikos	Adar or Odor	Adar
7. Artemisios	Nisan or Nison	Nisan
8. Daisios	Iyar or Ior	Iyyar
9. Panemos	Hasiran or Chirson	Sivan
10. Loos	Tamus or Tomus	Tammuz
11. Gorpiaios	Ab or Ov	Ab
12. Hyperberetaios	Elul or Ilul	Elul

121. Evidence that the calendar was, in fact, arranged thus and continued in use in this order until in the first Christian century is found at Dura-Europos. This was a fortress on the Euphrates at the eastern edge of the Syrian desert founded under Seleucus I Nicator, and it remained an important caravan city under the Parthians. In the excavations at Dura, in the temple of Zeus Kyrios, a cult relief was found with an inscription in both Palmyrene and Greek and a date corresponding to A.D. 31.[185] The Palmyrene inscription mentions the month of Tishri, the Greek inscription gives the month Appellaios. If it is the second month Tishri which is meant, this correspondence agrees with the tabulation just given and shows that the equation represented therein prevailed at least until this date.

TABLE 20. *The Macedonian Calendar in Babylonia (Earlier Correlation)*

Macedonian Months	*Babylonian Months*	*Jewish Months*
1. Artemisios	Nisanu	Nisan
2. Daisios	Aiaru	Iyyar
3. Panemos	Simanu	Sivan
4. Loos	Duzu	Tammuz
5. Gorpiaios	Abu	Ab
6. Hyperberetaios	Ululu	Elul
7. Dios	Tashritu	Tishri
8. Apellaios	Arahsamnu	Marheshvan
9. Audynaios	Kislimu	Chislev
10. Peritios	Tebetu	Tebeth
11. Dystros	Shabatu	Shebat
12. Xanthikos	Addaru	Adar

[185] *The Excavations at Dura-Europos: Preliminary Report of the Seventh and Eighth Seasons of Work,* plate XXXVII and 307–309.

122. In Babylonia at this time the Macedonian months were presumably equated with the Babylonian months according to the same scheme just observed but with the year beginning in the spring in accordance with Babylonian custom. This gives a calendar (Table 20), which again may be labeled as representing the earlier correlation.

123. Interesting confirmation of this arrangement of the calendar is found at Seleucia on the Tigris, a site opposite the later Ctesiphon and below the present Baghdad. Seleucia was founded by Seleucus I Nicator, and was an important center both in the Seleucid empire and the succeeding Parthian empire. In the exploration of this site a large number of coins were found, the greater number probably minted right here. Those of the Seleucid period did not bear dates, but in the Parthian period in the reign of Mithridates I, after 141 B.C., the coins begin to show dates and in later issues some coins show not only the year but also the month. One group (No. 136) giving both year and month is from the reign of Artabanus II (A.D. 11–30/31[?]). The year dates are ϛKT = 326, and ZKT = 327; assuming that the Seleucid era is intended they correspond to A.D. 15/16 and 16/17. The months mentioned are shown in Table 21.

TABLE 21. *The Macedonian Months at Seleucia in A.D. 15/16–16/17*

A.S. 326	Gorpiaios
	Hyperberetaios
	Apellaios
	Audynaios
	Peritios
	Dystros
	Xandikos
A.S. 327	Artemisios
	Panemos
	Peritios

The first four bear one monogram or countermark, which is the sign of the controller of the mint; the last six bear another monogram. Arranged in the order just given, the months stand in a proper sequence according to the Babylonian calendar (with Artemisios = Nisanu as the first month of the new year beginning in the spring), and the change in monograms indicates one change in mint administration during the period. This sequence will be more evident if the months are listed again by their number in the calendar as in Table 22. But if it were assumed that the Macedonian calendar, with Dios as the first month, were used, then the order would have to be as in Table 23. And, as the breaking up of the monogram groups indicates, it would be necessary to suppose a very unlikely alternation of mint controllers. A similarly unlikely breaking up of the simple sequence of the monograms would result if the coins were arranged on the supposition that a month other than Artemisios, say Xandikos, was equated with Nisanu as the first month of the year. Therefore it may be taken as established that at Seleucia at this time the Macedonian months were used according to the Babylonian calendar, with

Artemisios the equivalent of Nisanu as the first month of the year, as shown in Table 20 above.[186]

TABLE 22. *The Macedonian Months at Seleucia in A.D. 15/16–16/17*

A.S. 326	5.	Gorpiaios
	6.	Hyperberetaios
	8.	Apellaios
	9.	Audynaios
	10.	Peritios
	11.	Dystros
	12.	Xandikos
A.S. 327	1.	Artemisios
	3.	Panemos
	10.	Peritios

TABLE 23. *The Macedonian Months at Seleucia in A.D. 15/16–16/17*

A.S. 326	2.	Apellaios
	3.	Audynaios
	4.	Peritios
	5.	Dystros
	6.	Xandikos
	11.	Gorpiaios
	12.	Hyperberetaios
A.S. 327	4.	Peritios
	7.	Artemisios
	9.	Panemos

124. But both in Syria and in Babylonia, i.e., at Dura-Europos and at Seleucia on the Tigris, there is evidence for a shift in the calendar which probably took place before the middle of the first Christian century. At this time, due perhaps to the insertion of an extra intercalary month in the Greek and Macedonian calendar, the sequence of the Macedonian months shifted one place in relation to the Babylonian and Jewish months.

125. At Dura-Europos, a horoscope was found scratched in the plaster of a room of a private house. It consists essentially of an ellipse, divided by two lines at right angles. One line connects the zenith with the nadir; one line connects the point in the heavens which was rising (the ὡροσκόπος proper) at the time indicated, with the point which was setting. Around the outside of the ellipse the signs of the zodiac are given by abbreviations of their names, ΤΟΞ for Τοξότης (Sagittarius), etc. Among these signs the positions of the sun, moon, and planets are shown at the same time the horoscope was cast. For example, at ΔΙΔ = Δίδυμοι (Gemini) is marked ΦΑΙΝ, an abbreviation for Φαίνων, the Greek name for Saturn; and at ΛΕΩΝ (Leo) are three abbreviations: ΠΥ = Πυρόεις, Mars; ΦΩCΦ = Φωσφόρος, Venus; CΤΙΛΒ = Στίλβων, Mercury. At the top the

[186] McDowell, *Coins from Seleucia on the Tigris,* 103–104, 138–139, 147–153.

date is given as: ΖΠΥΠΑΝΘ. ΖΠΥ equals 487; ΠΑΝ is an abbreviation for Πανήμου, "of the month Panemos"; and Θ equals nine. The date is therefore the ninth day of the month of Panemos in the year 487, a year which it may be surmised is stated in terms of the Seleucid era.

126. Within the limits of the occupation of Dura from 300 B.C. to A.D. 275, the planets were in the positions indicated in this horoscope in July A.D. 176. This was the year 487 of the Seleucid era and proves that it was, in fact, this era which was employed for the year date. The position of the moon is lost in gaps in the plaster, but the possible places for it would be in Aquarius, Scorpio, or Cancer. For the year in question, Cancer would be impossible because the relations of the other planets would not hold. If the moon was in Scorpio the date was July 3–5, A.D. 176; if the moon was in Aquarius the date was July 10–12, A.D. 176. Shortly prior to those dates the new moon became visible at Babylon on the evening of June 25. This appearance began the month Duzu (June/July) in the Babylonian calendar. In the earlier correlation between the Babylonian and Macedonian calendars (Table 20) Duzu was equated with Loos. In the present inscription, however, the month is named Panemos. Therefore, the one month relative shift has taken place and the calendars are in what we may call their later correlation.[187]

127. At Seleucia on the Tigris another group of coins now comes into consideration.[188] This group (No. 92) is from the reign of Gotarzes II (A.D. c. 44–51) and, like the group just treated (§123), also gives dates with both year and month. The year date is ZNT = A.S. 357 = A.D. 46/47. The months mentioned can be listed satisfactorily from either Artemisios or Xandikos as the first month of the year. Since Dura provides the evidence of the shift just considered (§126), since Josephus will shortly be found equating Xanthikos with Nisan (§138), and since the evidence here at Seleucia fits equally well in this pattern, it is likely that at this time at Seleucia as well as at Dura the sequence of Macedonian months began with Xandikos as the equivalent of Nisanu. Therefore, we may list the months from these coins in the order shown in Table 24.

TABLE 24. *The Macedonian Months at Seleucia in A.D. 46/47*

1.	Xandikos	5.	Loos
2.	Artemisios	6.	Gorpiaios
3.	Daisios	7.	Hyperberetaios
4.	Panemos		

From the evidence here at Seleucia the change in the correlation of the months took place between A.D. 16/17 (§123) and A.D. 46/47. From the Palmyrene-Greek inscription in the temple of Zeus Kyrios at Dura-Europos (§121) the change must have come after A.D. 31, therefore between A.D. 31 and 46/47.[189]

---

[187]*Excavations at Dura-Europos: Second Season,* 161–164; Johnson, *Dura Studies,* 1–15.
[188]McDowell, *Coins from Seleucia on the Tigris,* 73–74, 119.
[189]Cf. Samuel, *Greek and Roman Chronology,* 140–143, who dates the introduction of the change from the earlier to the later correlation sometime between A.D. 15/16 and 46/47.

128. As valid, then, for shortly before the middle of the first century A.D. onwards, we may show this later correlation of the calendar in Tables 25 and 26 representing the beginning of the year, respectively, in the spring as in Babylonia, and in the fall as in Macedonia and Syria.

TABLE 25. *The Macedonian Calendar in Babylonia (Later Correlation)*

Macedonian Months	*Babylonian Months*	*Julian Months*
1. Xanthikos	Nisanu	Mar/Apr
2. Artemisios	Aiaru	Apr/May
3. Daisios	Simanu	May/June
4. Panemos	Duzu	June/July
5. Loos	Abu	July/Aug
6. Gorpiaios	Ululu	Aug/Sept
7. Hyperberetaios	Tashritu	Sept/Oct
8. Dios	Arahsamnu	Oct/Nov
9. Apellaios	Kislimu	Nov/Dec
10. Audynaios	Tebetu	Dec/Jan
11. Peritios	Shabatu	Jan/Feb
12. Dystros	Addaru	Feb/Mar

TABLE 26. *The Macedonian Calendar In Syria (Later Correlation)*

Macedonian Months	*Babylonian Months*	*Julian Months*
1. Hyperberetaios	Tashritu	Sept/Oct
2. Dios	Arahsamnu	Oct/Nov
3. Apellaios	Kislimu	Nov/Dec
4. Audynaios	Tebetu	Dec/Jan
5. Peritios	Shabatu	Jan/Feb
6. Dystros	Addaru	Feb/Mar
7. Xanthikos	Nisanu	Mar/Apr
8. Artemisios	Aiaru	Apr/May
9. Daisios	Simanu	May/June
10. Panemos	Duzu	June/July
11. Loos	Abu	July/Aug
12. Gorpiaios	Ululu	Aug/Sept

129. Returning now to the *Hemerologium* (§119), it is precisely this calendar which we have just established as in use in Syria in the later period (Table 26) which is given in *Hemerologium* as the "calendar of the Greeks," i.e., the calendar of the Syrian Greeks, especially the inhabitants of Antioch. In the *Hemerologium* this calendar is presented in the form in which it was brought into a fixed relationship to the Julian calendar, and the dates of the beginnings of the months and the number of days in the months are given.[190] This is shown in Table 27 where the year is made to begin, according to Macedonian and Syrian custom, in the fall.

[190] *Histoire de l'Académie Royale des Inscriptions et Belles-Lettres* 47 (1809): 81;

TABLE 27. *The Syro-Macedonian Calendar (Later Correlation) in Relation to the Julian Calendar*

Macedonian Months	*Beginning On*	*Number of Days*
1. Hyperberetaios	Oct 1	31
2. Dios	Nov 1	30
3. Apellaios	Dec 1	31
4. Audynaios	Jan 1	31
5. Peritios	Feb 1	28
6. Dystros	Mar 1	31
7. Xanthikos	Apr 1	30
8. Artemisios	May 1	31
9. Daisios	June 1	30
10. Panemos	July 1	31
11. Loos	Aug 1	31
12. Gorpiaios	Sept 1	30

(2) In Arabia

130. Among the numerous other calendars presented in the *Hemerologium* (§119) we will note that of Arabia only briefly and then turn to Egypt. The calendar of the province of Arabia also used the Macedonian month names but began in spring and followed the Egyptian pattern in that it had twelve months of thirty days each and then five epagomenal days before the beginning of the new year. On the basis of the *Hemerologium* it may be shown in Table 28.[191]

TABLE 28. *The Macedonian Calendar in Arabia*

Macedonian Months	*Beginning On*	*Number of Days*
1. Xanthikos	Mar 22	30
2. Artemisios	Apr 21	30
3. Daisios	May 21	30
4. Panemos	June 20	30
5. Loos	July 20	30
6. Gorpiaios	Aug 19	30
7. Hyperberetaios	Sept 18	30
8. Dios	Oct 18	30
9. Apellaios	Nov 17	30
10. Audynaios	Dec 17	30
11. Peritios	Jan 16	30
12. Dystros	Feb 15	30
Epagomenae	Mar 17	5

Ideler, *Handbuch* 1: 430, PW 10.2, col. 1595.

[191]*Histoire de l'Académie Royale des Inscriptions et Belles-Lettres* 47 (1809): 81; Ideler, *Handbuch* 1: 437; PW 10.2, col. 1595.

(3) In Egypt

LITERATURE: *The Tebtunis Papyri,* vol. 1, ed. by Bernard P. **Grenfell**, Arthur S. **Hunt**, and J. Gilbart **Smyly** (London, 1902); *The Hibeh Papyri,* vol. 1, ed. by Bernard P. **Grenfell** and Arthur S. **Hunt** (London, 1906); A. **Bouché-Leclercq**, *Histoire des Lagides* (4 vols.; Paris: E. Leroux, 1903–1907); George **Milligan**, *Selections from the Greek Papyri* (Cambridge : Cambridge University Press, 1910) ; Henry Norris **Russell**, *Astronomy,* vol. 1, *The Solar System* (Boston: Ginn, 1926–27); T. C. **Skeat**, "The Reigns of the Ptolemies," *Mizraim* 6 (1937): 7–40 and *Münchener Beiträge zur Papyrusforschung und antiken Rechtsgeschichte* 39 (1954); republished in *The Reigns of the Ptolemies* (2d ed.; Munich: Beck, 1969); idem, "Notes on Ptolemaic Chronology," in JEA 48 (1960): 91–94; Alan Edouard **Samuel**, *Ptolemaic Chronology* (Münchener Beiträge zur Papyrusforschung und antiken Rechtsgeschichte, 43; Munich: Beck, 1962), 46–47; idem, *Greek and Roman Chronology* (Munich: Beck, 1972), 145–151; Edwyn **Bevan**, *The House of Ptolemy: A History of Egypt under the Ptolemaic Dynasty* (Chicago: Argonaut, 1968); Peter **Green**, *Alexander of Macedon, 356–323 B.C.: A Historical Biography* (Berkeley: University of California Press, 1991).

131. In Egypt, the Macedonian calendar was introduced by Alexander the Great, who invaded with his Macedonian and Greek troops in the autumn of 332 B.C. and left in the spring of 331 B.C. As we have explained §§40, 41), the twelve thirty-day Egyptian months were Thoth, Phaophi, Hathyr, Choiak, Tybi, Mecheir, Phamenoth, Pharmuthi, Pachon, Pauni, Epeiph, and Mesore (Table 6), with five epagomenal days at the end of the year to make a total of 365 days. At the time of Alexander's conquest, the beginning of the civil year with the month of Thoth fell in mid-November and, with the loss of a day in every four years, the year fell steadily earlier (§45, Table 7). With the introduction of the Macedonian calendar, Macedonian month names are often found along with the Egyptian names in the Egyptian papyri, although at least at first synchronization can be difficult. By the time of Ptolemy V Epiphanes (203–181 B.C.) there was a complete assimilation and the equation of Macedonian and Egyptian month names was: Dystros/Thoth, Xanthikos/Phaophi, Artemisios/Hathyr, Daisios/Choiak, Panemos/Tybi, Loos/Mecheir, Gorpiaios/Phamenoth, Hyperberetaios/Pharmuthi, Dios/Pachon, Apellaios/Pauni, Audynaios/Epeiph, Peritios/Mesore.[192]

132. Two examples of attempted synchronization of Macedonian and Egyptian dates may be given (§§132, 133). The death of Alexander the Great was in the year 323 B.C. Plutarch,[193] citing Aristobulus, says he died on the thirtieth day of the month Daisios (τριακάδι Δαισίου). Again,[194] citing the ἐφημερίδες or royal journals, he places the death "on the twenty-eighth, towards evening (τῇ τρίτῃ φθίνοντος πρὸς δείλην)." With the Greek day beginning at sundown §115), the death could easily have been assigned to the twenty-ninth of Daisios. Also in a month of twenty-nine days, it is probable that the twenty-ninth day was, in effect, omitted and the last day of the month was called, instead of the twenty-ninth, the thirtieth (τριάκας). Hence there is probably no inconsistency and the

---

[192] Samuel, *Greek and Roman Chronology*, 149–150.

[193] *Alexander* 75.

[194] *Alexander* 76.

day was actually Daisios 29. Codex A of Pseudo-Callisthenes gives the date as Pharmuthi 4. Thus a synchronism is established and may be continued: Daisios 29 = Pharmuthi 4 (June 13, 323 B.C.); Panemos 1 = Pharmuthi 5, and so on. More recent study, however, finds in a contemporary Babylonian astronomical text the statement of a date for the death of Alexander in "month 2 (i.e., Aiaru, beginning May 12), Babylonian day 29, king died." Accepting the equation of Daisios 29 with Aiaru 29 (rather than with Pharmuthi 4 as in Pseudo-Callisthenes), therefore provides the true date of the evening of June 10, 323 B.C., for Alexander's death.[195]

133. The Rosetta Stone contains a decree in honor of Ptolemy V Epiphanes (c. 203–c. 181 B.C.) dated in the ninth year (196 B.C.) of his reign. This synchronism is given: "on the fourth day of the month Xandikos, which corresponds to the eighteenth day of the Egyptian month of Mecheir (μηνὸς Ξανδικοῦ τετράδι Αἰγυπτίων δὲ Μεχεὶρ ὀκτωκαιδεκάτηι)."[196] Accordingly, reckoning backward, we establish that Xanthikos 1 = Mecheir 15. From these and other attested synchronisms, tables of at least approximate correspondences may be compiled, and from them it may be concluded that the general tendency of the Macedonian months was to lose in relation to the Egyptian months, i.e., to fall later in the Egyptian year, although sometimes, presumably due to the manner of intercalation, they moved ahead.[197]

134. The assimilation of the Macedonian and Egyptian calendars described above (§131) continued into the reign of Ptolemy VIII Euergetes II, nicknamed Physkon (145–116 B.C.), but in his time a new equation of the two was established. Among the papyri found at Tebtunis in the Fayum is a portion of a letter written by an official under Euergetes II.[198] Line 7 contains this date: ἔτους νγ Ξαν ιζ Μεχεὶρ ιζ. The year date (νγ = 53) indicates the fifty-third year of Euergetes II. The future Euergetes II was first proclaimed king in Alexandria in 170 B.C.; his fifty-third year is 119/118 B.C.[199] Ξαν abbreviates Ξανδικοῦ, and the seventeenth day (ιζ = 17) of Xandikos is equated with the seventeenth day of Mecheir. This date—the seventeenth day of Xandikos and the seventeenth day of Mecheir in the fifty-third year of Euergetes II—shows an exact correspondence of the two calendars and also implies, as Table 29 will show, that at the beginning of the year Dios 1 (rather than Dystros 1) was equated with Thoth 1. From this time on, the two calendars remained in this exact agreement.

135. Under the Roman empire, the months in Egypt were also given names in honor of the Roman emperors, and a number of these names are

---

[195]For the date of June 13, 323 B.C., see Skeat in *Mizraim* 6 (1937): 28–29; idem, *Reigns of the Ptolemies,* 9; Grenfell and Hunt, *The Hibeh Papyri,* 1:334, 339; and also *EB* (1987), 1:240. For the corrected date of the evening of June 10 see Samuel, *Ptolemaic Chronology,* 46–47; Peter Green, *Alexander of Macedon*, 475.

[196]E. A. Wallis Budge, *The Rosetta Stone in the British Museum,* (London: Religious Tract Society, 1929), 53, 67.

[197]Grenfell and Hunt, *The Hibeh Papyri* 1:334, 336–337.

[198]Grenfell, Hunt, and Smyly, *The Tebtunis Papyri,* No.25, 102–103.

[199]Bouché-Leclercq, *Histoire des Lagides* 2:393; Samuel, *Greek and Roman Chronology,* 150.

known. We may call them the honorific imperial names. The several names of the months, and their equivalents in Julian dates (in exact agreement with the *Hemerologium* [§119]) are shown in Table 29.[200]

TABLE 29. *The Macedonian Calendar in Egypt*

MONTH NAMES

	Macedonian	*Egyptian*	*Roman*		*Julian Dates in a Common Year*
1.	Dios	Thoth	Σεβαστός	Sebastos	Aug 29–Sept 27
2.	Apellaios	Phaophi	Δομιτιανός	Domitianos	Sept 28–Oct 27
3.	Audynaios	Hathyr	Νέος Σεβαστός	Neos Sebastos	Oct 28–Nov 26
4.	Peritios	Choiak	Ἁδριανός	Hadrianos	Nov 27–Dec 26
5.	Dystros	Tybi			Dec 27–Jan 25
6.	Xanthikos	Mecheir			Jan 26–Feb 24
7.	Artemisios	Phamenoth			Feb 25–Mar 26
8.	Daisios	Pharmuthi	Νερώνειος	Neroneios	Mar 27–Apr 25
9.	Panemos	Pachon	Γερμανίκειος	Germanikeios	Apr 26–May 25
10.	Loos	Pauni	Σωτήριος	Soterios	May 26–June 24
11.	Gorpiaios	Epeiph			June 25–July 24
12.	Hyperberetaios	Mesore	Καισάρειος	Kaisareios	July 25–Aug 23
	Epagomenal days				Aug 24–Aug 28

136. Returning now to the time of Ptolemy III Euergetes I (247–221 B.C.), there was already then a great center of Hellenic learning and culture in the famous Museum and Library at Alexandria, where the noted Greek astronomer Eratosthenes (c. 276–c. 194 B.C.) was in charge. Among scientific undertakings there was concern with reformation of the calendar. As described above (§§40, 41, 131), the Egyptian civil year began on Thoth 1 and consisted of twelve thirty-day months with Egyptian and, after the coming of Alexander, Macedonian names, to which were added five epagomenal days, dedicated to the gods Osiris, Seth, and Horus and the goddesses Isis and Nephthys, to make a year of 365 days in all. Nonetheless, this year still slipped ahead of the season at the rate of one day every four years as measured by the heliacal rising of Sirius (Sothis), and thus by a whole year in a Sothic period of 1,460 years. By this time Greek science at Alexandria was advanced enough to know that what was wanted to counteract the discrepancy was to put in an extra day every fourth year. In ancient times the calendar was largely in the hands of the priesthood,[201] and Ptolemy evidently encouraged the Egyptian priests to take up the problem. In March 327 a synod of priests from all Egypt came together at Canopus and passed a decree. Three copies of this decree have been found inscribed on stone (one from Tanis now in Cairo, with hieroglyphic, Greek, and demotic texts; one also in Cairo, also with trilingual texts; and one now in the Louvre, very damaged). The text is known as the Decree of Canopus. It praises Ptolemy and Berenice,

[200]Bouché-Leclercq, *Histoire des Lagides* 4:287–289; Milligan, *Selections from the Greek Papyri,* xviii; Bischoff in PW 10.2, col. 1588.

[201]Russell, *Astronomy* 1:151.

his sister and wife, called the Brother-and-Sister Gods, for their many services to Egypt, and then takes up many topics, among them the matter of the year. It is recognized that "the rising of the [Sothis] star" may change to another day in four years, and it is proposed that

> in order that the seasons may correspond regularly according to the establishment of the world, and in order that it may not occur that some of the national feasts kept in winter may come to be kept in summer, the sun changing one day in every four years, and that other feasts now kept in summer may come to be kept in winter in future times, as has formerly happened, and now would happen if the arrangement of the year remained of 360 days, and the five additional days added; from now onward one day, a feast of the Benefactor Gods, shall be added every four years to the five additional days before the new year, in order that all may know that the former defect in the arrangement of the seasons and the year and the received opinions concerning the whole arrangement of the heavens has been corrected and made good by the Benefactor Gods.[202]

It was this rectification of the Egyptian calendar which prepared for the reformation of the Roman calendar by Julius Caesar (§§143–145).

(4) In Palestine

LITERATURE: Ludwig **Ideler**, *Handbuch der mathematischen und technischen Chronologie* (Berlin: A. Rucker, 1825–1826), 1:400–402; F.-M. **Abel**, *Les Livres des Maccabées* (Paris: LeCoffre, 1949), XLIX–LII; J. C. **Dancy**, *A Commentary on I Maccabees* (Oxford: Blackwell, 1954), 49–50.

137. Evidence of the use of the Macedonian calendar in Palestine appears in 2 Maccabees and in Josephus. In its account of the Maccabean period, the book of 2 Maccabees (considered to have been written in Greek in Alexandria in the middle of the first century B.C.) quotes a letter from King Antiochus to the Jewish senate and the rest of the Jews, and also a letter from the Romans to them in which the dates of Xanthikos 15 and Xanthikos 30 are given (2 Macc 11:30, 33, 38). Here we may suppose that the Syro-Macedonian calendar was in use in the earlier correlation (Table 19) which we have established as probably prevailing prior to sometime between A.D. 31 and 46/47 (§127). In this correlation Xanthikos was equivalent to Adar, and this and the other equivalences would appear as in Table 30.

138. In his *Jewish Antiquities* and *Jewish War,* Josephus commonly uses Macedonian month names and from time to time adds their Jewish equivalents. In *Ant.* 1.80–81 he states that Dios and Marheshvan are the same and that this was the second month. This means that in a year beginning in the fall Hyperberetaios = Tishri was the first month. He also says that Xanthikos and Nisan are the same and are the first month of the year for divine worship and for

---

[202]Bevan, *The House of Ptolemy,* 210–211; trans. Mahaffy, *History of Egypt under the Ptolemaic Dynasty.*

ordinary affairs. Again in *Ant.* 3.248 he equates Xanthikos and Nisan and states that this month begins the year. Also, in *Ant.* 11.148, 12.248, and 12.319, he equates Apellaios and Chislev and makes no difference between the twenty-fifth day in the one month and in the other. As would be expected in the time at the end of the first century A.D. when Josephus wrote, these correspondences agree with the later correlation between the Macedonian and Babylonian months established above (Tables 25, 26). In Josephus, therefore, the Macedonian months may be taken as fully and exactly equivalent to the Jewish months as shown in Table 31.

TABLE 30. *The Macedonian Calendar in Palestine (Earlier Correlation)*

Macedonian Months	*Jewish Months*	*Julian Equivalents*
1. Artemisios	Nisan	Mar/Apr
2. Daisios	Iyyar	Apr/May
3. Panemos	Sivan	May/June
4. Loos	Tammuz	June/July
5. Gorpiaios	Ab	July/Aug
6. Hyperberetaios	Elul	Aug/Sept
7. Dios	Tishri	Sept/Oct
8. Apellaios	Marheshvan	Oct/Nov
9. Audynaios	Chislev	Nov/Dec
10. Peritios	Tebeth	Dec/Jan
11. Dystros	Shebat	Jan/Feb
12. Xanthikos	Adar	Feb/Mar

TABLE 31. *The Macedonian Calendar in Palestine (Later Correlation)*

Macedonian Months	*Jewish Months*	*Julian Equivalents*
1. Xanthikos	Nisan	Mar/Apr
2. Artemisios	Iyyar	Apr/May
3. Daisios	Sivan	May/June
4. Panemos	Tammuz	June/July
5. Loos	Ab	July/Aug
6. Gorpiaios	Elul	Aug/Sept
7. Hyperberetaios	Tishri	Sept/Oct
8. Dios	Marheshvan	Oct/Nov
9. Apellaios	Chislev	Nov/Dec
10. Audynaios	Tebeth	Dec/Jan
11. Peritios	Shebat	Jan/Feb
12. Dystros	Adar	Feb/Mar

9. The Roman Calendar

LITERATURE: Walter F. **Wislicenus**, *Der Kalender in gemeinverständlicher Darstellung* (Leipzig: Teubner, 1905); H. J. **Rose**, "Calendar, Roman," in *EB* 4: 579; Agnes Kirsopp **Michels**, *The Calendar of the Roman Republic* (Princeton: Princeton University Press,

1967); Alan E. **Samuel**, *Greek and Roman Chronology: Calendars and Years in Classical Antiquity* (Munich: Beck, 1972), 153ff.

139. From an early time, the Roman calendar was lunisolar. The earliest year was supposed to have been introduced by Romulus, the legendary founder of Rome, and to have comprised only ten months. The introduction of a calendar of twelve lunar months was attributed to Numa Pompilius, second legendary king of Rome (715–672 B.C.). Livy (1.19.6–7) describes the work of Numa as follows:

> And first of all he divided the year into twelve months, according to the revolutions of the moon. But since the moon does not give months of quite thirty days each, and eleven days are wanting to the full complement of a year as marked by the sun's revolution, he inserted intercalary months in such a way that in the twentieth year the days should fall in with the same position of the sun from which they had started, and the period of twenty years be rounded out. He also appointed days when public business might not be carried on, and others when it might, since it would sometimes be desirable that nothing should be brought before the people.

140. The twelve months were supposed to have begun in the spring and to have had the order and number of days shown in Table 32. In Table 32 it is recognizable that the month names were derived in part from the Roman gods, as in the case of the first month, sacred to Mars; and in part from place in the sequence, as in the case of the fifth month, Quintilis, from *quinque,* "five." The length of the months—keeping to uneven numbers—may have been influenced by the wish to have a day exactly in the middle of each month. To bring this lunar year of 354 days at least approximately into harmony with the solar year, an intercalary month was inserted each second year.

TABLE 32. *The Early Roman Calendar*

	Name of Month	*Number of Days*
1.	Martius	31
2.	Aprilis	29
3.	Maius	31
4.	Junius	29
5.	Quintilis	31
6.	Sextilis	29
7.	Septembris	29
8.	Octobris	31
9.	Novembris	29
10.	Decembris	29
11.	Januarius	29
12.	Februarius	27
		354

141. In the division of the Roman month, the first day of the month was termed *kalendae,* that is kalends or calends. From Latin *calare* and Greek καλῶ, "to call," this meant "callings" and probably referred to an official calling out of the day. The full moon was called ides. In the long months—Martius, Maius, Quintilis, and Octobris—this was the fifteenth day; in the short months—the other eight—this was the thirteenth. The nones was the ninth day, counted inclusively, before the ides: therefore in the long months the seventh, in the short months the fifth day of the month. Other days were counted backward and inclusively from these fixed points. Thus, for example, *a d iii non Quint* abbreviates *ante diem iii nonas Quintiles,* meaning "the third day before the nones of Quintilis," and equals July 5. There was also a week of eight days, but it was independent of the months and simply marked the time from one market day to the next; and the seven-day week was only gradually introduced from the East and through its use by the Christians. Of the cumbersome system of kalends, ides, and nones, and related reckoning, Wislicenus remarks that it is fortunate nothing has survived in modern usage except the word "calendar" which comes from the Latin *kalendae.* As for what is now meant by "calendar," that was designated by the Romans as *fasti* (from Greek φάσκω, φημί, "to say") meaning, first, a day on which it is allowed to speak; hence a day on which judgment may be pronounced, i.e., a court day; and, finally, an enumeration of all the days of the year with their festivals, etc., especially including the *fasti consulares,* or lists of the magistrates according to their years of service.[203]

142. Although the Roman calendar just described (§140) began in the spring with Martius 1, we are told by Cassiodorus Senator[204] that in A.U.C. 601 = 153 B.C. the consuls, elected for one year, began to take office on Jan 1. Under the influence of this custom the beginning of the year was put back to Januarius 1, and the year continued to be reckoned regularly from this point.

143. By the end of the Roman republic the calendar had come into a state of confusion, particularly due to difficulties and inaccuracies in the system and practice of intercalation. In A.U.C. 691 = 63 B.C. (see Table 56) Julius Caesar became pontifex maximus and still followed the previous haphazard practice until the end of 47 B.C. Within this sixteen-year period the calendar months had receded by about 60 days from their customary position within the tropical year. In order to make up for the deficiency, and in preparation for a complete reform of the calendar, Caesar extended the length of the year A.U.C. 708 = 46 B.C. to 445 days. For the project he sought advice from the Alexandrian astronomer Sosigenes and in accordance with his suggestions established (in 45 B.C.) what is known as the Julian calendar. This calendar is still in use, with one small modification, among all Western nations.[205] All dependence upon the cycles of the moon was abandoned, and the true length of the year was accepted as 365¼ days. Caesar did not, however, impose this calendar throughout the empire (e.g.,

---

[203]Samuel, *Greek and Roman Chronology,* 151–155. For the *Fasti* in general, which were usually cut in stone and built into the walls of buildings, see Michels, *Calendar of the Roman Republic,* 22–33, 173–190.

[204]Ed. Theodor Mommsen, *Chronica minora* (Berlin: Weidmann 1892–1898), 2:130.

[205]Russell, *Astronomy* 1:152.

upon the Jews), many of whose peoples were unwilling to give up the long-familiar lunar relationship. As the outline (in Table 33) of a regular year in the Julian calendar shows, the beginning of the year was transferred to January 1 from March 1 where it had been (Table 32). What had been the "fifth" month and called Quintilis was now the seventh month and, by vote of the Senate, renamed Julius in honor of Julius Caesar, and later the former "sixth" month, Sextilis, was moved to eighth place and renamed Augustus in honor of that emperor. The lengths of the several months were changed from the former figures, which totaled 354 days (12 × 29.5, the average length of a moon month), to make the now required 365 full days.

TABLE 33. *The Julian Calendar*

	Name of Month	*Number of Days*
1.	Januarius	31
2.	Februarius	28
3.	Martius	31
4.	Aprilis	30
5.	Maius	31
6.	Junius	30
7.	Julius	31
8.	Augustus	31
9.	Septembris	30
10.	Octobris	31
11.	Novembris	30
12.	Decembris	31
		365

144. The year as just outlined was still one-fourth day short of the requisite 365¼-day year, and adjustment was also made for this fact. In the first year of the new calendar (i.e., 45 B.C.) Februarius was given twenty-nine days and the year had 366 days; in the three following years Februarius had twenty-eight days and the year 365 days; and this same pattern was repeated continuously with an added day every fourth year. In the Roman calendar the added day followed the twenty-fourth day in Februarius which was the sixth day before kalends of March, and hence was counted as a second sixth day; hence the year in which this was done was called *annus bisextus*. At present, the added day is at the end of the month—Feb 29—and the year is known as a leap year because in it any fixed date after February "leaps" over a day of the week and falls on the day following that on which it would normally fall. In the transition from B.C. to A.D. as far as leap years are concerned, 45 B.C. was a leap year and so too were 5 B.C. and 1 B.C.; then the leap years in the Christian era became A.D. 4, A.D. 8, and so on.

145. The small modification later recognized as necessary in the Julian calendar (§143), was instituted by Pope Gregory XIII in 1582. As modern astronomy tells, the true length of the tropical year is not exactly 365¼ days (= 365 days and 6 hours) but exactly 365 days, 5 hours, 48 minutes, and 46.0

seconds, which makes the Julian year 11 minutes and 14.0 seconds too long. This difference amounts to a little more than 9 days in 1,200 years, so in the Julian calendar the date of the vernal equinox (important for the establishment of the date of Easter in the Christian church, §§632–634) comes earlier and earlier as time goes on. By A.D. 1582 it had fallen back to the eleventh of March instead of occurring on the twenty-first, as it did at the time of the Council of Nicea in A.D. 325. Pope Gregory, therefore, took the advice of the distinguished astronomer of his time, Clavius, and ordered the calendar corrected by dropping ten days, so that the day following October 4, 1582, should be called the fifteenth instead of the fifth. After that, century years should be leap years only if they are exactly divisible by 400. Thus 1700, 1800, 1900, 2100, and so on are not leap years, but 1600 and 2000 are. This is the Gregorian calendar and the very precise form of the calendar accepted in most Western nations.[206]

C. OFFICIAL AND REGNAL YEARS

146. The question naturally arises as to how a particular year is to be designated. In general, this was done at first by reference to some important event in the year and later by reference to the year of a ruler or other official.

1. In Egypt

LITERATURE: Kurt **Sethe**, "Die Entwicklung der Jahresdatierung bei den alten Aegyptern," in *Untersuchungen zur Geschichte und Altertumskunde Aegyptens* 3 (1905): 60–100; Alan H. **Gardiner**, "Regnal Years and Civil Calendar in Pharaonic Egypt," in *JEA* 31 (1945): 11–28; Bettina **Schmitz**, "Jahreszählung," *LÄ* 3, cols. 238–240; T. C. **Skeat**, *Reigns of the Ptolemies* (2d ed.; Munich: Beck, 1969).

147. The earliest stages known in the development of the Egyptian system may be seen on the famous Palermo Stone.[207] On the front the first line gives the names in successive rectangles of predynastic kings of Lower Egypt without indication of how long each reigned. Beginning with line two the right side of each rectangle is marked by a vertical line which curls over at the top. This is the hieroglyphic sign for a palm tree and the symbol for a year. Each rectangle is therefore a year-compartment. The stone is a fragment, but as far as it is preserved, lines two and three record the First Dynasty; four and five the Second Dynasty; line six the Third Dynasty; the lost lines seven and eight on the front and the first line on the back the Fourth Dynasty; and the rest of the back the Fifth Dynasty. Within each year-compartment the hieroglyphs describe one or more outstanding occurrences of the year. In the record of the First Dynasty, for example, one year is designated as that of the "Smiting of the Troglodytes."[208]

---

[206]Ibid., 153.
[207]Finegan, *Light from the Ancient Past,* Fig. 27.
[208]Breasted, *Ancient Records* 1:104.

148. In the middle space above the long rows of year-compartments are written the names of kings. Thus the years are also years of their reigns. Several entries represent the transition from one reign to the next. One of these is found at the beginning of the first line on the back. Here the year-compartment is divided by a plain vertical line. To the right of this line the king's name has been lost but hieroglyphic signs are in part preserved and in part plainly to be restored in terms of the space that was available.[209] Four crescent moons indicate four months. A sun signifies days and is followed by two signs for ten (two vertical strokes joined by a curve at the top) and four vertical strokes for four units. Together the signs mean: "four months and twenty-four days." To the left of the plain vertical dividing line is to be read "seven months and eleven days," and in the middle space above and onto the left of the name of King Shepseskaf, one of the last kings of the Fourth Dynasty. Four months and twenty-four days plus seven months and eleven days equals twelve months (of thirty days each) and five days, which is exactly the length of the standard civil year in Egypt (§40). Therefore, this year was divided by the amounts specified between the last part-year of the reign of the preceding king and the first part of a year of the reign of King Shepseskaf. Further hieroglyphs to the left also call this part-year the "rising," i.e., the accession of the new king, and the "union of the two lands," a name for a feast celebrating the accession. At this time, therefore, the years of a king simply coincided with years of the civil calendar, plus such parts of years as were involved in the beginning and the ending of a given reign.

149. Furthermore, the Palermo Stone shows the first steps toward the numbering of regnal years. In the reign of a First Dynasty king is mentioned the "first occurrence of the Feast of Djet."[210] This can hardly have been the inauguration of this feast but only its first observance in the reign of this king. The numbered recording of events of regular occurrence in the several years of a king's reign is almost the same as the numbering of the regnal years themselves. That such numbering was continued is shown, not only by a "Second occurrence of the Feast of Djet" in the reign of another First Dynasty king[211] but also by this formula found in every other year of kings of the Second Dynasty: "fourth occurrence of the numbering"; "fifth occurrence of the numbering"; "sixth occurrence of the numbering"; and so on.[212] In some cases this is called a "numbering of gold and lands,"[213] and later it is a "numbering of large cattle."[214] Since the numbering took place only every second year, there is also such a designation as the "year after the seventh numbering."[215] Here, then, in the first dynasties and in the Old Kingdom are all the elements of the system which continued in use throughout most of Egyptian history: the years of the king are the same as the years of the civil calendar; the years are identified by a consecutive numbering.

---

[209]Gardiner, *JEA* 31 (1945): 12 and Fig. 1c.
[210]Breasted, *Ancient Records* 1:101.
[211]Ibid., §107.
[212]Ibid., §§120, 122, 124.
[213]Ibid., §§135, etc.
[214]Ibid., §157.
[215]Ibid., §161.

150. In the New Kingdom (Eighteenth to Twentieth Dynasties), however, a different manner of reckoning was introduced and for a time employed. Instead of equating a regnal year with a year of the standard civil calendar, each regnal year was reckoned from the actual accession day, whenever it was, to the anniversary of the same, and so on. This may be called a factual regnal year in distinction from a regnal year equated with a calendar year.

151. But again in the Saite period (Twenty-sixth Dynasty) and from then on, the old system was employed and the regnal years were the same as the years of the civil calendar, i.e., each regnal year began with New Year's Day, the first day of the first month of the first or Inundation season, the first day of the month of Thoth.

152. Given the system just described (§§149, 151) where the regnal year was counted as the calendar year, the question naturally arises as to how to treat portions of years. It must usually have been the case that a preceding ruler died with some portion of his last calendar year unfinished and a new ruler acceded to the throne at some point prior to the next New Year's day. At least from the time of the Ptolemies it is possible to see how the Egyptian scribes handled this problem. From his accession to the end of the then current calendar year was the new king's first regnal year. This fractional first regnal year and the unfinished part of the last regnal year of the preceding ruler occupied a single calendar year. In the texts such a year is referred to by some such phrase as "the last year which is also the first." Thus, for example, the year 52/51 B.C. in which Ptolemy XII Auletes was succeeded by his daughter Cleopatra VII is called ἔτος λ τὸ καὶ α, "the thirtieth year which is also the first."[216] Then the next calendar year, beginning Thoth 1, was also the new king's second regnal year.

153. In a consecutive tabulation this means that the last unfinished calendar year of a ruler, in which his successor begins to reign, is not credited to the expiring king but is counted to the new king. In the example just given (§152), the transition from Ptolemy XII Auletes to Cleopatra VII would have to be tabulated as in Table 34. By such a manner of reckoning, in giving consecutive totals, Ptolemy XII Auletes would be credited with twenty-nine years of reign.

154. Another interesting example of the manner of reckoning under discussion is found in Oxyrhynchus Papyrus No. 98.[217] This papyrus is an acknowledgment, written in the fifth year of Antoninus Pius, by a certain Chaeremon that he had received from Archias, a freedman, the sum of 168 drachmae, the balance due on a loan of 700 drachmae made four years earlier. This previous date on the original loan is stated thus in lines 12–15 of the papyrus:

τῷ Ἀθὺρ μηνὶ [τοῦ
δευτέρου καὶ ἰκοστοῦ ἔτους θεοῦ Ἀδρια[νοῦ,

---

[216]T. C. Skeat in *Mizraim* 6 (1937): 8; and in *JEA* 46 (1960): 91.
[217]*OxyP* 1:160–161.

ὅ ἐσ[τ]ι πρῶτον ἔτος Ἀντωνίνου Κ[αίσαρος
τοῦ κυρίου

in the month of Hathyr
in the twenty-second year of the deified Hadrian
which is the first year of Antoninus Caesar,
our sovereign

TABLE 34. *Egyptian Regnal Years at the Transition from Ptolemy XII Auletes to Cleopatra VII*

Regnal Year	*New Year's Day, Thoth 1*	*Calendar Year*	
		PTOLEMY XII AULETES	
29	Sept 5, 53 B.C.	53/52 B.C.	Last full regnal year = calendar year of Auletes's reign.
		CLEOPATRA VII	
1	Sept 5, 52 B.C.	52/51 B.C.	"The 30th year which is also the 1st," i.e. the 30th and uncounted year of Auletes in which this king died; the accession and 1st year of Cleopatra.
2	Sept 5, 51 B.C.	51/50 B.C.	2d year of Cleopatra.

155. This double date may be readily understood from the tabulation in Table 35 of the regnal years of Hadrian and the transition to the reign of Antoninus Pius in Egyptian reckoning. All years are shown as common years. The papyrus also mentions the month Hathyr. Since Hathyr falls in Oct/Nov, the date was in Oct/Nov A.D. 137.

156. The way just illustrated is the way reigns are recorded in the Canon or list of rulers given by the Alexandrian astronomer Claudius Ptolemaeus in the second century of the Christian era. This means that in an extended sequence of this sort, kings who inaugurated and terminated their reigns within a single calendar year are not even counted in the list, because it was the next king who was newly on the throne as the year ended to whom the year was credited. This accounts for the omission in the Canon of Ptolemy VII Neos Philopator, Berenice III, and Ptolemy XI Alexander II, as well as of Galba, Otho, and Vitellius.[218]

[218]Skeat in *Mizraim* 6 (1937): 7–8.

TABLE 35. *The Regnal Years of Hadrian in Egyptian Reckoning*

Egyptian Regnal Year	*Corresponding Julian Dates*	*Events*
1	Aug 29, 116–Aug 28, 117	On Aug 8 or 9, A.D. 117, Trajan died and Hadrian succeeded him. The balance of that year in the Egyptian calendar, i.e., through Epagomenae 5 = Aug 28, 117, constituted regnal year 1 of Hadrian.
2	Aug 29, 117–Aug 28, 118	Hadrian's regnal year 2 began with the beginning of the next calendar year on Thoth 1 = Aug 29, and so extended from Aug 29, 117, to Aug 28, 118. Succeeding regnal years were therefore:
3	Aug 29, 118–Aug 28, 119	
. . .	. . .	
20	Aug 29, 135–Aug 28, 136	
21	Aug 29, 136–Aug 28, 137	
22	Aug 29, 137–Aug 28, 138	In this calendar year Hadrian died on July 10, 138, and was succeeded by Antoninus Pius. This calendar year was therefore at the same time regnal year 22 of Hadrian and regnal year 1 of Antoninus.

2. In Mesopotamia

LITERATURE: Julius **Lewy**, "Forschungen zur alten Geschichte Vorderasiens," in *MVAG* 29 (1924): 2; A. **Ungnad**, "Datenlisten," in *RA* 2: 131–194; Arno **Poebel**, "The Duration of the Reign of Smerdis, the Magian, and the Reigns of Nebuchadnezzar III and Nebuchadnezzar IV," in *AJSL* 56 (1939): 121–145; idem, "The Use of Mathematical Mean Values in Babylonian King List B," in *Miscellaneous Studies* (Assyriological Studies 14; Chicago: University of Chicago Press, 1947), 110–122; P. van der **Meer**, *The Ancient Chronology of Western Asia and Egypt* (Leiden: Brill, 1947).

157. In Mesopotamia, as in Egypt, the oldest known way to designate a year was by an outstanding occurrence in it. In the Old Akkadian period (c. 2360–c. 2180 B.C.) and under King Naram-Sin, year designations such as these are found:[219]

> In the year that Naram-Sin laid the foundation of the temple of Enlil in Nippur and of Inanna in Zabalam.
> Year: Naram-Sin brought the mouth of the canal E-erina to Nippur.

In the later Third Dynasty of Ur there are such year-designations as these,[220] in the reign of Shulgi:

---

[219]Ungnad, in *RA* 2:133.

To Shulgi was strength given.
The high priest of Shulgi was installed and exalted.

And in the reign of Pur-Sin:

King Pur-Sin destroyed Urbilum.

In the First Dynasty of Babylon under Hammurabi (now probably to be dated around 1728–1686 B.C.), year-designations include ones such as these:[221]

Hammurabi (became) king.
He established justice in the country.
Uruk and Isin were conquered.
The canal Hammurabi-hegal (was dug).

For the reign of Samsuiluna, immediate successor of Hammurabi, a tablet in the British Museum[222] begins:

Year: Samsuiluna (became) king.
Year: He established freedom (from taxation) for Sumer and Akkad.

It continues with successive years, including:

Year: Canal "Samsuiluna is a source of prosperity (for the people)."
Year: All the enemies.
Year: The wall of Isin was demolished.
Year: Upon the command of Enlil.
Year following (the year): Upon the command of Enlil.
Year: He redug the canal Durul and Taban.

After all have been given there is a summary statement that thirty-eight year-names have been listed, and a concluding note giving the date when the list was written:

Thirty-eight year-(names) of king Samsuiluna.
(Written) Aiaru 2 (of)
the year: Ammisaduga (son of Samsuiluna, became) king.

158. As in the example just given, such lists of successive year-names can be totaled up to the number of years in the reign of a king, and then summaries of successive reigns can also be given. Another British Museum tablet gives this summary, for example, for the First Dynasty of Babylon.[223]

Sumuabi, king, 15 years.
Sumulail, 35 years.
Sabu, his son, same (i.e., king), 14 years.
Apil-Sin, his son, same, 18 years.
Sinmuballit, his son, same, 30 years.
Hammurabi, his son, same, 55 years.

---

[220]Ibid., 140, 143.
[221]Ibid., 178–179; *ANET* 270–271.
[222]Ungnad, in *RA* 2:182; *ANET* 271.
[223]*ANET* 271.

Samsuiluna, his son, same, 35 years.
Ebishum, his son, same, 25 years.
Ammiditana, same, 25 years.
Ammisaduga, same, 22 years.
Samsuditana, same, 31 years.
Eleven kings, dynasty of Babylon.

In this case it is at once noticeable, however, that Samsuiluna is credited with thirty-five years, whereas the list of year-names for his reign just previously considered (§157) totaled thirty-eight. Presumably the total where the actual year-names are listed one after the other is correct, and there is reason to think that, in the case of the summary tablet just quoted, a later scribe no longer had access to all the original figures and used some mean values to fill in his list.[224] After the compilation of lists such as the above, it was a natural development to number the years of a king's reign, and reckoning according to regnal years designated by number is found from the Kassite period (c. 1650–c. 1175 B.C.) on.[225]

159. In Assyria, however, a system of dating according to eponyms was used, and long lists of these eponyms are found in the cuneiform sources.[226] While the first full year of a king's reign is named after himself, each of the following years is designated with the name of a high official. The choice of the official who was to give his name to the year was first by lot, but later was a matter of his rank in the hierarchy, regular turns being taken from the king on down. In the lists the name of the official is introduced with the word *limmu,* hence these are also called limmu-lists, but the meaning is still eponym-year or eponymat. The extant sources make possible a reconstruction of the list beginning with Adad-nirari about 911 B.C. and continuing to the middle of the seventh century B.C. In the tenth year of Ashur-dan III, the year designated by the name of Bur-Sagale as eponym, a solar eclipse is mentioned. This has been identified with an astronomically computed eclipse of June 15, 763 B.C., so that a fixed point is established in the list.[227]

160. Returning now to the reckoning of years by the numbered years of kings' reigns, this was introduced according to present evidence, as noted above (§158), in the Kassite period (c. 1650–c. 1175 B.C.), was used in Assyria alongside the eponym dating, and continued in use in Babylonia until in the time of the Seleucid era.[228] As we have already seen in discussing Egyptian records of reigns, it is important to know how regnal years are related to calendar years, and how the years are counted at the point of transition from one reign to another. Already on the Palermo Stone we saw (§148) how a calendar year was divided between the last portion of the last year of the preceding king and the first portion of the first year of the new king. We noted also (§152) that the prevailing solution of the problem of how to count these part-years at such a

---

[224]Poebel, *Miscellaneous Studies,* 110–122.
[225]Ungnad, *RA* 2:132.
[226]Luckenbill, *Ancient Records* 2:1194–1198.
[227]Ungnad, *RA* 2: 412–457; *ANET* 274.
[228]Ungnad, *RA* 2: 132, 412; *ANET* 278–279.

transition point was to reckon the part of a year from a new king's accession to the next New Year's day—whether this part was long or short—as his first regnal year, and to count the next full calendar year as constituting already his second regnal year. In Mesopotamia the problem was handled in a different way. The part-year at the outset of a new reign was designated by a name of its own. Already the Sumerians call it *mu-sag-namlugal-a(k),* meaning "year (representing) the beginning of the kingship (of someone)," and the corresponding term in Babylonian is *resh sharruti.* The latter, in turn, is translated word for word in the Hebrew ראשית מלכות (*reshit malkut,* §421). In English the common and convenient rendering is "accession year."[229]

161. Using this term, the system of reckoning which prevailed in Babylonia, Assyria, and Persia may be called the accession-year system. This means that the balance of the calendar year in which a preceding king died or was removed and a new king came to the throne was counted as the accession year of the new king, and the first full year of his reign was reckoned as beginning with the next New Year's day, i.e., with the next Nisanu 1 in the Babylonian calendar. The calendar year in which the predecessor occupied the throne for only a part of the year and then died or was removed, could therefore still be counted as corresponding to his own last numbered regnal year. If we may most unambiguously designate the system just described, then, as the accession-year system, we may also use as the most unambiguous designation for the contrasting system discussed in relation to Egypt and summarized in the preceding paragraph (§160) as the non-accession-year system. To recapitulate: In the accession-year system, the portion of a year from the accession of the king to the end of the then current calendar year is only his "accession year" (and for chronological purposes remains a part of the last numbered regnal year of his predecessor), and the new king's year 1 begins only on the first day of the new calendar year after his accession. In the non-accession-year system, the portion of a calendar year, no matter how brief, remaining from the accession of the king to the end of the then current calendar year is treated not as an uncounted accession year but as already year 1 of the new king; therewith the preceding king fails to be credited with that calendar year as a regnal year in which he does not live out a full year on the throne. To convert an accession-year system into a non-accession-year system it is necessary to add a year to the accession-year number; hence the accession-year system is sometimes called postdating. Contrariwise, to convert a non-accession-year system into an accession-year system it is necessary to subtract one year from the non-accession-year number, hence the non-accession-year system is sometimes called antedating. This alternative terminology is, however, ambiguous and confusing, and is not used in the present book.[230]

162. The way in which the chronological data are presented in accordance with the accession-year system may be seen most clearly in the tables of Parker and Dubberstein, *Babylonian Chronology* (= PDBC) where, as we have

---

[229]Lewy, *MVAG* 29 (1924): 2, 25 n.3; Albright in *JBL* 51 (1932): 102; Poebel in *AJSL* 56 (1939): 121 n.3.

[230]THCK 16–17, 87–88; McFall, *BSac* 148 (589, Jan–Mar 1991): 7.

noted (§54), the data of the cuneiform sources and of astronomy are correlated. For a single example we may note the transition from the reign of Nabopolassar to that of Nebuchadrezzar II. From the annalistic references in the cuneiform document known as the Babylonian Chronicle (British Museum 21946) and from the astronomical reconstitution of the Babylonian calendar it can be established that Nabopolassar died on the eighth day of the month Abu in the twenty-first year of his reign, a date corresponding to Aug 15, 605 B.C.; and that Nebuchadrezzar II ascended the throne in Babylon soon thereafter on the first day of Ululu, a date corresponding to Sept 7, 605 B.C. The transition may therefore be tabulated as in Table 36.

TABLE 36. *Babylonian Regnal Years at the Transition from Nabopolassar to Nebuchadrezzar II*

Regnal Years	*New Year's Day, Nisanu 1*	*Calendar Year*	
		NABOPOLASSAR	
21	Apr 12, 605 B.C.	605/604 B.C.	Nabopolassar dies on Abu 8 = Aug 15 in his 21st regnal year. Nebuchadrezzar II ascends the throne on Ululu 1 = Sept 7, and the balance of this calendar year until the next New Year's day, i.e., Nisanu 1, is accounted his "accession year."
		NEBUCHADREZZAR II	
1	Apr 2, 604 B.C.	604/603 B.C.	This is now the 1st regnal year of Nebuchadrezzar, and successive years are counted consecutively onward in the same manner.
2	Mar 22, 603 B.C.	603/602 B.C.	

3. Among the Jews

LITERATURE: Julian **Morgenstern**, "The New Year for Kings," in *Occident and Orient: Gaster Anniversary Volume* (ed. Bruno Schindler; London, Taylor's Foreign Press, 1936), 439–456; Edgar **Frank**, *Talmudic and Rabbinical Chronology: The Systems of Counting Years in Jewish Literature* (New York, P. Feldheim, 1956).

163. In the foregoing discussion (§§146ff.) of materials reflecting practices in Egypt and in Mesopotamia in the reckoning of regnal years points have come into view, implicitly or explicitly, which must always be kept in mind in any consideration of the reckoning of such years in any land. In explication and recapitulation of such points, it is evident that at least the following items must be noticed in the attempt to understand any system of reckoning by regnal years. (1) *Accession.* At what point is the reign considered to begin? This point most often coincides, no doubt, with the death of the preceding ruler, yet there may be an interval before the new king is selected, installed, or confirmed in office. Other possibilities as to when his reign is considered actually to begin include the time when a coregency is established, when a capital is occupied, when a decisive victory is won, or when some remaining rival is eliminated. (2) *Factual year or calendar year.* Is the regnal year counted from the actual accession to the annual anniversary of the same? If so, it may be called a factual year. Is the regnal year counted as equivalent to the calendar year? The latter is probably much more often the case, and therewith additional questions arise. (3) *Accession year or non-accession year.* If the regnal year is equated with a calendar year, is the reckoning by the accession-year or the non-accession-year system? In the accession-year system the balance of the calendar year in which the point of the beginning of the reign falls is considered as an "accession year" and only the next full calendar year is considered as regnal year 1. In the non-accession-year system the calendar year in which the beginning point of the reign falls is itself counted as year 1 of the reign. (4) *Calendar.* If the regnal year is equated with a calendar year, which calendar year is in use? The calendars that have already been discussed in some detail (§§37ff.) are simply listed in Table 37 by their name and the date (in the order of the Julian year) of their New Year's day, which is the crucial point for reckoning by regnal year equated with calendar year.

TABLE 37. *Calendars and New Year's Days*

Calendar	*New Year's Day*
Roman (Julian; Table 33)	Jan 1
Babylonian (Table 9)	Nisanu (Mar/Apr) 1
Jewish (Table 38)	Nisan (Mar/Apr) 1
Macedonian in Babylonia (earlier correlation; Table 20)	Artemisios = Nisanu (Mar/Apr) 1
Macedonian in Babylonia (later correlation; Table 25)	Xanthikos = Nisan (Mar/Apr) 1
Macedonian in Palestine (earlier correlation; Table 30)	Artemisios = Nisan (Mar/Apr) 1
Macedonian in Palestine (later correlation; Table 31)	Xanthikos = Nisan (Mar/Apr) 1
Macedonian in Arabia (Table 28)	Xanthikos 1 = Mar 22
Greek (Attic; Table 16)	Hekatombaion (July) 1
Greek (Delphic; Table 17)	Apellaios (July) 1
Egyptian (fixed standard civil calendar; Table 8)	Thoth 1 = Aug 29
Macedonian in Egypt (fixed equation; Table 29)	Dios 1 = Thoth 1 = Aug 29
Honorific Imperial in Egypt (Table 29)	Sebastos 1 = Thoth 1 = Aug 29
Israelite (Tables 12, 39)	Tishri (Sept/Oct) 1
Macedonian in Syria (earlier correlation; Table 19)	Dios = First Tishri = Tishri (Sept/Oct) 1
Macedonian in Syria (later correlation; Table 26)	Hyperberetaios = Tishri (Sept/Oct) 1
Syro-Macedonian in relation to the Julian (Table 27)	Hyperberetaios 1 = Oct 1

164. Which of the methods just outlined (§163) were employed by the Jews is a question which must necessarily be raised in connection with many biblical dates. Some of the concrete problems in this regard will be taken up in Part Two of this book. In extra-biblical Jewish sources there is one passage in particular which, because of its relative antiquity and its relatively explicit statements as to how years are reckoned, must be considered in the present context. This passage is found in the Mishna and gives concise definitions of four different New Year's days; in the accompanying Gemara these definitions are elucidated and discussed at length; and the whole is now contained in the Babylonian Talmud in the division *Moed* ("Feasts") and in the tractate *Rosh Hashanah* ("New Year").[231] The Mishna reads as follows:

> There are four New Years. On the first of Nisan is New Year for kings and for festivals. On the first of Elul is New Year for the tithe of cattle. Rabbi Eleazar and Rabbi Simeon, however, place this on the first of Tishri. On the first of Tishri is New Year for years, for release and jubilee years, for plantation and for tithe of vegetables. On the first of Shebat is New Year for trees, according to the ruling of Beth Shammai; Beth Hillel, however, place it on the fifteenth of that month.

165. We are here concerned with two of the New Years thus defined in the Talmud, and the first is that which begins with the month Nisan in the spring (the new moon of Nisan ideally coinciding with the spring equinox, *1 Enoch* 72): "On the first of Nisan is New Year for kings and festivals." According to this statement one would suppose that regnal years always coincided with calendar years beginning Nisan 1. In the ensuing rabbinic discussion of the Gemara it is further explained:

> If a king ascends the throne on the twenty-ninth of Adar, as soon as the first of Nisan arrives he is reckoned to have reigned a year. This teaches us that Nisan is the New Year for kings, and that one day in a year is reckoned as a year. But if he ascended the throne on the first of Nisan he is not reckoned to have reigned a year till the next first of Nisan comes round.[232]

According to this statement, not only do regnal years coincide with calendar years beginning Nisan 1 but they are also reckoned by what we have called the non-accession-year method. Indeed we recognize here as a general or normal principle of Jewish reckoning that the part stands for the whole: a part of a month is considered a whole month and a part of a year is considered a whole year.[233] In reckoning the years of life of a person, however, this does not hold but it is completed years which are counted. Thus Rabbi Avadyah, elucidating another passage in the Mishna (*Para* 8:9), says: "Like a man whose son is born on passover. He has fulfilled his first year of life on passover of the next year."[234]

---

[231]*Rosh Hashanah* 1:1, Danby 188; 2a ff. Epstein, *BT* 2:7, 1ff.
[232]Epstein, *BT* 2.
[233]Cf. also *Rosh Hashanah* 10b, Epstein, *BT* 38.
[234]Quoted by Frank, *Talmudic and Rabbinical Chronology,* 18 n.17.

166. Returning to the passage in *Rosh Hashanah,* the fact that kings' reigns are always reckoned as commencing from Nisan 1 is substantiated in the rabbinic discussion by the citation of 1 Kgs 6:1. Here the year is given as at the same time the four hundred and eightieth after the Israelites came out of Egypt and the fourth year of Solomon, and the month is given only once as Ziv, the second month. Ziv, using the old Canaanite month name (§60). Since Ziv = Iyyar was the second month both in the four hundred and eightieth year reckoned from the exodus and in the fourth year of the reign of Solomon, both series of years were stated in terms of years reckoned from Nisan 1.

167. After that a considerable discussion ensues,[235] as to whether the rule that New Year for kings is Nisan 1 was meant to apply only to the kings of Israel, and it is strongly maintained at least by some that the years of non-Israelite kings are reckoned not from Nisan 1 but from Tishri 1. Here Neh 1:1 mentions the month of Chislev in the twentieth year; Neh 2:1 mentions the month of Nisan in the twentieth year of King Artaxerxes. Supposing that it is the same "twentieth year" that is meant in both cases, in one and the same year Nisan would come later than Chislev only if the year began with Tishri. Other rabbis, however, denied that this argument was conclusive. In spite of this uncertainty, however, it was affirmed as certain that the numbering of the months always commences with Nisan. Using the formula customary for the introduction of a Baraitha, it was said: "Our Rabbis taught: On the first of Nisan is New Year for months,"[236] i.e., the order of the months always begins with Nisan.

168. The second New Year mentioned in *Rosh Hashanah* with which we are here concerned is defined in the words: "On the first of Tishri is New Year for years, for release and jubilee years. . . . " The "release" is that of the Sabbatical year; for this and for the Jubilee year see below (§§224ff.). With regard to "years," the Gemara explains that this is the New Year which is used for reckoning cycles.[237] The cycles are the four *tequfot* (§34), which are the four dividing points of the year and the four seasons which they introduce: the *tequfah* of Tishri (autumnal equinox); the *tequfah* of Tebet (winter solstice); the *tequfah* of Nisan (vernal equinox); the *tequfah* of Tammuz (summer solstice).

169. In the same connection it is stated that the world was created in Tishri, a topic taken up again a little later in the discussion.[238] Among the rabbis who held this opinion, Rabbi Eleazar is quoted as saying:

> In Tishri the world was created; in Tishri the patriarchs [Abraham and Jacob] were born; in Tishri the patriarchs died; on passover Isaac was born; on New Year [Tishri 1] Sarah, Rachel, and Hannah were visited [i.e., remembered on high]; on New Year Joseph went forth from prison; on New Year the bondage of our ancestors in Egypt ceased [six months before the redemption which was exodus]; in Nisan they were redeemed and in Nisan they will be redeemed in the time to come.

---

[235] *Rosh Hashanah* 3a f., Epstein, *BT* 7ff.
[236] *Rosh Hashanah* 7a, Epstein, *BT* 23.
[237] *Rosh Hashanah* 8a, Epstein, *BT* 30.
[238] *Rosh Hashanah* 10b–11a, Epstein, *BT* 38–39.

This opinion that the world was created in Tishri was supported by Rabbi Eleazar by reference to Gen 1:11 where the putting forth of vegetation was held to imply the autumnal season of rainfall (§31); another rabbi, however, cited the same verse to show that the time was Nisan. In the reckoning of years from the creation of the world (§§204ff.) it was generally considered that the start should be made from Tishri. Another argument in support of Tishri as the month in which the world was created was based upon the first word in Genesis, בראשית, "In the beginning." The letters of this word can be rearranged to make א׳ בתשרי, "the first day in the month of Tishri."[239]

170. In summary, we find ourselves concerned chiefly with two Jewish years, one beginning in the spring on Nisan 1, one beginning in the fall on Tishri 1. Regardless of which year is used, numbering of the months is normally in sequence from Nisan (§167). The two Jewish years therefore appear as in Tables 38 and 39.

TABLE 38. *The Jewish Year with Nisan 1 as New Year's Day*

1.	Nisan	Mar/Apr
2.	Iyyar	Apr/May
3.	Sivan	May/June
4.	Tammuz	June/July
5.	Ab	July/Aug
6.	Elul	Aug/Sept
7.	Tishri	Sept/Oct
8.	Marheshvan or Heshvan	Oct/Nov
9.	Chislev	Nov/Dec
10.	Tebeth	Dec/Jan
11.	Shevat	Jan/Feb
12.	Adar	Feb/Mar

TABLE 39. *The Jewish Year with Tishri 1 as New Year's Day*

7.	Tishri	Sept/Oct
8.	Marheshvan or Heshvan	Oct/Nov
9.	Chislev	Nov/Dec
10.	Tebeth	Dec/Jan
11.	Shevat	Jan/Feb
12.	Adar	Feb/Mar
1.	Nisan	Mar/Apr
2.	Iyyar	Apr/May
3.	Sivan	May/June
4.	Tammuz	June/July
5.	Ab	July/Aug
6.	Elul	Aug/Sept

4. In Greece

LITERATURE: R. D. **Hicks**, "Chronology," in *A Companion to Greek Studies* (ed. Leonard Whibley; 3d ed.; Cambridge: Cambridge University Press, 1916), 69ff.

171. In regard to official and regnal years, the Greek system again is not of major concern in our area of investigation, but may be mentioned briefly as we make the transition to the Roman system. Throughout the historical period the custom was to date events by a local official or local officials in office at the time. Those particularly singled out to serve in this way were the first archon at Athens, the first ephor at Sparta, and the priestess of Hera at Argos, the last named being chosen for life. Thus, for a single example, the Athenian historian

[239]Frank, *Talmudic and Rabbinical Chronology,* 16 n.15.

Thucydides gives a date equivalent to April 431 B.C. by naming the following officials:

> When Chrysis was in the forty-eighth year of her priesthood at Argos, and Aenesias was ephor at Sparta, and Pythodorus had still four months to serve as archon at Athens, in the sixteenth month after the battle of Potidaea, at the opening of spring. (2.2.1)

5. In Rome

LITERATURE: T. **Mommsen**, *Chronica minora* (3 vols.; Monumenta Germaniae historica 9, 11, 13; Berlin: Weidmann, 1892–1898); Willy **Liebenam**, *Fasti consulares Imperii romani von 30 v. Chr. bis 565 n. Chr. mit Kaiserliste und Anhang* (KLT 41–43; Bonn: A. Marcus und E. Weber, 1909); J. S. **Reid**, "Chronology and Chronological Tables," in *A Companion to Latin Studies* (ed. John E. Sandys; 3d ed.; Cambridge: Cambridge University Press, 1925), 90–148; A. **Cappelli**, *Cronologia, cronografia e calendario perpetuo dal principio dell'êra cristiana ai giorni nostri* (2d ed.; Milan: Hoepli, 1930); "Chronological Tables," in *CAH*, vol. 10 (1934), at end; Arthur E. **Gordon**, *Album of Dated Latin Inscriptions*, vol. 1, *Rome and the Neighborhood, Augustus to Nerva,* Text and Plates (Berkeley: University of California Press, 1958).

(1) Consuls

172. In a method somewhat similar to that seen in the eponym lists of Assyria (§159) and the reference to various officials in Greece (§171), it was the custom in Rome to designate a year by mention of two officials, the consuls, who were in office in that year. When the ancient Roman monarchy fell, the king was replaced by two magistrates who, throughout the republic, were the heads of administration at home and abroad. Under the later rule of the Caesars the office continued and the emperor himself was often elected to the position. Since the post was held for one year—from 153 B.C. on, a year beginning on Jan 1 (§142)—a reference to the two consuls then in office sufficed to define a year-date.

173. The rise and use of this system are clearly shown by the Roman historian Livy. He tells how "the rule of the kings of Rome, from its foundation to its liberation, lasted two hundred and forty-four years" (1.9.4) and how then two consuls were chosen in the assembly of the people, those for the first year (A.U.C. 245 [for dating A.U.C. see §§188ff.] = 509 B.C.) being Lucius Junius Brutus and Lucius Tarquinius Collatinus. Collatinus resigned before his year of office ended, and was replaced by Publius Valerius (2.2.10–11). For the following year (A.U.C. 246 = 508 B.C.) Livy states: "Next Publius Valerius (for the second time) and Titus Lucretius were made consuls" (2.9.1). And so the framework of Roman history continues. Typical further references from Livy are:

> A.U.C. 249 = 505 B.C.
> *Consules M. Valerius P. Postumius. Eo anno bene pugnatum . . .*
> The consulship of Marcus Valerius and Publius Postumius.
> This year a successful war was waged . . . [240]

A.U.C. 254 = 500 B.C.
Consules Ser. Sulpicius M. Tullius; nihil dignum memoriae actum.
In the consulship of Servius Sulpicius and Manius Tullius nothing worthy of note occurred.[241]
A.U.C. 256 = 498 B.C.
Consules Q. Cloelius et T. Larcius, inde A. Sempronius et M. Minucius. His consulibus aedis Saturno dedicata.
The consuls Quintus Cloelius and Titus Larcius were followed by Aulus Sempronius and Marcus Minucius. In the latter year a temple to Saturn was dedicated.[242]
A.U.C. 432 = 322 B.C.
In sequenti anno, Q. Fabio L. Fulvio consulibus. . . .
In the following year, when Quintus Fabius and Lucius Fulvius were consuls. . . .[243]

174. For an example of consular dates in inscriptions, a marble tablet may be cited which was found on the Via Latina in Rome. It appears to be the epitaph of Scirtus, who was a slave charioteer, and it contains a list of his races dated by consuls. These dates begin (line 3) with L. Munatius and C. Silius (= A.D. 13); they include (line 8) Tiberius Caesar III and Germanicus Caesar II (= A.D. 18); and (line 11) Tiberius Caesar IIII and Drusus Caesar II (= A.D. 21); and they extend to (line 15) Cossus Cornelius Lentulus and M. Asinius (= A.D. 25).[244]

175. Lists of the consuls were compiled at an early date but often contained discrepancies or gaps. Livy tells of certain consuls whose names he could find *neque in annalibus priscis neque in libris magistratuum,* "neither in the ancient annals nor in the lists of magistrates" (4.7.10). Among the sources of this sort were the *Annales Maximi* or annals of the Pontifical College published by Mucius Scaevola in 130 B.C.; and the *Fasti capitolini* (for the *fasti* cf. §141), affixed to the wall of the *Regia* or official residence of the Pontifex Maximus and in extant fragments in the Museum on the Capitol.[245] The *Fasti capitolini,* in turn, were a source ultimately drawn upon, with revision, by the *Chronographer of the Year 354.*

176. *Chronographus anni CCCLIIII* or *Chronographer of the Year 354* is the title under which there has come down in two late copies of older manuscripts an anonymous work which may have been edited in the year indicated by Furius Dionysius Filocalus, later the calligrapher of Pope Damasus (A.D. 366–384). This work, which is available in Mommsen's *Chronica minora* 1, contains: (1) a list of the consuls beginning with Brutus and Collatinus (§173) and extending to A.D. 354;[246] (2) a list of the dates of Easter from 312 to 411;[247]; (3) a list of the prefects

---

[240] 2.16.1.
[241] 2.19.1.
[242] 2.21.1.
[243] 8.38.1.
[244] Gordon, *Album of Dated Latin Inscriptions* 1:67 No. 60.
[245] Reid, *Companion to Latin Studies,* 103f.
[246] Mommsen, *Chronica minora* 1:50–61.
[247] Ibid., 62–64.

of the city from 254 to 354;[248] (4) a list of the burial places of bishops *(Depositio episcoporum)* and martyrs *(Depositio martyrum)* and the days on which they were remembered;[249] and (5) a list of the bishops of Rome from Peter to Liberius.[250] The *Depositio martyrum* became the basis of the vast *Martyrologium hieronymianum* in the sixth century, and the *Catalogus liberianus* developed into the *Liber pontificalis* (§666) of the seventh century.[251]

177. The Roman monk and historian Cassiodorus Senator (A.D. c. 490–c. 585) also compiled in his *Chronica* (published in A.D. 519) a list of the consuls.[252] It begins with Junius Brutus and Lucius Tarquinius (A.U.C. 245 = 509 B.C.), then Publius Valerius II and Titus Lucretius (A.U.C. 246 = 508 B.C.), and so on down to the time of Cassiodorus himself.

178. For the time with which we are chiefly concerned in relation to such dates, the list of consuls given by *Chronographus anni CCCLIIII* appears in Table 40. In each case one is to understand *Caesare V et Antonio consulibus,* and so on, as in the example from Livy for A.U.C. 432 = 322 B.C. given above (§173).

(2) Honors

179. Roman dating also made use of reference to various honors received by the emperor from the senate in the course of his reign. Of these honors three were the most important. One is the honor of being elected consul, and in the list of consuls in Table 40 we see many examples where the emperor appears and the number of times he holds the consulship is given. A second honor is that called *tribunicia potestas,* δημαρχικὴ ἐξουσία, or "tribunician power." The Roman magistrates known as "tribunes" enjoyed a certain sacrosanctity and a similar privilege was conferred upon the emperor when he was granted this honor. Dio explains the matter in these words:

> The tribunician power (ἡ ἐξουσία ἡ δημαρχική), as it is called, which used to be conferred only upon men of the greatest influence, gives them the right to nullify the effects of measures taken by any other official, in case they do not approve it, and makes them immune from scurrilous abuse; and if they appear to be wronged in even the slightest degree, not merely by deed, but even by word, they may destroy the guilty party, as one accursed, without a trial. The emperors, it should be explained, do not think it right to be tribunes, inasmuch as they belong altogether to the patrician class, but they assume the power of the tribunes to its full extent, as it was when it was greatest; and in numbering the years they have held the imperial office they use the tribunician power to mark the stages, the theory being that they received it year by year along with those who are regularly made tribunes. (8.17.9–10)

[248]Ibid., 65–69.
[249]Ibid., 70–72.
[250]*Catalogus liberianus;* ibid., 73ff.
[251]Hans Lietzmann, *Die drei ältesten Martyrologien* (KLT 2; Bonn: A. Marcus und E. Weber, 1903), 3f.
[252]Mommsen, *Chronica minora* 2:109–161.

TABLE 40. *Roman Consuls from 44 B.C. to A.D. 135*

A.U.C.	*B.C.*	*Consuls*	*A.U.C.*	*A.D.*	*Consuls*
710	44	Caesare V et Antonio	762	9	Camerino et Sabino
711	43	Pansa et Hirstio (C. Pansa and A. Hirtius were killed and Octavius [later to be Augustus] was declared consul)	763	10	Dolabella et Silano
			764	11	Lepido et Tauro
			765	12	Caesare et Capitone
			766	13	Planco et Silano
712	42	Lepido et Planco	767	14	Duobus Sextis
713	41	Petate et Isaurico	768	15	Druso Caesare et Flacco
714	40	Calvino et Pollione	769	16	Tauro et Libone
715	39	Censorino et Sabino	770	17	Flacco et Rufo
716	38	Pulchro et Flacco	771	18	Tito Caesare III et Germanico Caesare II
717	37	Agrippa et Gallo			
718	36	Publicula et Nerva	772	19	Silano et Balbo
719	35	Cornificio et Pompeio	773	20	Messala et Cotta
720	34	Libone et Atratino	774	21	Tito Caesare IIII et Druso Caesare II
721	33	Augusto II et Tullo			
722	32	Henobulbo et Sossio	775	22	Agrippa et Galba
723	31	Augusto III et Messala	776	23	Pollione et Vetere
724	30	Augusto IIII et Grasso	777	24	Caethego et Varro
725	29	Augusto V et Apuleio	778	25	Agrippa et Lentulo
726	28	Augusto VI et Agrippa II	779	26	Getulico et Sabino
727	27	Augusto VII et Agrippa III	780	27	Grasso et Pisone
728	26	Augusto VIII et Tauro	781	28	Silano et Nerva
729	25	Augusto VIIII et Silano	782	29	Gemino et Gemino
730	24	Augusto X et Flacco	783	30	Vinicio et Longino
731	23	Augusto XI et Pisone	784	31	Tiberio Caesare V solo
732	22	Marcello et Arrutio	785	32	Arruntio et Ahenobarbo
733	21	Lollio et Lepido	786	33	Galba et Sulla
734	20	Apuleio et Nerva	787	34	Vitello et Persico
735	19	Saturnino et Lucretio	788	35	Camerino et Noniano
736	18	Lentulo et Lentulo	789	36	Allieno et Plautino
737	17	Turnio et Silato	790	37	Proculo et Nigrino
738	16	Henobarbo et Scipione	791	38	Iuliano et Asprenate
739	15	Libone et Pisone	792	39	C. Caesare II et Caesiano
740	14	Grasso et Augure	793	40	C. Caesare III solo
741	13	Nerone et Varo	794	41	C. Caesare IIII et Saturnino
742	12	Messala et Quirino	795	42	Tito Claudio II et Longo
743	11	Tuberone et Maximo	796	43	Tito Claudio III et Vitellio
744	10	Africano et Maximo	797	44	Crispo II et Tauro
745	9	Druso et Crispino	798	45	Vinicio et Corvino
746	8	Censorino et Gallo	799	46	Asiatico II et Silano
747	7	Nerone et Pisone	800	47	Tito Claudio IIII et Vitellio III
748	6	Balbo et Vetere	801	48	Vitellio et Publicula
749	5	Augusto XII et Sulla	802	49	Verannio et Gallo
750	4	Sabino et Rufo	803	50	Vetere et Nerviliano
751	3	Lentulo et Messalino	804	51	Tito Claudio V et Orfito
752	2	Augusto XIII et Silvano	805	52	Sulla et Othone
753	1	Lentulo et Pisone	806	53	Silano et Antonino
754	A.D. 1	Caesare et Paulo	807	54	Marcello et Aviola
755	2	Vinicio et Varo	808	55	Nerone Caesare et Vetere
756	3	Lamia et Servilio	809	56	Saturnino et Scipione
757	4	Catulo et Saturnino	810	57	Nerone II et Pisone
758	5	Voleso et Magno	811	58	Nerone III et Messala
759	6	Lepido et Arruntio	812	59	Capitone et Aproniano
760	7	Cretico et Nerva	813	60	Nerone IIII et Lentulo
761	8	Camello et Quintiliano	814	61	Turpillino et Peto

A.U.C.	*B.C.*	*Consuls*	*A.U.C.*	*A.D.*	*Consuls*
815	62	Mario et Gallo	852	99	Palma et Senecione
816	63	Regulo et Rufo	853	100	Traiano III et Frontino
817	64	Grasso et Basso	854	101	Traiano IIII et Peto
818	65	Nerva et Vestino	855	102	Servillo II et Sura II
819	66	Telesino et Paulo	856	103	Traiano V et Maximo II
820	67	Capitone et Rufo	857	104	Surano II et Marcello
821	68	Trachala et Italico	858	105	Candido II et Quadrato
822	69	Galva II et Vinio	859	106	Commodo et Cereale
823	70	Vespasiano II et Tito	860	107	Sura et Senecione
824	71	Vespasiano III et Nerva	861	108	Gallo et Bradua
825	72	Vespasiano IIII et Tito II	862	109	Palma II et Tullo
826	73	Domitiano II et Messalino	863	110	Priscina et Ortito
827	74	Vespasiano V et Tito III	864	111	Pisone et Bolano
828	75	Vespasiano VI et Tito IIII	865	112	Traiano VI et Africano
829	76	Vespasiano VII et Tito V	866	113	Celso et Crispino
830	77	Vespasiano VIII et Domitiano V	867	114	Vopisco et Asta
831	78	Commodo et Prisco	868	115	Messala et Pedone
832	79	Vespasiano VIIII et Tito VI	869	116	Aeliano et Vetere
833	80	Tito VII et Domitiano VII	870	117	Nigro et Aproniano
834	81	Silva et Pollione	871	118	Adriano II et Salinatore
835	82	Domitiano VIII et Sabino	872	119	Adriano II et Rustico
836	83	Domitiano VIIII et Rufo	873	120	Severo et Fulvo
837	84	Domitiano X et Sabino	874	121	Vero II et Augure
838	85	Domitiano XI et Furvo	875	122	Aviola et Pansa
839	86	Domitiano XII et Dolabella	876	123	Petino et Aproniano
840	87	Domitiano XIII et Saturnino	877	124	Glabrione et Torquato
841	88	Domitiano XIIII et Rufo	878	125	Asiatico II et Aquilino
842	89	Fulvo et Atratino	879	126	Vero III Ambibulo
843	90	Domitiano XV et Nerva	880	127	Titiano et Gallicano
844	91	Clabrione et Traiano	881	128	Asprenate et Libone
845	92	Domitiano XVI et Saturnino	882	129	Marcello II et Marcello II
846	93	Collega et Priscino	883	130	Catulino et Apro
847	94	Asprenate et Laterano	884	131	Pontiano et Rutino
848	95	Domitiano XVII et Clemente	885	132	Augurino et Sergiano
849	96	Valeriano et Vetere	886	133	Hibero et Sisenna
850	97	Nerva II et Rufo III	887	134	Serviano et Varo
851	98	Nerva III et Traiano II	888	135	Luperco et Attico

In the case of Augustus, there were occasional grants of honor earlier, but from 23 B.C. on, the tribunician power was renewed annually and was reckoned from July 1, 23 B.C. Thus, in his own record of his life and work, the *Res gestae,* completed in A.D. 14, he states that he was "in the thirty-seventh year of his tribunician power."[254] From then on at each change of reign the new emperor was accorded the honor at the moment of his accession to the throne. For the successors of Augustus up to Trajan, therefore, the first tribunician year was the actual year which began on the accession day and extended through the day prior to the anniversary day one year hence, and the further tribunician years were reckoned in like manner.[255]

[254]*CAH* 10:139.
[255]L. Hennequin in *Dictionnaire de la Bible,* Supplément 2:359.

180. The third honor to be mentioned was that of the "imperial acclamation" signified by the designation *imperator,* αὐτοκράτωρ. Originally this was an honorary appellation by which Roman soldiers saluted their general after a military victory. Subsequently, the designation was conferred by the senate and received at frequent intervals by Augustus and his successors. According to a description by Dio (52.41.3), the title was often conferred on account of achievements and sometimes also carried the sense of supreme power. Telling of the year when Augustus was consul for the fifth time (29 B.C.), Dio continues,

> And he assumed the title of *imperator.* I do not here refer to the title which had occasionally been bestowed, in accordance with the ancient custom, upon generals in recognition of their victories—for he had received that many times before this and received it many times afterwards in honor merely of his achievements, so that he won the name of *imperator* twenty-one times—but rather the title in its other use, which signifies the possession of the supreme power, in which sense it had been voted to his father Caesar and to the children of the descendants of Caesar.

As the sources also show, an emperor often received this imperial acclamation not only a number of times in the course of the years of his reign but also even several times within a single year.

181. In listing the three honors just discussed, usual practice was to put them in the order: tribunician power, imperial acclamation, and consulship. In illustration of the importance attached to them, we may recall the report of Tacitus[255] of the comments that were made upon the death of Augustus concerning his numerous honors:

> Much, too, was said of the number of his consulates (in which he had equaled the combined totals of Valerius Corvus and Caius Marius [i.e., 6 + 7 = 13]), his tribunician power unbroken for thirty-seven years, his title of imperator twenty-one times earned, and his other honors, multiplied or new.

(3) Years of Reign

182. As in other lands, there was also, of course, reference in Roman custom to the years of reign of the emperors, and in the interpretation of references to regnal years the same kind of problems arise which have already been noted elsewhere (§163). Such a reference to regnal years might also be combined with reference to consuls, to the consulship of the emperor, or to other of his honors. And in the provinces there might be added, too, some reference to some system of dating prevailing in the area. Thirty-five large papyrus documents found in a cave at Nahal Hever in the State of Israel provide interesting illustration of the combined methods of dating. These manuscripts are written in Greek, Aramaic, and Nabatean, and evidently constitute the archive of a Jewish family living at the south end of the Dead Sea in what was

---

[255] *Annals* 1.9.

the kingdom of Nabatea and what was made into Provincia Arabia by Trajan in A.D. 106. The manuscripts belong to the fifty-year period from near the end of the first century of the Christian era to just before the Bar Kokhba revolt, i.e., from A.D. 88 to 132. Most of them begin by stating the date according to the Roman consuls, the emperor (e.g., the ninth year of Hadrian = A.D. 125), and the local date of the province (e.g., the twenty-fifth year of the "New Arabian Province" = A.D. 130).[256]

(4) Tables of Emperors

183. In Tables 41–45, therefore, we provide for ready reference outlines of events and honors in the lives and reigns of the emperors from Augustus to Nero. Events are chiefly such as need to be kept in mind in relation to the question of when the reign was considered to begin. Honors, when held simultaneously, are listed in the usual order: tribunicia potestate, imperator, consul. Ultimate sources are ancient literary records and inscriptions; a compilation is provided by Liebenam, *Fasti consulares.*

TABLE 41. *Events and Honors in the Life and Reign (Mar 15, 44 B.C.–Aug 19, A.D. 14) of Augustus*

B.C./A.D.	*Month and Day*	*Chronology*
63 B.C.	Sept 23	Birth of C. Octavius
44	Mar 15	Assassination of Julius Caesar
43	Apr 15	Octavian Imperator I
	Aug 19	Octavian Consul I
42		
41		
40	Dec	Imperator II
39		
38		Imperator III
37		
36		Imperator IV
35		
34 (or 33)		Imperator V
33		Consul II
32		
31		Consul III
	Sept 2	Octavian defeated Antony at Actium
	Sept 2	Imperator VI
30		Consul IIII
	Aug	Death of Antony and Cleopatra
29		Imperator VII
		Consul V
28		Consul VI
27		Consul VII
	Jan 16	Octavian received title Augustus
26		Consul VIII

[256]Yigael Yadin in *BA* 24 (1961): 94–95; and in *IEJ* 12 (1962): 235–257; H. J. Polotsky in *IEJ* 12 (1962): 258–262.

B.C./A.D.	*Month and Day*	*Chronology*
25		Imperator VIII
		Consul VIIII
24		Consul X
23		Consul XI
	July 1, 23–June 30, 22	Tribunicia potestate I
22	July 1, 22–June 30, 21	Tribunicia potestate II
21	July 1, 21–June 30, 20	Tribunicia potestate III
20		Imperator VIIII?
	July 1, 20–June 30, 19	Tribunicia potestate IIII
19	July 1, 19–June 30, 18	Tribunicia potestate V
18	July 1, 18–June 30, 17	Tribunicia potestate VI
17	July 1, 17–June 30, 16	Tribunicia potestate VII
16	July 1, 16–June 30, 15	Tribunicia potestate VIII
15		Imperator X?
	July 1, 15–June 30, 14	Tribunicia potestate VIIII
14	July 1, 14–June 30, 13	Tribunicia potestate X
13	July 1, 13–June 30, 12	Tribunicia potestate XI
12		Imperator XI
	July 1, 12–June 30, 11	Tribunicia potestate XII
11		Imperator XII
	July 1, 11–June 30, 10	Tribunicia potestate XIII
10	July 1, 10–June 30, 9	Tribunicia potestate XIIII
9		Imperator XIII
	July 1, 9–June 30, 8	Tribunicia potestate XV
8		Imperator XIIII
	July 1, 8–June 30, 7	Tribunicia potestate XVI
7	July 1, 7–June 30, 6	Tribunicia potestate XVII
6	July 1, 6–June 30, 5	Tribunicia potestate XVIII
5		Consul XII
	July 1, 5–June 30, 4	Tribunicia potestate XVIIII
4	July 1, 4–June 30, 3	Tribunicia potestate XX
3	July 1, 3–June 30, 2	Tribunicia potestate XXI
2		Consul XIII
	July 1, 2–June 30, 1	Tribunicia potestate XXII
1 B.C.	July 1, 1 B.C.–June 30, A.D. 1	Tribunicia potestate XXIII
A.D. 1	July 1, 1–June 30, 2	Tribunicia potestate XXIIII
2		Imperator XV
	July 1, 2–June 30, 3	Tribunicia potestate XXV
3	July 1, 3–June 30, 4	Tribunicia potestate XXVI
4		Imperator XVI
	July 1, 4–June 30, 5	Tribunicia potestate XXVII
5	July 1, 5–June 30, 6	Tribunicia potestate XXVIII
6		Imperator XVII
	July 1, 6–June 30, 7	Tribunicia potestate XXVIIII
7	July 1, 7–June 30, 8	Tribunicia potestate XXX
8		Imperator XVIII
	July 1, 8–June 30, 9	Tribunicia potestate XXXI
9		Imperator XVIIII
	July 1, 9–June 30, 10	Tribunicia potestate XXXII
10	July 1, 10–June 30, 11	Tribunicia potestate XXXIII
11		Imperator XX
	July 1, 11–June 30, 12	Tribunicia potestate XXXIIII
12	July 1, 12–June 30, 13	Tribunicia potestate XXXV
13	July 1, 13–June 30, 14	Tribunicia potestate XXXVI
14		Imperator XXI
	July 1, 14–Aug 19, 14	Tribunicia potestate XXXVII
	Aug 19	Death of Augustus

TABLE 42. *Events and Honors in the Life and Reign (Aug 19, A.D. 14–Mar 16, A.D. 37) of Tiberius*

B.C./A.D.	*Month and Day*	*Chronology*
42 B.C.	Nov 16	Birth of Tiberius Claudius Nero
13		Tiberius Consul I
9		Tiberius Imperator I
8		Imperator II
7		Consul II
6	July 1, 6–June 30, 5	Tribunicia potestate I
5	July 1, 5–June 30, 4	Tribunicia potestate II
4	July 1, 4–June 30, 3	Tribunicia potestate III
3	July 1, 3–June 30, 2	Tribunicia potestate IIII
2	July 1, 2–June 30, 1	Tribunicia potestate V
1 B.C.		
A.D. 1		
2		
3		
4	June 26	Tiberius adopted by Augustus and designated as his successor; called Tiberius Julius Caesar
	July 1, 4–June 30, 5	Tribunicia potestate VI
5	July 1, 5–June 30, 6	Tribunicia potestate VII
6		Imperator III
	July 1, 6–June 30, 7	Tribunicia potestate VIII
7	July 1, 7–June 30, 8	Tribunicia potestate VIIII
8	July 1, 8–June 30, 9	Tribunicia potestate X
9		Imperator IIII
	July 1, 9–June 30, 10	Tribunicia potestate XI
10	July 1, 10–June 30, 11	Tribunicia potestate XII
10/11		Imperator V
11		Imperator VI
	July 1, 11–June 30, 12	Tribunicia potestate XIII
12		Tiberius governs the provinces jointly with Augustus
	July 1, 12–June 30, 13	Tribunicia potestate XIIII
13	July 1, 13–June 30, 14	Tribunicia potestate XV
14		Imperator VII
	Aug 19	Death of Augustus
	c. Sept 12	Funeral of Augustus
	Sept 17	Tiberius voted new head of state; called Tiberius Caesar Augustus
	July 1, 14–June 30, 15	Tribunicia potestate XVI
15	July 1, 15–June 30, 16	Tribunicia potestate XVII
16	July 1, 16–June 30, 17	Tribunicia potestate XVIII
17	July 1, 17–June 30, 18	Tribunicia potestate XVIIII
18		Consul III
	July 1, 18–June 30, 19	Tribunicia potestate XX
19	July 1, 19–June 30, 20	Tribunicia potestate XXI
20	July 1, 20–June 30, 21	Tribunicia potestate XXII
21		Imperator VIII
		Consul IIII
	July 1, 21–June 30, 22	Tribunicia potestate XXIII
22	July 1, 22–June 30, 23	Tribunicia potestate XXIIII
23	July 1, 23–June 30, 24	Tribunicia potestate XXV
24	July 1, 24–June 30, 25	Tribunicia potestate XXVI
25	July 1, 25–June 30, 26	Tribunicia potestate XXVII
26	July 1, 26–June 30, 27	Tribunicia potestate XXVIII

B.C./A.D.	Month and Day	Chronology
27	July 1, 27–June 30, 28	Tribunicia potestate XXVIIII
28	July 1, 28–June 30, 29	Tribunicia potestate XXX
29	July 1, 29–June 30, 30	Tribunicia potestate XXXI
30	July 1, 30–June 30, 31	Tribunicia potestate XXXII
31		Consul V
	July 1, 31–June 30, 32	Tribunicia potestate XXXIII
32	July 1, 32–June 30, 33	Tribunicia potestate XXXIIII
33	July 1, 33–June 30, 34	Tribunicia potestate XXXV
34	July 1, 34–June 30, 35	Tribunicia potestate XXXVI
35	July 1, 35–June 30, 36	Tribunicia potestate XXXVII
36	July 1, 36–Mar 16, 37	Tribunicia potestate XXXVIII
37	Mar 16	Death of Tiberius

TABLE 43. *Events and Honors in the Life and Reign (Mar 16, A.D. 37–Jan 24, A.D. 41) of Gaius (Caligula)*

A.D.	Month and Day	Chronology
12	Aug 31	Birth of Gaius (Caligula)
37		Gaius Consul I
	Mar 16	Death of Tiberius
	Mar 18	Gaius Imperator; as emperor called Gaius Caesar Augustus Germanicus
	Mar 18, 37–Mar 17, 38	Tribunicia potestate I
38	Mar 17, 38–Mar 17, 39	Tribunicia potestate II
39		Consul II
	Mar 18, 39–Mar 17, 40	Tribunicia potestate III
40		Consul III
	Mar 18, 40–Mar 17, 41	Tribunicia potestate IIII
41		Consul IIII
	Jan 24	Gaius killed

TABLE 44. *Events and Honors in the Life and Reign (Jan 25, A.D. 41–Oct 12, A.D. 54) of Claudius*

B.C./A.D.	Month and Day	Chronology
10 B.C.	Aug 1	Birth of Tiberius Claudius Drusus
A.D. 37		Claudius Consul I
41	Jan 24	Death of Gaius (Caligula)
	Jan 24	Claudius Imperator I; also II and III in 41?
	Jan 25	Claudius made emperor; called Tiberius Claudius Caesar Augustus Germanicus
	Jan 25, 41–Jan 24, 42	Tribunicia potestate I
42	Jan 25, 42–Jan 24, 43	Tribunicia potestate II
43		Imperator IIII–VIII
		Consul III
	Jan 25, 43–Jan 24, 44	Tribunicia potestate III
44	Jan 25, 44–Jan 24, 45	Tribunicia potestate IIII
45		Imperator VIIII–XI
	Jan 25, 45–Jan 24, 46	Tribunicia potestate V
46		Imperator XII

B.C./A.D.	Month and Day	Chronology
	Jan 25, 46–Jan 24, 47	Tribunicia potestate VI
47		Imperator XIII–XV
		Consul IIII
	Jan 25, 47–Jan 24, 48	Tribunicia potestate VII
48		Imperator XVI
	Jan 25, 48–Jan 24, 49	Tribunicia potestate VIII
49		Imperator XVII, XVIII
	Jan 25, 49–Jan 24, 50	Tribunicia potestate VIIII
50		Imperator XVIIII–XXI
	Jan 25, 50–Jan 24, 51	Tribunicia potestate X
51		Imperator XXII–XXV
		Consul V
	Jan 25, 51–Jan 24, 52	Tribunicia potestate XI
52		Imperator XXVI, XXVII
	Jan 25, 52–Jan 24, 53	Tribunicia potestate XII
53	Jan 25, 53–Jan 24, 54	Tribunicia potestate XIII
54	Jan 25, 54–Oct 12, 54	Tribunicia potestate XIIII
	Oct 12	Claudius poisoned

TABLE 45. *Events and Honors in the Life and Reign (Oct 13, A.D. 54–June 9, A.D. 68) of Nero*

A.D.	Month and Day	Chronology
37	Dec 15	Birth of Lucius Domitius Ahenobarbus
50	Mar 1	Claudius adopts Domitius; henceforth called Lucius Claudius Nero
54	Oct 12	Claudius poisoned
	Oct 13	Nero made emperor; called Nero Claudius Caesar Augustus Germanicus
	Dec 4	Tribunicia potestate granted to Nero, and reckoned from this date or from Oct 13, 54 until A.D. 59; then reordered so that the following figures finally prevail:
	Oct 13–Dec 9, 54	Tribunicia potestate I
	Dec 10, 54–Dec 9, 55	Tribunicia potestate II
54		Imperator I
55		Imperator II
		Consul I
	Dec 10, 55–Dec 9, 56	Tribunicia potestate III
56	Dec 10, 56–Dec 9, 57	Tribunicia potestate IIII
57		Imperator III
		Consul II
	Dec 10, 57–Dec 9, 58	Tribunicia potestate V
58		Consul III
	Summer	Imperator IIII, V
	Dec 10, 58–Dec 9, 59	Tribunicia potestate VI
	Dec 10, 59–Dec 9, 60	Imperator VI
59	Sept	Tribunicia potestate VII
60		Consul IIII
	Summer 60 (or 59)	Imperator VII
	Dec 10, 60–Dec 9, 61	Tribunicia potestate VIII
61		Imperator VIII, VIIII
	Dec 10, 61–Dec 9, 62	Tribunicia potestate VIIII
62	Dec 10, 62–Dec 9, 63	Tribunicia potestate X

A.D.	*Month and Day*	*Chronology*
63	Dec 10, 63–Dec 9, 64	Tribunicia potestate XI
64	Dec 10, 64–Dec 9, 65	Tribunicia potestate XII
	Between 64 and 66	Imperator X
65	Dec 10, 65–Dec 9, 66	Tribunicia potestate XIII
66		Imperator XI
	Dec 10, 66–Dec 9, 67	Tribunicia potestate XIIII
67		Imperator XII
	Dec 10, 67–Dec 9, 68	Tribunicia potestate XV
68		Consul V
	June 9	Suicide of Nero

D. ERAS

LITERATURE: **Kubitschek**, "Aera," in PW, vol. 1, cols. 606–666.

184. An era (Latin *aera*) is a sequence of years reckoned from a definite point of time which is called the epoch (Greek ἐποχή). There was at least some manner of idea of the use of an era in ancient Egypt for a stela found at Tanis attests a celebration at that place by a vizier named Seti (about 1330 B.C.) of a four-hundredth anniversary in the form of worship of the god Seth. The text reads in part: "Year 400, fourth month of the third season, day 4 . . . Seti . . . said: 'Hail to thee, O Seth. . . . ' "[257] There is also an enigmatic reference to "the era of Ishtar" in connection with Sargon king of Agade in the Sargon Chronicle, a cuneiform tablet written in the New Babylonian period, now in the British Museum.[258] In the course of time a great many eras were established, reckoned from many different epochs, events in political and military history and all other sorts of memorable points. These include, for example, the Macedonian era counted from 148 B.C. when Macedonia became a Roman province, and the era of Actium dated from the naval battle at Actium on Sept 2, 31 B.C., in which Octavian defeated Mark Antony.[259] The several more important and widely used eras will now be described.

1. The Era of the Olympiads

LITERATURE: R. D. **Hicks**, "Chronology," in *A Companion to Greek Studies* (ed. Leonard Whibley; 3d ed.; Cambridge: Cambridge University Press, 1916), 70; Hans **Lietzmann**, *Zeitrechnung der römischen Kaiserzeit, des Mittelalters und der Neuzeit für die Jahre 1–2000 nach Christus* (Berlin: De Gruyter, 1934), 11–12; E. J. **Bickerman**, *Chronology of the Ancient World* (London: Thames & Hudson, 1968), 75–76; Alan E. **Samuel**, *Greek and Roman Chronology* (Handbuch der Altertumswissenschaft; Munich: Beck, 1972), 183–194; Alden A. **Mosshammer**, *The Chronicle of Eusebius and Greek Chronographic Tradition* (London: Associated University Presses, 1979), 67–83.

185. Except for points in biblical history employed as epochs in later Jewish and Christian systems of chronology, the earliest epoch in any widely used ancient

[257] *ANET* 252–253; cf. Alan H. Gardiner, *JEA* 19 (1933): 124; 31 (1945): 28.
[258] *ANET* 266.
[259] Samuel, *Greek and Roman Chronology,* 246–247.

era was the traditional point of the beginning of the Olympic games which was so employed in the Greek era of the Olympiads. The Olympic games (τὰ Ὀλύμπια) were held every four years, and the period of four years from one celebration to the next was known as an Ὀλυμπιάς, or "Olympiad" (abbreviated Ol.). The time when the games were held was at the height of summer, and Consorinus, for example, says that the Olympic contest was celebrated in summer-like days *(ex diebus duntaxet aestivis, quibus agon Olympicus celebratur).*[260] As to the first year of the Olympiadic era, ancient historians differ, but modern scholars generally accept the year 776.[261] For the purpose of this reckoning, the year was usually the normal Greek calendar year, and we saw (§§113–114) that this began at Athens with Hekatombaion 1, at Delphi with Apellaios 1, both of which may be taken as approximately equivalent to July 1. The first year of the first Olympiad accordingly ran approximately from July 1, 776, to June 30, 775 B.C., and may be stated in brief form as 776/775 B.C. In other lands, it was presumably possible to maintain the dating by Olympiads but to state the years in terms of other calendars, for example the Egyptian beginning on Thoth 1 = Aug 29, or the Syro-Macedonian beginning on Hyperberetaios (Sept/Oct) 1. But normally in the homeland and wherever else standard Greek practice was followed, we may assume a year extending approximately from July 1 to June 30.

186. Dating by the Olympiadic system is used already by the Sicilian historian Timaeus (c. 352–c. 256 B.C.) and is found in many ancient sources. Oxyrhynchus Papyrus No. 12,[262] for example, which is a portion of a scroll written about A.D. 250, gives a list of events in Greek, Roman, and Oriental history covering the years 355–315 B.C., and the dating is by Olympiads and by the archons at Athens. A typical item (column 6, line 1–5) reads:

> In the 115th Olympiad Damasias of Amphipolis won the foot race. The archons at Athens were Neaechmus, Apollodorus, Archippus, Demogenes.

187. In Table 46 the Olympiadic years are listed for selected periods of particular relevance to our investigation. From the list it is obvious that one Olympiadic year occupies parts of two separate years in the Christian calendar, and the same was true in respect of other calendars of the ancient world. As we have seen, these included the Egyptian calendar year beginning on Thoth 1 = August 29 (§29, Table 8), the Syro-Phoenician year beginning on Hyperberetaios 1 = October 1 (§129, Table 27), the Roman consular year beginning from 153 B.C. on January 1 (§§142, 172, Table 40), and the Julian calendar year beginning from 45 B.C. on January 1 (§§143, 144, Table 33). In modern custom the parallel years of the Greek, Syrian, Roman, and Christian eras are listed in Table 56, and it is explained[263] that in the list the year of the Christian calendar is that in which the other years begin. Thus, for example, where Ol. 151, 1 is equated with the year 176 B.C. it means that the Olympiadic year runs from summer 176 to summer 175 B.C., A.S. 137 means autumn 176 to autumn 175 B.C., and A.U.C. 578 means winter 176 to winter 175 B.C.

---

[260]Censorinus, *De die natali liber,* ed. Otto Jahn (Amsterdam: Rodopi, 1964), 63.

[261]Bickerman, *Chronology of the Ancient World,* 76; Samuel, *Greek and Roman Chronology,* 194 n. 2.

[262]*OxyP* 1:25–36.

[263]Schürer, *History,* vol. 1.2, 393–398; Vermes/Millar, *History* 1:607–611.

TABLE 46. *Olympiads*

Ol.	*Julian*	*Ol.*	*Julian*
1, 1	July 1, 776–June 30, 775 B.C.	15, 1	July 1, 720–June 30, 719 B.C.
2	July 1, 775–June 30, 774 B.C.	2	July 1, 719–June 30, 718 B.C.
3	July 1, 774–June 30, 773 B.C.	3	July 1, 718–June 30, 717 B.C.
4	July 1, 773–June 30, 772 B.C.	4	July 1, 717–June 30, 716 B.C.
2, 1	July 1, 772–June 30, 771 B.C.	16, 1	July 1, 716–June 30, 715 B.C.
2	July 1, 771–June 30, 770 B.C.	2	July 1, 715–June 30, 714 B.C.
3	July 1, 770–June 30, 769 B.C.	3	July 1, 714–June 30, 713 B.C.
4	July 1, 769–June 30, 768 B.C.	4	July 1, 713–June 30, 712 B.C.
3, 1	July 1, 768–June 30, 767 B.C.	17, 1	July 1, 712–June 30, 711 B.C.
2	July 1, 767–June 30, 766 B.C.	2	July 1, 711–June 30, 710 B.C.
3	July 1, 766–June 30, 765 B.C.	3	July 1, 710–June 30, 709 B.C.
4	July 1, 765–June 30, 764 B.C.	4	July 1, 709–June 30, 708 B.C.
4, 1	July 1, 764–June 30, 763 B.C.	18, 1	July 1, 708–June 30, 707 B.C.
2	July 1, 763–June 30, 762 B.C.	2	July 1, 707–June 30, 706 B.C.
3	July 1, 762–June 30, 761 B.C.	3	July 1, 706–June 30, 705 B.C.
4	July 1, 761–June 30, 760 B.C.	4	July 1, 705–June 30, 704 B.C.
5, 1	July 1, 760–June 30, 759 B.C.	19, 1	July 1, 704–June 30, 703 B.C.
2	July 1, 759–June 30, 758 B.C.	2	July 1, 703–June 30, 702 B.C.
3	July 1, 758–June 30, 757 B.C.	3	July 1, 702–June 30, 701 B.C.
4	July 1, 757–June 30, 756 B.C.	4	July 1, 701–June 30, 700 B.C.
6, 1	July 1, 756–June 30, 755 B.C.	20, 1	July 1, 700–June 30, 699 B.C.
2	July 1, 755–June 30, 754 B.C.	2	July 1, 699–June 30, 698 B.C.
3	July 1, 754–June 30, 753 B.C.	3	July 1, 698–June 30, 697 B.C.
4	July 1, 753–June 30, 752 B.C.	4	July 1, 697–June 30, 696 B.C.
7, 1	July 1, 752–June 30, 751 B.C.	21, 1	July 1, 696–June 30, 695 B.C.
2	July 1, 751–June 30, 750 B.C.	2	July 1, 695–June 30, 694 B.C.
3	July 1, 750–June 30, 649 B.C.	3	July 1, 694–June 30, 693 B.C.
4	July 1, 749–June 30, 748 B.C.	4	July 1, 693–June 30, 692 B.C.
8, 1	July 1, 748–June 30, 747 B.C.	22, 1	July 1, 692–June 30, 691 B.C.
2	July 1, 747–June 30, 746 B.C.	2	July 1, 691–June 30, 690 B.C.
3	July 1, 746–June 30, 745 B.C.	3	July 1, 690–June 30, 689 B.C.
4	July 1, 745–June 30, 744 B.C.	4	July 1, 689–June 30, 688 B.C.
9, 1	July 1, 744–June 30, 743 B.C.	23, 1	July 1, 688–June 30, 687 B.C.
2	July 1, 743–June 30, 742 B.C.	2	July 1, 687–June 30, 686 B.C.
3	July 1, 742–June 30, 741 B.C.	3	July 1, 686–June 30, 685 B.C.
4	July 1, 741–June 30, 740 B.C.	4	July 1, 685–June 30, 684 B.C.
10, 1	July 1, 740–June 30, 739 B.C.	24, 1	July 1, 684–June 30, 683 B.C.
2	July 1, 739–June 30, 738 B.C.	2	July 1, 683–June 30, 682 B.C.
3	July 1, 738–June 30, 737 B.C.	3	July 1, 682–June 30, 681 B.C.
4	July 1, 737–June 30, 736 B.C.	4	July 1, 681–June 30, 680 B.C.
11, 1	July 1, 736–June 30, 735 B.C.	25, 1	July 1, 680–June 30, 679 B.C.
2	July 1, 735–June 30, 734 B.C.	2	July 1, 679–June 30, 678 B.C.
3	July 1, 734–June 30, 733 B.C.	3	July 1, 678–June 30, 677 B.C.
4	July 1, 733–June 30, 732 B.C.	4	July 1, 677–June 30, 676 B.C.
12, 1	July 1, 732–June 30, 731 B.C.	26, 1	July 1, 676–June 30, 675 B.C.
2	July 1, 731–June 30, 730 B.C.	2	July 1, 675–June 30, 674 B.C.
3	July 1, 730–June 30, 729 B.C.	3	July 1, 674–June 30, 673 B.C.
4	July 1, 729–June 30, 728 B.C.	4	July 1, 673–June 30, 672 B.C.
13, 1	July 1, 728–June 30, 727 B.C.	27, 1	July 1, 672–June 30, 671 B.C.
2	July 1, 727–June 30, 726 B.C.	2	July 1, 671–June 30, 670 B.C.
3	July 1, 726–June 30, 725 B.C.	3	July 1, 670–June 30, 669 B.C.
4	July 1, 725–June 30, 724 B.C.	4	July 1, 669–June 30, 668 B.C.
14, 1	July 1, 724–June 30, 723 B.C.	28, 1	July 1, 668–June 30, 667 B.C.
2	July 1, 723–June 30, 722 B.C.	2	July 1, 667–June 30, 666 B.C.
3	July 1, 722–June 30, 721 B.C.	3	July 1, 666–June 30, 665 B.C.
4	July 1, 721–June 30, 720 B.C.	4	July 1, 665–June 30, 664 B.C.

Ol.		Julian	Ol.		Julian
29,	1	July 1, 664–June 30, 663 B.C.	43,	1	July 1, 608–June 30, 607 B.C.
	2	July 1, 663–June 30, 662 B.C.		2	July 1, 607–June 30, 606 B.C.
	3	July 1, 662–June 30, 661 B.C.		3	July 1, 606–June 30, 605 B.C.
	4	July 1, 661–June 30, 660 B.C.		4	July 1, 605–June 30, 604 B.C.
30,	1	July 1, 660–June 30, 659 B.C.	44,	1	July 1, 604–June 30, 603 B.C.
	2	July 1, 659–June 30, 658 B.C.		2	July 1, 603–June 30, 602 B.C.
	3	July 1, 658–June 30, 657 B.C.		3	July 1, 602–June 30, 601 B.C.
	4	July 1, 657–June 30, 656 B.C.		4	July 1, 601–June 30, 600 B.C.
31,	1	July 1, 656–June 30, 655 B.C.	45,	1	July 1, 600–June 30, 599 B.C.
	2	July 1, 655–June 30, 654 B.C.		2	July 1, 599–June 30, 598 B.C.
	3	July 1, 654–June 30, 653 B.C.		3	July 1, 598–June 30, 597 B.C.
	4	July 1, 653–June 30, 652 B.C.		4	July 1, 597–June 30, 596 B.C.
32,	1	July 1, 652–June 30, 651 B.C.	46,	1	July 1, 596–June 30, 595 B.C.
	2	July 1, 651–June 30, 650 B.C.		2	July 1, 595–June 30, 594 B.C.
	3	July 1, 650–June 30, 649 B.C.		3	July 1, 594–June 30, 593 B.C.
	4	July 1, 649–June 30, 648 B.C.		4	July 1, 593–June 30, 592 B.C.
33,	1	July 1, 648–June 30, 647 B.C.	47,	1	July 1, 592–June 30, 591 B.C.
	2	July 1, 647–June 30, 646 B.C.		2	July 1, 591–June 30, 590 B.C.
	3	July 1, 646–June 30, 645 B.C.		3	July 1, 590–June 30, 589 B.C.
	4	July 1, 645–June 30, 644 B.C.		4	July 1, 589–June 30, 588 B.C.
34,	1	July 1, 644–June 30, 643 B.C.	48,	1	July 1, 588–June 30, 587 B.C.
	2	July 1, 643–June 30, 642 B.C.		2	July 1, 587–June 30, 586 B.C.
	3	July 1, 642–June 30, 641 B.C.		3	July 1, 586–June 30, 585 B.C.
	4	July 1, 641–June 30, 640 B.C.		4	July 1, 585–June 30, 584 B.C.
35,	1	July 1, 640–June 30, 639 B.C.	49,	1	July 1, 584–June 30, 583 B.C.
	2	July 1, 639–June 30, 638 B.C.		2	July 1, 583–June 30, 582 B.C.
	3	July 1, 638–June 30, 637 B.C.		3	July 1, 582–June 30, 581 B.C.
	4	July 1, 637–June 30, 636 B.C.		4	July 1, 581–June 30, 580 B.C.
36,	1	July 1, 636–June 30, 635 B.C.	50,	1	July 1, 580–June 30, 579 B.C.
	2	July 1, 635–June 30, 634 B.C.		2	July 1, 579–June 30, 578 B.C.
	3	July 1, 634–June 30, 633 B.C.		3	July 1, 578–June 30, 577 B.C.
	4	July 1, 633–June 30, 632 B.C.		4	July 1, 577–June 30, 576 B.C.
37,	1	July 1, 632–June 30, 631 B.C.	51,	1	July 1, 576–June 30, 575 B.C.
	2	July 1, 631–June 30, 630 B.C.		2	July 1, 575–June 30, 574 B.C.
	3	July 1, 630–June 30, 629 B.C.		3	July 1, 574–June 30, 573 B.C.
	4	July 1, 629–June 30, 628 B.C.		4	July 1, 573–June 30, 572 B.C.
38,	1	July 1, 628–June 30, 627 B.C.	52,	1	July 1, 572–June 30, 571 B.C.
	2	July 1, 627–June 30, 626 B.C.		2	July 1, 571–June 30, 570 B.C.
	3	July 1, 626–June 30, 625 B.C.		3	July 1, 570–June 30, 569 B.C.
	4	July 1, 625–June 30, 624 B.C.		4	July 1, 569–June 30, 568 B.C.
39,	1	July 1, 624–June 30, 623 B.C.	53,	1	July 1, 568–June 30, 567 B.C.
	2	July 1, 623–June 30, 622 B.C.		2	July 1, 567–June 30, 566 B.C.
	3	July 1, 622–June 30, 621 B.C.		3	July 1, 566–June 30, 565 B.C.
	4	July 1, 621–June 30, 620 B.C.		4	July 1, 565–June 30, 564 B.C.
40,	1	July 1, 620–June 30, 619 B.C.	54,	1	July 1, 564–June 30, 563 B.C.
	2	July 1, 619–June 30, 618 B.C.		2	July 1, 563–June 30, 562 B.C.
	3	July 1, 618–June 30, 617 B.C.		3	July 1, 562–June 30, 561 B.C.
	4	July 1, 617–June 30, 616 B.C.		4	July 1, 561–June 30, 560 B.C.
41,	1	July 1, 616–June 30, 615 B.C.	55,	1	July 1, 560–June 30, 559 B.C.
	2	July 1, 615–June 30, 614 B.C.		2	July 1, 559–June 30, 558 B.C.
	3	July 1, 614–June 30, 613 B.C.		3	July 1, 558–June 30, 557 B.C.
	4	July 1, 613–June 30, 612 B.C.		4	July 1, 557–June 30, 556 B.C.
42,	1	July 1, 612–June 30, 611 B.C.	56,	1	July 1, 556–June 30, 555 B.C.
	2	July 1, 611–June 30, 610 B.C.		2	July 1, 555–June 30, 554 B.C.
	3	July 1, 610–June 30, 609 B.C.		3	July 1, 554–June 30, 553 B.C.
	4	July 1, 609–June 30, 608 B.C.		4	July 1, 553–June 30, 552 B.C.

Ol.		*Julian*
57,	1	July 1, 552–June 30, 551 B.C.
	2	July 1, 551–June 30, 550 B.C.
	3	July 1, 550–June 30, 549 B.C.
	4	July 1, 549–June 30, 548 B.C.
58,	1	July 1, 548–June 30, 547 B.C.
	2	July 1, 547–June 30, 546 B.C.
	3	July 1, 546–June 30, 545 B.C.
	4	July 1, 545–June 30, 544 B.C.
59,	1	July 1, 544–June 30, 543 B.C.
	2	July 1, 543–June 30, 542 B.C.
	3	July 1, 542–June 30, 541 B.C.
	4	July 1, 541–June 30, 540 B.C.
60,	1	July 1, 540–June 30, 539 B.C.
	2	July 1, 539–June 30, 538 B.C.
	3	July 1, 538–June 30, 537 B.C.
	4	July 1, 537–June 30, 536 B.C.
61,	1	July 1, 536–June 30, 535 B.C.
	2	July 1, 535–June 30, 534 B.C.
	3	July 1, 534–June 30, 533 B.C.
	4	July 1, 533–June 30, 532 B.C.
62,	1	July 1, 532–June 30, 531 B.C.
	2	July 1, 531–June 30, 530 B.C.
	3	July 1, 530–June 30, 529 B.C.
	4	July 1, 529–June 30, 528 B.C.
63,	1	July 1, 528–June 30, 527 B.C.
	2	July 1, 527–June 30, 526 B.C.
	3	July 1, 526–June 30, 525 B.C.
	4	July 1, 525–June 30, 524 B.C.
64,	1	July 1, 524–June 30, 523 B.C.
	2	July 1, 523–June 30, 522 B.C.
	3	July 1, 522–June 30, 521 B.C.
	4	July 1, 521–June 30, 520 B.C.
65,	1	July 1, 520–June 30, 519 B.C.
	2	July 1, 519–June 30, 518 B.C.
	3	July 1, 518–June 30, 517 B.C.
	4	July 1, 517–June 30, 516 B.C.
66,	1	July 1, 516–June 30, 515 B.C.
	2	July 1, 515–June 30, 514 B.C.
	3	July 1, 514–June 30, 513 B.C.
	4	July 1, 513–June 30, 512 B.C.
. . .		. . .
110,	1	July 1, 340–June 30, 339 B.C.
	2	July 1, 339–June 30, 338 B.C.
	3	July 1, 338–June 30, 337 B.C.
	4	July 1, 337–June 30, 336 B.C.
111,	1	July 1, 336–June 30, 335 B.C.
	2	July 1, 335–June 30, 334 B.C.
	3	July 1, 334–June 30, 333 B.C.
	4	July 1, 333–June 30, 332 B.C.
112,	1	July 1, 332–June 30, 331 B.C.
	2	July 1, 331–June 30, 330 B.C.
	3	July 1, 330–June 30, 329 B.C.
	4	July 1, 329–June 30, 328 B.C.
113,	1	July 1, 328–June 30, 327 B.C.
	2	July 1, 327–June 30, 326 B.C.
	3	July 1, 326–June 30, 325 B.C.
	4	July 1, 325–June 30, 324 B.C.
114,	1	July 1, 324–June 30, 323 B.C.
	2	July 1, 323–June 30, 322 B.C.
	3	July 1, 322–June 30, 321 B.C.
	4	July 1, 321–June 30, 320 B.C.
115,	1	July 1, 320–June 30, 319 B.C.
	2	July 1, 319–June 30, 318 B.C.
	3	July 1, 318–June 30, 317 B.C.
	4	July 1, 317–June 30, 316 B.C.
116,	1	July 1, 316–June 30, 315 B.C.
	2	July 1, 315–June 30, 314 B.C.
	3	July 1, 314–June 30, 313 B.C.
	4	July 1, 313–June 30, 312 B.C.
117,	1	July 1, 312–June 30, 311 B.C.
	2	July 1, 311–June 30, 310 B.C.
	3	July 1, 310–June 30, 309 B.C.
	4	July 1, 309–June 30, 308 B.C.
118,	1	July 1, 308–June 30, 307 B.C.
	2	July 1, 307–June 30, 306 B.C.
	3	July 1, 306–June 30, 305 B.C.
	4	July 1, 305–June 30, 304 B.C.
119,	1	July 1, 304–June 30, 303 B.C.
	2	July 1, 303–June 30, 302 B.C.
	3	July 1, 302–June 30, 301 B.C.
	4	July 1, 301–June 30, 300 B.C.
120,	1	July 1, 300–June 30, 299 B.C.
	2	July 1, 299–June 30, 298 B.C.
	3	July 1, 298–June 30, 297 B.C.
	4	July 1, 297–June 30, 296 B.C.
. . .		. . .
150,	1	July 1, 180–June 30, 179 B.C.
	2	July 1, 179–June 30, 178 B.C.
	3	July 1, 178–June 30, 177 B.C.
	4	July 1, 177–June 30, 176 B.C.
151,	1	July 1, 176–June 30, 175 B.C.
	2	July 1, 175–June 30, 174 B.C.
	3	July 1, 174–June 30, 173 B.C.
	4	July 1, 173–June 30, 172 B.C.
152,	1	July 1, 172–June 30, 171 B.C.
	2	July 1, 171–June 30, 170 B.C.
	3	July 1, 170–June 30, 169 B.C.
	4	July 1, 169–June 30, 168 B.C.
153,	1	July 1, 168–June 30, 167 B.C.
	2	July 1, 167–June 30, 166 B.C.
	3	July 1, 166–June 30, 165 B.C.
	4	July 1, 165–June 30, 164 B.C.
154,	1	July 1, 164–June 30, 163 B.C.
	2	July 1, 163–June 30, 162 B.C.
	3	July 1, 162–June 30, 161 B.C.
	4	July 1, 161–June 30, 160 B.C.
155,	1	July 1, 160–June 30, 159 B.C.
	2	July 1, 159–June 30, 158 B.C.
	3	July 1, 158–June 30, 157 B.C.
	4	July 1, 157–June 30, 156 B.C.
. . .		. . .
180,	1	July 1, 60–June 30, 59 B.C.
	2	July 1, 59–June 30, 58 B.C.
	3	July 1, 58–June 30, 57 B.C.
	4	July 1, 57–June 30, 56 B.C.

Ol.		Julian	Ol.		Julian
181,	1	July 1, 56–June 30, 55 B.C.	195,	1	July 1, 1–June 30, A.D. 2
	2	July 1, 55–June 30, 54 B.C.		2	July 1, 2–June 30, A.D. 3
	3	July 1, 54–June 30, 53 B.C.		3	July 1, 3–June 30, A.D. 4
	4	July 1, 53–June 30, 52 B.C.		4	July 1, 4–June 30, A.D. 5
182	1	July 1, 52–June 30, 51 B.C.	196,	1	July 1, 5–June 30, A.D. 6
	2	July 1, 51–June 30, 50 B.C.		2	July 1, 6–June 30, A.D. 7
	3	July 1, 50–June 30, 49 B.C.		3	July 1, 7–June 30, A.D. 8
	4	July 1, 49–June 30, 48 B.C.		4	July 1, 8–June 30, A.D. 9
183,	1	July 1, 48–June 30, 47 B.C.	197,	1	July 1, 9–June 30, A.D. 10
	2	July 1, 47–June 30, 46 B.C.		2	July 1, 10–June 30, A.D. 11
	3	July 1, 46–June 30, 45 B.C.		3	July 1, 11–June 30, A.D. 12
	4	July 1, 45–June 30, 44 B.C.		4	July 1, 12–June 30, A.D. 13
184,	1	July 1, 44–June 30, 43 B.C.	198,	1	July 1, 13–June 30, A.D. 14
	2	July 1, 43–June 30, 42 B.C.		2	July 1, 14–June 30, A.D. 15
	3	July 1, 42–June 30, 41 B.C.		3	July 1, 15–June 30, A.D. 16
	4	July 1, 41–June 30, 40 B.C.		4	July 1, 16–June 30, A.D. 17
185,	1	July 1, 40–June 30, 39 B.C.	199,	1	July 1, 17–June 30, A.D. 18
	2	July 1, 39–June 30, 38 B.C.		2	July 1, 18–June 30, A.D. 19
	3	July 1, 38–June 30, 37 B.C.		3	July 1, 19–June 30, A.D. 20
	4	July 1, 37–June 30, 36 B.C.		4	July 1, 20–June 30, A.D. 21
186,	1	July 1, 36–June 30, 35 B.C.	200,	1	July 1, 21–June 30, A.D. 22
	2	July 1, 35–June 30, 34 B.C.		2	July 1, 22–June 30, A.D. 23
	3	July 1, 34–June 30, 33 B.C.		3	July 1, 23–June 30, A.D. 24
	4	July 1, 33–June 30, 32 B.C.		4	July 1, 24–June 30, A.D. 25
187,	1	July 1, 32–June 30, 31 B.C.	201,	1	July 1, 25–June 30, A.D. 26
	2	July 1, 31–June 30, 30 B.C.		2	July 1, 26–June 30, A.D. 27
	3	July 1, 30–June 30, 29 B.C.		3	July 1, 27–June 30, A.D. 28
	4	July 1, 29–June 30, 28 B.C.		4	July 1, 28–June 30, A.D. 29
188,	1	July 1, 28–June 30, 27 B.C.	202,	1	July 1, 29–June 30, A.D. 30
	2	July 1, 27–June 30, 26 B.C.		2	July 1, 30–June 30, A.D. 31
	3	July 1, 26–June 30, 25 B.C.		3	July 1, 31–June 30, A.D. 32
	4	July 1, 25–June 30, 24 B.C.		4	July 1, 32–June 30, A.D. 33
189,	1	July 1, 24–June 30, 23 B.C.	203,	1	July 1, 33–June 30, A.D. 34
	2	July 1, 23–June 30, 22 B.C.		2	July 1, 34–June 30, A.D. 35
	3	July 1, 22–June 30, 21 B.C.		3	July 1, 35–June 30, A.D. 36
	4	July 1, 21–June 30, 20 B.C.		4	July 1, 36–June 30, A.D. 37
190,	1	July 1, 20–June 30, 19 B.C.	204,	1	July 1, 37–June 30, A.D. 38
	2	July 1, 19–June 30, 18 B.C.		2	July 1, 38–June 30, A.D. 39
	3	July 1, 18–June 30, 17 B.C.		3	July 1, 39–June 30, A.D. 40
	4	July 1, 17–June 30, 16 B.C.		4	July 1, 40–June 30, A.D. 41
191,	1	July 1, 16–June 30, 15 B.C.	205,	1	July 1, 41–June 30, A.D. 42
	2	July 1, 15–June 30, 14 B.C.		2	July 1, 42–June 30, A.D. 43
	3	July 1, 14–June 30, 13 B.C.		3	July 1, 43–June 30, A.D. 44
	4	July 1, 13–June 30, 12 B.C.		4	July 1, 44–June 30, A.D. 45
192,	1	July 1, 12–June 30, 11 B.C.	206,	1	July 1, 45–June 30, A.D. 46
	2	July 1, 11–June 30, 10 B.C.		2	July 1, 46–June 30, A.D. 47
	3	July 1, 10–June 30, 9 B.C.		3	July 1, 47–June 30, A.D. 48
	4	July 1, 9–June 30, 8 B.C.		4	July 1, 48–June 30, A.D. 49
193,	1	July 1, 8–June 30, 7 B.C.	207,	1	July 1, 49–June 30, A.D. 50
	2	July 1, 7–June 30, 6 B.C.		2	July 1, 50–June 30, A.D. 51
	3	July 1, 6–June 30, 5 B.C.		3	July 1, 51–June 30, A.D. 52
	4	July 1, 5–June 30, 4 B.C.		4	July 1, 52–June 30, A.D. 53
194,	1	July 1, 4–June 30, 3 B.C.	208,	1	July 1, 53–June 30, A.D. 54
	2	July 1, 3–June 30, 2 B.C.		2	July 1, 54–June 30, A.D. 55
	3	July 1, 2–June 30, 1 B.C.		3	July 1, 55–June 30, A.D. 56
	4	July 1, B.C.–June 30 A.D. 1*		4	July 1, 56–June 30, A.D. 57

Ol.		Julian	Ol.		Julian
209,	1	July 1, 57–June 30, A.D. 58	211,	1	July 1, 65–June 30, A.D. 66
	2	July 1, 58–June 30, A.D. 59		2	July 1, 66–June 30, A.D. 67
	3	July 1, 59–June 30, A.D. 60		3	July 1, 67–June 30, A.D. 68
	4	July 1, 60–June 30, A.D. 61		4	July 1, 68–June 30, A.D. 69
210,	1	July 1, 61–June 30, A.D. 62	212,	1	July 1, 69–June 30, A.D. 70
	2	July 1, 62–June 30, A.D. 63		2	July 1, 70–June 30, A.D. 71
	3	July 1, 63–June 30, A.D. 64		3	July 1, 71–June 30, A.D. 72
	4	July 1, 64–June 30, A.D. 65		4	July 1, 72–June 30, A.D. 73

*A.D. 1 equals Ol. 194, 4 Jan–June, plus Ol. 195, 1 July-Dec.

2. The Era of the City of Rome

LITERATURE: Ludwig **Ideler**, *Handbuch der mathematischen Chronologie,* vol. 2 (Berlin: Rucker, 1826), 150ff.; J. S. **Reid**, "Chronology," in *A Companion to Latin Studies* (ed. John E. Sandys; Cambridge: Cambridge University Press, 1925), 105ff.; Hans **Lietzmann**, *Zeitrechnung der römischen Kaiserzeit, des Mittelalters und der Neuzeit für die Jahre 1–2000 nach Christus* (Berlin: W. de Gruyter, 1934), 12f.; Elias J. **Bickerman**, *Chronology of the Ancient World* (London: Thames and Hudson, 1968), 77; Alan E. **Samuel**, *Greek and Roman Chronology* (Munich: Beck, 1972), 250–276.

188. The era distinctively used among the Romans took for its epoch the foundation of the city of Rome, and the reckoning was *ab urbe condita,* "from the foundation of the city," or *anno urbis conditae,* "in the year of the founded city" (abbreviated A.U.C.). As to when Rome was founded, however, there were different opinions. Dionysius of Halicarnassus (54?-7? B.C.), the Greek historian who wrote on Ῥωμαϊκὴ Ἀρχαιολογία or "Roman Antiquities" in twenty books and also a lost work on chronology called Χρόνοι or "Times" which is cited by Clement of Alexandria,[264] discusses the problem at length, citing a number of authorities and several variant opinions.[265] He says that the Greek historian Timaeus of Sicily thought that Rome and Carthage were founded at the same time in the thirty-eighth year before the first Olympiad, or 814/813 B.C.; and Quintus Fabius placed it in the first year of the eighth Olympiad, or 748/747 B.C. Porcius Cato used a different type of reference and put the founding of Rome four hundred and thirty-two years after the Trojan war. At this point Dionysius cites the Chronicles of Eratosthenes, for which he expresses high regard. This work began with the fall of Troy, which Eratosthenes placed in 1184/1183 B.C. and considered the first datable event of human history, thus providing a line of demarcation between mythology and history.[266] Four hundred and thirty years after that brings us to 752/751 B.C. or to the Roman year which began in the first year of the seventh Olympiad, and this is the date which Dionysius himself accepts for the foundation of Rome.[267]

---

[264]*Stromata* 1.21.102.
[265]*Roman Antiquities* 1.74–75.
[266]Wacholder, *Essays,* 106.
[267]*Roman Antiquities* 1.75.3; Samuel, *Greek and Roman Chronology,* 198.

189. A yet slightly variant date, however, was calculated by the Roman antiquarian and writer, Varro (116–27 B.C.), whose *Antiquitatum rerum humanarum et divinarum* (in four parts, part 2, sects. 8–13 dealing with places, Rome, Italy; and part 3, sects. 14–19 dealing with times) is lost, but its second part on time and its divisions was apparently abstracted by Censorinus in *De die natali* (A.D. 238). From the middle of the first century B.C. onward, the era based on Varro's date (and hence known as the Varronian era) was the most widely accepted reckoning and that used by the chief Roman writers. In the twelfth chapter of his *Life of Romulus* Plutarch says that it was agreed that the city was founded on the twenty-first of April; mentions the third year of the sixth Olympiad; and describes the work of Varro in relation to the dating. Censorinus[268] also tells about Varro and then gives the date of his own writing in terms of both the Olympic games and the founding of Rome. In this double citation the 1,014th Olympiadic year is equated with the 991st year from the founding of Rome, making a difference of twenty-three years between the two eras. Since the Olympiadic year began about July 1 and the foundation of Rome, as we have just seen, on Apr 21, the period between the epochs of the two eras was actually less than twenty-three full years. Twenty-three full years from the beginning of the first Olympiad would only have passed at the end of Ol. 6, 3, i.e., about June 30, 753 B.C. Therefore Varro must have put the founding of Rome in Ol. 6, 3 (= 754/753) and to be exact on Apr 21, 753 B.C.[269] Between Dionysius's date of Ol. 7, 1 (=752/751) and Varro's date of Ol. 6, 3 (= 754/753) there is also evidence in yet other ancient writers for an epoch date for the founding of Rome in Ol. 6, 4 (=753/752).[270]

190. Assuming use of the Varronian era and strictly speaking, we should reckon A.U.C. from Apr 21, 753 B.C. By this factual reckoning A.U.C. 1 extended from Apr 21, 753 B.C., to Apr 20, 752; and if A.U.C. 1 is set parallel with 753 B.C. it means that A.U.C. 1 began in the year 753 B.C. But the Roman year came to be reckoned from Jan 1 (§142), therefore in practice the A.U.C. reckoning was also often counted from Jan 1. By this manner of reckoning A.U.C. 1 extended from Jan 1 to Dec 31, 753 B.C.; and in this case we have simple and exact equations, A.U.C. 1 = 753 B.C., A.U.C. 753 = 1 B.C., A.U.C. 754 = A.D. 1, and so on. Unless otherwise stated, it is this latter manner of equation which may be assumed in the present handbook. In either case a table of parallel years will show A.U.C. 1 in parallel with 753 B.C., A.U.C. 754 in parallel with A.D. 1, and so on (see Table 47).[271]

---

[268]*De die natali liber,* 21; ed. F. Hultsch 45; ed. Jahn, 63–64.
[269]Samuel, *Greek and Roman Chronology,* 250–251.
[270]Ibid., 251–252.
[271]Schürer, *History,* vol. 1.2, 393–398.

TABLE 47. *Years from the Founding of the City of Rome (Varronian Era)*

Ol.	*B.C.*	*A.U.C.*
6, 2	July 1, 755–June 30, 754	
3	July 1, 754–June 30, 753	0/1
4	July 1, 753–June 30, 752	1/2
7, 1	July 1, 752–June 30, 751	2/3
2	July 1, 751–June 30, 750	3/4
3	July 1, 750–June 30, 749	4/5
4	July 1, 749–June 30, 748	5/6
8, 1	July 1, 748–June 30, 747	6/7
2	July 1, 747–June 30, 746	7/8
3	July 1, 746–June 30, 745	8/9
4	July 1, 745–June 30, 744	9/10
9, 1	July 1, 744–June 30, 743	10/11
2	July 1, 743–June 30, 742	11/12
3	July 1, 742–June 30, 741	12/13
4	July 1, 741–June 30, 740	13/14
10, 1	July 1, 740–June 30, 739	14/15
2	July 1, 739–June 30, 738	15/16
3	July 1, 738–June 30, 737	16/17
4	July 1, 737–June 30, 736	17/18
11, 1	July 1, 736–June 30, 735	18/19
2	July 1, 735–June 30, 734	19/20
3	July 1, 734–June 30, 733	20/21
4	July 1, 733–June 30, 732	21/22
12, 1	July 1, 732–June 30, 731	22/23
2	July 1, 731–June 30, 730	23/24
3	July 1, 730–June 30, 729	24/25
4	July 1, 729–June 30, 728	25/26
. . .	. . .	
48, 1	July 1, 588–June 30, 587	166/167
2	July 1, 587–June 30, 586	167/168
3	July 1, 586–June 30, 585	168/169
4	July 1, 585–June 30, 584	169/170
49, 1	July 1, 584–June 30, 583	170/171
2	July 1, 583–June 30, 582	171/172
3	July 1, 582–June 30, 581	172/173
4	July 1, 581–June 30, 580	173/174
50, 1	July 1, 580–June 30, 579	174/175
2	July 1, 579–June 30, 578	175/176
3	July 1, 578–June 30, 577	176/177
4	July 1, 577–June 30, 576	177/178
51, 1	July 1, 576–June 30, 575	178/179
2	July 1, 575–June 30, 574	179/180
3	July 1, 574–June 30, 573	180/181
4	July 1, 573–June 30, 572	181/182
52, 1	July 1, 572–June 30, 571	182/183
2	July 1, 571–June 30, 570	183/184
3	July 1, 570–June 30, 569	184/185
4	July 1, 569–June 30, 568	185/186
53, 1	July 1, 568–June 30, 567	186/187
2	July 1, 567–June 30, 566	187/188
3	July 1, 566–June 30, 565	188/189
4	July 1, 565–June 30, 564	189/190
54, 1	July 1, 564–June 30, 563	190/191
2	July 1, 563–June 30, 562	191/192
3	July 1, 562–June 30, 561	192/193
4	July 1, 561–June 30, 560	193/194

Ol.	*B.C./A.D.*	*A.U.C.*
55, 1	July 1, 560–June 30, 559	194/195
2	July 1, 559–June 30, 558	195/196
3	July 1, 558–June 30, 557	196/197
4	July 1, 557–June 30, 556	197/
. . .	. . .	
117, 1	July 1, 312–June 30, 311	442/443
2	July 1, 311–June 30, 310	443/444
3	July 1, 310–June 30, 309	444/445
4	July 1, 309–June 30, 308	445/446
118, 1	July 1, 308–June 30, 307	446/447
2	July 1, 307–June 30, 306	447/448
3	July 1, 306–June 30, 305	448/449
4	July 1, 305–June 30, 304	449/
. . .	. . .	
150, 1	July 1, 180–June 30, 179	574/575
2	July 1, 179–June 30, 178	575/576
3	July 1, 178–June 30, 177	576/577
4	July 1, 177–June 30, 176	577/578
151, 1	July 1, 176–June 30, 175	578/579
2	July 1, 175–June 30, 174	579/580
3	July 1, 174–June 30, 173	580/581
4	July 1, 173–June 30, 172	581/
. . .	. . .	
194, 1	July 1, 4–June 30, 3	750/751
2	July 1, 3–June 30, 2	751/752
3	July 1, 2 B.C.–June 30, 1 B.C.	752/753
4	July 1, 1 B.C.–June 30, A.D. 1	753/754
195, 1	July 1, A.D. 1–June 30, A.D. 2	754/755
2	July 1, 2–June 30, 3	755/756
3	July 1, 3–June 30, 4	756/757
4	July 1, 4–June 30, 5	757/
. . .	. . .	
201, 1	July 1, 25–June 30, 26	778/779
2	July 1, 26–June 30, 27	779/780
3	July 1, 27–June 30, 28	780/781
4	July 1, 28–June 30, 29	781/782
202, 1	July 1, 29–June 30, 30	782/783
2	July 1, 30–June 30, 31	783/784
3	July 1, 31–June 30, 32	784/785
4	July 1, 32–June 30, 33	785/786
203, 1	July 1, 33–June 30, 34	786/787
2	July 1, 34–June 30, 35	787/788
3	July 1, 35–June 30, 36	788/789
4	July 1, 36–June 30, 37	789/
. . .	. . .	
211, 1	July 1, 65–June 30, 66	818/819
2	July 1, 66–June 30, 67	819/820
3	July 1, 67–June 30, 68	820/821
4	July 1, 68–June 30, 69	821/822
212, 1	July 1, 69–June 30, 70	822/823
2	July 1, 70–June 30, 71	823/824
3	July 1, 71–June 30, 72	824/825
4	July 1, 72–June 30, 73	825/

191. In making or interpreting an equation between a given a Roman year and an Olympiadic year, or contrariwise between an Olympiadic year and a Roman year, it is also necessary to be clear as to the method followed. The Roman year (and the corresponding year of the Christian era) may be set parallel with the Olympiadic year in the course of which it began or with the year in the course of which it ended. For example, the Roman year A.U.C. 1= 753 B.C. began in Ol. 6, 3 and ended in Ol. 6, 4, and hence might be set parallel with either. Stating the matter the other way around, the Olympiadic year may be set parallel with the Roman year and the Christian year in the course of which it began or with the year in the course of which it ended. Between the two possibilities the practice of ancient histories varied. For example, the first half of the Olympiadic year 180, 1 corresponded with the second half (from July 1 to December 31) of the year 60 B.C., and the second half of the same Olympiadic year corresponded with the first half (January 1 to June 30) of the year 59 B.C. For Diodorus and Polybius the equation was with 59 B.C., but for Dionysius of Halicarnassus the equation was with 60 B.C., and it is this latter practice which is now generally followed.[425] In this reckoning Ol. 1, 1 = 776 B.C.; Ol. 6, 4 = A.U.C. 1 = 753 B.C.; Ol. 151, 1 = A.U.C. 578 = 176 B.C.; Ol. 194, 4 = A.U.C. 753 = 1 B.C.; Ol. 195, 1 = A.U.C. 754 = A.D. 1. This is the custom which is to be understood in Schürer's full-scale tabulation of parallel years of the Greek, Syrian, Roman, and Christian eras (our Table 56)[426] and in Helm's edition of the *Chronicle* of Eusebius in Jerome's translation.[427]

3. The Seleucid Era

LITERATURE: A. **Bouché-Leclercq**, *Histoire des Séleucides* (2 vols.; Paris : E. Leroux, 1913–1914); Walther **Kolbe**, *Beiträge zur syrischen und jüdischen Geschichte* (Stuttgart: W. Kolhammer, 1926); Wilhelm **Kubitschek**, *Grundriss der antiken Zeitrechnung* (Handbuch der Altertumswissenschaft 1.7; Munich: Beck, 1928), 70–73; E. J. **Bickerman**, "Notes on Seleucid and Parthian Chronology, I, Seleucid Era," in *Berytus* 8 (1943–44): 73–76; idem, *Chronology of the Ancient World* (London: Thames and Hudson, 1968), 71–72; F.-M. **Abel**, *Les Livres des Maccabées* (Paris: LeCoffre, 1949); Sidney **Tedesche** and Solomon **Zeitlin**, *The First Book of Maccabees* (New York: Harper, 1950); J. C. **Dancy**, *A Commentary on I Maccabees* (Oxford: Blackwell, 1954); Alan Edouard **Samuel**, *Ptolemaic Chronology* (Munich: Beck, 1962); idem, *Greek and Roman Chronology* (Munich: Beck, 1972), 139–151; Ulrich **Wilcken**, *Alexander the Great* (trans. G. C. Richards; pref., "An Introduction to Alexander Studies, Notes, and Bibliography" by N. Borza; New York: W. W. Norton, 1967); Theodore Cressy **Skeat**, *The Reigns of the Ptolemies* (2d ed.; Munich: Beck, 1969); Peter **Green**, *Alexander of Macedon, 356–323 B.C.: A Historical Biography* (Berkeley: University of California Press, 1991).

192. When Philip II, king of Macedonia, was assassinated in 336 B.C. his son Alexander III the Great succeeded him, conquered virtually the whole

[425]Earnest Cary, *The Roman Antiquities of Dionysius of Halicarnassus* (LCL, 1937), xxxi; Bickerman, *Chronology of the Ancient World,* 76.

[426]Schürer, *History,* vol. 1.2, 393–398; cf. Vermes/Millar, *History* 1:607–611.

[427]See below §§304ff.

world, and died suddenly in Babylon on Daisios/Aiaru 29 = June 10, 323 B.C. (§132). No heir had been appointed, and the empire fell to Alexander's generals, known as the Diadochi or "successors." In the long and complex power struggles which ensued, Antigonus Cyclops (323–301) in Macedonia claimed all of Asia but, as Diodorus (18.2–3) tells us, the generals approved Philip Arrhidaeus, the half-witted, illegitimate son of Philip II, as king (323–316, and after him Alexander IV, the posthumous son of Alexander the Great, 316–312). This action was quickly followed by the division of the empire in satrapies, in which Egypt was allotted to Ptolemy I Soter I as satrap (governor) and Babylon to Seleucus I Nicator in the same capacity. It was only in 305 that Ptolemy assumed actual kingship so that his reign proper is dated 305–282, but he antedated the counting of his supposed royal years and in this retroactive regnal dating made his (fictitious) first year the same as the year of the death of Alexander the Great, beginning from June 10, 323.

193. As satrap in Babylon, Seleucus I Nicator experienced opposition and fled to Egypt for refuge with Ptolemy in 316–312, then in 312 the two together defeated Demetrius Poliorcetes, son of Antigonus, in the Battle of Gaza, after which Seleucus returned to Babylon and reconquered his satrapy. In an account of the decisive battle, Diodorus (19.80.5; cf. Plutarch, *Demetrius* 5) mentions that Demetrius had summoned his soldiers to Gaza from their winter quarters and thus awaited the approach of his opponents. Therefore the battle was presumably in the spring of the year, and the return of Seleucus was subsequent to that, so that the reconquest of Babylon is dated in August 312. It was only in 305 that Seleucus assumed the title of king of Babylon but, like Ptolemy I, he also antedated his regnal years. Ruling in Babylon, Seleucus accepted the Babylonian calendar with the year beginning on Nisanu 1 and with nineteen-year cycles of intercalation, and he equated his own (fictitious) first regnal year with the year in which Alexander IV died, namely, Alexander's seventh year beginning Nisanu 1 (April 3) 311 B.C. (Table 49). Accordingly, Seleucus's year 1 also begins in the Babylonian calendar from Nisanu 1 (April 3), 311; but, due to the difference between the Babylonian and the Macedonian calendars, in the latter the first year of Seleucus is dated from Dios 1 (October 7), 312 B.C. When Seleucus died and was succeeded by his son Antiochus I Soter, the latter continued from the same beginning point the numbering of his own regnal years and so too did the subsequent kings of the Seleucid kingdom (312–64 B.C.)[428] Thus the Seleucid era was instituted. Its designation is *anno Seleucidarum* (abbreviated A.S.) "in the year of the Seleucids," i.e., "in the Seleucid era," and it is reckoned from the two points as explained, from Dios 1 = Oct 7, 12 B.C., in the Macedonian calendar, from Nisanu 1 = Apr 3, 311 B.C., in the Babylonian calendar. Tables 48 and 49 show, for a few years at the beginning of the era, how the years are counted in terms of the two calendars.

---

[428]Bickerman, *Berytus* 8 (1944): 73–76; idem, *Chronology of the Ancient World,* 71, 159; PDBC 19–24, 36ff.; *EB* (1987), 617–618; 13: 248; Samuel, *Ptolemaic Chronology,* 14, 19, 24–25.

TABLE 48. *The Beginning of the Seleucid Era according to the Macedonian Calendar*

A.S.	*New Year's Day* *Dios 1 = Tishri 1*	*B.C.*
1	Oct 7, 312	312/311
2	Sept 26, 311	311/310
3	Oct 15, 310	310/309
4	Oct 4, 309	309/308
5	Sept 23, 308	308/307

TABLE 49. *The Beginning of the Seleucid Era according to the Babylonian Calendar*

A.S.	*New Year's Day* *Nisanu 1*	*B.C.*
1	Apr 3, 311	311/310
2	Apr 22, 310	310/309
3	Apr 10, 309	309/308
4	Mar 30, 308	308/307
5	Apr 18, 307	307/306

194. The Seleucid era is used in 1 Maccabees in many notations of date from 1:10 on. The reference in 1:10 states that Antiochus Epiphanes "began to reign in the 137th year of the kingdom of the Greeks." Other references also give days and months. The months are sometimes designated by name (e.g., 1:54), sometimes by number (e.g., 9:3), and sometimes by both, e.g., 4:52—"on the twenty-fifth day of the ninth month, which is the month of Chislev, in the 148th year"; and 16:14—"in the 177th year, in the eleventh month, which is the month of Shebat." Here where both number and name are cited it is evident that the months are numbered from the spring and it may be supposed that the year references in the same verses are also reckoned from the spring, i.e., are years of the Seleucid era according to the Babylonian-Jewish calendar. Then Chislev 25, in the year 148 (4:52), for example, will be interpreted thus: A.S. 148 = 164/163 B.C.; in this year Chislev 1 fell on Nov 20; therefore Chislev 25 was Dec 14, 164 B.C. If 1:10 is to be interpreted in the same way then the beginning of the reign of Antiochus Epiphanes in the 137th year was in the year beginning Mar 30, 175 B.C.

195. Some think, however, that while dates derived from a Jewish source are indeed reckoned in this way (namely: 1 Macc 1:29; 1:54; 1:59; 2:70; 4:52; 7:43; 9:3; 9:54; 10:21; 13:41; 13:51; 14:27; 16:14), other dates come from an official Seleucid source and are years of the Seleucid era as reckoned according to the Macedonian calendar, i.e., from a first year beginning Oct 7, 312 B.C. Dates which may come from such a source are 1 Macc 1:10; 3:37; 6:16; 7:1; 10:1; 10:57; 10:67; 11:19; 14:1; 15:10. In this case, the beginning of the reign of Antiochus Epiphanes (1:10) would be in the year beginning Oct 3, 176. In the same view,[429] four dates could fall in either class (namely: 1:20; 4:28; 6:20; 9:58); and one (6:20) is regarded as erroneous in either case. In 2 Maccabees similar problems are found and are presumably to be dealt with along the same lines.

196. Josephus likewise gives dates in the Seleucid era, and in two passages equates these with Olympiads:

> . . . in the 145th year, on the twenty-fifth day of the month which by us is called Chasleu (Χασλεύ = Chislev), and by the Macedonians Apellaios (Ἀπελλαῖος), in the 153d Olympiad[430]

> . . . the twenty-fifth of the month, Apellaios, in the 148th year, in the 154th Olympiad.[431]

The year A.S. 145 extended by the Macedonian reckoning from the fall of 168 B.C. to the fall of 167 B.C.; by the Babylonian reckoning from the spring of 167 B.C. to the spring of 166 B.C. Therefore Chislev 25 was Dec 27, 168, in the Macedonian reckoning; Dec 16, 167, in the Babylonian. Olympiad 153 began in the summer of 168 B.C. Therefore, the equivalence stated by Josephus is correct on either reckoning. The year A.S. 148 extended by the Macedonian reckoning from the fall of 165 B.C. to the fall of 164 B.C.; by the Babylonian reckoning from the spring of 164 B.C. to the spring of 163 B.C. Therefore, Chislev 25 was Dec 24, 165 B.C., in the Macedonian reckoning; Dec 14, 164 B.C., in the Babylonian. Olympiad 154 began in the summer of 164 B.C. Therefore, the equivalence stated by Josephus is correct only on the Babylonian reckoning and, assuming such reckoning, he is correct in both synchronisms.

197. In the *Chronicle* of Eusebius as translated by Jerome (§§259ff.),[432] the beginning of the reign of Seleucus Nicanor, as he is called, is placed in Ol. 117, 1. This Olympiadic year began July 1, 312 B.C., and the date is correct.

198. Of all the ancient eras the Seleucid became probably the one most widely and longest used. Examples of its employment in Jewish literature were given above (§§194–196), and among the Jews it continued in use for a long time. They called it not only "the Greek era" (מנין יונית, *minyan yewanit*), but also "the era of contracts" (מנין שטרות, *minyan shetarot*) because legal documents were dated by it. The era was also used by the followers of Muhammad, and it has continued in use by the Syrian Christians in Lebanon until the present.[433] In spite of the wide prevalence of the Seleucid era, there is also evidence for the employment of other less well-known eras at not a few cities in Syria-Palestine. For example, a "Pompeian" era with an epoch of 63 B.C. (when the Roman general Pompey took Jerusalem and Palestine) is attested at Gerasa in the Decapolis and is commonly known as the Gerasene era.[434] A "Caesarian" era

---

[429]Dancy, *A Commentary on I Maccabees,* 50–51.
[430]*Ant.* 12.248.
[431]*Ant.* 12.321.
[432]Helm 126.
[433]Kubitschek, *Grundriss der antiken Zeitrechnung,* 70.
[434]*Greek and Roman Chronology,* 180, 246 n.4.

with an epoch in 48 B.C. (the date of the defeat of Pompey by Gaius Julius Caesar at Pharsalus, also given as 49 B.C. due to the differences in local calendars) is found at Antioch on the Orontes.[435] Likewise there was an era of the Province of Arabia.[436]

4. The Jewish Eras

LITERATURE: Henry **Browne**, *Ordo saeclorum: A Treatise on the Chronology of the Holy Scriptures* (London: John W. Parker, 1844); Alexander **Marx**, *Seder 'Olam (Cap. 1–10)* (Berlin: H. Itzkowski, 1903); Eduard **Mahler**, *Handbuch der jüdischen Chronologie* (London: Gustav Fock, 1916); *Sefer Seder 'Olam. The Book of the Order of the World, being the Book Seder 'Olam Rabbah by Rabbi Yose ben Halafta, with comments and emendations by Rabbi Jacob Emden and Rabbi Elijah of Vilna . . . and now added to this edition to Seder 'Olam Zuta and the Sefer ha-Kabalah of Rabad, prepared for publication by Rabbi Samuel Waxman* ([5]712 = 1953); Edgar **Frank**, *Talmudic and Rabbinical Chronology* (New York: P. Feldheim, 1956); Ben Zion **Wacholder**, *Essays on Jewish Chronology and Chronography* (New York: Ktav, 1976); Chaim Joseph **Milikowsky**, "Seder Olam: A Rabbinic Chronography" (Ph.D. dissertation, Yale, 1981); Arthur **Spier**, *The Comprehensive Hebrew Calendar: Twentieth to Twenty-second Century, 5660–5860, 1900–2100* (3d ed.; Jerusalem: Feldheim, 1986).

(1) The Era of the Destruction of the Second Temple

199. The Jews employed the Seleucid era (§§192ff.) and called it by various names including Cessation of Prophecy (להפסקת הנבואה), Reign of the Greeks (למלכות יונים), and Contracts (לשטרות), this last name because in contracts and records of debts the year was reckoned according to the Seleucid calendar. Distinctive eras of their own were also developed. Of these one was that which took as its epoch the destruction of the Second Temple. In this era, dates are given as in a certain year of "the destruction of the temple" (לחרבן הבית, *lekhorban habayit*) or "from the destruction" (אחר החורבן, *'akhar hakhurban*). The era was used in Palestine and is still mentioned in Hebrew writings of the Middle Ages.

200. The great war of the Jews against the Romans began in A.D. 66 with Vespasian in charge of the Roman forces, then after Nero died (June 9, A.D. 68) and Vespasian became emperor (A.D. 69), he entrusted the continuance of the Jewish war to his son Titus. Shortly before Passover in the spring of A.D. 70, the Romans were in front of Jerusalem and their victory and the destruction of the temple ensued before the summer was over. In the Seleucid era the year of the destruction of the temple was 381, which corresponds to the year from the fall of A.D. 69 to the fall of A.D. 70 according to the Macedonian calendar; or to the year from the spring of A.D. 70, to the spring of A.D. 71 according to the Babylonian calendar. As to the month and day, the Jewish sources claim a striking

---

[435]Ibid., 247 n. 2.
[436]Ibid., 247 n. 8.

identity between the destruction of the Second Temple and of the First Temple. 2 Kgs 25:8 states that the First Temple was burned by Nebuzaradan on the seventh day of the fifth month, while Jer 52:12 gives the tenth day of the fifth month. The rabbis reconciled these data by explaining that the Babylonians entered the temple on the seventh day of Ab (which is the fifth month), ate and did damage to it on that day and the eighth, and on the ninth day toward dusk set fire to it; it then continued to burn through the whole of that day which is presumably extended through the tenth.[437] As to the reoccurrence of disaster at the identical time, they said, "The same thing too happened in the Second Temple."[438] For a single day, the ninth of Ab was taken as the exact date: "On the ninth of Ab . . . the Temple was destroyed the first and the second time."[439]

201. In his account of the second destruction Josephus gives the following sequence of events. On Xanthikos 14 Titus encamped before the city (*War* 5.99; 5.133; 5.567). On Panemos 17 the daily sacrifices ceased (6.94). On Loos 8 the Roman armies completed their earthworks (6.220) and Titus ordered the gates of the temple area set afire (6.228). On the following day, which was Loos 9, Titus resolved to spare the temple (6.241). On yet the following day, which was Loos 10, amidst the fighting, a soldier cast a firebrand into the temple and it was burned (6.244, 252). The date of the burning is stated explicitly by Josephus: "the tenth of the month Loos, the day on which of old it had been burnt by the king of Babylon" (6.250). In the later correlation of the Macedonian calendar as it was used in Palestine (Table 31), Loos was parallel to Ab, the fifth month. Therefore Josephus's date of Loos = Ab 10 is identical with Jeremiah's (52:12) date of the tenth day of the fifth month for the first destruction, and just one day later than the ninth day of Ab taken as the official date by the rabbis.

TABLE 50. *The Beginning of the Era of the Destruction of the Second Temple*

Year of the Destruction Era	*Beginning of the Year*	*End of the Year*	*A.D.*
1	Ab 9 = Aug 5, 70	Elul 30 = Sept 24, 70	70
2	Tishri 1 = Sept 25, 70	Elul 29 = Oct 13, 71	70/71
3	Tishri 1 = Oct 14, 71	Elul 30 = Oct 2, 72	71/72
4	Tishri 1 = Oct 3, 72	Elul 29 = Sept 21, 73	72/73
5	Tishri 1 = Sept 22, 73	Elul 29 = Oct 10, 74	73/74

202. Taking the ninth day of Ab as the standard date, in A.S. 381 this was equivalent to Aug 5, A.D. 70, and this was accordingly the epoch of the era of Destruction. The first year of the era would extend from the beginning point to

[437] *Taanith* 29a; Epstein, *BT* 2:7, 153–154.
[438] Ibid.
[439] *Taanith* 4:6; Danby 200.

the end of the then current calendar year. According to the passage already cited (§§164, 168) from *Rosh Hashanah,* the year which was used "for years"—which should include the reckoning of years in eras—was the year beginning on Tishri 1. Therefore, year 1 of the Destruction era extended from Ab 9 = Aug 5, A.D. 70, to the last day of Elul = Sept 24, A.D. 70; year 2 extended from Tishri 1 = Sept 25, A.D. 70, to the last day of the following Elul = Oct 13, A.D. 71; and so on. The first several years of the era were accordingly as shown in Table 50 from which any further years may also be calculated. An example of the use of this era is found in a Geniza fragment in the British Museum dated Tammuz 13, 987, after the destruction of the temple.[440] Since year 2 of this era equals A.D. 70/71, year 987 equals A.D. 1055/1056, and Tammuz 13 of that year was June 28, A.D. 1056.[441]

203. Along with Josephus's eyewitness account of the destruction of the temple by the Romans, there is also an account by Rabbi Yose ben Halafta in the *Seder 'Olam Rabbah* (30.86–97) and, since he was active around A.D. 150 (cf. our §206), only eighty years after the event, he is an important witness confirming Ab 9 as the standard remembered date and providing additional details. The passage reads:

> Rabbi Yose used to say: Propitiousness is assigned to a propitious day and calamity to a calamitous day. As it is found said: When the temple was destroyed, the first time, that day was immediately after the Sabbath, it was immediately after the Sabbatical year, it was (during the service of) the priestly division of Jehoiarib, and it was the ninth day of Ab; and so the second time (the temple was destroyed).[442]

From Josephus and Yose ben Halafta together, and from knowledge of the duty-periods of the priestly courses (§§237ff., Table 60) we can diagram the first ten days of the month of Loos/Ab in the summer of A.D. 70 as in Table 51.[443] Although not all of the coincidences may be as credible, it is also of interest to note how the Mishna associates yet other untoward events with the same date of the ninth day of Ab:

> On the ninth day of Ab it was decreed against our fathers that they should not enter into the land [of Israel] (Num 14:29–30; for this date see *Seder 'Olam Rabbah* 8.45–47, Milikowsky, *Seder 'Olam,* 473), and the temple was destroyed the first and the second time [by Nebuchadnezzar and by Titus], and Beth-Tor [or Bethar, modern Bettir southwest of Jerusalem, the scene of Bar Kokhba's final defeat in A.D. 135] was captured, and the City [Jerusalem] was ploughed up [by Hadrian]. (*Taanith* 4:6; Danby 200.)

---

[440] A. Marmorstein, *Zeitschrift der Deutschen Morgenländischen Gesellschaft* 67 (1913): 640 n.4, 643.

[441] Mahler, *Handbuch,* 152.

[442] Milikowsky, *Seder Olam,* 547.

[443] Cf. Mahler, *Handbuch,* 151–152.

TABLE 51. *Ab 1–10 and Equivalents in A.D. 70*

Day	*Hebrew*	*Julian*	*Event*
Sat	Ab 1	July 28	
Sun	Ab 2	July 29	
Mon	Ab 3	July 30	
Tue	Ab 4	July 31	
Wed	Ab 5	Aug 1	
Thu	Ab 6	Aug 2	
Fri	Ab 7	Aug 3	
Sat	Ab 8	Aug 4	Jehoiarib commenced
Sun	Ab 9	Aug 5	Temple destroyed (Rabbi Yose)
Mon	Ab 10	Aug 6	Temple burned (Josephus)

(2) *The Era of the World*

204. It will be noted below (§§253ff.) that Hellenistic-Jewish chronographers (Demetrius, before 200 B.C., and others) and also material at Qumran, employed a reckoning which counted years "from Adam" (ἀπὸ Ἀδάμ, *anno Adami*), and early rabbinic scholars also did the same. Somewhat similar to the reckoning from Adam and possibly, in part, an outgrowth from it, but largely an independent development and chronology, was the later system which reckoned from the creation of the world, out of which also developed the Byzantine creation era.[444] This later and more universally employed system is called the "era of creation" (מנין ליצירה, *minyan liyetsirah*) or the "era of the world" (מנין העולם, *minyan ha'olam*) or of the "creation of the world" (לבריאת העולם, *libriat ha'olam*). The epoch is the creation of the world, and dates are given "in the year of the world," often abbreviated A.M. for *anno mundi*.

205. The earliest mention of this era is in a *baraita* cited in the tractate *Avodah Zarah* in the Babylonian Talmud.[445] The whole passage, to which reference will be made again later (§208), begins with a quotation from Rabbi Hanina (third Christian century), who also employs this era and then cites the *baraita* for comparison.

> Said R. Hanina: From the year 400 after the destruction onwards, if one says unto you, "Buy a field that is worth one thousand denarii for one denar"—do not buy it. In a Baraitha it is taught: From the year 4231 of the Creation of the World onward, if one says unto you, "Buy thee a field that is worth a thousand denarii for one denar," do not buy it. What difference is there between these two [given periods]?—There is a difference of three years between them, the one of the Baraitha being three years longer.

206. In the tractate *Niddah,*[446] there is mention of a work called *Seder 'Olam* and of the author to whom it was attributed, Rabbi Yose. Rabbi Yose is

[444] Wacholder, *Essays,* 11 no. 8, 12 no. 11.
[445] *Avodah Zarah* 9b; Epstein, *BT* 4:7, 47.
[446] *Niddah* 46b; Epstein, *BT* 6:1, 325.

Yose ben Halafta (A.D. c. 150, d. c. 160), and the book is the *Seder 'Olam Rabbah* or "Book of the Order of the World." It is the oldest complete Jewish chronicle and lists events of the Hebrew Scriptures and of later history down to Bar Kokhba. In addition to Rabbi Yose's own work, it probably contains materials coming from several generations of rabbinic scholars both before and after Rabbi Yose.[447] A further and supplementary work of the eighth century, the *Seder 'Olam Zutta,* supplies the numbers of the years for the skeleton outline of *Seder 'Olam Rabbah* and continues it to around A.D. 800. *Seder 'Olam Rabbah* begins[448] with a tabulation from Gen 5 of which the opening lines are:

אדם	ק״ל = 130
שת	ק״ה = 105
נוש	צ״א = 90

These and the subsequent notations may be represented by Table 52.[449]

TABLE 52. *From Adam to Noah in* Seder 'Olam Rabbah

	Patriarch	*Year Born (A.M.)*	*Age at Birth of Son*
1.	Adam	0	130
2.	Seth	130	105
3.	Enosh	235	90
4.	Kenan	325	70
5.	Mahalalel	395	65
6.	Jared	460	162
7.	Enoch	622	65
8.	Methuselah	687	187
9.	Lamech	874	182
10.	Noah	1056	

207. Without giving these details, the *Seder 'Olam Zutta* begins at this point with the summary statement: "From Adam to Noah are 1,056 years." From here on Table 53 shows the main divisions of the chronicle (where *Seder 'Olam Rabbah* and *Seder 'Olam Zutta* diverge—as they sometimes do by a year—we follow *Seder 'Olam Rabbah*).

208. Returning to the passage quoted above (§205) from *Avodah Zarah,* we are now prepared to show that A.M. 3828 (the year of the second destruction) plus 400 (as in the formula of Rabbi Hanina) equals A.M. 4228; and that A.M. 4231 (cited in the *baraita*) minus 3 equals A.M. 4228. In other words, Rabbi Hanina and the *baraita* are in agreement in dating the second destruction in A.M. 3828 as does also *Seder 'Olam Rabbah.*

---

[447] Wacholder, *Essays,* 250.
[448] Ed. Waxman, 1.
[449] Frank, *Talmudic and Rabbinical Chronology,* 11–12.

TABLE 53. *From the Flood to the Destruction of the Second Temple in* Seder 'Olam Rabbah

	Event	*A.M.*	*Number of Years*
10.	(Continued from Table 52)		600 years, the age of Noah when the flood came (Gen 7:6)
11.	Flood	1656	340 years until the confusion of languages
12.	Confusion of languages	1996	52 years until the birth of Isaac
13.	Birth of Isaac	2048	400 years until the exodus from Egypt (Nisan 15) and the revelation on Sinai (7 weeks later)
14.	Exodus from Egypt (Nisan 15) and revelation on Sinai (7 weeks later)	2448	40 years of wandering in the wilderness until the entry into Canaan (Moses died [Deut 34:5) on Adar 7; the people mourned 30 days then, after 3 days [Jos 1:11; 3:2], passed over Jordan on Nisan 10)
15.	Entry into Canaan	2488	480 years from the exodus to the foundation of the temple (1 Kgs 6:1); therefore 440 years from the entry into Canaan to the foundation of the temple
16.	Foundation of the First Temple	2928	410 years the First Temple stood
17.	Destruction of the First Temple	3338	70 years of Babylonian captivity
18.	Consecration of the Second Temple	3408	420 years the Second Temple stood
19.	Destruction of the Second Temple	3828	

209. Since "the first of Tishri is New Year for years" (§§164, 168) and since the world was held by many to have been created in Tishri (§169), this year 3828 from the creation of the world was presumably reckoned as a year beginning on Tishri 1. Beginning thus in the fall, this year corresponds with year 381 of the Seleucid era also reckoned, by the Macedonian custom, from the fall and extending from the fall of A.D. 69 to the fall of 70. The following synchronism is hereby established: A.M. 3828 = A.S. 381 = A.D. 69/70 = year 1 of the era of Destruction.

210. The tabulation in Table 52 presumably places the creation of Adam near the beginning of the year zero and makes him one year old one year later, thus the years one, two, three, and so on, actually indicate the age of Adam[450] and after him the age of mankind. It would also be possible, however, to assign the number one to the year in which Adam was created rather than to the year when he became one year old. In that case, the year in which Adam was one year

[450]Cf. *Parah* 8:9, cited above in §165.

old would actually be year 2 of the era; and then the year of the second destruction would be A.M. 3829. But it would also be possible to assign the year one to the time when "the earth was without form and void" (Gen 1:2). In this case, Adam would be created near the beginning of year 2 and would be one year old in year 3; and then the year of the second destruction would be A.M. 3830.

TABLE 54. *The Era of Creation or the Era of the World*

		Creation Era			*Christian Era*	*Seleucid Era*	*Destruction Era*
		I	II	III	*B.C.*		
1.	Earth without form and void	1			3761/3760		
2.	Creation of Adam	2	1		3760/3759		
3.	Adam one year old	3	2	1	3759/3758		
4.	Flood	1658	1657	1656	2104/2103		
5.	Exodus	2450	2449	2448	1312/1311		
6.	Foundation of the First Temple	2930	2929	2928	832/831		
7.	Destruction of the First Temple	3340	3339	3338	422/421		
8.	Consecration of the Second Temple	3410	3409	3408	352/351		
9.	Beginning of the Seleucid Era	3450	3449	3448	312/311	1	
10.	Beginning of the Christian Era	3760 3761 3762	3759 3760 3761	3758 3759 3760	2/1 1 B.C./A.D. 1 A.D. 1/2	311 312 313	
11.	Destruction of the Second Temple and beginning of the Destruction Era	3830	3829	3828	69/70	381	1

211. Depending, therefore, upon which starting point is selected, the year of the destruction of the Second Temple is A.M. 3830, 3829, or 3828, and all three designations refer to the same year. Accordingly, Tables 52 and 53 may be expanded now to take account of these three possibilities (Table 54). The number of years to be added in the several steps, grouped here into larger units, may still be seen in Tables 52, 53; the three ways of counting are labeled Creation Era I, II, and III; and the correlation with the Christian, Seleucid, and Destruction eras is shown. Creation Era I (A.M. I) is used at present.[451] Note also (in

[451]Frank, *Talmudic and Rabbinical Chronology,* 7, 19.

Table 54) that from the destruction of the First Temple by Nebuchadnezzar in A.M. 3340/3339/3338 to the destruction of the Second Temple by Titus in A.M. 3830/3829/3828 is exactly 490 years or 70 Sabbatical cycles of 7 years each, and 10 Jubilee cycles of 49 years each (§§224, 231), making the same total found in Dan 9:24 (cf. §234) where Jeremiah's seventy years of exile (Jer 25:11–12) are interpreted as "seventy weeks of years" to the time of the ushering in of a new age of peace and the consecration of the holy place.[452]

212. It was also a concern of rabbinical chronology to establish the exact point of beginning of the first year of the era of Creation. In the language of these reckonings, the time of the new moon (the mean astronomical new moon, i.e., when the moon is in conjunction with the sun and its phase is new) is called the מולד (*molad,* plural *moladoth*). The day begins at our six o'clock p.m. which is called O h or 24 h, i.e., hour zero or hour twenty-four. So what we call Sunday 6 p.m. is by this system called Monday 0 h. The hour is divided into 1080 חלקים, *khalaqim* (from a word meaning "to divide"), or parts, so that each *kheleq* equals 3 1/3 seconds.

213. Using this system, the *molad* which marked the beginning of year 1 in Creation Era I is called Molad Tohu referring to the time when the earth was "without form" (תהו; Gen 1:2). It is also called Molad Beharad (בהר״ד). The latter name is derived as follows: ב = 2 and means the second day of the week, i.e., Monday. ה = 5 and means five hours after the beginning of Monday or what we would call Sunday 11 p.m.. ר״ד = 204 and means 204 *khalaqim* or 11 minutes and 20 seconds.

214. Astronomically, the moon actually was in conjunction (new phase) on Sunday, Oct 6, at eleven minutes after six o'clock in the morning, Jerusalem time, in the year 3761 B.C. Therefore, the crescent of the new moon would have been in the sky that evening to mark the first of Tishri and the beginning of the new year. By modern reckoning this was still Sunday evening but by Jewish reckoning it was the early hours of Monday, Oct 7. So, the Molad Beharad or Molad Tohu, the exact point of beginning of the first day of the first month (Tishri 1) of the first year of Creation Era I was placed on what present reckoning would give as Sunday, Oct 6, 3761 B.C., at eleven o'clock and eleven and one-third minutes p.m., but which Jewish reckoning specifies as on Monday, Oct 7, of the same year at five hours and 204 *khalaqim.*[453]

215. The point corresponding to Tishri 1, 3761 B.C., has continued to be that from which the World era is reckoned among the Jews. Accordingly, the formula for changing a date in the World era into the Christian era is to subtract 3,761 between the Jewish New Year's day (Tishri 1) and December 31, and to subtract 3,760 between Jan 1 and the Jewish New Year's day.[454] Thus Tishri 1, A.M. 5721, began at sundown at the time which the civil calendar calls Wednesday 6 p.m. but which the Jewish calendar calls Thursday 0 h, on Sept 21, A.D. 1960. To apply the

[452]Wacholder, *Essays,* 250.
[453]Mahler, *Handbuch,* 466–467.
[454]Frank, *Talmudic and Rabbinical Chronology,* 13.

formula: 5,721 – 3,761 = 1,960; after Jan 1, 5,721 – 3,760 = 1,961; in other words A.M. 5721 = A.D. 1960/1961. Note that in comparison with the Jewish date for the creation of the world in 3761 B.C. the Byzantine date was 5509 B.C. and the date calculated by Archbishop James Ussher (1650–1654) was 4004 B.C. (§299).[455]

216. In writing such a year date in Hebrew the 5 (ה) of the thousands is simply understood and not written. Next, for the date just given (§215), come ת and ש which have the numerical values of 400 and 300, respectively and total 700. Then come כ = 20 and א = 1. Thus, [ה]תשכ״א = [5]721.

5. The Era of Diocletian

LITERATURE: Carl **Bertheau**, "Era," in *NSH* 1:162–163.

217. Among eras with later epochs one may be mentioned briefly in transition to treatment of the Christian era. The reign of Diocletian (A.D. 284–305) was considered so important as to mark an era. Diocletian was proclaimed emperor by his troops at Chalcedon on Sept 17, A.D. 284. The reckoning of an era of Diocletian originated in Egypt and the epoch was taken as the Egyptian New Year's day immediately preceding his accession, namely Thoth 1 = Aug 29, A.D. 284. Accordingly, A.Diocl. 1 was Aug 29, 284–Aug 28, 285; A.Diocl. 100 was Aug 29, 383–Aug 28, 384, and so on. The era was often employed in the Christian church where, since Diocletian was the great persecutor of the Christians, it was also known as the *aera martyrum,* "era of the martyrs." Wide use of the era continued until in the eighth century, and it is still found among the Abyssinians and Copts in Egypt.[456]

6. The Christian Era

LITERATURE: Walter F. **Wislicenus**, *Der Kalender in gemeinverständlicher Darstellung* (Leipzig: Teubner, 1905), 14ff.; H. **Achelis**, "Dionysius Exiguus," in *NSH,* 3:441–442; **Bickerman**, *Chronology of the Ancient World* (1968), 10, 81, 90; Paul **Keresztes**, *Imperial Rome and the Christians,* vol. 1 (Lanham, Md.: University Press of America, 1989), 1.

218. When Cyril of Alexandria (died A.D. 444) computed his Easter-table, he employed the era just described (§217) and designated the separate years as so many years after Diocletian and his persecution. But when the prominent scholar of the next century, the Roman monk Dionysius Exiguus ("Dionysius the Little"), in A.D. 525 prepared a continuation of Cyril's Easter-table he did not count from Diocletian but *ab incarnatione Domini.* Feeling it inappropriate to reckon from the reign of the imperial enemy of Christianity, he explained:

> We have been unwilling to connect our cycle with the name of an impious persecutor, but have chosen rather to note the years from the incarnation of our Lord Jesus Christ.

---

[455]Wacholder, *Essays,* 107.
[456]Bickerman, *Chronology of the Ancient World,* 72, 104 n. 59.

219. For the year of the incarnation Dionysius accepted the year A.U.C. 753 (= 1 B.C., §190) and also for the day in that year of the nativity the date of December 25 (the day known in Rome already by Hippolytus [§562] and the *Chronographer of the Year 354* [§§563–564]). At the same time Dionysius went on to the immediately ensuing first day of January (seven days after December 25), which was the commencement of the regular Roman year A.U.C. 754 (= A.D. 1) to make this the beginning of the first year of his new era (a slight difference from the *Chronographer of the Year 354,* for whom the birth itself was in A.U.C. 754). Thus arose the still prevailing system of A.D. (*anno Domini,* "in the year of the Lord"), a system now sometimes referred to with the designation C.E. for Christian Era or Common Era.[457]

220. With the use of the Christian era and the reckoning *anno Domini* there arose also the possibility of counting backward from this beginning point as well as forward. While this possibility now seems obvious, it actually remained the custom for a long time to designate dates prior to the Christian era in terms of some of the older eras. But from the eighteenth century onward the use of a reckoning prior to the Christian epoch as well as following it became customary, and the designations *ante Christum* (A.C.), *anno ante Christum* (A.A.C.), and "before Christ" (B.C.) were employed.

221. In carrying the reckoning backward as well as forward, no year zero was established, but the first year of the period prior to Christ was placed immediately before the first year of the Christian era, that is the years 1 B.C. and A.D. 1 followed each other in immediate succession. Mathematically speaking, the omission of zero in a sequence of numbers involves an error and, accordingly, in astronomical reckoning, the first year before A.D. 1 is designated as year zero and from there on back the years are marked with a minus sign, while the years moving forward from year zero are marked with a plus sign. Thus, in the two systems, which we may call the historical and the astronomical, the years at the point of transition run as shown in Table 55.

TABLE 55. *The Transition from B.C. to A.D. in Historical and in Astronomical Reckoning*

Historical	*Astronomical*
4 B.C.	–3
3 B.C.	–2
2 B.C.	–1
1 B.C.	0
A.D. 1	+1
A.D. 2	+2
A.D. 3	+3
A.D. 4	+4

[457]Keresztes, *Imperial Rome and the Christians* 1:1.

TABLE 56. *Parallel Years of the Olympiadic, Seleucid, Roman, and Christian Eras*

Ol.	*A.S.*	*A.U.C.*	*B.C./A.D.*	*Ol.*	*A.S.*	*A.U.C.*	*B.C./A.D.*
187, 1	281	722	32	200, 1	333	774	21
2	282	723	31	2	334	775	22
3	283	724	30	3	335	776	23
4	284	725	29	4	336	777	24
188, 1	285	726	28	201, 1	337	778	25
2	286	727	27	2	338	779	26
3	287	728	26	3	339	780	27
4	288	729	25	4	340	781	28
189, 1	289	730	24	202, 1	341	782	29
2	290	731	23	2	342	783	30
3	291	732	22	3	343	784	31
4	292	733	21	4	344	785	32
190, 1	293	734	20	203, 1	345	786	33
2	294	735	19	2	346	787	34
3	295	736	18	3	347	788	35
4	296	737	17	4	348	789	36
191, 1	297	738	16	204, 1	349	790	37
2	298	739	15	2	350	791	38
3	299	740	14	3	351	792	39
4	300	741	13	4	352	793	40
192, 1	301	742	12	205, 1	353	794	41
2	302	743	11	2	354	795	42
3	303	744	10	3	355	796	43
4	304	745	9	4	356	797	44
193, 1	305	746	8	206, 1	357	798	45
2	306	747	7	2	358	799	46
3	307	748	6	3	359	800	47
4	308	749	5	4	360	801	48
194, 1	309	750	4	207, 1	361	802	49
2	310	751	3	2	362	803	50
3	311	752	2	3	363	804	51
4	312	753	1	4	364	805	52
195, 1	313	754	A.D. 1	208, 1	365	806	53
2	314	755	2	2	366	807	54
3	315	756	3	3	367	808	55
4	316	757	4	4	368	809	56
196, 1	317	758	5	209, 1	369	810	57
2	318	759	6	2	370	811	58
3	319	760	7	3	371	812	59
4	320	761	8	4	372	813	60
197, 1	321	762	9	210, 1	373	814	61
2	322	763	10	2	374	815	62
3	323	764	11	3	375	816	63
4	324	765	12	4	376	817	64
198, 1	325	766	13	211, 1	377	818	65
2	326	767	14	2	378	819	66
3	327	768	15	3	379	820	67
4	328	769	16	4	380	821	68
199, 1	329	770	17	212, 1	381	822	69
2	330	771	18	2	382	823	70
3	331	772	19	3	383	824	71
4	332	773	20	4	384	825	72

222. Mathematically, reckoning from B.C. to A.D. is simplified by the astronomical system. If we ask, for example, how many years there are from Jan 1, A.D. 2, to Jan 1, A.D. 4, simple subtraction gives the correct answer of 2 by either system. But if we ask how many years there are from Jan 1, 2 B.C., to Jan 1, A.D. 4, simple addition of these figures would give an answer of 6, which is incorrect. According to the astronomical system, however, one would still subtract the temporally prior date from the temporally following date. To subtract a negative number from a positive number their positive values are added. Accordingly, –1 subtracted from +4 is the same as 1 plus 4 equals 5, which is the correct answer.

223. In a table of parallel years (Table 56), which covers only a relatively few years at the transition from B.C. to A.D. but which can readily be extended as desired in either direction, the years of the Christian reckoning are shown as the standard and are, of course, years counted from Jan 1. The years reckoned from the founding of the city of Rome are considered to be counted from Jan 1 also and are, therefore, identical with the years B.C. and A.D. The Olympiadic years are years beginning on July 1 in the year B.C. or A.D. with which they are parallel, i.e., Ol. 184, 1 begins July 1, 44 B.C. and extends through June 30, 43 B.C. The years of the Seleucid era are considered to be reckoned according to the Macedonian system from Oct 1, i.e., A.S. 269 begins Oct 1, 44 B.C., and extends through Sept 30, 43 B.C. (By Babylonian reckoning A.S. 269 begins in the spring of 43 B.C. and extends to the spring of 42 B.C.)[305]

E. SABBATICAL YEARS, JUBILEES, AND PRIESTLY COURSES

1. Sabbatical Years

LITERATURE: Benedict **Zuckermann**, *A Treatise on the Sabbatical Cycle and the Jubilee: A Contribution to the Archaeology and Chronology of the Time Anterior and Subsequent to the Captivity* (trans. A. Löwy; London: Chronological Institute, 1866; repr. New York: Sepher Hermon Press, 1974); J. T. **Milik**, *Ten Years of Discovery in the Wilderness of Judaea* (Studies in Biblical Theology; Naperville, Ill.: Alec R. Allenson, 1959); P. **Benoit**, J. T. **Milik**, and R. de **Vaux**, *Les Grottes de Murabba'ât* (*DJD* 2; Oxford: Clarendon Press, 2 vols. 1961); Manfred R. **Lehmann**, "Studies in the Murabba'at and Nahal Hever Documents," *RQ* 4 (1963): 53–81; Ben Zion **Wacholder**, "The Calendar of Sabbatical Cycles During the Second Temple and the Early Rabbinic Period," *HUCA* 44 (1973), repr. idem, *Essays on Jewish Chronology and Chronography* (New York: Ktav, 1976), 1–44; Louis E. **Newman**, *The Sanctity of the Seventh Year: A Study of Mishnah Tractate Shebit* (Chico, Calif.: Scholars Press, 1983).

---

[305] Schürer, *History,* vol. 1.2, 393ff.

224. Jewish sources often reckon chronology in terms of Sabbatical years, the Jubilee, and priestly courses. The Sabbatical year (שנה השביעית, *shana hashevi'it*) also known as *shemitah* (שמטה, "release"), was considered to be the climax of a week of years in which the seventh year was, like the Sabbath of the ordinary week, a whole Sabbath year. Like the weekly Sabbath, the Sabbatical year was a time of rest for the land. In this year, according to Exod 23:10–11, the land should "rest and lie fallow" and the vineyard and olive orchard also remain uncultivated. According to Deut 15:1ff., 12ff., the Sabbatical year was also a time of "release." In this year every creditor should release what he has lent to a neighbor, and every Hebrew slave should be set free, nor should the slave be released empty-handed but rather should be furnished liberally out of flock, threshing floor, and wine press. "You shall remember that you were a slave in the land of Egypt, and the Lord your God redeemed you." As Exodus (23:11) states, the purpose of leaving the land to lie fallow was "that the poor of your people may eat; and what they leave the wild beasts may eat," apparently meaning that the poor and the wild animals might have what grew of itself. Leviticus repeats the ordinance (25:1–7) and promises (25:20–22) that there will be a very large harvest in the sixth year, which will provide food not only for the sixth but also for the seventh year, with even some old produce left into the eighth year. In the eighth year a new crop may again be planted, but of course it must grow to maturity before it can be harvested and supply fresh new food. It is important to see that this means that not the seventh, "fallow" year but rather the eighth year is a time of acute food scarcity and hunger. In the account of the institution of the law of the Sabbatical year in Leviticus 25:2 the Lord instructs Moses to say to the people of Israel, "When you come into the land which I give you, the land shall keep a sabbath to the Lord," and it is of course evident that the law could only have been actually observed when the people were in their own agricultural land. The *Seder 'Olam Rabbah* (11.69–70)[306] accordingly gives dates for related biblical events—the people spent fourteen years at Gilgal (Josh 5:9–10) and seven years in conquering the land (Josh 6:2ff.), then (in the fifteenth year) assembled at Shiloh and set up the tent of meeting (Josh 18:1) and, "at this time, they began to count (for the purpose of reckoning) tithes, Sabbatical years, and Jubilees." Somewhat similarly, in the chronology of Archbishop Ussher (§700, Table 196), after the exodus from Egypt in 1492 B.C. and entry into Canaan in 1452, it is seven years later, in 1445, that the first Sabbatical year was observed and then forty-nine years later that the first Jubilee was celebrated. Later, according to Neh 8:1ff., when Ezra read "the book of the law of Moses" to the people after the return from the Babylonian exile he called upon them to repent of much disobedience (Neh 9:33–34), and the people in response (Neh 10:29–31) covenanted to keep the law and promised among other things to "forego the crops of the seventh year and the exaction of every debt." Thus, the *Seder 'Olam Rabbah* (30.31–37)[307] says that Scripture compares the incoming of the people in the time of Ezra to their incoming in the time of Joshua: "Just as at their incoming in the time of Joshua they became subject to tithes, Sabbatical years, and Jubilees . . . so too at their incoming in the time of Ezra."

---

[306]Milikowsky, *Seder 'Olam,* 481.
[307]Ibid., 545.

225. There are many references to the Sabbatical year in the rabbinical and Talmudic literature, which provide basis for calculations on dates of the observance. As quoted above (§164) the tractate *Rosh Hashanah* (1.1) in the Mishna states that the first of Tishri is New Year for release and Jubilee years; therefore, it may be concluded that the Sabbatical year (and the Jubilee year, too) began regularly on the first day of Tishri and ended on the last day of Elul.[308] For simplicity's sake they year may be spoken of as extending from Tishri to Tishri or from autumn to autumn. In 1856 Benedict Zuckermann published a table of the Sabbatical years from 535/534 B.C. to A.D. 2238/2239, and this has been widely accepted.[309] In 1973, on the basis of recently discovered inscriptions and papyri, Ben Zion Wacholder published a revised table of the Sabbatical years from 519/518 B.C. to A.D. 440/441.[310] In 1979 Donald Wilford Blosser published a new study of Jubilee and Sabbatical years, with a calendar of Sabbatical years extending from 171/170 B.C. to A.D. 75/76, a tabulation which is contrary to Wacholder and in exact agreement with Zuckermann.[311] Excerpts adapted from the two tables are presented in the two columns of our Table 57,[312] and it may be seen that the two tabulations differ from each other by just one year, with Wacholder's dates being one year the later. For example, Zuckermann and Blosser have a Sabbatical year in 514/513 B.C., whereas the corresponding year in Wacholder is in 513/512.

TABLE 57. *Sabbatical Years according to Zuckermann, Blosser, and Wacholder*

Ruler		*Zuckermann, Blosser*	*Wacholder*
Cyrus	S.	535/534 B.C.	
538–530 B.C.	1.	534/533	
	2.	533/532	
	3.	532/531	
	4.	531/530	
Cambyses	5.	530/529	
529–522	6.	529/528	
	S.	528/527	
	1.	527/526	
	2.	526/525	
	3.	525/524	
	4.	524/523	
	5.	523/522	
Darius I	6.	522/521	
521–485	S.	521/520	

308Wacholder, *Essays,* 2–3.

309Zuckermann, *Sabbatical Cycle and Jubilee,* 60–64.

310Wacholder, *Essays,* 33–44.

311Donald Wilford Blosser, "Jesus and the Jubilee: Luke 4:16–30, The Year of Jubilee and Its Significance in the Gospel of Luke" (Ph.D. diss., St. Mary's College, The University of St. Andrews, Scotland, 1979), 113.

312Wacholder's tabulation from *Essays,* 33–34.

Ruler	*Zuckermann, Blosser*	*Wacholder*
(Darius I)	1. 520/519	
	2. 519/518	1. 519/518 B.C.
	3. 518/517	2. 518/517
	4. 517/516	3. 517/516
	5. 516/515	4. 516/515
	6. 515/514	5. 515/514
	S. 514/513	6. 514/513
		S. 513/512
	1. 44/43	
	2. 43/42	1. 43/42
	3. 42/41	2. 42/41
Herod	4. 41/40	3. 41/40
40 (37)–4 B.C.	5. 40/39	4. 40/39
	6. 39/38	5. 39/38
	S. 38/37	6. 38/37
		S. 37/36
	1. 37/36	
	2. 36/35	1. 36/35
	3. 35/34	2. 35/34
	4. 34/33	3. 34/33
	5. 33/32	4. 33/32
	6. 32/31	5. 32/31
	S. 31/30	6. 31/30
		S. 30/29
	1. 30/29	
	2. 29/28	1. 29/28
	3. 28/27	2. 28/27
	4. 27/26	3. 27/26
	5. 26/25	4. 26/25
	6. 25/24	5. 25/24
	S. 24/23	6. 24/23
		S. 23/22
	1. 23/22	
	2. 22/21	1. 22/21
	3. 21/20	2. 21/20
	4. 20/19	3. 20/19
	5. 19/18	4. 19/18
	6. 18/17	5. 18/17
	S. 17/16	6. 17/16
		S. 16/15
	1. 16/15	
	2. 15/14	1. 15/14
	3. 14/13	2. 14/13
	4. 13/12	3. 13/12
	5. 12/11	4. 12/11
	6. 11/10	5. 11/10
	S. 10/9	6. 10/9
		S. 9/8
	1. 9/8	
	2. 8/7	1. 8/7
	3. 7/6	2. 7/6
	4. 6/5	3. 6/5
	5. 5/4	4. 5/4
	6. 4/3	5. 4/3

Ruler	*Zuckermann, Blosser*		*Wacholder*	
	S.	3/2 B.C.	6.	3/2 B.C.
			S.	2/1 B.C.
	1.	2/1 B.C.		
	2.	1 B.C./A.D. 1	1.	1 B.C./A.D. 1
	3.	A.D. 1/2	2.	A.D. 1/2
	4.	A.D. 2/3	3.	A.D. 2/3
	5.	3/4	4.	3/4
	6.	4/5	5.	4/5
	S.	5/6	6.	5/6
			S.	6/7
	1.	6/7		
	2.	7/8	1.	7/8
	3.	8/9	2.	8/9
	4.	9/10	3.	9/10
	5.	10/11	4.	10/11
	6.	11/12	5.	11/12
	S.	12/13	6.	12/13
			S.	13/14
Tiberius				
A.D. 14–37	1.	13/14		
	2.	14/15	1.	14/15
	3.	15/16	2.	15/16
	4.	16/17	3.	16/17
	5.	17/18	4.	17/18
	6.	18/19	5.	18/19
	S.	19/20	6.	19/20
			S.	20/21
	1.	20/21		
	2.	21/22	1.	21/22
	3.	22/23	2.	22/23
	4.	23/24	3.	23/24
	5.	24/25	4.	24/25
	6.	25/26	5.	25/26
	S.	26/27	6.	26/27
			S.	27/28
	1.	27/28		
	2.	28/29	1.	28/29
	3.	29/30	2.	29/30
	4.	30/31	3.	30/31
	5.	31/32	4.	31/32
	6.	32/33	5.	32/33
	S.	33/34	6.	33/34
			S.	34/35
	1.	34/35		
	2.	35/36	1.	35/36
Caligula	3.	36/37	2.	36/37
37–41	4.	37/38	3.	37/38
	5.	38/39	4.	38/39
	6.	39/40	5.	39/40
Claudius	S.	40/41	6.	40/41
41–54			S.	41/42
	1.	41/42		
	2.	42/43	1.	42/43

Ruler	*Zuckermann, Blosser*		*Wacholder*	
	3.	43/44	2.	43/44
	4.	44/45	3.	44/45
	5.	45/46	4.	45/46
	6.	46/47	5.	46/47
	S.	47/48	6.	47/48
			S.	48/49
	1.	48/49		
	2.	49/50	1.	49/50
	3.	50/51	2.	50/51
	4.	51/52	3.	51/52
Nero	5.	52/53	4.	52/53
54–68	6.	53/54	5.	53/54
	S.	54/55	6.	54/55
			S.	55/56
	1.	55/56		
	2.	56/57	1.	56/57
	3.	57/58	2.	57/58
	4.	58/59	3.	58/59
	5.	59/60	4.	59/60
	6.	60/61	5.	60/61
	S.	61/62	6.	61/62
			S.	62/63
	1.	62/63		
	2.	63/64	1.	63/64
	3.	64/65	2.	64/65
	4.	65/66	3.	65/66
	5.	66/67	4.	66/67
	6.	67/68	5.	67/68
Vespasian	S.	68/69	6.	68/69
69–79			S.	69/70
Hadrian	1.	125/126		
117–138	2.	126/127	1.	126/127
	3.	127/128	2.	127/128
	4.	128/129	3.	128/129
	5.	129/130	4.	129/130
	6.	130/131	5.	130/131
	S.	131/132	6.	131/132
			S.	132/133
	1.	132/133		
	2.	133/134	1.	133/134
	3.	134/135	2.	134/135
	4.	135/136	3.	135/136
	5.	136/137	4.	136/137
Antoninus Pius	6.	137/138	5.	137/138
138–161	S.	138/139	6.	138/139
			S.	139/140

S = Sabbatical year

226. A Sabbatical year is mentioned at several important historical points, and the date of the Sabbatical year in question has elicited much discussion but without unanimous agreement as to the correct answer. For example, in regard to the very important historical event of the siege of Jerusalem by the Romans in the summer of A.D. 70 and the destruction of the Second Temple in the month of Ab (July/Aug), we have already (§201) followed Josephus's description of the sequence of events and (§203) have quoted the statement of Rabbi Yose ben Halafta (A.D. c. 150) that the day-date was Ab 9 (= Aug 5, A.D. 70) and the time was "immediately after the Sabbatical year." Reckoning years beginning on Tishri 1, the destruction was in 69/70 and the preceding year was 68/69; thus 68/69 was a Sabbatical year, and this is the way it is shown in the table by Zuckermann. Wacholder, however, thinks the statement attributed to Rabbi Yose is based not on factual information but on midrashic chronography, and is problematic. Wacholder's corresponding date is A.D. 69/70 (rather than 68/69), and in partial justification of this date he observes that Ab 9, A.D. 70, falls at least in the last part of the year Tishri 69/Elul 70, if not strictly after that year.[313] Since we have taken Yose ben Halafta as an early and dependable authority, we accept the date of 68/69 and also use it as basic for the determination of several other Sabbatical years in what follows, all thus, in fact, in accordance with Zuckermann (and Blosser).[314]

227. Josephus (*War* 1.343–357; *Ant.* 14.465–491; 15.5–7) tells of the long siege of Jerusalem by which Herod, having been appointed king of the Jews by the Romans in the consular year *Calvino et Pollione* (40 B.C., *Ant.* 14.389), took the city and assumed his actual kingship in the consular year *Agrippa et Gallo* (37 B.C., *Ant.* 14.487).[315] Jerusalem was still held by Antigonus, the last of the Hasmoneans, and Herod was assisted by the Roman general Sossius. The siege began in the spring, was in process in the summer (*Ant.* 14.473), and in all lasted for five (*War* 1.351) or six (*War* 5.398) months. The first city wall was taken in forty days, and the second in fifteen more (*Ant.* 14.476). In addition to the pressure from without, there was also "the stealthy approach of famine" within the city (*War* 5.343), and the inhabitants "were distressed by famine and the lack of necessities, for a sabbatical year happened to fall at that time" (*Ant.* 14.475). Finally, Jerusalem was taken by Herod and Sossius "on the day of the Fast" (*Ant.* 14.487). As in Acts 27:9 and in *Ant.* 18.94, "The Fast" is most probably a reference to the Day of Atonement on Tishri 10, which fell in the year 37 on Oct 6.[316] Since, according to *Ant.* 14.475, a Sabbatical year was in effect before Herod took the city, that Sabbatical year must have begun on Tishri 1 in the year 38, and this agrees with the tabulation by Zuckermann showing 38/37 as a Sabbatical year. Reckoned backward from the Sabbatical year A.D. 68/69 (the Sabbatical year immediately before the destruction of the Second Temple in the year 69/70 §226), sixteen cycles of seven years each or 112 years takes us back to a cycle beginning in 44/43 (A.D. 68/69 + 44/43 B.C. = 112 ÷ 7 = 16) with 38/37 as its seventh and Sabbatical year, and confirms the date just quoted. In *Ant.* 15.7,

---

[313]Wacholder, *Essays,* 19–24 no. 8.
[314]Blosser, "Jesus and the Jubilee," 112.
[315]For the consular years see §178 and Table 40.
[316]PDBC 44.

however, Josephus says that after Herod took Jerusalem there was no end to the troubles of the people because, on the one hand their "greedy master" plundered them, and on the other hand "the seventh year, which came round at that time, forced them to leave the land unworked, since we are forbidden to sow the earth in that year." Here the Sabbatical year would apparently have to be 37/36 B.C., as per the tabulation by Wacholder.[317] Since both cannot be correct, Josephus has evidently provided us with an inconsistency, which is, of course, not uncommon in Josephus. If we may think that the coincidence of the Sabbatical year would more likely have been remembered in connection with the major event of the protracted siege of Jerusalem, we will still prefer the Sabbatical year date of 38/37 B.C.[318] It is also possible that what Josephus here calls the seventh year was in fact the eighth year of extreme privation (cf. §224).

228. In *Ant.* 14.487 (already cited just above, §227, for the consular date of the taking of Jerusalem by Herod and Sossius), Josephus gives the most precise date yet for the event. Josephus writes:

> This calamity befell the city of Jerusalem during the consulship at Rome of Marcus Agrippa and Caninius Gallus, in the hundred and eighty-fifth Olympiad, in the third month, on the day of the Fast, as if it were a recurrence of the misfortune which came upon the Jews in the time of Pompey, for they were captured by Sossius on the very same day, twenty-seven years later.

The consulship of Agrippa and Gallus was in 37 B.C. (Table 40). What is meant by "in the third month" is not clear. The hundred and eighty-fifth Olympiad ended on June 30, 36 B.C. (Table 46). The capture of Jerusalem by Sossius (and Herod) "on the very same day, twenty-seven years later" than the prior capture of the city by Pompey refers back to the well-known conquest of Jerusalem by the Roman general in 63 B.C. Reckoned from that date we come to the year 36 B.C. for the taking of Jerusalem by Sossius and Herod (63 – 27 = 36). The precision of this reference leads to acceptance in the present book of 36 B.C. as the correct date of the event, along with which it may well also be implied that Herod's initial appointment as king of the Jews may have been in 39 rather than 40 B.C. In 36 B.C. the date of Tishri 10 for the Day of Atonement corresponds with October 25. Assuming that Herod's first regnal year began on the next Nisan 1 (accession-year system), i.e., on Nisan 1, 35 B.C., his death thirty-four years later (*War* 1.665; *Ant.* 17.191; cf. Table 140) was early in 1 B.C.

229. From written texts and other objects found in 1951–52 in caves, difficult of access, in Wadi Murabba'at (in the Judean desert fifteen miles east-southeast of Jerusalem) it is learned that this was a place of refuge at many different periods of Palestinian history.[319] A text found here (Mur 18), written on papyrus in Aramaic, bears a date in "year two of Nero Caesar," which suggests that it was left here during the First Revolt of the Jews against the Romans.[320]

---

[317]Wacholder, *Essays,* 13–15 no. 5.

[318]For discussion including yet other relevant data see Vermes/Millar, *History,* vol. 1, 284–286 n. 11; Ralph Marcus, LCL Josephus, notes to *Ant.* 12.378; 14.475; 15.7.

[319]Milik, *Ten Years of Discovery,* 14ff.

[320]Benoit, Milik, and de Vaux, *Grottes de Murabba'ât,* vol. 1, 100–104 no. 18.

The text constitutes an acknowledgment of a debt owed by a certain Zachariah bar Yehohanan to a certain Abshalom bar Hanin, and a promise to repay. For our present purpose the important fact is that, in addition to the date in the second year of Nero are also the words farther along in the text, "in this year of release (שנת שמטה)." The emperor Claudius died on Oct 13, A.D. 54, and was succeeded by Nero. In factual years of reign the first year of Nero was therefore Oct 13, 54, to Oct 12, 55, and the second year was Oct 13, 55, to Oct 12, 56. The editors therefore date the text in 55/56.[321] Wacholder[322] concurs in this date and, in accordance therewith, identifies this Sabbatical year mentioned in the text with 55/56, a year which appears in his tabulation as a Sabbatical year. Although it is repudiated by Wacholder, a different possibility arises when the photograph of the original document is considered.[323] The document is preserved in two fragments. On the *recto* are eight lines of legal text (the date is in L. 1, the mention of "this year of Shemitah" is in L. 7), written perpendicularly to the fibers of the papyrus; on the *verso* are four lines written after the page was turned by 90 degrees. The four lines contains (1) the name of Zachariah bar Yehohanan, (2) the name of the scribe who wrote the note for the principal, and who was himself the first of three witnesses, (3 and 4) the names of the other two witnesses. Among ancient Jewish notes, of which this is one, it is known that there were two types: (1) a "simple" note (גט פשוט, *get pashut*) with the signatures of the usual two witnesses in the interior; (2) a "folded" note (גט מקושר, *get mequshar*) with the signatures of three witnesses on the exterior.[324] Furthermore, if a king's name and date are used, the Talmud[325] says that in a simple note the king's first year is counted as year 1, but in a folded note the first year is counted as already his year 2, the explanation being that this is a gesture of respect to the young king.[326] Accordingly, the present text (Mur 18) may be recognized as a folded note with its three witnesses, and the date in the second year of Nero may be understood to refer respectfully to Nero's first year, i.e., to A.D. 54/55. Reckoning back from our point of reference in the Sabbatical year of 68/69 (§226) two cycles of seven years each we come to A.D. 54/55 (68/69 – 14 = 54/55) as the correct Sabbatical year at that time (as in the tabulation by Zuckermann). Wacholder[327] thinks that "there is no reason . . . to assume that our document was in fact antedated," but the evidence seems to be otherwise, so this can be regarded, in fact, as an interesting example of antedating (cf. §§517–518).

230. Most of the texts from Murabba'at belong to the period of the Second Jewish Revolt and the decades immediately preceding.[328] From coins and inscriptions it is known that, on his last great journey to the east, the emperor Hadrian (A.D. 117–138) was in Syria in A.D. 129/130, traveled to Egypt in 130,

---

321 Ibid., 67, 100.
322 Wacholder, *Essays,* 17–19 no. 7.
323 Benoit, Milik, and de Vaux, *Grottes de Murabba'ât,* vol. 2, Pl. XXIX.
324 Ibid., 104 under *Verso.*
325 *Baba Bathra* 164b; Epstein, *BT* 22:714.
326 Lehmann, *RQ* 4 (1963): 56–57; idem, *BAR* 5 (6, Nov/Dec 1979), 11.
327 Wacholder, *Essays,* 19 no. 7.
328 Milik, *Ten Years of Discovery,* 129–130.

and in 131 was again in Syria, having visited Jerusalem twice. In his *Roman History* (69.12.1–2) Dio Cassius gives an account of the same journey and tells that Hadrian founded a new pagan city at Jerusalem to be named Aelia Capitolina, and this brought on a war because the Jews felt it was intolerable for foreign races to be settled in their city and foreign religious rites to be planted there; as long as Hadrian was close by in Egypt and again in Syria they remained quiet, but when he went farther away they revolted openly. The foundation of Aelia Capitolina was therefore probably while Hadrian was in Syria in 130, but the outbreak of the revolt only after his second visit (131), while most of the building work was probably only after the revolt was crushed.[329] In the *Chronicle* of Eusebius[330] the outbreak of the uprising is dated in the 16th year of Hadrian or in the year of Abraham 2148 which is A.D. 132, and in Eusebius's *Church History* (4.6.3) we learn that the war only ended three and a half years later when the rebels' last stronghold, Beththera (probably Bettir, five miles southwest of Jerusalem) fell to the Romans in the 18th year of Hadrian (A.D. 134/135). Accordingly, the start of the revolt was taken as the beginning of a new era, and legal documents of the period, found in Wadi Murabba'at, are dated in terms of the year of "the liberation of Israel," the first, second, third and fourth years.[331]

231. Of special interest at the present point are a dozen smaller and larger papyrus fragments of rental contracts found at Murabba'at and known collectively as Mur 24; they are written in Hebrew, and each apparently contained originally the same date of issuance and a clause about the Sabbatical year.[332] The date is on the twentieth of the month Shebat (Jan/Feb) in the second year of the liberation of Israel. The contracts are simple notes, so the chronology is not to be antedated as in the folded note (§229), but taken at face value. Since the Bar Kokhba revolt began in A.D. 132 (§230) the first civil year (§164) of the liberation was 132/133 and this second year, when the contracts were written, was 133/134. As to the legal matter involved, the renter of a certain piece of land promises to deliver in payment of the rent a certain amount of wheat in each of five years "until the end of the eve of Shemitah,"[333] i.e., up to but not including the next Shemitah. As to Shemitah (Sabbatical) years at this time, the nearest preceding one was in 131/132, a date which was 63 years or nine Sabbatical cycles after our point of reference in 68/69, the Sabbatical year immediately before the destruction of the Second Temple (§226), and the next upcoming Sabbatical year, to which the legal promise refers, is therefore in 138/139.[334] The resultant chronology is outlined in Table 58. Wacholder[335] dates the first year of the liberation of Israel from Nisan 1, A.D. 132, to Adar 29, 133; the twentieth of Shebat in the second year of the liberation roughly in Feb 134; and counts the

---

329Vermes/Millar, *History,* vol. 1, 541–543, 553.

330Helm 200; Vermes/Millar, *History,* vol. 1, 542 n. 126.

331Vermes/Millar, *History,* 1, 546.

332Benoit, Milik, and de Vaux, *Grottes de Murabba'ât,* vol. 1, 122–134; Wacholder, *Essays,* 24–27 no. 9.

333Engl. trans. of Mur 24 E, Line 9, in Wacholder, *Essays,* 25, with list in n. 85 of the other fragments and Lines in which the same clause occurs.

334Lehmann, *RQ* 4 (1963): 56–57.

335Wacholder, *Essays,* 27.

time of the contract as five years, six months, and ten days, running to the last day of Elul (roughly Sept) in 139. Therefore, the next Shemitah, to which the contract refers, is Tishri 139 to Elul 140, which is in accordance with Wacholder's tabulation of Sabbatical years. Contrariwise, we maintain the analysis above, with the next Sabbatical year in 138/139, and this agrees with the tabulation by Zuckermann and Blosser.

TABLE 58. *Sabbatical Years in Papyri 24 from Murabba'at*

A.D.	131/132	Sabbatical year
	132/133	"first year of the liberation of Israel"
	133/134	"second year of the liberation of Israel" the date of Mur 24
	134/135	
	135/136	five years "until the end of the eve of Shemitah"
	136/137	
	137/138	
	138/139	Sabbatical year

2. Jubilees

LITERATURE: Benedict **Zuckermann**, *A Treatise on the Sabbatical Cycle and the Jubilee: A Contribution to the Archaeology and Chronology of the Time Anterior and Subsequent to the Captivity* (trans. A. Löwy; London: Chronological Institute, 1866; repr. New York: Sepher Hermon Press, 1974);R. H. **Charles**, *The Book of Jubilees, or, The Little Genesis* (London: Adam & Charles Black, 1902); idem, *APOT* vol. 2, 1–82; Eduard **Mahler**, *Handbuch der jüdischen Chronologie* (Grundriss der Gesamtwissenschaft des Judentums; Leipzig: Gustav Fock, 1916); Hermann L. **Strack** and Paul **Billerbeck**, *Kommentar zum Neuen Testament aus Talmud und Midrash,* vol.4 (Munich: Beck, 1928); A.S. van der **Woude**, "Melchisedek als himmlische Erlösergestalt in den neugefundenen eschatologischen Midraschim aus Qumran Höhle XI," in *Oudtestamentische Studien* 14 (1965):, 354–373; M. de **Jonge** and A.S. van der **Woude**, "11Q Melchizedek and the New Testament," *NTS* 12 (1965/66): 301–326; August **Strobel**, "Das apokalyptische Terminproblem in der sogen. Antrittspredigt Jesu (Lk 4.16–30)," *TLZ* 92 (4, 1967): 251–254; idem, *Ursprung und Geschichte des frühchristlichen Osterkalenders* (Texte und Untersuchungen 121; Berlin: Akademie, 1977); Ben Zion **Wacholder**, "Chronomessianism: The Timing of Messianic Movements and the Calendar of Sabbatical Cycles," in *HUCA* 46 (1975): 201–218; idem, *Essays on Jewish Chronology and Chronography* (New York: Ktav, 1976), 1–44; Robert Bryan **Sloan** Jr., *The Favorable Year of the Lord: A Study of Jubilary Theology in the Gospel of Luke* (Austin, Tex.: Schola Press, 1977); Donald Wilford **Blosser**, "Jesus and the Jubilee: Luke 4:16–30, The Year of Jubilee and Its Significance in the Gospel of Luke" (Ph.D. diss., St. Mary's College, University of St. Andrews, Scotland, 1979); Sharon Hilda **Ringe**, "The Jubilee Proclamation in the Ministry and Teaching of Jesus: A Tradition-Critical Study in the Synoptic Gospels and Acts" (Ph.D. diss., Union Theological Seminary, New York, 1981); Joseph A. **Fitzmyer**, "Further Light on Melchizedek from Qumran Cave 11," *JBL* 86 (1987): 25–41; David **Wenham**, "The Rediscovery of Jesus' Eschatological Discourse" (Gospel Perspectives 4; Sheffield: JSOT Press, 1984).

232. If the Sabbatical year was the climax of a week of seven years, the institution of the Jubilee involved a week of seven times seven years or forty-nine years. The name Jubilee comes from a Hebrew word for trumpet, יובל (*yovel*), literally "ram's horn," the instrument which was blown to announce the occasion. In the book of Leviticus the statement about the Sabbatical year (Lev 25:1–7, cf. above §224) is followed immediately by a long statement about Jubilee (25:8–16, 23–55). The passage begins:

> And you shall count seven weeks (or sabbaths, RSV mg.) of years, seven times seven years, so that the time of seven weeks of years shall be to you forty-nine years. Then you shall send abroad the loud trumpet on the tenth day of the seventh month; on the day of atonement you shall send abroad the trumpet throughout all your land. And you shall hallow the fiftieth year, and proclaim liberty throughout the land to all its inhabitants; it shall be a jubilee for you, when each of you shall return to his property and each of you shall return to his family.

Much detail follows about the redemption of property, and the like. Here it seems plain that the forty-nine years were followed by a separate fiftieth year, which was the Jubilee year proper, and this was the more usual reckoning,[336] but even among the rabbinic authorities there was disagreement and some considered that there were only forty-nine years in the program and the forty-ninth year was itself the Jubilee year.[337] Furthermore, the book of *Jubilees* (about 160–150 B.C., §95), which takes its name from the institution, always makes the Jubilee consist of forty-nine years and uses the name for this entire unit of time.[338] The name "Sabbath of Sabbaths" was also used and occurs in the *War Scroll* from Qumran (1QM 7.14) and the related *Damascus Document* (CD 16.4). In a discussion of the Sabbatical and Jubilee years in the tractate *'Arakin* in the Babylonian Talmud[339] certain rabbis are quoted as holding "that the fiftieth year is not included," meaning not included in the cycle of seven years; but Rabbi Judah is cited as holding "that the fiftieth year counts both ways," meaning counted as both the Jubilee year and the year beginning the next seven-year cycle. Most authoritatively Maimonides states:

> It is a command to count seven seven-year periods and (then) to sanctify the fiftieth year (as a Jubilee year). . . . the Jubilee year is not included in the number of the seven-year periods; the forty-ninth year is Shemitah, the fiftieth year is Jubilee, and the fifty-first year is the beginning of the (new) seven-year periods.[340]

233. In effect the Jubilee year is "a heightened and intensified sabbath year."[341] As in the Sabbatical year itself (§224), in the Jubilee year property is recovered, debts are canceled, slaves are released, and the land lies fallow. As to the underlying reason for all of this the Lord God says, "the land is mine; for you are strangers and sojourners with me," and "the people of Israel . . . are my servants whom I brought forth out of the land of Egypt" (Lev 25:23, 55).

336Charles, *Book of Jubilees,* lxvii.
337Wacholder, *Essays,* 2.
338Charles, *Book of Jubilees,* lxvii.
339Epstein, *BT* 31:196 for *'Arakin* 33a.
340Mahler, *Handbuch,* 107–108.
341Sloan, *Favorable Year,* 7.

The Jubilee not only looks back to the action of God in the past but also in some sense forecasts the future; it is associated with the language of Isa 61:1–2 about the "anointed," the proclamation of "liberty to the captives," and "the year of the Lord's favor," all of which are evidently yet in the future. Such association of the Jubilee with eschatological thought appears in a text found in 1956 in the form of thirteen small fragments in cave 11 at Qumran and published in 1965 by A. S. van der Woude under the designation 11Q Melchizedek, the name coming from the prominence in the document of the person and role of Melchizedek, the mysterious "King of Salem" (Gen 14:18) and/or "king of righteousness" (Heb 7:2), whose name appears here (in line 9) as equivalent to the name of God. The text is probably of the first half of the first century A.D.[342] As the fragments stand, in line 1 only one damaged word can be seen. In lines 2–3 two biblical texts are cited, namely, Lev 25:13, which deals with the year of Jubilee and the return in that year of every man to his possessions, and Deut 15:2, which deals with the Sabbatical year and the release in that year by the creditor of that which he has lent his neighbor. Elsewhere in the document there is further citation of the Torah (Lev 15:13), the Prophets (Isa 52:7), and the Writings (Psa 82:1–2). While Isa 61:1–2 is not actually quoted, the interpretative comments throughout are all related to this passage so that the whole work is virtually a commentary *(pesher)* on the passage. Explanation follows in terms of eschatology in lines 4–7: "Its interpretation, at the end of days, concerns those in exile. . . . Melchizedek will bring them back . . . and he will proclaim liberty for them to set them free and make atonement for their sins." This will be "in the last year of Jubilee . . . the tenth year of Jubilee." Here the chronology of the end time is apparently based on the prophecy of Jer 29:10 that God would visit his people after seventy years and bring them back to their own country, as interpreted in Dan 9:24 to mean seventy weeks of years, i.e., a period of 490 years or ten Jubilee periods. Lines 8–13 go on to say that that time "is the time of the acceptable year of Melchizedek," but also the time when Melchizedek "will avenge with the vengeance of the judgments of God" (the phraseology plainly coming from Isa 61:2, "the year of the Lord's favor" and "the day of vengeance of our God"), the objects of the vengeance being Belial (in Psa 18:4, "perdition," parallel with "death") and all the spirits of his lot. Finally in line 18 he "who brings good tidings" (quoted from Isa 52:7) is identified as "the anointed" (משיח, *mashiakh,* from which the word *messiah* is derived) by the Spirit (derived from Isa 61:1, "the Spirit of the Lord God is upon me, because the Lord has anointed me. . . ."). In the present context this must be the Messiah of whom it was said by Daniel (9:25) that until the coming of the anointed one, a prince, there should be seven weeks (i.e., seven Jubilee periods).[343] In the translation by de Jonge and van der Woude,[344] line 18 reads: "*And he that bringeth good tidings:* that is the anointed by the Spirit, from whom He (?) says . . . and that which He says: *He that bringeth good tidings* of good. . . ." In the transcription and translation of the text by Fitzmyer[345] a partially destroyed

---

[342]Van der Woude, "Melchisedek als himmlische Erlösergestalt," 357.

[343]Merrill P. Miller, "The Function of Isa 61:1–2 in 11Q Melchizedek," *JBL* 88 (1969): 467–469; Wacholder, "Chronomessianism," 210–211.

[344]*NTS* 12 (1965/66): 303.

[345]*JBL* 86 (1987): 27, 29, 40.

word is restored as *dn[y'l],* i.e., the name of Daniel, and the translation reads: "and the herald i[s th]at [An]ointed One (about) whom Dan[iel] said . . ." The whole context, therefore, must envision the Messiah of whom Daniel said (9:25) that "until the coming of an anointed one, a prince, there shall be seven weeks" (i.e., seven Jubilee periods, with the final climax of the end time in the tenth Jubilee, line 7).

234. There is uncertainty as to how regularly and how literally the Jubilee year was observed. According to one rabbinic source, the institution was abolished after the fall of Samaria (723 B.C., §426), since the words of Lev 25:10 (in the passage just above) require the Jubilee only when it can be proclaimed "throughout the land to all its inhabitants," which was no longer possible after the deportation of the people of Northern Israel, and most Talmudic authorities are said to grant that the Jubilee was not observed in the Jewish calendar after the Babylonian exile.[346] On the other hand, the Sabbatical year and the Jubilee were so closely related in the book of Leviticus and in their significance that it is difficult to think that the latter would fall away all together.[347] Also, the existence of the book of *Jubilees* (which probably dates in the original Hebrew from the second century B.C. and was found in Hebrew fragments in Cave 1 at Qumran [§95]) and the more recently published Melchizedek text from Qumran Cave 11 (§233) attest to the importance of the idea of Jubilee in that time.

235. Although dates such as have been found for the Sabbatical cycles have not survived for the Jubilee years, Ben Zion Wacholder has proposed a reconstruction of fifteen 49-year cycles running from a first cycle in 603/602–555/554 B.C., believed to be traceable in the book of Daniel (9:24–27, cf. our §211), to a fifteenth cycle in A.D. 84/85–132/133, extending into the Bar Kokhba period, and this is reproduced in our Table 59.[348]

TABLE 59. *Calendar of Jubilee Cycles*

No.	*Julian Years*	*No.*	*Julian Years*
1.	603/602–555/554 B.C.	9.	211/210–163/162 B.C.
2.	554/553–506/505	10.	162/161–114/113
3.	505/504–457/456	11.	113/112–65/64
4.	456/455–408/407	12.	64/63 B.C.– A.D. 16/15
5.	407/406–359/358	13.	A.D. 15/14–34/35
6.	358/357–310/309	14.	35/36–83/84
7.	309/308–261/260	15.	84/85–132/133
8.	260/259–212/211		

346Wacholder, *Essays,* 2 and n. 4, citing *y. Shevi'it* 10:3, 39c, as well as *'Arakin* 326.
347Cf. Josephus, *Ant.* 3.280–281.
348Wacholder, *Essays,* 246–248, 256–257, and Table Three on p. 257, which is reproduced by permission of Hebrew Union College Press, Cincinnati. In Table 59 note our correction in no. 13, reckoning back from the Jubilee year of 132/133 when the Bar Kokhba rebellion commenced (§231) 132/133 – 49 = 83/84 – 49 = 34/35.

236. We have seen above (§231) that Wacholder dates the beginning of the Bar Kokhba rebellion and the first year of the liberation of Israel in A.D. 132/133 and, according to his tabulations, 132/133 was both a Sabbatical year and a Jubilee year, which, he suggests, may have contributed to the religious fervor of the uprising.[349] Our own date (following Lehmann and Zuckermann) for the Sabbatical year in question is 131/132 (rather than 132/133), and if at this point the Sabbatical and Jubilee years indeed fell at the same time our own estimate of the Jubilee year would also be that much different. August Strobel[350] depends upon Ezra 7:8 for a different reckoning. According to that text, Ezra came to Jerusalem in the seventh year of Artaxerxes (458/457 B.C.) and a solemn penitential service was held (§458). At least in later Jewish tradition this was held to have been a Sabbatical year *(shemitah)* from which later Sabbatical and also Jubilee years could be counted. Thus Maimonides writes:

> With Ezra the Shemitah began to be counted and after seven of them they sanctified the fiftieth year; for even though the Jubilee year was not observed [i.e., not in the economy but in the liturgy], these years were nevertheless counted in order to be able to sanctify the Shemitah.[351]

Later the point from which to start the count was taken to be the first year of Artaxerxes (464/463) rather than the seventh. Counting from this point for ten Jubilee periods totaling 490 years establishes A.D. 26/27 as a Sabbatical year (464/463 B.C. + 490 years = A.D. 26/27) and also makes the following year, A.D. 27/28, a Jubilee year.[352] Although Blosser agrees with Strobel in making A.D. 26/27 a Sabbatical year (our Table 57), Blosser[353] doubts the adequacy of the evidence to support the Jubilee chronologies developed by either Wacholder or Strobel and concludes that it is not possible to construct a Jubilee cycle nor to prove that any specific year during the Second Temple period or New Testament period was in fact a Jubilee year.

3. Priestly Courses

LITERATURE: Henry **Browne**, *Ordo saeclorum: A Treatise on the Chronology of the Holy Scriptures* (London: John W. Parker, 1844); Thomas **Lewin**, *Fasti sacri, or A Key to the Chronology of the New Testament* (London: Longmans, Green, 1865); M. **Avi-Yonah**, "A List of Priestly Courses from Caesarea," *IEJ* 12 (1962): 137–139; Roger T. **Beckwith**, "St. Luke, the Date of Christmas and the Priestly Courses at Qumran," *RQ* 9 (1977): 73–96; additional refs. in **Finegan**, *Archeology NT* 1:46 no. 44; 142–143 no. 132.

237. According to the Hebrew Scriptures, Aaron, along with his younger brother Moses (Exod 7:7), was descended from Jacob and Leah's

---

349Ibid., 256.
350Strobel, *TLZ* 92 (4, 1967): 252–254; *Ursprung und Geschichte*, 93–95.
351Strobel, *Ursprung und Geschichte*, 94.
352Strobel, *TLZ* 92 (4, 1967): 252; *Ursprung und Geschichte*, 92 n. 3.
353Blosser, "Jesus and the Jubilee," 115–116.

third son Levi (Levi–Kohath–Amram–Aaron, Gen 29:34; Exod 6:16–20), and Aaron and his four sons (Nadab, Abihu, Eleazar, Ithamar) were consecrated by Moses as priests (Lev 8:30). After the death of Nadab and Abihu (Lev 10:1–2), Eleazar and Ithamar continued as priests (Lev 10:12), then when David was old and made his son Solomon king (1 Chron 23:1), with the help of Zadok of the sons of Eleazar, and of Abimelech of the sons of Ithamar, David organized sixteen descendants of Eleazar and eight descendants of Ithamar as the heads of twenty-four divisions of priests, the choice being by lot (1 Chron 24:3, 7–18). Likewise in the Mishna (m. *Ta'an.* 4, 2; Danby 199) the origin of the twenty-four priestly divisions is attributed to the "First Prophets" (meaning David and Solomon).

TABLE 60. *Twenty-four Priestly Courses*

1.	Jehoiarib	13.	Huppah
2.	Jedaiah	14.	Jeshebeab
3.	Harim	15.	Bilgah
4.	Seorim	16.	Immer
5.	Malchijah	17.	Hezir
6.	Mijamin	18.	Happizzez
7.	Hakkoz	19.	Pethahiah
8.	Abijah	20.	Jehezkel
9.	Jeshua	21.	Jachin
10.	Shecaniah	22.	Gamul
11.	Eliashib	23.	Delaiah
12.	Jakim	24.	Maaziah

238. Reflecting the work of the priests in the daily services of the temple, in Hebrew (as in 2 Chron 31:16) a priestly division is called משמר (*mishmar,* pl. *mishmarot*), a word which literally means "watch" and can be any serving division; in Greek it is ἐφημερία (from ἐπί, "upon," and ἡμέρα, "day"; 1 Chron 23:6 LXX; Josephus, *Life* 2; *Ant.* 12.265); and in English in addition to "division" (RSV) a familiar translation is "course" (KJV). The head or chief of a division or course is the ראש המשמר *(rosh hamishmar)* or ἄρχων *(archōn)*. Of the courses we will later be concerned in particular with Jehoiarib (no. 1) and Abijah (no. 8). Within the main divisions or courses there were also various subdivisions, and insofar as the members of a subdivision were of one family these were called "fathers' houses" (בית אבות, as in 1 Chron 24:4), and in Greek "families" (πατριαί, as in Josephus, *Ant.* 7.365) or "clans" (φυλαί, as in Josephus, *Life* 2).[354] Of the clans Josephus gives an example as he relates that at a time in the Jewish War with the Romans when Vespasian had subdued Galilee (*War* 4.120) and the Zealots had occupied the temple in Jerusalem, the latter undertook to choose a new high priest by lot from the clan Eniachin (*War* 4.155). but neither his clan name nor the name of the course of which it was a part is known. The sequence of all twenty-four courses, known by the names of their supposedly original heads as given in 1 Chron 24:7–18, is shown in Table 60.

[354]Vermes/Millar, *History,* vol. 2, 248–249.

239. From the critical point of view, it may be questioned whether there actually were twenty-four priestly courses in the time of David; at any rate, the priesthood probably suffered disruption in the time of the Babylonian exile, and according to the Palestinian Talmud (*y. Ta'an.* 68a), only four priestly families returned from the exile with Zerubbabel and Joshua.[355] These were those of the children of Jedaiah, Harim, Pashur, and Immer, and, except for Pashur, the names correspond with names in the list of twenty-four just given (Table 60), namely, Jedaiah no. 2, Harim no. 3, and Immer no. 16. The four families were then subdivided. In the book of Nehemiah there are three lists of the priestly divisions, each called by the name of its original head; in Neh 12:1–7 the heads are called "the chiefs of the priests," who came up with Zerubbabel and Jeshua (the late form of the name Joshua), and they are twenty-two in number (with the same number in Neh 10:3–9); while in Neh 12:12–21 there are twenty divisions under Joshua's successor, the high priest Joiakim. Although there is variation in the names in the several lists, in each list the name of Abijah appears, and in two of the lists the name of Joiarib (Jehoiarib). Whether as the completion of a gradual process or the restoration of an original arrangement,[356] the number of the courses soon became twenty-four and continued thus thereafter. Josephus, who (*Life* 2) considered it a "peculiar distinction" that his ancestors belonged to the first of the twenty-four courses (Jehoiarib) and to the most eminent of its constituent clans, and who (*Ant.* 7.365–366) gives the same account as Leviticus and 1 Chronicles (§237) of the origin of the priestly institution, says that the original apportionment of the twenty-four courses had lasted down to his day (*Ant.* 7.366). Also, in Mishnaic times there were groups of representatives from outlying districts, organized in correspondence with the twenty-four courses and called by the name of Maamad, part of whom went up to the temple to witness the offering of the sacrifices and part of whom assembled in their own town to hold prayers at fixed times during the day coinciding with the fixed times of sacrifices in the temple (*m. Ta'an.* 4.2; Danby 199, cf. 794 no. 21).

240. It is also to be noted that, in the ruins of a synagogue built at Caesarea at the end of the third or beginning of the fourth century A.D., fragments of an inscription carved on marble at about the same date preserve the names of four of the priestly courses together with the names of the towns or villages in Galilee where they were then settled (a transfer of location to the north, no doubt after the destruction of the temple in A.D. 70 and the expulsion of the Jews from Aelia Capitolina—Hadrian's name for Jerusalem—by Hadrian after 132–135). As far as they survive, the course names are exactly the same as those in the full list of twenty-four, with which we are already familiar (Table 60); they are:

The 17th course Hezir: Mamliah
The 18th course Happizzez: Nazareth
The 19th course Pethahiah: Akhlab Arab
The 20th course Jehezkel: Migdal Nunaiya.[357]

---

[355]Ibid., 245–247.
[356]R. W. Moss, HDCG vol. 1, 6.

Further in connection with this priestly courses list, in a lecture at Caesarea in 1990 on the 2,000th anniversary of the founding of Caesarea, Lee Levine pointed out that the practice of inscribing such texts relating to the Mishmarot and placing them on the walls of synagogues continued until very recent times among the Yemenite Jews.[358]

241. As for the length of the periods of service in the temple of the twenty-four priestly courses, the Hebrew Scriptures do not explain how this matter was arranged, but Josephus (*Ant.* 7.365) states that in the original institution of the divisions by David, "he further arranged that one family should minister to God each week from Sabbath to Sabbath." From the Tosephta (*t. Sukka* 4.24–25) and Mishna (*m. Sukka* 5.8; Danby 181; *m. Tamid* 5.1; Danby 586–587) it is learned that in the Sabbath-day changeover from one course to the next the outgoing priests offered the morning sacrifice and the incoming priests offered the evening sacrifice. The Mishna (*m. Sukka* 5.7) also states that at the three great festivals of the year—i.e., at Passover, Pentecost, and Tabernacles—all the courses of priests performed service together.[359] This presumably means that, because of the heavier-than-usual duties involved, the course normally on duty at the time was assisted by all the others. Since each course served for seven days and a new course came on duty each Sabbath day, it is evident that it would take exactly 24 weeks or 168 days (7 × 24 = 168) to complete one rotation of the whole cycle of twenty-four courses, figures that are important for chronological calculations.

242. For chronology it is also important to ask whether (1) there was a fresh start of the whole series of twenty-four priestly courses each year at the beginning of a new year, probably at either of the two main new years, i.e., either at the beginning of the first month, Nisan, in the spring or at the beginning of the seventh month, Tishri, in the fall, or (2) whether the courses followed each other in continuous unbroken succession without any regard to the end of the old year or the beginning of the new. A saying of Rabbi Abbahu (A.D. c. 300) recorded in the Jerusalem Talmud (*y. Sukka* 5.7–8)[360] appears to imply supposition (no. 2) of unbroken succession of the courses. It was a Jubilee-year custom that a piece of arable land previously owned by a particular priestly course would revert to the priesthood as a whole and then be assigned for the next Jubilee period of 49 to 50 years to the course which was on duty at the beginning of the new Jubilee. Abbahu made a calculation and found that, at the beginning of each new Jubilee year, a different course was on duty until each of the twenty-four had had a turn, a situation which would not follow if the sequence of the courses always began at the same time (a new year) each year. Thus, the system of unbroken succession would provide equal fairness to each of the priestly courses, and Abbahu believed that this bore witness to the wisdom of David in supposedly having instituted such an arrangement. The supposition of this system is accepted, for example, by Lewin in his *Fasti sacri* (see LITERA-

[357]Avi-Yonah, *IEJ* 12 (1962): 137–139.
[358]Written communication from Jerry Vardaman, January 14, 1993.
[359]Vermes/Millar, *History,* vol. 2, 292.
[360]Strack-Billerbeck 2:62–63.

TURE). It is difficult to see, however, how such a system could have been carried out without confusion about the calendar, or how it could have been reestablished accurately after such a time as when the temple was desecrated by Antiochus Epiphanes on Dec 15, 167 B.C. (1 Macc 1:54), and lay desolate for three years.

243. Other and earlier evidence makes a beginning again of the sequence of the courses at each new year (supposition no. 1) more likely than a continuous succession. A Midrashic saying attributed to Rabbi Hiyya (A.D. c. 200)[361] seems to imply that the series began anew at each Nisan 1. On the other hand, the already quoted (§164) statement in the Mishnaic tractate *Rosh Hashanah* (1:1; Danby 188) that the first of Tishri is new year for release (i.e., Sabbatical) years and for Jubilee years, suggests, rather, that Tishri 1 was the point for the courses, too, to start again. At two very important earlier events, it was precisely at this point that we hear especially of the priests and the sacrifices. At the dedication of Solomon's temple there were many sacrifices and the priests were active; the date was "in the month of Etanim [the earlier name for Tishri, Table 12], which is the seventh month" (1 Kgs 8:2), and the beginning of the festivities was probably on the first day of the month because it was on the eighth day (1 Kgs 8:66) that the people were finally sent away at the end. In the first year of Cyrus (538/537 B.C., §340), the king ordered that the exiles might return to Jerusalem, "From the first day of the seventh month (i.e., Tishri 1 = Sept 17, 538 B.C.)[362] they began to offer burnt offerings to the Lord." In tables drawn up by Roger T. Beckwith it is, in fact, established that in New Testament times the cycle of the priestly courses commenced each year at the beginning of Tishri and that this was its one fixed point in the year. At Qumran the same was true, but with the difference that Jerusalem began the cycle not on the Sabbath on or next after Tishri 1, but on the Sabbath on or next before Tishri 1, so that the first course (Jehoiarib) would always be on duty on Tishri 1 itself, whereas Qumran began the cycle from the Sabbath next after Tishri 1.[363] This is the solution which is accepted in the present book as to the cycles of the priestly courses.

4. Qumran and Jerusalem

LITERATURE: J. T. **Milik**, "Le travail d'édition des manuscrits du désert de Juda," *Volume du Congrès Strasbourg 1956* (VTSup 4; Leiden: Brill, 1957), 24–26; idem, *Ten Years of Discovery* (Naperville, Ill.: Allenson, 1959), 107–109; Robert H. **Eisenman** and Michael **Wise**, *The Dead Sea Scrolls Uncovered: The First Complete Translation and Interpretation of 50 Key Documents Withheld for Over 35 Years* (Shaftesbury, Dorset; Rockport, Mass.; Brisbane, Queensland: Element Books, 1992), 92–134. See also LITERATURE on the calendar of *Jubilees* at §94.

244. At Qumran the lunisolar calendar of Babylonia and Jerusalem may have been in use for most everyday purposes, but for liturgical purposes

[361]Ibid., 59; J. Van Goudoever, *Biblical Calendars* (Leiden: Brill, 1961), 24.
[362]PDBC 29.
[363]Beckwith, *RQ* 9 (1977): 81, 85–90.

the Qumran calendar was that which we know from *Jubilees* (§§94ff.), namely, a solar calendar of 52 weeks and 364 days, in which the dates in the month always fall on the same day of the week, Nisan 1 and Tishri 1 always on a Wednesday, and the main religious festivals always on Wednesday (with Passover on Tuesday evening), Friday, and Sunday. Although the year begins on Wednesday, as far as numbering the days of the week is concerned Wednesday is still the fourth day, Saturday or the Sabbath is the seventh, Sunday is the first, and so on. The nature of the solar calendar made possible different relationships to it of the priestly courses. The *War Scroll* from Qumran mentions twenty-six divisions: "The chiefs of the courses, twenty-six, in their courses they shall serve" (1QM 2.2).[364] The two courses additional to the usual twenty-four are not named and it is not known how they were fitted into the sequence of the divisions, but the addition of the two is no doubt intended, at least in theory, to make the series agree with the calendar, for going through the twenty-six courses twice would fill out the year of 52 weeks exactly (2 × 26 = 52). It must be said, however, that in texts found at Qumran which deal with the priestly courses, no names appear other than those of the otherwise-known twenty-four courses, and those that are listed stand in the normal sequence.[365] As for the twenty-four courses, they went through a six-year cycle in which thirteen rotations of the twenty-four, with each course on duty for one week, exactly filled out six years of the Qumran calendar (13 × 24 weeks = 312 weeks, and 6 × 52 weeks = 312 weeks; see below §245, the second example of a text published early).

245. A number of texts, all fragmentary, dealing with chronology, the calendar, and the priestly courses, were found in Cave 4 at Qumran, a few of which were published early and others only much later. Two examples of texts published early are the following.[366] The first is the liturgical calendar already mentioned (§94), which gives festival dates in relation to the day of the week in the priestly course on duty in the Jerusalem temple. The fragment covers part of a first year, presumably in the Qumran six-year cycle explained just above (§244), and the terse notations may be filled out and explained as follows:[367]

> The first year . . . its festivals.
>
> On the third (day) in Maaziah: the Passover (i.e., on Tuesday in the week of the 24th course, falls the Passover. observed on Nisan 14, Exod 12:2–6).
>
> On the first (day) in Jedaiah: the Waving of the Omer (this sentence is partially restored but the meaning is unmistakable): on Sunday in the week of the 2nd course, falls the waving of the "sheaf" (עמר, *'omer*), the first sheaf of harvested

---

[364]Yigael Yadin, *The Scroll of the War of the Sons of Light against the Sons of Darkness* (Oxford University Press, 1962), 262.

[365]J. C. VanderKam, *Textual and Historical Studies in the Book of Jubilees* (HSM 14; Missoula: Scholars Press, 1977), 275 n. 118.

[366]Milik, "Travail d'édition," 24–26; idem, *Ten Years of Discovery,* 107–109.

[367]VanderKam, *Textual and Historical Studies in the Book of Jubilees* (Missoula, Mont.: Scholars Press, 1977), 273–274. Quoted by permission of Scholars Press, Atlanta, Ga. Cf. Vermes/Millar, *History,* vol. 2, 248.

barley, as per Lev 23:11, 15: "the priest . . . shall wave the sheaf before the Lord. . . . the sheaf of the wave offering").

On the fifth (day) in Seorim: the Passover (i.e., on Thursday in the week of the 4th course, falls the [Second] Passover, observed one month later, on Iyyar 14, for those ritually unclean and unable to keep the [First] Passover, *Seder 'Olam Rabbah* 8.15–19).[368]

On the first (day) in Jeshua: the Festival of Weeks (i.e., on Sunday in the week of the ninth course, falls the Feast of Weeks, Exod 34:22; Lev 23:15–16, in Greek called Pentecost, 2 Macc 12:32; Acts 2:1).

On the fourth (day) in Maaziah: the Day of Remembrance (i.e., on Wednesday in the week of the twenty-fourth course, falls the memorial day [זכרון, *zikaron*] observed at the new year on Tishri 1, Lev 23:24).[369]

On the sixth (day) in Jehoiarib: the Day of Atonement (i.e., on Friday in the week of the first course, the day described in Lev 16).

On the fourth (day) in Jedaiah: the Festival of Tabernacles (i.e., on Wednesday in the week of the second course, the Feast of Booths, Lev 23:34; Deut 16:13).

246. The second text also presents an almanac for six years. It begins with Nisan and preserves ten entries of course-names for the first year: Gamul (no. 22), Maaziah (no. 24), Jedaiah (no. 2), Seorim (no. 4), Malchijah (no. 5), Jeshua (no. 9), Maaziah (no. 24) again, Jehoiarib (no. 1), Jedaiah (no. 2) again, and Jehezkel (no. 20). It is to be noted that, although the course of Gamul (no. 22) is on duty at the beginning of Nisan, if the intervening entries are filled in, Jehoiarib (no. 1) is on duty at the beginning of Tishri. Thus, although Nisan was New Year for most purposes at Qumran, including Sabbatical and Jubilee years, Tishri 1 must have been New Year for the priestly courses. As already noted (§243), however, in contrast with Jerusalem, where the changeover took place on the Sabbath on or next before Tishri 1, Qumran made the change on the Sabbath on or next after Tishri 1.[370]

247. Out of eighteen texts published later from Qumran Cave 4, which deal with chronology, the calendar, and the priestly courses, the following are a few examples:[371] 4Q559 is the designation which covers three fragments of a biblical chronology.[372] Fragments 1 and 3 begin with mention of Terah as seventy years old when he became the father of Abraham (Gen 11:26, MT and LXX), Abraham ninety-nine years old when he became the father of Isaac (Gen 21:5, 100 years old, MT and LXX), and so on down to when Aaron went out from Egypt, at which point a summary gives a total of 11,536 years, which, if reckoned from the creation, is far more than figures given even by Demetrius and Eupolemus

---

[368]Joseph Milikowsky, "*Seder Olam:* A Rabbinic Chronography" (Ph.D. dissertation, Yale, 1981).

[369]*JE* 9: 256.

[370]Beckwith, *RQ* 9 (1977): 87–90.

[371]Eisenman and Wise, *Dead Sea Scrolls Uncovered,* 92–134.

[372]Ibid., 92–93.

(below §§254ff., 261ff.). Fragment 3 preserves a few more names, including Cushan-rishathaim and Othniel, with a figure of eight years (Judg 3:8, MT and LXX) for the subjugation of Israel by the former until deliverance by the latter.

248. 4Q321 and 4Q320 are the numbers assigned to two groups of calendrical fragments which not only reckon by months (begun by lunar observation) and by the rotation of the priestly courses, but also set forth synchronisms between the lunisolar calendar of Jerusalem and the solar calendar of Qumran. As in the texts described above (§244), in 4Q321 the six-year cycle is in view.[373] Fragment 1 contains the equivalences of the months beginning with the seventh solar month of the first year and ending with the second solar month of the fourth year, while Fragment 2 begins with the fifth solar month of the sixth year and goes on to the twelfth solar month of that year, thus completing the cycle. The way the equivalences of the months in the two systems are stated can be seen in the translation, restorations, and clarifying parentheses of Frag. 1, col. 1, vv. 1–2: "(The next lunar month ends) on the second of Abi[jah, on] the twe[nty-fifth of the eighth (solar) month. Lunar observation takes place on the third of Mijamin, on the seventeenth] of it (i.e., of solar month eight)."[374] The other notations follow in similar compact style. In Fragment 2 (from col. 1 v. 8 to col. 2, v. 6) a cycle of six years is again in view, and the first days of the months and festivals that take place in the months are identified in terms of the priestly courses in which they fall. In compact form and without indication of the translators' restorations, we are told about the first year:

> The first year: the first month begins in Delaiah. In Maaziah is the Passover. In Jedaiah is the Lifting of the Omer. The second month begins in Jedaiah. In Seorim is the Second Passover. The third month begins in Hakkoz. In Jeshua is the Festival of Weeks. The fourth month begins in Eliashib. The fifth month begins in Bilgah. The sixth month begins in Jehezkel. The seventh month begins in Maaziah. That day is the Day of Remembrance. In Joiarib is the Day of Atonement. In Jedaiah is the Festival of Booths. The eighth month begins in Seorim. The ninth month begins in Jeshua. The tenth month begins in Huppah. The eleventh month begins in Hezir. The twelfth month begins in Gamul.[375]

249. Like the first part of 4Q321, 4Q320 is also concerned to set out the correspondence between the lunisolar calendar of Jerusalem and the solar calendar of Qumran. 4Q320 is a fragment with three columns and, in the three columns, covers three years. The notations are very concise, but with the following translation of col. 1, v. 6 is explanation in parentheses which provides guidance for understanding the other similarly arranged dates, as follows:

> The fifth day of the course of Jedaiah = the twenty-ninth day (of the lunar month) = the thirtieth day (of the solar month) in it (i.e., in the first month of the solar year).[376]

---

[373]Ibid., 109–116.
[374]Ibid., 112.
[375]Ibid., 115.
[376]Ibid., 118.

According to Josephus (*Ant.* 18.19) the Essenes were excluded from the temple at Jerusalem, and there is no doubt that Qumran was in opposition to Jerusalem, wherefore it is a question why the compilers of these calendrical texts were concerned to synchronize their own solar calendar with the lunisolar calendar of Jerusalem. To explain the concern the translators of the texts here dealt with emphasize the belief at Qumran that all time is holy and its measurement ordained by God (cf. Gen 1:14, "And God said, 'Let there be lights in the firmament of the heavens . . . and let them be for signs and for seasons and for days and years' "); therefore the authors at Qumran could feel responsible to know both systems and to bring to light the errors of their opponents as well as to maintain their own correct understanding. Further, the people of Qumran surely expected to win out at last and to come to power in Jerusalem, where they would presumably expect to impose their own chronological system, but to do so with precision they would need to know both the lunisolar date (which they considered false) and the real solar date. However that may be, there is no doubt that the Qumran texts have provided valuable information about the two systems and have revealed remarkably sophisticated knowledge of such subjects.

Chapter 3

EARLY CHRONICLERS AND CHRONOGRAPHERS

1. Chronicles and Chronographies

(1) Greek and Roman

250. Works devoted to chronology were familiar in the Greek and Roman world and are frequently referred to under names often related to the Greek word χρονικός or χρονικόν. Derived from the noun χρόνος (§i in the Preface) these are adjectives which mean "concerning time" and they, in turn, give us names such as the following: τὰ χρονικά, with which βιβλία may be understood, are "chronological books" and are mentioned by Plutarch (*Themistocles* 27). αἱ χρονικαί, with which γραφαί may be understood, are "chronological writings" and are mentioned by Dionysius of Halicarnassus (1.8.3). χρονικοὶ κανόνες are "chronological canons" and are mentioned by Plutarch (*Solon* 27). A χρονογραφία is a "chronography," and Dionysius of Halicarnassus (1.74.2) gives χρονογραφίαι, "chronographies," as the title of a work of Eratosthenes. Similarly a χρονογράφος (Latin *chronographus*) is a writer of chronology, a chronographer, or a chronicler, and Strabo (1.2.9) mentions the writers of chronicles (οἱ χρονογράφαι) whose works he used.

251. In Latin τὰ χρονικά were *chronica* and Pliny (*Natural History* 35.34.58), for example, speaks of "the chronicles undoubtedly being in error" (*chronicorum errore non dubio*). Likewise Aulus Gellius (*Attic Nights* 17.4.5; 17.21.1) mentions a work of Apollodorus entitled with the same plural, *Chronica,* and tells of making notes for his own work "from the books known as Chronicles" *(ex libris qui chronici apellantur)*. In Latin the same word came to be used as a singular form, and Aulus Gellius (17.21.3.) cites a passage, for example, in the first chronicle of Cornelius Nepos *(in primo Chronico)*. So a χρονικά or *chronica (-ae)* is also such a work, and in English we may speak of chronicles or of a chronicle or a chronicon.

252. As for the word "canon" (κανών) found in Plutarch's mention (§224) of "chronological canons" (χρονικοὶ κανόνες), it could apply to the whole work or might apply particularly to the tabular summary or "table" which might follow upon introductory materials. Also, in the singular or plural, the word could have the sense of a whole system of chronology, as when Dionysius of Halicarnassus (1.74.2), in parallelism with his mention of the *Chronographies* (χρονογραφίαι) of Eratosthenes, says that "the canons (οἱ κανόνες) of Eratosthenes are sound."

(2) Jewish

LITERATURE: Nikolaus **Walter**, *Fragmente jüdisch-hellenistischer Historiker,* which is part 2 of *Historische und legendarische Erzählungen,* which is in turn volume 1 of the series Jüdische Schriften aus hellenistische-romanischer Zeit (= JSHRZ, vol. 1.2; Gütersloh: Gerd Mohn, 1973ff.); *Unterweisung in Lehrhafter Form* which is volume 3 of the same series (= JSHRZ, vol. 3; Gütersloh: Gerd Mohn, 1974ff.); Ben Zion **Wacholder**, "Biblical Chronology in the Hellenistic World Chronicles," in *Essays on Jewish Chronology and Chronography* (New York: Ktav, 1976), 106–136; Lester L. **Grabbe**, "Chronography in Hellenistic Jewish Historiography," *SBLSP* 17 (1979): 43–68.

253. Beginning in the late third, second and first centuries B.C., Jewish (and Samaritan) scholars, living in the Hellenistic and Roman world (and in Palestine) undertook chronographical and chronical studies. For their works we are largely dependent upon Cornelius Alexander Polyhistor, a Hellenistic-Roman author of the middle of the first century B.C., whose *Concerning the Jews* consisted almost entirely of excerpts from Hellenistic-Jewish as well as anti-Jewish and neutral sources, which work is quoted occasionally in the *Stromata (Miscellanies)* of Clement of Alexandria,[1] and the *Praeparatio evangelica (Preparation of the Gospel)* of Eusebius.[2] Of the Jewish scholars thus known, especially of interest are Demetrius, Eupolemus, Artapanus, and Pseudo-Eupolemus, while for the related information which they also provide we will speak, too, of the two books of *Enoch,* the book of *Jubilees,* the *Genesis Apocryphon,* and Josephus.

a. Demetrius

254. The excerpts of the work of Demetrius made by Alexander Polyhistor are preserved in Clement's *Stromata* (1.141.1–2) and Eusebius's *Praeparatio*

---

[1] Ed. Otto Stählin, *Clemens Alexandrinus,* vol. 2, *Stromata* 1–6 (GCS; new ed., Ludwig Früchtel; 4th ed., Ursula Treu; Berlin: Akademie, 1985); vol. 3, *Stromata* 7–8 (2d ed., Ludwig Früchtel; Berlin: Akademie, 1970); trans. William Wilson, *The Writings of Clement of Alexandria* (2 vols.; Edinburgh: T. & T. Clark, 1867, 1869).

[2] For Eusebius's *Praeparatio evangelica* see the Greek text ed. Karl Mras and Edouard des Places, *Eusebius Werke,* vol. 8, 1 and 2 (GCS; Berlin: Akademie, 1982–1983); trans. Edwin Hamilton Gifford (Oxford: Clarendon, 1903; repr. Grand Rapids: Baker, 1981).

evangelica (2.17–39).[3] In the fragment in Clement the title of Demetrius's writing is *Concerning the Kings of Judea,* but the fragments in Eusebius begin with Abraham, Isaac, and Jacob, and go on from that early point, so there may have been a fuller title for the entire work. A date in Clement's fragment names Ptolemy IV (Philopator, 221–205 B.C.),[4] so Demetrius must have been active in the last two decades before 200 B.C., and Alexandria was in all probability his city. Demetrius is, therefore, the earliest datable Alexandrian-Jewish author whom we know. The Bible text on which Demetrius's studies are based is unmistakably and exclusively that of the Greek Septuagint,[5] which was itself probably brought to completion in Alexandria in the middle of the third century B.C. (under Ptolemy II Philadelphus [285–246 B.C.] according to the *Letter of Aristeas),*[6] and Demetrius is the earliest known witness for the use of the Septuagint. As far as the extant excerpts from Demetrius go, he covered biblical history from Abraham to the capture of Jerusalem by Nebuchadnezzar, and worked largely as an exegete, raising many interesting questions of interpretation. Along therewith, however, he also introduced his system of biblical chronology and established dates in terms of that chronology for many events and personages.

255. In relation to biblical persons and events Demetrius usually sets down ages, spans of time, and the like, in agreement with the Septuagint text, but upon occasion appears to invent figures to make some total he wishes to reach.[7] In the details of his system, Demetrius notes that Abraham, who was 75 years old when he went to Canaan (Gen 12:4), was in the land for 25 years until the birth of Isaac (Gen 21:5), Isaac was there for 60 years until Jacob was born (Gen 25:26), and Jacob was there for 130 years until he went down into Egypt (Gen 47:9), thus the period of the patriarchs in Canaan totaled 215 years.[8]

256. In his earlier life, as Demetrius relates, Jacob, son of Isaac, spent 20 years with Laban in Haran (7 years to his marriage with Leah, 7 years more as required to pay for his marriage with Rachel, and 6 years more as Laban demanded [Gen 31:41]).[9] Then, as Demetrius relates further, Jacob came back to Canaan where he reached the city of Shechem (Gen 33:18) and stayed there for 10 years and was 107 years old when his sons, Simeon and Levi, slew Hamor and his son Shechem and the men of the city in revenge for Shechem's treatment of their sister Dinah (Gen 34), after which Jacob went on to Bethel where his name was changed to Israel (Gen 35:10).[10] In accordance with these figures,

---

[3] Walter, JSHRZ, vol. 3.2, 280–292.

[4] For the lives and dates of the Ptolemies see Alan Edouard Samuel, *Ptolemaic Chronology* and T. C. Skeat, *The Reigns of the Ptolemies*; Edwyn Bevan, *The House of Ptolemy: A History of Egypt under the Ptolemaic Dynasty* (Chicago: Argonaut, 1968).

[5] Walter, JSHRZ, vol. 3.2, 281.

[6] Henry Barclay Swete, *An Introduction to the Old Testament in Greek* (Cambridge: Cambridge University Press, 1914; repr. Peabody, Mass.: Hendrickson, 1989), 16–17.

[7] Wacholder, *Essays,* 112.

[8] Walter, JSHRZ, vol. 3.2, 288 F2, 16.

[9] Ibid., 284–285 F2 3–6.

[10] Ibid., 286 F2 7–10.

Demetrius's chronology makes Jacob 77 years old when he first went to Haran and Laban (107 – [10 + 20] = 77).[11]

257. In Haran, where Jacob was married to Leah and Rachel, he had eleven sons and one daughter (by Leah, Reuben, Simeon, Levi, Judah, Issachar, Zebulun, and the daughter Dinah; by Bilhah, maid of Rachel, Dan, Naphtali; by Zilpah, maid of Leah, Gad, Asher; and finally by Rachel, the eleventh son, Joseph [Gen 29:32–30:13]; while a twelfth son, Benjamin, was borne by Rachel as Jacob later journeyed on from Bethel [Gen 35:18, 22–26]); and for all of those born in Haran Demetrius gives the year and month of birth (e.g., in the eighth year and tenth month, Reuben; in the ninth year and eighth month, Simeon; in the twentieth year and sixth month, Levi, and so on down to the fourteenth year and eighth month, Joseph).[12]

258. Demetrius also follows the descendants of Jacob/Israel in Egypt (Gen 46:8–27), where Jacob himself died at the age of 147 years (Gen 47:28). Out of seventy persons of the house of Jacob, that came into Egypt (Gen 46:27), Demetrius singles out the following in particular, with their years: Levi, third son of Jacob and Leah (Gen 29:34), was 34 years old when he came to Egypt with Jacob, was in Egypt for 17 years and was 60 years old when he became the father of Kohath (contrary to Gen 46:11 where Kohath and two brothers all came with Levi to Egypt); Kohath was 40 years old when he became the father of Amram (Exod 6:18); Amram was 78 years old when he became the father of Moses (Exod 6:20); and Moses was 80 years old when, with his eighty-three-year-old brother Aaron, he confronted Pharaoh (Exod 7:7) and led the Israelites out of Egypt. The result of these figures is that the Israelites were in Egypt for 215 years (17 + 40 + 78 + 80 = 215), exactly the same as the 215 years that the patriarchs were in Canaan. Whereas the Hebrew text of Exod 12:40–41 states that the people of Israel were in Egypt for 430 years, the Septuagint version of Exod 12:40 reads: "The time that the people of Israel dwelt in Egypt and in the land of Canaan was 430 years," and Demetrius divides that total time into two exactly equal parts of 215 years each for Canaan and for Egypt.[13]

259. As for the long sweep of time, Demetrius began at the beginning and established the so-called *annus Adami,* in which years are counted in sequence "from Adam (ἀπὸ Ἀδάμ),"[14] abbreviated A.Ad. In this system, the birth of Abraham was 3,334 years after Adam, exactly as in Septuagint text of Genesis and much longer than the 1,948 years found in the Hebrew text,[15] and the coming of Jacob and his family into Egypt was 3,624 years from Adam, corresponding with the LXX (and contrasting with 2,238 in the Hebrew text)[16] (3,334 [birth of Abraham] + 75 [age of Abraham when he came to Canaan] + 215 [patriarchal period in Canaan] = 3,624), and 1,360 years from the flood, also

[11] Ibid., 284 F2 1.
[12] Ibid., 284–285 F2 3–5.
[13] Ibid., 289–290 F2 19.
[14] Wacholder, *Essays,* 113,.
[15] Ibid., 111 (on p. 112 this figure is given as 3,234, but 3,334 is correct).
[16] Walter, JSHRZ, vol. 3.2, 289 and n. to F2 18 c.

corresponding with the LXX (and contrasting with 580 in the Hebrew text),[17] which figure places the flood in A.Ad. 2264 (3,624 – 1,360 = 2,264). Adding to the coming of Jacob and his family into Egypt in A.Ad. 3624 the 215 years of the sojourn of the Israelites in Egypt brings the chronology of Demetrius to A.Ad. 3839 as the date of the exodus.[18] In sequence from Adam the dates are flood 2264, birth of Abraham 3334, entry of Jacob into Egypt 3624, exodus of the Israelites under Moses 3839. For the equation of these A.Ad. dates with dates B.C., see below (§264).

260. Finally (in the badly preserved fragment in Clement of Alexandria, *Stromata* 1.141.1–2), Demetrius comes to the exile of the ten tribes of the Northern Kingdom of Samaria (by Shalmaneser V in 722 B.C., 2 Kgs 17:6) and the exile of the people of Jerusalem by Nebuchadnezzar (in 586 B.C.), and, with an error of some seven years, puts 128 years and 6 months between the two events and, with a larger error, puts 573 years and 9 months between the fall of Samaria and his own contemporary, Ptolemy IV (221–204 B.C.).[19] Since Clement says that Demetrius's book was entitled *Concerning the Kings of Judea,* Demetrius must have told much more than this about the Southern Kingdom, but whatever it was has been lost.

b. Eupolemus

261. The extensive excerpts of the work of Eupolemus made by Alexander Polyhistor are preserved by Eusebius *(Praeparatio evangelica)* 9.30.1–9.34.18 and 20; 9.39.2–5), while Clement of Alexandria (*Stromata* 1.141. 4–5) preserves a short fragment which probably comes from the same source but is not specifically identified by Clement as to the source from which it was derived.[20] According to Alexander Polyhistor (in *Praeparatio evangelica* 9.30.1) Eupolemus's writing was entitled *Concerning the Prophetic Work of Elijah,* but this is surely incorrect, and Clement (*Stromata* 1.141.4) says that Eupolemus's work corresponded with the presentation by Demetrius, so Clement presumably means that Eupolemus's book was also called *Concerning the Kings of Judea.* In contrast with the Alexandrian Demetrius, who used the Septuagint exclusively, Eupolemus uses the Hebrew text as well as the Septuagint, and is recognizable as probably a Palestinian Jew and probably to be identified with the Eupolemus of 1 Maccabees (8:17–18; cf. 2 Macc 4:11), who was sent by Judas Maccabeus on an embassy to Rome around 160 B.C. From references in the fragment in Clement to the fifth year of Demetrius (I Soter, 162–150 B.C.) and the twelfth year of Ptolemy (VIII Euergetes, regnal years officially counted from accession in 170 B.C.), Eupolemus composed his work in 158 B.C. This date, stated thus in Ptolemaic terms, is confirmed in an addition in the same fragment which refers to the two Roman consuls of the year 40 B.C. and gives 120 years as the time from Eupolemus on to them (from 158 to 40 counted inclusively).[21]

---

[17] Ibid., 289 and n. to F2 18 d.
[18] Wacholder, *Essays,* 117.
[19] Walter, JSHRZ, vol. 3.2, 292 F6 1–2.
[20] Walter, JSHRZ, vol. 1.2, 93–108.

262. Like Demetrius, Eupolemus is interested in exact figures for the history he narrates and, like Demetrius, his long-range chronology is based on counting from Adam *(anno Adami).* Perhaps thinking of them as predecessors of the Judean kings, Eupolemus begins (as known from the excerpts from his work)[22] with Moses and Joshua, who worked—as he says—as prophets, Moses for 40 years and Joshua for 30 years.[23] In a fragment of Eupolemus's work preserved by Clement in his *Stromata* (1.153.4) and Eusebius in his *Praeparatio evangelica* (9.26.1), Eupolemus says that Moses was the first wise man (σοφός), and he was the first who imparted the alphabet (γράμματα) to the Jews, the Phoenicians received it from the Jews, the Greeks from the Phoenicians. Moses was also the first who wrote laws for the Jews.[24] Along the same line, Clement (*Stromata* 1.150.4) and Eusebius (*Praeparatio evangelica* 9.6.9) also quote the second century A.D. Pythagorean philosopher, Numenius, in the saying, "For what is Plato but Moses speaking in Attic Greek?"

263. After perhaps saying something about the judges of Israel which Alexander Polyhistor may have just passed over, Eupolemus says that Samuel was a prophet and by Samuel Saul was chosen king and died after a reign of 21 years (here the text of 1 Sam 13:1 is defective; Acts 13:21 gives 40 years, as does Josephus in *Ant.* 6.378, but 20 years in *Ant.* 10.143). Then Eupolemus goes on to David and Solomon with many details, especially about the temple as prepared for by David and built by Solomon and with long quotations of letters between Solomon and an Egyptian king, who is called by the otherwise unknown name of Vaphres but may have been thought of by Eupolemus as the pharaoh whose daughter was married to Solomon (1 Kgs 3:1). As to later history, Eupolemus makes relatively brief mention of events related to the conquest of Jerusalem by Nebuchadnezzar.[25]

264. Like that of Demetrius (§259), Eupolemus's long-range chronology is based on counting from Adam *(anno Adami).* In the fragment preserved by Clement,[26] the date there given, equivalent to 158 B.C. (§261), is said to be 5,149 years from Adam, which places Adam in 5307 B.C. (5,149 + 158 = 5,307). Likewise, from the time when Moses led the Jews out of Egypt to the same terminus of 158 B.C. is said to be 2,580 years, thus Eupolemus's date for the exodus is 2738 B.C. (2,580 +158 = 2,738), and this for Eupolemus is also A.Ad. 2569 (5,307 – 2,738 = 2,569).[27] Assuming the foregoing results and that Eupolemus's dates are earlier than those of Demetrius by 1,270 years in the whole time on back from the exodus to the flood, Table 61 provides a summary of their respective *anno Adami* and B.C. dates.

---

[21] Ibid., 95–96, 107–108 and n. to F5 4 c and d.
[22] Ibid.
[23] Ibid., 99–107.
[24] Ibid., 99, F1, 1.
[25] Ibid., 99–107.
[26] Ibid., 107–108 F5, 4–5.
[27] Wacholder, *Essays,* 117 and n. 40.

TABLE 61. *Dates A. Ad. and B.C. in Demetrius and Eupolemus*

	DEMETRIUS		EUPOLEMUS	
	A.Ad.	*B.C.*	*A.Ad.*	*B.C.*
Adam		5307		5307
Flood	2264	3043	994	4037
Birth of Abraham	3334	1973	2064	3243
Entry of Jacob into Egypt	3624	1683	2354	2953
Exodus under Moses	3839	1468	2569	2738

c. Artapanus

265. Relatively extensive excerpts from the work of the Hellenistic-Jewish historian Artapanus (c. 100 B.C.), made by Alexander Polyhistor, are preserved by Eusebius (*Praeparatio evangelica* 9.18.1; 9.23.1–4; 9.27.1–37).[28] Here Artapanus's book is said to have been called *Concerning the Jews* and also *Judaica.*[29] As far as the material is preserved, however, it deals chiefly with Moses. At the outset there is a brief mention of Abraham as predecessor of Moses, as follows:

> Artapanus in his *Jewish History* says that the Jews . . . were called Hebrews from Abraham. And he, they say, came with all his household into Egypt, to Pharethothes (Φαρεθώθης) the king of the Egyptians and taught him astronomy/astrology (ἀστρολογία). In Greek ἀστρολογία is from ἀστρολόγος (ἄστρον, λέγω), so as geology is the science of the earth this is properly the science of the stars, while the related word ἀστρονομία is from ἀστρονόμος (ἄστρον, νέμω), classing the stars, thus both words have to do with astronomy and later astrology. Then, after remaining in Egypt for twenty years, Abraham removed again into the region of Syria. . . .[30]

The word "Pharethothese," which Artapanus apparently intends as the name of the Egyptian king, is no doubt the Hellenized form of "Pharaoh," which Josephus also uses both normally and in particular in his version of Abraham's visit to Egypt in *Ant.* 1.163; in another version in *War* 5.379, Josephus names "Nechaos, also called Pharaoh" (Νεχαώς . . . ὁ δ'αὐτὸς ἐκαλεῖτο καὶ Φαραώ) as the reigning king of Egypt who had to do with Sarah and Abraham, but the well-known Pharaoh Necho II (610–595 B.C.) was much later in the time of Josiah (2 Kgs 23:29; 2 Chron 35:21). As for Artapanus's statement that Abraham lived in Egypt for twenty years, this seems an exaggerated claim and in every way unlikely.[31]

---

[28] Walter, JSHRZ, vol. 1.2, 121–136.
[29] Ibid., 127–128 F1 1; F2 1; F3 1.
[30] *Praeparatio evangelica* 9.18.1; Walter, JSHRZ, vol. 1.2, 127; trans. Gifford, Tome vol. 3, Pars Prior, 451.
[31] Wacholder, *Essays,* 46.

266. After the brief notice of Abraham there is also a short account of Joseph, and then Artapanus continues with a relatively full narrative of the life of Moses from birth to death at the age of eighty-nine (compared with a hundred and twenty in Deut 34:7). The basis of the account is Gen 1–17 but the narrative is greatly elaborated and adorned with may fanciful details. In particular, Moses gave the Egyptians many useful things: in technology (ships, stone cutting), in culture (philosophy, writing), in political organization (division of the land into 36 regions) and in religion (referral of the regional cults to reverence for the true God). On account of these things Moses was loved by the people and by the priests was accorded divine honor and named "Hermes," the Hellenistic equivalent of the Egyptian Thoth, the scribe of the gods. In spite of his attribution to Moses of such extensive educational missions in Egypt, and in contrast with his assignment to Abraham of a twenty-year stay in Egypt, Artapanus does not provide chronological information about Moses, except to say that he was a grown-up man at the time of his good works in Egypt, and (as noted just above) that he was eighty-nine years of age at death. Artapanus also gives the names of several pharaohs and of the pharaoh's daughter (Merris), who raised Moses, but otherwise the names are unknown.[32]

d. Pseudo-Eupolemus

267. Next to be mentioned is an unknown writer commonly called Pseudo-Eupolemus. In explanation of the name,[33] there is a fragment of some length in *Praeparatio evangelica* 9.17.2–9 which begins with the formula, "Eupolemus in his book *Concerning the Jews of Assyria* says. . . . " In the text which follows, however, it is plain that the author here quoted is not the Palestinian-Jewish historian named Eupolemus, who used the Hebrew text of the Torah as well as the Septuagint and was much interested in the Jewish temple in Jerusalem (§§261, 263), but rather an anonymous writer who depends upon the Septuagint and apparently does not know Hebrew, who speaks about Phoenicia—the name is literally equivalent to Canaan but hardly likely to have been used by a Jewish writer—and who is especially interested in Mount Gerizim, the sacred center of the Samaritans, and thus is very probably himself a Samaritan. For example, the scene about Abraham and Melchizedek in Gen 14:18–20 is transferred to Mount Gerizim and altered to say about Abraham that he was "admitted as a guest into the temple of the city called Argarizin [i.e., Gerizim], which being interpreted is 'Mount of the Most High,' and received gifts from Melchizedek [which of the two gave to the other is not unambiguously marked in the Hebrew text], who was king and the priest of God."[34] Since there is no apparent knowledge of the destruction of the Samaritan temple on Mount Gerizim around 129 B.C. by John Hyrcanus (135–104 B.C.), the date of the Pseudo-Eupolemus is perhaps in the first half of the second century B.C.[35]

---

[32] Walter, JSHRZ, vol. 1.2, 122, 129–130 F3 1, 3, 4 and n. 1 c and d, 3 a, 4 c and d.

[33] Ben Zion Wacholder, "Pseudo-Eupolemus' Two Greek Fragments on Abraham," *HUCA* 34 (1963): 83–113; Walter, JSHRZ, vol. 1.2, 137–143.

[34] *Praeparatio evangelica* 9.17.5–6; Walter, JSHRZ, vol. 1.2, 142, F1 5–6.

[35] Walter, JSHRZ, vol. 1.2, 138–140.

268. The Pseudo-Eupolemus fragment[36] begins with a short mention of the city of Babylon, which was first founded, the writer says, by those who were saved from the cataclysm (i.e., the flood); they were giants (Gen 6:4) and built the famous tower, but it was destroyed by the action of God and they were scattered over the whole earth (Gen 11:4–9). According to Gen 11:10–32, Abraham lived in the tenth generation after the flood (Shem, Arpachshad, Shelah, Eber, Peleg, Reu, Serug, Nahor, Terah, Abraham), but as it stands, the present text in unexplained self-contradictory-wise gives both the tenth and thirteenth generation for the time of Abraham's birth. It also states that the place of his birth was the Babylonian city of Camarina, which some call the city Urie (Οὐρίη), which is translated as the city of the Chaldeans (Χαλδαίων). This is, of course, the biblical Ur of the Chaldeans (Gen 11:28 Hebrew; χώρα τῶν Χαλδαίων LXX). As for the otherwise unknown name Camarina, one hypothesis connects it with the Arabic *qamar* ("moon") and interprets it as meaning City of the Moon, appropriate to Ur as a seat of the moon god, Sin/Nannar.[37] Here Abraham himself, it is affirmed, surpassed all men in nobility and wisdom, was the inventor of astronomy and Chaldean art (ἀστρολογία καί Χαλδαϊκή), and was well pleasing to God because of his zeal toward religion. By reason of God's commands he came and dwelt in Phoenicia. He taught the Phoenicians the changes of the sun and the moon and all things of that sort, and found favor with their king. Afterwards the Armenians invaded the Phoenicians (cf. Gen 14:1–12), but when they had been victorious and had taken Abraham's nephew [Lot] prisoner, Abraham came to the rescue (Gen 14:13–16); thereafter Abraham was received as a guest in the temple at Mount Gerizim (the incident cited above, §267); but when there was famine Abraham removed into Egypt with all his household and dwelt there and the incident of his wife Sarah and Pharaoh took place (Gen 12:10–20). How long Abraham stayed in Egypt is not stated, but the main narrative concludes:

> And Abraham dwelt with the Egyptian priests in Heliopolis [the famous city of the Sun] and taught them many things; and it was he who introduced astronomy/astrology and the other sciences (ἀστρολογία καί τὰ λοιπά) to them, saying that the Babylonians and himself had found these things out, but tracing back the first discovery to Enoch, and saying that he, and not the Egyptians, had first invented astronomy/astrology.[38]

Thus, what Abraham communicated to the Egyptians and what Enoch was the first to discover (εὑρηκέναι, find out, discover) was astronomy/astrology and the other sciences (τὰ λοιπά, the rest).

e. *Enoch*

269. For Enoch as the first discoverer of astral science there is a probable reflection of this status in the biblical assignment to him of a lifespan

---

[36] Ibid., 141–143.

[37] Ibid., 141 n. to F1 3 b.

[38] *Praeparatio evangelica* 9.17.8; Walter, JSHRZ, vol. 1.2, 142 F1 8; trans. Gifford, vol. 1, 451.

of 365 years, the same number as the round number of days in a solar year. Two pseudepigraphical books bear his name. *1 Enoch,* as it is commonly designated, is considered a composite work of the last two centuries B.C.[39] It was written originally in a Semitic language, perhaps part in Aramaic and part in Hebrew. Fragments of the original Aramaic were found in Cave 4 at Qumran, where the work was obviously valued.[40] Portions are in a Greek translation,[41] and the entirety is preserved in Ethiopic.[42] In the so-called "Astronomical Chapters" (72–82),[43] Enoch was shown "the motion of the luminaries of heaven" (72:1)[44] and himself recounted and wrote down all that he learned for his son Methuselah (Gen 5:21) so that the latter might pass it down to all later generations (82:1–3). Included is an account of the sun in its progress through the signs of the zodiac, called "portals," and the resultant increase and decrease of the days and nights (72:2ff.),[45] an account of the moon and its phases (73:1ff.), and a recognition of the difference between a lunar year of twelve months (alternately of 29 and of 30 days, making a year of 354 days), and a solar year of 12 months of 30 days = 360 days, with four intercalary days in the equinoxes and solstices), making a year of 364 days (74:1ff.).[46]

270. The book of *2 Enoch,*[47] preserved only in Slavonic, is recognized as the work of a Hellenistic Jew who lived in Egypt, probably in Alexandria, and wrote in Greek, but also drew upon some Hebrew sources; the date of composition was probably between 30 B.C. and A.D. 70.[48] In the book, Enoch, already 365 years old (1:1), is taken up to view the secrets of the seven heavens. In the first (3:1ff.) he sees the treasure-houses of the snow and the dew; in the second (7:1ff.) he witnesses the dreadful punishment of the apostates; in the third (8:1ff.) he sees paradise (cf. 2 Cor 12:2–4); in the fourth (11:1ff.) he observes the courses of the sun and moon, and understands that the solar year has 365¼ days, while the lunar year has 354 days (16:4–5); in the fifth (18:1ff.) he sees the "watchers" (Ἐγρήγοροι), who, with their prince Satanail, were agents of evil before the fall of the angels (Gen 6:1); in the sixth (19:1ff.) he sees the angels together with the cherubim and seraphim (six-winged ones, Isa 6:2), all singing at the footstool of the Lord; and in the seventh heaven (20:1ff.) he sees the heavenly hosts and views from afar the Lord sitting on his very high throne. Finally (64:1; 67:1–2), Enoch speaks of all of this to his sons and the people, and

---

[39]*APOT* 2.163–177.

[40]J. T. Milik, *The Books of Enoch: Aramaic Fragments of Qumran Cave 4* (Oxford: Clarendon, 1976).

[41]Matthew Black, *Apocalypsis Henochi Graece* (Leiden: Brill, 1970), 1–44.

[42]Michael A. Knibb in consultation with Edward Ullendorff, *The Ethiopic Book of Enoch: A New Edition in the Light of the Aramaic Dead Sea Fragments* (2 vols.; Oxford: Clarendon, 1978); Matthew Black, *The Book of Enoch or I Enoch: A New English Edition with Commentary and Textual Notes, in consultation with James C. VanderKam, with an Appendix on the 'Astronomical Chapters' (72–82) by Otto Neugebauer* (Leiden: Brill, 1985).

[43]Black, *Book of Enoch,* 386–419 (Neugebauer).

[44]Knibb, *Ethiopic Book of Enoch,* vol. 2, 167; Black, *Book of Enoch,* 389.

[45]Cf. *APOT* vol. 2, 237, n. to v. 2.

[46]Cf. *APOT* vol. 2, 240, n. to vv. 10–11.

[47]*APOT* vol. 2, 425–469.

[48]*APOT* vol. 2, 425–426, 428–429.

then, like Elijah later (2 Kgs 2:1–11), is taken up bodily to the highest heaven. See also about Enoch in the book of *Jubilees,* below §272.

f. *Jubilees*

271. The book of *Jubilees* has been described above (§§95–110) in terms of date of composition (c. 160–150 B.C.), form (a communication from "the angel of the presence" to Moses on Mount Sinai), and calendar (a solar calendar of 364 days in the year). In theological character the book is a call to its readers to a reformation based on obedience to the authority of Enoch in correct time-reckoning and to the authority of the patriarchs and Moses in the normative law, all in order that the expected time of salvation may come.[49] The span of time covered in the book extends from the creation of the world to the entry of Israel into the land of Canaan and, as the title of the book suggests, dates are given throughout in terms of the Jubilee system. It is to be noted that the book always makes the Jubilee consist of forty-nine years, rather than fifty which was otherwise the more usual reckoning among the Jews.[50] So the account of the life of Adam begins: "In the first week [i.e., a "week" of seven years] of the first Jubilee Adam and his wife were in the garden of Eden for seven years tilling and keeping it" (*Jub.* 3:15). In the margins of *Jubilees* as edited by Charles[51] these seven years in the life of Adam are marked at this point as equivalent to the first seven years *anno mundi* (A.M. 1–7) and such equivalences are continued throughout the entire book all the way to the fiftieth Jubilee when Israel is to cross the Jordan and enter the land of Canaan (*Jub.* 50:4); accordingly, Charles's equivalences in the *anno mundi* system are reproduced in such chronological notations as follow.

272. In the sequence of the immediately following events, it was after the completion of exactly seven years as just described (§271), in the second month of the next year, that the serpent approached the woman with the temptation to eat of the forbidden fruit of the tree that was in the midst of the garden (Gen 3:1; *Jub.* 3:17), therefore this was in the year A.M. 8. An interesting further example of the employment of the Jubilee system of dating is at the point where the birth and reputation of Enoch, son of Jared (Gen 5:18; *Jub.* 4:16–18), are described:

> And in the eleventh jubilee Jared took to himself a wife, and her name was Baraka, . . . in the fourth week of this jubilee, and she bare him a son in the fifth week, in the fourth year of the jubilee, and he called his name Enoch. And he was the first among men that are born on earth who learnt writing and knowledge and wisdom and who wrote down the signs of heaven according to the order of their months in a book, that men might know the seasons of the year according to the order of their months in a book, that men might know the seasons of the year according to the order of their separate months. And he

---

[49] Berger, *Buch der Jubiläen,* 279–285 (see the LITERATURE for the calendar of *Jubilees* at §94).

[50] Charles, *Book of Jubilees,* lxvii.

[51] Ibid., 25–268; and *APOT* vol. 2, 16–81.

was the first to write a testimony, and he testified to the sons of men among the generations of the earth, and recounted the weeks of the jubilees, and made known to them the days of the years, and set in order the months and recounted the Sabbaths of the years as we made (them) known to him.

273. In *Jubilees* the life of Abraham is of special interest. It is said that Abraham was born in Ur of the Chaldeans (*Jub.* 11:8) in the seventh year in the second week in the thirty-ninth Jubilee (*Jub.* 11:14–15; A.M. 1876). Already as a child he began to understand the error of idolatry and, when he was two weeks of years (i.e., fourteen years) old (A.M. 1890), he separated himself from his father Terah that he might not worship idols with him (*Jub.* 11:16). In the fortieth Jubilee, in the second week, in its seventh year (A.M. 1925), Abraham took a wife named Sarai, who was the daughter of his father (but not of his mother, according to Gen 20:12; *Jub.* 12:9). In the third year of the third week (A.M. 1928) Abraham's brother, Haran, took a wife and in the seventh year of this week (A.M. 1932) she bore him a son who was named Lot (*Jub.* 12:10); and Nahor, also a brother of Abraham, also married a wife (*Jub.* 12:11). At the age of sixty, in the fourth week, in its fourth year (A.M. 1936), Abraham arose in the night and burned the house of idols; when worshipers tried to rescue their gods from the fire, Haran rushed in to save them and was burned to death (*Jub.* 12:12–14). Then Terah left Ur with his sons to go into Lebanon and Canaan but settled in Haran for two weeks of years (*Jub.* 12:15). In the sixth week, in its fifth year (A.M. 1951), Abraham sat up throughout the night to observe the stars, and it came into his heart to say that all the signs of the stars and moon and sun are in the hand of the Lord, so that night he prayed and said: "My God, God Most High, Thou alone art my God, and Thee and Thy dominion have I chosen" (*Jub.* 12:15–19).

274. From Haran, Abraham went on with his wife Sarai and nephew Lot and came to Shechem in Canaan, where the Lord said to him: "To thee and to thy seed will I give this land" (Gen 12:6–7; *Jub.* 13:1–3); then in the first year, in the seventh week, on the new moon of the first month (A.M. 1954), Abraham built an altar on a mountain between Bethel and Ai and called on the name of the Lord (Gen 12:8), saying, "Thou, the eternal God, art my God" (*Jub.* 13:8). Going towards the south, Abraham came to Hebron, which was built at that time, and dwelt there for two years (*Jub.* 13:10). In the third year of the week (A.M. 1956)—i.e., after two years in Canaan—and with famine driving him from the land, Abraham and Sarai went down into Egypt, where he dwelt for five years before his wife was torn away from him (*Jub.* 13:10–11).[52] Referring to the Egyptian city Tanis (LXX Τάνιν, Hebrew צען, Zoan, represented by the modern village of San el-Hagar on the second eastern or Tanitic branch of the Nile), and presumably meaning that this was Abraham's place of residence in Egypt, Num 13:22 is cited at this point in the remark that "Tanais in Egypt was at that time built—seven years after Hebron," and thus Abraham's two years at Hebron and five years at Tanis/Tanais come to the very same seven years. After Abraham's five years at Tanais, two more years passed before his wife was restored to him

[52] Wacholder, *Essays,* 45–55, "How Long Did Abram Stay in Egypt?"

and, in the third year of the first week of the forty-first Jubilee (A.M. 1963), Abraham returned to Canaan (*Jub.* 13:16), where, a year later—in the fourth year of the same week—the Lord came to him in a dream with the promise of protection and reward (Gen 15:1; *Jub.* 14:1). Finally, after more experiences and trials Abraham died at the age of 175 years (Gen 25:7; *Jub.* 21:2). Since Abraham was born in A.M. 1876 (*Jub.* 11:15) and lived 175 years he must have died in A.M. 2051, but the dates in *Jub.* 21:1 and 22:1 do not agree with this, and emendation is proposed to read "in the sixth week in the forty-second Jubilee, in the seventh year, which would give the proper year A.M. 2051."[53]

g. *Genesis Apocryphon*

275. The so-called *Genesis Apocryphon* (1QApoc) was found in Cave 1 at Qumran and is an Aramaic text of considerable length,[54] which is probably to be dated in the first century B.C.[55] The largest part of the text deals with Abraham and is based on Gen 12–17, with much similarity to the corresponding part of the book of Jubilees (§§273–274). In a number of places the Aramaic is a direct translation of the Hebrew text more often it is a paraphrase and also an extension and development of the biblical stories. In the *Genesis Apocryphon* Abraham speaks in the first person and tells the story himself. Thus the narrative of the visit of the patriarch to Egypt begins: "So I set out . . . and I kept going southward . . . until I reached Hebron (19.8–9; cf. Gen 12:9, "And Abram journeyed on, still going toward the Negeb"). Hebron was built at that time, Abraham says further, and he stayed there for two years. Then, because of famine, he proceeded to Egypt, where he crossed the seven heads of the river (the traditional seven branches of the Nile), and went to Zoan (19.22). Abraham stayed in Zoan for five years and three of the nobles of Egypt came to him there and asked of him "kindness, wisdom, and truth" (19.23–24), which is different from Pseudo-Eupolemus, in which account Abraham dwelt with the Egyptian priests in Heliopolis (§268). After that Sarah was taken into the house of Pharaoh but, after two years (20.18), was returned to Abraham unharmed, and they returned to Canaan. Following the war of the kings and the rescue of Lot, and before the surviving text breaks off unfinished, God appears to Abraham in a vision (Gen 15:1) with promise of blessing, and the promise is introduced with a chronological summary of Abraham's experiences: "Look, ten years have elapsed since the time you departed from Haran; you passed two (years) here

---

[53]Charles, *Book of Jubilees,* 132 n. to 21:1 and 137 n. 22:1.

[54]Nahman Avigad and Yigael Yadin, *A Genesis Apocryphon, A Scroll from the Wilderness of Judaea: Description and Contents of the Scroll, Facsimiles, Transcription and Translation of Columns II, XIX-XXII* (Jerusalem: Magnes Press of the Hebrew University and Heikhal ha-Sefer, 1956); Joseph A. Fitzmyer, *The Genesis Apocryphon of Qumran Cave 1: A Commentary* (2d rev. ed.; Rome: Biblical Institute Press, 1971).

[55]Avigad and Yadin, *Genesis Apocryphon,* 38; E. Y. Kutscher, "The Language of the 'Genesis Apocryphon:' A Preliminary Study," *Aspects of the Dead Sea Scrolls* (Scripta Hierosolymitana 4; Jerusalem: Magnes Press, Hebrew University, 1958), 1–35, esp. 22: "I would therefore venture to date the scroll on the basis of its language to the 1st century B.C.E.–1st century C.E.)"; Fitzmyer, *Genesis Apocryphon,* 16–19.

[in Canaan], seven in Egypt [five years in Zoan, two years while Sarah was in the house of Pharaoh], and one since you returned from Egypt (22.27–28).

h. Josephus

276. The Jewish historian, Josephus, writing at Rome at the end of the first century A.D. was, of course, interested in chronology in relation to the history he wrote, and the more so because he particularly wished to demonstrate the high antiquity of Jewish traditions in comparison with pagan, presumably on the hypothesis that priority implies superiority. In *Against Apion* (1.1) he makes it plain that such a demonstration of the great age of the Jewish race was a prime purpose in the writing of the *Antiquities,* and he claims that the history of his people embraces, in fact, a period of five thousand years. Josephus there says:

> In my history of our Antiquities, most excellent Epaphroditus, I have, I think, made sufficiently clear to any who may peruse that work the extreme antiquity of our Jewish race, the purity of the original stock, and the manner in which it established itself in the country which we occupy today. That history embraces a period of five thousand years, and was written by me in Greek on the basis of our sacred books.

Also, like Artapanus (§265) and Pseudo-Eupolemus (§268) who said that Abraham taught the Egyptians astral and other science, and Eupolemus (§262) who said that Moses gave the alphabet to the Jews, from whom it went on to the Phoenicians and Greeks, Josephus (*Ant.* 1.165, 167–168) declares that Abraham "consorted with the most learned of the Egyptians" and "introduced them to arithmetic and transmitted to them the laws of astronomy (ἀστρονομία). For before the coming of Abraham the Egyptians were ignorant of these sciences, which thus traveled from the Chaldeans into Egypt, whence they passed to the Greeks." As for the philosophical import of astronomy, like *Jubilees* (§273), which relates that it was after Abraham sat up all night to observe the star that he declared the Lord alone to be his God, Josephus (*Ant.* 1.155–156) says it was from "the course of sun and moon, and from all the celestial phenomena" that Abraham inferred the monotheistic doctrine, namely, "that God, the creator of the universe, is one."

277. As for rabbinic chronography and specifically chronological works as such, we have already had occasion (§206) to deal with the relatively old and very important *Seder 'Olam Rabbah* of the second Christian century and also with the eighth century continuation of the same, the *Seder 'Olam Zutta.* Although not directly dependent on the Hellenistic-Jewish chronographers surveyed just above (§§253ff.), there are similarities but also differences in their schemes. The date of the exodus, for example, is the year 2448 from the creation of the world in *Seder 'Olam Rabbah* (Table 52) as compared with 2569 in Eupolemus and 3839 in Demetrius (Table 61). As already stated (§215), it is the reckoning of the Era of the World from 3761 B.C. in *Seder 'Olam Rabbah* that is most universally accepted among the Jews. Also, in proceeding shortly to consider certain early Christian chronicles (§§278ff.), we will find that they tabulate the chronological data of the Hebrew Scriptures in much the same manner as the *Seder 'Olam.*

(3) Early Christian

278. As for early Christian writers, there was a not improper reticence about chronology and an awareness of its uncertainties. As noted earlier (§v in the Preface), this attitude was expressed by Eusebius even in the introduction to his Chronicle where he quoted Acts 1:7—"it is not for you to know times or seasons"—and applied this saying not only to the eschatological end-time but also to all times, thus emphasizing the factor of uncertainty in all chronological reckoning. Nevertheless, early Christian writers, including Eusebius himself, were led to be interested in chronology for various reasons.

279. There was concern to comprehend the whole sweep of God's administration of the world and the time of the world's end. The *Epistle of Barnabas* (15) observes that God made the works of his hands in six days (Gen 1), recalls that with him one day is as a thousand years (Psa 90:4; 2 Pet 3:8), and concludes that he will finish all things in six thousand years.

280. As was true of Josephus (§276) and presumably for similar reasons, there was also an interest among Christians in demonstrating the high antiquity of biblical traditions over against pagan ones. In his *Address to the Greeks* (31–41, especially 31), Tatian undertakes to show by chronological considerations that "philosophy [i.e., the Christian] is older than the system of the Greeks." Clement of Alexandria also wishes to prove that biblical institutions and laws are far more ancient than the philosophy of the Greeks. He cites the work of Tatian in this regard, and devotes a long section of his own *Stromata* (1.21) to an outline of history with tables and dates.

281. Chronological studies were pursued in connection with trying to show the fulfillment of prophecy. In *An Answer to the Jews* (8), Tertullian inquires into "the times . . . of the predicted and future nativity of the Christ, and of his passion, and of the extermination of the city of Jerusalem."

282. And chronological investigation was necessary in relation to the determination of the date of church festivals, particularly of Easter. Eusebius (*Ch. Hist.* 6.22.1) states that Hippolytus of Rome (A.D. 170–236) wrote a work on the Passover in which he gave a chronological table and set forth a paschal canon of sixteen years. Jerome (*Lives of Illustrious Men* 61) likewise says that Hippolytus wrote *A Reckoning of the Paschal Feast and Chronological Tables,* in which he discussed the cycle of sixteen years, which the Greeks knew, and through which he gave the cue to Eusebius for the construction of a cycle of nineteen years. In 1551 a marble statue was found on the Via Tiburtina at Rome of a person (the upper part of the body is missing) seated in a chair, probably none other than Hippolytus, for on the back of the chair is inscribed a list of works agreeing well with what he is known to have written, and on either side is an Easter canon. The latter gives astronomical full moons and Easter dates as calculated for the sixteen years from A.D. 222 to 237.[56]

---

[56] *DACL,* vol. 6.2, cols. 2425–2428.

283. Thus, chronological statements and passages are to be found in various early Christian writers such as those we have cited and others, and eventually longer and entire works on chronology arose. Among the earliest and most important are those of Africanus (§§284ff.) and Eusebius (§§294ff.).

2. The *Chronographies* of Africanus

LITERATURE: M. J. **Routh**, *Reliquiae sacrae* (Oxford, 1846), 238–309, 357–509; George **Salmon**, "Africanus, Julius," in *DCB* 1: 53–57; E. **Schwartz**, "Die Königslisten des Eratosthenes und Kastor mit Excursen über die Interpolationen bei Africanus und Eusebios," in *Abhandlungen der Königlichen Gesellschaft der Wissenschaften zu Göttingen: Mathematisch-physikalische Klasse* 40 (1894–1895):1–96, especially 22–54.

284. Julius Africanus was a Christian writer who spent much of his life (A.D. c. 170–c. 240) at Emmaus (Nicopolis, not the Emmaus of Luke 24:16) in Palestine. The church historian Socrates (*Ch. Hist.* 2.35) mentions him along with Clement and Origen as "eminent for . . . information on every department of literature and science." Eusebius (*Ch. Hist.* 6.31.2) says that among his numerous writings were "five blocks of Chronographies (πέντε Χρονογραφιῶν), a monument of labor and accuracy." The title of the work was therefore presumably Χρονογραφίαι, *Chronographies.* As a whole it has been lost, but there are quotations and extracts from it in Eusebius and other writers, while Eusebius himself probably based his own *Chronicle* upon it. The fragments, in all quite extensive, are edited by Routh.

285. As his starting point Africanus takes the creation of Adam, and he reckons his years ἀπό Ἀδάμ, "from Adam." In references we may use the designation A. Ad., *anno Adami,* "in the year of Adam." As he deals with the Old Testament Africanus uses the Septuagint text. The first interval is from the creation of Adam to the time when he became the father of Seth. Gen 5:3 states in the Hebrew text that "When Adam had lived 130 years he became the father of . . . Seth"; but the Septuagint gives the figure as 230 years. Here it is unnecessary to decide whether the time of the conception or the time of the birth of the child is meant, but there are chronological computations (§§554, 559, 560) where the distinction must be taken into account. Seth, in turn, was 105 years old, according to the Hebrew, when he became the father of Enosh, but 205 according to the Septuagint (Gen 5:6). Following the Septuagint, Africanus begins:[57]

> Ἀδὰμ γενόμενος ἐτῶν σλ′ γεννᾷ τὸν Σήθ . . .
> When Adam is 230 years old he begets Seth . . .
>
> Σὴθ γενόμενος ἐτῶν σε′ ἐγέννησεν τὸν Ἐνώς.
> When Seth was 205 years old he begot Enosh.
>
> Ἀπὸ Ἀδὰμ τοίνυν μέχρι γενέσεως Ἐνὼς ἔτη τὰ σύμπαντα υλε′
> From Adam, therefore, to the begetting (or birth)
> of Enosh was all together 435 years.

[57] Excerpt 6, Routh 240.

At the outset this gives us the tabulation in Table 62.

TABLE 62. *From Adam to Enosh in the* Chronographies *of Africanus*

	Patriarch	Born A.Ad.	Begot the Son at the Age of
1.	Adam	0	230
2.	Seth	230	205
3.	Enosh	435	

Africanus then goes on in this same manner, makes certain adjustments in his data, and arrives at the dates in Table 63.

TABLE 63. *From the Flood to the Death of Joseph in the* Chronographies *of Africanus*

	Event	A.Ad.
4.	Flood[58]	2262
5.	Entry of Abraham into the Promised Land[59]	3277
6.	Death of Joseph[60]	3563

286. After that, Africanus puts Moses and the exodus from Egypt (which he also equates with the time of the flood of Ogygos in Greek legend) [61] under the first king of the Egyptian Eighteenth Dynasty, whom he calls Amos.[62] The year of the exodus is not preserved in the fragments of Africanus, but he gives the final year of the judges as ͵δσϙβʹ = 4292, and from the intervals involved, the date of the exodus can be calculated as having been A.Ad. 3707 in the system of Africanus.[63] From the exodus (and the flood of Ogygos) to the first Olympiad was ͵ακʹ = 1020 years;[64] therefore in the reckoning of Africanus A.Ad. 4727 = Ol. 1, 1.

287. Here and from this point onward Africanus could correlate his dates with the well-established Greek system of dating by Olympiads (§§185ff.). In the Greek calendar, it will be remembered (§185), the year began in the summer, and Ol. 1, 1 was the year from approximately July 1, 776, to June 30, 775 B.C. In the case of Africanus, writing in Palestine, it seems likely that he

58 Excerpt 8, Routh 243, cf. 507.
59 Excerpt 9, Routh 245, cf. 507.
60 Excerpt 21, Routh 269, cf. 508.
61 Ogygos ("Ωγυγος) was the first king of Thebes (chief city of Boeotia). In his reign came a great deluge. The account is one of the two Greek versions of the flood, the other being the story of Deucalion.
62 Excerpt 28, Routh 281.
63 Schwartz in *AKGWG* 40 (1894–95): 22–23.
64 Excerpt 22, Routh 273, 275.

would have used the Syro-Macedonian calendar with the year beginning on Oct 1 (§129).[65] If he took the Oct 1 nearest July 1, 776, it would be Oct 1, 776, and would make Ol. 1, 1, equivalent to Oct 1, 776–Sept 30, 775 B.C. At all events, for present purposes it will suffice to indicate the equivalent year as 776/775 B.C. So the synchronism is: A. Ad. 4727 = Ol. 1, 1 = 776/775 B.C.

288. Also, in terms of Olympiads it was possible to indicate a positive synchronism with secular history. Citing Diodorus and others as his authorities, Africanus places the first year of Cyrus in Ol. 55, 1. In his own *Library of History* Diodorus of Sicily does, in fact, say: "Cyrus became king of the Persians in the opening year of the fifty-fifth Olympiad" (9.21). Africanus says:[66] Κῦρος δ'οὖν τῷ πρώτῳ τῆς ἀρχῆς ἔτει, ὅπερ ἦν 'Ολυμπιάδος νε' ἔτος τὸ πρῶτον; "Cyrus was in the first year of his reign which was the fifty-fifth Olympiad the first year." Therefore the synchronism exists: Cyrus year 1 = Ol. 55, 1 = 560/559 B.C. Recapitulating, Africanus says in the same passage[67] that from the first Olympiad (i.e., Ol. 1, 1) to Ol. 55, 1 and the first year of Cyrus is σιζ' = 217 years, which is correct (i.e., 54 × 4 = 216 + 55, 1 = 217, counted inclusively). So, since Ol. 1, 1 = A.Ad. 4727 (§287), Ol. 55, 1 = A.Ad. 4943. Likewise Africanus says that from Ogygos (= from Moses and the exodus) to Cyrus is ͵ασλζ' = 1,237 years.[68] If the exodus was in A.Ad. 3707, and if we count these 1,237 years inclusively (as we saw we had to do with the 217 years just above), then we reach the figure of 4,943. Accordingly, Cyrus's year 1 = Ol. 55, 1 = A.Ad. 4943, and Ol. 55, 1 = 560/559 B.C.

289. This point where Africanus is able to synchronize his system with a well-fixed point in secular history is also a very important point in biblical history since Cyrus was the king who terminated the captivity of the Jews in Babylonia. In that same passage from which we have just been quoting, Africanus brings his reckoning to the first year of Cyrus with the words: ἐπὶ Κύρου βασιλείας ἔτος πρῶτον, ὅπερ ἦν αἰχμαλωσίας τέλος; "to the first year of the reign of Cyrus when there was an end to the captivity." Actually 560/559 B.C. is the year when Cyrus became king of Persia, but he did not take Babylon and free the Jewish captives until 539 B.C. From the dates just surveyed (§§286–289) our tabulation representing Africanus may be continued as shown in Table 64.

290. Fortunately, the fragments of Africanus also preserve his dates for the life of Jesus. Counting as usual from Adam, he says that the number of years to the appearing of the Savior is 5,500 (ἀριθμὸν ἐτῶν πεντάκις χιλίων πεντακοσίων [in alphabetical numerals the figures would be written ͵εφ'] εἰς τὴν ἐπιφάνειαν τοῦ Σωτηρίου Λόγου);[69] and the number to the presence of the Lord and the resurrection is 5,531 (Συνάγονται δὲ τοίνυν οἱ χρόνοι ἐπὶ τὴν τοῦ Κυρίου παρουσίαν ἀπὸ 'Αδάμ, καὶ τῆς ἀναστάσεως ἔτη ͵εφλα').[70] In view of the synchro-

[65] Schwartz, *AKGWG*, 24.
[66] Excerpt 22, Routh 271.
[67] Ibid., 273.
[68] Ibid., 273, 274, 275.
[69] Excerpt 10, Routh 246.

nism previously established (§288) for the first year of Cyrus where A.Ad. 4943 = Ol. 55, 1 = 560/559 B.C., we can also establish that A.Ad. 5500 = Ol. 194, 2 = 3/2 B.C. which must be Africanus's date for the birth of Christ.

TABLE 64. *From the Exodus to the First Year of Cyrus in the* Chronographies *of Africanus*

	Event	*A.Ad.*	*Ol.*	*B.C.*
7.	Exodus under Moses and flood of Ogygos	3707		
8.	End of the period of the Judges	4292		
9.	First Olympiad	4727	1, 1	776/775
10.	First year of Cyrus	4943	55, 1	560/559

291. The understanding just stated (§290) of the dates of Africanus for the death and resurrection of Christ is confirmed by another statement which Africanus makes. Following the date given for the resurrection he says:[71] ἀφ' οὗ χρόνου ἐπὶ 'Ολυμπιάδα σν' ἔτη ρϙβ'; *a qua temporis epocha ad Olympiadem 250 anni 192;* that is, it was 192 years from the resurrection of Christ to the 250th Olympiad. This terminal point of Ol. 250 is presumably given because Africanus was closing his work at that time, perhaps in the last days of Ol. 249, 4 = A.D. 220/221. If we add 192 years to A.Ad. 5531 we get A.Ad. 5723 and this, by the statement just quoted, has to equal Ol. 250, 1 = A.D. 221/222. Therefore, as Table 65 shows, Africanus's date for the resurrection in A.Ad. 5531 must equal Ol. 202, 1 = A.D. 29/30; and his date for the birth of Jesus in A.Ad. 5500 must equal Ol. 194, 2 = 3/2 B.C.[72] The years of the life of Jesus must then appear as shown in Table 65 according to the chronology of Africanus.

292. In a recapitulatory table (Table 66) we may now bring together the major points which we have determined in the *Chronographies* of Africanus. Since, in this scheme, 4,726 years lie before Ol. 1, 1 = 776/775 B.C. we conclude that the date of Africanus for year 1 of Adam is equivalent to 5502/5501 B.C.[73]

---

[70] Excerpt 50, Routh 306.
[71] Ibid.
[72] E. Schwartz, *Eusebius Werke,* vol. 2.3, 222 n. 1.
[73] Schwartz in *AKGWG* 40 (1894–95): 23.

TABLE 65. *The Years of the Life of Jesus according to the* Chronographies *of Africanus*

Ol.	*B.C./A.D.*	*A.Ad.*	*Event*
194, 1	4/3 B.C.	5499	
2	3/2 B.C.	5500	Birth of Jesus
3	2/1 B.C.	5501	
4	1 B.C./A.D. 1	5502	
195, 1	A.D. 1/2	5503	
2	A.D. 2/3	5504	
3	3/4	5505	
4	4/5	5506	
196, 1	5/6	5507	
2	6/7	5508	
3	7/8	5509	
4	8/9	5510	
197, 1	9/10	5511	
2	10/11	5512	
3	11/12	5513	
4	12/13	5514	
198, 1	13/14	5515	
2	14/15	5516	
3	15/16	5517	
4	16/17	5518	
199, 1	17/18	5519	
2	18/19	5520	
3	19/20	5521	
4	20/21	5522	
200, 1	21/22	5523	
2	22/23	5524	
3	23/24	5525	
4	24/25	5526	
201, 1	25/26	5527	
2	26/27	5528	
3	27/28	5529	
4	28/29	5530	
202, 1	29/30	5531	Death and resurrection of Christ
2	30/31	5532	
3	31/32	5533	
4	32/33	5534	
...	...	...	
249, 4	220/221	5722	
250, 1	221/222	5723	

293. In comparison with the scheme (Table 66) of Africanus (A.D. c. 170–c. 240), the work of his contemporary, Hippolytus of Rome (A.D. c. 170–c. 236) may be mentioned only briefly. The *Chronicle* of Hippolytus was published in Rome in the thirteenth year of Severus Alexander, the date to which its tables are carried. Severus Alexander began to reign on Mar 11, A.D. 222,[74] and his thirteenth factual year of reign extended from Mar 11, A.D. 234, to Mar 10, 235.

[74]Willy Liebenam, *Fasti consulares Imperii romani* (KLT 41–43; Bonn: A. Marcus und E. Weber, 1909),111.

TABLE 66. *Recapitulation of Major Points in the* Chronographies *of Africanus*

	Patriarchs and Events	*A.Ad.*	*Ol.*	*B.C./A.D.*
1.	Adam	0		
2.	Seth	230		
3.	Enosh	435		
4.	Flood	2262		
5.	Entry of Abraham into the Promised Land	3277		
6.	Death of Joseph	3563		
7.	Exodus under Moses and flood of Ogygos	3707		
8.	End of the period of the Judges	4292		
9.	First Olympiad	4727	1, 1	776/775 B.C.
10.	First year of Cyrus	4943	55, 1	560/559 B.C.
11.	Birth of Jesus	5500	194, 2	3/2 B.C.
12.	Resurrection of Christ	5531	202, 1	A.D. 29/30

TABLE 67. *The Chronology of Hippolytus of Rome*

	Period	*Number of Years in the Period*	*Cumulative Years from Adam*
1.	From Adam to the flood	2,242	
2.	From the flood to Abraham's Entry into Canaan	1,141	3,383
3.	From Abraham's entry into Canaan to the Death of Joshua	501	3,884
4.	From the death of Joshua through the reign of Zedekiah	958	4,842
5.	From the exile to the birth of Christ	660	5,502
6.	From the birth of Christ to the passion	30	5,532
7.	From the passion to the thirteenth year of Severus Alexander	206	5,738

TABLE 68. *The Chronology of "Hippolytus of Thebes"*

	Period	*Years*
1.	From Adam to Noah	2,242
2.	From Noah to Abraham	1,170
3.	From Abraham to Moses	444
4.	From Moses to David	599
5.	From David to Christ	1,045
	Total:	5,500

The original work of Hippolytus is probably preserved only in one incomplete manuscript (Codex Matritensis 4701), but is also transmitted in various translations and revisions, some of which in particular represent the work of later chronographers in Alexandria. As reconstructed from these sources, the chronological system of Hippolytus appears in its presumed original form as shown in

Table 67.[75] Since the year 5738 reckoned from Adam falls in the thirteenth year of Severus Alexander, i.e., in A.D. 234/235, the year 5502 (to which the birth of Jesus is assigned) must have been equivalent to 3/2 B.C. In terms of the Christian era this is the same date for the birth of Christ which we found the chronology of Africanus to indicate (Table 66), although it is there equivalent to the year 5500 (rather 5502) from Adam. In his *Commentary on Daniel* (4.24),[76] however, Hippolytus gives the year as A.Ad. 5500, and another text which goes under the name of "Hippolytus of Thebes" and presumably represents one of the Egyptian revisions of the work of Hippolytus of Rome, also gives A.Ad. 5500,[77] so the latter figure is shown in Table 68.

3. The *Chronicle* of Eusebius

LITERATURE: Alfred **Schoene**, *Eusebii Chronicorum libri duo* (2 vols.; Berlin: Weidmann, 1875–1876); idem, *Die Weltchronik des Eusebius in ihrer Bearbeitung durch Hieronymus* (Berlin: Weidmann, 1900); George **Salmon**, "Eusebius, Chronicle of," in *DCB* 2: 348–355; John K. **Fotheringham**, *The Bodleian Manuscript of Jerome's Version of the Chronicle of Eusebius Reproduced in Collotype with an Introduction* (Oxford: Clarendon, 1905); Eduard **Schwartz**, *Eusebius Werke,* vol. 2.3 (GCS; Berlin: Akademie, 1909), 215–248; Josef **Karst**, *Eusebius Werke,* vol. 5, *Die Chronik aus dem Armenischen überbsetzt mit textkritischem Commentar* (GCS; Leipzig: Hinrichs, 1911); John K. **Fotheringham**, *Eusebii Pamphili Chronici canones latine vertit, adauxit, ad sua tempora produxit* (London: Humphrey Milford, 1923); Rudolf **Helm**, *Eusebius Chronik und ihre Tabellenform* (Abhandlungen der Preussischen Akademie der Wissenschaften: Philosophisch-historische Klasse 4; Berlin: W. de Gruyter, 1924); idem, *Hieronymus Zusätze in Eusebius Chronik und ihr Wert für die Literaturgeschichte* (Philologus: Supplementband 21, Heft 2; Leipzig: Dieterich, 1929); idem, "Die neuesten Hypothesen zu Eusebius (Hieronymus) Chronik," in *Sitzungsberichte der Preussischen Akademie der Wissenschaften: Philosophisch-Historische Klasse* 1929: 371–408; idem, *Eusebius Werke,* vol. 7, *Die Chronik des Hieronymus* (GCS; 2d ed.; Berlin: Akademie, 1956); Alan E. **Samuel**, *Greek and Roman Chronology* (Munich: Beck, 1972), 194 n.2; Alden A. **Mosshammer**, *The Chronicle of Eusebius and Greek Chronographic Tradition* (Lewisburg: Bucknell University Press, 1979); Harold W. **Attridge** and Gohei **Hata**, eds., *Eusebius, Christianity, and Judaism* (Studia Post-Biblica 42; Leiden: E. J. Brill, 1992), esp. pp. 467–491, "Eusebius' *Chronicle* and Its Legacy," by William **Adler**.

294. In his *Eclogae propheticae* (1)[78] Eusebius mentions a work of his own which he calls Χρονικοὶ κανόνες, *Chronological Canons,* and speaks of as ἐπιτομὴ παντοδαπῆς ἱστορίας, an "epitome of universal history." In his *Praeparatio evangelica*[79] he refers to the same work and uses some material from it. As he begins his *Church History* and explains the plan of it, he says, in effect, that the *Church History* is an expansion of the same earlier work:

---

[75] *Hippolytus Werke,* vol. 4, *Die Chronik* (ed. Adolf Bauer, Rudolf Helm; GCS; Berlin: Akademie, 1955), 193–196.

[76] *Commentaire sur Daniel* (trans. Maurice Lefèvre; SC 14; Paris: Cerf, 1947), 309.

[77] Ed. Jo. Albertus Fabricius, *S. Hippolyti episcopi et martyris Opera non antea collecta* (Hamburg: Chr. Liebezeit, 1716–1718), 46.

[78] MPG 22:1024.

[79] 10.9.11; ed. Karl Mras, *Eusebius Werke,* vol. 8.1, 587.

> I have already given an epitome of these things in the Chronological Canons which I have composed, but notwithstanding that, I have undertaken in the present work to write as full an account of them as I am able. (1.1.6)

In the *Church History* Eusebius also refers in very full, complimentary terms, as we have seen (§284), to the *Chronographies* of Africanus, and his acquaintance with and high regard for that work make it probable that it provided much of the basis for his own *Chronicle.* From his own work in the *Chronicle* and the *Church History* it is evident that he also drew directly from the Scriptures, from Josephus, and from other sources.

(1) Chronology in the Church History

295. Of the Χρονικοί κανόνες of Eusebius the Greek text unfortunately has been lost, but there are extant Armenian and Latin versions, which will be discussed below (§§303ff.). Since the *Church History* is preserved in Greek and since it is—as Eusebius himself says—based upon the *Chronicle,* it may be useful to look briefly at the *Church History* to see how the author uses his chronological sources.[80] In the *Church History* he mentions "those Greek historians who have recorded the Olympiads, together with the respective events which have taken place in each period" (2.7.1). Therefore, he was familiar with this manner of reckoning and with sources which employed it. In the *Chronicle* he cites the Olympiads regularly; that he does not do so in the *Church History* may be because he thought it unnecessary to weight this narrative with a repetition of the citations.

296. In quoting the supposed correspondence of Abgar, ruler of Edessa, and Jesus, and also a further Syriac account of how, after the Ascension, the apostle Thaddeus came to preach at Edessa, Eusebius reproduces a date in this way: "These things were done in the three hundred and fortieth year" (1.13.22). This is presumably a date in the Seleucid era,[81] but he does not regularly employ this era.

297. A regular practice of Eusebius in the *Church History* is to give dates in terms of rulers, particularly the Roman emperors. When he cites documents and sources of a particular local area, we may suppose that he reproduces the system there in use. When he quotes an Easter letter of the Alexandrian bishop Dionysius (7.23.4), for example, with a date in the ninth year of the emperor Gallienus, we may suppose that this date is to be interpreted according to Egyptian practice. In Egypt the calendar year began Aug 29 (§49) and the non-accession-year system prevailed, that is, the period from accession to the end of the then current calendar year was counted as year 1, the ensuing calendar year was year 2, and so on (§152). Since Gallienus was declared Augustus about September A.D. 253,[82] his first nine regnal years would be reckoned in the Egyptian system as shown in Table 69. According to this reckoning, then, an Easter letter dated in the ninth year of Gallienus would belong at Easter A.D. 262. Likewise not a few other citations by

---

[80] E. Schwartz, *Eusebius Werke,* vol. 2.3, 215–248.
[81] Ibid., 217 n.3.
[82] *CAH* 12:169.

Eusebius appear to give dates in accordance with the local systems in the areas represented by the sources.[83]

TABLE 69. *Regnal Years of Gallienus in Egyptian Reckoning*

Egyptian Regnal Years	*A.D.*
1	Sept 253–Aug 28, 254
2	Aug 29, 254–Aug 28, 255
3	Aug 29, 255–Aug 28, 256
4	Aug 29, 256–Aug 28, 257
5	Aug 29, 257–Aug 28, 258
6	Aug 29, 258–Aug 28, 259
7	Aug 29, 259–Aug 28, 260
8	Aug 29, 260–Aug 28, 261
9	Aug 29, 261–Aug 28, 262

298. It was noted (§294) that Eusebius had high regard for the work of Africanus, and it seems likely that for as important a date as the birth of Jesus, Eusebius would have the same date as Africanus. According to Africanus, as we saw (§§290, 291), the date of the birth of Jesus is A.Ad. 5500 = Ol. 194, 2 = 3/2 B.C.; and we judged it probable (§287) that he counted an Olympiadic year as running from Oct 1 to Sept 30, so that the year just given was, in fact, the year from Oct 1, 3 B.C., to Sept 30, 2 B.C.

299. In the *Church History* Eusebius gives the date of the birth of Jesus thus:

> It was in the forty-second year of the reign of Augustus and the twenty-eighth after the subjugation of Egypt and the death of Antony and Cleopatra, with whom the dynasty of the Ptolemies in Egypt came to an end, that our Savior and Lord Jesus Christ was born in Bethlehem of Judea. (1.5.2)

In this statement the twenty-eighth year has to do with the rule of Egypt by Augustus after the death of Antony and Cleopatra and is presumably to be computed according to the same principles just used in establishing the regnal years of Gallienus in Egyptian reckoning (§297). The death of Antony was on Aug 1, 30 B.C., and that of Cleopatra followed later in the same month.[84] Year 1 of Augustus was therefore, in Egyptian reckoning, only the balance of that calendar year, namely Aug 1 to Aug 28, 30 B.C., and the new calendar year then ensuing was already year 2 of the reign. The beginning of the reign and the resultant date for year 28 are shown in Table 70.

300. According to the same passage in Eusebius (§299) this twenty-eighth year after the subjugation of Egypt was parallel with the forty-second year of the reign of Augustus. For the factual years of the reign of Augustus the beginning point was presumably provided by the death of Julius Caesar on

[83] Schwartz, *Eusebius Werke,* vol. 2.3, 219–220.
[84] *CAH* 10:108.

Mar 15, 44 B.C. (Table 41). Counted from this point, factual years of reign went as shown in Table 71, where the resultant date for year 42 is also given.

TABLE 70. *Regnal Years of Augustus in Egyptian Reckoning*

Egyptian Regnal Years	*B.C.*
1	Aug 1, 30–Aug 28, 30
2	Aug 29, 30–Aug 28, 29
. . .	. . .
28	Aug 29, 3–Aug 28, 2

TABLE 71. *Factual Years of Reign of Augustus*

Factual Regnal Years	*B.C.*
1	Mar 15, 44–Mar 14, 43
2	Mar 15, 43–Mar 14, 42
. . .	. . .
42	Mar 15, 3–Mar 14, 2

301. The manner of counting given (Table 71) already satisfies, with an equivalence during a considerable part of the two years, the equation of the twenty-eighth year in Egyptian reckoning and the forty-second year of the reign. If Eusebius used the Syro-Macedonian calendar and equated regnal years with calendar years in that calendar, the regnal years would have been counted from Oct 1 (Table 37). If they were counted from Oct 1 prior to Mar 15, 44 B.C. (i.e., from Oct 1, 45 B.C.), the equation of the forty-second year (which would then be Oct 1, 4–Sept 30, 3 B.C.) with the twenty-eighth year in Egyptian reckoning would be almost destroyed. The alternate possibility is, therefore, to be preferred, namely, that the regnal years were counted from Oct 1 following Mar 15, 44 B.C. (i.e., from Oct 1, 44 B.C.). In this case, the period from Mar 15 to Oct 1, 44 B.C., constituted, in effect, an accession year (§163), and the ensuing regnal years ran as in Table 72 with a resultant date for the forty-second year as shown there, too.

TABLE 72. *Regnal Years of Augustus in the Syro-Macedonian Calendar as Presumed Used by Eusebius*

Regnal Years	*B.C.*
Accession year	Mar 15, 44–Sept 30, 44
Year 1	Oct 1, 44–Sept 30, 43
. . .	. . .
Year 42	Oct 1, 3–Sept 30, 2

In this case, year 42 (Oct 1, 3–Sept 30, 2 B.C.) coincides even more extensively with year 28 in the Egyptian reckoning (Aug 29, 3–Aug 28, 2 B.C.) than the factual year 42 (Mar 15, 3–Mar 14, 2 B.C.). Either the calendar year just described or the factual year must be what Eusebius means by the forty-second year of Augustus. In either case, the date of Eusebius for the birth of Jesus is 3/2 B.C., the same as that given by Africanus (§§290–291).

302. A further check on this date is possible from two other references of Eusebius in the *Church History.* Referring to the action of Diocletian against the Christian church, he says that "from the birth of our savior to the destruction of the places of worship" was "a period of three hundred and five years" (7.32.32); and later he dates the persecution and the destruction of churches by Diocletian as follows:

> It was in the nineteenth year of the reign of Diocletian, in the month Dystros, called March by Romans, when the feast of the Savior's passion was near at hand, that royal edicts were published everywhere, commanding that the churches be leveled to the ground. . . . (8.2.4)

Diocletian became emperor in the late autumn—probably Nov 17—in A.D. 284; he celebrated his vicennalia (a festival on the twentieth anniversary of reign) in Rome on Nov 20, 303.[85] In this case, factual years (from November to November) and Syro-Macedonian calendar years (Oct 1 to Sept 30) were not far apart and there is little doubt that Eusebius would have normally counted the regnal years of Diocletian as extending from autumn to autumn, beginning with the autumn of his accession. If, to be precise, he used the Syro-Macedonian calendar years, they would have run as shown as Table 73.

TABLE 73. *Regnal Years of Diocletian in the Syro-Macedonian Calendar*

Regnal Years	*A.D.*
1	Nov 17, 284–Sept 30, 285
2	Oct 1, 285–Sept 30, 286
. . .	. . .
19	Oct 1, 302–Sept 30, 303

The month Dystros = March, mentioned by Eusebius, in this nineteenth year of Diocletian was, therefore, March A.D. 303. A date for the birth of Jesus in 3/2 B.C. means that approximately two years—slightly more or slightly less—had elapsed at the turn of the era; here, at the point of the persecution, we are in the three hundred and third year after the beginning of the Christian era; together, counting inclusively, the total is three hundred and five years, and a date by Eusebius for the birth of Jesus 3/2 B.C. is confirmed.[86]

---

[85] *CAH* 12:323, 340.

[86] Schwartz in *AKGWG* 40 (1894–1895): 30. It must be noticed, however, that in the consecutive tabulation of the *Chronicle* itself, at least as edited by Jerome (Helm 225–228), the beginning of the reign of Diocletian is placed in A.D. 285, his first regnal year is equated with A.D. 286, and his nineteenth year and the first year of the persecution is equated with A.D. 304. The historically correct date of the inauguration of the persecution,

(2) *The Armenian Version of the* Chronicle

303. Turning now to the *Chronicle* itself, we have already noted (§295) that the Greek text is lost but that Armenian and Latin versions are extant. The Armenian version is found in two late codices of the thirteenth-fourteenth centuries, and has been edited by Karst. It is now believed that the Armenian derives from a Greek redaction prepared about a quarter of a century after Jerome composed the Latin version. The Armenian version contains a lengthy introductory portion, often spoken of as the *Chronicle* proper, which deals with the chronology of the Chaldeans, Hebrews, Egyptians, Greeks, and Romans (most of this material survives only in Armenian); then follow the chronological tables themselves, often called the Canon.[87] As found in the Armenian, the tables are confined within the horizontal limits of the breadth of a page. On each side of the page is a column in which events are listed. Events in biblical history are almost always on the left side; events in secular history are distributed on both sides. In the center of the page are several narrow columns of dates. One of these numbers the years from Abraham. Another column, after that point is reached, gives the Olympiadic dates. Other columns, as many as are needed, list the successive years of kings of various nations. As now preserved, the Armenian Canon begins with year 344 of Abraham, which is equated with the time of Joseph in Egypt, and comes down to Constantine and Maximian, that is to the time of Eusebius himself.

(3) *The Latin Version of the* Chronicle *by Jerome*

304. The Latin version of the *Chronicle* was the work of Jerome. In his Letter 57 to Pammachius written in A.D. 395, Jerome refers to what he had done "in translating the *Chronicle* of Eusebius of Caesarea into Latin"; and there is reason to think the translation was made in Constantinople in A.D. 381.[88] This version is represented in nearly a dozen manuscripts, the two earliest probably from the fifth century, and has been edited by Helm.

305. In this version Jerome made additions of his own, particularly enlarging the notices which pertained to Roman history and continuing the tables to Valentinian and Valens, that is, to his own time. The long introductory section dealing with the chronology of the various nations, found in the Armenian, is not in the Latin version. It opens instead with only a brief introduction by Jerome and the Latin translation of a brief introduction by Eusebius. The chronological tables themselves have a somewhat different arrangement from the Armenian. Down to the end of the Jewish captivity the columns are spread over two adjacent pages. On each page there is a column of events in the center place which is sometimes called the *spatium historicum.* On each side thereof is a column or columns of dates. Since these consist for the most part of successive

---

however, is A.D. 303 and probably on Feb 23 (*CAH* 12:666).

[87] Mosshammer, *Greek Chronographic Tradition,* 78; William Adler, "Eusebius' Chronicle and Its Legacy," 467.

[88] Schoene, *Weltchronik des Eusebius,* 249–252.

years of successive kings, they are sometimes called *fila regnorum.* After the point indicated there is only one column of events, with columns of dates on either side of it, and the whole is kept within the limits of one page. After the fall of Jerusalem (A.D. 70), there is no longer a column of dates on the right side.

306. Since the form of the tables is more complex and more carefully arranged in the Latin than in the Armenian, and since Jerome says in his preface[89] that he dictated his translation to a stenographer *(notarius)* at very high speed *(velocissime),* we can hardly think that he was responsible for the invention of this complicated form, and we must suppose that the Latin version, in fact, represents the original arrangement of the Canon better than the more simply arranged Armenian.[90] Also, when compared with the *Church History* of Eusebius, the figures in the Armenian version are found to diverge more widely than those in the Latin, so from this point of view also Helm's 1956 edition of Jerome's translation may be taken, as far as it extends, as the preferred source.[91]

307. In his chronological tables Eusebius provided a running framework in the form of two universal standards. He considered Abraham the most ancient personage whose date could be ascertained with some accuracy and therefore used years of Abraham *(anni Abraham)* as his first universal standard. The years *ab Abraham* are brought together at ten-year intervals, as Eusebius says in his preface *(omnem annorum congeriem in decadas cecidimus),*[92] and continued throughout the Canon as if Abraham had lived the entire time and these were the years of his continuing life (and in occasional summaries Eusebius also gives recapitulations from Adam). The Olympiads are introduced as I Olymp., II Olymp., and so on, and are marked in at four-year intervals. Alongside the years of Abraham and the Olympiadic years are columns for the monarchs and their years of three great lines: Persian kings, Egyptian Ptolemies, and Roman emperors. The figures for the years of Abraham are underscored (X, XX, etc.) and so too are the figures for the years of reign of the first king set immediately alongside. At the extreme right Helm gives the years B.C. and A.D. in continuous sequence.[93]

308. With regard to the Olympiadic year, it was noted above (§185) that 776 B.C. is generally accepted as the starting point of the reckoning, and in brief form the first year is given as 776/775 B.C. It may be assumed that Eusebius knew that the Olympic games were celebrated in the summer so that an Olympiadic year extended over parts of two years in some other calendars with which he was concerned, and that he introduced his Olympiadic dates accordingly. Referring again to Schürer's table of the Greek, Syrian, Roman, and Christian eras (our Table 56),[94] and taking the Olympiadic year strictly, Ol. 151, 1, for example, is

---

[89] Helm 2.

[90] Helm, *Eusebius Chronik und ihre Tabellenform*, 45.

[91] Schwartz, *Eusebius Werke,* vol. 2.3, 238; and "Die Königslisten des Eratosthenes und Kastor," in *AKGWG* 40 (1894–1895): 27, 44.

[92] Helm 18.

[93] George Salmon in *DCB* 2:353; Mosshammer, *Greek Chronographic Tradition,* 15, 35.

[94] Schürer, *History,* vol. 1.2, 393–398; Vermes/Millar, *History* 1:607–611.

equivalent to summer 176–summer 175 B.C. and A.S. 137 is equivalent to autumn 176–autumn 175 B.C. The portion of the *Chronicle* of Eusebius (Jerome) in question here is reproduced in Table 74.

TABLE 74. *Some Parallel Years around the Year 176 B.C. in the* Chronicle *of Eusebius (Jerome)*

B.C.	*A.Abr.*	*Ol.*	*Alexandrians*	*Syria and Asia*
			Of Egypt the 5th, Ptolemy Epiphanes, 24 years	Seleucus, also called Philopator, 12 years
180	1837	150	24	8
			Of Egypt the 6th, Ptolemy Philometor, 35 years	
179	1838		1	9
178	1839		2	10
177	1840		3	11
176	1841	151	4	12
				Antiochus Epiphanes, 11 years
175	1842		5	1

To explicate and add modern dates of rulers, in some cases slightly different from those given by Eusebius (Jerome): The Olympiads are

Ol. 150, 1 = summer 180 to summer 179
2 = summer 179 to summer 178
3 = summer 178 to summer 177
4 = summer 177 to summer 176
Ol. 151, 1 = summer 176 to summer 175
2 = summer 175 to summer 174

The presently accepted regnal years of the Alexandrians are Ptolemy V Epiphanes (205–180 B.C.), and Ptolemy VI Philometor (180–145 B.C.). The Syrians/Asians are Seleucus IV Philopator (187–175) and Antiochus Epiphanes (175–164), and the *Chronicle* dates are reasonably close.[95]

309. Rather than understanding an Olympiadic year as beginning strictly in the summer, as the preceding elucidation does (§308), Mosshammer says that Eusebius of course knew that the Olympic games took place in the summer but, for the purpose of chronographic synchronization with other calendars, made the Olympiadic year begin "several months later," supposedly meaning in the autumn. In support of this theory Mosshammer notes that the first Olympiad was celebrated in the second year of Aeschylus (Greek tragic poet and participant in the Persian wars) but is synchronized in the *Chronicle* with the third year of Aeschylus.[96] Samuel goes farther and says that Eusebius seems to have equated the Olympiadic year to the Julian, beginning January 1. The example Samuel

[95] *EB* (1987) ad. loc.
[96] Mosshammer, *Greek Chronographic Tradition*, 79–80; citing Helm 85a–86a.

adduces to validate this theory, namely, the Olympiadic date of the death of Julius Caesar, will be noted below (§320, Table 85).[97]

310. With regard to the years of Abraham in Helm's edition of the *Chronicle* of Eusebius: like the Olympiadic dates (§308), the Abrahamic dates are stated in single-year figures but are to be understood as overlapping two years. Thus the generally accepted date of the first year of Abraham, which is marked as equivalent to 2016 B.C.,[98] is to be understood as 2016/2015 B.C.; and the further years of Abraham in our Table 75 are all to be understood in the same way.[99] The correctness of the initial dates of 776/775 B.C. for the sequence of Olympiadic years (§308 Table 46) and of 2016/2015 B.C. for the sequence of years of Abraham (§309 Table 75) in the *Chronicle* of Eusebius (Jerome) will be confirmed at the place where the *Chronicle* comes to a well-known point in Babylonian and biblical chronology, namely, the second year of the Persian king, Darius I (§§330–333, Tables 89, 90). Theoretically an overlap could be either forward or backward; e.g., the year A.D. 68 could mean either 68/69 or 67/68 (cf. §671).

TABLE 75. *Years of Abraham in the* Chronicle *of Eusebius*

A.Abr.	*Julian*
1	2016
2	2015
3	2014
. . .	. . .
2014	3
2015	2
2016	1 B.C.
2017	A.D. 1
2018	2
2019	3
. . .	. . .
2086	70
2087	71
2088	72
2089	73
2090	74

For extrapolating years not shown in this table, note that (a) the sum of any year B.C. and the corresponding A.Abr. year is 2017; and (b) any A.D. year is always 2016 less than the corresponding A.Abr. year.

(4) From Adam to Abraham in the Chronicle

311. For the biblical chronology prior to Abraham we have what is in the long introductory portion of the Armenian version and what is in the very

[97] Samuel, *Greek and Roman Chronology,* 194 n. 2.

[98] Helm 20a–20b.

[99] William Adler, "Eusebius' *Chronicle* and Its Legacy," in Attridge and Hata, *Eusebius, Christianity, and Judaism,* 474.

brief introduction of Eusebius, translated by Jerome, in the Latin version. According to the Armenian version, Eusebius notices that there are differences in the figures in the Hebrew, Septuagint, and Samaritan texts. In general, he thinks that mistakes and inconsistencies are evident in the extant Hebrew text and that the Septuagint was translated from ancient and accurate copies of the Hebrew text and was therefore to be preferred.[100] The Septuagint text used by Eusebius must have differed from that available now, however, as may be noted for example in its omission of Elon in the list of Judges (Table 79). From Adam to the flood[101] the figures given by the several texts are: LXX—2,242 years; Hebrew—1,656 years; Samaritan—1,307 years. Africanus, who also followed the Septuagint, has 2,262 years here (Table 63), the difference perhaps being due to different figures for Methuselah. In the brief Latin introduction[102] the figure is also 2,242. From the flood to Abraham, as the Armenian version notes,[103] the several texts give these figures: LXX—942; Hebrew—292; Samaritan—942. Again the Latin introduction gives 942 years from the flood to the nativity of Abraham. The several totals from Adam to Abraham are therefore: LXX—3,184; Hebrew—1,948; and Samaritan—2,249. Accepting the Septuagint as the standard, the skeletal tabulation in Table 76 results (cf. Africanus, Table 66; Hippolytus of Rome, Table 67; "Hippolytus of Thebes," Table 68).

TABLE 76. *From Adam to Abraham in the* Chronicle *of Eusebius*

Event	*A.Ad.*	*Number of Years Intervening*
Adam	0	2,242
Flood	2242	942
Birth of Abraham	3184	

(5) From Abraham through the Egyptian Servitude

312. At this initial point the tables of the Canon are spread across two adjacent pages and, in the four columns of successively numbered years, the first year of Abraham is synchronized with the years of the reign of Assyrian, Greek, and Egyptian kings.[104] The first column at the left-hand side gives the years of rule of the Assyrian kings. In the view of Greek writers, the first historical king of Asia was Ninus. Herodotus (1.7) names Ninus (Νίνος) as the son of Belus, and Diodorus (2.1–7) gives an extended account of his life and accomplishments. Opening his record of "the events which took place in Asia in the ancient period, beginning with the time when the Assyrians were the dominant power," Diodorus writes: "The first to be handed down by tradition to history and memory for us as one who achieved great deeds is Ninus, king of the Assyrians." He goes on to tell

[100]Karst 45.
[101]Karst 38–41.
[102]Helm 15.
[103]Karst 41–45.
[104]Helm 20 a–b.

how Ninus conquered most of Asia between the Tanais or Don River and the Nile, and then founded a very great city to which he gave his own name, Ninus. Eusebius is, therefore, simply following the standard Greek view of the history of Asia when he begins the first column of the Canon with Ninus son of Belus and says that he ruled all of Asia except India. He also notes that he founded the city of Ninus in the region of the Assyrians, which the Hebrews call Nineveh. To Ninus he attributes a reign of fifty-two years and he says, presumably following some further established tradition, that it was in the forty-third year of Ninus that Abraham was born. Thus, he places the beginning of Hebrew history against the backdrop of the history of Asia and, in fact, at the beginning of that history.

313. In his second column, accordingly, Eusebius shows this beginning of Hebrew history by placing year 1 of Abraham over against year 43 of Ninus. Extending the correlation to Greece and to Egypt he shows in the third column the rule of the Sicyonians and in the fourth column the rule of the Egyptians. At Sicyon, a city of the Peloponnesus also known as Aegialeia ("beach-town"), the second king of the dynasty was ranked as the ruler of Europe and was in the twenty-second year of a forty-five year reign. In Egypt the identical year was the first of the first king of the Sixteenth Dynasty, a dynasty which Eusebius says reigned in Thebes for one hundred and ninety years and was followed by the Seventeenth Dynasty of "shepherd kings."[105] This first year of the Canon, which is the first year of Abraham, appears, therefore, as in Table 77.

TABLE 77. *Year 1 of Abraham in the* Chronicle *of Eusebius*

Kingdom of the Assyrians	*Beginning of the Hebrew people*	*Kingdom of the Sicyonians*	*Kingdom of the Egyptians*
Ninus, son of Belus Year 43	Abraham Year 1	The second king of Sicyon Year 22	The Sixteenth Dynasty Year 1

314. From Abraham to Moses and the exodus from Egypt, Eusebius finds that the Septuagint, Hebrew, and Samaritan texts all agree on a total of 505 years, and he gives this figure (DV) in the Latin introduction.[106] This is counted as follows: In the seventy-fifth year of Abraham God made the promise (Gen 12:1–4) to him.[107] This "first year of the promise of God to Abraham" is also used as a point of cumulative reckoning, and ten years later the "tenth year of the promise" is noted, and so on for some time.[108] When Abraham was one hundred years old he became father of Isaac.[109] When Isaac was sixty years old he became the father of Jacob.[110] When Jacob was 121 years old, Joseph became

[105]Helm 28 b.
[106]Karst 45–46, 156–161; Helm 17.
[107]Helm 23 n.
[108]Ibid., 23 a 24 a, etc.
[109]Ibid., 24 a.

the chief of the land of Egypt and continued in that position for eighty years.[111] After the death of Joseph the servitude of the Israelites in Egypt began and continued for 144.[112] Moses was born in the sixty-fourth year of the servitude, which was also the 350th year of the promise (25 + 60 + 121 + 80 + 64 = 350).[113] At this point a cumulative reckoning from Moses is also introduced, and is noted at ten year intervals.[114] Here we notice that Moses was eighty years old in the 144th and last year of the servitude, which was also the 430th year of the promise,[115] a figure likewise used by Paul (Gal 3:17). This portion of the Canon may therefore be recapitulated briefly as shown in Table 78.

TABLE 78. *From Abraham through the Servitude in Egypt in the* Chronicle *of Eusebius*

Year of Abraham	*Year of the Promise*	*Year of Moses*	*Year of Hebrew History*	*Events*	*Number of Years Intervening*
		ABRAHAM			
1			1	Born	75
75	1		75	Receives promise	
100	25		100	Becomes father of Isaac	25
		ISAAC			
101	26		1	Born	
160	85		60	Becomes father of Jacob	60
		JACOB			
161	86		1	Born	
281	206		121	Becomes chief of Egypt	121
		JOSEPH THE CHIEF OF EGYPT			
282	207		1	Becomes chief	
361	286		80	Dies	80
		SERVITUDE OF THE HEBREWS IN EGYPT			
362	287		1		
425	350	1	64	Moses born	64
505	430	80	144	Last year of servitude	80
					505

[110]Ibid., 27 a.
[111]Ibid., 32 a.
[112]Ibid., 36 a.
[113]Ibid., 39 a.
[114]Ibid., 40 a, etc.
[115]Ibid., 43 a.

TABLE 79. *From the Wandering in the Wilderness to the Building of the Temple in the* Chronicle *of Eusebius*

Year of Abraham	*Year of Hebrew History*	*Event*	*Number of Years Intervening*
	Moses leads the Hebrew people in wilderness for 40 years		
506	1		40
545	40	Death of Moses	
	After Moses, Joshua leads the people for 27 years		
546	1		27
572	27		
	The Judges		
	Othniel, 40 years		
	Ehud, 80 years		
	Deborah and Barak, 40 years		
	Gideon, 40 years		
	Abimelech, 3 years		
	Tola, 22 years		
	Jair, 22 years		
	Jephthah, 6 years		328
	Ibzan, 7 years		
	[Here it is noted that in the Hebrew text (Judg 12:11–12) has Elon 10 years, but that this is not in the LXX, hence is omitted in the table (cf. above §263).]		
	Abdon, 8 years		
	Samson, 20 years		
	Eli, 40 years		
	Samuel and Saul, 40 years		
901	1		40
940	40		
	David, 40 years		
941	1		40
980	40		
	Solomon, 40 years		
981	1		
982	2		4
983	3		
984	4	Foundation of the temple	
			479

(6) From the Wandering in the Wilderness to the Foundation of the Temple in the Fourth Year of Solomon

315. The next portion of the Canon continues from the forty years in the wilderness to the fourth year of Solomon in which the building of the temple in Jerusalem was begun.[116] In brief, and continuing the cumulative reckonings of only the years of Abraham, this portion of the tabulation provides the outline in Table 79.

316. The period just summarized totals 479 years, and in the Latin introduction Eusebius gives the same figure as the time from Moses to Solomon and the first building of the temple.[117] At the beginning of this part of the tabulation there is a note in the Canon,[118] however, which gives the period as 480 years. In 1 Kgs 6:1, the Hebrew text says that it was the 480th year after the people came out of Egypt and in the fourth year of Solomon's reign that he began to build the temple. In the same passage the Septuagint, as available today, has the 440th year; one manuscript has the 480th.[119] If one counts, inclusively, from A.Abr. 505, the last year of the servitude, to A.Abr. 984, the fourth year of Solomon, the period was indeed 480 years long. But the note in the Canon appears to be intended as reckoning from the first year in the wilderness (A.Abr. 506) and, in that case, the 480 years total is one in excess of what the tabulation actually shows. Also, at the end of this period there is a note in the Canon[120] which recapitulates the years from Adam to this point and uses the figure of 480 years in the same way. It gives the figures in Table 80.

TABLE 80. *A Summary Note in the* Chronicle *of Eusebius from Adam to the Building of the Temple*

Period	*Number of Years*
From Adam to the flood	2,242
From the flood to Moses (942 + 505)	1,447
From Moses and the egress of the Israelites from Egypt to the 4th year of Solomon and the building of the temple	480
	4,169

According to our understanding of the tabulation, the summary figures should be those shown in Table 81. Since the two notes with the figure of 480 years are, thus, in disagreement with the actual tables by one year, they may be editorial and in error to this extent.

[116]Ibid., 43–70.
[117]Ibid., 17.
[118]Ibid., 43 a.
[119]LXX, ed. Rahlfs, vol. 1, 638.
[120]Helm 70 a.

TABLE 81. *A Corrected Summary Note in the* Chronicle *of Eusebius from Adam to the Building of the Temple*

	Number of Years
From Adam to the flood	2,242
From the flood to Moses (942 + 505)	1,447
From Moses and the egress of the Israelites from Egypt to the fourth year of Solomon and the building of the temple	479
	4,168

(7) From the Fifth Year of Solomon to the Destruction of the Temple

317. From the fifth year of Solomon, with which the Canon continues, down to the eleventh year of Zedekiah and the destruction in that year of the temple, the years of reign of the kings of Judah are given in Table 82.[121] The eleventh year of Zedekiah, with which that table closes, was the year in which

TABLE 82. *The Years of the Kings of Judah in the* Chronicle *of Eusebius*

	King	*Number of Years of Reign*
1.	Solomon (beginning, inclusively, with his 5th year)	36
2.	Rehoboam	17
3.	Abijam	3
4.	Asa	41
5.	Jehoshaphat	25
6.	Jehoram	8
7.	Ahaziah	1
8.	Athaliah	7
9.	Joash	40
10.	Amaziah	29
11.	Azariah, or Uzziah	52
12.	Jotham	16
13.	Ahaz	16
14.	Hezekiah	29
15.	Manasseh	55
16.	Amon	12
17.	Josiah	32
18.	Jehoahaz (3 months)	1
19.	Jehoiakim	11
20.	Jehoiachin (3 months)	1
21.	Zedekiah	11
		442

[121]Helm 70a–99a.

the temple was destroyed (2 Kgs 25:2ff.; Jer 52:5ff.). Without listing these individual reigns, our main tabulation may be continued in brief in Table 83. At this point in the text of the *Chronicle*[122] it is correctly noted that from its first erection to its burning by Nebuchadnezzar the temple had endured for 442 years.

TABLE 83. *From the Fifth Year of Solomon to the Eleventh Year of Zedekiah in the* Chronicle *of Eusebius*

A. Abr.	*Year of Hebrew History*	*B.C.*	*Number of Years Intervening*
	Solomon		
985	5	1032	
	Zedekiah		
1426	11	591	442

318. Within the period just summarized (§317) we come to the point where the Greek era of the Olympiads (§§185ff.) begins. The way this is shown, at the outset, in the Canon[123] may be indicated in Table 84. As stated already (§307), the Olympiadic number is regularly set at the left side of the page and the Olympiadic years are aligned with regnal years. The B.C. dates, shown in the right-hand column, will be discussed in §319.

TABLE 84. *The First Olympiadic Notations in the* Chronicle *of Eusebius*

A. Abr.	*Ol.*	*Year of Hebrew History*	*B.C.*
		Azariah, or Uzziah, is king for 52 years	
1240	1	49	777
1241		50	776
1242		51	775
1243		52	774
		Jotham is king for 16 years	
1244		1	773
1245	2	2	772
1246		3	771
1247		4	770
1248		5	769
1249	3	6	768
1250		7	767

[122]Helm 100 a.
[123]Helm 86a–87b.

319. In the standard Greek reckoning, Ol. 1, 1 began about July 1, 776 B.C., and extended to about June 30, 775 B.C. (§§307, 309).[124] Whether the Olympiadic years are to be taken strictly or as beginning several months later than July 1, they cover parts of two Julian years and therefore such a date as 776 B.C. set opposite must be understood as in fact 776/775 B.C.; alternatively, if the Olympiadic year is understood as coinciding with a Julian year, then 776 B.C. means January 1 to December 31, 776.[125] Regnal years set alongside of course have their own durations, and Eusebius/Jerome presumably had the opportunity to know these accurately.[126]

320. In Table 85[127] we reach the point of Ol. 184, 1 adduced by Samuel (§307) as showing that Eusebius equated the Olympiadic year to the Julian, beginning Jan 1. The date in question is that of the death of Julius Caesar. Caesar is here said correctly to have had a rule of four years and seven months; Olympiad 184 is named between years four and five of Caesar; and a note opposite his fifth year states that he was killed in the senate house on the ides of March *(Idibus Martiis C. Julius Caesar in curia occiditur),* a date confirmed in Roman history as Mar 15, 44 B.C. Helm's date in the right margin is 44 B.C. The question of present concern is the identification of this date with Ol. 184, 1. If Ol. 184, 1 extended from July 1, 44, to June 30, 43 (the standard Greek reckoning), or from autumn 44 to autumn 43 (the beginning of the Olympiadic year moved several months later), in neither case would March 15, 44 B.C., fall within the Olympiadic year. But if the Olympiadic year was the same as the Julian year and extended from Jan 1 to Dec 31, 44 B.C., the Mar 15 date would fall within the year.

TABLE 85. *The Olympiadic Date of the Death of Julius Caesar in the* Chronicle *of Eusebius*

Regnal Year	*Ol.*	*Event*
C. Julius Caesar, 4 years, 7 months		
1	183	Begins to rule
2		
3		
4		
5	184	Is killed on the ides of March

321. At the same time we note that in the Armenian version of the *Chronicle* year 5 of Julius Caesar is equated with Ol. 184, 2.[128] Here, too, Samuel finds the same arrangement as in the Latin *Chronicle* and the same equation of

[124]George Salmon in *DCB* 2:353 col. 2.
[125]Samuel, *Greek and Roman Chronology,* 194 n. 2.
[126]Fotheringham, *The Bodleian Manuscript,* 16.
[127]Helm 156–157.
[128]Karst 209.

the Olympiadic year to the Julian year, but with the epoch being 777 B.C. instead of 776.[129]

322. If the Olympiadic years in the Canon are equivalent to Julian years so that Ol. 1, 1 = Jan 1–Dec 31, 776 B.C., and so on, it does not necessarily follow that regnal years are also equivalent to Julian years. Presumably, they coincide at least in some part with the Julian year indicated but, in particular cases, we may still try to determine if possible, within those limits, the beginning and ending points of the regnal year. It is for this reason that we have said, for example, that the notation of Azariah's year 50 in Table 84 means that that year of that king must have either begun or ended in Ol. 1, 1 = 776 B.C.

323. If we continue the enumeration of the years of Abraham, as we have done in Table 84, down to the year 50 of Azariah we have the equation: A.Abr. 1241 = Azariah's year 50 = Ol. 1, 1 = 776 B.C. From this point it is possible to reckon backwards and establish the equivalent B.C. dates of earlier events. Doing this, we establish that A.Abr. 1 = 2016 B.C. (cf. §307). From Adam to Abraham was 3,184 years according to the figures of the Septuagint (1,948 according to the Hebrew text; §311). This would place the creation of Adam in 5200 B.C. (3964 according to the Hebrew).

(8) The Seventy Years of Captivity

324. The portion of the *Chronicle* which we have just discussed brought us to year 11 of Zedekiah, the year in which the temple was destroyed by Nebuchadnezzar (Table 83). In his major left-hand column of secular history, in succession to the Assyrians, Eusebius has now for some time been showing the rule of the Medes and will shortly go on with the Persians. Thus year 11 of Zedekiah was equated with year 8 of Astyages the Median king.[130] Continuing from this point the *Chronicle* covers next the seventy years of captivity (Jer 25:11–12; 29:10; Dan 9:2).[131] The period may be summarized as shown in Table 86. Also see Table 89 and §§331, 333 for explanation of the duplication of year 2 of Darius due to overlap with the seven months of the magi. It is plain, therefore, that Eusebius counts the captivity as extending from the destruction of the temple in A.Abr. 1427 = 590 B.C. to the time when the returned exiles were free to resume the rebuilding of the temple in A.Abr. 1497 = 520 B.C., making seventy years.

325. In Jeremiah 29:10 the promise of the Lord is to bring the people back "when seventy years are completed for Babylon." In the history of the ancient Orient the defeat in 609 B.C. of Ashur-uballit II, ruler in the western city of Haran of the last remnant of the Assyrian empire, by Nabopolassar of Babylon, marked the end of that empire and the rise to power of the Babylonian empire (§430). Then in 539 Cyrus the Persian marched in victory into Babylon

---

[129]Samuel, *Greek and Roman Chronology,* 194 n.2.
[130]Helm 99 a.
[131]Helm 100–105.

(§329) and the seventy years of Babylon and the seventy years of Jewish captivity were "completed" (709 – 539 = 70).[132]

TABLE 86. *The Seventy Years of Captivity in the* Chronicle *of Eusebius*

A. Abr.	*Media/Persia*	*Year of Hebrew History*	*B.C.*	*Number of Years Intervening*
	KINGDOM OF THE MEDES Astyages reigns for 38 years			
1426	8	Year 11 of Zedekiah; the temple in Jerusalem is destroyed and the people of Judea are in captivity for 70 years	591	
1427	9	1	590	
1456	38	30	561	30
	KINGDOM OF THE PERSIANS The 1st, Cyrus, reigns for 30 years			
1457	1	31	560	
1486	30	60	531	30
	Of the Persians the 2d, Cambyses, reigns for 30 years			
1487	1	61	530	
1494	8	68	523	8
	Of the Persians the 3d, the magi brothers reign 7 months after whom Darius reigns 36 years			
1495	1	69	522	
1496	2	70	521	
1497	2	70	520	2
				70

326. The reign of Cyrus falls within the preceding tabulation (Table 86), and it may be recalled (§288) that Africanus took from Diodorus the equation of year 1 of Cyrus with Ol. 55, 1. Eusebius elsewhere[133] quotes Africanus and Diodorus in the same respect, and in the Canon makes the same equation. This also means that he shows the thirtieth and last year of the reign of Cyrus in relation to Ol. 62, 2. The tabulation of the *Chronicle* at these two points may be reproduced as in Table 87.[134]

[132]See Ross E. E. Winkle, "Jeremiah's Seventy Years for Babylon: A Re-assessment, II: The Historical Data," in *Andrews University Seminary Studies* 26 (Aug 1987): 289–299.

[133]*Praepar. evang.* 10.10.4, *Eusebius Werke,* vol. 8.1, 591.

TABLE 87. *The Beginning and the End of the Reign of Cyrus in the* Chronicle *of Eusebius*

Ol.	*Kingdom of the Persians*
54, 4	Year 38 of Astyages
55, 1	Year 1 of Cyrus
...	...
62, 1	Year 29 of Cyrus
62, 2	Year 30 of Cyrus
62, 3	Year 1 of Cambyses

327. By the reckoning of Olympiadic dates which we have accepted (§320) as probably used by Eusebius, Ol. 55, 1 equals 560 B.C., Ol. 62, 2 equals 531 B.C. For the reign of Cyrus quite precise information is now available from the cuneiform sources and in terms of the Babylonian calendar.[135] The latest date attested in his reign is the twenty-third day of Abu in his ninth year (mentioned on a tablet from Borsippa), which (counting his years of reign in Babylon) is equivalent to Aug 12, 530 B.C. The earliest date attested in the reign of his successor Cambyses is the twelfth day of Ululu in the latter's accession year, and this is equivalent to Aug 31, 530. It is to be concluded that the death of Cyrus, fighting on the northeastern frontier, was reported in Babylon in August 530 B.C.

328. According to the *Chronicle*, the reign of Cyrus ended in his thirtieth and last year and this year was related to Ol. 62, 2, i.e., to 531 B.C. If the regnal year of Cyrus was considered to begin in the spring, in line with Mesopotamian custom, his year 30 could extend from Mar/Apr 531 to Mar/Apr 530, and it would end a few months ahead of his actual death as just established (§327). But if the regnal year was counted as beginning on the following Oct 1, then year 30 extended from Oct 1, 531, to Sept 30, 530 B.C., and included the time when the death of Cyrus became known in Babylon in August 530 B.C. By the same interpretation year 1 of Cyrus, related to Ol. 55, 1 = 560 B.C., would mean more exactly the year from Oct 1, 560, to Sept 30, 559 B.C.

329. The biblical references to the first year of Cyrus when he made the proclamation which allowed the Jewish exiles to return from Babylon to Jerusalem (2 Chron 36:22f.; Ezra 1:1ff.) are presumably stated in terms of his reign in Babylon since they deal with an event in that city. According to the cuneiform evidence and the Babylonian calendar, Babylon fell on Tashritu 16 = Oct 12, 539 B.C., and Cyrus entered the city two and one-half weeks later on Arahsamnu 3 = Oct 29. His Babylonian regnal years began, therefore, as shown in Table 88,[136] and his first year, in which he made the proclamation, was 538/537 B.C.

134Helm 102 a, 104 a.
135PDBC 14.
136PDBC 29.

TABLE 88. *Babylonian Regnal Years of Cyrus at the Beginning of His Reign*

Regnal Year	*B.C.*
Accession	539/538
Year 1	538/537
Year 2	537/536

330. In the second year of the return of the exiles to Jerusalem, Zerubbabel began the rebuilding of the temple (Ezra 3:8). Then the work was interrupted and not resumed until the second year of Darius (Ezra 4:24) and it was completed in the sixth year of Darius on the third day of the month Adar (Ezra 6:15). The same dates are also given by Josephus.[137] The beginning of the reign of Darius has been shown in Table 86. If we now expand and continue our summary of the *Chronicle* at the point of the transition to and beginning of the reign of Darius, we have Table 89.[138]

TABLE 89. *The Beginning of the Reign of Darius I in the* Chronicle *of Eusebius*

A.Abr.	*Ol.*	*Kingdom of the Persians*	*B.C.*
		Cambyses reigns for 8 years	
1493	Ol. 64	7	524
1494		8	523
		The magi brothers reign 7 months, then Darius reigns 36 years	
1495		1	522
1496		2	521
1497	Ol. 65	2	520
1498		3	519
1499		4	518
1500		5	517
1501	Ol. 66	6	516

331. In Table 89 the unusual fact is that year 2 of Darius is shown twice in succession. At this point a note in the Canon[139] calls attention to this fact and explains that it is because one of the years is comprised with the seven months of the magi. Actually, according to the Behistun inscription,[140] the magian Gaumata, who claimed to be Bardiya, son of Cyrus, and who is also known as Smerdis, seized the entire Persian empire on Duzu 9 = July 1, 522 B.C., and was

[137]*Against Apion* 1.154.
[138]Helm 104 a–106.
[139]Helm 105 a.
[140]§§11, 13.

killed by Darius on Tashritu 10 = Sept 29, 522.[141] Cambyses himself is still mentioned in a text of Nisanu 23 = Apr 18, 522, and may not have died until after July 1, 522. Therefore in Babylonian chronology the transition from Cambyses to Darius I and the early years of reign of the latter are usually shown as in Table 90 with the first year of Darius in 521/520 and the second year in 520/519.[142]

TABLE 90. *The Beginning of the Reign of Darius I in Babylonian Chronology*

Year 8 of Cambyses (including the reign of Gaumata)	522/521
Year 1 of Darius	521/520
Year 2	520/519
Year 3	519/518
Year 4	518/517
Year 5	517/516
Year 6	516/515

332. Since the arrangement of the *Chronicle* reflected in Table 89 with two successive listings of "year 2" of Darius is obviously confusing, it is not surprising to find that this arrangement has been altered in the Armenian version. Here[143] the magi are allowed a separate year to themselves as is shown in Table 91.

333. In Helm's edition of the *Chronicle* of Eusebius (105a–106), the second year of Darius is equated with Olympiad 65, 1, A.Abr. 1497, which is equivalent to A.D. 520 (our Table 89). As seen in our Table 46, Ol. 65, 1 is 520/519 B.C. As seen in our Table 75, Abraham's year 1497 is 520 B.C. and is to be understood as 520/519 B.C. As seen in our Table 90, in Babylonian chronology (PDBC, our Table 90) the second year of Darius (I) was 520/519, so the agreement is exact. This second year of Darius was of special significance because then it was first possible for the Jews who had returned from Babylonian exile to resume the rebuilding of the temple in Jerusalem (Ezra 4:5; Hag 1:1; Zech 1:1). That point could be considered to round out the years of captivity (§324), for the people were not really free until they were free to reconstruct their sanctuary at home; only then was it "the end of the desolations of Jerusalem, namely, seventy years" (Dan 9:2). So in the *Chronicle* the seventy completed years are the *anni Abraham* from 1427 (Table 86) to 1497 (Table 89). Likewise, counted inclusively from 2016/2015 B.C., Abraham's year 1427 is 520/519 (2,016 – 1,497 = 519 + 1 = 520; 2,015 – 1,497 = 518 + 1 = 519, hence 520/519).

[141]Arno Poebel in *AJSL* 55 (1938): 42–165, 285–314; 56 (1939):121–145.
[142]PDBC 30.
[143]Karst 189–190.

TABLE 91. *The Beginning of the Reign of Darius I in the Armenian Version of the* Chronicle *of Eusebius*

A.Abr.	*Kingdom of the Persians*
	Cambyses reigns for 8 years
1494	8
	The magi, 2 brothers, rule for 7 months
1495	1
	Darius reigns for 36 years
1496	1
1497	2
1498	3
1499	4
1500	5
1501	6

(9) From the Rebuilding of the Temple to the Birth of Jesus

334. Likewise year 6 of Darius is related to Ol. 66, 1 = 516 B.C. (Table 89). In similar fashion this will mean 516/515 and is thus again in agreement with the same date in Table 90. In this year the temple was completed on Adar 3 (Ezra 6:15), and in Babylonian chronology this date is equivalent to Mar 12, 515 B.C.

335. Beginning with the resumption of the rebuilding of the temple (§334) the next period covered by the *Chronicle* may be taken as extending to the birth of Jesus which is placed in the forty-second year of Augustus. The numbering of the intervening years may be seen in Table 92, which takes consecutive years from several parallel columns in the *Chronicle* in succession.[144]

336. As Table 92 shows, the period from the second year of Darius to the forty-second year of Augustus comprised five hundred and nineteen years and extended from A.Abr. 1497 to 2015, and at this point in the *Chronicle* a note indicates that the years from Abraham to the nativity of Christ are 2,015.

[144]Helm 106–169.

TABLE 92. *From the Rebuilding of the Temple in the Second Year of Darius to the Birth of Jesus in the Forty-second Year of Augustus in the* Chronicle *of Eusebius*

A.Abr.	*Regnal Year*	*B.C.*	*Number of Years Intervening*
	KINGDOM OF THE PERSIANS		
	Darius, 36 years		
1497	Year 2	520	
	Year 36		
	Xerxes, 20 years		
	Artabanus, 7 months		
	Artaxerxes Longimanus, 40 years		191
	Darius Nothus, 19 years		
	Artaxerxes Mnemon, 40 years		
	Artaxerxes Ochus, 26 years		
	Arses, 4 years		
	Darius son of Arsames, 6 years		
	KINGDOM OF THE MACEDONIANS		
	[Alexander had already reigned 7 years (his year 1 = Arses year 4 = 336 B.C.) and the tabulation continues now with his year 8]		
1688	Year 8	329	5
	Year 12		
	[Thereafter the table continues with the Ptolemaic dynasty]		
	KINGDOM OF THE ALEXANDRIANS		
1693	Ptolemy Lagus, 40 years	324	
	Ptolemy Philadelphus, 38 years		
	Ptolemy Euergetes, 26 years		
	Ptolemy Philopator, 17 years		
	Ptolemy Epiphanes, 24 years		
	Ptolemy Philometor, 35 years		
	Ptolemy Euergetes, 29 years		
	Ptolemy Physkon, 17 years		276
	Ptolemy Alexander, 10 years		
	Ptolemy who was exiled by his mother, 8 years		
	Ptolemy Dionysos, 30 years		
	Cleopatra then reigned for 22 years, but of those years we will here count only 2		
	[Year 3 of Cleopatra is equated with year 1 of Julius Caesar and from here on we follow the column of the Romans, also adding again the Olympiads]		
	KINGDOM OF THE ROMANS		
	C. Julius Caesar, 4 years, 7 months		
	Ol. 183		
1969	Year 1	48	
1970	Year 2	47	
1971	Year 3	46	
1972	Year 4		
	Ol. 184		
1973	Year 5	44	

A.Abr.	*Regnal Year*	*B.C.*	*Number of Years Intervening*
	In this year Julius Caesar was killed on the ides of March = Mar 15		
	Octavian Caesar Augustus, 56 years, 6 months		
1974	Year 1	43	
	Ol. 194		
2013	Year 40	4	
2014	Year 41	3	47
2015	Year 42	2	
	Jesus Christ the son of God is born in Bethlehem of Judea		
			519

TABLE 93. *The Birth of Jesus Christ in the* Chronicle *of Eusebius*

A.Abr.	*Ol.*	*Romans*	*B.C./A.D.*
		Octavian (Augustus), 56 years, 6 months	
2010		37	7 B.C.
		38	6
		39	5
	194	40	4
		41	3
		42	2
		Jesus Christ, son of God, born in Bethlehem of Judea	
		43	1 B.C.
	195	44	A.D. 1

337. We have seen that in the *Church History* Eusebius assigns the birth of Jesus to year 42 of Augustus and that this year can be taken either as a factual year from Mar 15, 3 B.C., to Mar 14, 2 B.C. (Table 71), or as an autumn year from Oct 1, 3 B.C., to Sept 30, 2 B.C. (Table 72), the latter after the probable precedent of Africanus (Table 65), so that Eusebius agrees with Africanus on a date of 3/2 B.C. for the birth of Jesus (Table 92). For the essential details in the *Chronicle,* see Table 93.[145] These are A.Abr. 2015, Ol. 194, 3, year 42 of Augustus.[146]

(10) The Period of the Life of Jesus

338. The *Chronicle* now continues[147] from the year after the birth of Jesus, i.e., from the forty-third year of Augustus, to the fifteenth year of Tiberius when John the Baptist began to preach and Jesus began his public ministry (Luke

[145]Helm 168–169.
[146]Mosshammer, *Greek Chronographic Tradition,* 78.
[147]Helm 169–174.

3:1ff.), and to the eighteenth year of Tiberius in which year Eusebius places the death of Jesus. Table 94 is an outline of the Canon for this period.

TABLE 94. ***The Period of the Life of Jesus from the Forty-third Year of Augustus to the Eighteenth Year of Tiberius in the Chronicle of Eusebius***

A.Abr.	*Ol.*	*Romans*	*B.C./A.D.*	*Number of Years Intervening*
		Augustus		
2016	194, 4	Year 43	1. B.C.	14
2029	198, 1	Year 56	A.D. 13	
		Tiberius, 23 years		
2030	198, 2	Year 1	14	15
2044	201, 4	Year 15	28	
		John the Baptist preaches in the wilderness		
2045	202, 1	Year 16	29	
2046	202, 2	Year 17	30	3
2047	202, 3	Year 18	31	
		The death of Jesus Christ		32

TABLE 95. ***From the Nineteenth Year of Tiberius to the Second Year of Vespasian and the Final Destruction of Jerusalem in the Chronicle of Eusebius***

A.Abr.	*Romans*	*A.D.*	*Number of Years Intervening*
	Tiberius		
2048	Year 19	32	5
2052	Year 23	36	
	Gaius, 3 years, 10 months		
2053	Year 1	37	4
2056	Year 4	40	
	Claudius, 13 years, 8 months, 28 days		
2057	Year 1	41	14
2070	Year 14	54	
	Nero, 13 years, 7 months, 28 days		
2071	Year 1	55	14
2084	Year 14	68	
	Vespasian, 9 years, 11 months, 22 days		
2085	Year 1	69	2
2086	Year 2	70	
			39

(11) From after the Death of Jesus to the Final Destruction of Jerusalem in the Second Year of Vespasian

339. From the nineteenth year of Tiberius, which was the first year after the death of Jesus, to the second year of Vespasian, which was the year in which Jerusalem was finally destroyed, the *Chronicle* may be outlined as shown in Table 95.[148]

(12) The Tables of the Chronicle *from Julius Caesar to Vespasian*

340. The period from Julius Caesar to Vespasian, outlined in brief in Tables 92, 94, and 95, is of special interest in relation to the New Testament and may now be shown (Table 96) somewhat more fully as it actually appears in the tables of the *Chronicle*.[149] Julius Caesar was in power for four years and seven months, and we will begin with his last year shown as his fifth. The same year is shown as the seventh of Cleopatra (who reigned for twenty-two years) and the twenty-fourth of Hyrcanus (who held the high priesthood of the Jews for thirty-four years). After Hyrcanus comes the thirty-seven year reign of Herod the Great, the beginning of the reign being placed several years too late (§501ff.) with a consequent displacement of his successors, too. The years of Abraham are shown in the left-hand margin at ten-year intervals, the Olympiadic years are noted between regnal years, and the brief historical notices follow the years to which they appear to relate. Our understanding of the interrelationships of the Olympiadic dates, regnal years, and dates before and after the Christian era has been set forth above (§§307, 319–320, etc.).

TABLE 96. *The Tables of the* Chronicle *from Julius Caesar to Vespasian*

A.Abr.	*Ol.*	*Romans*	*Alexandrians*	*Jews*	*B.C.*
		Julius Caesar	Cleopatra	Hyrcanus	
	184	5	7	24	44
		Julius Caesar is killed on the ides of March. Octavian Caesar Augustus reigns 56 years, 6 months			
		1	8	25	43
		2	9	26	43
		3	10	27	41
	Ol. 185	4	11	28	40
		5	12	29	39
		6	13	30	38
1980		7	14	31	37
	Ol. 186	8	15	32	36
		9	16	33	35
		10	17	34	34
				Herod reigns 37 years	

[148] Helm 174–187.

[149] Helm 157–187.

A.Abr.	*Ol.*	*Romans*	*Alexandrians*	*Jews*	*B.C./A.D.*
		11	18	1	33
	Ol. 187	12	19	2	32
		13	20	3	31
		14	21	4	30
		15	22	5	29
			End of the empire of the Alexandrians		
	Ol. 188	16		6	28
1990		17		7	27
		18		8	26
		19		9	25
	Ol. 189	20		10	24
		21		11	23
		22		12	22
		23		13	21
	Ol. 190	24		14	20
		25		15	19
		26		16	18
2000		27		17	17
	Ol. 191	28		18	16
		29		19	15
		30		20	14
		31		21	13
	Ol. 192	32		22	12
		33		23	11
		34		24	10
		35		25	9
	Ol. 193	36		26	8
2010		37		27	7
		38		28	6
		39		29	5
	Ol. 194	40		30	4
		41		31	3
		42		32	2
Jesus Christ the son of God is born in Bethlehem of Judea					
All the years from Abraham to the birth of Christ total 2,015					
		43		33	1 B.C.
	Ol. 195	44		34	A.D. 1
		45		35	2
		46		36	3
2020		47		37	4
				Archelaus leader of the Jews for 9 years	
	Ol. 196	48		1	5
		49		2	6
		50		3	7
		51		4	8
	Ol. 197	52		5	9
		53		6	10
		54		7	11
		55		8	12
	Ol. 198	56		9	13
		Tiberius reigns 23 years		Herod the tetrarch holds chief place for 24 years	

A.Abr.	*Ol.*	*Romans*	*Alexandrians*	*Jews*	*A.D.*
2030		1		1	14
		2		2	15
		3		3	16
	Ol. 199	4		4	17
		5		5	18
		6		6	19
		7		7	20
	Ol. 200	8		8	21
		9		9	22
		10		10	23
2040		11		11	24
	Ol. 201	12		12	25
		13		13	26
		Pilate is sent by Tiberius as procurator of Judea			
		14		14	27
		15		15	28
John the son of Zechariah preaches in the desert by the Jordan river					
From the second year of Darius and the rebuilding of the temple, 548 years; from Solomon and the first building of the temple, 1,060 years; from Moses and the exodus of the Israelites from Egypt, 1,539 years; from Abraham, 2,044 years; from the flood to Abraham, 942 years; from Adam to the flood, 2,242 years					
	Ol. 202	16		16	29
		17		17	30
		18		18	31
Jesus Christ, according to the prophecies which were spoken ahead of time concerning him, comes to his passion in the 18th year of Tiberius					
		19		19	32
	Ol. 203	20		20	33
2050		21		21	34
		22		22	35
		23		23	36
		Gaius (Caligula) reigns 3 years, 10 months			
	Ol. 204	1		24	37
				Agrippa, chief of the Jews, 7 years	
		2		1	38
		3		2	39
		4		3	40
		Claudius reigns 13 years, 8 months, 28 days			
	Ol. 205	1		4	41
		2		5	42
		3		6	43
2060		4		7	44
				Agrippa, king of the Jews, 26 years	
	Ol. 206	5		1	45
		6		2	46
		7		3	47
		8		4	48
	Ol. 207	9		5	49
		10		6	50
		11		7	51

A.Abr.	Ol.	Romans	Alexandrians	Jews	A.D.
		12		8	52
2070	Ol. 208	13		9	53
		14		10	54
		Nero reigns 13 years, 7 months, 28 days			
		1		11	55
		2		12	56
		Festus succeeds Felix			
	Ol. 209	3		13	57
		4		14	58
		5		15	59
		6		16	60
	Ol. 210	7		17	61
		8		18	62
		9		19	63
2080		10		20	64
		Nero burns the larger part of the city of Rome			
	Ol. 211	11		21	65
		12		22	66
		13		23	67
		14		24	68
		First persecution of the Christians by Nero, in which Peter and Paul die			
	Ol. 212	Vespasian reigns 9 years, 11 months, 22 days			
		1		25	69
		2		26	70
		Titus destroys Jerusalem			
From the 15th year of the reign of Tiberius Caesar and from the beginning of the preaching of the gospel, 42 years; from the 2d year of Darius, under whom the temple was built again, 590 years; from the first building of the temple under Solomon to the most recent destruction of it which was carried out under Vespasian, 1,102 years					

(13) Summary of the Chronicle

341. In accordance with the foregoing analysis we may summarize the *Chronicle* in abbreviated form from Adam to the final destruction of the temple as it stands in the Latin version of Jerome (Table 97). We give the number of years in the several major periods, cumulative reckonings from Adam and from Abraham, the Olympiadic dates of Eusebius, and equivalents B.C. or A.D. as found in Helm.

342. That Table 97 does, in fact, represent correctly the way Eusebius counts the years from Adam to the final destruction of Jerusalem is confirmed by the comparison with cumulative summaries of years contained in the *Chronicle*, typical examples of which were reproduced in Table 96. The figures given in several of these summaries are shown in Tables 98–101, and their correspondence with the figures in Table 97 may be seen at a glance.

TABLE 97. *Summary of the* Chronicle *of Eusebius in the Latin Version of Jerome*

Event	*Number of Years*	*A.Ad.*	*A.Abr.*	*Ol.*	*B.C./A.D.*
Adam	2,242	0			5200 B.C.
Flood		2242			
1st year after the flood	942	2243			
Birth of Abraham		3184	0		
1st year of Abraham	505	3185	1		2016
Last year of servitude in Egypt		3689	505		1512
1st year in the wilderness	479	3690	506		1511
Foundation of the temple in the 4th year of Solomon		4168	984		1033
5th year of Solomon	442	4169	985		1032
50th year of Azariah or Uzziah				1, 1	776
Destruction of the temple in the 11th year of Zedekiah		4610	1426	47, 2	591
1st year of captivity	70	4611	1427	47, 3	590
70th year of the captivity and (1st) 2d year of Darius		4680	1496	64, 4	521
Rebuilding of the temple in the (2d) 2d year of Darius	519	4681	1497	65, 1	520
Birth of Jesus in the 42d year of Augustus		5199	2015	194, 3	2 B.C.
43d year of Augustus	29	5200	2016	194, 4	1 B.C.
Beginning of the public ministry of Jesus in the 15th year of Tiberius		5228	2044	201, 4	A.D. 28
16th year of Tiberius	3	5229	2045	202, 1	A.D. 29
Death of Jesus in the 18th year of Tiberius		5231	2047	202, 3	31
19th year of Tiberius	39	5232	2048	202, 4	32
Final destruction of Jerusalem in the 2d year of Vespasian		5270	2086	212, 2	70
	5,270				

343. In the Introduction of Eusebius as translated by Jerome the figures in Table 98 are included.[150]

[150] Helm 15, 17.

TABLE 98. *Cumulative Summary Figures in the Introduction of the Chronicle of Eusebius*

Period	*Number of Years*
From Adam to the flood	2,242
From the flood to the nativity of Abraham	942
From Abraham to Moses and the exodus from Egypt	505
From Moses to Solomon and the building of the temple	479
From Solomon to the restoration of the temple under Darius	512 (442 + 70 = 512)
From Darius to the preaching of Jesus Christ in the 15th year of Tiberius	548 (519 + 29 = 548)
From Abraham to the 15th year of Tiberius	2,044

344. At the fourth year of Solomon the figures in Table 99 are given.[151]

TABLE 99. *Cumulative Summary of the Fourth Year of Solomon in the Chronicle of Eusebius*

Period	*Number of Years*
From Adam to the flood	2,242
From the flood to Moses	1,447 (942 + 505 = 1,447)
From Moses to Solomon and the building of the temple	480
Total	4,169

It has already been explained (§316) that while this note gives the conventional figure of 480 years (1 Kgs 6:1) from Moses to Solomon and the building of the temple, the figure in the Introduction (Table 98) and the actual listing of the sequential years in the Canon give 479, and the total therefore should really be 4,168 (Table 97) instead of 4,169.

345. At the birth of Jesus the cumulative figure is a total of 2,015 years from Abraham to the Nativity.[152]

346. At the beginning of the public ministry of Jesus in the fifteenth year of Tiberius, it is marked that this point was removed, as shown in Table 100, from certain earlier historic points.[153]

---

[151]Helm 70 a.
[152]Helm 169.
[153]Helm 173–174.

TABLE 100. *Cumulative Summary at the Fifteenth Year of Tiberius in the* Chronicle *of Eusebius*

Period	*Number of Years*
From the rebuilding of the temple under Darius	548 (519 + 29 = 548)
From Solomon and 1st building of the temple	1,060 (442 + 70 + 548 = 1,060)
From Moses and the exodus from Egypt	1,539 (479 + 1,060 = 1,539)
From Abraham	2,044 (505 + 1,539 = 2,044)

Here it is also recalled that from the flood to Abraham was 942 years, and from Adam to the flood, 2,242 years. Therefore, although the total is not given, from Adam to the beginning of the public ministry of Jesus Christ must have been 5,228 (2,242 + 942 + 2,044 = 5,228) years.

347. At the final destruction of the temple there is a brief recapitulation of the number of years of this point from previous points, as shown in Table 101.[154]

TABLE 101. *Cumulative Summary at the Final Destruction of the Temple in the* Chronicle *of Eusebius*

Period	*Number of Years*
From the 15th year of Tiberius	42 (39 + 3 = 42)
From the 2d year of Darius and the rebuilding of the temple	590 (519 + 29 + 42 =590)
From Solomon and the 1st building of the temple	1,102 (442 + 70 + 590 = 1,102)

[154]Helm 187.

PART TWO

Problems of Chronology in the Bible

Chapter 4

I. THE OLD TESTAMENT

1. From Abraham to Jacob and Joseph

LITERATURE: Y. **Aharoni**, "The Land of Gerar," a paper published in Hebrew in *Eretz-Israel* 3 (1954): 108–11, and in English in *IEJ* 6 (1956): 26–32, especially 31; Nelson **Glueck** in *The Holy Land: New Light on the Prehistory and Early History of Israel* (Antiquity and Survival 2.2–3; The Hague; Luctor et Emergo, 1957), 275; F. **Cornelius**, "Chronology, Eine Erwiderung," in *JCS* 12 (1958) 101–104; Nelson **Glueck**, *Rivers in the Desert: A History of the Negev* (New York: Farrar, Straus, and Cudahy, 1959), 68–69; Friedrich **Cornelius**, "Genesis XIV," *ZAW* 72 (1960): 1–7; Roland de **Vaux**, *Die hebräischen und die modernen Entdeckungen* (Düsseldorf: Patmos, 1961); idem, *Die Patriarchenerzählungen und die Geschichte* (Stuttgart Bibelstudien 3; Stuttgart: Katholisches Bibelwerk, 1965); idem, *The Early History of Israel* (Philadelphia: Westminster, 1978); A. R. **Millard** and D. J. **Wiseman** eds., *Essays on the Patriarchal Narratives* (Leicester, England: InterVarsity, 1960; Winona Lake: Eisenbrauns, 1983); A. R. **Millard**, "Methods of Studying the Patriarchal Narratives as Ancient Texts," in Millard and Wiseman, *Essays,* 35–51; J. J. **Bimson**, "Archaeological Data and the Dating of the Patriarchs," in Millard and Wiseman, *Essays,* 53–89; M. J. **Selman**, "Comparative Customs and the Patriarchal Age," in Millard and Wiseman, *Essays,* 91–139; K. A. **Kitchen**, *Ancient Orient and Old Testament* (London: Tyndale Press, 1966); idem, *The Bible in Its World* (Exeter, England: Paternoster Press, 1977; Downers Grove, Ill.: InterVarsity, 1978); idem, "The Patriarchal Age: Myth or History?" in *BAR* 21 (2, Mar/Apr 1995), 48ff.; D. J. **Wiseman**, ed., *Peoples of Old Testament Times* (London: Oxford University Press, 1973); Eugene H. **Merrill**, "Fixed Dates in Patriarchal Chronology," *BSac,* (Jul–Sept 1980): 241–251; idem, *Kingdom of Priests: A History of Old Testament Israel* (Grand Rapids: Baker, 1987), 25–55.

348. In the study of biblical chronology it is necessary to seek as far as possible to correlate the biblical record with the findings of ancient history and archaeology (cf. §703). For this purpose the preliminary materials of the present book include an outline (page xxxv) of archaeological and cultural periods in the Holy Land,[1] and a list (page xxxvi) of Egyptian dynasties with minimal and maximal dates at the present stand of research.[2] As to dates in the Old Testament, the texts reflected in the works of the Jewish and Samaritan chronologists and chronographers surveyed above (§253ff.) show that there were at least three systems of biblical chronology in the main biblical texts of the last few centuries B.C., namely, those of the Hebrew text, which was later standardized by the Masoretes and is normally translated in modern Bibles (the MT); that of the Septuagint, which was the Bible used in Egypt (the LXX); and that of the Hebrew Pentateuch preserved by the Samaritans. A comparative study of these concludes that the system found in the MT is original as compared with the Septuagint and that the differences in the LXX are rational alterations at points when the chronology in the MT is difficult to understand or appears to be self-contradictory; while the Samaritan system mainly follows the MT until the flood and then the LXX although with several modifications.[3]

TABLE 102. *Biblical Personages from Adam to Abraham with Ages according to MT and LXX*[4]

PERSON	MT		LXX	
	Age at Birth of First Son	*Remaining Years*	*Age at Birth of First Son*	*Remaining Years*
Adam	130	800	230	700
Seth	105	807	205	707
Enosh	90	815	190	715
Kenan	70	840	170	740
Mahalalel	65	830	165	730
Jared	162	800	162	800
Enoch	65	300	165	200
Methuselah	187	782	187	782
Lamech	182	595	188	565
Noah	500	450	500	450
Shem	100	500	100	500
Arpachshad	35	403	135	430 (400)
Cainan (only LXX)	—	—	130	330
Shelah	30	403	130	330
Eber	34	430	134	370 (270)
Peleg	30	209	130	209
Reu	32	207	132	207
Serug	30	200	130	200
Nahor	29	119	79 (179)	129 (125)
Terah	70	135	70	—
Abraham	100	75	100	75

[1] *NEAE* 4:1529.

[2] Jürgen von Beckerath, "Chronologie," *LÄ* 1, cols. 967–971.

[3] Gerhard Larsson, "The Chronology of the Pentateuch: A Comparison of the MT and LXX," *JBL* 102 (1983): 401–409.

[4] Ibid., 402–403.

349. As compiled in the study just cited (§348), in the genealogical line from Adam up to Abraham the MT and the LXX (according to the most accepted manuscripts) give the ages shown in Table 102 of every man when he became the father of his first son and the number of his remaining years, the sum of the two figures of course giving the total length of life of the person in question. While the very long lives attributed to the earlier personages in this line have led to critical doubts about their existence, it may be remembered that the Sumerian King List[5] from ancient Mesopotamia also gives names from before and after the flood, with even more extreme figures of reigns, and yet inscriptional and other evidence makes it likely that among these, for example, Enmebaragisi was a real ruler of the city of Kish and Gilgamesh a real ruler of the city of Uruk,[6] thus high numbers of years in lifespans or in reigns in later texts do not necessarily prove that the persons named were unhistorical.[7]

350. Although the name of Shem, the oldest son of Noah (Gen 5:32), has provided modern philologists with the name "Semitic" for the family of related languages of which Hebrew is a part, and Eber, the great-grandson of Shem (1 Chron 1:17–18, Shem, Arpachshad, Shelah, Eber), is the eponym for the Hebrew people, it is on down the line (Eber, Peleg, Reu, Serug, Nahor, Terah, Abram/Abraham, Gen 11:10–26; 1 Chron 1:24–27) that the first person to be called a Hebrew is the tenth in descent from Noah (Josephus, *Ant.* 2.148), namely, "Abram the Hebrew" (Gen 14:13). Thus it is he who is revered as the "patriarch" (πατριάρχης, father of a nation) of his people (Heb 7:4) and the ancestor of Israel (Acts 13:16, 26), and his journey from Ur of the Chaldeans (probably the famous Ur in southern Babylonia)[8] to Haran and on to the land of Canaan is considered the first date of Hebrew history.[9] Further, Abraham became the father of Isaac, Isaac became the father of Jacob, and Jacob the father of "the twelve patriarchs" (Acts 7:8–9), thus the so-called "patriarchal age" encompassed the lifespans of Abraham, Isaac, Jacob, and the twelve sons of Jacob. These twelve sons (Reuben, Simeon, Levi, Judah, Issachar, Zebulun, sons of Leah; Dan, Naphtali, sons of Bilhah; Gad, Asher, sons of Zilpah; Joseph, Benjamin, sons of Rachel) were collectively "the sons of Jacob" (Gen 34:7, KJV, RSV) and, when Jacob received the name of Israel (Gen 32:28), they were "the children of Israel" (Gen 32:32; Josh 18:3 KJV) or "the people of Israel" (Josh 18:3 RSV), "the tribes (or the twelve tribes) of Israel" (Gen 49:16, 28 KJV, RSV), and "the Israelites" (Gen 32:32 RSV) or simply "Israel" (Exod 5:2 KJV, RSV).

351. Concerning the patriarchal age, it may be recalled that in the later nineteenth century the German scholar Julius Wellhausen spoke repeatedly of "the patriarchal legend," and said that in this legend "we attain to no historical knowledge of the patriarchs, but only of the time when the stories about them arose in the Israelite people; this later age is here unconsciously projected, in

---

[5] Thorkild Jacobsen, *The Sumerian King List* (*AS* 11; Chicago: University of Chicago Press, 1939).

[6] For both Enmebaragisi and Gilgamesh see A. Falkenstein, *RA* 3 (1968): 359.

[7] Kitchen, *Bible in Its World,* 33.

[8] Alan Millard, *BR* 8, 4 (Aug 1992): 8.

[9] Wacholder, *Essays,* 51.

its inner and its outward features, into hoary antiquity, and is reflected there like a glorified mirage."[10] Even until now essentially similar opinion is expressed, for example, by Donald B. Redford, who speaks about the biblical narratives concerning the origins of early Israel as "the historical pastiche that ancient Israel fabricated to justify its ingress" into Canaan.[11] In the light of archaeological discovery about the ancient world in the regions of the Bible, however, the picture looks very different, and what is told in the Bible about the patriarchs fits in many ways into what is known about life in Palestine and related lands (including Mesopotamia and Egypt) in round numbers around 2000 B.C. By this time and in these regions what we call civilization was already ancient. During thousands of years towns, cities, city-states, kingdoms, and empires had succeeded each other. Writing in several forms made record-keeping and literature possible, what we know as sciences developed, laws were promulgated, and the common culture was shared to a greater or lesser degree by pastoralists, farmers, and city dwellers alike. It is in this world and in particular in what archaeology calls the Middle Bronze Age (2200–1550 B.C.) that the patriarchs move as ordinary human beings delineated with very individual characteristics. They bear names of the type found in texts of the Middle Bronze Age, they follow social and legal usages otherwise attested (marriage, adoption, purchase of property), they live in tents and use camels (these items of course not limited to Middle Bronze), they travel widely, as others did, and they visit places also otherwise known to have existed at the time.[12] John Bright has written: "As the early second millennium has emerged into the light of day, it has become clear that the patriarchal narratives, far from reflecting the circumstances of a later day, fit precisely in the age of which they purport to tell."[13]

(1) Early Dating

352. As just remarked (§351), many facts point to the patriarchs belonging around the early second millennium B.C. and, archaeologically speaking, to the Middle Bronze Age, on account of which this age if often spoken of as the patriarchal age.[14] In the archaeology of Palestine the Middle Bronze Age is usually divided into Middle Bronze Age I (MB I) and Middle Bronze Age II (MB II), for which the usually accepted divisions are MB I 2200–2000 B.C. and MB

---

[10]Julius Wellhausen, *Prolegomena to the History of Israel* (Edinburgh: Adam & Charles Black, 1885), 318–319.

[11]Donald B. Redford, *Egypt, Canaan, and Israel in Ancient Times* (Princeton: Princeton University Press, 1992), 237, quoted in a review of this book by Kenneth A. Kitchen, *BAR* 19 (1, Jan/Feb 1993): 6, 8.

[12]For details see J. A. Thompson, *NBD* (1962) 939–941; De Vaux, *Patriarchenerzählungen und Geschichte,* 21; idem, *Bible and Ancient Near East,* 114–115, 119; Kitchen, *Ancient Orient and Old Testament,* 79–80; idem, *Bible in Its World,* 52–53, 59–60, 68, 73; Millard, *BR* 8, 4 (Aug 1992): 8. For mention of camels as not anachronistic in the patriarchal narratives, although only limited use is presupposed in the Bible and in external evidence until the 12th century, see Joseph P. Free, "Abraham's Camels," *JNES* 3 (1944): 187–193.

[13]John Bright, *A History of Israel* (Philadelphia: Westminster Press, 1989), 63.

[14]Kitchen, *Bible in Its World,* 135.

II 2000–1550 B.C.[15] A modified dating of the two divisions is employed by John J. Bimson together with David Livingston, who cite William F. Albright for MB I in 2100–1900 and MB II 1900–1550, and in addition propose to lower the end of the Middle Bronze period from the 16th century to the second half of the 15th century, specifically from 1550 to 1420.[16] Then in relation to the chronology

TABLE 103. *Topographical References in Palestine in the Patriarchal Narratives*

Sites	*Genesis*
SITES ASSOCIATED WITH ABRAHAM	
*Shechem	12:6
*Bethel	12:8; 13:3
Ai	12:8; 13:3
Zoar/Bela	13:10; 14:2
Sodom	13:10–13; 14:2; 18:20; 19:24, 28
Gomorrah	13:10; 14:2; 18:20; 19:24, 28
*Hebron	13:18; 23:2
Oaks of Mamre	13:18; 18:1
Admah	14:2
Zeboiim	14:2
Ashtaroth-karnaim	14:5
Ham	14:5
Shaveh-kiriathaim	14:5
Kadesh	14:7; 16:14; 20:1
Salem	14:18
Shur	16:7; 20:1; 25:18
*Beer-lahai-roi	16:14; 24:62
*Gerar	20:1–18
*Beer-sheba	21:14, 31–33; 22:19
The Negeb	12:9; 13:1; 20:1; 24:62
The land of the Philistines	21:32, 34
SITES ASSOCIATED WITH ISAAC, JACOB, AND JACOB'S SONS	
*Beer-lahai-roi	25:11
*Gerar	26:1–20
*Beer-sheba	26:23, 33; 28:10
*Bethel/Luz	28:11–22; 35:1, 6–8, 14–16
Galeed/Mizpah	31:49
Peniel/Penuel	32:30
Succoth	33:17
*Shechem	33:18–20; 34:1–31; 35:4; 37:12–14
Bethlehem/Ephrathah	35:16, 19; 48:7
*Kiriath-arba/Hebron	35:27
Tower of Eder	35:21
Dothan	37:17
Timnah	38:13–14

[15] *NEAE* 4:1529.

[16] John J. Bimson, *Redating the Exodus and Conquest* (JSOT Supplement Series, 5; Sheffield, England: University of Sheffield, 1978), 115, 147; John J. Bimson and David Livingston, "Redating the Exodus," *BAR* 13 (5, Sept/Oct 1987): 52.

of the patriarchs Bimson undertakes to establish in which of the two divisions of the Middle Bronze Age the patriarchs are datable, respectively.[17] For this purpose Bimson lists excavated sites in Palestine in two groups, (1) sites associated with the life of Abraham in Palestine, and (2) sites associated with Isaac and Jacob and Jacob's sons in Palestine.[18] Table 103 is adapted from his list.[19] Then excavation reports are adduced from many of the sites to establish relevant times of occupation in terms of MB I or MB II,[20] and finally appropriate conclusions are drawn as to the dating of the respective patriarchs.[21] In Table 103, asterisks (*) call attention to sites which appear in both groups.

353. Out of the sites listed in Table 103 a very few examples may be noted very briefly. In connection with Abraham: Kadesh or Kadesh-barnea is identified with the region in the Sinai Peninsula with the springs/oases of Ain el-Qudeirat, Ain Qadeis, El-Qusaima, and El-Muweilah. Within the period in question, a survey by Israeli archaeologists in 1956/1957 found the remains of an agricultural settlement on the hill overlooking the Qudeirat spring, and here in the whole region MB I finds were numerous but nothing was found of MB II.[22] In the Negeb, explorations in the 1950s by Nelson Glueck found that many settlements were founded in cultivable valleys and along routes of travel in the 21st century B.C. but destroyed in the 19th century and for the most part never again reoccupied, thus a time about the beginning of the 20th century MB (I) would have been a feasible time for Abraham to travel through the Negeb (Gen 12:9) from Canaan to Egypt and to return with his entourage of people and animals (Gen 12:10–20), whereas later he would have found only a wasteland.[23] As for the Philistines in the time of Abraham, the name is best known as the name of the sea people whom the Egyptians called Peleste, who settled on the coast of Canaan (and ultimately gave the land its name of Palestine) in the time of Ramses II not long before 1200 B.C., but it is reasonably surmised that the name is simply used in the book of Genesis for an earlier people who had also come in from the sea.[24] Of places associated with Jacob and his sons an example is Dothan (now Tel Dothan, thirteen miles north of Samaria). Here excavations have found nothing from MB I but have uncovered the remains of an urban center of the MB II period, including a city wall, storage jars next to the wall, and a complex of rooms. Thus, the excavator, Joseph P. Free, can speak of "abundant evidence of a Middle Bronze city in Joseph's day (Genesis 37:17ff.)."[25]

---

[17] J. J. Bimson, "Archaeological Data and the Dating of the Patriarchs," in Millard and Wiseman, *Essays* (1980, 1983), 53–89.

[18] Bimson, "Archaeological Data," 66.

[19] By permission of Eisenbrauns, Winona Lake.

[20] Bimson, "Archaeological Data," 65–66.

[21] Ibid., 81–82.

[22] Benno Rothenberg, *God's Wilderness: Discoveries in Sinai* (New York: Thomas Nelson, 1961, 1962), 33–46, esp. 39.

[23] Nelson Glueck, "The Age of Abraham in the Negeb," *BA* 18 (1955): 2–9; idem, *Rivers in the Desert,* 66–76.

[24] K. A. Kitchen, "The Philistines," in *Peoples of the Old Testament Times* (ed. D. J. Wiseman; Oxford: Clarendon, 1973), 55–57; Millard, "Methods of Studying," 44.

[25] Joseph P. Free, "The Fifth Season at Dothan," *BASOR* 152 (Dec 1958): 10–18, quotation on 18.

Another example is Shechem (identified with Tel Balata, near the later Nablus between Mounts Gerizim and Ebal). The single reference to Shechem in the Abraham narratives (Gen 12:6) refers only to the oak of Moreh which is described as "the place at Shechem," and there is no mention of a settlement or town nor of any contact with any inhabitants of the place. In the Jacob narratives, however, Shechem is a "city" (Gen 33:18), and Jacob, his daughter Dinah and his sons, are involved in unhappy dealings with the inhabitants. In correspondence with this situation reflected in the biblical records, archaeological work at Tel Balata/Shechem finds no occupation of the site in MB I but the remains of the walled city in MB II.[26]

354. In his analysis of the evidence Bimson finds that the places associated with Abraham were occupied in MB I and that the life of Abraham in Palestine may therefore be dated largely, if not entirely, before 2000 B.C., while the places associated with Jacob were occupied in MB II and therefore Jacob and his sons were in Palestine in that time, these conclusions, he holds, being in accord with the biblical dating of the patriarchs.[27]

(2) Later Dating

355. In a measure of contrast with this early dating of the patriarchal period and with the life of Abraham in Palestine placed largely before 2000 B.C. (§354), other studies of the evidence from sites and written materials in Mesopotamia and Egypt as well as from sites in Palestine point to a time somewhat later for the patriarchal period in general and for the life of Abraham in particular. For example, William F. Albright notes that practically every town mentioned in the biblical narratives of the patriarchs was in existence in the Middle Bronze Age (Shechem, Bethel, Ai, Jerusalem [Salem], Gerar, Dothan, Beer-sheba) and also adduces evidence from ancient Nuzi in Mesopotamia and from the Hyksos period in Egypt, and concludes:

> If we accept the probable hypothesis of some connection between the Hebrew entrance into Egypt and the Hyksos movement, and add three or four generations, we arrive at a date somewhere between 1900 and 1750 B.C. for Abraham's migration. The Patriarchal Age of Hebrew history would then fall somewhere in the latter part of the Middle Bronze Age in Palestine and during the late Middle Empire and the Hyksos period in Egypt.[28]

Roland de Vaux assembles onomastic, linguistic, and sociological factors from the Mesopotamian regions Abraham left to go to Canaan, and writes:

---

[26]G. Ernest Wright, *Shechem: The Biography of a Biblical City* (New York: McGraw-Hill, 1964, 1965), 128–133; idem, *EAE* 4:1086–1088; Edward F. Campbell, *NEAE* 4:1345–1354.

[27]Bimson, "Archaeological Data," 81–82, 86, 88.

[28]William Foxwell Albright, *From the Stone Age to Christianity* (Baltimore: Johns Hopkins Press, 1940), 150; cf. idem, *The Archaeology of Palestine and the Bible* (3d ed.; Cambridge: American Schools of Oriental Research, 1974), 137–139, 143.

> According to the information which we have at our disposal at present, then, it would seem that during the whole of the second millennium, the nineteenth and eighteenth centuries B.C. formed the most suitable period for Israel's first settlement in Canaan.[29]

> If I should dare to give a date, I would say that Abraham was in Hebron [Gen 13:18] around 1850 or perhaps a little later.[30]

Likewise K. A. Kitchen deals with details of the patriarchal narratives (personal names, legal usages, and the like) in the Middle Eastern context, possible links with major events in external history, and possible chronological links between the patriarchal and later epochs, and concludes:

> The total evidence, therefore, accords very well with a date for the Patriarchs in the twentieth to eighteenth centuries B.C., and shows a reasonable degree of consistency when properly interpreted.[31]

> A total evaluation of all the available lines of evidence would best place the patriarchs Abraham to Jacob somewhere in the first half of the second millennium B.C. (c. 1900–1700?).[32]

Very similarly John Bright says that the events of Genesis 12–50 fit best in the time between about the twentieth and seventeenth centuries (Middle Bronze II).[33] This substantial consensus is taken as convincing in the present book.

(3) Biblical Numbers

356. It might seem possible to get a simple solution to the problem of the date of Abraham and the patriarchs from biblical figures as they stand. In the first place, 1 Kgs 6:1 (MT) states that Solomon began to build the temple in the second month of the fourth year of his reign, which was in the four hundred and eightieth year after the people of Israel came out of the land of Egypt. It will be explained more fully below (§424) that the fourth year of Solomon was probably 968/967 B.C. and that this leads to the date of 1446 for the exodus. In the second place, Exod 12:40 (MT) states that the time that the people of Israel dwelt in Egypt was four hundred and thirty years. Together, the two statements give a date of 1876 B.C. (1,446 + 430 = 1,876) for when Jacob/Israel came down to Egypt (Gen 47:1–12). Further, Jacob was 130 years old when he came to Egypt (Gen 47:9), therefore he was born in 2066 (1,876 + 130 = 2,006). Jacob's father Isaac was 60 years old when Jacob was born (Gen 25:26), therefore Isaac was born in 2066 (2,006 + 60 = 2,066). Isaac's father Abraham was 100 years old when Isaac was born (Gen 21:6), therefore Abraham was born in 2166 (2,066 + 100 = 2,166). Abraham was 75 years of age when he went on from Haran to

---

[29] Roland de Vaux, *The Early History of Israel* (Philadelphia: Westminster Press, 1978), 265.

[30] De Vaux, *Die hebräischen Patriarchen,* 43.

[31] Kitchen, *Ancient Orient and Old Testament,* 56.

[32] Kitchen in Wiseman, ed., *Peoples,* 72 n. 20.

[33] John Bright, *A History of Israel* (3d ed.; Philadelphia: Westminster, 1981), 58.

Canaan (Gen 12:4), therefore he came to Canaan in 2091 (2,166 – 75 = 2,091). The death of Abraham was at the age of 175 (Gen 25:7), therefore he died in 1991 (2,166 – 175 = 1,991). The death of Isaac was at the age of 180 (Gen 35:28), therefore in 1886 (2,066 – 180 = 1,886). Jacob died at the age of 147, 17 years after he came to Egypt (Gen 47:28), therefore the death of Jacob was in 1859 (2,006 – 147 = 1,859). These dates thus arrived at in the patriarchal period are listed in our Table 104, and are in agreement with similar calculations on the respective items by Eugene H. Merrill.[34]

TABLE 104. *Dates in Lives of Patriarchs, Reckoned from Exodus in 1446 and with Egyptian Sojourn of 430 Years*

B.C.	*Event*	*Age*	*Genesis*
2166	Abraham born		
2091	Abraham goes from haran to Canaan	Abraham 75	12:4
2066	Isaac born	Abraham 100	21:5
2006	Jacob born	Isaac 60	25:26
1991	Abraham dies	Abraham 175	25:7
1886	Isaac dies	Isaac 180	35:28
1876	Jacob and family move to Egypt	Jacob 130	47:9
1859	Jacob dies	Jacob 147	47:28

357. The exodus date of 1446 B.C., derived from 1 Kgs 6:1, however, is not beyond question. It has been suggested that 1 Kgs 6:1 may be an editorial expansion of 1 Kgs 6:37,[35] arrived at by calculation,[36] 480 years being equal to 12 generations of 40 years each. In Num 32:13 it is stated that the children of Israel were made to "wander in the wilderness forty years, until all the generation that had done evil in the sight of the Lord was consumed," and this could suggest that "forty years" (itself in some instances apparently a conventional round number) was the normal span of a generation. In 1 Chron 6:50–53 the genealogy of the sons of Levi contains 12 names from Aaron (brother and contemporary of Moses, Exod 6:20; 7:7) to Ahimaaz (father of Azariah, a priest contemporary with Solomon, 1 Kgs 4:2), so 12 generations at 40 years each would be 480 years. Alternatively, in 1 Chron 6:3–12 from Aaron to Zadok (the priest who anointed Solomon, 1 Kgs 1:39, who was himself anointed along with Solomon, 1 Chron 29:22, and who became the chief priest of the Jerusalem temple, 1 Kgs 2:27, 35) was 11 generations and would give 440 years, the variant figure found in the LXX version of 1 Kgs 6:1. It will also be explained more fully below (§402ff.) that the mention of the city of Raamses in Exod 1:1 makes it likely that the oppression and exodus of the Israelites was under Ramses II, and that the only mention of Israel in an Egyptian inscription by Ramses II's

[34]Merrill, "Fixed Dates," *BSac* 137, 547 (July–Sept 1980): 242–243 and Table 1 on p. 248; idem, *Kingdom of Priests,* Table 2 on p. 31. For permission to print the figures in our table 97 in agreement with the figures by Merrill in *Kingdom of Priests,* acknowledgment is made to Baker Book House, Grand Rapids.

[35]*OAB* ad loc.

[36]*ABC* ad loc.

successor, Merneptah, helps to establish a probable exodus date of 1250 B.C. This date is 196 years later than the exodus date of 1446 B.C., and if we count back from 1250 (rather than from 1446), but still assume an Egyptian sojourn of 430 years, then all the patriarchal dates are correspondingly later, as shown in Table 105.

TABLE 105. *Dates in Lives of the Patriarchs, Reckoned from Exodus in 1250 and with Egyptian Sojourn of 430 Years*

B.C.	*Event*
1970	Abraham born
1895	Abraham goes from Haran to Canaan
1870	Isaac born
1810	Jacob born
1795	Abraham dies
1690	Isaac dies
1680	Jacob and family move to Egypt
1663	Jacob dies

358. The statement in Exod 12:40 that the people of Israel dwelt in Egypt for 430 years (352) is also not without question.[37] In this connection genealogical lists of persons said to have lived in the time of the Egyptian sojourn, and the number of generations involved, may be considered, but there are variations in the meaning of "generation" and in the available lists. The common Hebrew word for "generation" is דר (*dor,* usually translated as γενεά in the LXX) and is derived from a Hebrew verb which means "to move in a circle," and is thus a "circle of time," which can be of different lengths. In the most literal sense a generation is the period from a man's birth to the birth of his first son; collectively, it is all the people who live in that period; and in the plural it is a list of the successive births of a family history.[38] In Greek chronography, intellectual maturity was at the age of forty and, with the thought of the birth of a pupil at that point in the master's life, the forty-year interim until the pupil also reached maturity constituted a sort of intellectual "generation" (so Apollodorus [middle of second century B.C.], whose influence is traceable in Eusebius's *Chronicle*).[39]

359. In Gen 15:13 (MT, LXX) Abraham is told that his descendants will sojourn in a land that is not theirs and be oppressed for four hundred years and (15:16) will come back "in the fourth generation," so here a generation is equated broadly with a hundred years, and we have already mentioned (§358) a round figure of 400 years for the Egyptian sojourn. In three detailed genealogies

---

[37]The figure of 400 years for the same period found in Gen 15:13 (MT and LXX), in Acts 7:6, and in Josephus (*Ant.* 2.204; *War* 5.382), is most simply explained as a round number for the 430 figure. For a more complex assessment see Harold Hoehner, "The Duration of the Egyptian Bondage," *BSac* 126 (1969): 308–316.

[38]T. C. Mitchell, *NBD* 460; S. J. De Vries, *IDB* 2:366.

[39]Mosshammer, *Chronicle* of Eusebius, 115–121 (for this work see LITERATURE at §294).

several persons who were with Moses in the exodus stand in relatively long generational sequences from the inception of the Egyptian sojourn, namely, (1) Bezalel (Exod 31:2–5), seventh generation from Jacob (Israel, Judah, Perez, Hezron, Caleb [Chelubai], Hur, Uri, Bezalel, 1 Chron 2:1–20); (2) Elishama (Num 1:10), tenth generation from Jacob (Israel, Joseph, Ephraim, Beriah, Rephah, Resheph, Telah, Tahan, Ladan, Ammihud, Elishama, Gen 41:50, 52; 1 Chron 7:23–26); (3) Joshua (Exod 33:11), twelfth generation from Jacob (. . . Elishama, Nun, Joshua, 1 Chron 7:27). If these seven, ten, and twelve generations are reckoned at forty years each they run to 280, 400, and 480 years and thus are, on the whole, not in contradiction of a 430-year period of the sojourn.[40] If, however, a shorter and presumably more realistic estimate is made of the probable length of these generations a shorter sojourn can be supposed. A shorter genealogical sequence which can also point to a shorter sojourn is found in Exod 6:16–20; since it provides the names of the grandfather and father of Moses it may be supposed that it has preserved relatively accurate information. We learn that Kohath (son of Levi [Exod 6:16] and grandson of Jacob [Gen 29:34]) was one of those who went down into Egypt [Gen 46:11], and he lived 133 years (Exod 6:18); his son was Amram who lived 137 years; Amram's son was Moses (Exod 6:20) who, when he confronted Pharaoh was 80 years of age (Exod 7:7). To accord with longer sequences it has been suggested that intermediate names have been omitted (which is of course not unusual in ancient genealogies), and even that only tribe (Levi), clan (Kohath), and family-group (Amram) are given here.[41] As the names stand, however, even though we are not told the age of Kohath when he went down into Egypt, if we suppose that his grandson, Moses, was born 80 years later, and if Moses was 80 years old at the exodus (Exod 7:7), we have a total of only 160 years for the sojourn in Egypt.[42]

360. In Exod 12:40 an actual textual variant in the Septuagint adds several words, so that the statement reads: "The time that the people of Israel dwelt in Egypt *and in the land of Canaan* was four hundred and thirty years." Pierre Montet supposes that the Alexandrian scholars who prepared the Septuagint might have had access to some lost source such as a complete and authentic Manetho and might have derived the reading in question from that source.[43] However that may be, we have already seen (§254) that the Alexandrian-Jewish chronographer, Demetrius (before 200 B.C.), who used the LXX exclusively, understood that there was an exact division of the 430 years into 215 years in Canaan and 215 years in Egypt. The LXX text is apparently reflected also in Gal 3:17, which makes the 430 years cover the time from the promises to Abraham (Gen 12:7; 13:15; 17:8; 22:18; 24:7) to the exodus and the giving of the law. Similarly, and perhaps in dependence upon Demetrius,[44] Josephus states in one passage (*Ant.* 2:318) that the Israelites left Egypt "430 years after the coming of our forefather Abraham to Canaan, Jacob's migration to Egypt having taken place 215 years later."

---

[40] Kitchen, *Ancient Orient and Old Testament,* 55.
[41] Ibid., 54.
[42] H. H. Rowley, *From Joseph to Joshua* (London: Oxford University Press, 1950), 70–71.
[43] Pierre Montet, *Egypt and the Bible* (Philadelphia: Fortress Press, 1966), 7.
[44] H. St. J. Thackeray, *Josephus* (LCL), vol. 4, 305 n. c.

361. In relation to the MT 430/LXX 215 figures, Gerhard Larsson (whose comparison of chronology in the MT and the LXX indicates that alterations in the LXX are at points where the MT is difficult to understand or self-contradictory, see above §348 and n. 3) finds a 430-year sojourn-period "impossible" in the light of the Kohath/Amram/Moses sequence (§359), and concludes that "at most the period [of the sojourn] could be a little more than 300 years."[45] How much Larsson would call "a little more" than the 300 years he mentions is not known, but for the sake of an interesting possibility in connection with Joseph in Egypt (§389 and Table 114) we will add 14 years (15 years would be 5 percent of 300 years, a not unreasonable amount) and set down the figure of 314 years. In comparison with the 430-year Egyptian sojourn in our Tables 104 and 105 we therefore have the figures of 215 and 314 years for the sojourn to consider in our remaining tabulations (Tables 106, 107, 108).

362. In comparison with Table 104 (exodus 1446, sojourn 430 years) the figures in Table 106 (exodus 1446, sojourn 215 years) are 215 years later. In comparison with Table 105 (exodus 1250, sojourn 430 years), the figures in Table 107 (exodus 1250, sojourn 215 years) are 215 years later and 411 years later than the figures in Table 104. In comparison with Table 105 (exodus 1250, sojourn 430 years), the figures in Table 108 (exodus 1250, sojourn 314 years) are 116 years later and 312 years later than the figures in Table 104.

TABLE 106. *Dates in Lives of the Patriarchs, Reckoned from Exodus in 1446 and with Egyptian Sojourn of 215 Years*

B.C.	*Event*
1951	Abraham born
1876	Abraham goes from Haran to Canaan
1851	Isaac born
1791	Jacob born
1776	Abraham dies
1671	Isaac dies
1661	Jacob and family move to Egypt
1644	Jacob dies

363. In summary of the chronological outline of the patriarchal age in general and of the life of Abraham in particular, there are variables in the two dates for the exodus derived from 1 Kgs 6:1 (1446 B.C.) and from Exod 1:11 (1250 B.C.) and in the three periods of the Egyptian sojourn based upon Exod 12:40 MT (430 years), Exod LXX (215 years), and our hypothetical figure based upon Gerhard Larsson's comparison of MT and LXX (314 years). Taking account of these variables results in the figures in Tables 104–108. In evaluation of the results, in Table 104 Abraham goes to Canaan in 2091 B.C., and this is best in line at least broadly with, the chronology advanced by John J. Bimson (our §354), according to which the life of Abraham in Palestine was largely, if not

[45]Larsson, *JBL* 102 (1983): 406.

entirely, before 2000 B.C. In Tables 105 and 106 the dates for Abraham's going to Canaan are in 1895 and 1876, respectively, well in accord with the later dating of the patriarchal age (§355), in which Roland de Vaux, for example, thinks of Abraham in Hebron around 1850 B.C. In Tables 107 and 108 Abraham goes to Canaan in 1680 and 1779, respectively; 1680 is probably too late for consideration, but 1779 is within the limits suggested by Albright ("between 1900 and 1750 for Abraham's migration") and by Kitchen and Bright ("in the twentieth to eighteenth centuries B.C."). Our preference is for exodus in 1250 (see below §419) and sojourn of 314 years, and the resultant figures are those in Table 108.

TABLE 107. *Dates in Lives of Patriarchs, Reckoned from Exodus in 1250 and with Egyptian Sojourn of 215 Years*

B.C.	*Event*
1755	Abraham born
1680	Abraham goes from Haran to Canaan
1655	Isaac born
1595	Jacob born
1580	Abraham dies
1475	Isaac dies
1465	Jacob and family move to Egypt
1448	Jacob dies

TABLE 108. *Dates in Lives of Patriarchs, Reckoned from Exodus in 1250 and with Egyptian Sojourn of 314 Years*

B.C.	*Event*
1854	Abraham born
1779	Abraham goes from Haran to Canaan
1754	Isaac born
1694	Jacob born
1679	Abraham dies
1574	Isaac dies
1564	Jacob and family move to Egypt
1547	Jacob dies

2. Joseph

364. Coming now to Joseph (Gen 37ff.), it must be noted that some critical opinion judges that the Egyptian personal names in the biblical account of Joseph's time in Egypt are characteristic of the Eighteenth and the Ramesside (Nineteenth and Twentieth) Dynasties or later, and that what we have about Joseph is little more than a story composed in those later times.[46] For example,

[46]Jürgen Ebach, "Josephsgeschichte," *LÄ* 3: 270–273; Donald B. Redford, "A Study of the Biblical Story of Joseph," VTSup 20 (1970): 205ff.

the title Pharaoh literally means "great house" [written with the hieroglyphic signs for a house and a wooden column, the latter meaning "great"], originally designated the king's palace, and was probably only used for the king himself from Thutmose III (Eighteenth Dynasty) onward;[47] therefore the title may be anachronistic in the Joseph story (Gen 39:1, etc.; cf. Gen 12:15ff. where it is surely anachronistic in the time of Abraham). On the other hand, the Joseph account certainly has "an authentic Egyptian ring,"[48] and will be taken as it stands in what follows.

TABLE 109. *Dates in the Life of Joseph, Reckoned from Exodus in 1446 and with Egyptian Sojourn of 430 Years*

B.C.	*Event*	*Age*	*Genesis*
1916/1915	Joseph born		
1899	Joseph sold into Egypt	Joseph 17	37:2
1886	Joseph enters the service of Pharaoh	Joseph 30	41:46
1886–1879	Seven years of plenty in Egypt		41:47
1879–1872	Seven years of famine in Egypt		41:54
1876	Descent of Jacob to Egypt	Joseph 39	
1859	Jacob dies	Joseph 57	
1806	Joseph dies	Joseph 110	50:22

365. For the chronology of the life of Joseph in Egypt the book of Genesis provides these notations: Joseph was seventeen years old when sold into Egypt (Gen 37:2), and thirty years of age when he entered the service of Pharaoh the king of Egypt (41:46). Under Joseph's administration and thus presumably beginning at the time he entered the service of Pharaoh there were seven years of plenty in Egypt (41:47), followed by seven years of famine (41:54). It was when two years of famine were past and five more years of famine were yet to come (45:6) that Joseph sent for his father Jacob to come with all his household to live in Egypt. The foregoing discussion of the patriarchal age (§§356ff. and Tables 104–108) takes account of variables in exodus-date (1446, 1250 B.C.) and sojourn-period in Egypt (430, 215, 314 years), and in each of the five tables one item is the date when Joseph came down into Egypt—the crucial date from which to translate the above years in the life of Joseph into dates B.C. We begin with Table 104 (reckoned from exodus in 1446 and with Egyptian sojourn of 430 years). in this table the descent of Jacob and his family to Egypt was in 1876 B.C. Since Joseph was thirty years old when he rose to power under Pharaoh and beginning then had lived through seven years of plenty and two years of famine, he was at the time Jacob and his family came thirty-nine years of age. Being of that age in 1876 he was born around 1916, and the years of plenty were 1886–1879 and the years of famine 1879–1872. Joseph finally died at the age of a hundred and ten years (50:22) in 1806. These figures are listed in our Table

---

[47]Jürgen Osing, "Pharo," *LÄ* 4:1021.

[48]W. Gunther Plaut, *The Torah,* vol. 1, *Genesis* (New York: Union of American Hebrew Congregations, 1974), 379.

109, and, like the figures in Table 104, are in agreement with the calculations of Eugene H. Merrill.[49]

(1) In the Middle Kingdom

366. If, as shown in Table 109, Joseph was in Egypt in 1899–1806 and entered the service of Pharaoh in 1866, these dates fall in the Egyptian Middle Kingdom (2040–1674) and in particular in the Twelfth Egyptian Dynasty (1991–1785). For perspective at salient points we will very briefly recall Egyptian dynastic history, the basic outline of which is provided by the *Egyptian History* of Manetho, an Egyptian priest in the temple at Heliopolis (under Ptolemy II Philadelphus, 285–246 B.C.), whose work survives in fragments in Josephus, Africanus (A.D. c. 221), and the history of the world by George Syncellus (A.D. c. 800).[50] Around 3150 B.C., the first king of the first dynasty, Menes, united Upper and Lower Egypt (Manetho, 27ff.) and founded the capital later known as Memphis (Herodotus 2.99) near the apex of the Delta (10 miles south of modern Cairo).[51] Building on the basis of the first two dynasties (3150–2700), the Third to Sixth Dynasties established the splendid Old Kingdom and the Pyramid Age (2700–2200), but were followed by the First Intermediate Period (2200–2040) of the Seventh to Tenth Dynasties, when disintegration ensued and local rulers divided the country among themselves.[52] In the following Middle Kingdom (2040–1674), Egypt entered the second great period of its history. Kings of the Eleventh Dynasty (2040–1991) at Thebes (modern Luxor and Karnak) in Upper Egypt accomplished the reunion of Upper and Lower Egypt, and the rule of the whole country was continued by the kings of the Twelfth Dynasty (1991–1785).[53] With probable reign dates including overlapping coregencies, the rulers of the Twelfth Dynasty are listed in Table 110.

367. In view of his rule of the whole country Amenemhet I (1991–1962).[54] the founder and first king of the Twelfth Dynasty, established a new fortified palace city near the border between Upper and Lower Egypt (location uncertain, but probably between Maidum and Memphis).[55] The new city was named Itj-taui, meaning "he has taken possession of the Two Lands,"[56] and this was the

---

[49] Merrill, *Kingdom of Priests,* Table 2 on p. 31, by permission of Baker Book House, Grand Rapids; idem, "Fixed Dates," *BSac* 137 (547, Jul–Sept 1980) 244–245, 247, 248 Table 1, 250 n. 13.

[50] *Manetho,* trans. W. G. Waddell (LCL, 1940). See Jürgen von Beckerath, *Abriss der Geschichte des alten Ägypten* (Munich-Vienna: Oldenbourg, 1971); Nicolas Grimal, *Histoire de l'Egypte ancienne* (Paris: Fayard, 1988); idem, *A History of Ancient Egypt* (Oxford: Blackwell, 1992); for geographical sites see John Baines and Jaromír Málek, *Atlas of Ancient Egypt* (New York: Facts on File, 1980, 1982); for religion see Finegan, *Myth and Mystery,* 39–64 with references.

[51] Christiane M. Zivie, "Memphis," *LÄ* 4: 24–41.

[52] Hanns Stock, *Die erste Zwischenzeit Ägyptens* (Rome: Pontifical Biblical Institute, 1949).

[53] H. E. Winlock, *The Rise and Fall of the Middle Kingdom in Thebes* (New York: Macmillan, 1947).

[54] Jürgen von Beckerath, "Amenemhet I," *LÄ* 1, cols. 189–190.

[55] Baines and Málek, *Atlas,* 47.

"Residence City" while Thebes continued as the second chief city and was the "Southern City."[57] Amenemhet I also built a fortress at el-Khata'na in the Qantir district of the East Delta.[58] This shift of residence and interest to the north and northeast continued under Sesostris I (1962–1928), the second and perhaps the most important king of the Twelfth Dynasty.[59] In his reign there was an extraordinary amount of building throughout Egypt, and his monuments are still found all the way from Aswan to Alexandria.

TABLE 110. *The Rulers of the Twelfth Dynasty*

Name	*B.C.*
Amenemhet I	1991–1962
Sesostris I	1962–1928
Amenemhet II	1928–1895
Sesostris II	1895–1878
Sesostris III	1878–1842
Amenemhet III	1842–1797
Amenemhet IV	1797–1790
Nefrusobek	1790–1785

368. Between Egypt and the lands to the northeast, relatively peaceful relations prevailed for the most part during the Twelfth Dynasty, and are exemplified in the Story of Sinuhe.[60] This work is preserved in many texts from the late Twelfth to the Twenty-first Dynasty and, although often viewed as fiction, nevertheless is regarded as providing an accurate picture of the times both in Egypt and abroad.[61] The story begins at the apparently unexpected death of Amenemhet I and the succession of Sesostris I (1962–1928) when, for unexplained but presumably political reasons, Sinuhe, a noble of high rank then out with the army on a campaign in the west, fled the country. He found a damaged barge and crossed the Nile in the nighttime, then passed by the east of the quarry above Gebel Ahmar (the Red Mountain, northeast of Cairo). "Going northward," as Sinuhe did, the first exit route from the Delta to be reached would be Wadi Tumilat (§§385, 411) while the farther-north coastal road was the military route, on which Sinuhe would surely not have wished to be. Proceeding eastward, presumably in Wadi Tumilat, Sinuhe came to the Wall-of-the-Ruler, "made to oppose the Asiatics and to crush the Sand-Crossers." This was a line of fortified towers set at a distance from each other,[62] and at such a fortification, presumably in Wadi Tumilat, Sinuhe crouched in a bush, then slipped past in the night. He reached Peten at daybreak and later, near death

---

[56]Wolfgang Helck, "Itj-taui," *LÄ* 3: 211.

[57]William C. Hayes, "Notes on the Government of Egypt in the Late Middle Kingdom," *JNES* 12 (1953): 31–39,

[58]Baines and Málek, *Atlas,* 18, 41, 167.

[59]William K. Simpson, "Sesostris I," *LÄ* 5: 890–899.

[60]*ANET* 18–22.

[61]William K. Simpson, "Sinuhe," *LÄ* 5: 950–955.

[62]Wolfgang Helck, "Grenze, Grenzsicherung," *LÄ* 2: 896–897.

from thirst, halted at the Island of Kem-wer (literally the Great Black, probably the area of the Bitter Lakes).[63] Rescued by an Asiatic Sheikh, he went on toward Qedem (the East in general) and eventually reached Upper Retenu (Palestine/Syria). There, during a stay of many years, he became commander of the king's army and, in connection with military affairs, we hear of the *hega khoswe,* "rulers of foreign lands," the term from which the later name Hyksos was derived.[64] In old age and upon pardon by Sesostris I, Sinuhe returned, no longer by surreptitious travel as long before, but apparently down the main coastal road (the biblical "way of the land of the Philistines," Exod 13:17) between Egypt and Palestine, for he arrived openly and proudly at the "Ways of Horus."[65] This was the northeastern border-fortress (Sile, probably at Tell Abu Sefa, nearly 2 miles east of el-Qantara),[66] named for the route on which the Horus-king marched triumphantly, the military road illustrated in reliefs of Seti I on the outer north wall of the Hypostyle hall in the temple of Karnak.[67] From the Ways of Horus Sinuhe proceeded by sailing boat with a kitchen boat alongside, and so came home to the Residence City (Itj-taui).

369. Under Amenemhet II (1928–1895)[68] and Sesostris II (1895–1878),[69] the third and fourth kings of the Twelfth Dynasty, a noble, Khnumhotep II, had a tomb at Beni Hasan in Middle Egypt, and a wall painting in his tomb reflects and illustrates the movement of peoples in this time from the northeast toward the Nile Valley. The painting depicts a group of persons who have come to Khnumhotep, evidently bringing gifts and desiring trade. The accompanying inscription reads: "The arrival, bringing eye-paint, which 37 Asiatics brought to him." The leader of the group is labeled as a "ruler of foreign lands" *(hega khoswe),* the same title as in the Story of Sinuhe (§368), and his name is Ibsha. The date is appended as the sixth year of Sesostris II, about 1890. All the men in the party appear as Semites with thick black hair falling to the neck, and pointed black beards. The usual garment of the men is long and highly colored in vertical patterns, worn leaving one shoulder free, and the women also wear long garments of colored material with vertical patterns. Four warriors carry spears, throw sticks, and a bow. One man, with garment reaching to the knees, water-skin on his back, and making music on a lyre, walks behind his donkey, while on the donkey's gay saddle-cloth are spear, throw-stick, and bellows, the last item leading to the suggestion that these are traveling metalworkers. Another donkey carries two children.[70]

370. Under Sesostris III (1878–1842)[71] and later there was not only acceptance of foreigners but also fear and antipathy toward them. This is

---

[63] Baines and Málek, *Atlas,* 135, 167.

[64] Adolf Erman and Hermann Grapow, *Wörterbuch der ägyptischen Sprache,* vol. 3 (Leipzig: Hinrichs, 1929), 171, 29; Manfred Bietak, "Hyksos," *LÄ* 3: 93.

[65] Manfred Bietak, "Horuswege," *LÄ* 3: 62–64.

[66] Farouk Gomas, "Sile," *LÄ* 5: 946–947; Baines and Málek, *Atlas,* 43, 167.

[67] Alan H. Gardiner, "The Ancient Military Road between Egypt and Palestine," *JEA* 6 (1920): 99–116.

[68] Jürgen von Beckerath, "Amenemhet II," *LÄ* 1: 189–190.

[69] William K. Simpson, "Sesostris II," *LÄ* 5: 899–903.

[70] P. E. Newberry, *Beni Hasan* (London, 1893), Pl. XXX; *ANEP* No. 3; *ANET* 229.

reflected in the Execration texts, which have been found on broken bowls, apparently smashed to break the power of the foes, and these inscriptions especially name Asiatics and many places in Palestine and Syria.[72] On the other hand, the increased incoming of outsiders, especially from Palestine/Syria and for the most part with peaceful acceptance in Egypt, is again attested under Amenemhet III (1842–1797), and we hear in texts of the time of outsiders who are workers on the land, soldiers, artisans, and persons purchased on the Asiatic slave market.[73] Similarly, a papyrus attributed to the late Middle Kingdom preserves the names of seventy-seven persons with their titles and occupations, of whom forty-eight are Asiatics, including men, women, and children; the adults have retained their Asiatic names, the children already have Egyptian names; the women are employed in weaving, the men and children work as household servants, gardeners, brewers, and store-keepers.[74] Finally, the Twelfth Dynasty came to an end with its last two rulers, Amenemhet IV (1797–1790) and, after his death, his surviving sister-wife, Nefrusobek (1790–1785).[75]

371. In view of such items as the foregoing (§§363–366) in the picture of the Middle Kingdom, it is possible to think that the account about Joseph fits here satisfactorily. In socio-economic regard, it is hardly an unlikely event that a caravan of traders came from beyond the Jordan on the way down to Egypt and found a young man who was sold on the Asiatic slave market in Egypt. In cultural regard an item of comparison, for example, is in fact that when Sinuhe returned to Egypt after living for years among the Semites of Syria/Palestine, it was said of him: "See, this is Sinuhe, who has come back as an Asiatic, a creature of the Bedouins," and on account of this appearance, before Sinuhe went into the presence of the king, he was cared for in Egyptian facilities, and he says: "Years were made to pass away from my body. I was shaved, and my hair was combed."[76] So also Joseph, upon release from the dungeon after years of imprisonment, "shaved himself" (Gen 41:14) before he came before Pharaoh, an action which Eugene H. Merrill holds was entirely correct if Joseph was presenting himself before a native Egyptian ruler of the Twelfth Dynasty, but would hardly have been necessary if Joseph were, at a later date, going before a bearded Hyksos king.[77] Merrill also notes[78] that it was "apparently" the Hyksos who introduced or popularized in Egypt the use of the horse and chariot, but does not discuss this fact further, yet it is this fact which actually provides major reason for consideration of a different date for Joseph, namely in the period of the Hyksos, as does also the fact that a "bearded Hyksos king" of Asiatic and perhaps Semitic background might be more ready than a native Egyptian to welcome another of such a background into his court.

---

[71] William K. Simpson, "Sesostris III," *LÄ* 5: 903–906.

[72] *ANET* 328–329.

[73] Jürgen von Beckerath, "Amenemhet III," *LÄ* 1: 190–191.

[74] Montet, *Egypt and the Bible,* 12.

[75] Jürgen von Beckerath, "Amenemhet IV," *LÄ* 1: 191–192; idem, "Sobeknofru," *LÄ* 5: 1050–1051.

[76] Trans. Adolf Erman, *The Literature of the Ancient Egyptians* (London: Methuen, 1927), 27–28.

[77] Merrill, *Kingdom of Priests,* 52–53.

[78] Ibid., 54.

372. With continuing allowance for the variables explained above (§365), in addition to Table 109, Tables 111–114 are also possible.

TABLE 111. *Dates in the Life of Joseph, Reckoned from Exodus in 1250 and with Egyptian Sojourn of 430 Years*

B.C.	*Event*	*Age*	*Genesis*
1720/1719	Joseph born		
1703	Joseph sold into Egypt	Joseph 17	37:2
1690	Joseph enters the service of Pharaoh	Joseph 30	41:46
1690–1683	Seven years of plenty in Egypt		41:47
1683–1676	Seven years of famine in Egypt		
1680	Descent of Jacob to Egypt	Joseph 39	
1663	Jacob dies	Joseph 57	
1610	Joseph dies	Joseph 110	50:22

TABLE 112. *Dates in the Life of Joseph, Reckoned from Exodus in 1446 and with Egyptian Sojourn of 215 Years*

B.C.	*Event*	*Age*
1701/1700	Joseph born	
1684	Joseph sold into Egypt	Joseph 17
1671	Joseph enters the service of Pharaoh	Joseph 30
1671–1664	Seven years of plenty in Egypt	
1664–1657	Seven years of famine in Egypt	
1661	Descent of Jacob to Egypt	Joseph 39
1644	Jacob dies	Joseph 57
1591	Joseph dies	Joseph 110

TABLE 113. *Dates in the Life of Joseph, Reckoned from Exodus in 1250 and with Egyptian Sojourn of 215 Years*

B.C.	*Event*	*Age*
1505/1504	Joseph born	
1488	Joseph sold into Egypt	Joseph 17
1475	Joseph enters the service of Pharaoh	Joseph 30
1475–1468	Seven years of plenty in Egypt	
1468–1461	Seven years of famine in Egypt	
1465	Descent of Jacob to Egypt	Joseph 39
1448	Jacob dies	Joseph 57
1395	Joseph dies	Joseph 110

TABLE 114. *Dates in the Life of Joseph, Reckoned from Exodus in 1250 and with Egyptian Sojourn of 314 Years*

B.C.	*Event*	*Age*
1604/1603	Joseph born	
1587	Joseph sold into Egypt	Joseph 17
1574	Joseph enters the service of Pharaoh	Joseph 30
1574–1567	Seven years of plenty in Egypt	
1567–1560	Seven years of famine in Egypt	
1564	Descent of Jacob to Egypt	Joseph 39
1547	Jacob dies	Joseph 57
1494	Joseph dies	Joseph 110

(2) In the Hyksos Age

373. In the life of Joseph in Egypt the crucial date is that of his entry into the service of Pharaoh. In Table 109 that date is 1886 B.C., which is in the Middle Kingdom (2040–1674) and in the Twelfth Dynasty (1991–1785; above §366). In Tables 111–114, now under consideration, Joseph's entry into Pharaoh's service is much later, the dates extending from 1690 to 1475 B.C. Again for perspective, it is necessary to look at Egyptian history in this later time. After the Middle Kingdom, Egypt experienced a Second Intermediate Period (1674–1553)[79] which lasted until the foundation of the New Kingdom, beginning with the Eighteenth Dynasty inaugurated by the reign of Ahmose (1552–1526).[80] In general, the Second Intermediate Period was characterized by the increasing infiltration of Egypt and ultimate attainment of power in Egypt by force by foreigners from the lands northeast.[81] In Egyptian texts these people are generally designated as Asiatics,[82] and many of their individual names are given, names which are often plainly Semitic. Some of the incomers are found occupying high positions in government;[83] many settle in communities and start to unite and gain control over territories of their own.[84] Among them are certainly the *heqa khoswe* or "rulers of foreign lands," a term we have met already with Sinuhe in Syria/Palestine (§368) and in the tomb of Khnumhotep II at Beni Hasan (§369). In Greek in Manetho the term is rendered as Ὑκσώς and explained as meaning "king-shepherds" (Josephus, *Ag. Apion* 1.82; Manetho, 85).[85]

---

[79]Grimal, *Ancient Egypt,* 392.

[80]Jürgen von Beckerath, *Untersuchungen zur politischen Geschichte der Zweiten Zwischenzeit in Ägypten* (Glückstadt: J. J. Augustin, 1964); idem, "Zwischenzeit," *LÄ* 6: 1442–1448.

[81]Jürgen von Beckerath, "Fremdherrschaft," *LÄ* 2: 312–313.

[82]Raphael Giveon, "Asiaten," *LÄ* 1: 462–471, esp. 464.

[83]Herschel Shanks, *BAR* 7 (5, Sept/Oct 1981) 42.

[84]Grimal, *Ancient Egypt,* 182.

[85]For the Hyksos see T. Säve Söderbergh, "The Hyksos Rule in Egypt," *JEA* 37 (1951): 53–71; R. M. Engberg, *The Hyksos Reconsidered* (Chicago: University of Chicago Press, 1939); John van Seters, *The Hyksos: A New Investigation* (New Haven: Yale University Press, 1966); Manfred Bietak, "Hyksos," *LÄ* 3: 93–103.

374. In terms of Manetho's dynasties, the Second Intermediate Period comprises the Thirteenth Dynasty at Thebes, the Fourteenth Dynasty at Xois in the West Delta, the Fifteenth Dynasty at Memphis and Avaris, the Sixteenth Dynasty at Thebes, and the Seventeenth Dynasty with two divisions, (native) Egyptian kings at Thebes and "shepherd kings" at Memphis and Avaris.[86] What we have thus far (§373) described as a gradual infiltration of Egypt by Asiatics,. especially the Hyksos, preparing the way for eventual takeover by force, brings us to the point where Manetho begins his account of the Hyksos, namely, where he describes their outright invasion and conquest, albeit without their having to strike a blow, but nevertheless doing much damage to the country and people, a view which no doubt reflects the later generally hostile, Egyptian remembrance of the Hyksos (e.g., compare the opinion of Hatshepsut, §399). In his text as given by Josephus, Manetho begins his account (Manetho, 79–87):

> Tutimaeus. In his reign, for what cause I know not, a blast of God smote us; and unexpectedly, from the regions of the East, invaders of obscure race marched in confidence against our land.

375. As to King Tutimaeus (Τουτίμαιος in Greek), whom Manetho names to date the invasion, his name has often been identified with that of Dedumose/Dedumesiu (Egyptian *Ddw-msjw,* cf. §387), which was the name of two Egyptian kings distinguished by two throne names (or one king who changed his throne name) of the Thirteenth Dynasty. Jürgen von Beckerath holds the identification to be linguistically and historically impossible.[87] Manfred Bietak thinks the identification only "perhaps" *(vielleicht)* correct.[88] Nicolas Grimal names Dedumesiu I as the thirty-third or thirty-fourth king of the Thirteenth Dynasty with a date of about 1675 B.C., and says that "if this king is to be identified with Manetho's Tutimaeus," it would have been during his reign that the Hyksos became rulers of Egypt.[89] If the identification were correct it would be an important date in the history of the Hyksos in Egypt.

376. Another small item which can possibly attest the presence of the Hyksos even earlier in the Thirteenth Dynasty is in connection with the Egyptian king of that dynasty known as Sobekhotep IV and dated around 1730–1720.[90] His Egyptian name *(Hʿ-nfr-Rʿ)* is rendered in Greek as Chenephres (Χενεφρῆς), and the Hellenistic-Jewish writer Artapanus (c. 100 B.C., §265) records that in the time of Chenephres Egypt was divided into various kingdoms,[91] a brief notice which can perhaps be taken to reflect the existence of both the independent state of Xois in the West Delta and also of a small domain of the Hyksos in the East Delta, possibly already then, in view of what we know of the importance of the place otherwise, at Avaris.[92] As for yet one more king of the early Thirteenth

---

[86]Manetho, 73–97.
[87]Von Beckerath, "Tutimaios," *LÄ* 6: 816; idem, "Dedumose," *LÄ* 1: 1003.
[88]Bietak, "Hyksos," *LÄ* 3: 101 n. 5.
[89]Grimal, *Ancient Egypt,* 185.
[90]Anthony Spalinger, "Sobekhotep IV," *LÄ* 5: 1041–1048 and n. 45.
[91]Eusebius, *Praeparatio evangelica* 9. 27.3; *Eusebius Werke*, vol. 8.1, 519.
[92]Grimal (*Ancient Egypt,* 184), says that Avaris passed into Hyksos control during the reign of Sobekhotep IV. T. O. Lambdin ("Hyksos," *IDB* 2: 667) gives the date of 1730

Dynasty, named Hornedjheritef, his name is connected with a word which can mean "Asiatic," but in the case of the king the name probably has only something to do with the pursuit of a vigorous foreign policy.[93]

377. Finally, Manetho continues,

> the invaders appointed as king one of their number whose name was Salitis. He had his seat at Memphis, levying tribute from Upper and Lower Egypt, and always leaving garrisons behind in the most advantageous positions. Above all, he fortified the district to the east. . . .
>
> In the Saite [Sethroite, cf. Africanus, Manetho, 91, immediately below] he found a city very favorably situated on the east of the Bubastite branch of the Nile, and called Avaris after an ancient religious tradition. This place he rebuilt and fortified with massive walls, planting there a garrison of as many as 240,000 heavy-armed men to guard his frontier. . . .

Manetho states that Salitis ruled for nineteen years, then lists five more kings with their respective lengths of reign, and goes on to say of the six collectively:

> These six kings, their first rulers, were ever more and more eager to extirpate the Egyptian stock. Their race as a whole was called Hyksos, that is, "king-shepherds" [Manetho's explanation of the etymology of *hega khoswe* rather than "rulers of foreign lands," as in our §374].

Then Josephus himself, who preserves the above quotation in the words of Manetho, adds:

> These kings whom I have enumerated above, and their descendants, ruling over the so-called Shepherds, dominated Egypt, according to Manetho, for 511 years [surely a very exaggerated figure].

In the text of Manetho as given by Africanus (Manetho, 91) six Hyksos kings are also listed, but with some different names and different lengths of reign and with the incorrect statement that they founded (rather than rebuilt and fortified, Manetho, 83, just above) the city [Avaris] which was their base; also it is stated that the six kings constituted the Fifteenth Egyptian Dynasty:

> The Fifteenth Dynasty consisted of Shepherd Kings. There were six foreign kings from Phoenicia, who seized Memphis; in the Sethroite nome they founded a town, from which as a base they subdued Egypt.
>
> The first of these kings, Saites, reigned for 19 years; the Saite nome is called after him.

After completing this list of the six kings, Manetho, according to Africanus and Eusebius (Manetho, 93–95), goes on to the Sixteenth and Seventeenth Egyptian

---

but says that this was when the first Hyksos dynasty—the fifteenth according to traditional Egyptian accounts—was established in the Delta with it capital at Avaris.

[93]Jürgen von Beckerath, "Hornedjheritef," *LÄ* 3: 11; Grimal, *Ancient Egypt,* 183–184.

Dynasties and includes them in the Hyksos Age, but with the Seventeenth Dynasty divided between Hyksos kings and native Egyptian kings at Thebes:

> The Sixteenth Dynasty were Shepherd Kings again, 32 in number.
>
> The Seventeenth Dynasty were Shepherd Kings again, 43 in number; and kings of Thebes or Diospolis, 43 in number. Total of the reigns of the Shepherd Kings and the Theban kings, 151 years.

378. Other than for the occurrence of their names in the lists of Manetho as just cited (§377), identification of the six kings of the Fifteenth Dynasty—who are sometimes called the "Great Hyksos"[94]—is only partially possible. Salitis (Saites), the first in the lists who, according to Manetho (above §377), rebuilt and fortified Avaris, may have been already an Asiatic military leader with a small territory under his control in the East Delta. No monuments of his are known, but he is to be equated with Shalek who will be named below (§380).[95] Enon and Apachnan are also not to be identified from any known monuments. Apophis and Iannas are mistakenly reversed in order and, as the sequence of historical events shows, Apophis should be no. 5 immediately before Assis as no. 6. Apophis is the most important of the six Hyksos kings and stands at the high point of Hyksos rule in Egypt. His was the longest rule of any (61 years in Manetho according to Josephus, although this figure should probably be corrected to 41 [§379]). In different texts Apophis appears with three different throne names (Aqenenre, Auserre, Nebkhepeshre, all compounded with the name of the Egyptian god, Re, as were many other Hyksos names). The three throne names have been thought to indicate three different kings[96] but more probably were assumed at different points in Apophis's reign and if so they also attest to the length of his rule. The thirty-third year of the reign of Apophis is mentioned in the Rhind Mathematical Papyrus (now in the British Museum), and he is named on the stela of Kamose at Thebes as the Hyksos king upon whom Kamose imposed a severe defeat.[97] The name of Apophis also appears on various other monuments, including a lintel at Qantir and a granite vessel from a later king's grave at Thebes where it may have been taken as booty of war.[98] It is also of interest that under Apophis there was a "chancellor" named Yakob-el, *Yakob* being the name of Jacob in Hebrew, and *el* a name for God often used in the Hebrew Scriptures.[99] After Apophis it must have been Assis (= Khamudy = Archles, see §379) who took the throne, for he is named by Manetho, according to Josephus, as the last of the six kings of the Fifteenth Dynasty (Manetho, 83) and given a reign of 49 years and 2 months, a figure which should perhaps be

---

[94] Margaret Stefana Drower, *EB* (1966), 983.

[95] Wolfgang Helck, *Untersuchungen zu Manetho und den ägyptischen Königslisten* (Untersuchungen zur Geschichte und Altertumskunde Ägyptens 18; Berlin: Akademie, 1956), 37; Von Beckerath, *Abriss,* 31; Helck, "Schalek," *LÄ* 5: 528.

[96] So, still, Grimal, *Ancient Egypt,* 186, Apophis I; 192, Apophis II, throne name Aqenenre on a dagger bought in Luxor; 194, Apophis III, placed as the last of the Sixteenth Dynasty Hyksos vassal kings, name on a dagger from Saqqara.

[97] Claude Vandersleyen, "Kamose," *LÄ* 3: 306–308.

[98] Von Beckerath, *Abriss,* 32; idem, "Apophis," *LÄ* 1: 352.

[99] Shanks, *BAR* 7 (5, Sept–Oct 1981): 42–43.

corrected to a more likely 9 years.[100] Meanwhile, Kamose, who defeated Apophis, was succeeded by his younger brother, Ahmose, for a reign of twenty-five years (Manetho, 101 with n. 3, and 111), in 1552–1526 B.C., and it was Ahmose who completed the expulsion of the Hyksos from Egypt.[101]

379. In contrast with the various and very long year-totals assigned to the reigns of the Hyksos kings in the passages of Manetho quoted above (§377), the Turin Canon of Kings (a papyrus in the Museo Egizio, Turin, compiled in the time of Ramses II with king lists back to the beginning of the New Kingdom and very fragmentary items for the First and Second Intermediate Periods),[102] provides a much shorter period for six Hyksos kings, presumably the same six of the Fifteenth Dynasty of Manetho. Although very badly preserved at the point of the Hyksos period, the papyrus contains (10.19) the name of Apophis and gives him 40 years of reign, which supports the proposed correction of Manetho's 61 years to 41 (§378). Also the papyrus contains (10.20) the name of Khamudy as the last of the Hyksos kings, which means that Khamudy and Assis must be identical (§378).[103] The parallel king in Manetho, according to Africanus (Manetho, 91), would appear to be Archles since he is credited with the same number of full years (49) as Assis, probably to be corrected to 9,[104] and a further identification of Assis/Khamudy/Archles is also proposed with Assehre, whose name appears on an obelisk at Tanis.[105]

380. Immediately following the name of Khamudy in the Turin Canon of Kings there is a summary statement such as is familiar in other examples in the better-preserved New Kingdom portions of the papyrus. This statement reads (10.21): "[Total, rulers of] foreign lands, 6, they made 108 years." This figure of 108 years for the six kings is usually taken as more likely than any of the other much longer totals. Support for the shorter period is found in a late genealogical table of priests of Memphis which gives not only their own ancestors but also the kings under whom those ancestors served; in the time of the Hyksos it names as a generation apart King Shalek, then Apophis, and then Ahmose (who expelled the Hyksos), and is ground for equating Shalek with Salitis in Manetho according to Josephus, as mentioned above (§378), as well as for accepting the shorter period of time for the Great Hyksos. Accordingly, the six kings of Manetho's Fifteenth Dynasty may be listed as in Table 115, which shows the names, their order, and their reported lengths of reign (with hypothetical corrections in the Josephus column), together with the totals thereof, as given by (1) the Turin Canon of Kings, by (2) Josephus (who is generally believed to have the best forms of the names), and (3) by Africanus.[106]

---

[100]Jürgen von Beckerath, "Chamudi," *LÄ* 1: 903–904.

[101]Claude Vandersleyen, "Ahmose," *LÄ* 1: 99–101.

[102]Alan H. Gardiner, *The Royal Canon of Turin* (Oxford: University Press, 1959); Alessandro Roccati, "Turiner Königspapyrus," *LÄ* 6: 809–810.

[103]Von Beckerath, "Chamudi," *LÄ* 1: 903–904.

[104]Helck, *Untersuchungen zu Manetho,* 63.

[105]Manetho, 91 n. 6; Grimal, *Ancient Egypt,* 194.

[106]Helck, *Untersuchungen zu Manetho,* Table on 36, 37 for superiority of forms in Josephus.

TABLE 115. *Hyksos Kings (Fifteenth Dynasty) in Egypt*

Turin Canon		*Josephus*			*Africanus*		
No.	*Name*	*No.*	*Name*	*Years*	*No.*	*Name*	*Years*
		1.	Salitis	19	1.	Saites	19
		2.	Bnon	44/31?	2.	Bnon	44
		3.	Apachnan	36/7?	3.	Pachnan	61
		4.	Apophis	61/41?	4.	Staan	50
		5.	Iannas	50/1?	5.	Archles	49
6.	Khamudy	6.	Assis	49/9?	6.	Apophis	61
Total, 108			Total, 259/108?			Total, 284	

As for the statements of Manetho quoted above (§377) that the six kings and their descendants remained master of Egypt for 511 years, and that there were Hyksos kings in the Sixteenth and one part of the Seventeenth Dynasty, the references may be to contemporaries and vassals of the Great Hyksos, who held sway in lesser territories.[107]

381. As for the year dates for the Hyksos Age in Egypt, we have seen that already in the Thirteenth Dynasty, around 1675 B.C. (in the reign of Tutimaeus/Dedumose, §375) and around 1730–1720 (in the reign of Sobekhotep IV, §376), there are possible signs of the growing presence and significance of the Hyksos in the Delta,[108] while it is in the Fifteenth Dynasty that the six main Hyksos kings rule in full power, the end of their sway only coming when Ahmose (1552–1526), founder of the Eighteenth Dynasty and the New Kingdom, conquers their capital of Avaris (§373). The date of this decisive event was probably between the tenth and fifteenth years of Ahmose.[109] If we accept year 10 for the purpose of our reckoning, this means that the end of the Hyksos domination of Egypt was in 1542 (1,552 – 10 = 1,542). Since the six main Hyksos kings of the Fifteenth Dynasty ruled, according to the Turin Canon of Kings, for 108 years (§379), they must have begun to rule in 1650 (1,542 + 108 = 1,650), and they and the probably contemporary Sixteenth and Seventeenth Dynasties belong therefore in 1650–1542.[110] With the end of the Hyksos rule in 1542, counting inclusively the probable nine-year reign of Assis, the sixth and last of the main

---

[107]Redford, *History and Chronology of the Eighteenth Dynasty,* 45.

[108]Von Beckerath, "Zwischenzeit, Zweite," *LÄ* 6: 1444–1445, dates the Thirteenth Dynasty in 1781–1650/1645, and describes the kings of the Fourteenth Dynasty, "as far as they are real," as ruling in various parts of the Delta between 1710/1700 and 1650/1645.

[109]Von Beckerath, ibid.; cf. K. A. Kitchen, *Pharaoh Triumphant* (Warminster, England: Aris & Phillips, 1982), 9, for the storming of Avaris by Ahmose "after ten years of inconclusive activity."

[110]Bietak, "Hyksos," *LÄ* 3: 93, for the Hyksos rule as 1650–1542. Von Beckerath, "Zwischenzeit, Zweite," *LÄ* 6: 1444–1445, puts the Fifteenth and the contemporary Sixteenth and Seventeenth Dynasties c. 1650/1645–1540/1535.

Hyksos kings (§379), would have been 1550–1542, and the preceding probable 41-year reign of Apophis (§378) would have been 1590–1550.[111]

382. It was intimated above (§371) that we think we should look for historical circumstances appropriate to Joseph in Egypt in the time of the Hyksos. In this connection we are interested in the "city called Avaris [Egyptian *Hat-wa'ret,* perhaps "house of the River Arm"][112] after an ancient religious tradition," which Manetho says was very favorably situated on the east of the Bubastite branch of the Nile [the easternmost branch, therefore of great strategic significance in relation to the frontier], which Salitis [the first of the six main Hyksos kings] rebuilt and fortified [making it the main Hyksos center]. Having thus been the Hyksos capital, Avaris later became the site of Pi-Ramesse/Per-Ramses, the famous residence city and capital of Ramses II, bearing his own name (§407). It was long supposed that the location of Avaris and Per-Ramses was at Tanis (Greek for Egyptian *Dja'net,* modern San el-Hagar) in the northeastern Delta,[113] a supposition largely based on the many Ramesside stones and statues excavated and still to be seen at Tanis.[114] Now, however, the site in question has almost certainly been found at Tell el-Dab'a and nearby locations (12 mi south of Tanis), and it is realized that the Ramesside materials at Tanis probably originated in the Tell el-Dab'a region and were brought from there to Tanis when Tanis was the residence and burial place of the kings of the Twenty-first and Twenty-second Dynasties.

383. Among the materials found at Tanis is the so-called Stela of the Year 400.[115] This monument was made by Ramses II (1279–1212) and must have been set up originally at Per-Ramses. It was found at Tanis in 1863 by Auguste Mariette,[116] reburied and only rediscovered at Tanis seventy years later by Pierre Montet.[117] In a relief in the upper part of the stela, Ramses II stands in the center offering a libation to the god Seth, who is shown in Asian garb and designated "Seth of Ramses," thus evidently was at home in Ramses II's city. In the text below the relief, Ramses II is named with a long titulary and is said to have commanded the making of the stela, while a date is given in "Year 400," fourth day of the fourth month of the third session. This presumably means that this "Year 400" is the 400th anniversary of the "ancient religious tradition" (§377) of the worship of the god Seth at this place. In extended discussion of the monument,[118] it has been held that this points to the foundation of the worship and the temple of Seth at Avaris around 1720 B.C. and that it was also around 1730–1720 that Hyksos seized Avaris and made it their

---

[111]Von Beckerath, "Apophis," *LÄ* 1: 352, for Apophis c. 1590–1550.

[112]Fritz Hommel, *Ethnologie und Geographie des alten Orients* (Handbuch der Altertumswissenschaft, 3.1.1; Munich: Beck, 1926), 962.

[113]Baines and Málek, *Atlas,* 167, 176–177.

[114]Malte Roemer, "Tanis," *LÄ* 6: 194–209.

[115]Trans. in Breasted, *Ancient Records* 3:538–542; *ANET* 252–253.

[116]Mariette, "La stèle de l'an 400," *Revue archéologique* 11 (1865): 169ff. and Pl. 4.

[117]Montet, "La stèle de l'an 400 retrouvée," *Kemi* 4 (1933): 192–215 and Pls.

[118]Kurt Sethe, "Der Denkstein mit dem Datum des Jahres 400 der Ära von Tanis," *Zeitschrift für ägyptische Sprache und Altertumskunde* 65 (1930): 85–89; Raymond Weill, "The Problem of the Site of Avaris," *JEA* 21 (1935): 10–25.

political and religious center.[119] It is true that discrepancies and contradictions have been observed in identification of persons other than Ramses II on the stela and, for this and other reasons, it has now been said that "in regard to this date [the 400th year] it is at most a matter of a jubilee celebration of the Seth temple of Avaris, in which connection was sought with the family history of the Ramessides, but that it is not a matter of a historical datum of the beginning of the Hyksos rule is now generally taken for granted."[120] Nevertheless, we have also seen at least some other small items of evidence possibly suggesting the organized presence and even some domain of the Hyksos in the Egyptian Delta in about the time just mentioned, namely, around 1675 (§375) and around 1730–1720 (§376), and the rule of the six main Hyksos kings in Avaris is, of course, well established in the 108-year period 1650–1542 (§381). At any rate, the Stela of the Year 400 shows that the worship of the god Seth was ancient in Lower Egypt (where his name was pronounced Sutekh), and this is also confirmed by the fact that a son of Sobekhotep IV of the Thirteenth Dynasty, named Nehesi, and himself a minor king of the Fourteenth Dynasty from the East Delta (c. 1710), is the first king known with the title "beloved of Seth, lord of Avaris."[121] Since Seth was known as the "lord of foreign lands" and was recognized as much like the Canaanite storm god, Baal, it is not surprising, especially when Avaris became the main center of the Hyksos, that Seth became the chief god of the Hyksos in Egypt.[122]

384. Turning now to specific biblical dates for Joseph in Egypt and in particular to his entry into the service of Pharaoh as shown in our Tables 109, 111–114: In Table 109, this particular date is in 1886 B.C., a very early date which requires a time for Joseph in the Middle Kingdom and on that account has, in our opinion, been judged unlikely (§371). At the other end of the scale of dates, in Table 113 Joseph's entry into Pharaoh's service is in 1475, and this is after the foundation of the Eighteenth Dynasty by Ahmose (1552–1526) and in the time of Thutmose III and Hatshepsut (Table 116) and is therefore entirely unlikely. In Tables 111 and 112 the dates in question are 1690 and 1671, which fall in the Thirteenth and Fourteenth Dynasties (see above §381 and esp. n. 108). Although there are probably increasing signs of the Hyksos presence in these times, these dynasties are relatively obscure and we lack specific information to connect with Joseph, such as we will (in §385ff.) find in the Fifteenth Dynasty. There is one item of interest, however, already at the present point as well as a little later, too (§385). In the biblical account Joseph was sold into slavery in Egypt for twenty shekels of silver (Gen 37:28) and it has been established from ancient sources that this was the correct average price in the Middle East for a slave in 1700 B.C., earlier the price was less (average ten to fifteen shekels), by the fifteenth century it was thirty or even forty shekels and later rose even higher.[123]

---

[119]Grimal, *Ancient Egypt,* 185; cf. T. O. Lambdin, "Hyksos," *IDB* 2: 667.

[120]Rainer Stadelmann, "Sethos I," *LÄ* 5: 911–917, esp. col. 912; idem, "Satre," *LÄ* 5: 493–494; idem, "Vierhundertjahrstele," *LÄ* 6: 1039–1043, quoted statement in German in col. 1042.

[121]Jürgen von Beckerath, "Nehesi," *LÄ* 4: 392.

[122]Herman te Velde, "Seth," *LÄ* 5: 908–911; *ANET* 231 n. 9.

[123]K. A. Kitchen, *Ancient Orient and Old Testament,* 52–53; idem, "Slave, Slavery,"

385. We come therefore to Table 114, in which Joseph is sold into Egypt in 1587 (still probably within the time range for twenty shekels of silver as the price for a slave, §384), and enters into the service of Pharaoh in 1574. Now we are in the main Hyksos period in Egypt, with the six main Hyksos kings ruling for 108 years in 1650–1542 (§381). In the accounts by Manetho (our §377) the main Hyksos base was at Avaris, a city "very favorably situated" (doubtless meaning in strategic respect to guard the frontier), on the east of the easternmost branch of the Nile. In the service of Pharaoh, this would no doubt have been the residence of Joseph. From here at Avaris, as located now at Tell el-Dab'a (§382), there was direct access along the Nile branch to Pelusium and the coastal road to Palestine/Syria, and much closer access overland (for perhaps 15 miles) to the entrance to Wadi Tumilat.[124] We have already seen (§368) that Wadi Tumilat was probably the route of Sinuhe when he went out from Egypt to Palestine/Syria, and we will later (§411) read the report of a frontier official when Bedouin tribes were allowed to come in—almost certainly through Wadi Tumilat—from Edom to keep them and their cattle alive. In the light of such examples, Wadi Tumilat was probably the way of ingress for Jacob and his household in their descent into Egypt. The valley is 35 miles in length but scarcely a half dozen miles in width, with land suited for grazing but bounded by desert on either side. It is almost certainly to be identified with biblical Goshen, where Israel was thereafter allowed to settle with the flocks and herds for which this was the best of the land (Gen 47:1, 6).[125] In Avaris, therefore, Joseph was relatively close at hand to go out to meet his incoming father, and it is notable that he traveled overland in the chariot with which he had already been provided by way of honor by the king (Gen 41:43; 46:29), otherwise long journeys in Egypt were ordinarily by water on the Nile and its numerous channels and canals (e.g., Sinuhe, taking boat upon his return to Egypt to proceed to the Residence City).[126]

386. As to the history of the horse-drawn chariot and the time when it would have been natural for Joseph to use such conveyance (§385), from illustrations, literary references, and archaeological remains, the chariot hitched to two horses was introduced for battle in Mesopotamia in the first half of the third millennium B.C. (before Abraham), and is well known in the Fertile Crescent beginning from the eighteenth century (around the time of the patriarchs). In Egypt the horse-drawn chariot was not yet in use in the twentieth and nineteenth centuries and is not yet shown in wall paintings of the Twelfth Dynasty (1991–1785), which often illustrate other aspects of military matters.[127]

NBD, 1195–1196 with references to ancient Middle Eastern sources and citing I. Mendelsohn, *Slavery in the Ancient Near East* (1949): 117–115, and *IEJ* 5 (1955): 68.

[124]Hans Goedicke, "Wadi Tumilat," *LÄ* 6: 1124–1126.

[125]For Goshen as equivalent to part or all of Wadi Tumilat, although no Egyptian equivalent of the name has been found, see Alan H. Gardiner, "The Supposed Egyptian Equivalent of the Name of Goshen," *JEA* 5 (1918): 218–223; de Vaux, *Early History of Israel,* 302–303; Jürgen Ebach, "Gosen," *LÄ* 2: 755–756.

[126]Montet, *Egypt and the Bible,* 8.

[127]Yigael Yadin, *The Art of Warfare in Biblical Lands in the Light of Archaeological Study* (2 vols.; New York: McGraw Hill, 1963), 1:37, 74–76, 86–90; Silvio Curto, "Krieg," *LÄ*

After that, the horse-drawn chariot becomes known and it is generally accepted that it was through the Hyksos that it became known in Egypt.[128] That the horse-drawn chariot was brought in through Canaan is supported by the facts that the Egyptian words for chariot and horse are borrowed from the Canaanite and the early Egyptian chariots are exactly like the light Canaanite chariot.[129]

387. Indirect evidence of the use of the light chariot is recognized on a stela found at Edfu. In the scene on the stela, a personage identified as "king's son and commander" is seated together with his wife and underneath their seat is shown a pair of heavy gloves. Certainly not needed in Egypt because of climatic conditions, the gloves are probably such as protected the hands of a chariot driver as he held the reins of his horses, an identification which is the more likely because the owner of the stela was a military officer. For comparison there is a scene in the grave at Amarna of the "god's father," Eje (perhaps the mother of Nofretete), in which Akhenaten gives many gifts to Eje, among which are similar gloves, these being appropriate here, too, inasmuch as Eje had a title marking him as General of battle-chariot troops. The Edfu stela is dated under Dedumose (Egyptian *Dwd-msjw*), whom we have already met (§375) as a king of the late Thirteenth Dynasty.[130] Direct archaeological evidence about the horse in Egypt includes the following: In the excavation of a fortification at Buhen opposite Wadi Halfa[131] (in Lower Nubia, under Egyptian control in the Thirteenth and Fourteenth Dynasties),[132] on a level dated c. 1675 B.C., the skeleton of a horse was found with teeth showing the effects of a bit, giving proof that the horse was used under control.[133] In excavation at Tell el-Dab'a (Avaris) horse teeth were found in Level E-2 of early Hyksos time.[134] In 1994 it was reported that eight rare Hyksos tombs had been found in the desert near Tell el-Kebir, not far from Avaris (Tell el-Dab'a). In one tomb already opened were four human skeletons, with alabaster jars and scarabs. As described by Ali Hassan, head of the Pharaonic sector at the Egyptian Antiquities Organization, the pots are of high quality and the scarabs suggest that the tombs belonged to important persons, possibly Hyksos rulers. Buried a few yards from the tomb, was uncovered the earliest intact skeleton of a horse yet found in Egypt, confirming the connection of the horse with the Hyksos.[135]

388. In literary texts in Egypt the first mention of the horse and chariot is at the end of the period of the six main Hyksos kings and, in particular, in

---

3: 773, 783 n. 77.

[128]Wolfgang Decker, "Wagen," *LÄ* 6: 1130–1135, esp. col. 1130; Eugen Strouhal, *Life of the Ancient Egyptians* (London: OPUS; Norman, University of Oklahoma Press, 1992), 113.

[129]For pictures of the Egyptian chariot see *ANEP,* Index.

[130]Wolfgang Helck, "Ein indirekter Beleg für die Benutzung des leichten Streitwagens in Ägypten zu Ende der 13. Dynastie," *JNES* 37 (1938): 337–340. For Eje see Jürgen von Beckerath, "Eje," *LÄ* 1: 1211–1212.

[131]Baines and Málek, *Atlas,* 20, 186.

[132]Grimal, *Ancient Egypt,* 184.

[133]"Editorial Foreword," *JEA* 45 (1959): 1–2.

[134]Lothar Störk, "Pferd," *LÄ* 4: 1010; Wolfgang Helck, *JNES* 37 (1938): 337.

[135]Reuters in *San Francisco Chronicle,* Jan 31, 1994.

connection with Kamose, the last native Egyptian king of the Seventeenth Dynasty at Thebes, who began the war against the Hyksos, and his brother the king Ahmose (1552–1526), who won the decisive victory over the Hyksos at Avaris in 1542 (§381 and below §392). In Carnarvon Tablet I (found in Western Thebes and probably copied from a stela of Kamose himself), Kamose records his battle against the Hyksos and at the point of a certain stronghold of the Hyksos says: "Their horses [presumably chariot horses] were fled inside."[136] There was also a certain naval officer named Ahmose and known as the son of Abina (his mother—his father was Bibi),[137] who served under the just-mentioned king Ahmose, and in his tomb at el-Kab in Upper Egypt there are biographical inscriptions in which he tells not only of his participation in the conquest of Avaris, but also of his own earlier life under the same king. Of this he says: "I used to accompany the Sovereign—life, prosperity, health—on foot, following his excursions in his chariot."[138] Thus, it can be concluded that as the danger from the battle-chariot equipped Hyksos became apparent the Egyptians took over the same for themselves but also used the horse-drawn chariot for peaceful purposes as well. Thus, in terms of historical circumstances, Joseph in Egypt fits best toward the end of the period of the six main Hyksos kings (1650–1542).

389. Furthermore, explicit placement of Joseph in the time of the main Hyksos kings is found in Manetho, according to Eusebius (in the Armenian version of his *Chronicle*[139] and as quoted by Syncellus [Manetho, 95–97]), where four of the kings are named and said to have been of the Seventeenth Dynasty—Saites for 19 years, Bnon for 40 years, Apophis for 14 years, Archles for 30 years, total 103 years close to the 108 years of the Turin Canon—and it is said: "It was in their time that Joseph was appointed king of Egypt." Exact naming of the king under whom Joseph served is found in the *Book of Sothis* (Manetho, 239), a work which was attributed to Manetho in antiquity and transmitted by Syncellus in the belief that it was from Manetho, an attribution which is no longer accepted. Here also four Hyksos kings are named and said to have been of the Seventeenth Dynasty—Silites, Baion, Apachnan, Apophis (whom we, of course, know as kings of the Fifteenth Dynasty, see our Table 115). Concerning Apophis it is stated:

> Some say that this king was at first called Pharaoh, and that in the fourth year of his kingship Joseph came as a slave to Egypt. He appointed Joseph lord of Egypt and all his kingdom in the seventeenth year of his rule, having learned from him the interpretation of the dreams and having thus proved his divine wisdom.

From the fourth to the seventeenth year of Apophis is 14 years, inclusively, and from Joseph's age 17 when he was sold into Egypt (Gen 37:2) to his age 30 when he entered the service of Pharaoh (Gen 41:46, cf. our Tables 109, 111–114) is

---

[136]*ANET* 232–233. Alan H. Gardiner, "The Defeat of the Hyksos by Kamose: The Carnarvon Tablet, No. 1," *JEA* 3 (1916): 95–110; *ANET* 232–233.

[137]Wolfgang Helck, "Ahmose, son of Abina," *LÄ* 1: 110–111.

[138]*ANET* 233–234.

[139]Karst 68.

likewise 14 years, inclusively, therefore the tradition in the *Book of Sothis* can be seen as congruent in this respect with biblical tradition. On this basis, Apophis may be taken as the Pharaoh under whom Joseph served. The probable date of the reign of Apophis is 1590–1550 (§381), so his year 4 is 1587 and his year 17 is 1574, and in our Table 114 these are the dates when Joseph was sold into Egypt (1587) and when he entered the service of Pharaoh (1574). This is the specific time which seems the most fitting for Joseph in Egypt.

3. The Exodus

LITERATURE: J. S. **Griffiths**, *The Exodus in the Light of Archaeology* (London: Scott, 1923); J. W. **Jack**, *The Date of the Exodus* (Edinburgh, T. & T. Clark, 1925); W. M. Flinders **Petrie**, *Palestine and Israel* (London: S.P.C.K., 1934), 54–58; William F. **Albright**, *From the Stone Age to Christianity* (2d ed.; Baltimore: Johns Hopkins Press, 1946), 194ff.; H. H. **Rowley**, *From Joseph to Joshua* (London: Oxford University Press, 1950), 129ff.; M. B. **Rowton**, "The Background of the Treaty between Ramesses II and Hattušiliš III," in *JCS* 13 (1959): 1–11; idem, "Comparative Chronology at the Time of Dynasty XIX," in *JNES* 19 (1960): 15–22; K. A. **Kitchen**, *Ancient Orient and Old Testament* (London: Tyndale; Chicago: InterVarsity, 1966); idem, *The Bible in Its World: The Bible and Archaeology Today* (Downers Grove, Ill.: InterVarsity, 1978), 75–79; idem, *Pharaoh Triumphant: The Life and Times of Ramesses II* (Warminster: Aris & Phillips, 1982); Donald B. **Redford**, *History and Chronology of the Eighteenth Dynasty of Egypt* (Toronto: University of Toronto Press, 1967); John J. **Bimson**, *Redating the Exodus and Conquest* (JSOT Suppl. 5; Sheffield: University of Sheffield Press, 1978); idem, *Redating the Exodus and Conquest* (2d ed.; Sheffield: Almond Press, 1981); Hershel **Shanks**, "The Exodus and the Crossing of the Red Sea According to Hans Goedicke," *BAR* 7 (5, Sept/Oct 1981): 42–50; Douglas MacCallum Lindsay **Judisch**, "Critical Chronology and the Exodus," in *CTQ* 49 (1985): 267–271; John J. **Bimson** and David **Livingston**, "Redating the Exodus," *BAR* 13 (5, Sept/Oct 1987): 40–53, 66–68; Baruch **Halpern**, "Radical Exodus Redating Fatally Flawed," *BAR* 13 (6, Nov/Dec 1987): 56–61; Eugene H. **Merrill**, *Kingdom of Priests: A History of Old Testament Israel* (Grand Rapids: Baker Book House, 1987), 57–91; Wally G. **Vaughn**, *From the Descent to the Exodus: Five Unresolved Issues* (Portsmouth, N.H.: Peter E. Randall, 1991).

390. In some recent works the biblical account of the exodus is reinterpreted in a theory of a "peasant revolt" against the Canaanite city states, an "indigenous revolutionary social movement," a theory which reduces an actual exodus to inconsequence or denies that it took place, and, thus, is little interested in any particular dates.[140] In biblical tradition, however, the exodus of the Israelite people from Egypt and the establishment of the twelve tribes in Canaan marked the beginning of the nation of Israel, and from that point of view the events of the exodus and their dating are of historical importance. The

---

[140]George E. Mendenhall, "The Hebrew Conquest of Palestine," *BA* 25 (Sept 1962): 66–87; Norman K. Gottwald, "Were the Early Israelites Pastoral Nomads?" *BAR* 4, 2 (June 1978): 2–7; idem, *The Hebrew Bible: A Socio-literary Introduction* (Philadelphia: Fortress Press, 1985); P. Kyle McCarter, Jr., "Major New Introduction to the Bible: Norman Gottwald's Sociological-Literary Perspective," *BR* Summer 1986, 42–50; Bernard W. Anderson, "Mendenhall Disavows Paternity: Says He Didn't Father Gottwald's Marxist Theory," *BR* Summer 1986, 46–50.

factors bearing on the date of the exodus and the entry into Canaan are numerous and complex, and not a few solutions to the problems have been proposed by various scholars.[141] Broadly speaking, two major theories have emerged, one which places the events in the Eighteenth Egyptian Dynasty and the fifteenth century B.C., and one which places the events in the Nineteenth Egyptian Dynasty and the thirteenth century B.C.

(1) Exodus in the Eighteenth Dynasty and the Fifteenth Century B.C.

391. It has been mentioned (§356) and will be explained more fully below (§424) that the statement in 1 Kgs 6:1 that Solomon built the temple in his fourth year and in the 480th year after the people of Israel came out of Egypt leads to the date of 1446 B.C. for the exodus. As seen in Table 116 the year 1446 B.C. falls in the Eighteenth Egyptian Dynasty and in the reign of Thutmose III (1479–1425).

TABLE 116. *Rulers of the Eighteenth Dynasty*

	Name	*Dates of Reign*
1.	Ahmose	1552–1526
2.	Amenhotep I	1526–1506
3.	Thutmose I	1506–1493
4.	Thutmose II	1493–1479
5.	Thutmose III	1479–1425
6.	Hatshepsut	1478–1458
7.	Amenhotep II	1425–1401
8.	Thutmose IV	1401–1390
9.	Amenhotep III	1390–1352
10.	Amenhotep IV	1352–1348
	Akhenaten	1348–1338
11.	Smenkhkare	1338–1336
12.	Tutankhaten/Tutankhamen	1336–1327
13.	Ay	1327–1323
14.	Horemheb	1323–1295

392. For perspective it will be remembered that the largely Semitic Hyksos came gradually into Egypt, by probably around 1730 B.C. took Avaris in the East Delta as their main base, and ruled in Manetho's Fifteenth and contemporary Sixteenth and part of the Seventeenth Dynasties from 1650 to 1542 (§381). In spite of the fact that the Hyksos respected and adopted much in Egyptian civilization and religion (e.g., they were devoted to the Egyptian god Seth with his ancient center at Avaris [§383], they came to be hated and Kamose, the last native Egyptian king of the Seventeenth Dynasty at Thebes, began the war against them and against their king Apophis, as Kamose tells on a stela at Karnak [§378]).[142] The date of the stela is the third year of Kamose's reign, and

[141]Vaughn, *Five Unresolved Issues*.
[142]Claude Vandersleyen, "Kamose," *LÄ* 3: 306–308.

this is the probable date of the war. Kamose himself probably did not long survive the campaign, for his make-shift burial suggests that his death came suddenly and unexpectedly.[143] After Kamose, his younger brother, Ahmose (1552–1526), won the decisive victory over the Hyksos at Avaris and Manetho, using the name of Tethmosis for Ahmose, describes him as "the king who drove [them] the Hyksos out of Egypt," and shows him as the founder of the Eighteenth Dynasty (Manetho, 101).[144] The biography of Ahmose, son of Abina (described above §388), tells not only how, under King Ahmose, he himself commanded a ship in battle at Avaris and participated in the three-year siege of the withdrawing Hyksos at Sharuhen (in southern Palestine), but also how he went with Ahmose on a campaign southward against the Nubians, and then continued to serve under Amenhotep I,[145] with whom he went into Kush, and under Thutmose I,[146] with whom he went both to Kush and to Retenu (Syria/Palestine) and as far as Naharin (the common name in Egyptian for Mesopotamia, probably equivalent to the Hebrew dual, נהרים "the Two Rivers"). Among various exploits for which Ahmose, son of Abina, was awarded gold for valor, in Naharin, he says: "I carried off a chariot, its horse, and him who was in it as a living prisoner. They were presented to his majesty." Mesopotamian armament was matched now by what the Egyptians had learned from the Hyksos—the composite bow and other weapons, and especially the horse-drawn chariot (§388)—and Egypt was beginning to build an empire that would reach from the Fourth Cataract of the Nile to beyond the Euphrates. In spite of such indebtedness to the Hyksos, the Egyptians, at least in retrospect, looked back upon the Second Intermediate Period and the Hyksos age as a time of disruption and disaster (note, for example, the opinion of Hatshepsut cited below [§399]), but now the Eighteenth Dynasty emerged in the start of a new age of brilliant achievements and great prosperity and was parallel in many respects to the scarcely less splendid times of the Twelfth Dynasty after the First Intermediate Period.[147]

393. When Thutmose I died (1493) at the end of a reign of a dozen years, the only surviving son of the king and his first queen, Ahmose Nofretere,[148] was Hatshepsut,[149] while a son of the king and his second queen, Mutnofret, succeeded as Thutmose II (1493–1479)[150] and, presumably to strengthen his claim to the throne, he was married to Hatshepsut, his half-sister. While still the queen of Thutmose II, Hatshepsut began a tomb for herself but never completed it, and inside, on an unfinished sarcophagus, are the titles which belonged to her at this stage of her career: "King's daughter, king's sister, wife of the god, great wife of the king . . . Hatshepsut."[151] In turn Thutmose II

---

[143]Redford, *Eighteenth Dynasty,* 40–41.

[144]Claude Vandersleyen, "Ahmose," *LÄ* 1: 99–101.

[145]Erik Hornung, "Amenophis I," *LÄ* 1: 201–203.

[146]Christine Meyer, "Thutmosis I," *LÄ* 6: 536–539.

[147]Gunn and Gardiner, *JEA* 5 (1918): 56.

[148]Meyer, "Thutmosis I," *LÄ* 6: 536; Michel Gitton, "Ahmose-Nofretere," *LÄ* 1: 102–109.

[149]Wilfred Seipel, "Hatschepsut I," *LÄ* 2: 1045–1052.

[150]Christine Meyer, "Thutmosis II," *LÄ* 6: 539–540.

[151]For the tomb and sarcophagus see Howard Carter, *JEA* 4 (1917): 107–118; for the title "god's wife" see Redford, *Eighteenth Dynasty,* 71–72.

died relatively young and was succeeded by his only son, Thutmose III (1479–1425),[152] whose mother was a member of Thutmose II's harem named Isis. Thutmose III evidently came to the throne while still very young, and Hatshepsut became regent (1478), controlled the affairs of the country, and between Years 2 and 7 of Thutmose's reign took the title "king," then, in the fashion of the great kings, built her still-famous mortuary temple at Deir-el-Bahri. In the twenty-second year (1458) of the reign of Thutmose III, Hatshepsut disappears from the records, probably simply by death,[153] but was later regarded with such disfavor that her figure and name were destroyed on many monuments throughout Egypt and her name replaced by the name of Thutmose III or that of her father (Thutmose II) or her grandfather (Thutmose I). Thutmose III then reigned as pharaoh alone (1458–1425), conducted seventeen Asiatic campaigns (for campaigns in Asia the months were from April to October),[154] and did building works (in the other part of the year) in both Upper and Lower Egypt. At Heliopolis, third city of importance in ancient Egypt after Thebes and Memphis,[155] Thutmose III, like many other kings, built, and erected obelisks, and two of the obelisks were taken to Alexandria by Augustus in the year 22 B.C. and again in the nineteenth century carried away and placed, one on the Thames embankment in London, the other in Central Park, New York City.[156] Elsewhere in the Delta Thutmose III's engineer, Minmose, cites extensive projects, but of these little survives.[157]

394. Coming now to the biblical narrative of the exodus and possible correlation with the background of Egyptian history just outlined (§§392–393), the book of Exodus begins with recapitulation of the names of Jacob's family who came to Egypt, and then recounts (1:8–11):

> Now there arose a new king over Egypt, who did not know Joseph. And he said to his people, "Behold, the people of Israel are too many and too mighty for us. Come, let us deal shrewdly with them, lest they multiply, and, if war befall us, they join our enemies and fight against us and escape from the land." Therefore they set taskmasters over them to afflict them with heavy burdens; and they built for Pharaoh store-cities, Pithom and Ramses [to which the LXX adds: and On, which is Heliopolis].

The mention of "a new king" suggests the rise of a new dynasty, and (as observed above §391) in terms of an exodus date of 1446 B.C. this would be the Eighteenth Dynasty (1552–1295). The fact that the king "did not know [acknowledge] Joseph" and was apprehensive of increasing numbers and growing power of the Israelites, can reflect the position of the Eighteenth Dynasty as the first Egyptian dynasty after the expulsion of the Hyksos and the increased suspicion

---

152Donald B. Redford, "Thutmosis III," *LÄ* 6: 540–548.
153Redford, *Eighteenth Dynasty,* 87.
154Curto, *LÄ* 3, 774.
155Baines and Málek, *Atlas,* 167, 173–174; László Kákósy, "Atum," *LÄ* 1: 550–552; Finegan, *Myth and Mystery,* 51–52.
156Breasted, *Ancient Records* 2:632–636.
157Redford, *LÄ* 6: 543. For Minmose see Redford, *Eighteenth Dynasty,* 65 n. 140.

thereafter of other Asiatics and Semitics.[158] As to the identity of the "new king," he could have been the first king of the dynasty, namely, Ahmose (1552–1526).

395. As for Moses and the possibility of his connection with the period just described, chronological points in his life are birth (Exod 2:2); flight to Midian at the age of forty from the pharaoh who sought to kill him (Exod 2:11–15; Acts 7:23–29); the time forty years later (Acts 7:30) when he returned to Egypt and, at the age of eighty, spoke to Pharaoh, was involved with the miracles of the plagues of Egypt and accomplished the exodus (Exod 7:7ff.),[159] the forty years that he led Israel in the wilderness (Exod 16:35; Num 14:33–34; 32:13; Deut 1:3; Acts 7:36); and his death at the age of one hundred twenty on Mount Nebo in Moab opposite Jericho (Deut 34:7). Taking the figures as they stand and reckoning from Moses' age of eighty at the theoretical time of the exodus in 1446, his birth was in 1526 (1,446 + 80 = 1,526). This was the last year of Ahmose and he could have been the pharaoh under whom the newborn child was under the threat of death (Exod 1:22). If the unnamed "Pharaoh's daughter," who appears in Exod 2:5–10, was the daughter of Ahmose, she might have been born in the early part of the king's reign of twenty-five years and four months[160] and have been around twenty years of age when she found the baby, which would seem appropriate to the narrative. Adopted by the daughter of Pharaoh and by her given the name of Moses, the child grew up in safety and was instructed in all the wisdom of the Egyptians (Exod 2:10; Acts 7:21–22). Meanwhile the oppression of the people of Israel continued and evidently intensified. When Moses was grown up he went out and saw the burdens of his people and took their side by killing an Egyptian who was beating a Hebrew. When Pharaoh heard of it, he sought to kill Moses and Moses fled to Midian, being forty years of age at the time (Exod 2:11–15; Acts 7:23–29); reckoned from birth in 1526 this would have been in 1486 and the pharaoh from whom he fled would have been Thutmose II (1493–1479). When forty years had passed (Acts 7:30) and the former king of Egypt had died (Exod 2:23), Moses was sent back to Egypt (Exod 3:10; Acts 7:34) where in 1446 (according to the present theory), at the age of eighty, Moses confronted Pharaoh—Thutmose III (1479–1425)—and the exodus ensued. Then, after forty years in the wilderness, in 1406, Israel reached the edge of Canaan and Moses passed away there at the age of one hundred twenty. If the king of Egypt whom Moses confronted was Thutmose III it is appropriate that he is called Pharaoh, for it is precisely from Thutmose III that this term ("great house") was used for the person of the king (§364).[161]

396. By way of comparison with the trial scheme worked out just above (§§394–395), other studies also place the exodus in the Eighteenth Dynasty and the fifteenth century B.C. but vary in details. John J. Bimson and David Living-

---

[158] W. Gunther Plaut, *The Torah,* vol. 2, *Exodus* (New York: Union of American Hebrew Congregations, 1983), 6.

[159] For the plagues as phenomena ecologically possible in the Egyptian environment, see Greta Hort, *ZAW* 69 (1957): 84–103; 70 (1958): 48–59. See also Robert R. Stieglitz, "Ancient Records and the Exodus Plagues," *BAR* 13 (6, Nov/Dec 1987): 46–49.

[160] Vandersleyen, "Ahmose," *LÄ* 1: 99–101.

[161] Jürgen Osing, "Pharo," *LÄ* 4: 1021.

ston also place the flight of Moses to Midian under Thutmose II[162] and the exodus under Thutmose III.[163] The reign of Thutmose III is given as 1490–1436 for which Borchardt-Egerton followed by Albright, Wright, Pritchard, and others are cited, and the fourth year of Solomon is given as 967 with the exodus 480 years earlier placed in 1447 or say 1450 for convenience or 1460 during the sole reign of Thutmose III, and the Israelite entry into Canaan in 1410–1400 or 1420. It is held further that archaeological evidence at excavated sites in the land of Israel (Jericho, Bethel, Hazor, Debir, Lachish, Hebron, Hormah, Dan) agrees with Israelite conquest in the fifteenth century B.C. and not in the thirteenth century,[164] giving "almost perfect correlation between the archaeological evidence and the Biblical account of the conquest of Canaan." Involved also is a proposed change of the date of the end of the Middle Bronze Age, but in a rejoinder Baruch Halpern (see LITERATURE) affirms that the archaeological evidence does not support either the change about the Middle Bronze Age nor the proposed redating of both exodus and conquest.

397. Eugene H. Merrill[165] gives similar biblical dates, but in his chronology, the birth of Moses was in 1526,[166] and Hatshepsut, the daughter of Thutmose I (dated in 1526–1512) is surmised to have been in her early teens by that date and "the general picture of . . . this bold queen" leads to identification of her as the daughter of Pharaoh who rescued Moses.[167] Moses fled to Midian in the year 1486 at age forty; the pharaoh was Thutmose III (dated in 1504–1450), then in his eighteenth year, and the elderly Hatshepsut, who died three years later, was no longer able to protect Moses. It was after the death of Thutmose III that Moses felt free to return to Egypt, and Amenhotep II (dated in 1450–1425) was the pharaoh of the exodus.[168] Likewise, on the basis of 1 Kgs 6:1, Douglas MacCallum Lindsay Judisch affirms the date of 1446 B.C. for the Israelite exodus from Egypt.[169]

398. The question of the way the Israelites went from Egypt to Canaan is also relevant to the present consideration and in at least one theory (Goedicke, see §399) is connected with an exodus date in the Eighteenth Dynasty and the fifteenth century B.C. Otto Eissfeldt[170] located the exodus-route site of Baal-zephon (Exod 14:2, 9) on the Mediterranean coast east of Port Said, where a spit of land separates a lagoon anciently called Lake Sirbonis (also Lake Bardawil) from the sea, and where the sea has been known to break through from time to time, and the suggestion was that such an event could have been what overwhelmed Pharaoh's army (Exod 14:28). A survey of the region begun in 1972 by

---

162Bimson, *Redating the Exodus and Conquest,* 250.

163*BAR* 13 (5, Sept/Oct 1987): 42, 44–45, 52, 67 n. 27.

164*Redating* (1978), 230.

165Merrill, *Kingdom of Priests;* for his dates of Egyptian rulers he follows the *Cambridge Ancient History* (1973), see p. 58 Table 4 and 59–60 and n. 5.

166Ibid., 59.

167Ibid., 60.

168Ibid., 62.

169*CTQ* 49 (1985): 267–271.

170Otto Eissfeldt, *Baal Zaphon, Zeus Kasios und der Durchzug der Israeliten durchs Meer* (Halle: Max Niemeyer, 1932).

E. Oren of Ben Gurion University at Beersheba, however, showed that the archaeological presuppositions of the Eissfeldt theory are incorrect, and that the traditional view which locates the route of Israel as going to Mount Sinai in the south of the Sinai Peninsula is still most likely.[171]

399. A slightly different theory of a marine happening on the eastern Mediterranean coast, with a specific exodus date, is proposed by Hans Goedicke.[172] Goedicke refers to the volcanic eruption which is believed to have destroyed the Greek island of Thera/Santorini around 1475 B.C. and to have sent a tidal wave (tsunami) to devastate the Minoan civilization on Crete thirty miles to the south. Goedicke thinks that this tidal wave also swept through Lake Menzaleh (a southern bay of the Mediterranean Sea, west of Port Said), and to the plain south of the Pelusiac branch of the Nile,[173] where it was responsible for the "miracle at the sea." The resultant date proposed for the exodus is therefore the year 1477. Dating the reign of Queen Hatshepsut in 1487–1468, Goedicke holds that Hatshepsut was the "king" of the exodus. This conclusion is supported by reference to Semitic inscriptions at Serabit el-Khadem in Sinai, which can be dated to the reign of Hatshepsut, and to the Speos Artemidos Inscription. The latter inscription is on the façade of the rock temple of this name (just south of Beni Hasan in Middle Egypt),[174] which was built by Hatshepsut and dedicated to the local lion goddess Pakhet. As translated by Gardiner,[175] the text is a denunciation by Hatshepsut of the Hyksos and a claim that it was she herself who restored order in Egypt after the disruption they caused. Referring to the time "when the Asiatics were in Avaris," Hatshepsut says, "I have banished the abomination of the gods." Goedicke believes, however, that the reference is to the destruction of the Israelites at the exodus, and therefore Hatshepsut, as the author of the inscription was the ruler of Egypt at that time. Actually, however, the place where Goedicke thinks the Israelites crossed the sea is 30 miles inland and, from the standpoint of oceanography as represented by Doron Nof of the Department of Oceanography, Florida State University, and Nathan Paldor of the Hebrew University of Jerusalem, the supposed tsunami would have been dissipated long before reaching the point.[176] Furthermore, the record in Exod 13:17–18 is that the Israelites did not go on the coast route and up through the land of the Philistines, which was the route on which the armies of Egypt regularly marched and on which the Israelites might "see war and return to Egypt," but rather they went "by the way of the wilderness toward the Red Sea." As for this wilderness, its traditional location in the southern Sinai peninsula was supported by Israeli scholars who explored the Sinai mountains during a

---

[171]G. I. Davies, "The Wilderness Itineraries and Recent Archaeological Research," *Studies in the Pentateuch* (VTSup 41; Leiden: Brill, 1990), 161–167, 172.

[172]See Hershel Shanks, "The Exodus and the Crossing of the Red Sea, According to Hans Goedicke," *BAR* 7 (5, Sept/Oct 1981): 42–50.

[173]Baines and Málek, *Atlas,* 167.

[174]Ibid., 43, 121, 128.

[175]Alan H. Gardiner, *JEA* 32 (1946): 43–56.

[176]Doron Nof and Nathan Paldor, "Are there Oceanographic Explanations for the Israelites' Crossing of the Red Sea?" *Bulletin of the American Meteorological Society* 73 (3, Mar 1992): 308.

brief period of Israeli occupation (1956) and came to believe that it was indeed in this region that the Israelites encamped when the Law was given,[177] an opinion also supported by E. Oren as cited just above.

400. Likewise, instead of any incursion of the Mediterranean from the west (as per Eissfeldt and Goedicke) to overwhelm the pursuing Egyptians, Exod 14:21, 26–27 speaks of "a strong east wind all night," which drove the sea back and made it possible for the Israelites to cross, then allowed the water to come back upon the Egyptians. In a computer calculation based on oceanographic and atmospheric sciences, Nof and Paldor recognized that the Gulf of Suez is unique in that it is a long, narrow, and shallow northern extension of the much larger body of water, the Red Sea proper, and assumed that the Israelite crossing was at the northern edge of the present gulf. They also assumed that the "east wind" (רוח קדים, Exod 14:21) was actually a northeast wind, which was entirely possible since in biblical Hebrew there are only four wind directions (E, W, N, S) and "east" can also mean northeast or southeast. In analysis of the possible oceanographic and atmospheric processes involved, it was reckoned that a northeast wind of about 40 to 45 miles per hour, blowing constantly for about 10 hours, could push the water of the gulf back from the northern shore by as much as a mile, lowering its depth by 10 feet or more, thus leaving dry land where the Israelite crossing occurred. Abrupt relaxation of the wind would allow the water to return as a gravity wave that could flood the entire temporarily dry zone within minutes. It is thus suggested that the Israelite crossing occurred while the water receded and that the drowning of the Egyptians was the result of the rapidly returning wave.[178]

401. In some other theories which place the exodus in the Eighteenth Dynasty, Moses is brought into connection with Amenhotep IV/Akhenaten (1352–1348/1348–1338). The chief support for this view is the similarity of the "monotheism" of Moses and of Akhenaten.[179] The latter was devoted to the Aten, the power manifest in the Sun Disk, for whom the king changed his own name from Amenhotep ("Amen/Amun Is Content") to Akhenaten ("Well-Pleasing to Aten") and named his own new capital city Akhetaten ("Horizon of the Aten," now Tell el-Amarna).[180] Akhenaten's teaching is preserved in a hymn to the Aten, the longest copy of which was inscribed in the tomb at Amarna of Ay, private secretary and chief official of the king. In the text Aten is called the "sole god" and described as universal and beneficent.[181] Likewise biblical tradition attributes monotheistic doctrine to Moses (Exod 20:2–3; Deut 6:4, etc.), and it has been said that "if . . . the term 'monotheist' means one who teaches the existence of only one God, the creator of everything, the source of justice, who

---

177 Yohanan Aharoni in Benno Rothenberg, *God's Wilderness* (New York: Thomas Nelson, 1962), 126.

178 Nof and Paldor, "Oceanographic Explanations," 305–314.

179 Sigmund Freud, *Moses and Monotheism* (New York: Knopf, 1939), 28–40; Tertius Chandler, *Godly Kings and Early Ethics* (Hicksville, N.Y.: Exposition, 1976), 27–28; idem, "Nota: 'Dating Moses's Exodus,' " *BO* 35 (2, Apr–June 1993): 88.

180 Baines and Málek, *Atlas,* 123–125.

181 *ANET* 369–371.

is equally powerful in Egypt, in the desert, and in Palestine . . . " then Moses is certainly a monotheist.[182] In spite of the similarities, however, the antecedents to which Moses appealed (Exod 3:6, 15, etc.) were those of the patriarchal period, and it was presumably from those sources that the distinctive Israelite heritage was most directly derived.[183]

(2) Exodus in the Nineteenth Dynasty and the Thirteenth Century B.C.

402. With such serious studies in the foregoing (§§391ff.) diverging as they do—e.g., Hatshepsut as the pharaoh's daughter who found Moses, or Hatshepsut as the pharaoh of the exodus, Akhenaten as the pharaoh under whom Moses lived, and so on—it is evident that the data available for placing the exodus in the Eighteenth Dynasty and the fifteenth century B.C. are not without ambiguity or contradiction. The probably most serious problem of all in our opinion, however, is the statement of Exod 1:11 that the people of Israel "built for Pharaoh store-cities, Pithom and Raamses [and On, which is Heliopolis, according to the LXX]." The biblical city-name of Raamses must be the Hebrew form of the Egyptian Pi-Ramesse/Pi-Ramses or Per-Ramses, where Egyptian *pi/per* means "house" or "domain." This name is best known as that of the great East Delta residence and capital city constructed (§382) by Ramses II (1279–1212 B.C.). It is of course possible that the name remained in later usage as the common name for the site even when referring to earlier times too. An example of such retrospective usage is in the account of how, long before, Joseph brought his father and brothers to live in Egypt and settled them in the land of Goshen, and this is called "the land of Raamses" (Gen 47:11). Also there was earlier occupation at the sites of Ramses and Pithom (§§409, 412), and building work by Thutmose III at Heliopolis has already been noted (§393). Therefore, Exod 1:11 does not pose an insuperable difficulty in the way of placement of the exodus in the Eighteenth Dynasty and the fifteenth century B.C.; nevertheless, burdensome labor by the Israelites at Ramses probably, first of all, suggests work at the great city when it was being built by Ramses II, and the appropriateness of the exodus date in the Nineteenth Dynasty and the thirteenth century B.C. is therefore now to be considered.

403. To continue for perspective our brief review of Egyptian history, we may glance again at Table 116 and note that in the closing period of the Eighteenth Dynasty Amenhotep IV (1352–1348)/Akhenaten (1348–1338)[184] was followed for short reigns by his close associates Smenkhkare (1338–1336),[185] Tutankhaten/Tutankhamen (1336–1327),[186] and Ay (1327–1323),[187] and for a

---

[182]William F. Albright, *From the Stone Age to Christianity* (Baltimore: Johns Hopkins Press, 1940), 207.

[183]William F. Albright, *The Biblical Period* (Pittsburgh: privately distributed, 1950), 9; reprinted from Louis Finkelstein, ed., *The Jews: Their History, Culture and Religion* (4 vols.; Philadelphia: Jewish Publication Society of America, 1949).

[184]Steffen Wenig, "Amenophis IV," *LÄ* 1: 210–219.

[185]Wolfgang Helck, "Semenchkare," *LÄ* 5: 837–841.

[186]Marianne Eaton-Krauss, "Tutanchamun," *LÄ* 6: 812–816.

[187]Jürgen von Beckerath, "Eje," *LÄ* 1: 1211–1212.

much longer reign by Horemheb (1323–1295).[188] As we learn from the "Restoration Stela" of Tutankhamen and from the stela of Ay where Ay offers flowers to Hathor,[189] and from other monuments, the solar monotheism of Akhenaten was soon left behind by his successors in favor of a return to the old gods and the previously established order, and the city of Akhenaten was abandoned for return to Thebes and Memphis. Most of all the break with Akhenaten's rule was effectuated by Horemheb as he reformed the government and revitalized the military. At this point Manetho's dynastic lists as given by Africanus and Eusebius are in bad order and it has been thought that, in view of his accomplishments, Horemheb should be considered not the last king of the Eighteenth Dynasty as in our Table 116 but as the first king of the Nineteenth Dynasty;[190] nevertheless, the accepted list of the first half-dozen kings of the Nineteenth Dynasty is as shown in our Table 117.

TABLE 117. *Kings of the Nineteenth Dynasty*

	Name	*Dates of Reign*
1.	Ramses I	1295–1294
2.	Seti I	1294–1279
3.	Ramses II	1279–1212
4.	Merneptah	1212–1202
5.	Amenmesse	1202–1199
6.	Seti II	1202–1196

404. To return to Horemheb (§403) and the transition from the Eighteenth to the Nineteenth Dynasty, before he became king Horemheb prepared a tomb for himself at Saqqara near Memphis, and fragments of reliefs from his tomb and from other monuments provide information on his early career. He was a military man, under Tutankhamen was commander-in-chief of the army and in charge of foreign affairs, and under Ay had the titles of King's Deputy in the Whole Land and Royal Scribe. In some of the reliefs from the Saqqara tomb Horemheb acts as King's Deputy (although the reliefs were later altered to make him appear as king) and various groups of Asiatics present themselves before him, some of them refugees, whose town has been laid waste and whose countries are starving, who beg a home in Egypt, as they say, "after the manner of your fathers' fathers since the beginning."[191] In the position of king, Horemheb made a new tomb for himself in the Valley of Kings in Western Thebes,[192] and in his sixteenth regnal year he conducted a major campaign in Western Asia in which he went as far as Carchemish.[193] Under earlier pharaohs Memphis,

---

[188]Jürgen von Beckerath, "Haremheb," *LÄ* 2: 962–964.

[189]Breasted, *Ancient Records* 2:1042–1043.

[190]*Manetho,* trans. Waddell (LCL, 1940), 148–153 and 148–149 n. 1 .

[191]Breasted, *Ancient Records* 3:11.

[192]Erik Hornung and Frank Teichmann, *Das Grab des Haremhab im Tal der Könige* (Bern: Francke, 1971).

[193]Breasted, *Ancient Records* 3: 45–67; Donald B. Redford, "New Light on the Asiatic Campaigning of Horemheb," *BASOR* 211 (1973): 36–49.

Egypt's traditional capital, was base for wars in Western Asia, but already in the Middle Kingdom there was increased interest in the East Delta (§367) and now, under Horemheb, there was even more interest and especially so in the East Delta's principal town of Avaris where the Hyksos had ruled. Avaris was very possibly the place of origin of Horemheb's family,[194] and in Horemheb's extensive building activity from Upper to Lower Egypt he restored the temple of Seth at Avaris,[195] the local god whom the Hyksos had worshiped too (§383).

405. Horemheb had no son, or at least no surviving son, of his own, and before he died he designated a successor who also came from a long line of military men in the East Delta. This person was the son of an officer named Seti ("Seth's man") who had served under Akhenaten. The son was called by the Egyptian name of Peramesse (Pa-Ramses, the Ramses), and he became Ramses I (1295–1294) and the founder of the Ramesside dynasties (Manetho's Nineteenth and Twentieth), but by then was aged and died after a reign of only a year and four months.[196] Already in earlier life Peramesse had a son, born probably about the time of Horemheb's accession to the throne,[197] and the son was named Seti after the grandfather and eventually took the throne as Seti (Sethos) I (1294–1279).[198] As king Seti I campaigned successfully in Palestine and Syria and as far as Qadesh on the Orontes. At home he did large building works, especially at the great religious centers of Thebes, Abydos, and Heliopolis. Memphis was his administrative capital as it had often been from ancient times, and in the East Delta he also planned and began a palace near what is now the village of Qantir,[199] as his summer residence (and perhaps at the same time headquarters for his Asiatic campaigns).[200]

406. Upon the death of Seti I his son, Ramses II, named after the fashion of the family for the grandfather, and still relatively young, acceded to the throne for what became a reign of sixty-six years and two months.[201] For the crucial date of the beginning of the reign of Ramses II, upon which many other dates hinge, three years have been considered, namely, 1304, 1290, and 1279, depending upon how the Sothic date in Papyrus Ebers (a medical papyrus dated in the ninth year of the reign of Amenhotep I [r. 1526–1506], found at Luxor and now in the Leipzig Museum)[202] is interpreted. The year 1304 has been accepted,[203] but is now rejected, leaving the real choice between 1290 and 1279, eleven years apart.[204] The year 1290, with the entire reign 1290–1224, was

---

[194] Alain-Pierre Zivie, " Ramses I," *LÄ* 5:101.
[195] Manfred Bietak, "Ramsesstadt," *LÄ* 5:130.
[196] Zivie, "Ramses I," *LÄ* 5:100–108.
[197] Kitchen, *Pharaoh Triumphant,* 18.
[198] Rainer Stadelmann, "Sethos I," *LÄ* 5: 911–917.
[199] Baines and Málek, *Atlas,* 167, 175–176.
[200] Von Beckerath, *Abriss,* 42.
[201] Marianne Eaton-Krauss, "Ramses II," *LÄ* 5:106–114.
[202] Von Beckerath, *Abriss,* 35.
[203] M. B. Rowton, "Comparative Chronology of the Time of Dynasty XIX," *JNES* 19 (1960):16–22.
[204] K. A. Kitchen, *JEA* 61 (1975): 266, in a highly critical review of J. D. Schmidt, *Ramses II: A Chronological Structure for His Reign* (Near Eastern Studies 3; Baltimore: Johns

formerly preferred,[205] but the year 1279, with the reign 1279–1212, is now preferred,[206] and is now accepted in the present book together with the other dates congruent therewith.

407. In military respect Ramses II fought repeatedly against the Hittites, the climactic battle being against the Hittite king Muwatallish at Qadesh on the Orontes in Ramses II's fifth regnal year (1275/1274), and the ultimate outcome was a treaty of peace with the Hittite king Hattushilish III in Ramses II's twenty-first year of reign (1259/1258), further confirmed by his marriage to the daughter of Hattushilish III in Ramses II's thirty-fourth year of reign (1246/1245).[207] In building work the many and massive monuments of Ramses II are still to be seen in Egypt all the way from Abu Simbel between the First and Second Cataracts of the Nile to the Delta. Of greatest interest for our present consideration is his building of a great new residence city and capital in the East Delta. This city superseded the earlier Avaris of the Hyksos at Tell el-Dab'a (§§382, 385) which, after the expulsion of the Hyksos, had remained a deserted city (Manetho, according to Josephus, 125), and the new city also incorporated and expanded the summer palace of Seti I at Qantir (§405) and reached into the place of the present village of Khata'na as well. The first mention of the city is in a long inscription which Ramses II carved in the temple of his father, Seti I, at Abydos. This tells how, in the first year of his reign (1279/1278) Ramses II visited Thebes and erected a statue of his father there, then went to Abydos where he undertook to complete the temple of Seti I which had been left unfinished. In the account of his sailing down the Nile from Thebes and by a connecting canal to Abydos there is a reference which apparently indicates that he was also going on farther north to the Delta, and it is in this passage that the name of his new city occurs: "[He] began the way, to make the voyage, while the royal barges illuminated the flood, turning downstream to the seat of might, 'Per-Ramses Meri-Amen Great of Victories.' "[208] In this full name of the city, Per-Ramses is the "House" or "Domain" of Ramses, and Beloved-of-Amen and Great-of-Victories are epithets of the king. There is also mention of the city in a record of the treaty of Ramses II with the Hittites which is carved on a wall of the temple at Karnak. Here the arrival of the Hittite messengers who came to negotiate the treaty is introduced by this statement: "On this day, while his majesty was in the town of Per-Ramses Meri-Amen, doing the pleasure of his father Amen-Re; Harakhti; Atum, Lord of the Two Lands, the Heliopolitan;

Hopkins University Press, 1973); Grimal, *Ancient Egypt,* 250.

[205]K. A. Kitchen, *NBD* (1962), 214; Erik Hornung, *Untersuchungen zur Chronologie und Geschichte des Neuen Reiches* (Wiesbaden: O. Harrassowitz, 1964), 108; Redford, *Eighteenth Dynasty,* 208, with correlations with Hittite, Assyrian, and Babylonian records; von Beckerath, *Abriss* (1971), 42; Finegan, *Archaeological History*, 293–295 and Table 31; Baines and Málek, *Atlas* (1980, 1982), 36.

[206]Kitchen, *Pharaoh Triumphant,* 214; Marianne Eaton-Krauss, "Ramses II," *LÄ* 5:108; Grimal, *Ancient Egypt,* 392.

[207]S. Langdon and Alan H. Gardiner, "The Treaty of Alliance between Hattusili, King of the Hittites, and the Pharaoh Ramesses II of Egypt," *JEA* 6 (1920): 175–205. For the regnal years of Ramses II see Kitchen, *Pharaoh Triumphant,* 240–243.

[208]Breasted, *Ancient Records* 3:261.

Amen of Ramses Meri-Amen; Ptah of Ramses Meri-Amen; and [Seth], the Great of Strength, the Son of Nut, according as they give him an eternity of jubilees and an infinity of years of peace, while all lands and all foreign countries are prostrate under his soles forever—there came the Royal Envoy and Deputy. . . ."[209] Here the city is plainly Ramses II's capital and the king is present there when the Hittite delegates come. Also the gods Amen and Ptah are mentioned in the forms in which they are worshiped there, and thus the name of the city occurs three times. Again, on a stela in the first hall of the great temple of Ramses II at Abu Simbel, the god Ptah makes address to the king and refers to the construction of the city: "Thou hast made an august residence, to make strong the boundary of the Two Lands [named]: 'Per-Ramses Meri-Amen Given Life,' that it may flourish on earth like the four pillars of heaven."[210] The famous city was also praised in poetical compositions which are preserved on papyri of the end of the thirteenth century.[211] Papyrus Anastasi II (British Museum 10243) uses Ramses II's epithet "Great of Victories" as a name by itself for the city; locates it broadly as between Djahi, which means the coastal plain of Palestine, and Egypt; describes it as full of provisions in a way that reminds one of the biblical term "store-cities" (Exod 1:1); and engages in a doubtless pardonable exaggeration of its vast extent:

> His majesty—life, prosperity, health!—has built himself a castle, the name of which is "Great of Victories." It is between Djahi and Egypt, and is full of food and provisions. . . . The sun rises in its horizon, and sets within it. All men have left their towns and are settled in its territory.

The text also names four temples in the four quarters of the city—the House of Amen in the west, the House of Seth in the south, that of Astarte in the east (the direction appropriate to her as a Semitic goddess), and that of Buto (cobra goddess and protectress of the northern kingdom) in the north. In Papyrus Anastasi III (B.M. 10246) a scribe tells of reaching Per-Ramses, as he names of the city, and reports that the district is beautiful. He writes of the abundantly productive fields, the lakes abounding with fish and birds, the Shi-Hor ("Waters of Horus") which has salt and natron (probably the otherwise unnamed stretch of water north of the Isthmus of Qantara, connected with Per-Ramses by the Pelusiac arm of the Nile, cf. Josh 13:3 which speaks of the Shi-Hor "which is before Egypt"),[212] and the ships which constantly go out and come back to mooring, to insure unfailing supplies. Then the writer portrays the fortunate inhabitants who feel no lack of anything, and who rejoice when their ruler comes into the city, and he concludes with an apostrophe to the king himself:

> One rejoices to dwell within it, and there is none who says: "Would that" to it. The small in it are like the great. . . . The young men of "Great of Victories" are dressed up every day, with sweet oil upon their heads and newly dressed hair. They stand beside their doors, their hands bowed down with flowers . . . on the day when User-maat-Re Setep-en-Re . . . enters in. . . .

---

[209]Ibid., 371; *ANET* 199.
[210]Breasted, *Ancient Records* 3: 406.
[211]Gardiner in *JEA* 5 (1918): 185–187; *ANET* 470–471.
[212]Manfred Bietak, "Schi–Hor," *LÄ* 5: 623–626.

(So) dwell content of heart and free, without stirring from it, O User-maat-Re Setep-en-Re . . . Ramses Meri-Amen . . . thou god![213]

408. It was stated briefly above (§382) that the site of Ramses II's capital of Per-Ramses and the preceding Hyksos capital of Avaris was earlier thought to be at Tanis largely because of the many Ramesside monuments found there (but actually brought from elsewhere), and this was the opinion of Pierre Montet who excavated at Tanis in 1929–1951.[214] In the meantime, Alan H. Gardiner proposed Pelusium (Tell el-Farama), at the mouth of the ancient Pelusiac branch of the Nile,[215] as the site,[216] later retracted this view in favor of Tanis,[217] and yet again[218] regarded this as uncertain because of the rival claims of the region of the villages of Khata'na and Qantir (12 mi south of Tanis).[219] At Qantir (9 km/5.6 mi north of Faqus) in 1929 Mahmud Hamza, on behalf of the Egyptian Department of Antiquities, found the remains of a large palace of Seti I, Ramses II, and their successors, and of the factory which made the colored glazed tiles and glazed statues with which this palace was adorned. In addition, five inscribed fragments of pottery jars were uncovered which bore the name Per-Ramses.[220] From this evidence Hamza concluded that this was the site of Ramses II's capital, and was supported on this by William C. Hayes of the Metropolitan Museum of Art, New York.[221] Labib Habachi of the Cairo Museum agreed and suggested further that the Hyksos capital of Avaris was probably to the south at the village of Kata'na (6 km/3.75 mi north of Faqus) and at Tell el-Dab'a (7 km/4.4 mi north of Faqus).[222] Writing about the Hyksos in 1966 John Van Seters made a thorough assessment of the evidence and concluded that there is little doubt that Khata'na-Qantir is to be preferred to Tanis as the location of Avaris and Pi-Ramesse.[223] In 1966 the Institute of Egyptology of the University of Vienna started excavations at Tell el-Dab'a and continued until 1969, then resumed the excavations in 1975 under the newly-established Austrian Archaeological Institute in Cairo, and in 1981 the work was still in progress

---

[213]For the five titles or names of Ramses II and for these two as his first name *(praenomen)* and main name *(nomen)* see Hugo Müller, *Die formale Entwicklung der Titular der ägyptischen Könige* (Glückstadt: J. J. Augustin, 1938); Finegan, *Let My People Go,* 24–25; Finegan, *Archaeological History,* 170–180.

[214]Pierre Montet, *Le Drame d'Avaris* (Paris: P. Geuthner, 1941), and other publications by Montet.

[215]Baines and Málek, *Atlas,* 167.

[216]Alan H. Gardiner, *Recueil d'études égyptologiques dédiées à la mémoire de Jean-François Champollion* (Paris: E. Champion, 1922), 215.

[217]Alan H. Gardiner, "Tanis and Pi-Ra'messe: A Retractation," *JEA* 19 (1933): 122–128.

[218]Alan H. Gardiner, *Egypt of the Pharaohs* (London: Weidenfeld & Nicolson, 1968), 258. For Tanis (Montet), Pelusium (Gardiner), and Qantir, see also B. Couroyer, "La résidence Ramesside du Delta et la Ramsès biblique," *RB* 53 (1946): 75–98.

[219]Baines and Málek, *Atlas,* 167.

[220]Mahmud Hamza, *ASAE* 30 (1930): 31–68.

[221]W. C. Hayes, *Glazed Tiles from a Palace of Ramesses II at Kantir* (Metropolitan Museum of Art Papers 3; New York, 1937).

[222]Labib Habachi, *ASAE* 52 (1954): 443–559.

[223]John Van Seters, *The Hyksos: A New Investigation* (New Haven: Yale University Press, 1966), 132–137, 149, and Fig. 21, Map of the region of Tell el-Dab'a and Qantir.

when the director, Manfred Bietak, published a full report as given in 1979 to the British Academy in London.[224]

409. As now understood,[225] the whole district just described (§408) was once a vast town site, with its main focus at Tell el-Dab'a. In earlier time Tell el-Dab'a was occupied already in the First Intermediate Period (2200–2040), and experienced a new foundation in the Middle Kingdom (2040–1674) and the Twelfth Dynasty (1991–1785). In the Fourteenth Dynasty (as we have already learned, §383) a king named Nehesi ruled here briefly—for only a few months according to the Turin King List (8.3)—and had the title "beloved of Seth, lord of Avaris."[226] In the fighting when the Hyksos were driven out of Egypt (§392) Avaris was evidently destroyed, for in Manetho's record of the Eighteenth Dynasty, according to Josephus (Manetho, 125), he calls it a "deserted city." Seth, however, was still a very important god, as is shown by the names of important personages in the late Eighteenth Dynasty (the officer Seti under Akhenaten, the father of Ramses I, §405), in the Nineteenth Dynasty (Seti I, Seti II), and in the early Twentieth Dynasty (Sethnakhte). Also, a new development ensued at Tell el-Dab'a at least from the time of Horemheb (1323–1295), under whom a new temple of Seth was built, and the name of Horemheb has been found on a temple lintel, which tends to confirm Kurt Sethe's interpretation (see our §383 n. 118) of the Stela of the Year 400.[227] Seti I (1294–1279) also did more for the temple of Seth, and the name of Seti I was found frequently in the area. Finally, in the climax of the long development centered on Tell-el-Dab'a it was Seti I's son, Ramses II (1279–1212) who carried out the essential enlargement of the city to make it worthy of his own name, Per-Ramses, Great of Victories.[228] A provisional drawing of the city-plan shows the former town of Avaris to the south with the temple of Seth, the temple of Amen to the west, the temple of Buto to the north, and the temple of Astarte to the east (as described in Papyrus Anastasi II, above §407), while the palace is toward the center and military and port installations are around the periphery.[229] In the conclusion of his report on Avaris and Piramesse (his spelling), Manfred Bietak states that it seems to him certain that Avaris and Piramesse were situated at Tell el-Dab'a and Qantir.[230]

410. Turning to the question of biblical references, there is no doubt that the geographical term "the land of Ramses" in Gen 47:11, the store-city name Raamses in Exod 1:1, and the exodus starting-point name Rameses in Exod

---

[224]Manfred Bietak, *Avaris and Piramesse: Archaeological Exploration in the Eastern Nile Delta* (from the Proceedings of the British Academy, London, vol. 65 [1979]; London: Oxford University Press, 1981); see now Manfred Bietak, *Avaris, the Capital of the Hyksos: Recent Excavations at Tell el-Daba* (London: British Museum Press, 1996).

[225]Rainer Stadelmann, "Auaris," *LÄ* 1: 552–554; Manfred Bietak, *Avaris and Piramesse;* idem, "Tell el-Dab'a," *LÄ* 6: 321–323; idem, "Ramsesstadt," *LÄ* 5: 120–146.

[226]For Seth as "lord of Hat-wa'ret/Avaris" see W. M. Flinders Petrie, *Tanis* (London: Trübner, 1885–1888), *Part I,* Pl. II no. 5; *Part II,* 16, no. 5; Stadelmann, *LÄ* 1: 553.

[227]Bietak, *LÄ* 5: 129–130.

[228]Marianne Eaton-Krauss, "Ramses II," *LÄ* 5: 108–114.

[229]Bietak, "Ramsesstadt," *LÄ* 5: 137–138; Kitchen, *Pharaoh Triumphant,* 123 illus. 42.

[230]Bietak, *Avaris and Piramesse,* 283.

12:37; Num 33:3, 5 all embody the name of Ramses II. While retrospective use of the name for an earlier time is admittedly possible (§402), the more immediate impression which is given by the passages which name the city where the Israelites labored and from which they departed, is that that city was the city built by Pharaoh Ramses (II), and if the date which this implies is coherent with other evidence bearing on the time of the Israelite exodus from Egypt and entrance into Canaan, this conclusion may be accepted as the more likely, and it is so accepted in the present book. Pithom and Heliopolis must also be considered.

411. As to Pithom (Exod 1:11), the name is almost certainly a writing in Hebrew of the Egyptian name Per-Tum, meaning the House or Domain of Atum, referring to the very important creator god of that time, a form of the sun god (Re-Atum), in the Heliopolitan theology.[231] Likewise the name of the Wadi Tumilat preserves in Arabic the name of the same god attached to this valley which provides a route from the eastern Delta out to Lake Timsah and beyond (§§368, 385). The valley begins about 5 mi east of Saft el-Hinna (east of Zaqaziq), which was the ancient Per-Sopdu, "the Domain of Sopd," the Egyptian god who was "the lord of the East."[232] In the Second Intermediate Period (1674–1553) and the Hyksos Age camp sites and burial grounds show that the valley was a dwelling area of Syro-Palestinian semi-nomads.[233] In the New Kingdom (1552–1069) the name Tjeku (Egyptian *T-k-w*) is found basically meaning Wadi Tumilat and perhaps referring especially to the eastern part of the valley (from Ras el-Wadi near Tell er-Retabeh eastward).[234] The name Tjeku is of uncertain derivation, but comparison has been suggested with an African word *thukka,* which means "pasture," so that the name correctly describes the character of the wadi as a "pastureland."[235] In this time the god Atum is regularly titled "lord of Tjeku,"[236] and in Tjeku (Wadi Tumilat) there was a fortress to guard this eastern approach to Lower Egypt (perhaps where Sinuhe slipped past the "Wall of the Ruler," §368), and through Ramesside times the name of the fortress incorporated the name of whoever was then the reigning pharaoh.[237] So in Papyrus Anastasi 6 (B. M. 10245, late Nineteenth Dynasty) a frontier official reports:

> [We] have finished letting the Bedouin tribes of Edom pass the Fortress of Merneptah . . . which is (in) Tjeku, to the pools of Per-Atum [of] Mer[ne]ptah . . . which are (in) Tjeku, to keep them alive and to keep their cattle alive. . . . [238]

It is obvious that Egypt is here in its traditional role of a place of refuge for people and animals from regions to the northeast, hard-pressed by famine in their homelands, and Wadi Tumilat is the route of ingress to Lower Egypt.

---

[231]László Kakósy, "Atum," *LÄ* 1: 550–552; Finegan, *Myth and Mystery,* 51–52.

[232]Edouard Naville, *The Shrine of Saft el Henneh and the Land of Goshen* (London: Trübner, 1887), 6ff.

[233]Hans Goedicke, "Wadi Tumilat," *LÄ* 6:1124–1126.

[234]Hans Goedicke, "Tjeku," *LÄ* 6: 609–610.

[235]Edouard Naville, *The Store-City of Pithom and the Route of the Exodus* (London: Trübner, 1888), 7; idem, *JEA* 10 (1924): 34.

[236]Carl Küthmann, *Die Ostgrenze Ägyptens* (Leipzig: W. Druglin, 1911): 30.

[237]Donald B. Redford, "Pithom," *LÄ* 4: 1055.

[238]Breasted, *Ancient Records* 3:272–273; *ANET* 259.

412. In the eastern half of Wadi Tumilat there are two main archaeological sites, each of which has, upon occasion, been considered the probable location of biblical Pithom: 21 mi in from Saft el-Hinna is Tell er-Retabeh, 8.5 mi farther east is Tell el-Maskhuta, and from there it is another 9.5 mi on to the eastern end of the wadi and Lake Timsah.[239] It is Tell er-Retabeh that is now the more likely site for biblical Pithom.[240] In a brief exploration of Tell er-Retabeh reported by W. M. Flinders Petrie in 1906,[241] stone vases of the Old Kingdom and a weight and scarabs of the Ninth to Twelfth Dynasties were found, which led Petrie to call this the oldest site known east of Bubastis. There were extensive fortifications, the earliest of which were of gray brick and black brick; a child's burial beside the wall appeared to be a foundation sacrifice which suggested Asian rather than Egyptian custom. Findings included a large house containing scarabs of the Eighteenth Dynasty, a temple of Ramses II of the Nineteenth Dynasty, and a brick wall built by Ramses III of the Twentieth Dynasty. The temple of Ramses II had been brilliantly painted in red, blue, and yellow, and was of special interest for a relief sculptured on the front which shows Ramses II smiting an Asiatic in the presence of a god who is identified in the accompanying label as "Tum, Lord of Tju."[242] Tum is of course the god Atum, and Tju should undoubtedly be Tjeku, a name found on other of the temple fragments too.[243] There were also two statues carved in a block of red granite, believed to be Ramses II and Atum, with an accompanying inscription speaking of the work of Ramses II in "building cities upon which his name is to eternity."[244] The extensive fortifications at Tell er-Retabeh suggest that at least in Ramesside times this was primarily a fortress city guarding the eastern entrance to the Egyptian Delta through Wadi Tumilat. Presumably, therefore, it may be identified with the Fortress of Merneptah named in the frontier official's report (§411), and the pools of Per-Atum of Merneptah were probably nearby. Prior to Merneptah the fortress and pools were presumably called by the name of Merneptah's father, Ramses II. The prominence of Atum and the work of Ramses II at this place are well in accord with the identification of Tell er-Retabeh as the ancient Per-Atum, the biblical Pithom.

413. The second main archaeological site in Wadi Tumilat, Tell el-Maskhuta, was excavated by Edouard Naville in 1883.[245] As recorded by Naville,[246] the hieroglyphic inscriptions found here make frequent reference to Atum and to Tjeku. The following are a few examples: A fragment which preserves part of the name of Ramses II contains also the words "the lord of Tjeku." A statue of around the Twenty-second Dynasty mentions "all the priests who go into the temple of Tum, the great and living god in the midst of Tjeku." A Saite fragment names an "official of the temple of Tum of Tjeku." A stela of Ptolemy II

---

[239]Baines and Málek, *Atlas,* 167.

[240]Donald B. Redford, "Pithom," *LÄ* 4: 1054–1058.

[241]W. M. Flinders Petrie, *Hyksos and Israelite Cities* (London: School of Archaeology, 1906), 28–34.

[242]Ibid., 29, 31, and Pls. XXIX, XXX.

[243]Alan H. Gardiner, "The Delta Residence of the Ramessides," *JEA* 5 (1918): 266.

[244]Petrie, *Hyksos and Israelite Cities,* 31 and Pl. XXXII.

[245]Naville, *Store-City of Pithom.*

[246]Ibid., esp. 15–21 and Pl. XI.

Philadelphus was erected "in front of Tum, the great living god of Tjeku," and describes the return of the gods from Persia, saying that "the gods of Pithom and Theku came to rest there."[247] From these quotations it may be seen that Tell el-Maskhuta was primarily centered upon a temple of Atum, and it is not surprising that Naville and not a few others have wished to identify Tell el-Maskhuta with Pithom.[248] Now, however, new excavation of Tell el-Maskhuta was inaugurated in 1978 by the Wadi Tumilat Project under the leadership of John S. Holladay of the University of Toronto, and it has been established that the foundation of Tell el-Maskhuta does not antedate the 7th century B.C. when Tell el-Maskhuta replaced declining Tell er-Retabeh.[249] It is therefore most probable that it is not Tell el-Maskhuta but Tell er-Retabeh that is to be identified with the biblical Pithom.[250]

414. With the Israelites settled in the land of Goshen (Wadi Tumilat, §385) they were conveniently available for Ramses II to press them into labor in his building works at Raamses (Per-Ramses in the region of Tell el-Dab'a, §§408–409) and Pithom (Per-Atum at Tell er-Retabeh, §412). As for Heliopolis (Exod 1:11 LXX), it was farther away, but still in Lower Egypt (at the southeastern apex of the Delta at Tell Hisn, now under the urban expansion of modern Cairo) and surely not too far away for Ramses II to take Israelite laborers there too, if he wished. Heliopolis (Egyptian On) was the ancient city of the sun god Re,[251] and Atum as a form of the sun god, whom we have just met (§413) as the "lord of Tjeku [Wadi Tumilat]," was at home in Heliopolis where he was the "lord of Heliopolis"[252] and was the first of the nine gods who comprised "the Great Ennead which is in Heliopolis."[253] At Heliopolis many Egyptian kings, including Thutmose III (§393) and Ramses II, built temples whether as buildings in their own right or as parts of the one great temple of Re, and erected obelisks.[254] Like the names of others, the name of Ramses II is found on granite blocks of the ruined temple(s); in one carving he is offering a libation to Atum.[255] Since Ramses II built at Per-Ramses (Raamses), Per-Atum (Pithom), and Heliopolis, there is no apparent contradiction with the statement of Exod 1:11 that the Israelites were constrained to labor at all three places and no intrinsic difficulty with the supposition that it was under Ramses II that this and the ensuing exodus occurred. It remains to note the imediately following events and to ask if they are congruent with the same supposition.

415. As named and pictured on his monuments Ramses II had at least seventy-nine sons and fifty-nine daughters and of these at the time of his death

---

[247]Ibid., 15–21.

[248]Baines and Málek, *Atlas,* 167, 177.

[249]Burton MacDonald, "Excavations at Tell el-Maskhuta," *BA* 43 (1980): 49–58, with summary by John S. Holladay on 51.

[250]Donald B. Redford, "Pithom," *LÄ* 4:1054–1058.

[251]László Kakósy, "Heliopolis," *LÄ* 2: 1111–1113.

[252]Breasted, *Ancient Records* 3:100.

[253]*ANET* 3.

[254]Baines and Málek, *Atlas,* 135, 173–174.

[255]Karl Baedeker, *Ägypten und der Sudan* (8th ed.; Leipzig: Karl Baedeker, 1928), 124.

the oldest surviving son and the one to inherit the throne was the thirteenth, named Merneptah. He was probably of considerable age at accession, and his highest attested date is his regnal year 10, so he may have had a reign as short as nine years and six months (1212–1202 B.C.).[256] In Western Thebes Merneptah demolished the funerary temple of Amenhotep III to build his own, and in the ruins of Merneptah's temple Flinders Petrie found in 1896 a stela which Merneptah had appropriated from Amenhotep III and carved on the reverse side a record of his own reportedly successful military engagements. The inscription on the stela, now in the Cairo Museum, is dated in Merneptah's year 5. The text is poetic and mainly about a war in this year 5 in which Merneptah repulsed an invasion of Egypt by the Libyans, then a final passage lists other defeated foreigners as well as the Libyans and reads as follows:

> The princes are prostrate, saying: "Mercy!"
> Not one raises his head among the Nine Bows.
> Desolation is for Tehenu, Hatti is pacified;
> Plundered is the Canaan with every evil;
> Carried off is Ashkelon; seized upon is Gezer;
> Yanoam is made as that which does not exist;
> Israel is laid waste, his seed is not;
> Hurru is become a widow for Egypt.
> All lands together, they are pacified;
> Everyone who was restless, he has been bound
> by the King of Upper and Lower Egypt, Merneptah, given life like Re every day.[257]

In elucidation of the allusions and information, we note that the salutation translated "Mercy" is the Canaanite word *shalam* meaning "Peace!" (Hebrew *shalom*); the Nine Bows is a traditional term used inclusively for the enemies of Egypt on its borders; Tehenu is a name for Libya; Hatti is the land of the Hittites, with whom the peace made by Ramses II still prevailed (§407). In Canaan are four names: Ashkelon (on the Palestinian coast between Joppa [Jaffa] and Gaza, Judg 14:19, etc.); Gezer (on the road from Joppa to Jerusalem, Josh 10:33, etc.); Yanoam (a town probably in northern Palestine, but location debatable[258]); and Israel. Israel is in parallel with Hurru, the land of the Hurrians (biblical Horites) which, before the Hittite conquest, included Syria, here Hurru is essentially equivalent to Palestine,[259] so Israel is in Canaan/Palestine. The first three names (Ashkelon, Gezer, Yanoam) are marked with the Egyptian determinative sign usual to designate a city-state. In contrast with these three Canaanite city-states so indicated, Israel is marked with the determinative for a people without a city-state, thus they were a known people in Canaan but were not yet organized in cities, were perhaps yet only tribes occupying the highlands.[260] This is the only known occurrence of the name of Israel in Egyptian records.[261]

---

[256]Rolf Krauss, "Merneptah," *LÄ* 4: 71–76.
[257]*ANET* 378; Breasted, *Ancient Records* 3:617; illustrations *ANEP* nos. 342–343.
[258]Raphael Giveon, "Januammu," *LÄ* 3: 244–245.
[259]W. F. Albright, *BASOR* 74 (Apr 1939): 21–22 and n. 42.
[260]Von Beckerath, *Tanis und Theben,* 67.

416. As to the date of year 5 on the stela of Merneptah, the king's father, Ramses II, died after 66 years and 2 months as sole pharaoh, probably in August of 1213 B.C. In the New Kingdom regnal years were reckoned factually, i.e., each regnal year began on the actual accession day (§150), therefore Merneptah's first regnal year can be shown as 1213/1212.[262] Beginning in August (or September) 1213, the larger part of Merneptah's first regnal year was in 1212. Accordingly, we may follow the usage which lists his entire reign as 1212–1202 (Table 117) and make his year 5 equivalent to 1208 (Table 118).[263]

TABLE 118. *The First Five Years of the Reign of Merneptah*

1.	1212
2.	1211
3.	1210
4.	1209
5.	1208

If the date of Merneptah's year 5 on his stela is equivalent to 1208 B.C., his Libyan war, which is the main subject of the stela, was probably in the summer of that year.[264] The king's campaign in "the Canaan," however, was probably before the Libyan war, therefore not later than his fourth year; likewise it was hardly as early as his first year of reign, therefore was probably between his second year (1211) and fourth year (1209),[265] let us say in a round figure in 1210 B.C.

417. On account of the poetic nature of the description of Merneptah's campaign in Canaan (§415) and for other reasons it has in the past been questioned whether such a military action in Canaan actually took place, but other evidence including an Egyptian inscription which names the king "the one who reduced Gezer"[266] confirms the fact and there is now no reason to doubt the Palestinian campaign.[267] Furthermore, Merneptah's campaign is now believed to be illustrated in relief carvings in the great temple of Amen-Re in Karnak. Adjoining the Hypostyle Hall there is a wall which was erected by Ramses II with an inscription containing the peace treaty he made with the Hittites (§407). On either side of this text are two carved reliefs of battle scenes, and these have naturally been supposed to be of battles of Ramses II.[268] New

---

[261]Jürgen Ebach, "Israel, Israelstele," *LÄ* 3: 205.

[262]Kitchen, *Pharaoh Triumphant,* 207, 215, 239, gives Aug 1213 for Ramses II's last illness and death, 1213–1204 for Merneptah's reign, and 1212 for Merneptah's year 2 and so on, which equates Merneptah's year 5 with 1209.

[263]So Grimal, *Ancient Egypt,* 393; Frank J. Yurco, "3,200-year-Old Picture of Israelites Found in Egypt," *BAR* 16 (5, Sept/Oct 1990): 24.

[264]Kitchen, *Pharaoh Triumphant,* 215, gives the summertime but puts it in the year 1209.

[265]Yurco, *BAR* 16 (5, Sept/Oct 1990): 34.

[266]Breasted, *Ancient Records* 3:606; *ASAE* 58 (1964): 273ff.; Roland de Vaux, *The Early History of Israel* (Philadelphia: Westminster, 1978), 490.

[267]Krauss, *LÄ* 4: 75.

study, however, has found that the cartouches which contain the name of the pharaoh originally associated with these four battle scenes give the name of Merneptah, while Merneptah's name was partially erased and replaced by the name of his successor, Amenmesse, and that cartouche, in turn, was usurped by the next pharaoh, Seti II. With this discovery the battle scenes were recognized as corresponding with Merneptah's battles with Ashkelon, Gezer, Yanoam, and Israel, and therewith as containing 3,200-year-old pictures of Israel in Canaan.[269]

418. According to the foregoing (§§415–416), Merneptah was in Canaan in 1210 B.C. and there met the not-yet-settled-down people of Israel. Prior to that Israel was in the wilderness for forty years (Exod 16:35; Num 14:33–34; 32:13; Deut 1:3; Acts 7:36), a number which need not be an imaginary round number, for it is made up of several dated periods (e.g., Exod 16:1; 19:1; 40:2; Num 1:1; 9:1; 20:1) plus thirty-eight years of wandering after leaving Kadesh-barnea (Deut 2:14), a total of forty years all together.[270] Accordingly, the exodus may be placed in about 1250 (1,210 + 40 = 1,250). If the exodus was in 1250, it was in the thirtieth year (1250/1249) of Ramses II.[271] Recalling the chronological points in the life of Moses (§394) and taking the biblical figures as they stand, if the exodus was in 1250 and if Moses was eighty years old when he and Aaron spoke to Pharaoh (Exod 7:7) and the exodus ensued, Moses was born in 1330 (1,250 + 80 = 1,330) and the king at that time was Tutankhaten/Tutankhamen (1336–1327); at the age of forty Moses fled to Midian (Acts 7:23), so this was in 1290 (1,330 – 40 = 1,290) and the king from whom he fled was Seti I (1294–1279); when forty years of Moses' exile had passed (Acts 7:30) it was 1250 (1,290 – 40 = 1,250), the former king of Egypt had died (Exod 2:23), it was in the reign of Ramses II (1279–1212), and the exodus took place; forty years thereafter spent in the wilderness extended to 1210 (1,250 – 40 = 1,210) and Moses died on the edge of Canaan in 1210 at the age of a hundred and twenty years (1,330 – 120 = 1,210).

419. In terms of archaeological periods, if the exodus was in 1250 B.C. and Israel was in Canaan in 1210, this was at the very end of the Late Bronze Age (around 1200) and almost at the beginning of Iron Age I (1200–1000). According to a number of reports of archaeological exploration and excavation, the findings are in harmony with such a time. Exploration in Jordan has been reported as indicating that an Early Bronze Age civilization disappeared in that region about 1900 B.C., then was replaced by the civilization of the Edomites, Moabites, and others only about the beginning of the thirteenth century; hence, only then would the king of Edom have been in strong position to refuse passage to Moses and make necessary the hard passage of the Israelites out around the

---

[268]Donald B. Redford, "The Ashkelon Relief at Karnak and the Israel Stele," *IEJ* 36 (1986): 188–200.

[269]Yurco, *BAR* 16 (5, Sept/Oct 1990): 20–38.

[270]Kitchen, *NBD* 215; idem, *Ancient Orient,* 60–61.

[271]For a year-by-year outline of the reign of Ramses II see Kitchen, *Pharaoh Triumphant,* 240–243; here the exodus is placed in the seventeenth year (1263/1262) of the king, or slightly later.

land of Edom (Num 20:16; 21:4).[272] Likewise excavation reports about a number of Canaanite cities said in the books of Joshua and Judges to have been taken by the Israelites—Debir, Lachish, Bethel, Hazor—give evidence of destruction in the second half of the thirteenth century, at which time the destruction could have been wrought by the recently come Israelites.[273] Likewise the settlement of the early Israelites themselves in the central hill country of Canaan is generally associated with the discovery there of many examples of a typical four-room house, often called the "Israelite-type house," dating in Iron Age I (1200–1000 B.C.). Interestingly enough, Manfred Bietak has noted in the report of excavation at Thebes in the 1930s by the Oriental Institute of the University of Chicago the very similar plan of a four-room house which is completely different from that of adjacent Egyptian houses and which dates sometime between the middle of the twelfth century and the first part of the eleventh century B.C., in the reigns between Ramses IV and Ramses XI, and Bietak supposes some connection of this house of this date with early Israelite settlers of this time in Canaan.[274] In terms of historical relationships, the dates of 1250 B.C. for the exodus and 1210 B.C. for the entry of Israel into Canaan are therefore well supported.

4. The Kings of Judah and Israel

LITERATURE: Joachim **Begrich**, *Die Chronologie der Könige von Israel und Juda und die Quellen des Rahmens der Königsbücher* (Tübingen: Mohr, 1929); Edwin R. **Thiele**, "The Chronology of the Kings of Judah and Israel," *JNES* 3 (1944):137–186; idem, *The Mysterious Numbers of the Hebrew Kings* (Chicago: University of Chicago Press, 1951); idem, "A Comparison of the Chronological Data of Israel and Judah," *VT* 4 (1954): 187–191; idem, *Mysterious Numbers* (2d ed.; Grand Rapids: Eerdmans, 1965); idem, *A Chronology of the Hebrew Kings* (Grand Rapids: Zondervan, 1977); idem, *Mysterious Numbers* (3d ed.; Grand Rapids: Zondervan, 1983); W. F. **Albright**, "The Chronology of the Divided Monarchy of Israel," in *BASOR* 100 (Dec 1945): 16–22; M. B. **Rowton**, "The Date of the Founding of Solomon's Temple," in *BASOR* 119 (Oct 1950): 20–22; W. F. **Albright**, "Alternative Chronology" (review of Thiele, *Mysterious Numbers*), *Interpretation* 6 (1952): 101–103; John L. **McKenzie**, Review of Thiele, *Mysterious Numbers, CBQ* 14 (1952): 300; J. **Liver**, "The Chronology of Tyre at the Beginning of the First Millennium B.C.," in *IEJ* 3 (1953): 113–122; Hayim **Tadmor**, "The Campaigns of Sargon II of Assur: A Chronological-Historical Study," in *JCS* 12 (1958): 22–40, 77–100; William W. **Hallo**, "From Qarqar to Carchemish: Assyria and Israel in the Light of New Discoveries," in *BA* 23 (1960): 34–61; Walter R. **Witfall**, Review of Thiele, *Chronology*, *JBL* 98 (Mar 1979): 118–119; Leslie **McFall**, "A Translation Guide to the Chronological Data in Kings and Chronicles," *BSac* 148 (589, Jan–Mar 1991): 3–45; Peter **James**, et al., *Centuries of Darkness* (New Brunswick: Rutgers University Press, 1993).

---

[272]Nelson Glueck, *The Other Side of Jordan* (New Haven: American Schools of Oriental Research, 1940): 125–147; Kitchen, *NBD* 215; idem, *Ancient Orient,* 61–62.

[273]Kitchen, *NBD* 215; idem, *Ancient Orient,* 62–69; Finegan, *Light from the Ancient Past,* 160–166.

[274]Hershel Shanks, "An Ancient Israelite House in Egypt?" *BAR* 19 (4, July/Aug 1993): 44–45, citing Manfred Bietak, "An Iron Age Four-Room House in Ramesside Egypt," *Eretz-Israel* 23 (1992): 10–12.

420. The biblical records of the reigns of the kings of Judah and Israel provide more detailed chronological information than is available for earlier biblical records. In attempting to understand the data found here it is essential to keep in mind many of the fundamental principles of time reckoning in the ancient world already discussed (esp. §163), in particular the differences of the Jewish calendar year beginning on Tishri 1 in the fall or on Nisan 1 in the spring (§170 and Tables 38, 39) and the distinctions between factual-year, accession-year, and non-accession-year dating. The relationship of the Hebrew (MT) to the Greek (LXX) texts also comes into consideration, and in addition translations into English vary. Amidst the complexities opinions have varied, and it is not easy to find correct solutions. At an earlier time the work on the chronology of the kings of Israel and Judah by Joachim Begrich (see LITERATURE) was regarded as complex but the most successful to that point, and Edwin R. Thiele's system was considered to be too elaborate, by W. F. Albright.[427] Nevertheless Thiele's system has since been increasingly accepted as the basic work on the subject,[428] his vindication of the Masoretic text (MT) has been widely influential,[429] and his tabulation of dates is often set forth as it is, or with minor adjustments.[430] Along this line, Leslie McFall has made a fresh presentation of Thiele's work together with modifications by McFall himself as well as notes on the proper translation of relevant texts in the books of Kings, Chronicles, and Jeremiah, and the present book accepts the Thiele/McFall system.

421. On the fundamental principles (§420) Thiele establishes the following:[431] (1) As to the reckoning of the regnal year: From 1 Kgs 6:1, 37, 38 it can be seen that in the reign of Solomon the regnal year was reckoned from Tishri to Tishri, and the successors of Solomon in the southern kingdom employed the same method to the end of the kingdom, as may be seen from 2 Kgs 22:3 and 23:23.[432] Again when Neh 1:1 and 2:1 refer to the month of Chislev and the following Nisan, both in the twentieth year of Artaxerxes, it seems plain that Nehemiah is using a year beginning in Tishri, even though he is referring to a Persian king.[433] Like Ezra-Nehemiah, Daniel also uses Tishri-to-Tishri years (Dan 1:1). With regard to the regnal year in the northern kingdom of Israel, Thiele observes that Jeroboam was a political refugee in Egypt for a time during the reign of Solomon (1 Kgs 11:40), and Egypt's "wandering" year began at that time in the middle of April, so when Jeroboam returned to become the first king of Israel (1 Kgs 12:2, 20) he would naturally be inclined to use a year beginning in the spring as in both Egypt and Mesopotamia, rather than in the fall as in the rival kingdom of Judah, so the Nisan to Nisan regnal year became the continuing

---

[427]W. F. Albright, *BASOR* 100 (Dec 1945): 17–18.

[428]See reviews in the LITERATURE by McKenzie and Witfall.

[429]McKenzie, "Review," *CBQ* 14 (1952): 300.

[430]James, *Centuries of Darkness,* ch. 8 by Peter James, Nikos Kokkinos, and John Frankish; see 166–167 and Table 8:1.

[431]Thiele, *Mysterious Numbers* (1965), 16ff.

[432]From the same verses Julian Morgenstern deduces a regnal year beginning with Nisan 1 (*Occident and Orient: Gaster Anniversary Volume,* 446).

[433]On this point Morgenstern agrees (*Occident and Orient,* 441) but Hayim Tadmor (*JNES* 15 [1956]: 227 n. 10) thinks that Nehemiah simply carried over "the twentieth year" by mistake when the month of Nisan was actually the beginning of the twenty-first year or, alternatively, that the text should read, "the twenty-fifth year," as in Josephus (*Ant.* 11.168).

usage in Israel.[434] Nisan years are also employed in Jeremiah, Ezekiel, Haggai, and Zechariah for the Hebrew kings and likewise for the rulers of Babylon and Persia.[435] While it is a common manner of speech to refer to a Tishri year or a Tishri-to-Tishri year (and to a Nisan year or a Nisan-to-Nisan year), it is obvious that such a year would be more exactly described as a year running from the first day of Tishri to the last day of Elul (or from the first day of Nisan to the last day of Adar; §170 and Tables 38, 39). It is obvious too that with the two systems of regnal years, one beginning in the fall and one beginning in the spring, one will overlap the other, but which is the earlier will have to be determined in the given case. Likewise a full year beginning in the fall or a full year beginning in the spring overlaps parts of two of our calendar years, and the only accurate designation in our calendar of the year in question is to identify its exact opening and closing dates in our calendar. In a less precise designation, a dual symbol may be used, such as 931/930, and more simply still this may be written as 930 (as Thiele usually does), although as he says 931 would be as good or better (cf. §424 n. 295).[436] It is also to be noted that in the Hebrew Scriptures the months of the year are always numbered from Nisan, regardless of whether the reckoning of the year is from the spring or the fall.[437] (2) As to how the years of reign are counted: In the factual-year system the first year of reign begins on the day of the king's accession to the throne, the second year begins exactly a year later, and so on. In the non-accession-year system the year in which the ruler comes to the throne is counted as his first year regardless of how many days or months remain in that year, and his second year begins with the first new year's day (Tishri 1 or Nisan 1) after his accession; this system is also called "antedating," a confusing term which is not employed in the present book. In the accession-year system the year in which the king comes to the throne is called his accession year and for the purpose of counting his years of reign, his first official year is that which begins with the new year's day after his accession; this system is also called "postdating," a confusing term avoided in the present book.[438] In Hebrew the word ראש *(rosh)* means "head" or "front" and in relation to time it and the related noun ראשית *(reshit)* and adjective ראשני *(roshoni)* mean "beginning" or "first." The phrase בראשית מלכות *(bereshit malkut)* occurs in Jer 26:1 in relation to Jehoiakim and in Jer 27:1; 28:1; and 49:34 in relation to Zedekiah. The phrase is commonly translated "in the beginning of the reign of . . . " (RSV) and is doubtless to be recognized as the Hebrew equivalent of the Babylonian *resh sharruti* (§160) and the normal designation of an accession year. Related but variant forms are found in Jer 25:1 and in 2 Kgs 25:27 = Jer 52:31 and will require special notice later to determine, if possible, whether they mean "beginning" and refer to an accession year (§434), or mean "first" and refer to an official first year of reign. According to Thiele, Judah followed the accession-year system from Rehoboam to Jehoshaphat inclusive, the non-accession-year system from Jehoram to Joash, and the accession-year system again from Amaziah to

---

[434]Thiele, *Mysterious Numbers* (1965), 28–30, 166.

[435]Thiele, *Chronology,* 68 n. 3.

[436]Ibid., 15.

[437]Thiele, *Mysterious Numbers* (1965), 28, and see n. 11 for the references from which this fact is known.

[438]Thiele, *Chronology,* 87–88.

Zedekiah; and Israel followed the non-accession-year system from Jeroboam I to Jehoahaz, and the accession-year system from Jehoash to Hoshea.[439] If this is correct, then in the later period of the two monarchies both were using the accession-year system, and at the same time the biblical writers would presumably also use the accession-year system in their references to Babylonian or Persian kings. Thiele also recognizes coregencies and overlapping reigns of Hebrew kings and the occurrence of what he calls "dual dating," defined as counting both years of overlap and years of sole reign, but giving the year of accession as the year when the overlap ends and the sole reign begins.[440] (3) As to the relative priority of the Hebrew text (MT) and the Greek text (LXX): Thiele finds that the Greek manifests confusion against the consistency of the Hebrew pattern, and this shows clearly that the Hebrew preceded the Greek.[441]

422. Within even the earlier part of the period of the Hebrew kings, certain synchronisms with Middle Eastern chronology otherwise are available.[442] On any reckoning, Ahab king of Israel, must have been on the throne about the middle of the ninth century B.C. In the Monolith Inscription[443] of Shalmaneser III (858–824 B.C.) his victory over a Syrian coalition of twelve kings at Qarqar on the Orontes River is recorded and "Ahab, the Israelite" is named among the allied leaders. The battle is placed in the sixth year of the Assyrian king and it is stated that he left Nineveh on the fourteenth day of Aiaru (Apr/May) and crossed the Euphrates at its (spring) flood, hence the event at Qarqar is probably to be placed in the summer of 853 B.C. This provides independent confirmation of the rule of Ahab at this time.[444]

423. On the Black Obelisk of Shalmaneser III the Assyrian king records the taking of tribute from Jehu king of Israel,[445] and in a fragment of his annals dates this event in the eighteenth year of his reign, 841 B.C.[446] Between Ahab who fought Shalmaneser III at Qarqar in 853 (§305) and Jehu who paid tribute to him in 841, the rulers of Israel were Ahaziah and Joram who are credited with reigns of two years and twelve years respectively in 1 Kgs 22:51 and 2 Kgs 3:1. By the non-accession-year system these two reigns actually total twelve years, which is the time between Qarqar and the paying of tribute by Jehu. Therefore, the death of Ahab at Ramoth-gilead (1 Kgs 22:3, 35) must have taken place in 853 B.C. soon after Qarqar, and the accession of Jehu have been in 841 B.C.[447]

424. Counting backward from the battle of Qarqar and the death of Ahab (§423), if the reigns of the kings of Israel are reckoned according to the non-accession-year system, and those of the kings of Judah according to the accession-year system, the period of the division of the kingdom of Rehoboam

---

[439]Ibid., 17–19.
[440]Ibid., 33ff., 88.
[441]Ibid., 62–63.
[442]McFall, "Translation Guide," 9–10.
[443]Luckenbill, *Ancient Records* 1: 610–611; *ANET* 278–279; *ANEA* 188.
[444]Thiele, *Mysterious Numbers* (1983), 72–76.
[445]Luckenbill, *Ancient Records* 1:590; *ANET* 281; *ANEA* 192.
[446]Luckenbill, *Ancient Records* 1:672; *ANET* 280; *ANEA* 192.
[447]Thiele, *Mysterious Numbers* (1983), 76; McFall, "Translation Guide," 9, 17 no. 16.

and Jeroboam totals seventy-eight years and leads to placing the disruption in 931/930. If the first year of Rehoboam and Jeroboam I in the separated kingdoms was 931/930, then Solomon's fortieth and last year was 932/931, his first year was 971/970 and his fourth year in which the temple was founded was 968/967.[448] If Solomon's first year of reign was 971/970 then the death of David, his predecessor, can be put in 972/971. If David was then seventy years old, he was born in 1042/1041, and his forty-year reign (7 years in Hebron, 33 years in Jerusalem, 1 Kgs 2:11) began in 1012/1011. Prior to David, the defective text of 1 Sam 13:1 leaves us to say only that Saul reigned in the early tenth century B.C. (Table 119). Returning to Solomon, his fourth year of reign was from Tishri (Sept/Oct) 968 to the end of Elul (Aug/Sept) 967, and according to 1 Kgs 6:1, 37 it was in this year that Solomon laid the foundation of the house of the Lord in the month of Ziv, this month being the second month (equivalent therefore to the later Iyyar, Apr/May, our Tables 12, 13), and this point of time was in the 480th year after the people of Israel came out of Egypt. Since the Israelites left Egypt in the first month of the year (Exod 12:1), in the month of Abib (Exod 23:15, the equivalent of the later Nisan, Mar/Apr), the date here indicated for the exodus is Nisan (Mar/Apr) 1446 B.C.[449]

425. In one of his inscriptions Tiglath-pileser III (744–727 B.C.) mentions receiving tribute from a number of kings including Azariah of Judah.[450] The reference belongs to the third year of the reign of Tiglath-pileser; since he departed from the traditional system of counting regnal years and included his accession year (745 B.C.) in the numbering, his third year was 743 B.C.[451] In another text, dated according to the eponym lists in 732 B.C., he speaks

---

[448]Thiele, *JNES* 3 (1944): 147, 184; *VT* 4 (1954): 187–191; Thiele, *Mysterious Numbers* (1965), 52, stating the date as 931; Thiele, *Chronology,* 31–32, stating the date as 931/930; Thiele, *Mysterious Numbers* (1983), stating the date as 930 for simplicity but noting that 931 might have been equally appropriate or even more accurate than 930, depending on the season of the year when Jeroboam's rebellion took place. Begrich (*Chronologie der Könige,* 155) places the division of the kingdom in 926 B.C. Albright (in *BASOR* 100 [Dec 1945]:16–22; and in *Interpretation* 6 [1952]:101–103) puts it in 922 B.C. The latter date, with a correlative of 959 B.C. for the founding of Solomon's temple, is supported by M. B. Rowton (in *BASOR* 119 [Oct. 1950]: 20–22) from evidence in the king list of Tyre as cited by Josephus from Menander of Ephesus. Dealing with the same materials, however, Liver (in *IEJ* 3 [1953], 113–122) accepts the date of 825 B.C. for the foundation of Carthage as given by Pompeius Trogus (rather than 814 B.C. as given by Timaeus), puts the beginning of the reign of Hiram of Tyre in 979/978 B.C., and arrives at the date of 968/967 for the commencement of work on the temple, and 931/930 for the separation of the kingdom. McFall, "Translation Guide," 43, cites William H. Barnes, "Studies in the Chronology of the Divided Monarchy of Israel" (Ph.D. diss., Harvard Divinity School, 1986) for 932 B.C. as the date of the death of Solomon and the division of his kingdom, but McFall himself (ibid., 10) lists Solomon as dying in Sept 931–Apr 930, and gives these same dates for the first year of reign of Jeroboam and the first year of reign of Rehoboam.

[449]McFall, "Translation Guide," 12 no. 1 and Chart 1; Merrill, "Fixed Dates," *BSac* 137 (July–Sept 1980): 242, for the same date of the exodus in 1446.

[450]Luckenbill, *Ancient Records* 1:770; *ANET* 282; *ANEA* 193.

[451]A. Poebel, *JNES* 2 (1943): 89 n. 23.

of the defeat of Rezon.[452] This is probably the same event as that mentioned in 2 Kgs 16:9 ("he [Tiglath-pileser] killed Rezin") and provides a date for the submission of Ahaz of Judah to the Assyrian king (2 Kgs 16:7) as well as for the deportation of Northern Israelites by Tiglath-pileser III (2 Kgs 15:29) and the change of rule from Pekah to Hoshea (2 Kgs 15:30), the assassination of Pekah and the accession of Hoshea falling between Tishri (Sept/Oct) 732 and Nisan (Mar/Apr) 731.[453]

TABLE 119. *Years of Saul, David, and Solomon*

King	*B.C.*
Saul	Early 10th century
David	Birth 1042/1041, reign 1012/1011 to death 972/971
Solomon	
Regnal years	
1	Tishri (Sept/Oct) 971–Elul (Aug/Sept) 970
2	Tishri (Sept/Oct) 970–(Aug/Sept) 969
3	Tishri (Sept/Oct) 969–Elul (Aug/Sept) 968
4	Tishri (Sept/Oct) 968–Elul (Aug/Sept) 967
. . .	. . .
40	Tishri (Sept/Oct) 932–(Aug/Sept) 931

426. Since the accession year of Hoshea was 732/731 (§425), his ninth and last year, in which Samaria fell to the Assyrians and the northern kingdom came to an end (2 Kgs 17:6; 18:10), was 723/722, and the specific date was after Nisan 1, 723, therefore probably in the summer fighting season of 723.[454] The Assyrian king was Shalmaneser V (2 Kgs 18:9). A Babylonian Chronicle (B. M. 92502) states (1.27–31) as the noteworthy event in the reign of Shalmaneser V that the city of Shamarain was destroyed, surely a cuneiform record of the fall of the capital of Northern Israel, as per the biblical account. The Babylonian Chronicle goes on to say that Shalmaneser (V) died in his fifth year, in the month of Tebetu (Dec/Jan), and that on the twelfth day of that month (Dec 20, 722) his successor Sargon (II) acceded to the throne of Assyria, with Sargon's first year beginning in Nisan 721.[455] In some of his own late inscriptions Sargon II claims that at the beginning of his rule, in his first year of reign, he captured Samaria, carried off 27,290 people from it, and resettled the city.[456] This is probably an appropriation of honor for himself of what his predecessor had done in a three-year siege (2 Kgs 17:6; 18:10), and may reflect the idea that an Assyrian

[452]Luckenbill, *Ancient Records* 1:779; *ANET* 283; *ANEA* 194; cf. Thiele, *Mysterious Numbers* (1951), 90, 106, 121; Albright, *BASOR* 100 (Dec 1945): 22 n. 26.

[453]McFall, "Translation Guide," 31, nos. 45, 46; cf. Nadav Na'aman, "Historical and Chronological Notes on the Kingdoms of Israel and Judah in the 8th Century BC," in *VT* 36 (July 1986): 71–82: Pekah twenty years from 749 to 731/730 and Hoshea nine years 731/730–723/722.

[454]Thiele, *Chronology,* 53, 59; Thiele, *Mysterious Numbers* (1983), 163; McFall, "Translation Guide," 33 nos. 49, 50.

[455]*ANET* 301–303; Thiele, *Mysterious Numbers* (1983), 163–164.

[456]Luckenbill, *Ancient Records* 2: 4, 55; *ANET* 284–285.

king must always have accomplished something militarily significant immediately at the outset of his reign, and it has been shown to be probable that it was only late in 720 as a part of a western campaign, that Sargon first came to Samaria to deport the people and to rebuild the city as the center of a new province called Samarina.[457]

427. In the annals of Sennacharib (704–681 B.C.) the record of his "third campaign" (701 B.C.) describes a siege of Jerusalem, doubtless conducted during the summer of that year, which must be the same as the siege which 2 Kgs 18:13 and Isa 36:1 put in the fourteenth year of King Hezekiah (Tishri [Sept/Oct] 702 to the end of Elul [Aug/Sept] 701).[458]

5. The Closing Period of the Kingdom of Judah

LITERATURE: C. J. **Gadd**, *The Fall of Nineveh* (London: Oxford University Press, 1923); W. F. **Albright**, "The Seal of Eliakim and the Latest Preëxilic History of Judah, with Some Observations on Ezekiel," *JBL* 51 (1932): 77–106; Waldo H. **Dubberstein**, "Assyrian-Babylonian Chronology (669–612 B.C.)," *JNES* 3 (1944): 38–42; W. F. **Albright**, "A Brief History of Judah from the Days of Josiah to Alexander the Great," *BA* 9 (1946): 1–16; D. Winton **Thomas**, "The Age of Jeremiah in the Light of Recent Archaeological Discovery," *PEQ* 1950: 1–15; D. J. **Wiseman**, *Chronicles of Chaldaean Kings (626–556 B.C.) in the British Museum* (London: Trustees of the British Museum, 1956); J. Philip **Hyatt**, "New Light on Nebuchadrezzar and Judean History," *JBL* 75 (1956): 277–284; A. **Malamat**, "A New Record of Nebuchadrezzar's Palestinian Campaigns," *IEJ* 6 (1956): 246–256; Hayim **Tadmor**, "Chronology of the Last Kings of Judah," *JNES* 15 (1956): 226–230; Edwin R. **Thiele**, "New Evidence on the Chronology of the Last Kings of Judah," *BASOR* 143 (Oct 1956): 22–27; Martin **Noth**, "Die Einnahme von Jerusalem im Jahre 597 v. Chr.," *ZDPV* 74 (1958): 133–157; Elias **Auerbach**, "Der Wechsel des Jahres-Angangs in Juda im Lichte der neugefundenen babylonischen Chronik," *VT* 9 (1959): 113–121; E. **Auerbach**, "Die Umschaltung vom judäischen auf den babylonischen Kalender," *VT* 10 (1960): 69–70; Alberto R. **Green**, "The Chronology of the Last Days of Judah: Two Apparent Discrepancies," *JBL* 101 (1982): 57–73; Gershon **Galil**, "The Babylonian Calendar and the Chronology of the Last Kings of Judah," *Biblica* 72 (1991): 367–378; Leslie **McFall**, "A Translation Guide to the Chronological Data in Kings and Chronicles," *BSac* 72 (1991): 367–378.

428. Assyria, which had deported Northern Israelites (§§425, 426) and threatened Jerusalem (§427), fell but was replaced by the Chaldean or New Babylonian empire, which ultimately destroyed the kingdom of Judah. Babylonian Chronicles in the British Museum cover much of what was the closing period of the kingdom of Judah.[459] By the correlation of such extra-biblical evidence with biblical data it is possible to state dates in this period with relatively great precision and assurance.

---

[457]Thiele, *Mysterious Numbers* (1983), 163–168, citing Hayim Tadmor, "Campaigns of Sargon II," 38.

[458]Luckenbill, *Ancient Records* 2:240; *ANET* 288; *ANEA* 200; Thiele, *Mysterious Numbers* (1983), 78; McFall, "Translation Guide," 36 no. 55.

[459]For bibliography of the translated chronicles and of many studies thereof see Green, "Last Days of Judah," 57–58 n. 1, 2.

429. British Museum Tablet No. 25127 records the accession of the Chaldean Nabopolassar to the throne of Babylon: "On the twenty-sixth day of the month of Arahsamnu, Nabopolassar sat upon the throne in Babylon. This was the 'beginning of reign' of Nabopolassar."[307] The date of this "beginning of reign" or accession of Nabopolassar corresponds to Nov 23, 626 B.C., and the ensuing twenty-one regnal years of Nabopolassar extend from 625/624 to 605/604.[308] British Museum Tablet No. 21901 records the destruction of Nineveh, the great Assyrian capital, by Nabopolassar and his allies (cf. Zeph 2:13–15; Nah 3:1–3).[309] This was in the fourteenth year of Nabopolassar, in the month Abu, but the day is missing in a gap in the text. The date was therefore sometime in July/Aug 612 B.C.

430. In the western city of Haran a remnant of Assyrian empire was maintained a few years longer by Ashur-uballit II (611–608 B.C.). British Museum Tablet No. 21901 records that in his sixteenth year (610/609 B.C.) Nabopolassar drove Ashur-uballit out of Haran; in the next year (609/608) between Duzu (June/July) 609 and Ululu (Aug/Sept) 609 Ashur-uballit and "a large army of Egypt" tried to reconquer Haran.[310] The "army of Egypt" is surely the expeditionary force of Pharaoh Necho II (609–595), mentioned also in 2 Kgs 23:29 and 2 Chron 35:21, which King Josiah tried vainly to oppose at Megiddo. The purpose of Necho was evidently to assist the Assyrians and resist the New Babylonians; the intent of Josiah was to keep help from reaching the Assyrians, the old enemy of Judah. The death of Josiah in his own thirty-first year, in his ill-fated attempt at Megiddo, is therefore to be dated in the seventeenth year of Nabopolassar and in the month of Duzu/Tammuz (June 25–July 23) 609 B.C.[311] The endeavor of the Egyptians to assist the Assyrians evidently failed, for the attackers "afterwards . . . retired from the siege," and Ashur-uballit disappeared from the scene.[312] This event in 609 was the final end of the Assyrian empire.

431. The Egyptians stayed in the north for some years. British Museum Tablet No. 22047 reports that in the twentieth year of Nabopolassar (606/605 B.C.) they successfully attacked a Babylonian garrison in the city of Kimuhu on the Euphrates.[313] British Museum Tablet No. 21946 tells how, in the twenty-first year of Nabopolassar (605/604), the Babylonian king sent his son Nebuchadnezzar against the Egyptians. Nebuchadnezzar met the Egyptian army in Carchemish on the bank of the Euphrates, accomplished their defeat, and conquered the whole area of "the Hatti-country." In the record of Nebuchadnezzar's seventh year, soon to be quoted (§437), "the Hatti-land" includes "the

---

[307]Wiseman, *Chronicles,* 50–51, cf. 7, 93.

[308]PDBC 27.

[309]Luckenbill, *Ancient Records* 2:1177–1178; *ANET* 304; *ANEA* 202.

[310]Luckenbill, *Ancient Records* 2:1183; *ANET* 305; *ANEA* 202.

[311]PDBC 27; *JNES* 15 (1956): 228–229; Thiele, *Mysterious Numbers* (1983), 180–181; McFall, "Translation Guide," 38 no. 68; Green, "Last Days of Judah," *JBL* 101 (1982): 72 n. 50.

[312]W. F. Albright, "The Seal of Eliakim and the Latest Preëxilic History of Judah, with Some Observations on Ezekiel," *JBL* 51 (1932): 77–106, esp. 86–87.

[313]Wiseman, *Chronicles,* 67.

city of Judah," therefore the term is a general designation for Syria-Palestine. Soon after the victories at Carchemish and in the Hatti-country, Nebuchadnezzar learned that his father had died and returned to Babylon to ascend the throne. The chronicle puts the death of Nabopolassar on Abu 8 = Aug 15, 605, and the accession of Nebuchadnezzar on Ululu 1 = Sept 7, 605 B.C. The crucial battle of Carchemish must have taken place between Nisanu 1 (= Apr 12) when Nabopolassar's twenty-first year began and Abu 8 (= Aug 15) when he died, therefore say in Simanu in late May to early June 605 B.C.[314] The accession year of Nebuchadnezzar extended from Ululu 1 = Sept 7, 605 to the end of the current calendar year. His first regnal year began on the next Nisanu 1 (Apr 2) 604 (cf. Table 10). Thiele notes that two eclipses confirm 605 as the year of accession for Nebuchadnezzar. The first occurred on Apr 22, 621, in the fifth year of Nabopolassar, which puts Nabopolassar's death in the twenty-first year of his reign in 605 and thus the beginning of Nebuchadnezzar's reign in that year too. The second eclipse was on July 4, 568, in the thirty-seventh year of Nebuchadnezzar, which also counts correctly from accession in 605. Thiele concludes that no date in ancient history is more firmly established than this.[315]

432. As we go on to consider the further sequence of dates of the kings of Judah it is to be remembered that, according to Thiele (above §421), in the southern kingdom the regnal year was reckoned in terms of the year which began in the fall in the month of Tishri, and that the accession-year system was again in use in Judah from Amaziah to Zedekiah, i.e., to the end, while Ezra-Nehemiah use Tishri years even for the kings of Persia and Daniel also employs Tishri years, but Jeremiah, Ezekiel, Haggai, and Zechariah use Nisan years for the Hebrew kings as well as for the rulers of Babylon and Persia. Confirmation of reckoning by the fall beginning of the year is found as late as in the eighteenth year of King Josiah. In his eighteenth ear (2 Kgs 22:3) the "book of the law" was found in the house of the Lord (2 Kgs 22:8) and in the selfsame eighteenth year the Passover was celebrated (2 Kgs 23:23). The numerous intervening events between the finding of the law book and the observance of the Passover could hardly have been concentrated within the two weeks between Nisan 1 and Nisan 14 as would have been necessary if Josiah's eighteenth year had only begun on Nisan 1; therefore his eighteenth year must have begun the preceding Tishri 1. We have dated the death of Josiah at Megiddo in Duzu/Tammuz (June 25–July 23) 609 B.C. (§430). After him the people put on the throne his son Jehoahaz, and the latter reigned for three months (2 Kgs 23:31). The reign of Jehoahaz began, therefore, in Tammuz and ended three months later in Tishri (Sept 21–Oct 19) 609 B.C.[316] The end of the short reign of Jehoahaz came because Pharaoh Necho deposed him and in his place installed Eliakim, also a son of Josiah, in the kingship, changing his name to Jehoiakim, and Jehoiakim reigned for eleven years (2 Kgs 23:36). Because the three months of the reign of Jehoahaz extended over into Tishri 609, the first month of the next new year, Jehoiakim had an accession year of about eleven months in the balance of that year (609/608), and

[314]Green, "Last Days of Judah," 68 n. 37.
[315]Thiele, *Chronology,* 69.
[316]Thiele, *Mysterious Numbers* (1983), 182; Green, "Last Days of Judah," 72 n. 50.

his first regnal year began on yet the next Tishri 1 (Sept 10), 608.[317] The sequence of Josiah, Jehoahaz, and Jehoiakim is shown in Table 120.

TABLE 120. *The Transition from Josiah to Jehoahaz and to Jehoiakim, and the Regnal Years of Jehoiakim*

Name	*B.C.*
Josiah: died at Megiddo	Sometime in Tammuz (June 25–July 23) 609
Jehoahaz: 3 months reign	
Month 1	Tammuz (June 25–July 23)–Ab (July 24–Aug 22) 609
Month 2	Ab (July 24–Aug 22)–Elul (Aug 23–Sept 20) 609
Month 3	Elul (Aug 23–Sept 20)–Tishri (Sept 21–Oct 19) 609
Jehoiakim: accession year	Sometime in Tishri (Sept 21–Oct 19) 609–end of Elul (Sept 9) 608
Year 1	Tishri 1 (Sept 10) 608–end of Elul II (Sept 28) 607
Year 2	Tishri 1 (Sept 29) 607–end of Elul (Sept 18) 606
Year 3	Tishri 1 (Sept 19) 606–end of Elul (Oct 6) 605
Year 4	Tishri 1 (Oct 7) 605–end of Elul (Sept 25) 604
Year 5	Tishri 1 (Sept 26) 604–end of Elul (Oct 14) 603
Year 6	Tishri 1 (Oct 15) 603–end of Elul (Oct 3) 602
Year 7	Tishri 1 (Oct 4) 602–end of Elul (Sept 21) 601
Year 8	Tishri 1 (Sept 22) 601–end of Elul (Oct 9) 600
Year 9	Tishri 1 (Oct 10) 600–end of Elul (Sept 30) 599
Year 10	Tishri 1 (Oct 1) 599–end of Elul (Oct 19) 598
Year 11	Tishri 1 (Oct 20) 598–end of Elul (Oct 8) 597

433. We have already seen (§431) that the battle of Carchemish must have taken place in May/June 605 B.C., after which Nebuchadnezzar made conquests in "the Hatti-land," i.e., in Syria-Palestine, and then went back to Babylon to take the theone on Ululu 1 (Sept 7), 605. The book of Daniel (1:1) states that in the third year of Jehoiakim Nebuchadnezzar besieged Jerusalem and carried off temple treasures together with Daniel and others of the tribe of Judah to Babylon. Although this taking of Jerusalem and first deportation of some of its people to Babylon is otherwise unknown, the event must have taken place in the time soon after the battle of Carchemish, when Nebuchadnezzar accomplished his other victories in Syria-Palestine. Since the book of Daniel uses Tishri years (Thiele, above §421, 425), and since in those terms the third year of Jehoiakim (Table 120) extended to the end of Elul/Ululu on Oct 6, 605, the date in Dan 1:1 includes correctly the time soon after Carchemish (May/June 605). Since Jeremiah uses Nisan years the same date is stated in Jer 46:2 as in the fourth year of Jehoiakim.[318]

---

[317]McFall, "Translation Guide," 39, no. 61 and Charts 29–30.

[318]Thiele, *Mysterious Numbers* (1983), 183. For a long discussion of the whole problem involved see Green, "Last Days of Judah," 68–73.

434. As in Jer 46:2 so also in Jer 25:1 the word of the Lord which came to Jeremiah is assigned the same date that was explained just above (§433) as shortly after Carchemish (605 B.C.) when Nebuchadnezzar was about to attack Jerusalem and carry off Daniel and others. In the expectation of that disaster (Jer 25) Jer 25:11–12 predicts that Judah and its neighbors will serve the king of Babylon for seventy years, and only after seventy years will Babylon and its king be punished for their iniquity. Again in Jer 29:10 the seventy years are cited: "For thus says the Lord: When seventy years are completed for Babylon, I will visit you, and I will fulfill to you my promise and bring you back to this place." The "seventy years . . . for Babylon," of which Jeremiah speaks are therefore the seventy years of Babylonian rule, and the return of Judah from exile is contingent upon the end of that period. Since the final fall of the Assyrian empire was in 609 B.C. (§430), and the New Babylonian empire endured from then until Cyrus the Persian took Babylon in 539, the period of Babylonian domination was in fact seventy years (609 – 539 = 70). Other mentions of the seventy years are 2 Chron 36:21 and Dan 9:2, which refer specifically to the prophecies of Jeremiah and Isa 23:15–18 and Zech 1:12 and 7:5, which do not refer to Jeremiah. Finally, in Dan 9:24, the seventy years are understood to be "seventy weeks of years" (i.e., 70 × 7 = 490 years).[319]

435. The first regnal year of Nebuchadnezzar (§431) extended from Nisanu 1 (Apr 2), 604, to the last day of Addaru (Mar 21) 603, and in that year, in the month of Simanu (May 30–June 28) 604, the new king of Babylon returned to the west, evidently to cement his supremacy, and the Babylonian Chronicle (B.M. 21946) goes on to tell us that "all the kings of the Hatti-land came before him and he received their heavy tribute."[320] It may well be supposed that Jehoiakim was among the kings making submission at that time, and a reference to Jehoiakim's submission is probably to be recognized in 2 Kgs 24:1, which says that Jehoiakim became the servant of Nebuchadnezzar for three years, but then turned and rebelled against him. According to our Table 120 this submission to Nebuchadnezzar would have been in Jehoiakim's fourth regnal year, the three years of subserviency would have been Jehoiakim's fifth, sixth, and seventh years, and the act of rebellion would have fallen in Jehoiakim's eighth year (601/600), which corresponds with half of Nebuchadnezzar's fourth year (601/600). In his fourth year, according to B.M. 21946, Nebuchadnezzar suffered a virtual defeat on the borders of Egypt, and this could well be the event which caused Jehoiakim to venture upon rebellion.

436. As we are told in 2 Kgs chap. 24, in his eleventh year Jehoiakim "slept with his fathers, and Jehoiachin his son reigned in his stead" (v. 6). In evident emulation of his father (v. 9) Jehoiachin also rebelled against the king of

---

[319]For the above interpretation of the seventy years see Ross E. Winkle, "Jeremiah's Seventy Years for Babylon: A Re-assessment," Part I: The Scriptural Data, *AUSS* 25 (1987): 201–214; Part II: The Historical Data, *AUSS* 25 (1987): 289–299. For other proposed solutions see C. F. Whitley, "The Term Seventy Years Captivity," *VT* 4 (1954): 60–72; Avigdor Orr, "The Seventy Years of Babylon," *VT* 6 (1956): 304–306; C. F. Whitley, "The Seventy Years Desolation—A Rejoinder," *VT* 7 (1957): 416–418. For a discussion of the seventy weeks of years see Hoehner, *Chronological Aspects,* 115–139.

[320]Wiseman, *Chronicles,* 67–69, cf. 25.

Babylon and in response the forces of Nebuchadnezzar besieged Jerusalem (v. 10) and Nebuchadnezzar came and took Jehoiachin prisoner, this being in the eighth year of Nebuchadnezzar (v. 12). At this time Nebuchadnezzar carried off temple and kingly treasures and "carried away all Jerusalem," ten thousand captives including seven thousand men of valor and one thousand craftsmen and smiths, as well as Jehoiachin himself, with his mother and wives, and officials and chief men of the land (vv. 13–16). In succession to Jehoiachin, Nebuchadnezzar made Mattaniah, Jehoiachin's uncle (or brother, 2 Chron 36:10), king, and changed his name to Zedekiah (2 Kgs 25:17).

437. British Museum Tablet 21946 (already cited in our §§431, 435) provides this record for the seventh year of Nebuchadnezzar:

> In the seventh year, the month of Kislimu, the king of Akkad mustered his troops, marched to the Hatti-land, and encamped against the city of Judah and on the second day of the month of Addaru he seized the city and captured the king. He appointed there a king of his own choice, received its heavy tribute and sent them to Babylon.[321]

The "king of Akkad" is Nebuchadnezzar, the "city of Judah" must be Jerusalem, and the newly chosen king must be Zedekiah, so this is unmistakably the Babylonian record of the fall of Jerusalem to Nebuchadnezzar, corresponding on the whole to the account just summarized from 2 Kgs chap. 24 (§436). The seventh year of Nebuchadnezzar began on Nisanu 1 (Mar 27) 598 B.C. The month of Kislimu began on Dec 18, 598. The second day of the month of Addaru was Mar 16, 597 B.C.[322] The last is the most exact information to come from cuneiform records for an event recorded in the Bible, and gives us a precise day for the fall of Jerusalem and the capture of Jehoiachin.[323]

438. There is an apparent discrepancy in the chronology in the fact that 2 Kgs 24:12 dates the taking of Jerusalem and the capture of Jehoiachin in the eighth year of Nebuchadnezzar (§435) rather than the seventh year as per the Babylonian Chronicle (§437). But it will be remembered (§432) that in Judah the kings' years were counted from Tishri 1 in the fall (rather than from Nisan 1 in the spring as the Babylonians did), and if the Tishri year was applied to Nebuchadnezzar his first regnal year would begin a half-year earlier on Tishri 1 (Oct 7) 605, his eighth year would start Tishri 1 (Oct 20) 598 and extend to the last day of Elul (Oct 8) 597 (thus being exactly parallel to the eleventh year of Jehoiakim), and the campaign of Nebuchadnezzar beginning in Kislimu (Nov/Dec) 598 and the fall of Jerusalem, capture of Jehoiachin, and appointment of Zedekiah would all fall within this year correctly.[324]

439. As for the deportation of Jehoiachin, 2 Chron 36:10 states that Nebuchadnezzar brought him to Babylon "in the spring of the year" (RSV) or "at

---

321 Wiseman, *Chronicles,* 73.
322 PDBC 27.
323 Green, "Last Days of Judah," 58 n. 4.
324 Ibid., 62 and n. 14.

the turn of the year" (Berkeley Version). The Hebrew used here, לתשובת השנה *(litshubat hashanah)* could possibly mean shortly before the new year and refer to the date of the second day of Addaru, Mar 16, 598, in the seventh year of Nebuchadnezzar, given in the Babylonian Chronicle for the capture of Jehoiachin (our §437).[325] More likely, however, is a time at or after Nisan 1, since that is the date of the Babylonian new year and thus most naturally the beginning of "the spring of the year." If 2 Kgs 24:14 is correct that the total number of persons selected for deportation was ten thousand, and if much booty was taken and prepared for transport, even to the cutting in pieces of the vessels of gold from the temple as 2 Kgs 24:13 states, then it may readily be supposed that it was a number of weeks before the captives and goods were assembled and the caravan could depart. In fact Ezek 40:1 speaks of what seems to be an exact anniversary ("that very day") of the inauguration of the exile and dates it "at the beginning of the year, on the tenth day of the month." This must mean the tenth day of Nisan in the eighth year of Nebuchadnezzar, which was on Apr 22, 597, and was a little more than a month after the fall of Jerusalem on Mar 16. Nisan 10 (Apr 22), 597, is therefore thc probable date of the actual deportation of Jehoiachin and the beginning of his exile, and this was already in the eighth year of Nebuchadnezzar.[326]

440. In connection with the foregoing (§439) the question may be raised as to the official point of termination of the reign of Jehoiachin and the accession of Zedekiah. In B.M. 21946 the date of Addaru 2 (Mar 16), 597 B.C., is in the sentence that states that the king of Akkad seized the city (Jerusalem) and captured the king (Jehoiachin), and conceivably the capture of Jehoiachin could also be considered the official end of his reign. Since the duration of his reign was three months (2 Kgs 24:8) or more exactly three months and ten days (2 Chron 36:9), we could count back three months and ten days from Addaru/Adar 2 (Mar 16), 597, and come to Arahsamnu/Heshvan 22 (Dec 9), 598, for the commencement date of Jehoiachin's reign and the date of the death of Jehoiakim, his father and predecessor.[327] It is a separate sentence in B.M. 21946, however, which describes the appointment of Zedekiah as the king of Nebuchadnezzar's "own choice" and the deportation of the many persons ("them"). Rather than thinking of Jehoiachin's reign as having ended while he was still a king, albeit a captured king, in Jerusalem, it seems more likely that his reign ended officially and that Zedekiah was officially installed in his place only when Jehoiachin was actually carried away, which was probably on Nisanu/Nisan 10 (Apr 22), 597 (§439). Counting back from this date for three months and ten days we come to Tebetu/Tebeth 1 (Jan 16), 597, for the beginning of the reign of Jehoiachin and the death of Jehoiakim. In either case, the date (Dec 9, 598, or preferably Jan 16, 597) falls properly within the eleventh year of the eleven-year reign of Jehoiakim (Table 120), and the implied winter time agrees with the prophecy of Jeremiah (36:30) that Jehoiakim's dead body would be cast out to the frost by night.[328]

---

[325]Noth, *ZDPV* 74 (1958): 133–157.

[326]Thiele, *Mysterious Numbers,* 187; McFall, "Translation Guide," 39 no. 63.

[327]Green, "Last Days of Judah," *JBL* 101 (1982): 58.

[328]McFall, "Translation Guide," 39 no. 63; in n. 30 McFall observes that if Jehoiachin's reign began on or around Dec 9 it would have ended around Mar 18 and not

441. While the Babylonian Chronicle (B.M. 21946) has given us the exact date of the fall of Jerusalem to Nebuchadnezzar on Addaru 2 (Mar 16) 597, and also continues to report several succeeding expeditions of Nebuchadnezzar to the Hatti-land, the extant text of the Chronicle terminates with the eleventh year (594/593) of the Babylonian king and does not extend far enough to record the final fall of Jerusalem. The city's final fall is related, however, along with relevant dates in the reign of Zedekiah and the reign of Nebuchadnezzar, in 2 Kgs 25, and there are several parallels in 2 Chron 36:11–21; Jer 39:1–10; 52 (and some other passages); and in Ezek 17:11–21. As seen above (§440), we assume that the appointment of Zedekiah as king in Jerusalem was at the time of the deportation of Jehoiachin, i.e., on Nisan 10 (Apr 22), 597. Accordingly, assuming the accession-year system and the regnal year beginning on Tishri 1 (§432), the accession year of Zedekiah began on Nisan 10 (Apr 22), 597, and extended to the end of Elul on Oct 8 of the same year, while his first regnal year began on Tishri 1 (Oct 9), 597, and extended to the end of Elul II on Oct 27, 596.[329] According to 2 Kgs 24:18; 2 Chron 36:11; Jer 52:1 Zedekiah was twenty-one years old when he became king and he reigned eleven years in Jerusalem. Preceding dates for Jehoiakim and Jehoiachin and dates of accession year and regnal years for Zedekiah are shown in Table 121.[330]

TABLE 121. *The Transition from Jehoiakim to Jehoiachin to Zedekiah, and the Accession and Regnal Years of Zedekiah*

Name	*B.C.*
Death of Jehoiakim and accession of Jehoiachin	Heshvan 22 (Dec 9), 598, or preferably Tebeth 1 (Jan 16) 597
Fall of Jerusalem and capture of Jehoiachin	Adar 2 (Mar 16), 597
Deportation of Jehoiachin	Nisan 10 (Apr 22), 597
Zedekiah: Accession Year	Nisan 10 (Apr 22) 597–Elul 30 (Oct 8) 597
Year 1	Tishri 1 (Oct 9) 597–Elul II 30 (Oct 27) 596
Year 2	Tishri 1 (Oct 28) 596–Elul 29 (Oct 15) 595
Year 3	Tishri 1 (Oct 16) 595–Elul 30 (Oct 5) 594
Year 4	Tishri 1 (Oct 6) 594–Elul 29 (Oct 22) 593
Year 5	Tishri 1 (Oct 23) 593–Elul 30 (Oct 12) 592
Year 6	Tishri 1 (Oct 13) 592–Elul 29 (Oct 1) 591
Year 7	Tishri 1 (Oct 2) 591–Elul 29 (Oct 20) 590
Year 8	Tishri 1 (Oct 21) 590–Elul 30 (Oct 9) 589
Year 9	Tishri 1 (Oct 10) 589–Elul 30 (Sept 28) 588
Year 10	Tishri 1 (Sept 29) 588–Elul 30 (Sept 17) 587
Year 11	Tishri 1 (Oct 18) 587–Elul 30 (Oct 6) 586

442. Nebuchadnezzar exacted an oath of allegiance from Zedekiah (Ezek 17:13) as the king he had chosen (§437) but, in spite of warnings from

around Apr 22, which agrees with our preference for Jehoiachin's accession on Jan 16 rather than on Dec 9.

[329]PDBC 27.

[330]McFall, "Translation Guide," 39 no. 63; 40 no. 65, Charts 30–31.

Jeremiah (Jer 27:8) and Ezekiel (Ezek 17:16), Zedekiah engaged in negotiations for help from Egypt (Ezek 17:15) and other nations (Jer 27:3–7) and, in spite of the help which never came, like Jehoiakim and Jehoiachin, he too rebelled against the king of Babylon (2 Kgs 24:20; 2 Chron 36:13). The warning by Jeremiah was issued already "in the beginning of the reign of Zedekiah" (Jer 17:1 RSV), presumably meaning in Zedekiah's accession year (Table 121), so his plotting to forswear his oath evidently began at once. In Zedekiah's ninth regnal year, in the tenth month, on the tenth day of the month, Nebuchadnezzar came against his faithless appointee and with his whole army laid siege to Jerusalem (2 Kgs 25:1). The ninth year of Zedekiah was Tishri 1 (Oct 10), 589, to Elul 30 (Sept 28), 588; the tenth month is Tebeth (Dec/Jan), and in that year the tenth day of this month was equivalent to Jan 15, 588.[331] The siege went on for slightly more than two and one-half years until at last famine was unbearably severe in the city, a breach was made in the city, the king and men of war fled by night but were overtaken in the plains of Jericho, and Zedekiah was captured and taken to Nebuchadnezzar at Riblah (east of Baalbek in the plain of Coelesyria), where his sons were slain before his eyes and he was blinded and taken off to Babylon and to prison until the day of his death (2 Kgs 25:3–7; Jer 52:5–11). The date of this the final fall of Jerusalem was in the eleventh year of Zedekiah, on the ninth day of the fourth month (2 Kgs 25:2–3; Jer 52:5–6). The eleventh year of Zedekiah was from Tishri 1 (Oct 18), 587, to Elul 30 (Oct 30), 586. The fourth month is Tammuz (June/July) and in 586 the ninth day was equivalent to July 18 and is identified as a Saturday.[332] This, then, is the highly probable date of the final fall of Jerusalem—July 18, 586 B.C.

443. In the fifth month, on the seventh day of the month—which was the nineteenth year of Nebuchadnezzar—Nebuzaradan, Nebuchadnezzar's captain of the bodyguard, came to Jerusalem; he burned the house of the Lord, and the king's house and all the houses of Jerusalem, and his army broke down the walls around the city; he carried away to Babylon both treasures and people, and left behind only some of the poorest of the land (2 Kgs 25:8–12; Jer 52:12–16). The date of his coming, specified as the seventh day of the fifth month in 2 Kg 25:8, is given in Jer 52:12 as the tenth day of the fifth month. The fifth month of the year is Ab (July/Aug); in 586, Ab 7 was Aug 14, and Ab 10 was Aug 17. As for the equivalence with the nineteenth year of Nebuchadnezzar (2 Kgs 25:8), the placement of the capture of Jehoiachin in the eighth year of Nebuchadnezzar in 2 Kgs 24:12 was explained above (§438) by the supposition that the year of Nebuchadnezzar was considered to begin in Tishri after the manner of Judah rather than in Nisan after the Babylonian manner. With a similar supposition at the present point, the nineteenth year of Nebuchadnezzar would begin on Tishri 1 (Oct 18), 587, and extend to the last day of Elul (Oct 6) 586, and this regnal year would include Ab 7 (Aug 14) and Ab 10 (Aug 17). In the present case, however, the nature of the overlap is such that the nineteenth year of Nebuchadnezzar counted from Nisan 1 (Apr 13) to Adar 30 (Apr 1), 586, would equally well include Ab 7 and Ab 10.[333] At any rate, rabbinic tradition dealt with the two

[331]PDBC 28; Finegan, *Archaeological History,* 388 n. 18.
[332]Thiele, *Mysterious Numbers* (1983), 190; McFall, "Translation Guide," 40 no. 67.

specific days of Ab 7 and Ab 10 by supposing that they encompassed a certain sequence of events and focused on Ab 9 as the beginning of the major conflagration of the temple, thus it is this day in particular, identified as a Saturday, which has remained in melancholy remembrance (see §§200ff., 468).

444. As for the several deportations of people of Judah during these terrible times, we have noted in 2 Kgs 24:12, 14 the carrying away by Nebuchadnezzar of ten thousand captives along with Jehoiachin in the eighth year of Nebuchadnezzar (§436), and in 2 Kgs 25:8, 11 the coming of Nebuzaradan to Jerusalem in the nineteenth year of Nebuchadnezzar and the burning of the city and the carrying away of an unspecified number of captives (§443). In Jer 52:28–30 three deportations by Nebuchadnezzar are listed: in the seventh year 3,023 Jews; in the eighteenth year of Nebuchadnezzar 832 persons from Jerusalem; and in the twenty-third year of Nebuchadnezzar 745 persons carried away by Nebuzaradan; in all 4,600. Since the regnal years in Jeremiah are probably in terms of the Nisan year, and those in 2 Kings in terms of the Tishri year (§432), the seventh and eighteenth years in Jeremiah are probably identical with the eighth and nineteenth years in 2 Kings (§§438, 443).[334] On the other hand, the numbers of captives differ and are more precise in Jeremiah, therefore some hold that Jeremiah has only preserved record of some otherwise unknown minor events unconnected with the two major deportations described in 2 Kings, and this of course must be the case with the event reported in the twenty-third year of Nebuchadnezzar, which is without biblical parallel.[335]

445. After the final fall of Jerusalem (586 B.C., §§442–443), Nebuchadnezzar appointed as governor over those who remained in the land, or were able to come back from elsewhere, Gedaliah, the son of Ahikam, who made his seat of government at Mizpah. Ahikam had been an adviser of Josiah (2 Kgs 22:12) and a friend of Jeremiah (Jer 26:24), and Jeremiah himself, given freedom by Nebuzaradan, dwelt with Gedaliah at Mizpah (Jer 40:6). But a certain Ishmael, member of the deposed royal family and evidently unwilling that one who was not of the house of David should sit on even the little that was left of David's throne, assassinated Gedaliah. Thereupon, all the people, frightened of the probable response of the Babylonians, fled to Egypt, taking Jeremiah with them (2 Kgs 25:25–26; Jer 41:1–2; 43:6). The date when Gedaliah was slain was in the seventh month (2 Kgs 25:25; Jer 41:1); the seventh month is Tishri (Sept/Oct); in 586 Tishri began on Oct 7.[336]

446. In summary, a listing of the kings of Judah and Israel is adapted from Thiele and McFall and shown in Table 122.[337]

---

[333]PDBC 28; Galil, *Babylonian Calendar,* 378, for the dates of the ninth of Tammuz and the seventh and tenth of Ab in 586.

[334]Cf. W. F. Albright, "The Nebuchadrezzar and Neriglissar Chronicles," *BASOR* 143 (1956): 28–33.

[335]Green, "Last Days of Judah," 63–67.

[336]McFall, "Translation Guide," 40 no. 65.

[337]As compared with Thiele, McFall makes four minor alterations in the dates of reign of (1) Jehoahaz/Jehoash, and (2) Hoshea in Israel, and (3) Azariah/Jotham and

TABLE 122. *Dates of the Rulers of Judah and Israel*

Ruler	*Year of Accession*	*Year of Death*
	JUDAH	
Rehoboam	Sept/Oct 931–Mar/Apr 930	Mar/Apr–Sept/Oct 913
Abijam	Mar/Apr–Sept/Oct 913	Sept/Oct 911–Mar/Apr 910
Asa	Sept/Oct 911–Mar/Apr 910	Sept/Oct 870–Mar/Apr 869
Jehoshaphat	Sept/Oct 870–Mar/Apr 869	Mar/Apr–Sept/Oct 848
Jehoram	Mar/Apr–Sept/Oct 848	Mar/Apr–Sept/Oct 841
Ahaziah	Mar/Apr–Sept/Oct 841	Mar/Apr–Sept/Oct 841
Athaliah	Mar/Apr–Sept/Oct 841	Mar/Apr–Sept/Oct 835
Joash	Mar/Apr–Sept/Oct 835	Mar/Apr–Sept/Oct 796
Amaziah	Mar/Apr–Sept/Oct 796	Mar/Apr–Sept/Oct 767
Azariah	Mar/Apr–Sept/Oct 767	Mar/Apr–Sept/Oct 739
Jotham	Mar/Apr–Sept/Oct 739	Sept/Oct–Sept/Oct 731
Ahaz	Sept/Oct 732–Sept/Oct 731	c. Mar/Apr 715
Hezekiah	c. Mar/Apr 715	Sept/Oct 687–Sept/Oct 686
Manasseh	Sept/Oct 687–Sept/Oct 686	Sept/Oct 643–Sept/Oct 642
Amon	Sept/Oct 643–Sept/Oct 642	Sept/Oct 641–Sept/Oct 640
Josiah	Sept/Oct 641–Sept/Oct 640	c. July 609
Jehoahaz	c. July 609	c. Oct 609
Jehoiakim	c. Oct 609	Dec 9 598
Jehoiachin	Dec 598–Apr 597	after Apr 561
Zedekiah	Apr 597–Aug 586	c. Aug 586
	ISRAEL	
Jeroboam I	Sept/Oct 931–Mar/Apr 930	Sept/Oct 910–Mar/Apr 909
Nadab	Sept/Oct 910–Mar/Apr 909	Sept/Oct 909–Mar/Apr 908
Baasha	Sept/Oct 909–Mar/Apr 908	Sept/Oct 886–Mar/Apr 885
Elah	Sept/Oct 886–Mar/Apr 885	Sept/Oct 885–Mar/Apr 884
Zimri	Sept/Oct 885–Mar/Apr 884	Sept/Oct 885–Mar/Apr 884
Tibni	Sept/Oct 885–Mar/Apr 884	Mar/Apr 880–Sept/Oct 880
Omri	Sept/Oct 885–Mar/Apr 884	Sept/Oct 874–Mar/Apr 873
Ahab	Sept/Oct 874–Mar/Apr 873	Mar/Apr–Sept/Oct 853
Ahaziah	Mar/Apr–Sept/Oct 853	Mar/Apr–Sept/Oct 852
Joram	Mar/Apr–Sept/Oct 852	Mar/Apr–Sept/Oct 841
Jehu	Mar/Apr–Sept/Oct 841	Sept/Oct 814–Mar/Apr 813
Jehoahaz	Sept/Oct 814–Mar/Apr 813	Sept/Oct 798–Mar/Apr 797
Jehoash	Sept/Oct 798–Mar/Apr 797	Sept/Oct 782–Mar/Apr 781
Jeroboam II	Sept/Oct 782–Mar/Apr 781	Aug/Sept 753
Zechariah	Aug/Sept 753	Mar 752
Shallum	Mar 752	late Apr 752
Menahem	late Apr 752	Sept/Oct 742–Mar/Apr 741
Pekahiah	Sept/Oct 742–Mar/Apr 741	Sept/Oct 740–Mar/Apr 739
Pekah	Sept/Oct 740–Mar/Apr 739	Sept/Oct 732–Mar/Apr 731
Hoshea	Sept/Oct 732–Mar/Apr 731	Mar/Apr–Sept/Oct 723

(4) Ahaz/Hezekiah in Judah, which are incorporated in our table; and four major and five minor modifications in respect of coregencies, which are not shown in our table (see "Translation Guide," 11), nor are Thiele's coregencies shown in our table (see Thiele, *Mysterious Numbers* [1983], 219).

6. The Exile of Jehoiachin

LITERATURE: Ernst F. **Weidner**, "Jojachin, König von Juda, in babylonischen Keilschrift-texten," in *Mélanges Syriens offerts a Monsieur René Dussaud* (Paris: Geuthner, 1939), 2:923–927; W. F. **Albright**, "King Joiachin in Exile," in *BA* 5 (1942): 49–55; K. S. **Freedy** and D. B. **Redford**, "The Dates in Ezekiel in Relation to Biblical, Babylonian, and Egyptian Sources," *JAOS* 90 (1970): 462–485.

447. It will be remembered (§439) that, although Jerusalem fell and Jehoiachin was captured on Addaru 2 (Mar 16), 597 B.C., in the last month of the seventh year of Nebuchadnezzar, there is reason to think that Jehoiachin was not actually carried away from the city until a little more than a month later on Nisanu 10 (Apr 22), 597, which was already in the eighth year of Nebuchadnezzar. Surely this is the probable time to think of as the beginning of Jehoiachin's actual exile, even as we have also thought that this was the official point of the termination of his reign and the accession of his successor Zedekiah (§440). At the other end of the period within which we can trace the fate of Jehoiachin we have in only slightly variant passages in Second Kings and Jeremiah information about the thirty-seventh year of his exile and about the treatment he experienced from then on until the end of his life.

> And in the thirty-seventh year of the exile of Jehoiachin king of Judah, in the twelfth month, on the twenty-seventh day of the month, Evil-merodach king of Babylon, in the year that he began to reign, graciously freed Jehoiachin king of Judah from prison; and he spoke kindly to him, and gave him a seat above the seats of the kings who were with him in Babylon. So Jehoiachin put off his prison garments. And every day of his life he dined regularly at the king's table; and for his allowance, a regular allowance was given him by the king, every day a portion, as long as he lived (2 Kgs 25:27–30).

> And in the thirty-seventh year of the captivity of Jehoiachin king of Judah, in the twelfth month, on the twenty-fifth day of the month, Evil-merodach king of Babylon, in the year that he became king, lifted up the head of Jehoiachin king of Judah and brought him out of prison; and he spoke kindly to him, and gave him a seat above the seats of the kings who were with him in Babylon. So Jehoiachin put off his prison garments. And every day of his life he dined regularly at the king's table; as for his allowance, a regular allowance was given him by the king according to his daily need, until the day of his death as long as he lived (Jer 52:31–34).

448. The biblical Evil-merodach is the Babylonian Amel-Marduk, the son and successor of Nebuchadnezzar, and the chronology of his reign is based on cuneiform sources.[338] The last tablet dated in the reign of Nebuchadnezzar is from Uruk with the date Ululu 26 in his forty-third year, which is equivalent to Oct 8, 562 B.C.; and the first tablet dated to Amel-Marduk is perhaps from Sippar and has the same date equivalent to Oct 8, 562. The death of Nebuchad-

---

[338] PDBC 12, 28.

nezzar and the accession of Amel-Marduk were therefore in the early days of Oct 562, and the extent of the year prior to that date belonged to the last and forty-third year of Nebuchadnezzar, while the balance of the year constituted the accession year of Amel-Marduk. The whole year was 562/561, and with this as Amel-Marduk's accession year, his first year of reign was 561/560.

TABLE 123. *Nisan Years of the Captivity of Jehoiachin in Parallel with Nisan Years of Nebuchadnezzar and Amel-Marduk*

B.C.		*Regnal Years of Nebuchadnezzar*	*Captivity Years of Jehoiachin*
597/596		8	1
596/595		9	2
595/594		10	3
594/593		11	4
593/592		12	5
592/591		13	6
591/590		14	7
590/589		15	8
589/588		16	9
588/587		17	10
587/586		18	11
586/585		19	12
585/584		20	13
584/583		21	14
583/582		22	15
582/581		23	16
581/580		24	17
580/579		25	18
579/578		26	19
578/577		27	20
577/576		28	21
576/575		29	22
575/574		30	23
574/573		31	24
573/572		32	25
572/571		33	26
571/570		34	27
570/569		35	28
569/568		36	29
568/567		37	30
567/566		38	31
566/565		39	32
565/564		40	33
564/563		41	34
563/562		42	35
562/561	Nebuchadnezzar	43	36
	Amel-Marduk accession		
561/560	Amel-Marduk	1	37

449. According to the above translations (RSV, §447), Amel-Marduk's gracious action for Jehoiachin was "in the year that he began to reign" (2 Kgs 25:27) or "in the year that he became king" (Jer 52:31), which can suggest

Amel-Marduk's accession year (562/561, §448). The Hebrew in the two passages (בשנת מלכו את־ראש, *bishnat malko 'et-rosh*) is not the same, however, as what we have recognized as the normal designation of an accession year (§421). Rather the present phrase is more probably to be translated as James Moffatt does, "in the first year of his reign," and the first year, following the accession year, was 561/560. In accordance with Babylonian custom the years of Nebuchadnezzar and Amel-Marduk are, of course, "Nisan years" beginning on Nisan/Nisanu (for the terminology §421) and, since Jehoiachin's exile began on Nisan 10, so near the beginning of the Nisan year, and his exile was in Babylonia, we may reasonably disregard the ten days difference and simply cite Jehoiachin's captivity years as Nisan years too. The resulting tabulation appears in Table 123, and it is evident that the thirty-seventh year of Jehoiachin's captivity does not agree with Amel-Marduk's accession year but does agree exactly with his first full regnal year.[339]

7. The Dates in Ezekiel

LITERATURE: Julius A. **Bewer**, "Das Datum in Hes 33:21," *ZAW* 54 (1936): 114–115; C. F. **Whitley**, "The Thirtieth Year in Ezekiel I, 1," *VT* 9 (1959): 326–330; K. S. **Freedy** and D. B. **Redford**, "The Dates in Ezekiel in Relation to Biblical, Babylonian, and Egyptian Sources," *JAOS* 90 (1970): 462–485; Edwin R. **Thiele**, *The Mysterious Numbers of the Hebrew Kings* (2d ed.; Grand Rapids: Eerdmans, 1965), 169; idem, *Mysterious Numbers* (3d ed.; Grand Rapids: Zondervan, 1983), 187–191.

450. When Jerusalem fell to Nebuchadnezzar on Addaru 2 (Mar 16) 597 all "except the poorest people of the land:" (2 Kgs 24:14) were carried off with Jehoiachin into the Babylonian captivity, and the priest Ezekiel was presumably among those taken away at that time.[340] In Ezek 1:1 he describes himself as "among the exiles by the river Chebar" (a canal which is also mentioned in business documents found at Nippur, southeast of Babylon),[341] by which river there was a place called Telabib where the deportees (or at least part of them) were settled, with Ezekiel having a house of his own (Ezek 8:1). The same opening verse (Ezek 1:1) gives a date "in the thirtieth year, in the fourth month, on the fifth day of the month," and 1:2–3 cites "the fifth day of the month" (presumably the same fourth month) in "the fifth year of the exile of King Jehoiachin" as the time when "the word of the Lord came to Ezekiel the priest," apparently meaning the time of his initial commissioning as a prophet. On the basis of the probable manner of reckoning the years of the exile of Jehoiachin (Table 123) the fifth year was 593/592, the fourth month is Tammuz (June/July), and in 593 the fifth day of Tammuz was July 31.[342] While the significance of the thirtieth year in 1:1 is not explained, it could be that this was the thirtieth year after Ezekiel's call as a prophet and was the date of the initial composition of his book by Ezekiel himself in the year 563.[343]

---

[339]Although independently reached, the results agree with Freedy and Redford, "Dates in Ezekiel," *JAOS* 90 (1970): 467, Table I.

[340]*ABC* 714.

[341]W. F. Albright, *JBL* 51 (1932): 100.

[342]PDBC 28; Thiele, *Mysterious Numbers* (1983), 187–188.

[343]*OAB* 1000.

451. Throughout the book of Ezekiel there is a further series of dates (8:1; 20:1; 24:1; 26:1; 29:1, 17; 30:20; 31:1; 32:1, 17; 33:21; 40:1) of the same exactitude as in 1:1–3 and, as there, many but not all of these identify times when "the word of the Lord" came to Ezekiel. Because the initial dating is in "the fifth year of the exile of King Jehoiachin" (1:2) it may reasonably be assumed that the other dates too are stated in terms of years of Jehoiachin's exile, and this is confirmed in 33:21; 40:1 where Ezekiel gives dates "of our exile." Dated points of special significance in relation to the contemporary history will be noted in what follows. In the sixth year, in the sixth month, on the fifth day of the month (Ezek 8:1), Ezekiel was brought by the Spirit "in visions of God" to Jerusalem where he saw the abominations at the gate of the temple, in which women wept for Tammuz and men with their backs to the temple and their faces toward the east worshiped the sun. The sixth year of the exile of Jehoiachin was 592/591 (Table 123), the sixth month is Elul (Aug/Sept), and in 592 the fifth day of Elul was Sept 17. In the ninth year, in the tenth month, on the tenth day of the month, the word of the Lord came to Ezekiel telling him that the king of Babylon had laid siege to Jerusalem "this very day" (Ezek 24:1). The ninth year of the exile of Jehoiachin was 589/588 (Table 123), the tenth month is Tebeth (Dec/Jan), and in 588 the tenth day of Tebeth was Jan 15.[344] The identical date is recorded in identical words in 2 Kgs 25:1 but in terms of the reign of Zedekiah (where the regnal years are Tishri years), and the result is the same.

452. The date of the final fall of Jerusalem to Nebuchadnezzar has been established above (§442) as Tammuz 9 (July 18) 586. In the twelfth year of what Ezekiel calls "our exile," in the tenth month, on the fifth day of the month, a man who had escaped from Jerusalem came to him and said, "the city has fallen" (Ezek 33:21). The twelfth year of the exile was 586/585 (Table 123), the tenth month is Tebeth (Dec/Jan), and in 585 the fifth day of Tebeth was Jan 8. From July 18 to the following Jan 8 the man had taken somewhat less than six months for the journey. The time compares favorably with a full four months required by Ezra for a journey in the reverse direction under peaceful circumstances (Ezra 7:9, see below §459).[345]

453. The date of Ezekiel's vision of the temple in Ezek 40:1 has already been identified (§439) as evidently marking the anniversary of the "very day" of the inauguration of the exile. The date, Ezekiel says, is in the twenty-fifth year "of our exile," at the beginning of the year [evidently in the first month, Nisan], on the tenth day of the month, and in the fourteenth year after the city was conquered. The twenty-fifth year of the exile was 573/572, and in 573 the tenth day of Nisan was Apr 28. Inasmuch as Jerusalem fell according to our reckoning (§442) on Tammuz 9 (July 18), 586, in the nineteenth year of Nebuchadnezzar (586/585), the fourteenth year from that date, counted inclusively, was 573/572 and the exact anniversary date is Apr 28, 573 B.C.[346]

---

[344]PDBC 28; *OAB* 1029.
[345]Finegan, *Archaeological History,* 388–389 n. 18.
[346]Finegan, *Archaeological History,* 389 n., 18; *OAB* 1052.

8. Post-Exilic Dates

LITERATURE: R. P. **Dougherty**, *Nabonidus and Belshazzar* (New Haven: Yale University Press, 1929); Norman H. **Smith**, "The Date of Ezra's Arrival in Jerusalem," *ZAW* 63 (1951): 53–66; H. H. **Rowley**, "The Chronological Order of Ezra and Nehemiah," in *The Servant of the Lord and Other Essays on the Old Testament* (London: Lutterworth, 1952), 131–159; Kurt **Galling**, "Von Naboned zu Darius," in *ZDPV* 69 (1953): 42–64; 70 (1954): 4–32; Peter R. **Ackroyd**, "Two Old Testament Historical Problems of the Early Persian Period," in *JNES* 17 (1958): 13–27; J. **Morgenstern**, "The Dates of Ezra and Nehemiah," in *JSS* 7 (1962): 1–11.

454. The fall of Babylon to Cyrus the Persian led to the return of the Jewish exiles to their homeland. The fall of Babylon is recorded in a cuneiform document known as the Nabonidus Chronicle.[347] Referring to the seventeenth and last year of King Nabunaid (Nabonidus) of Babylon, this source gives dates which may be summarized, with their equivalents, as follows: The Persian forces took Sippar on Tashritu 14 = Oct 10, 539 B.C.; they took Babylon on Tashritu 16 = Oct 12; and Cyrus entered the city on Arahsamnu 3 = Oct 29. The decree allowing the exiles to return to Jerusalem was published in the first year of Cyrus (2 Chron 36:22; Ezra 1:1; 6:3). His first official year as king of Babylon was 538/537.[348] As quoted in Ezra 1:3 the intent of the Cyrus decree was that the exiles returned to Jerusalem should "rebuild the house of the Lord," i.e., should rebuild the temple which Nebuchadnezzar and Nebuzaradan had destroyed. The spirit of the decree is confirmed in the Cyrus Cylinder, a cuneiform document in which Cyrus says, among other things, that he returned foreign exiles to their former homes and in place of sanctuaries which were in ruins for a long time he established permanent sanctuaries for their images.[349]

455. As per the references just cited (§454), the book of Chronicles (2 Chron 36:22–23) and the book of Ezra (Ezra 1:1–4) begin with slightly variant quotations of the decree by Cyrus allowing the return of the exiles and the rebuilding of the Jerusalem temple, and the books of Ezra and Nehemiah continue about the ensuing events, to which the books of Haggai and Zechariah are also related (Ezra 6:14). According to the present order of the books of Ezra and Nehemiah, the priest Ezra came back to Jerusalem first and instituted a great religious reform, then Nehemiah came later and as governor accomplished the rebuilding of the walls of Jerusalem. The matter is complicated, however, because where the Persian king Artaxerxes is named (Ezra 7:7; Neh 2:1) it is not clear whether this is the first or the second king of this name, and for this and other reasons some prefer a theoretical rearrangement of the materials of the two books and of the order of Ezra 1–6, then Nehemiah 1–7, 11–13, and then Ezra 7–10, and Nehemiah 8–10, and is followed immediately below (§§456ff.), with dates where stated or inferred.

---

[347] *ANET* 305–306; *ANEA* 203–204.
[348] PDBC 29.
[349] *ANET* 315–316.

456. While many exiles did not wish to go away from the possessions they had acquired in Babylonia (Josephus, *Ant.* 11.8), a first contingent of returnees was made up of "everyone whose spirit God had stirred to go up to rebuild the house of Lord which is in Jerusalem," and over these Cyrus appointed as leader "Sheshbazzar the prince of Judah" and gave to him the treasures of gold and siver Nebuchadnezzar had taken from Jerusalem and put in the house of his own gods (Ezra 1:5–11). The name of Sheshbazzar is probably to be recognized as a variant of Shenazzar, named in 1 Chron 3:18 as one of the sons of Jeconiah the captive.[350] Many of the exiles no doubt still considered Jeconiah the legitimate king of Judah, and thus in the choice of Sheshbazzar Cyrus allowed for the return to be under a prince of the Davidic line and to that extent allowed for the restoration of the identity of the nation.[351] The date of Sheshbazzar's going is not given, but it was no doubt not far from the time of Cyrus's decree for the return, i.e., about 538/537. Under Sheshbazzar the foundations of the temple were laid, but opposition arose from "the people of the land" (Ezra 4:4) and the temple was still unfinished in the time of Darius (Ezra 5:16).

457. In turn, under Zerubbabel and Jeshua, many more came back to Jerusalem and Judah, each to his own town (Ezra 2:1). Zerubbabel was the grandson of Jeconiah (either the son of Pedaiah [1 Chron 3:18] or the son of Shealtiel [Ezra 3:2]) and thus also, like Sheshbazzar, whom he succeeded as leader of the community, was of the royal house of David, while his name ("sown in Babylon") attested to his birth in the land of the exile. Doubtless also born during the exile, Jeshua the son of Jozadak (also Joshua son of Jehozadak) was the high priest of the returned community (Hag 1:1). Under Zerubbabel and Jeshua the rebuilding of the temple was resumed in the second year of Darius (Ezra 4:24), Darius having confirmed that Cyrus issued the original decree for the rebuilding (Ezra 6:1–3), and the prophets Haggai and Zechariah encouraging the work with their preaching (Ezra 5:1). The second regnal year of Darius I was 520/519 B.C. In that year in the sixth month, on the first day of the month, the prophet Haggai exhorted Zerubbabel to rebuild the house of the Lord (Hag 1:1f.). This date was Aug 29, 520. The beginning of the work was in the sixth month, on the twenty-fourth day of the month (Hag 1:15). This was Sept 21, 520. In the same year in the eighth month the first address of Zechariah was given (Zech 1:1). This was in Oct/Nov 520. The completion of the rebuilding of the temple was on the third day of the month of Adar in the sixth year of the reign of Darius (Ezra 6:15). The date was Mar 12, 515.

458. Nehemiah, cupbearer (Neh 1:11) to Artaxerxes in Susa, winter capital of the Persian empire, learned with sorrow from some who came from Judah of the deplorable state of those living in Jerusalem where the wall of the city was still broken down (1:1–3). In the month of Nisan in the twentieth year of Artaxerxes, the king sent Nehemiah, with armed escort (1:9) and with the authority of a governor of Judah, to Jerusalem, and he was there in that position

---

[350] Bernhard W. Anderson, *Understanding the Old Testament* (Englewood Cliffs, N.J.: Prentice-Hall, 1957), 430–463; *OAB* 573.

[351] W. F. Albright, *The Biblical Period,* 48–49.

for twelve years (5:14). If the king was Artaxerxes I Longimanus (464–424 B.C.), the year of Nehemiah's going was 445/444 and the first day of Nisan was Apr 13, 445, and the twelve years of his stay are counted as extending to the thirty-second year of Artaxerxes (433/432). After surveying the state of the walls of Jerusalem by night (2:15), Nehemiah rallied the people to work (2:17–18), each laboring with one hand holding a weapon in the other hand because of enemies (4:17), and the rebuilding of the wall was completed in fifty-two days on the twenty-fifth day of the month Elul (6:15); the date was equivalent to Oct 2, 445 B.C., and the event was celebrated with much gladness (12:27). When the wall was completed Nehemiah enrolled the people by genealogy (7:5), evidently to establish true membership in the community, and lots were cast to bring one out of ten to live in Jerusalem, in order to strengthen the population of the holy city (11:1). In the thirty-second year of Artaxerxes I (433–432) Nehemiah was back with the Persian king, but "after some time" asked leave and returned to Jerusalem for a second period of administration (13:7). Finding that various evils had arisen (13:7ff.), he instituted further social and religious reforms, including insistence on strict observance of the tithe (13:12) and the Sabbath (13:15ff.) and the abandonment of foreign marriages (13:23ff.), and he established the duties of the priests and Levites (13:30). How long this period of service by Nehemiah continued we are not told, save that Darius is mentioned in Neh 12:22, and this must be Darius II Nothus, who reigned in 423–405. Josephus (*Ant.* 11.183) says only that Nehemiah died at an advanced age.

459. In the probably correct sequence of its parts, the narrative concerning Ezra the scribe (Ezra 7:6, not the Ezra who was among the priests and Levites who came up with Zerubbabel, Neh 12:1) tells of his journey (Ezra 7–8), of his reading of the Law (Neh 8), of the expulsion of foreign wives (Ezra 9–10), and of the renewal of the covenant (Neh 9).[352] It was by permission of Artaxerxes king of Persia that Ezra led a band of returning exiles from Babylonia to Jerusalem, leaving Babylonia on the first day of the first month, in the seventh year of the king (Ezra 7:1, 8–9). If the king was Artaxerxes I (464–424) the seventh year was 458/457, the departure was on Apr 8, 458, and the arrival was on Aug 4, 458, just four months of travel in all (§452). In this case Ezra came to Jerusalem some thirteen years before the arrival of Nehemiah (§458). If, however, the king was Artaxerxes II Memnon (404–359), the seventh year was 398/397, the departure on the first day of the first month was on Apr 5, 398, and the arrival in Jerusalem on the first day of the fifth month was on July 31, 398.[353] In this case Nehemiah's first twelve years of governorship in Jerusalem (445–433) were already past as well as his return soon thereafter, and a prayer by Ezra (Ezra 9:9) can reflect as already accomplished both the rebuilding of the temple by Zerubbabel and also the repair of the walls by Nehemiah, but Neh 8:9 and 10:1 represent Nehemiah and Ezra as there together.

460. As for Ezra's own work, he was "a scribe skilled in the law of Moses" (Ezra 7:6), and he brought with him from Babylonia "the book of the

---

[352] Anderson, *Understanding the Old Testament,* 454, n. 19.
[353] PDBC 34.

law of Moses" (Neh 8:1), and at the request of the people, on the first day of the seventh month, he began the reading of the book in public assembly, and the Levites "gave the sense, so that the people understood the reading" (Neh 8:8). In accordance with the law the Feast of Booths (Tabernacles) was observed for seven days with a solemn assembly on the eighth day (Neh 8:14ff.). Further, in a penitential assembly on the twenty-fourth day of the same month "the Israelites separated themselves from all foreigners, and stood and confessed their sins and the iniquities of their fathers" (Neh 9:2). Because of all this a firm covenant was made and written, and the princes, Levites, and priests set their seal to it (Neh 9:38). Although there are other traditions, Josephus (*Ant.* 11.158) says that Ezra died soon after the celebration of the Feast of Tabernacles and was buried at Jerusalem with great magnificence. Thus, in the years just surveyed (§§454ff.) the work of Sheshbazzar, Zerubbabel, Nehemiah, and Ezra ensured the survival and marked out the major characteristics of post-exilic Judaism.

Chapter 5

II. THE NEW TESTAMENT

LITERATURE: Rudolf **Bultmann**, *Die Geschichte der synoptischen Tradition* (2d ed., Göttingen: Vandenhoeck & Ruprecht, 1931); idem, *The History of the Synoptic Tradition* (trans. John Marsh; reprint, Peabody, Mass.: Hendrickson, 1993); F. F. **Bruce**, *The New Testament Documents: Are They Reliable?* (5th rev. ed.; London and Downers Grove, Ill.: InterVarsity, 1960); idem, "The Acts of the Apostles Today," *BJRL* 65 (1982/1983): 35–56; Bo **Reicke**, *The New Testament Era: The World of the Bible from 500 B.C. to A.D. 100* (Philadelphia: Fortress, 1968); Ernst **Haenchen**, *The Acts of the Apostles: A Commentary* (Oxford: Blackwell, 1971); Pierre **Benoit**, *Jesus and the Gospel* (New York: Seabury, 1973), 11–45, "Reflections on 'Formgeschichtliche Methode' "; W. Ward **Gasque**, *A History of the Criticism of the Acts of the Apostles* (Beiträge zur Geschichte der biblischen Exegese 17; Tübingen: J. C. B. Mohr [Paul Siebeck], 1975); R. T. **France** and David **Wenham**, eds., *Gospel Perspectives: Studies of History and Tradition in the Four Gospels* (6 vols.; Sheffield: JSOT Press, 1980–1986); David **Wenham**, *The Rediscovery of Jesus' Eschatological Discourse* (Gospel Perspectives 4; Sheffield, England: JSOT Press, 1984); R. T. **France**, *The Evidence for Jesus* (Downers Grove, Ill.: InterVarsity, 1986); Donald L. **Jones**, "Luke's Unique Interest in Historical Chronology," SBLSP 1989, 378–387; James H. **Charlesworth**, ed., *The Messiah: Developments in Earliest Judaism and Christianity* (Minneapolis: Fortress, 1992; papers from an international symposium held at Princeton Theological Seminary in 1987); James D. G. **Dunn**, "Messianic Ideas and Their Influence on the Jesus of History," in Charlesworth, *The Messiah,* 365–381; John P. **Meier**, *A Marginal Jew: Rethinking the Historical Jesus,* vol. 1, *The Roots of the Problem and the Person* (ABRL; New York: Doubleday, 1991); Hershel **Shanks**, Stephen J. **Patterson**, Marcus J. **Borg**, and John Dominic **Crossan**, *The Search for Jesus: Modern Scholarship Looks at the Gospels* (Symposium of the Smithsonian Institution, September 11, 1993; Washington, D.C.: Biblical Archaeological Society, 1994); Klaus **Berger**, *Theologiegeschichte des Urchristentums: Theologie des Neuen Testaments* (Tübingen and Basel: Francke, 1994); Ben **Witherington** III, *The Jesus Quest: The Third Search for the Jew of Nazareth* (Downers Grove, Ill.: InterVarsity, 1995).

461. In the New Testament, chronological notations in relation to the lives of John the Baptist, Jesus, Peter, and Paul, are found chiefly in the Four Gospels and the Book of the Acts of the Apostles. As for the Gospels and their accounts of the life of Jesus, it is now possible to speak of three phases of the modern search for the historical Jesus. In 1906 under the title *Von Reimarus zu Wrede,* Albert Schweitzer published an analysis of the works of a whole series of German scholars extending from Hermann Samuel Reimarus (1694–1768) to Wilhelm Wrede (1859–1906). This was translated by W. Montgomery as *The Quest of the Historical Jesus,*[1] providing the name by which the search in question has been best known ever since. According to Reimarus, Jesus believed God would help him establish an earthly kingdom and deliver the Jews from political oppression, a hope which ended on the cross. Following this disappointment his followers invented the resurrection and hoped for a second coming of Christ. According to Wrede the early Christians believed that Jesus was only made the Messiah by the resurrection and that is why he is represented in the Gospels as forbidding the disciples to divulge this "messianic secret." In his book Schweitzer also includes his own understanding of the teaching of Jesus in terms of "thoroughgoing eschatology." This thoroughgoing eschatology led to an "interim ethic" for the brief time before the coming of the kingdom of heaven.

462. In the first half of the twentieth century this first search for the historical Jesus was continued even more radically by Martin Dibelius (Berlin 1908–1915, Heidelberg 1915–1947), whose *Die Formgeschichte des Evangeliums,* translated by Bertram Lee Woolf as *From Tradition to Gospel*[2] earned him the title of "the founder of the school of form criticism"; and by Rudolf Bultmann (Marburg 1921–1951), whose *Die Geschichte der synoptischen Tradition,* translated by John Marsh as *The History of the Synoptic Tradition,* has been highly influential ever since. Bultmann argued that the early church had no interest in the history of Jesus as such but only in what would serve the concrete needs and interests of its own life and faith, and to that end sayings of Jesus and narratives of his life were freely modified or freely invented. Sayings, it is held, are often tied to no particular place or time, or at most only accidentally so or as the result of the play of the imagination. For example, Bultmann says that the details about the situation in the stories of the calling of the disciples (Mark 1:16–20) only derive from the metaphor of "fishers of men," and have no historical value. Similar skepticism is addressed to such indications of time as the tradition contains.[3] As for the written form in which we have the Gospels, the evangelists were editors rather than authors and the framework in which they assembled the materials has no value either geographical or chronological. For example, the indications of time in Mark 1:32, 35 belong to this editorial stage.[4] Furthermore, according to Bultmann, the New Testament expresses itself in prescientific mythological terminology drawn from Jewish apocalyptic literature and Gnostic redemption

---

[1] Schweitzer, *The Quest of the Historical Jesus* (trans. W. Montgomery; London: A. & C. Black, 1910; repr. New York: Macmillan, 1968).

[2] Heidelberg, *From Tradition to Gospel* (trans. B. L. Woolf; New York: Scribners, 1935).

[3] Bultmann, *Geschichte der synoptischen Tradition,* 67f., 258, 365; idem, *History of Synoptic Tradition,* 63–64.

[4] Bultmann, *History of Synoptic Tradition,* 243.

legends. To make it understandable to the modern person, whatever is mythological must be eliminated, hence Bultmann's program involves demythologization *(Entmythologisierung)*. Ultimately, Bultmann's approach makes such a distinction between "the Christ of faith" and "the Jesus of history" as to make the search for the latter seem almost impossible. Some other scholars, however, have judged that neither this sharp a distinction between the two nor the concomitant pessimism regarding the historicity of the Gospels is warranted.[5]

463. As for the dating of the four canonical Gospels, the Synoptics are usually placed after A.D. 70 and John after these. These datings have not, however, gone unchallenged. For example, John A. T. Robinson argued that all of the books of the New Testament might be dated prior to the fall of Jerusalem in A.D.[6] W. F. Albright and C. H. Dodd both argued that John relied on pre–A.D. 70 sources, and Robinson went on to argue for Johannine priority.[7] J. D. G. Dunn has found many indications that John's portrayal of Jesus draws upon good historical information about what Jesus said and did,[8] and the Dead Sea Scrolls have provided further evidence for this point of view.[9] Furthermore, a papyrus fragment of John (Papyrus Rylands Greek 457, generally known as $\mathfrak{P}^{52}$) has been dated to not later than A.D. 125[10] and perhaps A.D. 100 or a decade earlier,[11] which gives a date by which the Gospel would have been already in circulation in Egypt. The most recent full-scale consideration of the date of composition of John in terms of its historical relationships places it shortly after the death of Peter and before the destruction of Jerusalem.[12] Such is the best conclusion about the Fourth Gospel and certainly makes possible its apostolic authorship. The present author concurs with the judgment of R. T. France that "some, and perhaps all, of the gospels were written in substantially their present form within thirty years of the events,"[13] so that their contents should be regarded not as the product of a long folk-tradition but as accounts of recent happenings.

---

[5] See, e.g. William Hendriksen, *Matthew* (NTC; Grand Rapids: Baker Book House, 1973), 65–76, esp. 72; J. D. G. Dunn, "Messianic Ideas," 366, 371–72.

[6] *Redating the New Testament* (Philadelphia: Westminster, 1976). For a survey regarding the Synoptic Gospels, see esp. John Wenham, *Redating Matthew, Mark and Luke: A Fresh Assault on the Synoptic Problem* (London: Hodder & Stoughton, 1991).

[7] W. F. Albright, *The Archaeology of Palestine* (Hammondsworth, Middlesex: Penguin, 1949), 240, 244ff.; C. H. Dodd, *Historical Tradition in the Fourth Gospel* (Cambridge: Cambridge University Press, 1963); J. A. T. Robinson, *The Priority of John* (Philadelphia: Westminster, 1986).

[8] "Let John Be John" in Peter Stuhlmacher, ed., *Das Evangelium und die Evangelien* (Tübingen: Mohr, 1983).

[9] James H. Charlesworth, "Reinterpreting John: How the Dead Sea Scrolls Have Revolutionized Our Understanding of the Gospel of John," *BR* 9 (1, Feb 1993): 18ff. Cf. Craig Blomberg, *The Historical Reliability of the Gospels* (Downers Grove, Ill.: InterVarsity, 1987), 161; and see further F. F. Bruce, *The Gospel of John* (Grand Rapids: Eerdmans, 1983).

[10] C. H. Roberts, *An Unpublished Fragment of the Fourth Gospel* (Manchester: Manchester University Press, 1935).

[11] Charlesworth, "Reinterpreting John," 19.

[12] Berger, *Theologiegeschichte des Urchristentums,* 653–57. Berger dates the death of Peter to A.D. c. 66.

[13] *The Evidence for Jesus,* 103, 121.

464. A series of scholars has considered the Acts of the Apostles a late writing of undependable historical worth. In a two-volume work on Paul (1873–75) Ferdinand Christian Baur of Tübingen described the book of Acts as a tendentious and subjective composition aimed at reconciling the supposedly antithetic Petrine (Jewish-Christian) and Pauline (Gentile) parties, a book which must have been composed far along in the second century. In an Introduction to the New Testament (1904) Adolf Jülicher dated the Book of Acts after the beginning of the second century and considered its picture of the apostolic age an idealization representing the nebulous conceptions of a later generation and showing that only meager information was then available to the author of this later time. In his very influential commentary,[14] Ernst Haenchen holds that the entire picture in Acts of the missionary situation shows that no co-worker of Paul is speaking but rather a person of a later generation, who is trying to set forth things on which he no longer possesses true perspective. On the other hand, it may be remembered that the Book of Acts is the second volume of a two-volume work (Luke–Acts). In the introduction to the first volume the author refers to what eyewitnesses have delivered "to us," and affirms his own intention, "having followed all things closely for some time past," to write an orderly account so that his addressee "may know the truth." It can hardly be supposed that the qualifications and intentions of the author were any less in the second volume of his work. In fact he appears therein as a companion of Paul (cf. "Luke the beloved physician," Col 4:14) on a number of occasions of which he can speak in the first person plural ("we"), in particular on the shipwreck journey (Acts 27:1–28:16) of which he tells so accurately that his description is a classic source of information on Mediterranean seafaring in the first century of the Christian era. Thus in his commentary on the Greek text of Acts,[15] F. F. Bruce points to the precision of the historical and geographical references characteristic of Acts as making attribution to Luke highly acceptable. Bruce remarks elsewhere[16] that "Haenchen's commentary . . . fails to reckon seriously and critically enough with Luke's claim to relate what actually happened, on the basis of personal research and, where possible of eyewitness testimony," and of Luke himself Bruce reiterates that "his real purpose . . . was to record what actually happened." Numerous other scholars have expressed similar confidence in the historical value of Acts.[17]

465. As to the date of the book of Acts, it may be remembered that Adolf von Harnack came finally to the judgment that the closing words of the book (Acts 28:30–31) require the conclusion that the work was completed very soon after the "two whole years" there mentioned.[18] To assume that a book was

---

[14] *The Acts of the Apostles: A Commentary* (Philadelphia: Westminster, 1971).

[15] *The Acts of the Apostles: The Greek Text with Introduction and Commentary* (2d ed.; London: Tyndale, 1952).

[16] "The Acts of the Apostles Today" (44, 56).

[17] E.g., Alfred Wikenhauser, *Die Apostelgeschichte und ihr Geschichtswert* (Münster: Aschendorff, 1921); A. N. Sherwin-White, *Roman Society and Roman Law in the New Testament* (Oxford: Clarendon, 1963), 189; J. N. Geldenhuys, *Commentary on Luke* (Grand Rapids: Eerdmans, 1950); idem, in *New Bible Dictionary* (Grand Rapids: Eerdmans, 1962), 756; Donald L. Jones, "Luke's Unique Interest in Historical Chronology"; W. Ward Gasque, *A History of the Criticism of the Acts of the Apostles*.

written near the end of the time of the last event it records is a normal way of determining the date of an ancient writing. In this case this time was the two years of Paul's house arrest in Rome (Acts 28:30–31), in our reckoning A.D. 58–60. Since Acts is the second volume of a two-volume work, of which the first volume is the Gospel according to Luke, that Gospel must necessarily be earlier, and the Gospel according to Mark (if used by Luke, as usually believed), necessarily earlier still. Harnack writes:

> . . . the concluding verses of the Acts of the Apostles, taken in conjunction with the absence of any reference in the book to the result of the trial of St. Paul and to his martyrdom, make it in the highest degree probable that the work was written at a time when St. Paul's trial in Rome had not yet come to and end. . . . then the date of the Lukan Gospel must be earlier, and that of the Gospel of St. Mark earlier still.

466. It is not the intention of the present book to say that there are no problems in the chronological items in the Gospels and Acts; it is also not the intention to deny that many of the problems are so complex that there is room for many differences of opinion about them; but it is the intention to affirm that in these fields there are significant materials with which to work and that such work is important.

A. THE LIFE OF JOHN THE BAPTIST

LITERATURE: Walter **Wink**, *John the Baptist in the Gospel Tradition* (Cambridge: University Press, 1968); Robert L. **Webb**, *John the Baptizer and Prophet* (Sheffield: JSOT Press, 1991).

467. The life of John the Baptist and the life of Jesus are closely interrelated. In the person of John, Mark 1:2 sees fulfilled the prophecy of Mal 3:1 about the messenger who would prepare the way of the Lord, even as John's father, Zechariah, prophesied that the child would go before the Lord to prepare his ways (Luke 1:76), as John himself said that he was sent before the Christ (John 3:28), and as Jesus also identified John as he of whom it was written, "I send my messenger . . . who shall prepare thy way" (John 3:28), all of which led Christians later to designate John as the "forerunner" (πρόδρομος, going, lit. running, before), using the word which occurs in the New Testament only in Heb 6:20, where it describes Jesus as having gone on ahead of his followers into heavenly places. In identification of the parents of John, his father Zechariah is called a priest of the division of Abijah, and John's mother Elizabeth was also of priestly descent, being of the daughters of Aaron (Luke 1:5). The lineage of Mary, the mother of Jesus, is not identified but Elizabeth, the mother of John, is described as Mary's kinswoman (Luke 1:36). Mary's husband, Joseph, was of the house of David (Luke 1:27) and his trade was that of a carpenter (Matt 3:55) as was that of Jesus too (Mark 6:3). Points of special importance in the relationship of John and Jesus (§§468ff.) are when they were born, when they began their public work, and when John was put to death.

---

[18] Adolf von Harnack, *The Date of the Acts and of the Synoptic Gospels* (New York: G. P. Putnam's Sons, 1911), 93–99, 125.

1. The Birth of John and the Course of Abijah

LITERATURE: Henry **Browne**, *Ordo saeclorum: A Treatise on the Chronology of the Holy Scriptures* (London: John W. Parker, 1844); Thomas **Lewin**, *Fasti sacri, or A Key to the Chronology of the New Testament* (London: Longmans, Green, 1865); Roger T. **Beckwith**, "St. Luke, The Date of Christmas and the Priestly Courses at Qumran," *RQ* 9 (1977): 73–94.

468. At the time when it was made known to Zechariah that his wife Elizabeth would bear him a son, to be called John, Zechariah's priestly division of Abijah was on duty and Zechariah himself had the honor to be chosen by lot to burn incense in the temple on the altar of incense within the Holy Place (Exod 30:1–10; 37:25–28; 1 Macc 4:49), and it was there that he received the announcement. Somewhat later ("after these days," Luke 1:24) Elizabeth conceived and presumably some nine months thereafter bore the promised son (Luke 1:57), who became John the Baptist. In the meantime, in Elizabeth's sixth month, it was announced to Mary that she too would bear a son who should be called Jesus, and Mary came at that time to visit Elizabeth (Luke 1:26, 9–40). Therefore it was presumably about nine months after Mary's visit to Elizabeth, and about fifteen months after the initial announcement to Zechariah, that Jesus was born (Luke 2:7). Since the announcement to Zechariah came when he was on duty in the temple as a priest in the course of Abijah, this fact would be of significance for the chronology of both John the Baptist and Jesus, if it could be known when the course of Abijah was then on duty. The basic facts in the Hebrew Scriptures, Josephus, and the rabbinic sources about the priestly courses (the first course Jehoiarib, the eighth course Abijah, and so on) have been explained above (§§237 and following, and Table 60), together with the tradition that the First and Second Temples were destroyed on a day after the Sabbath, during a post-Sabbatical year, and during the weekly service of the course of Jehoiarib, on the calendar date of the ninth day of Ab equivalent in the year A.D. 70 to Aug 5 (§§200ff. and Table 50).

469. An example of an attempt to establish the date of the birth of Jesus in relation to the course of Abijah, and with the assumption that the priestly courses followed each other in continuous succession without regard to the beginning of a new year, is found in Thomas Lewin, *Fasti sacri,* who also cites Henry Browne, *Ordo saeclorum.* Although Lewin's other dates for the events in A.D. 70 are slightly divergent from ours, he gives the same date of Aug 4, A.D. 70, as the day when the course of Jehoiarib entered upon its office. From Aug 4, A.D. 70 (exclusive), back to Aug 4, 7 B.C. (inclusive), he counts 27,759 days (76 × 365.25 = 27,759). Assuming continuous succession of the 24 priestly courses, each cycle occupying 168 days (24 × 7 = 168), Lewin divides 27,759 days by 168 and finds 39 days left over. So on Aug 4, 7 B.C., the 24 courses still had 39 days to run before completing their cycle of 168 days, and must therefore have begun their cycle 129 days before, that is, on Mar 28, 7 B.C.; but if the first course began on Mar 28, 7 B.C., the eighth course, that of Abijah, would begin on May 16, 7 B.C. The conception of John the Baptist was at the close of Zechariah's course of seven days (Luke 1:23), and therefore about May 22, 7 B.C.; and the annunciation to the Virgin Mary was on the sixth month current (not the sixth month complete) after that (Luke 1:36), and therefore in Nov 7 B.C. The nativity, at the end of nine months from that time, would fall early in Aug 6 B.C., say for the sake of simplicity, on Aug 1, 6 B.C.[19]

470. In the present book, on the contrary, it is accepted with Roger T. Beckwith that the cycle of the twenty-four priestly courses began anew each year at the autumnal new year, with the first course, Jehoiarib, coming on duty on the Sabbath on or next before Tishri 1 (§243).[20] Since each course served one week and the next course came on duty on the next Sabbath/Saturday, it is evident that Abijah, as the eighth course, came on duty seven weeks after Jehoiarib, while it was seventeen weeks after Abijah when Jehoiarib came on duty again. Reckoning backward from the commencement of Jehoiarib's weekly service on the Sabbath/Saturday of Ab 8 equivalent to Aug 4, A.D. 70, using the tables of Babylonian Chronology, and showing both the Jewish month names and dates and also the equivalents in our calendar, the sequence would have been as shown in Table 124.[21]

TABLE 124. *From Jehoiarib Back to Abijah in A.D. 70*

	Course	*First Sabbath on Duty*
1.	Jehoiarib	Ab 8 = Aug 4
24.	Maaziah	Ab 1 = July 28
23.	Delaiah	Tammuz 24 = July 21
22.	Gamul	Tammuz 17 = July 14
21.	Jachin	Tammuz 10 = July 7
20.	Jehezkel	Tammuz 3 = June 30
19.	Pethahiah	Sivan 25 = June 23
18.	Happizzez	Sivan 18 = June 16
17.	Hezir	Sivan 11 = June 9
16.	Immer	Sivan 4 = June 2
15.	Bilgah	Iyyar 26 = May 26
14.	Jeshebeab	Iyyar 19 = May 19
13.	Huppah	Iyyar 12 = May 12
12.	Jakim	Iyyar 5 = May 5
11.	Eliashib	Nisan 28 = Apr 28
10.	Shecaniah	Nisan 21 = Apr 21
9.	Jeshua	Nisan 14 = Apr 14
8.	Abijah	Nisan 7 = Apr 7

Similarly, if the temple had stood and the priestly courses had continued as before, the sequence, reckoned in the same way, would have been as shown in Table 125.

[19] Lewin, *Fasti sacri,* xxviii–xxix; 109 no. 836; 360 no. 2149.

[20] Beckwith, *RQ* 9 (1977): 81, 85–86.

[21] PDBC 47. The tabulation in Beckwith, *RQ* 9 (1977): 83, Table 1, is essentially the same as in our Table 124 but counts in reverse from Abijah to Jehoiarib, uses Jewish month names and dates without equivalents in our calendar, assumes that the months were of 29 and 30 days alternately and reaches dates one day different in Iyyar, but exactly as in our tabulation shows Saturday Ab 8 for the commencement of Jehoiarib and Saturday Nisan 7 for the commencement of Abijah.

TABLE 125. *From Jehoiarib Forward to Jehoiarib in A.D. 70*

	Course	First Sabbath on Duty
1.	Jehoiarib	Ab 8 = Aug 4
2.	Jedaiah	Ab 15 = Aug 11
3.	Harim	Ab 22 = Aug 18
4.	Seorim	Ab 29 = Aug 25
5.	Malchijah	Elul 7 = Sept 1
6.	Mijamin	Elul 14 = Sept 8
7.	Hakkoz	Elul 21 = Sept 15
[8.	Abijah	Elul 28 = Sept 22]
9.	Jehoiarib	Elul 28 = Sept 22

If the priestly courses ran in unbroken succession without regard for the beginning of the new year (as some suppose, §242), course 7, Hakkoz, would have been followed by course 8, Abijah (as shown in Table in brackets), but if the cycle of courses began afresh at each autumnal new year (as is accepted in the present book), course 7, Hakkoz, would have been followed by Course 1 Jehoiarib to start the sequence over again, and Jehoiarib would have commenced on the Sabbath/Saturday Elul 28 = Sept 22 in order to be on duty already on Tishri 1 = Sept 25, A.D. 70.[22]

471. As for the sequence of the priestly courses from Jehoiarib (no. 1) to Abijah (no. 8) at the annual beginning again of the whole cycle on the Sabbath on or next before Tishri 1, Beckwith shows in his tables 1–4 that the course of Abijah (no. 8) probably came on duty each year on the Sabbaths falling on or about Heshvan 17 and Iyyar 8 (or, when there was a Second Adar, on Nisan 7).[23] The sequence leading to Heshvan 17 is reproduced in our Table 126.[24]

TABLE 126. *Annual Beginning Again of the Cycle of Priestly Courses from Jehoiarib to Abijah*

	Course	First Sabbath on Duty
1.	Jehoiarib	Elul 27
2.	Jedaiah	Tishri 4
3.	Harim	Tishri 11
4.	Seorim	Tishri 18
5.	Malchijah	Tishri 25
6.	Mijamin	Heshvan 3
7.	Hakkoz	Heshvan 10
8.	Abijah	Heshvan 17

[22]Our Table 125 begins with Jehoiarib and gives equivalent dates in our calendar, otherwise cf. Beckwith, *RQ* 9 (1977): 85, Table 3.

[23]Beckwith, *RQ* 9 (1977): 90.

[24]This excerpt is from Beckwith, *RQ* 9 (1977): 84, with acknowledgment to *Revue de Qumran*.

472. Assuming that the annual beginning again of the complete cycle of priestly courses was about the same in the time of Zechariah's service, Abijah would have been on duty the week of Heshvan 17–24 = Nov 10–17, which would therefore be the time when Zechariah received the announcement that Elizabeth would bear him a son to be named John. According to the references in Luke (§468), it should have been about fifteen months thereafter that Jesus was born. The ensuing fifteen Jewish months (shown in Table 127 with month-equivalents in our calendar) would lead to the week of Shebat 17–24 or, in a leap year (§78), to the week of Tebeth 17–24.[25]

TABLE 127. *Fifteen Months from the Course of Abijah to the Nativity*

	Ordinary Year		*Leap Year with Second Adar*
	Heshvan (Oct/Nov)		Heshvan (Oct/Nov)
1.	Chislev (Nov/Dec)	1.	Chislev (Nov/Dec)
2.	Tebeth (Dec/Jan)	2.	Tebeth (Dec/Jan)
3.	Shebat (Jan/Feb)	3.	Shebat (Jan/Feb)
4.	Adar (Feb/Mar)	4.	Adar (Feb/Mar)
5.	Nisan (Mar/Apr)	5.	Second Adar (Second Feb/Mar)
6.	Iyyar (Apr/May)	6.	Nisan (Mar/Apr)
7.	Sivan (May/June)	7.	Iyyar (Apr/May)
8.	Tammuz (June/July)	8.	Sivan (May/June)
9.	Ab (July/Aug)	9.	Tammuz (June/July)
10.	Elul (Aug/Sept)	10.	Ab (July/Aug)
11.	Tishri (Sept/Oct)	11.	Elul (Aug/Sept)
12.	Heshvan (Oct/Nov)	12.	Tishri (Sept/Oct)
13.	Chislev (Nov/Dec)	13.	Heshvan (Oct/Nov)
14.	Tebeth (Dec/Jan)	14.	Chislev (Nov/Dec)
15.	Shebat (Jan/Feb)	15.	Tebeth (Dec/Jan)

473. If we take the course of Abijah as beginning service on or about Heshvan 17 (rather than at the other possibility of Iyyar 8), then the sequence of the priestly periods of service (Table 127) leads to Tebeth (Dec/Jan) or Shebat (Jan/Feb) for the nativity of Jesus. In the year 3/2 B.C. (Seleucid year 309), to translate the dates into terms of our own calendar and using the figures in the Babylonian calendar,[26] the month Tebetu (Tebeth) began on Jan 8, 2 B.C., and Tebeth 17–24 was equivalent to Jan 24–31, 2 B.C., and the month Shabatu (Shebat) began on Feb 7, 2 B.C. Stating the figures more generally, Beckwith suggests that the Tebeth and Shebat dates point to a time for the nativity of Jesus between mid-January and fairly early February in 2 B.C. At any rate it is wintertime and is not far from the date of Nov 18 of Clement of Alexandria for the birth of Jesus (our §488). Beckwith thinks that this must have been a date handed down in the Egyptian church, which Clement believed to be historical tradition, and from which Hippolytus of Rome *(Commentary on Daniel)* derived his similar dating. "If so," Beckwith concludes, "it was a traditional belief in Clement's time that Christ was born in the winter (though not at the winter solstice). It may be that Clement, and through him Hippolytus, were in posses-

[25]Beckwith, *RQ* 9 (1977): 90.
[26]PDBC 45.

sion of a genuine historical tradition to this effect, which in the course of time had been mistakenly narrowed down to a particular day."[27] This conclusion—for simplicity say mid-winter—is therefore accepted in the present book. The two specific days (Dec 25 and Jan 6) which are now so well known, and possible contributory causes of their selection, will concern us at a later point (§§554–569).

B. THE LIFE OF JESUS

LITERATURE: Urban **Holzmeister**, *Chronologia vitae Christi* (Rome: Pontifical Biblical Institute, 1933); Damiano **Lazzarato**, *Chronologia Christi seu discordantium fontium concordantia ad juris normam* (Neapoli : M. d'Auria, 1952); Ethelbert **Stauffer**, *Jesus and His Story* (New York: Alfred A. Knopf, 1960); S. **Dockx**, *Chronologies néotestamentaires et vie de l'église primitive: Recherches exégétiques* (Paris: Duculot, 1976); Harold W. **Hoehner**, *Chronological Aspects of the Life of Christ* (Grand Rapids: Zondervan, 1977); Ernest L. **Martin**, *The Birth of Christ Recalculated* (Pasadena, Newcastle-upon-Tyne, England: Foundation for Biblical Research, 1978); idem, *The Star That Astonished the World* (2d ed.; Portland: ASK Publications, 1996); Paul **Keresztes**, *Imperial Rome and the Christians,* vol. 1, *From Herod the Great to about 200 A.D.* (Lanham, Md.: University Press of America, 1989); Paul L. **Maier**, *In the Fullness of Time: A Historian Looks at Christmas, Easter, and the Early Church* (San Francisco: Harper San Francisco, 1991); John P. **Meier**, *A Marginal Jew: Rethinking the Historical Jesus,* vol. 1, *The Roots of the Problem and the Person* (ABRL; New York: Doubleday, 1991); David W. **Beyer**, "Josephus Reexamined: Unraveling the Twenty-second Year of Tiberius" (presentation to the Society for Biblical Literature, Nov. 19, 1995).

1. The Birth of Jesus

(1) Caesar Augustus

474. In relation to world history, Luke 2:1 notes that Jesus was born under the rule of Caesar Augustus, but the year is not given. Early Christian sources give specific years of Augustus, but the way in which the years are reckoned is not always evident. There are in fact various possibilities. In our earlier Table 41 chief events and honors in the life and reign of Augustus were shown. In Table 128 a preliminary numbering of regnal years is given, following three possible starting points. Julius Caesar died on the ides of March, i.e., Mar 15, in A.U.C. 710 = 44 B.C., and Octavian, his grand-nephew and adopted heir, succeeded him. Regnal years beginning with that date are numbered in column 1, and with the first full year after that date in column 2. Octavian defeated Antony at Actium on Sept 2 in A.U.C. 723 = 31 B.C. Years beginning with that date are numbered in column 3. Antony and Cleopatra died sometime in the month of August in A.U.C. 724 = 30 B.C., and this date was presumably determinative of the beginning of the reign of Augustus in Egypt. Regnal years beginning with this date are numbered in column 4, and with the first full year after that date in column 5.

---

[27] Beckwith *RQ* 9 (1977): 92, 94.

TABLE 128. *Regnal Years of Caesar Octavian Augustus*

A.U.C.	*B.C./A.D.*		*Col. 1*	*Col. 2*	*Col. 3*	*Col. 4*	*Col. 5*
710	44 B.C.	Mar 15, death of Julius Caesar	1				
711	43		2	1			
712	42		3	2			
713	41		4	3			
714	40		5	4			
715	39		6	5			
716	38		7	6			
717	37		8	7			
718	36		9	8			
719	35		10	9			
720	34		11	10			
721	33		12	11			
722	32		13	12			
723	31	Sept 2, defeat of Antony at Actium	14	13	1		
724	30	Aug, death of Antony and Cleopatra	15	14	2	1	
725	29		16	15	3	2	1
726	28		17	16	4	3	2
727	27		18	17	5	4	3
728	26		19	18	6	5	4
729	25		20	19	7	6	5
730	24		21	20	8	7	6
731	23		22	21	9	8	7
732	22		23	22	10	9	8
733	21		24	23	11	10	9
734	20		25	24	12	11	10
735	19		26	25	13	12	11
736	18		27	26	14	13	12
737	17		28	27	15	14	13
738	16		29	28	16	15	14
739	15		30	29	17	16	15
740	14		31	30	18	17	16
741	13		32	31	19	18	17
742	12		33	32	20	19	18
743	11		34	33	21	20	19
744	10		35	34	22	21	20
745	9		36	35	23	22	21
746	8		37	36	24	23	22
747	7		38	37	25	24	23
748	6		39	38	26	25	24
749	5		40	39	27	26	25
750	4		41	40	28	27	26
751	3		42	41	29	28	27
752	2		43	42	30	29	28
753	1 B.C.		44	43	31	30	29
754	A.D. 1		45	44	32	31	30
755	2		46	45	33	32	31
756	3		47	46	34	33	32
757	4		48	47	35	34	33
758	5		49	48	36	35	34
759	6		50	49	37	36	35
760	7		51	50	38	37	36
761	8		52	51	39	38	37
762	9		53	52	40	39	38
763	10		54	53	41	40	39
764	11		55	54	42	41	40
765	12		56	55	43	42	41
766	13		57	56	44	43	42
767	14	Aug 19, death of Augustus	58	57	45	44	43

475. Referring to columns 1 and 2 of Table 128 and counting from the death of Julius Caesar on Mar 15, 44 B.C., to the death of Augustus on Aug 19, A.D. 14, it would appear that Augustus had a factual reign of fifty-seven years, five months, and four days. The fact that reckoning was actually made in this way is shown by Josephus (*War* 2.168; *Ant.* 18.32), who states that Augustus reigned fifty-seven years, six months, and two days. The figure of six months can hardly be correct and may occur in the present text of Josephus because some copyist confused the Greek numeral five (ε´) for the numeral six (ϛ´). The figure of two days, on the other hand is probably more precise than the four days of our preliminary reckoning, for the will of Julius Caesar was not opened until Mar 17 and that date therefore, rather than Mar 15, should probably be taken as the starting point of the reign.[28] Fifty-seven years, five months and two days is, accordingly, the factual length of the reign of Augustus in Rome, and his factual regnal years were as indicated in Table 129.

TABLE 129. *Factual Regnal Years of Augustus in Rome*

Number of Regnal Year	*Duration of Regnal Year*
1	Mar 17, 44–Mar 16, 43 B.C.
2	Mar 17, 43–Mar 16, 42 B.C.
. . .	. . .
36	Mar 17, 9–Mar 16, 8
37	Mar 17, 8–Mar 16, 7
38	Mar 17, 7–Mar 16, 6
39	Mar 17, 6–Mar 16, 5
40	Mar 17, 5–Mar 16, 4
41	Mar 17, 4–Mar 16, 3
42	Mar 17, 3–Mar 16, 2
43	Mar 17, 2–Mar 16, 1
44	Mar 17, 1 B.C.–Mar 16, A.D. 1
45	Mar 17, A.D. 1–Mar 16, 2
. . .	. . .
56	Mar 17, 12–Mar 16, 13
57	Mar 17, 13–Mar 16, 14
Additional months and days	Mar 17, 14–Aug 19, 14

476. Turning to Egypt and referring to columns 4 and 5 in Table 128, Antony and Cleopatra died at a not exactly known date in August 30 B.C. and the rule of Augustus in Egypt ensued. If we assume that the unknown exact date in August of the death of Antony and Cleopatra was at least somewhat prior to the beginning of the next Egyptian calendar year on Thoth 1 = Aug 29, and that this period, short as it was, was counted as the first regnal year of Augustus in Egypt (non-accession-year system), then his full span of regnal years in Egypt, extending to his death on Aug 19, A.D. 14, may be outlined as in Table 130. In such a manner of counting, the reign reached into a forty-fourth year. The forty-second year of his reign is mentioned in Oxyrhynchus Papyrus 2277 ([ἔτους] μβ Καίσαρος).

[28]*Josephus* (LCL), vol. 2, 388 note a.

Since the exact day in August which was taken as the beginning of the reign is unknown, it is possible only to show each regnal year as extending from an undetermined date in August of one year to an undetermined date in August of the next year. If the exact beginning date of the regnal year in the month of August was later than Aug 19 (the date of the death of Augustus in the year 14), then the forty-third regnal year was that much short of a full year; if the exact beginning date of the regnal year was prior to Aug 19, then the forty-third regnal year came to a close and there were some additional days before Aug 19. In reading the table observe, therefore, that "Aug 30 B.C.–Aug 29 B.C.," means from an undetermined date in the month of August in the year 30 B.C. to an undetermined date in the month of August in the year 29 B.C., and so on; but at the end "Aug A.D. 13–Aug 19, A.D. 14," means from an undetermined date in the month of August in the year A.D. 13 to the exact date of Aug 19 in the year A.D. 14.

TABLE 130. *Factual Regnal Years of Augustus in Egypt*

Number of Regnal Year	*Duration of Regnal Year*
1	In Aug 30 B.C.
2	Aug 30 B.C.–Aug 29 B.C.
. . .	. . .
22	Aug 10 B.C.–Aug 9 B.C.
23	Aug 9 B.C.–Aug 8 B.C.
24	Aug 8 B.C.–Aug 7 B.C.
25	Aug 7 B.C.–Aug 6 B.C.
26	Aug 6 B.C.–Aug 5 B.C.
27	Aug 5 B.C.–Aug 4 B.C.
28	Aug 4 B.C.–Aug 3 B.C.
29	Aug 3 B.C.–Aug 2 B.C.
30	Aug 2 B.C.–Aug 1 B.C.
31	Aug 1 B.C.–Aug A.D. 1
32	Aug A.D. 1–Aug A.D. 2
. . .	. . .
42	Aug A.D. 11–Aug A.D. 12
43	Aug A.D. 12–Aug A.D. 13

477. Instead of counting factual regnal years, however, it was also possible as we have seen (§163) to reckon regnal years as equivalents of calendar years. To use the Julian calendar in initial example, this would mean counting the regnal year as coterminous with the calendar year which extends from Jan 1 to Dec 31. If the reckoning was by what we have called the non-accession-year system, the first regnal year of Augustus in Rome comprised the period from Mar 15 to Dec 31, 44 B.C., the second regnal year was the calendar year from Jan 1 to Dec 31, 43 B.C., and so on, in other words column 1 of Table 128 may be used directly for the reckoning. If the reckoning was by what we have called the accession-year system, the period from Mar 17 to Dec 31, 44 B.C., was only an "accession year," and the first regnal year of Augustus in Rome was the ensuing calendar year, namely the year from Jan 1 to Dec 31, 43 B.C., and so on, in other words column 2 in Table 128 may be used directly for the reckoning.

478. In terms of the Julian calendar and the non-accession-year system, then, the regnal years of Augustus in Rome may be shown as in Table 131.

TABLE 131. *Regnal Years of Augustus Counted as Julian Calendar Years according to the Non-Accession-Year System*

Number of Regnal Year	*Duration of Regnal Year*
1	Mar 17–Dec 31, 44 B.C.
2	Jan 1–Dec 31, 43 B.C.
...	...
36	Jan 1–Dec 31, 9
37	Jan 1–Dec 31, 8
38	Jan 1–Dec 31, 7
39	Jan 1–Dec 31, 6
40	Jan 1–Dec 31, 5
41	Jan 1–Dec 31, 4
42	Jan 1–Dec 31, 3
43	Jan 1–Dec 31, 2
44	Jan 1–Dec 31, 1 B.C.
45	Jan 1–Dec 31, A.D. 1
46	Jan 1–Dec 31, 2
...	...
57	Jan 1–Dec 31, 13
58	Jan 1–Aug 19, 14

479. In terms of the Julian calendar and the accession-year system, the regnal years of Augustus in Rome may be shown as in Table 132.

TABLE 132. *Regnal Years of Augustus Counted as Julian Calendar Years according to the Accession-Year System*

Number of Regnal Year	*Duration of Regnal Year*
Accession year	Mar 17–Dec 31, 44 B.C.
1	Jan 1–Dec 31, 43
2	Jan 1–Dec 31, 42
...	...
36	Jan 1–Dec 31, 8
37	Jan 1–Dec 31, 7
38	Jan 1–Dec 31, 6
39	Jan 1–Dec 31, 5
40	Jan 1–Dec 31, 4
41	Jan 1–Dec 31, 3
42	Jan 1–Dec 31, 2
43	Jan 1–Dec 31, 1 B.C.
44	Jan 1–Dec 31, A.D. 1
45	Jan 1–Dec 31, 2
...	...
56	Jan 1–Dec 31, 13
57	Jan 1–Aug 19, 14

480. In Egypt a reckoning of regnal years as calendar years would presumably have been in terms of the Egyptian calendar. In its standardized form (Table 8) and in a common year this calendar year began on Thoth 1 = Aug 29. Since the deaths of Antony and Cleopatra took place at a not precisely determined time in the month of August 30 B.C., it may be assumed that it was at least some time prior to Aug 29 (§476). Therefore, in terms of the Egyptian calendar and the non-accession-year system the regnal years of Augustus must have appeared as in Table 133.

481. In terms of the Egyptian calendar and the accession-year system, the regnal years of Augustus would appear as shown in Table 134.

482. In Syria we believe (§§128–129, Table 27) that the Macedonian calendar was used from shortly before the middle of the first century of the Christian era onwards in its later correlation in which the year began on Hyperberetaios 1 = Oct 1. Counted as years of this calendar, according to the non-accession-year system, the regnal years of Augustus would be as shown in Table 135.

483. In terms of the same Macedonian calendar in Syria but according to the accession-year system the regnal years of Augustus would be as shown in Table 136.

484. In the Jewish calendar (Table 13) the year began with the month Nisan, equivalent to Mar/Apr of the Julian calendar. In 44 B.C. when Julius Caesar was killed on Mar 15 and Octavian succeeded him on Mar 17, the first day of Nisan should have fallen by lunar observation on Apr 20.[29] By the non-accession-year system, therefore, the first regnal year of Augustus would have extended from Mar 17 to Apr 19, with his second regnal year beginning on Apr 20, 44 B.C. In the accession-year system the same period, Mar 17 to Apr 19, 44 B.C., would have constituted the "accession year" and the first regnal year would have begun on Apr 20, 44 B.C. After that, in Tables 137 and 138, to allow for the variation from year to year in the exact date of Nisan 1, we simply show the regnal year as extending from Mar/Apr to Mar/Apr.

485. In the Jewish calendar and according to the accession-year system the regnal years of Augustus would be shown as in Table 138.

486. In what now follows we will identify dates for the birth of Jesus given in terms of years of Augustus by early Christian scholars and historians who lived from the second to the sixth centuries.[30] In §§487–499 the writers are treated in chronological order; in Table 139 the dates they give are listed in the chronological order of the dates.

---

[29] PDBC 44.

[30] Martin, *Birth of Christ,* 4; idem, *Star,* 34; Keresztes, *Imperial Rome,* 1. For precise details now see especially David W. Beyer, "Year of the Nativity: The Early Church Fathers Reexamined." Presentation to the American Academy of Religion, March 28, 1996 (copy sent by the author to the present writer on Oct 12, 1996). Beyer places "the birth of Christ at the end of the forty-first year of Augustus counting from his accession (August, 43 B.C.), that is, approximately August, 2 B.C." (op. cit., 3, cf. 5, 9).

TABLE 133. *Regnal Years of Augustus Counted as Egyptian Calendar Years according to the Non-Accession-Year System*

Number of Regnal Year	*Duration of Regnal Year*
1	From the deaths of Antony and Cleopatra sometime in Aug to Aug 28, 30 B.C.
2	Aug 29, 30–Aug 28, 29
. . .	. . .
22	Aug 29, 10–Aug 28, 9
23	Aug 29, 9–Aug 28, 8
24	Aug 29, 8–Aug 28, 7
25	Aug 29, 7–Aug 28, 6
26	Aug 29, 6–Aug 28, 5
27	Aug 29, 5–Aug 28, 4
28	Aug 29, 4–Aug 28, 3
29	Aug 29, 3–Aug 28, 2
30	Aug 29, 2–Aug 28, 1
31	Aug 29, 1 B.C.–Aug 28, A.D.1
32	Aug 29, A.D. 1–Aug 28, 2
. . .	. . .
42	Aug 29, 11–Aug 28, 12
43	Aug 28, 12–Aug 29, 13
44	Aug 29, 13–Aug 19, 14

TABLE 134. *Regnal Years of Augustus Counted as Egyptian Calendar Years according to the Accession-Year System*

Number of Regnal Year	*Duration of Regnal Year*
Accession year	From the deaths of Antony and Cleopatra sometime in Aug to Aug 28, 30 B.C.
1	Aug 29, 30–Aug 28, 29
2	Aug 29, 29–Aug 28, 28
. . .	. . .
22	Aug 29, 9–Aug 28, 8
23	Aug 29, 8–Aug 28, 7
24	Aug 29, 7–Aug 28, 6
25	Aug 29, 6–Aug 28, 5
26	Aug 29, 5–Aug 28, 4
27	Aug 29, 4–Aug 28, 3
28	Aug 29, 3–Aug 28, 2
29	Aug 29, 2–Aug 28, 1 B.C.
30	Aug 29, 1 B.C.–Aug 28, A.D. 1
31	Aug 29, A.D. 1–Aug 28, 2
. . .	. . .
42	Aug 29, 12–Aug 28, 13
43	Aug 29, 13–Aug 19, 14

Table 134 may be taken as the usual Egyptian reckoning of the years of rule of Augustus in Egypt. Accordingly his twenty-eighth year of rule in Egypt, with which we shall be specially concerned (in §488), was from Aug 29, 3 B.C., to Aug 28, 2 B.C.

TABLE 135. *Regnal Years of Augustus Counted as Syro-Macedonian Calendar Years according to the Non-Accession-Year System*

Number of Regnal Year	*Duration of Regnal Year*
1	Mar 17–Sept 30, 44 B.C.
2	Oct 1, 44–Sept 30, 43
. . .	. . .
36	Oct 1, 10–Sept 30, 9
37	Oct 1, 9–Sept 30, 8
38	Oct 1, 8–Sept 30, 7
39	Oct 1, 7–Sept 30, 6
40	Oct 1, 6–Sept 30, 5
41	Oct 1, 5–Sept 30, 4
42	Oct 1, 4–Sept 30, 3
43	Oct 1, 3–Sept 30, 2
44	Oct 1, 2–Sept 30, 1
45	Oct 1, 1 B.C.–Sept 30, A.D. 1
46	Oct 1, 1–Sept 30, 2
. . .	. . .
57	Oct 1, 12–Sept 30, 13
58	Oct 1, 13–Aug 19, 14

TABLE 136. *Regnal Years of Augustus Counted as Syro-Macedonian Calendar Years according to the Accession-Year System*

Number of Regnal Year	*Duration of Regnal Year*
Accession year	Mar 17, 44–Sept 30, 44 B.C.
1	Oct 1, 44–Sept 30, 43
2	Oct 1, 43–Sept 30, 42
. . .	. . .
36	Oct 1, 9–Sept 30, 8
37	Oct 1, 8–Sept 30, 7
38	Oct 1, 7–Sept 30, 6
39	Oct 1, 6–Sept 30, 5
40	Oct 1, 5–Sept 30, 4
41	Oct 1, 4–Sept 30, 3
42	Oct 1, 3–Sept 30, 2
43	Oct 1, 2–Sept 30, 1
44	Oct 1, 1 B.C.–Sept 30, A.D. 1
45	Oct 1, 1–Sept 30, 2
. . .	. . .
56	Oct 1, 12–Sept 30, 13
57	Oct 1, 13–Aug 19, 14

TABLE 137. *Regnal Years of Augustus Counted as Jewish Calendar Years according to the Non-Accession-Year System*

Number of Regnal Year	*Duration of Regnal Year*
1	Mar 17–Apr 19, 44 B.C.
2	Apr 20, 44 B.C.–Mar/Apr 43 B.C.
. . .	. . .
36	Mar/Apr 10 B.C.–Mar/Apr 9 B.C.
37	Mar/Apr 9 B.C.–Mar/Apr 8 B.C.
38	Mar/Apr 8 B.C.–Mar/Apr 7 B.C.
39	Mar/Apr 7 B.C.–Mar/Apr 6 B.C.
40	Mar/Apr 6 B.C.–Mar/Apr 5 B.C.
41	Mar/Apr 5 B.C.–Mar/Apr 4 B.C.
42	Mar/Apr 4 B.C.–Mar/Apr 3 B.C.
43	Mar/Apr 3 B.C.–Mar/Apr 2 B.C.
44	Mar/Apr 2 B.C.–Mar/Apr 1 B.C.
45	Mar/Apr 1 B.C.–Mar/Apr A.D. 1
46	Mar/Apr A.D. 1–Mar/Apr A.D. 2
. . .	. . .
57	Mar/Apr A.D. 12–Mar/Apr A.D. 13
58	Mar/Apr A.D. 13–Mar/Apr A.D. 14 with the death of Augustus on the following Aug 19

TABLE 138. *Regnal Years of Augustus Counted as Jewish Calendar Years according to the Accession-Year System*

Number of Regnal Year	*Duration of Regnal Year*
Accession year	Mar 17–Apr 19, 44 B.C.
1	Apr 20, 44 B.C.–Mar/Apr 43 B.C.
2	Mar/Apr 43 B.C.–Mar/Apr 42 B.C.
. . .	. . .
36	Mar/Apr 9 B.C.–Mar/Apr 8 B.C.
37	Mar/Apr 8 B.C.–Mar/Apr 7 B.C.
38	Mar/Apr 7 B.C.–Mar/Apr 6 B.C.
39	Mar/Apr 6 B.C.–Mar/Apr 5 B.C.
40	Mar/Apr 5 B.C.–Mar/Apr 4 B.C.
41	Mar/Apr 4 B.C.–Mar/Apr 3 B.C.
42	Mar/Apr 3 B.C.–Mar/Apr 2 B.C.
43	Mar/Apr 2 B.C.–Mar/Apr 1 B.C.
44	Mar/Apr 1 B.C.–Mar/Apr A.D. 1
45	Mar/Apr A.D. 1–Mar/Apr A.D. 2
. . .	. . .
56	Mar/Apr A.D. 12–Mar/Apr A.D. 13
57	Mar/Apr A.D. 13–Mar/Apr A.D. 14 with the death of Augustus on the following Aug 19

487. Writing *Against Heresies* in approximately A.D. 180, Irenaeus states: "Our Lord was born about the forty-first year of the reign of Augustus" (3.21.3). In the immediately following §§488, 489 on Clement of Alexandria and Tertullian it is shown that the forty-first year of Augustus was 3/2 B.C. and it is thus this date within which Irenaeus also places the birth of Christ.

488. In the *Stromata,* written about A.D. 194,[31] Clement of Alexandria says: "And our Lord was born in the twenty-eighth year . . . in the reign of Augustus" (1.21.145). In the same passage he also says very precisely: "From the birth of Christ . . . to the death of Commodus are, in all, 194 years, one month, thirteen days." The emperor Commodus was murdered Dec 31, A.D. 192.[32] From Jan 1, 2 B.C., to Dec 31, A.D. 192, is 194 years. One month and thirteen days before that is Nov 18, 3 B.C.[33] This is Clement's date for the birth of Christ. This date was in the twenty-eighth year of the Egyptian reign of Augustus. According to the usual reckoning of the years of Augustus's rule in Egypt (Table 134), his twenty-eighth year was from Aug 29, 3 B.C., to Aug 28, 2 B.C., and this is the year here indicated.

489. In *An Answer to the Jews,* written about A.D. 198,[34] Tertullian makes these statements (ch. 8):

> After Cleopatra, Augustus reigned forty-three years.
> All the years of the empire of Augustus were fifty-six years.
> In the forty-first year of the empire of Augustus, when he has been reigning for twenty-eight years after the death of Cleopatra, the Christ is born.
> And the same Augustus survived, after Christ is born, fifteen years.

After the death of Cleopatra Augustus reigned almost exactly forty-three factual years in Egypt (Table 130) as well as forty-three Egyptian calendar years according to the accession-year system (Table 134). In Rome, after the part year in which Julius Caesar died and before the part year in which he himself died, Augustus reigned fifty-six full calendar years (Table 132). By the reckoning just indicated (Table 132) the forty-first year of Augustus was the year 3 B.C.; the twenty-eighth Egyptian year (Table 134) was 3/2 B.C. After the year 3 B.C. = A.U.C. 751, fifteen full years of reign remained, namely A.U.C. 752–766 or 2 B.C.–A.D. 13; after the twenty-eighth Egyptian year there were fifteen years remaining, namely the twenty-ninth to the forty-third inclusive. Accordingly, Tertullian's date for the forty-first year of Augustus and the birth of Jesus is 3/2 B.C.

490. In his *Chronographies* Julius Africanus (A.D. c. 170–c. 240; §284) placed the birth of Christ in A.Ad. 5500 = Ol. 194, 2 = 3/2 B.C., as established above (§291). His contemporary, Hippolytus of Rome (A.D. c. 170–236) also indicates in his Chronicle the same date of 3/2 B.C., although in his scheme this is shown as the year 5502 from Adam (in an alternate text the year 5500; cf. §293).

---

[31] *ANF* 2:168.
[32] *EB* 6: 122.
[33] Holzmeister, *Chronologia vitae Christi,* 43.
[34] *ANF* 3:151 n. 1.

491. Origen (A.D. c. 185–c. 253) left Alexandria for Caesarea in A.D. 231. He had perhaps written some of his *Homilies on Luke* by then; the rest were written later in Caesarea.[35] In a Greek fragment of the *Homilies* Origen says that Christ was born in the forty-first year of Caesar Augustus, that Augustus reigned fifty-six years, and that after the birth of Christ there remained fifteen years.[36] The figures seem to be the same as those of Tertullian and to give the same result (§489), namely, 3/2 B.C.

492. Eusebius of Caesarea (A.D. c. 325) says in the *Church History*:

> It was, then, the forty-second year of the reign of Augustus, and the twenty-eighth year after the submission of Egypt and the death of Antony and Cleopatra . . . when our Savior and Lord Jesus Christ . . . was born. (1.5.2)

Likewise in Eusebius's *Chronicle* as translated by Jerome it is stated that Augustus reigned fifty-six years and six months (in round numbers fifty-seven years) and the birth of Jesus is placed in the forty-second year of Augustus.[37] It is therefore readily explainable that Eusebius simply placed the first year of Augustus one year earlier, making the year here in question the forty-second rather than the forty-first of Augustus (cf. Table 128, col. 1; Table 129). As already established (§§487–489), the year was 3/2 B.C.

493. Epiphanius (A.D. c. 315–403) was born in Palestine and became bishop of Salamis or Constantia on the island of Cyprus in A.D. 357. In his *Panarion* or "medicine chest" for the healing of all heresies, he states, like Eusebius (§492), that Augustus reigned fifty-six years and six months,[38] and that Jesus was born in his forty-second year.[39] He also says that this was the year when the consuls were Octavian for the thirteenth time and Silvanus (*Panarion* 51.22.3; for his list of consuls see 51.22.24). This indicates, therefore, the year 2 B.C., when the consul listing is: *Augusto XIII et Silvano* (Table 40). Epiphanius is in agreement, therefore, with the preceding sources in the date of 3/2 B.C. for the birth of Christ.

494. Epiphanius also mentions a different date for the birth of Christ which he says was given by the Alogi. The Alogi, as he calls them, were a group in Asia Minor around A.D. 180 who were opposed to the Montanists. Because the Montanists used the Johannine writings to support their doctrine of the Spirit, this group rejected these writings. Epiphanius explains the name he gives them: "They reject the books of John. Accordingly since they do not receive the Logos proclaimed by John they shall be called Alogi (Ἄλογοι)" (*Panarion* 51.3.2).

---

[35] F. C. Grant, *The Earliest Lives of Jesus* (London: S.P.C.K., 1962), 52.

[36] Frag. 82 on Luke 3:1; *Origenes Werke*, vol. 9, *Die Homilien zu Lukas,* ed. Max Rauer (GCS; 2d ed.; Berlin: Akademie, 1959), 260.

[37] Helm 157, 169.

[38] *Ancoratus* 60.4. The texts of Epiphanius have been edited by Karl Holl in *Ancoratus und Panarion* (GCS 25; Leipzig: J. C. Hinrichs, 1915–1933). Frank Williams has translated in *Panarion* in *The Panarion of Epiphanius of Salamis* (NHMS 35, 36; Leiden: Brill, 1987, 1994).

[39] *Panarion* 20.2 (*Chris.* 2.1).

According to the Alogi, Christ was born around (περί) the fortieth year of Augustus (51.29.1). Assuming the equation by Epiphanius of the forty-second year of Augustus with the year 2 B.C. (§493), the fortieth year must have been the year 4 B.C. In the same passage (51.29.2), however, he says that the Alogi put the birth of Christ under the consuls S. Camerinus and B. Pompeianus. Assuming that the latter name means Poppaeus Sabinus, these were the consuls of A.D. 9 (Table 40): *Camerino et Sabino.* The dates given by the Alogi therefore diverge inexplicably from the consensus date noted in the preceding discussion.

495. In fragments of "Hippolytus of Thebes" (§293) the birth of Christ is put one time in the forty-second year of Augustus,[40] but another time in the forty-third year of Augustus.[41] If the forty-second year means 3/2 B.C. (cf. §337), this is the same date given by Hippolytus of Rome (§490). Then the forty-third year would presumably mean the year 2/1 B.C.

496. The *Chronographer of the Year 354* (§176) lists as consuls Gaius Caesar and Lucius Aemilius Paullus, which indicates A.U.C. 754 = A.D. 1 (Table 40), and writes: "Hoc cons. dominus Iesus Christus natus" ("When these were consuls the Lord Jesus Christ was born"). This, however, is simply incorrect.

497. In his *Seven Books of History against the Pagans* (Ch. 6),[42] a work completed in 418, Paulus Orosius (born in Spain and associated with Augustine and Jerome) says that it was in "the seven hundred and fifty-second year after the founding of the City" that "Christ was born." In the equation of years from the founding of the city of Rome with Roman consular dates (Table 40), the year A.U.C. 752 is the year 2 B.C., and this is therefore to be taken as the date of Orosius for the birth of Jesus.

498. Cassiodorus Senator (A.D. c. 490–585; §177) carries his list of consuls to C. Lentulus and M. Messala and then notes: "His conss. dominus noster Iesus Christus filius dei in Bethlehem nascitur anno imperii Augusti XLI" ("When these were consuls our Lord Jesus Christ the Son of God was born in Bethlehem in the forty-first year of the reign of Augustus"). *Lentulo et Messalino* is the consular listing for A.U.C. 751 = 3 B.C. (Table 40), which was the forty-first year of Augustus in the Julian calendar according to the accession-year system (Table 132).

499. The Roman monk Dionysius Exiguus (A.D. 525), as explained above (§219), accepted A.U.C. 753 or 1 B.C. as the year of the incarnation and December 25 as the day of the nativity of Jesus, and at the same time counted A.U.C. 754 as *anno Domini* 1, in the new era intended to replace the older counting from Diocletian in the "era of the martyrs."

---

[40] Ed. Jo. Albertus Fabricius, *S. Hippolyti episcopi et martyris Opera non antea collecta* (Hamburg: Chr. Liebezeit, 1716–1718), 52.

[41] Frag. 13; MPG 117:1056.

[42] Orosius, *Seven Books of History against the Pagans* (trans. Roy J. Deferrari; FC50; Washington, D.C.: Catholic University of America Press, 1964), 280–281.

TABLE 139. *Dates of the Birth of Christ in Early Christian Sources*

Source	*Year of Augustus*	*Consuls*	*A. Ad.*	*Ol.*	*A.U.C.*	*B.C./A.D.*
Alogi	40	Camerino et Sabino				4 B.C. or A.D. 9
Irenaeus	41					3/2 B.C.
Clement of Alexandria	28					3/2 B.C.
Tertullian	41/28					3/2 B.C.
Africanus			5500	194, 2		3/2 B.C.
Hippolytus of Rome			5500, 5502			3/2 B.C.
"Hippolytus of Thebes"			5500			3/2 B.C.
Origen	41					3/2 B.C.
Eusebius	42/28					3/2 B.C.
Epiphanius	42	Augusto XIII et Silvano			752	3/2 B.C.
Cassiodorus Senator	41	Lentulo et Messalino			751	3 B.C.
Orosius					752	2 B.C.
Dionysius Exiguus					753	1 B.C.
Chronographer of the Year 54		Caesare et Paullo			754	A.D. 1

500. In Table 139 the sources and dates identified above (§§ 487ff.) are listed in the chronological order of the dates. Apart from the dates of 4 B.C. and A.D. 9, and of 3, 2, and 1 B.C. and A.D. 1, there is a remarkable consensus of the nine most important authorities for the year 3/2 B.C. So, from this evidence, the date of the nativity of Jesus is to be sought within the period of 3/2 B.C. Further evidence is also to be considered.

(2) Herod the Great

LITERATURE: Thomas **Corbishley**, "The Chronology of the Reign of Herod the Great," in *JTS* 36 (1935): 22–32; Stewart **Perowne**, *The Life and Times of Herod the Great* (London: Hodder & Stoughton, 1956); Stewart **Perowne**, *The Later Herods: The Political Background of the New Testament* (London: Hodder & Stoughton, 1958), later published under the subtitle; W. E. **Filmer**, "The Chronology of the Reign of Herod the Great," *JTS* 17 (1966): 283–298; Abraham **Schalit**, *König Herodes: Der Mann und sein Werk* (Studia Judaica 4; Berlin: Walter de Gruyter, 1969), 637–644; Michael **Grant**, *Herod the Great* (New York: American Heritage Press, 1971); Harold H. **Hoehner**, *Herod Antipas* (Cambridge: University Press, 1972); Timothy D. **Barnes**, "The Date of Herod's Death," *JTS* 19 (1968): 204–209; **Vermes/Millar**, *History,* vol. 1, 326–328 n. 165; S. **Safrai** and M. **Stern** in cooperation with D. **Flusser** and W. C. van **Unnik,** *The Jewish People in the First Century: Historical Geography, Political History, Social, Cultural and Religious Life and Institutions* (CRINT 1.1-2; Assen: Van Gorcum, 1974–76); Ernest L. **Martin**, *The Birth of Christ Recalculated* (Pasadena: Foundation for Biblical Research, 1978); idem, "The Nativity and Herod's Death," *CKC* 85–92; idem, *The Star That Astonished the World* (2d ed.; Portland: ASK Publications, 1996); Ormond **Edwards**, "Herodian Chronology," *PEQ* 1982: 29–42; P. M. **Bernegger**, "Affirmation of Herod's Death," *JTS* 34 (1983): 526–531; Donald L. **Jones**, "Luke's Unique Interest in Historical Chronology," SBLSP 1989,

378–379; Harold W. **Hoehner**, "The Date of the Death of Herod the Great," *CKC* 101–111; Paul L. **Maier**, "The Date of the Nativity and the Chronology of Jesus' Life," *CKC* 116–118; Paul **Keresztes**, *Imperial Rome and the Christians,* vol. 1, *From Herod the Great to about 200 A.D.* (Lanham, Md.: University Press of America, 1989); David W. **Beyer**, "Josephus Reexamined: Unraveling the Twenty-second Year of Tiberius" (presentation to the Society for Biblical Literature, Nov 19, 1995).

501. In terms of Jewish history, Matthew 2:1 states that Jesus was born "in the days of Herod the king"; and Luke 1:15 likewise places the annunciation to Zechariah and to Mary "in the days of Herod, king of Judea." Both references presuppose that Herod was still living when John and Jesus were born; therefore the date of the death of Herod is the crucial chronological point. A date of 4 B.C. for the death of Herod was established by Emil Schürer in his *History of the Jewish People in the Time of Jesus Christ* (1897–1898) with arguments that have long been accepted and are recapitulated in the new version of that work by Vermes and Millar. The main points are the following: (1) Josephus (*Ant.* 14.389) states that Herod received the kingship from Antony and Octavian "in the hundred and eighty-fourth Olympiad, the consuls being Gnaeus Domitius Calvinus, for the second time, and Gaius Asinius Pollio." The consular date *Calvino et Pollione* corresponds with the year 40 B.C. (Table 40). Ol. 184, 4 ended on June 30, 40 B.C. (Table 46). Another reference of Josephus indicates, however, that Herod did not actually go to Rome until winter (*Ant.* 14.376). Therefore, the date was actually in Ol. 185, 1. So Herod was named king late in 40 B.C.[43]

502. Josephus (*Ant.* 14.487) also states that Herod took Jerusalem and thus actually began his reign there, his rival Antigonus being slain, "during the consulship at Rome of Marcus Agrippa and Caninius Gallus, in the hundred and eighty-fifth Olympiad." The consular date *Agrippa et Gallo* signifies the year 37 B.C. (Table 40). Ol. 185, 4 extended from July 1, 37, to June 30, 36 B.C., and the city was probably taken in the summer or fall. Dio Cassius (49.22–23) places the event in the consulship of Claudius and Norbanus who were the predecessors in his list of Agrippa and Gallus, hence in 38 B.C., but is probably less accurate in this than Josephus. Herod therefore became king in fact by conquest of Jerusalem in the summer or fall of 37 B.C.[44]

503. Josephus (*War* 1.665; *Ant.* 17.191) says further that Herod died "after a reign of thirty-four years, reckoning from the date when, after putting Antigonus to death, he assumed control of the state; of thirty-seven years, from the date when he was proclaimed king by the Romans." From these two possible starting points Herod's years of reign may be numbered as in Table 140 to make the totals of thirty-seven and thirty-four years, respectively, and to come to 4 B.C. for his death. In the light of the definition of Jewish new years in *m. Rosh Hashanah* (above §164), which states that "the

---

[43] Vermes/Millar, *History* 1:281 n. 3.
[44] Ibid., 284 n.11.

first of Nisan is New Year for kings," Herod's years of reign were presumably reckoned as beginning on Nisan 1. If we take the consular date of 37 B.C. and probably the summer or fall of that year (§502) as the beginning date of the rule in fact of Herod and allow the time on to the following Nisan 1 of 36 B.C. to be his first year of rule, and Nisan 1, 36 B.C., to Nisan 1, 35, to be his second year, and so on, we have a list of his regnal years as in Table 141.

TABLE 140. *Regnal Years of Herod the Great*

B.C.	*Years of Reign from Being Named King*	*Years of Reign from the Taking of Jerusalem*
40	1	
39	2	
38	3	
37	4	1
36	5	2
35	6	3
34	7	4
33	8	5
32	9	6
31	10	7
30	11	8
29	12	9
28	13	10
27	14	11
26	15	12
25	16	13
24	17	14
23	18	15
22	19	16
21	20	17
20	21	18
19	22	19
18	23	20
17	24	21
16	25	22
15	26	23
14	27	24
13	28	25
12	29	26
11	30	27
10	31	28
9	32	29
8	33	30
7	34	31
6	35	32
5	36	33
4	37	34

TABLE 141. *Regnal Years of Herod the Great from His Taking of Jerusalem in 37 B.C.*

1	Nisan 37–Nisan 36 B.C.
2	Nisan 36–Nisan 35
3	Nisan 35–Nisan 34
4	Nisan 34–Nisan 33
5	Nisan 33–Nisan 32
6	Nisan 32–Nisan 31
7	Nisan 31–Nisan 30
8	Nisan 30–Nisan 29
9	Nisan 29–Nisan 28
10	Nisan 28–Nisan 27
11	Nisan 27–Nisan 26
12	Nisan 26–Nisan 25
13	Nisan 25–Nisan 24
14	Nisan 24–Nisan 23
15	Nisan 23–Nisan 22
16	Nisan 22–Nisan 21
17	Nisan 21–Nisan 20
18	Nisan 20–Nisan 19
19	Nisan 19–Nisan 18
20	Nisan 18–Nisan 17
21	Nisan 17–Nisan 16
22	Nisan 16–Nisan 15
23	Nisan 15–Nisan 14
24	Nisan 14–Nisan 13
25	Nisan 13–Nisan 12
26	Nisan 12–Nisan 11
27	Nisan 11–Nisan 10
28	Nisan 10–Nisan 9
29	Nisan 9–Nisan 8
30	Nisan 8–Nisan 7
31	Nisan 7–Nisan 6
32	Nisan 6–Nisan 5
33	Nisan 5–Nisan 4
34	Nisan 4–Nisan 3

504. Josephus (*Ant.* 17.167) mentions an eclipse of the moon shortly before the death of Herod. There is also mention shortly afterward of "the Feast of Unleavened Bread, which the Jews call Passover" (*War* 2.10; *Ant.* 17.213). The reference to the Passover indicates spring. In 4 B.C. the month of Nisan began on Mar 29 and Nisan 14 = Apr 11.[45] As for the eclipse, this is the only eclipse of moon or sun mentioned by Josephus in any of his writings.[46] On the night of Mar 12/13, 4 B.C., there was a partial lunar eclipse, and there was no such phenomenon in 3 or 2 B.C. (see Table 142).[47] Thus if 4 B.C. is accepted

[45] PDBC 45.

[46] William Whiston, *The Works of Flavius Josephus* (repr. Peabody, Mass.: Hendrickson, 1987), 462 note c.

[47] Schürer, *History*, vol. 1.1, 465 n. 1; Vermes/Millar, *History* 1:327 n. 1. Table 142 is from Martin, *Star*, 121, where reference is made to Manfred Kudlek and Erich H. Mickler, *Solar and Lunar Eclipses of the Ancient Near East from 3000 B.C. to 0 with Maps* (Alter Orient und Altes Testament: Sonderreihe 1; Kevelaer: Butzon & Bercker, 1971). The table by

as the year of Herod's death it is usually concluded that the death occurred between Mar 12/13 (the eclipse) and Apr 11 (the Passover), an interval of twenty-nine days.

TABLE 142. *Lunar Eclipses from 7 B.C. to 1 B.C.*

Astronomical	*B.C.*	*Eclipses*
–6	7	None
–5	6	None
–4	5	Mar 23. Total eclipse. Central at 8:30 p.m. (elapsed time between eclipse and Passover, twenty-nine days)
–4	5	Sept 15. Total eclipse. Central at 10:30 p.m. (elapsed time between eclipse and Passover, seven months)
–3	4	Mar 13. Partial eclipse. Central at 2:20 a.m. (elapsed time between eclipse and Passover, twenty-nine days)
–2	3	None
–1	2	None
0	1	Jan 10. Total eclipse. Central at 1:00 a.m. (elapsed time between eclipse and Passover, twelve and a half weeks).

505. Barnes and Bernegger prefer 5 B.C. as a date for the death of Herod.[48] In this case the eclipse of the moon of *Ant.* 17.167 can be identified with a total lunar eclipse in the night of Sept 15/16, allowing seven months until Passover on Apr 17, 5 B.C. With this longer period for intervening events, Barnes prefers the 5 B.C. date to 4 B.C., but he still affirms that all the evidence "proves beyond a doubt that Herod died in 5 or 4 B.C."[49]

506. Barnes[50] also cites the Jewish tractate *Megillat Ta'anit (Scroll of Fasting),* composed originally not long after the destruction of Jerusalem (in A.D. 70). This work lists the days when "any joyous event could not be celebrated," i.e., days when fasting is appropriate, but also includes two semi-festival days when no mourning is permitted. These days are Chislev 7 (in 2 B.C.–Dec 5, before the lunar eclipse of Jan 10, 1 B.C.) and Shebat 2 (in 1 B.C.–Jan 28, eighteen days after the same eclipse). At the point of Chislev 7 a Jewish commentator, probably of the seventh century, has put in a concise notation: "on that day Herod died." Since the Chislev 7 date is before the eclipse of Jan 10, 1 B.C., after which Herod died, some think the note should belong with Shebat 2, in which

---

Martin is reproduced in our Table 142 by permission of Ernest L. Martin and ASK Publishers, Portland, Or. All the items in the table have been verified by the present writer in Bao-Lin Liu and Alan D. Fiala, *Canon of Lunar Eclipses 1500 B.C.–A.D. 3000* (Richmond, Va.: Willmann-Bell, 1992), courtesy of Professor Emeritus of Astronomy Harold Weaver, University of California, Berkeley.

[48] Barnes, *JTS* 19 (1968): 209; Bernegger, *JTS* 34 (1983): 526–531).

[49] Barnes, *JTS* 19 (1968): 209.

[50] Ibid.

case the eighteen days from then to Passover would be a short time for the events Josephus speaks of (§515). However, an early one of those events was the destruction of the golden eagle at the temple and the burning of the two rabbis, and Herod was already then so ill that a rumor went out that the king was dying (Josephus, *War* 1.651) or even that the king had died (Ant. 17.155), and perhaps it was this that the date of Shebat 2/Jan 28, 1 B.C. commemorated. Nevertheless Barnes says: "The only precise evidence which exists for the day of Herod's death gives 7 Kislev."[51]

507. If Herod died in 4 B.C. (§504) this was in the year 750 from the founding of Rome (A.U.C.) and if Jesus was born two years before that (in A.U.C. 748 = 6 B.C.) then there is the familiar anomaly of saying that he was born several years "before Christ." The explanation is of course that Dionysius Exiguus (§§218, 219) chose to place the birth of Christ in A.U.C. 753 and to make A.U.C. 754 the first year (A.D. 1) in the new Christian era.[52]

508. The visit of the wise men (μάγοι) from the East took place while Herod was still ruling (Matt 2:3).[53] When the wise men came to Bethlehem "they saw the child with Mary his mother" (Matt 2:11). Here the word in Greek is τὸ παιδίον (diminutive of παῖς, "child"). Normally translated "child," παιδίον can mean a "very young child," "infant." Justin Martyr (*Dialogue with Trypho,* 88) would apparently support this meaning in Matt 2:11, for he speaks of "the magi from Arabia, who as soon as the child was born came to worship him." On the other hand, as far as age is concerned, the word can also mean a somewhat older child, as would appear to be the case in the use of the same word in Matt 18:2 where, to illustrate an answer to a question of his disciples, Jesus called to himself a child and "put him in the midst of them." So it is relevant to note that, "according to the time which he had ascertained from the wise men," Herod "sent and killed all the male children in Bethlehem and in all that region who were two years old or under" (Matt 2:16).

509. As to the likelihood of Herod's perpetrating such a crime, Stewart Perowne affirms:

> That Herod, in the awful physical and mental decay into which he had fallen, and in this atmosphere of fervid Messianism, should have ordered the massacre of the Innocents of Bethlehem is wholly in keeping with all that we know of him. Bethlehem was but a few miles distant from his palace-fortress of Herodium: there least of all could any subversive cell be tolerated. Such an act was by no means unheard of. In pagan antiquity, the life of a new-born child was at the mercy of its father or of the state. As Abel points out, a few months before the birth of Augustus, a prodigy having presaged the birth of a king for the Roman people, the affrighted Senate decreed that none of the children born that year were to be brought up. Later on Nero, fearing the consequences of the

---

[51] Ibid.; Martin, *Birth of Christ*, 46–48; Keresztes, *Imperial Rome*, 7.

[52] Perowne, *Life and Times of Herod,* 174.

[53] For the story of the wise men in Matthew as based on a historical happening, see Edwin M. Yamauchi, "The Episode of the Magi," *CKC* 15–39.

> appearance of a comet, ordered the execution of leading aristocrats of Rome. Their children were driven from the city and died from hunger or poison.[54]

Likewise Paul L. Maier surveys current scholarly opinion, much of which considers the episode legend or myth. He points out the inconsistencies in the case for myth, and writes:

> If one reads Josephus's portrait of Herod in his last years (*Antiquities* 16 and 17) and then studies Matthew 2, one will be overwhelmed by the identical personality profiles that emerge of Herod, who, in his younger years, had every right to the epithet "the Great." Compare the infant massacre at Bethlehem with other Herodian atrocities and it correlates convincingly. . . . Particularly in his last days, Herod was anxious to nip any potential sedition in the bud. . . . Bethlehem, too, lay just northwest of the Herodium, the fortress-palace . . . where he was arranging his own tomb. . . . There, least of all, then, would he tolerate any sedition in the name of an infant "king of the Jews."[55]

510. As to the bearing on chronology of Herod's slaughter of the male children of Bethlehem "who were two years old or under" (Matt 2:16), this suggests that what the wise men told Herod made him think that Jesus was already anything up to two years old, thus was born up to two years before. That time was obviously somewhat prior to Herod's death, and if that death was early in the year 4 B.C. (§504) the two years or less would point back to 6 or 5 B.C. That the magi came when Jesus was two years old was an opinion held by some of the early Christian writers. Passages found in Origen,[56] Eusebius,[57] and Epiphanius (*Panarion* 51.10.1) state that Jesus was two years old when the wise men came and when he was taken to Egypt, that he remained in Egypt for two years and was four years old when he returned from there, and that the return was in the first year of Archelaus and the forty-first year of Augustus. Since Origen and Eusebius put the birth of Jesus in 3/2 B.C. (Table 139), these earliest events must have fallen into the following pattern (Table 143) in their view.

TABLE 143. *The Earliest Events in the Life of Jesus according to Origen*

Event	*Regnal Year of Augustus*	*B.C./A.D.*
Birth of Jesus	41	3/2 B.C.
	42	2/1 B.C.
Flight to Egypt at age of 2	43	1 B.C./A.D. 1
	44	A.D. 1/2
Return from Egypt at age of 4	45	A.D. 2/3

[54] Perowne, *Life and Times of Herod,* 172.

[55] Paul L. Maier, "Herod and the Infants of Bethlehem," paper at Nativity Conference II: 1992, San Francisco, November 21, 1992, quotation by permission of Professor Maier, Western Michigan University, Kalamazoo, Michigan.

[56] *Commentary on Matthew.* Frag. 23 ed. Erich Klostermann, vol. 12 (= GCS 41), 25.

[57] *Quaestiones ad Stephanum* 16.2. MPG 22:934.

According to Matt 2:19, 22, however, the return from Egypt took place upon the death of Herod and the succession of Archelaus, therefore in the spring of 4 B.C. or later according to the view here explored.

511. The figures of Epiphanius may be tabulated as shown in Table 144 (cf. §500).

TABLE 144. *The Earliest Events in the Life of Jesus according to Epiphanius*

Event	*Regnal Year of Augustus*	*Regnal Year of Herod*
Birth of Jesus	42	33
Coming of the magi	46	35
Death of Herod and succession of Archelaus	48	37

Also according to Epiphanius (*Panarion* 51, 22, 13) the star appeared in the East to the magi in the hour when Jesus was born and two years before they arrived in Jerusalem and Bethlehem.

512. The foregoing (§501ff.) has summarized the widely accepted dating of the death of Herod the Great in 4 (or possibly 5) B.C. Referring to the LITERATURE above, in 1966 W. E. Filmer raised a serious question about the 4 B.C. date and proposed a date in 1 B.C. instead, and in 1978 and 1996 Ernest L. Martin advanced detailed arguments for the same date of 1 B.C. The subject of the date of Herod's death was thus brought to the front again, and much discussion has ensued. In brief, the date of 4 or 5 B.C. is maintained by Barnes and Bernegger, and supported by Daniel Schwartz, who says that Filmer's system has been "universally rejected," and by Vermes and Millar and by Safrai, Stern, Flusser, and Van Unnik.[58] Along with Filmer and Martin, the date of 1 B.C. is set forth by Edwards and Keresztes.[59]

513. With acknowledgement of indebtedness to Filmer and Martin for discussion above and now further, it was observed (§227) from Josephus that Herod the Great took Jerusalem in a Sabbatical year, on the Day of Atonement, and exactly twenty-seven years from the day Pompey took Jerusalem (in 63 B.C.), hence on Oct 25, 36 B.C. With Herod's accession year beginning then, his first full year of reign began on Nisan 1, 35 B.C. On this basis we can go on from our Table 140, column 3, to list the factual years of Herod's reign with dates as in Table 145.

---

[58] Barnes, *JTS* 19 (1968): 209; Bernegger, *JTS* 34 (1983): 526–531; Daniel R. Schwartz, *Agrippa I: The Last King of Judaea* (Tübingen: J.C.B. Mohr, 1990), 205; Vermes/Millar, *History* 1:326 and n. 165; Safrai, Stern, Flusser, and Van Unnik, CRINT 1:68.

[59] Filmer, *JTS* 17 (1966): 283–298; Martin; Edwards, *PEQ* 1982: 29–42; Keresztes, *Imperial Rome,* 12–15.

TABLE 145. *Factual Years of Reign of Herod the Great with Dates*

Regnal year	*B.C.*	*Beginning Date of Year*
Accession	36/35	Tishri 10 = Oct 25, 36 B.C.
1	35/34	Nisan 1 = Apr 11, 35
2	34/33	Nisan 1 = Apr 1, 34
3	33/32	Nisan 1 = Apr 18, 33
4	32/32	Nisan 1 = Apr 7, 32
5	31/30	Nisan 1 = Mar 28, 31
6	30/29	Nisan 1 = Apr 16, 30
7	29/28	Nisan 1 = Apr 4, 29
8	28/27	Nisan 1 = Mar 25, 28
9	27/26	Nisan 1 = Apr 13, 27
10	26/25	Nisan 1 = Apr 2, 26
11	25/24	Nisan 1 = Apr 20, 25
12	24/23	Nisan 1 = Apr 9, 24
13	23/22	Nisan 1 = Mar 29, 23
14	22/21	Nisan 1 = Apr 17, 22
15	21/20	Nisan 1 = Apr 5, 21
16	20/19	Nisan 1 = Mar 26, 20
17	19/18	Nisan 1 = Apr 14, 19
18	18/17	Nisan 1 = Apr 4, 18
19	17/16	Nisan 1 = Apr 22, 17
20	16/15	Nisan 1 = Apr 11, 16
21	15/14	Nisan 1 = Mar 31, 15
22	14/13	Nisan 1 = Apr 19, 14
23	13/12	Nisan 1 = Apr 7, 13
24	12/11	Nisan 1 = Mar 28, 12
25	11/10	Nisan 1 = Apr 16, 11
26	10/9	Nisan 1 = Apr 5, 10
27	9/8	Nisan 1 = Mar 25, 9
28	8/7	Nisan 1 = Apr 13, 8
29	7/6	Nisan 1 = Apr 2, 7
30	6/5	Nisan 1 = Apr 20, 6
31	5/4	Nisan 1 = Apr 8, 5
32	4/3	Nisan 1 = Mar 29, 4
33	3/2	Nisan 1 = Apr 17, 3
34	2/1	Nisan 1 = Apr 6, 2

514. Proceeding now to look in greater detail at the last months and days of the life of Herod the Great, we remember (our §504) that Josephus tells us (*Ant.* 17.167) that an eclipse of the moon took place shortly before Herod died, and (*War* 2.10; *Ant.* 17.213) that the Jewish Passover came not long after his death. If the death of Herod is placed in 4 B.C. the eclipse in question can be identified with a partial lunar eclipse on Mar 12/13, allowing twenty-nine days until the Passover on Apr 11 (so e.g., Schürer/Vermes/Millar, our §504). Or if the death of Herod is placed in 5 B.C. the eclipse can be identified with a total lunar eclipse on Sept 15/16, allowing some seven months until Passover on Apr 17, 5 B.C. (so Barnes, Bernegger, our §505). If the death of Herod was in 1 B.C.—the year we are now exploring as probable for the death of Herod—the relevant eclipse of the moon was a total eclipse on the night of Jan 9/10,[60] and the full paschal moon of Nisan 14 was on Apr 8,[61] twelve and a half weeks later.

515. In the last period of Herod's life, between the eclipse shortly before he died and the Passover soon after his death, Josephus (*Ant.* 17.156–191) narrates many events. These are the following: (1) on the night of the eclipse Herod had two rabbis burned alive for involvement in the destruction of his golden eagle at the temple gate; (2) with his health worsening he traveled from Jericho to the hot baths of Callirrhoe near the northeast end of the Dead Sea; (3) when numerous baths and additional immersion in a vat of warm oil failed to bring relief he returned to Jericho; (4) at Jericho, knowing that death was near and being well aware that most of the Jewish people hated him, he sent officers into all areas of his kingdom to bring prominent Jewish elders to Jericho where he had them shut up in the hippodrome with instructions that upon his demise they be executed, so that there would be mourning throughout the nation at the time of his death; (5) receiving a letter from Augustus allowing him to either exile or execute his son Antipater, Herod sent his bodyguards to do the latter; (6) he then altered his will and designated Archelaus to have Judea, Samaria, and Idumea; Antipas to be tetrarch of Galilee and Perea; and Philip to be tetrarch of Gaulanitis and related regions; and (7) on the fifth day after having Antipater killed, he died. It is plain that it would have been difficult for all this to transpire within the twenty-nine days between the eclipse of Mar 12/13 and the Passover of Apr 11 in the year 4 B.C. The seven months in 5 B.C. would of course be more than sufficient, but that date is not otherwise strongly supported. In 1 B.C. the time would be adequate and not excessive, and this fact is an additional reason for preferring the 1 B.C. date for the death of Herod the Great.

516. The matter of the reigns of Herod's three sons and successors is also relevant to the question of the date of Herod's death, and has usually been taken as the major reason for accepting 4 B.C. as the correct date, on which basis the three rulers are usually listed as Archelaus, 4 B.C.–A.D. 6; Antipas, 4 B.C.–A.D. 39; Philip, 4 B.C.–A.D. 34.[62] As for the end point of each reign, the references or evidences seem plain: Herod Archelaus, ruler of Judea, Samaria, and Idumea, was banished in A.D. 6 in the tenth year of his reign (Dio 55, 27, 6; *Ant.* 17.342). Herod Antipas, tetrarch of Galilee and Perea, lost his tetrarchy during the second year of the emperor Gaius (38/39) and had reigned according to the evidence of coins for forty-three years (*Ant.* 18.252). Herod Philip, tetrarch of Gaulanitis and related regions, died in the twentieth year of Tiberius, A.D. 33/34, after a reign of thirty-seven years (*Ant.* 18.106). Calculating backward from these points, all seem to have begun to reign in 5 or 4 B.C.

517. Filmer however, considers that this kind of evidence can be misleading because coregency and antedating were common.[63] As he points out, in the case of the kings of Israel and Judah there were several occasions when a king appointed a son as coregent and the son's reign overlapped the father's by several years, thus the reign could appear longer than it actually was. In the time

---

[60] Bao-Lin Liu and Fiala, *Canon of Lunar Eclipses*, 89.
[61] Goldstine, *New and Full Moons*, 84 (April 7).
[62] E.g., Perowne, *Later Herods*.
[63] Filmer, *JTS* 17 (1966): 296–298.

after Alexander the Great we have seen specific examples of the antedating of reigns in the cases of Ptolemy I Soter I of Egypt and Seleucus I Nicator I in Babylon (§192), and there were other examples in the Hellenistic and early Roman period.[64] On an occasion when Herod was testifying to the Roman general and governor of Syria, Quintilius Varus, about his son Antipater, he spoke of him "to whom I have in a manner yielded up my royal authority while I am alive," and in his reply Antipater said that he had no reason to conspire against his father since "I was a king already . . . you proclaimed me king in your lifetime" (*War* 1.624, 625, 631–632). See below (§654) for antedating in the reign of Herod Agrippa II. Similar antedating could, therefore, easily have been practiced in the reigns of Herod Archelaus and Herod Antipas. In regard to Herod Philip there is now specific evidence (§518).

518. As cited just above (§516), the currently known text of Josephus's *Ant.* 18.106 states that Philip died in the twentieth year of Tiberius (A.D. 33/34; for the regnal years of Tiberius see Tables 151ff., especially 158, 167) after ruling for thirty-seven years. This points to Philip's accession at the death of Herod in 4 B.C. (4 years B.C. + 33 years A.D. = 37 years). But Filmer suspected that a figure had dropped out and that the text should probably read the twenty-second, rather than the twentieth, year of Tiberius (A.D. 35/36). Barnes rejected this reading as "comparatively ill-attested," although he agreed with Filmer that it was a pivotal point of the debate. In fact, however, already in the nineteenth century Florian Riess reported that the Franciscan monk Molkenbuhr claimed to have seen a 1517 Parisian copy of Josephus and an 1841 Venetian copy in each of which the text read "the twenty-second year of Tiberius." The antiquity of this reading has now been abundantly confirmed. In 1995 David W. Beyer reported to the Society for Biblical Literature his personal examination in the British Museum of forty-six editions of Josephus's *Antiquities* published before 1700 among which twenty-seven texts, all but three published before 1544, read "twenty-second year of Tiberius," while not a single edition published prior to 1544 read "twentieth year of Tiberius."[65] Likewise in the Library of Congress five more editions read the "twenty-second year," while none prior to 1544 records the "twentieth year." It was also found that the oldest versions of the text give variant lengths of reign for Philip of 32 and 36 years. But if we still allow for a full thirty-seven-year reign, then "the twenty-second year of Tiberius" (A.D. 35/36) points to 1 B.C. (1 year B.C. + 36 years A.D. = 37 years) as the year of death of Herod.[66] This is therefore the date which is accepted in the present book. Accordingly, if the birth of Jesus was two years or less before the death of Herod in 1 B.C., the date of the birth was in 3 or 2 B.C., presumably precisely in the period 3/2 B.C., so consistently attested by the most credible early church fathers (see above Table 139). Furthermore, we have seen evidence for a time of Jesus' birth in the mid-winter (Beckwith, our §473), therefore mid-winter in 3/2 B.C. appears the likely date of the birth of Jesus.

---

[64] Bickerman, in *Berytus* 8 (1943–44): 75, 77.

[65] Filmer, *JTS* 17 (1966): 298; Barnes, *JTS* 19 (1968): 205; Riess, *Das Geburtsjahr Christi* (Freiburg: Herder, 1880); Beyer, "Josephus Reexamined."

[66] Beyer, "Josephus Reexamined," 4.

(3) The Enrollment of Quirinius

LITERATURE: W. M. **Ramsay**, *Was Christ Born at Bethlehem?* (New York: Putnam, 1898); idem, *The Bearing of Recent Discovery on the Trustworthiness of the New Testament* (London: Hodder and Stoughton, 1915); Lily R. **Taylor**, "Quirinius and the Census of Judaea," in *AJP* 54 (1933): 120–133; Egbert C. **Hudson**, "The Principal Family at Pisidian Antioch," in *JNES* 15 (1956): 103–107; Ethelbert **Stauffer**, *Jesus and His Story* (New York: Knopf, 1960), 21–32; A. N. **Sherwin-White**, *Roman Society and Roman Law in the New Testament* (Oxford: Clarendon, 1963), 162–171; Harold W. **Hoehner**, *Chronological Aspects of the Life of Christ* (Grand Rapids: Zondervan, 1977), 13–23; *Res gestae divi Augusti: The Achievements of the Divine Augustus,* eds. P. A. Brunt and J. M. Moore (London: Oxford University Press, 1967); Paul **Keresztes**, *Imperial Rome and the Christians* (Lanham, Md.: University Press of America, 1989), vol.1, 5, 8–12, 19–21; Ernest L. **Martin**, *The Star That Astonished the World* (2d ed.; Portland: ASK Publications, 1996), 169–199, 232–234. See also very extensive bibliographies in Vermes/Millar, *History* 1:399–427; and *Josephus* (LCL), vol. 9, 556–557.

519. According to Luke 2:2 the birth of Jesus was at the time of "the first enrollment, when Quirinius was governor of Syria." The usually accepted sequence of governors of Syria runs as shown in Table 146.[67]

TABLE 146. *Governors of Syria*

B.C./A.D.	*Governor*
10–9 B.C.	M. Titius
9–6	C. Sentius Saturninus
6–4	P. Quintilius Varus
3–2 (?)	P. Sulpicius Quirinius
1 B.C.–A.D. 4	C. Caesar
A.D. 4–5	L. Volusius Saturninus
6–7	P. Sulpicius Quirinius

520. Of the life of P. Sulpicius Quirinius, Tacitus gives a brief outline as he tells of his funeral which took place in A.D. 21.

> About this time Tiberius wrote to the senate, requesting that a public funeral might be decreed to Sulpicius Quirinius. . . . He was born at Lanuvium, a municipal town: he distinguished himself by his military services, had considerable talents for business, and was raised by Augustus to the honor of the consulship. Having afterwards stormed and taken the strongholds of the Homanadensians in Cilicia, he obtained triumphal honors. He attended Gaius Caesar in his expedition to Armenia. . . . But the character of Quirinius was held in no esteem . . . and the sordid avarice of the man, even in old age, and in the height of his power, left a stain upon his memory. (*Annals* 3.48)

[67] Schürer, *History,* vol. 1.1, 350–357; PW, Zweite Reihe 4.2, col. 1629.

Chief points in this outline may be explicated as follows: (1) Quirinius was consul in 12 B.C. and appears in the list of consuls (Table 40) at this point: *Messala et Quirino*. (2) Sometime between 12 B.C. and A.D. 1 he conducted the Homanadensian War.[68] The resistance of the Homanadensians must have been broken by the time the net of Roman roads was laid out in the province of Galatia in 6 B.C., therefore at least the major part of this war must have been over by that date.[69] By around that date Quirinius could have been free to attend to other business in the East. (3) In A.D. 2–3 Quirinius was adviser to Gaius Caesar in Armenia.[70]

521. Concerning the occurrence of the name of Sulpicius Quirinius in Table 146 at the point of the years of A.D. 6–7: Josephus (*Ant.* 18.1–2) records that Quirinius was sent to Syria as governor at the same time that Coponius was sent to Judea as procurator.

> Now Cyrenius, a Roman senator, and one who had gone through other magistracies, and had passed through them till he had been consul, and one who, on other accounts, was of great dignity, came at this time into Syria, with a few others, being sent by Caesar to be a judge of that nation, and to take an account of their substance. Coponius also, a man of the equestrian order, was sent together with him, to have the supreme power over the Jews.

Upon the death of Herod the Great, Judea, Samaria, and Idumea were given to his son Archelaus who ruled 4 B.C.–A.D. 6. When Archelaus was deposed he was replaced by the first of the procurators, and this was Coponius who probably held office A.D. 6–9. Since Quirinius and he came out to their respective posts together, Quirinius must have assumed the governorship of Syria in A.D. 6, and thus he appears in the list above (§519) as governor in A.D. 6–7. The taxing for which Quirinius was responsible at this time was resisted by the Jews, and a revolt was attempted by Judas the Gaulonite, as Josephus (*Ant.* 18.4) states. The taxing was made "in the thirty-seventh year of Caesar's victory over Antony at Actium" (*Ant.* 18.26). This year was A.D. 6 (Table 128, column 3). If the fourteen-year census periods known in Egypt in A.D. 34, 48, and 62 (§523) are projected backward they come to A.D. 6, exactly the year here involved (34 – 14 = 20 – 14 = 6). It is probably this census which is referred to in Acts 5:37 along with mention of "Judas the Galilean." An inscription found over three hundred years ago on a gravestone in Venice and known as Lapis Venetus[71] records the career of a Roman officer named Q. Aemilius Secundus. He states that by order of P. Sulpicius Quirinius, whom he calls legatus Caesaris Syriae, he himself conducted a census of Apamea, a city-state of 117,000 citizens on the Orontes in Syria.[72] This is ordinarily taken to refer to the just-mentioned census by Quirinius in A.D. 6,[73] as attested in Josephus and Acts 5:37. But it should be noted that, in line with his date for the birth of Jesus in 12 B.C. (§543) E. Jerry

68 *CAH* 10:271.
69 Groag in PW, Zweite Reihe 4.1, col. 831.
70 *CAH* 10:276.
71 *CIL* 3.6687.
72 T. Mommsen, *Ephemeris epigraphica* 4 (1881): 538.
73 Vermes/Millar, *History* 1:259, 405.

Vardaman finds reason, supported by other inscriptional evidence at Corinth, to believe that the Lapis Venetus inscription is actually mentioning a census conducted by Quirinius in 12/11 B.C. and thus is the census of Luke 2:2.[74]

522. Tertullian (*Against Marcion* 4.19) states that the enrollment at the time of the birth of Jesus was "taken in Judea by Sentius Saturninus," and we remember that for Tertullian, as for many other early Christian scholars (§489), the date of the nativity was 3/2 B.C. Josephus (*Ant.* 17.89) refers to the time when Herod the Great had opportunity to speak about his son, Antipater, to Varus, and says: "At this time there happened to be in Jerusalem Quintilius Varus, who had been sent to succeed Saturninus as governor of Syria." These references make possible a revised table of governors of Syria, as in Table 147.[75]

TABLE 147. *Revised List of Governors of Syria*

B.C./A.D.	*Governor*
Prior to 7 B.C.	M. Titius
7 or 6–4 B.C.	P. Quintilius Varus
4 B.C.–2 B.C.	C. Sentius Saturninus
2 B.C.–A.D. 1	P. Quintilius Varus (a second time)
A.D. 1–4	C. Caesar

In connection with this listing of Varus as Syrian governor on two separate occasions a Latin inscription found in 1784 on a stone near Tibur (Tivoli, about twenty miles east of Rome) and known as the Lapis Tiburtinus[76] is of probable significance. The inscription contains the statement of a high Roman official that when he became governor of Syria he entered upon the office for the second time (Lat. *iterum*). It has even been thought[77] that this personage might have been Quirinius, but of that there is no other proof,[78] and the fact that the inscription was found near the remains of what is almost certainly the grand residential villa of Varus at Rome lends plausibility to the theory that the inscription is indeed from Varus.[79] As to Quirinius, the statement about him in Luke 2:2 is in Greek ἡγεμονεύοντος τῆς Συρίας. The first word is a present participle and can mean, as in the usual translation, that the enrollment was when Quirinius was governor of Syria, but can be taken literally and mean that it was when he was *hēgemōn* of Syria, and in Luke 3:1 the same word means when Pontius Pilate was procurator of Judea. Using the word in this sense, Justin Martyr (*Apology* 1.34) says that Quirinius was the Roman emperor's "first procurator in Judea." A procurator was ordinarily appointed directly by the emperor and was not a governor of a province but could be associated with a governor with a degree of independence. With such an understanding of his position

[74] Vardaman, *CKC* 61–63; idem, personal letter, July 10, 1993.
[75] Based on Martin, *Star,* 180.
[76] *CIL* 14.3613.
[77] Schürer, *History,* vol. 1.1, 352–354; Sherwin-White, *Roman Society,* 164–166.
[78] F. F. Bruce, "Quirinius," *NBD,* 1069.
[79] Martin, *Star,* 174–179, 232–234.

Quirinius could have been associated with Saturninus, the latter being the governor of Syria at the time in question (Table 147). In view of Luke's general accuracy in other chronological matters there seems no sufficient reason to question his accuracy in speaking of the position of Quirinius in relation to an enrollment at the time of the birth of Jesus.[80] But the question can remain as to what sort of an enrollment it was that took place at this time.

523. As for Roman census-practice, a census of Roman citizens was held periodically under the Republic, and Augustus conducted censuses in 28 and 8 B.C. and on later occasions.[81] In his own reorganization of the empire in 27 B.C. Augustus undertook to acquire exact knowledge of the available resources, and it was necessary to obtain full information about the number and legal status of the inhabitants of each province and the amount and sources of their wealth. To do this he had to hold a census similar to but distinct from the old census of the Republican period. In Gaul, where there was much resistance to the procedure, there was a census in 27 B.C., another in 12 B.C., and a third immediately after the death of Augustus.[82] In Cyrene exact information on the number and wealth of the inhabitants was available by 7 B.C.[83] In Egypt there are dated census returns from A.D. 34, 48, 62, and other years, suggesting a regular census every fourteen years.[84]

524. The question has been raised whether the Romans would have instituted census and taxation procedures in Palestine while Herod the Great was ruling as king of the Jews. That they would not have hesitated to do so is suggested by comparison with Apamea, where the autonomy of the city-state is shown by the fact that it minted its own coins,[85] and yet Quirinius himself had a census taken there (as described above §521). As for Herod, Josephus reports that in the time when Saturninus and Volumnius were the presidents of Syria (*Ant.* 16.277), Caesar Augustus demoted him from "friend" (φίλος = *amicus*) to "subject" (*Ant.* 16.290). Saturninus was listed above as governor of Syria in 9–6 B.C. (§519) and Volumnius was evidently associated with him. By comparison with Apamea and especially from the time of Herod's demotion by Augustus, Roman procedures of census and taxation might have been possible in Palestine. Nevertheless during the lifetime of Herod it is more likely that Jews in Judea paid their taxes not to Rome but directly to Herod himself, and the latter's grandiose building projects surely required large income. So there could have been other kinds of Roman "enrollment" which were not related to taxation.

525. In Luke 2:2 the Greek word for the first "enrollment," which took place at the time of the birth of Jesus, is ἀπογραφή. This word comes from the verb ἀπογράφω, which means "to write out," "enter in a list," "register,"

---

[80] Keresztes, *Imperial Rome,* 10–11.
[81] *CAH* 10:192; Martin, *Star,* 193.
[82] *CAH* 10:193.
[83] Ibid., 192–193.
[84] Finegan, *Light from the Ancient Past,* 260.
[85] A. R. Bellinger, *The Coins* (Excavations at Dura-Europos: Final Report 6; New Haven: Yale University Press, 1949), 86 nos. 1832, 1833.

therefore can be translated either as "census" or as "registration." Translated as "census" it is usually taken to have to do with taxation, but translated as "registration" it can be understood to have to do with some other matter for which people were required to register. In fact there was an event at precisely the time with which we are here concerned that could well have called for an empire-wide registration and could have been what we are concerned with at Bethlehem. In the *Res gestae divi Augusti,* a record of the public life and work of Augustus composed by himself at the age of seventy-six and preserved in Latin and Greek on the walls of a temple in Ankara (ancient Ancyra), known as the Monumentum Ancyranum, the emperor says (*Res gestae* 35):

> In my thirteenth consulship the senate, the equestrian order and the whole people of Rome gave me the title of Father of my Country (Pater Patriae).[86]

For "the whole people of Rome" to bestow the honor there must have been some kind of universal registration, perhaps an oath of loyalty such as that of which Josephus (*Ant.* 17.41–45) tells "when . . . the whole Jewish nation took an oath to be faithful to Caesar," but which six thousand Pharisees refused to swear. The date of the honor for Augustus in his thirteenth consulship is the year 2 B.C. (Table 41); the conferring of the title was on Feb 5, 2 B.C.; the registering of the people must have been ordered and carried out sometime in 3 B.C. or at least before Feb 5, 2 B.C. Referring to Luke 2:2, Orosius describes the entire matter in much the same manner as set forth above:

> Augustus ordered that a census be taken of each province everywhere and that all men be enrolled. . . . This is the earliest and most famous public acknowledgment which marked Caesar as the first of all men and the Romans as lords of the world, a published list of all men entered individually. . . . This first and greatest census was taken, since in this one name of Caesar all the peoples of the great nations took oath, and at the same time, through the participation in the census, were made a part of one society.

526. From relatively early times Christian writers declared that it was possible to verify the "census" in official Roman records. Justin Martyr (A.D. c. 114–165) speaks of "the registers of the taxing made under Cyrenius" (*Apology* 1.34) and Tertullian (A.D. c. 145–220) mentions the records of the census "kept in the archives of Rome" (*Against Marcion* 4.7). These records have not been found.

(4) The Star

LITERATURE: John **Williams**, *Observations of Comets from 611B.C. to A.D. 1640 Extracted from the Chinese Annals* (London: Stangeways and Walden, 1871; repr. Hornchurch, Essex, England: Science and Technology, 1987); J. K. **Fotheringham**, "The New Star of Hipparchus and the Dates of Birth and Accession of Mithridates," in *Monthly Notices of the Royal Astronomical Society* 79 (1919): 162–167; Knut **Lundmark**, "Suspected New Stars Recorded in Old Chronicles and Among Recent Meridian Observations," in *Publications*

[86] P. A. Brunt and J. M. Moore, eds., *Res gestae divi Augusti* (London: Oxford University Press, 1967), 57.

of the Astronomical Society of the Pacific 33 (1921): 225–238; idem, "The Messianic Ideas and Their Astronomical Background," in *Actes du VIIe Congrès International d'Histoire des Sciences, Jérusalem 4–12 Août 1953* (ed. F. S. Bodenheimer; Paris: Académie internationale d'histoire des sciences, [1953?]), 436–439; Paul **Schnabel**, "Der jüngste datierbare Keilschrifttext," in *ZA* 36 (1925): 66–70; *The Christmas Star* (Morrison Planetarium, California Academy of Sciences, 1954); Hsi **Tsê-tsung**, "A New Catalog of Ancient Novae," translated from *Acta Astronomica Sinica* 3 (1955): 183, and published in *Ancient Novae and Meteor Showers* (Smithsonian Contributions to Astrophysics 2.6; Washington, D.C.: Smithsonian Institution, 1958), 109–130; H. W. **Montefiore**, "Josephus and the New Testament," in *NovT* 4 (1960): 139–160; Konradin **Ferrari-D'Occhieppo**, *Der Stern der Weisen* (2d ed.; Vienna; Herold, 1977); idem, "The Star of the Magi and Babylonian Astronomy," *CKC* 41–53; E. C. **Krupp**, ed., *In Search of Ancient Astronomies* (Garden City, N.Y.: Doubleday, 1978); idem, *Echoes of the Ancient Skies* (New York: Harper & Row, 1983); idem, *Beyond the Blue Horizon: Myths and Legends of the Sun, Moon, Stars, and Planets* (New York: HarperCollins, 1991); Ernest L. **Martin**, *The Birth of Christ Recalculated* (Pasadena: Foundation for Biblical Research, 1978); idem, *The Star That Astonished the World* (Portland: ASK Publications, 1996); Ruth S. **Freitag**, *The Story of Bethlehem: A List of References* (Washington, D.C.: Library of Congress, 1979); A. J. **Sachs** and C. B. F. **Walker**, "Kepler's View of the Star of Bethlehem and the Babylonian Almanac for 7/6 BC," *Iraq* 46 (1984): 43–55; John **Mosley**, *The Christmas Star* (Los Angeles: Griffith Observatory, 1987); Jerry **Vardaman**, "Jesus' Life: A New Chronology," *CKC* 66; Nikos **Kokkinos**, "Crucifixion in A.D. 36: The Keystone for Dating the Birth of Jesus," *CKC* 157–162; Paul **Keresztes**, *Imperial Rome and the Christians,* vol. 1, *From Herod the Great to about 200 A.D.* (Lanham, N.Y.: University Press of America, 1989), 27–35; Edwin M. **Yamauchi**, "The Episode of the Magi," *CKC* 15–39; idem, *Persia and the Bible* (Grand Rapids: Baker Book House, 1990), 467–491; Paul L. **Maier**, *In the Fullness of Time: A Historian Looks at Christmas, Easter, and the Early Church* (San Francisco: Harper San Francisco, 1991), 51–61; Jack V. **Scarola**, *A Chronographic Analysis of the Nativity* (New York: Vantage Press, 1991); Dale C. **Allison**, Jr., "What Was the Star that Guided the Magi?" *BR* 9 (6, Dec 1993): 20ff.

527. When Jesus was born in Bethlehem wise men from the East came asking for the king of the Jews and saying that they had seen his star in the East (Matt 2:1–2). Some may regard the star as entirely mythical,[87] some as completely miraculous, but it is also possible to suppose and inquire after an actual celestial phenomenon back of the account.

528. The study of the celestial bodies which we call astronomy was already advanced in the ancient world, and the idea that the heavenly bodies might provide portents of events upon earth, which idea is basic to what we term astrology, also existed from early times. That the two were often intermingled is not surprising. In Mesopotamia the Sumerians identified the heavenly bodies with deities. The moon was Sin or Nanna, the sun was Utu, Venus was Inanna. The planets were "the big ones who walk about [the moon] like wild oxen"; the

---

[87]Allison, *BR* 9 (6, Dec 1993) 24: " . . . any investigation of what modern astronomy might tell us about Bethlehem's star amounts to a search for what was never there."

stars were "the little ones who are scattered about [the moon] like grain."[88] From the Old Babylonian period onward many astrological and astronomical texts are available. In the reign of Ammisaduga the appearances and disappearances of Venus were recorded. In the Kassite period, texts describe a division of the sky into three zones and record the names of constellations and planets. In texts dated c. 70 B.C. but doubtless copied from older material the fixed stars are arranged in three "roads" and the moon and planets are listed. By this time (c. 700 B.C.) and under the Assyrian empire court astronomers were making and recording systematic observations. Summarizing the "prehistory" of Babylonian astronomy (from c. 1800 to c. 400 B.C.), Neugebauer enumerates the "tools" which had become available:

> The zodiac of 12 times 30 degrees as reference system for solar and planetary motion. A fixed luni-solar calendar and probably some of the basic period relations for the moon and the planets. An empirical insight into the main sequences of planetary and lunar phenomena and the variation of the length of daylight and night. The use of arithmetic progressions to describe periodically variable quantities. And, above all, a complete mastery of numerical methods which could immediately be applied to astronomical problems.[89]

With the availability of these "tools" came the great development of mathematical astronomy in the Hellenistic period and the last three centuries of the pre-Christian era.

529. In Matthew 2:1ff. in connection with the birth of Jesus we are told about wise men from the East. In Greek a μάγος is a magus or magian (plural μάγοι, magi). The magi were originally one of the six tribes of the Median empire (Herodotus 1.101) and became a hereditary class of learned priests, with a high rank among them known as a *magupat* or "master of the magi." Possibly related was the *rabmag,* who was a high official of Nebuchadnezzar at his taking of Jerusalem (Jer 39:3, 13). In the Persian empire the magi were associated with Zoroastrianism, and one chief *magupat* was regarded as the successor of Zarathustra. When Tiridates was made king of Armenia by Nero he was a priest (Tacitus, *Annals* 15.24) and a magian and was so scrupulous in observance of the regulations of his faith that when he traveled to Rome to pay homage to Nero he went all the way by land in order to avoid defiling the sea (Pliny, *Nat. Hist.* 30.61). The name of the magi is related to the word

---

[88] Samuel N. Kramer, *From the Tablets of Sumer* (Indian Hills, Col.: Falcon's Wing Press, 1956), 79.

[89] For the summary of Babylonian astronomy see Otto Neugebauer, *The Exact Sciences in Antiquity* (2d ed.; Providence: Brown University Press, 1957), 97–144; for the Venus tablets see Arthur Ungnad, *Die Venustafeln und das neunte Jahr Samsuilunas (1741 v. Chr.)* (1940); for Babylonian texts in astronomy and astrology see, e.g., *The Cuneiform Inscriptions of Western Asia,* vol. 3 (London: R. E. Bowler, 1870), pls. LI-LXIV; and *Late Babylonian Astronomical and Related Texts,* copied by T. G. Pinches and J. N. Strassmeier (Providence: Brown University Press, 1955); for astrology see C. J. Gadd, *Ideas of Divine Rule in the Ancient East* (London: Oxford University Press, 1948), 53; for the *Astronomica,* a work on astronomy and astrology written by Marcus Manilius in part while Augustus was still alive and in part after his death, see the introduction and translation by G. P. Goold (LCL, 1977).

"magic," and in some cases was synonymous with Greek γοής, *goēs,* meaning "wizard," "sorcerer." In the Roman empire there were many impostors, also known as *Chaldaei* and *mathematici,* i.e., soothsayers, astrologers, and the like. One of the less reputable was Simon in the city of Samaria, who had practiced magic (μαγεύων) and for a long time had amazed the nation with his magic (μαγεία) (Acts 8:9ff.). At Paphos on Cyprus a Jewish false prophet and magus was at the court of Sergius Paulus, the proconsul (Acts 13:6, 8). "In Babylon" Strabo (16.1.6) reports, "a settlement is set apart for the local philosophers, the Chaldeans, as they are called, who are concerned mostly with astronomy." In Babylon Daniel spoke disparagingly of the "wise men, enchanters, magicians, and astrologers," but the king made Daniel himself "chief prefect over all the wise men of Babylon" (Dan 2:27, 48). So with Daniel and many other Jews living at Babylon the magi may well have been familiar with Jewish expectations of a future king and kingdom and been alert to signs recognizable in the heavens pointing thereto. So it is that magi journeyed to Jerusalem and in audience with King Herod asked, "Where is he who has been born king of the Jews? For we have seen his star in the East, and have come to worship him" (Matt 2:2).

530. Those who have believed that Herod the Great died in 4 B.C. (§§501ff.) have undertaken many explorations of astronomical events in the several years before that date which might be associated with the "star of Bethlehem." In China many astronomical records are available.[90] In the Shang period and the fourteenth and thirteenth centuries B.C. the famous Oracle Bones represent the practice of divination but also record astronomical observations. They report lunar and solar eclipses and other celestial phenomena. One inscription dating about 1300 B.C. gives this notice of a new star in the constellation Scorpio: "On the seventh day of the month . . . a great new star appeared in company with Antares." In the succeeding Chou period (c. 1100–221 B.C.) and particularly in its latter part observational work was continued and refined. In the Han period (202 B.C.–A.D. 220) cosmological theories were developed and astronomical records were carefully kept. One important source of this period is the *Shih Chi (Historical Records)* of Ssu-ma Ch'ien who lived c. 140–c. 80 B.C. and completed this great work between 100 and 90 B.C.[91] Somewhat later this massive undertaking was continued in a further important historical treatise, the *Ch'ien-Han Shu.*[92] This was the work of the Pan family, father, son, and daughter. Revising and continuing the work of Ssu-ma Ch'ien, the father Pan Piao (A.D. 3–54) compiled annals of emperors and biographies of notable men. The son, Pan Ku (A.D. 32–92) used materials

---

[90] For Chinese astronomy see Joseph Needham, *Science and Civilisation in China*, vol. 3, *Mathematics and the Sciences of the Heavens and Earth* (Cambridge: Cambridge University Press, 1959). Note that he uses minus and plus signs for B.C. and A.D., but does not insert a year zero as the astronomers do (§221); his dates are historical and not astronomical, and -40 is 40 B.C. and so on.

[91] Edouard Chavannes, *Les mémoires historiques de Se-Ma Ts'ien, traduits et annotés* (5 vols.; Paris: Leroux, 1895–1905); Burton Watson, *Records of the Grand Historian of China: Translated from the Shih chi of Ssu-ma Ch'ien,* vol. 1, *Early Years of the Han Dynasty, 209–141 B.C.* (New York: Columbia University Press, 1961).

[92] Homer H. Dubs, *The History of the Former Han Dynasty by Pan Ku* (3 vols.; Baltimore: Waverly Press, 1938–1955).

from his father and from Ssu-ma Ch'ien, compiled annals and biographies, and wrote nine of the ten treatises which make up the *History*. The daughter, Pan Chao (born A.D. 45–51, died 114–120), shared in the compilation of the tenth treatise, on astronomy.[93] Later still, toward the end of the thirteenth century of the Christian era, Ma Tuan-Lin (flourished A.D. 1240–1280) in his work *Wên-hsien t'ung-k'ao* in Chapter 286 dealt with observed comets down to A.D. 1222, and in Chapter 294 made a list of extraordinary stars. From these and other sources we have information on Chinese astronomical observations, including comets and novae, observations which have often proved to be of such accuracy that they are used seriously in present-day astronomy, e.g., in the search for radio stars.[94]

531. A nova is a star which suddenly, perhaps as a result of an explosion, increases very greatly in brightness, perhaps ten thousandfold or a millionfold. If the occurrence is exceptionally great the term supernova is used. The Oracle Bone inscription quoted above (§530) presumably describes a nova and is the oldest record of such a phenomenon. The word used is *hsin hsing,* meaning "fire star." From the middle of the Han period the usual name for a nova is *kho hsing* or "guest star." A comet is known to us as a luminous heavenly body, often with a long tail. The English term is derived from the Greek κομήτης, "long-haired." In China from early times the technical term was *hsi hsing* or *sao hsing,* now translated "brush star" or "sweeping star," suggesting how it brushes past or sweeps by. When a comet is in opposition, i.e., in line with the earth and sun, its tail is not visible. For a comet in opposition the Chinese uses a special term *po hsing*. Understandably enough, particularly with regard to tailless comets, a clear distinction is not always made between comets and novae. As to identifying the position of objects in the sky, the Chinese divided the visible heavens into thirty-one portions, of which twenty-eight were designated by the term *hsiu* or "stellar division." For example, the stellar division Fang is the part of the sky which includes our constellations Libra, Lupus, Ophiuchus, and Scorpio. As far as comets are concerned, John Williams has compiled a list of 372 comets in the Chinese sources from 611 B.C. to A.D. 1640; and as far as novae are concerned, Knut Lundmark made a list running from 134 B.C. to A.D. 1828, and Hsi Tsê-tsung published a revised list (see LITERATURE above).

532. In relation to the star in Matt 2:2, supposed parallels in pagan literature have been cited to suggest the mythical character of such an account.[95] Virgil,[96] for example, tells how on one occasion "a star shot from heaven" and provided a significant omen. Even in pagan records, however, actual phenomena of nature may sometimes be involved. A good example is provided by the study by J. K. Fotheringham of the new star of Hipparchus and the dates of the birth and accession

---

[93] *Food and Money in Ancient China: The Earliest Economic History of China to A.D. 25, Han Shu 24, with Related Texts, Han Shu 91 and Shih-Chi 129* (trans. Nancy Lee Swann; Princeton: Princeton University Press, 1950), 3.

[94] W. Baade in *Astrophysical Journal* 97 (1943): 126.

[95] E.g., Erich Klostermann, *Das Matthäusevangelium* (HZNT 4; 2d ed.; Tübingen: J. C. B. Mohr, 1927), 16; Rudolf Bultmann, *Die Geschichte der synoptischen Tradition* (2d ed.; Göttingen: Vandenhoeck & Ruprecht, 1931), 318.

[96] *Aeneid* 2.692–704.

of Mithridates.[97] Mithridates VI Eupator, famous king of Pontus and opponent of the Romans, died in 63 B.C. while Pompey was on the march toward Petra.[98] Pliny, who speaks of the fabulous achievements of Mithridates in linguistics and medicine, mentions that he reigned fifty-six years.[99] If these were full years of reign between the year of accession and the year of death, his accession was in 120 B.C. Memnon[100] states that he was thirteen years old at accession. Therefore, his birth was in 133 B.C. and his conception in the preceding year, 134 B.C.

533. Concerning Mithridates, Justin, Roman historian of the second century of the Christian era, quotes from the *Historiae philippicae* of Pompeius Trogus, a Roman historian of the time of Augustus, as follows:[101]

> His future greatness was also predicted by celestial portents. For both in the year in which he was begotten and in that in which he first began to reign, a star, a comet (stella cometes), so shone on each occasion for seventy days that the whole sky seemed to be on fire. For in its magnitude it occupied a fourth part of the sky, and in its brightness it overcame the brightness of the sun; and in rising and setting it took up a space of four hours.

534. Such an account might easily be dismissed, and has been, as entirely imaginary. But the question naturally arises whether there really were comets at the times indicated, by our calculation in 134 and in 120 B.C. Actually, there are relevant astronomical records in China. Since exact dates are involved, it may be explained that at this point in the Han period, in the reign of the emperor Wu (Mar 10, 141 B.C.–Mar 29, 87 B.C.),[102] a change was made in the calendar and names were given to periods of the reign signifying outstanding events of the respective periods. The first of these reign-periods are listed in Table 148.

TABLE 148. *Reign-Periods in the Reign of the Emperor Wu*

Period	*B.C.*
chien-yüan	140–135
yüan-kuang	134–129
yüan-shou	122–117

[97] *Monthly Notices of the Royal Astronomical Society* 79 (1919): 162–167.
[98] *CAH* 9:391.
[99] *Natural History* 25.3.6.
[100] Ch. 32, in the *Bibliotheca of Photius* (A.D. c. 820–891), Cod. 224; MPG 103:9050.
[101] Justin, *Pompei Trogi Historiarum epitoma* 37.2.1–3; ed. Otto Seel (Stuttgart: Teubner, 1935), 252.
[102] These are the exact dates for Wu, but he is commonly shown as reigning 140–87 B.C. because the reign of a Han emperor was reckoned by the number of calendar years in which he was nominally on the throne. Even if he died immediately after the ceremonies he performed on the first day of the new year which declared him emperor, his successor would not begin to reign officially until the New Year's day of the following Han calendar year. The Chinese year, of course, did not begin and end at the times of the western world. For the dating see Swann, *Food and Money in Ancient China,* 8.

535. In the *Shih Chi* of Ssu-ma Ch'ien, mentioned above (§530) as living c. 140–c. 80 B.C. and, therefore, at about the same time as Mithridates, there are these notices:

> The Standard of Ch'ih-yu resembles a comet. . . . [103]

> In the years *yüan-kuang* and *yüan-shou* the Standard of Ch'ih-yu appeared twice; its size was such that it filled half the sky.[104]

So the *Shih Chi* records a comet that appeared twice, once in *yüan-kuang* = 134–129, and once in *yüan-shou* = 122–117 B.C. The two appearances correspond to Comets No. 31 and No. 32 in Williams's list (§531). Another reference probably describes Comet No. 31:

> In the first year of the epoch *yüan-kuang,* the sixth month, a strange star was seen in Stellar Division Fang.[105]

This provides the date, which is equivalent to June 134 B.C., and indicates the part of the sky (§531) where the phenomenon was visible. An additional reference in the *Ch'ien-Han Shu* (§530) probably describes Comet No. 32. In the annals of the reign-period *yüan-shou* it is stated:

> In the third year, in the spring, there was a comet in the eastern quarter [of the sky].[106]

Here the date is spring 120 B.C. The dates of the two comets, therefore, the first (Williams No. 31) in 134 B.C. and the second (Williams No. 32) in 120 B.C., agree with the historically probable dates of the conception and the accession of Mithridates.

536. The position given for the comet of 134 B.C. in the stellar division Fang (§535) locates it in the area of the sky marked by the constellation Scorpio and others (§531). Astronomically, therefore, the appearance would have been visible also at Sinope, the birthplace of Mithridates. In fact there is evidence that this very phenomenon was observed in the Mediterranean world as well as in China. Pliny (*Natural History* 2.24.95) states that the Greek astronomer Hipparchus (who flourished 146–126 B.C.) "detected a new star *(novam stellam)* that came into existence during his lifetime." Pliny also mentions "the movement of this star in its line of radiance," and the fact that it moved thus probably means that it was a comet. He also says that this experience led Hipparchus to undertake the construction of his famous catalogue of the stars. In this catalogue he recorded this "new star" in the constellation Scorpio even as the Chinese noted it in their equivalent stellar division Fang. This agreement and a consideration of the time when Hipparchus began his catalogue both point to identification of the "new star" of Hipparchus and the comet of 134 B.C. in the Chinese records. "In any case," writes Needham,[107] "it was carefully watched at both

---

[103]Chavannes, *Les Mémoires historiques de Se-Ma Ts'ien* 3:392.
[104]Ibid., 408.
[105]Fotheringham in *Monthly Notices of the Royal Astronomical Society* 79 (1919): 163.
[106]Dubs, *The History of the Former Han Dynasty* 2:62.

ends of the Old World." So a comet, precisely dated in Chinese sources, was visible in the Mediterranean in 134 B.C., as was another in 120 B.C.—precisely the years of the begetting and the accession to the kingship of Mithridates according to the historical evidence (§532). The record of Pompeius Trogus (§533) about the *stella cometes* which appeared to signalize those events seems to be substantiated.

537. Speaking now directly about the star connected with the birth of Christ (Matt 2:2), it may be noted that the thought of a star in connection with the Messiah is attested as anciently as in the oracle of Balaam, supposedly delivered when Israel was come up out of Egypt and was encamped in the plains of Moab (Num 22:1):

> I see him, but not now;
> I behold him, but not nigh;
> a star shall come forth out of Jacob,
> and a scepter shall rise out of Israel.

It is interesting to observe that the expression of this idea is attributed to a man whose home was "near the River" (Num 22:5), i.e., in Mesopotamia where, as we pointed out (§528), there was such early and great interest in the heavenly bodies. Likewise, in later time and in the time of the magi, the influence of the messianic hopes of diaspora Jews still resident in Mesopotamia (and also in Arabia, from whence Justin Martyr said the magi came, §508), no doubt had to do with the expectation of the imminent rise of a supreme "king of the Jews" (Matt 2:2).

538. In regard to a possible astronomical event to connect with the star (ἀστήρ) of Matt 2:2, a conjunction of planets has been considered—a thought originally and most famously associated with the name of Johannes Kepler. On Dec 17, 1603, at Prague, Kepler, who was court astrologer under the Holy Roman Emperor Rudolph II (1576–1612), observed a conjunction of Jupiter and Saturn, then known as a "great conjunction," with Mars soon after moving into the vicinity of the other two, to make what in modern terminology is called a "massing" of the planets. Then in 1604–1605 a supernova appeared in the neighborhood of the three planets. Kepler calculated that a similar conjunction of Jupiter and Saturn, with Mars coming close too, had occurred in the year 7 B.C., on which occasion it was a triple, rather than a normal single conjunction. According to modern calculations, the three conjunctions of Jupiter and Saturn took place on May 27, Oct 6, and Dec 1, 7 B.C.[108] Although the triple conjunction was a striking event, the two planets did not come close enough to each other to present the appearance of a single star, but passed each other at a distance approximately equal to twice the diameter of the moon.[109] The appearance of the supernova, however, which Kepler observed soon after the conjunction was seen, made the total event even more impressive, and Kepler was inspired to write about the new star (*De stella nova,* 1606) and about the year of the birth of

---

[107]*Science and Civilisation in China* 3:425.
[108]Sachs and Walker, "Kepler's View," 43 n. 7.
[109]Ibid., 45.

Christ (*De anno natali Christi,* 1614).[110] Insofar as he dealt with the star of Matt 2:2 it has often been thought that it was the conjunction of Jupiter and Saturn which Kepler identified as the star of Bethlehem, but his view is more accurately expressed in his question: "Does not the star, which after the birth of Christ led the Wise Men out of the Orient to Him, form a highly significant counterpart to the new star which just appeared, which also shone forth at the time of a great conjunction?"[111]

539. As for a "new star," which might be either a nova or a comet (the two being not always distinguishable in Chinese sources), two items in the Chinese records fall near the time with which we are here concerned. Both fall in the reign of the Han emperor Ai-Ti (6–1 B.C.). Comet No. 52 in Williams's list is recorded by Ma Tuan-Lin (§530):

> In the reign of Emperor Ai-Ti, the second year of the epoch *chien-p'ing,* the second month, a comet appeared in Ch'ien-niu for about seventy days.

Also in the *Ch'ien-Han Shu* (chap. 26, p. 34b) of Pan Ku (§530) it is said to have appeared "for more than seventy days." The reign-period *chien-p'ing* is equivalent to 6–3 B.C., therefore the second year of the period is 5 B.C. The second month is March, so the appearance of the comet took place in March of 5 B.C. The *Ch'ien-niu* or stellar division Niu is the area of the sky including the constellation Capricorn.

540. The second comet in question is No. 53 in Williams's list. It is recorded in the *Tung Keen Kang Muh,* a compilation of Chinese history from the earliest times to the end of the Yüan dynasty (A.D. 1368). Referring again to the reign-period *chien-p'ing,* this record states:

> In the third year of the same epoch, the third month, there was a comet in Ho-ku.

Also in the *Ch'ien-Han Shu* (chap. 11, p. 6b)[112] it is recorded:

> In the third month, on [the day] *chi–yu.* . . . A comet appeared in the [constellation] Ho-ku.

The third year of the reign-period *chien-p'ing* (6–3 B.C.) is 4 B.C. The third month is April, so the date of the comet's appearing is April of 4 B.C. The stellar division Ho-ku corresponds with the constellation Aquila which is visible in Palestine and Babylonia for almost the entire year.

541. The object seen in March of 5 B.C. (Williams No. 52; §539) is called a *hui hsing* or "sweeping star" (§531); that in April of 4 B.C. (Williams No.

---

[110]Max Caspar, ed., *Johannes Keplers gesammelte Werke,* vols. 1–4 (Munich: Beck, 1937–), cited by Sachs and Walker, "Kepler's View," 43 n. 2.

[111]Max Caspar, *Kepler* (trans. and ed. C. Doris Hellman; London: Abelard-Schuman, 1959), 156, quoted by Sachs and Walker, "Kepler's View," 44; cf. Ideler, *Handbuch der mathematischen und technischen Chronologie* 2:400–401.

[112]Dubs, *The History of the Former Han Dynasty,* vol. 3.1, 33.

53; §540) is called a *po hsing,* properly a comet without a tail (§531). The latter, at least, it would seem, might have been a nova, and these objects are in fact taken account of by Hsi Tsê-tsung in "A New Catalog of Ancient Novae," as well as in *Observation of Comets* by Williams.

542. So there was a remarkable planetary conjunction in 7 B.C. (§538) and in 5 B.C. and again in 4 B.C. a comet or nova, certainly an "extraordinary" star, appeared as well (§§539–541). It would be possible, therefore, to theorize that some or all of these events had something to do with the star of Bethlehem and the journey of the wise men, and several scenarios to that effect have in fact been proposed (see in the LITERATURE above). (1) Knut Lundmark:

> The hypothesis that the Star of the Magi was a nova gains much in strength when we learn that in the year 5 B.C. there appeared a nova, which has been observed by Chinese star-gazers. There are two different sources about this very likely splendid phenomenon: the one tells that the nova was seen during 70 days, the second that it was seen during more than 70 days. Thus the Magi could have proper time to make a trip from any Eastern country to Jerusalem during the time of visibility of this nova.[113]

(2) H. W. Montefiore writes:

> It is certain that in B.C. 7 there were three conjunctions of Jupiter and Saturn in Pisces. It is certain that in B.C. 4 and B.C. 5 an unknown star or stars were visible in China and also in Babylonia or Palestine. It is possible that Babylonian astrologers, noting the conjunctions in B.C. 7, and moved by a prophecy of a coming world ruler in the East, possibly knowing the tradition that a star would appear two years before the birth of the Messiah, set out for Jerusalem. It is possible that, confirmed in their expectations by the appearance of a comet in B.C. 5 and guided by local information, they may have found the infant Jesus in a house in Bethlehem. Herod died in March B.C. 4, and Jesus, according to Matthew's story, must have been born before Herod's death. He may well have been born in B.C. 5 or early B.C. 4.[114]

(3) Jack V. Scarola[115] cites David H. Clark, John H. Parkinson, and F. Richard Stephenson,[116] adding his own quite detailed reconstruction of the sequence of events.

543. On either side of the comet/nova of 5 B.C. and of 4 B.C. in Williams, *Observations of Comets* (§531), the nearest comet after is No. 54 of A.D. 13, which is too late for our consideration. The nearest one before is No. 51, and it is dated in 12 B.C. The date of 12 B.C. is in fact proposed for the birth of Jesus by both Jerry Vardaman and Nikos Kokkinos[117] (but on totally separate grounds, cf.

---

[113] *Actes du VIIe Congrès*, 438.

[114] *NovT* 4 (1960): 143–144.

[115] *Chronographic Analysis*.

[116] "An Astronomical Re-appraisal of the Star of Bethlehem—A Nova in 5 B.C.," *Journal of the Royal Astronomical Society* 18 (1977): 443–449.

[117] Jerry Vardaman, "Jesus' Life: A New Chronology," *CKC* 57, 66; Nikos Kokkinos,

below §§585–586), and both agree likewise in identifying the comet of 12 B.C. as the star of Bethlehem. The comet of this year is best known as Halley's Comet, named after the English astronomer Edmund Halley (1656–1742), who observed it in 1682. It is one of the brightest comets known. Its orbit brings it back to the vicinity of the earth approximately every seventy-six years, most recently in 1909–1910 and in 1985–1986. In 12 B.C. it passed near the earth between Aug 24 and Oct 17, rising in the east but after early September being seen only in the west. For dates within this general period Vardaman supposes Jesus born in the general period of late 12 B.C. or spring 11 B.C.; Kokkinos thinks the magi should have reached Herod by mid-September 12 B.C.[118]

544. Those who still date the death of Herod the Great to 4 B.C. and the killing of the male children of Bethlehem (Matt 2:16) to 5 or 6 B.C. (§510) may be interested in the conjunction of Jupiter and Saturn in the year 7 B.C. and the nearness of Mars soon thereafter (§538). In this connection it is of special interest to note that four broken cuneiform tablets found at Babylon (three now in the British Museum and one in the Berlin Museum) contain a Babylonian *ephēmeris* or "almanac" (a publication of the computed positions of celestial bodies) for the very time in question. As now available in English translation,[119] the text is dated in the year 241 of the Arsacid Era of the Parthians (who were then ruling in Ctesiphon in Babylonia, with their era beginning in 247/246 B.C.), which is the year 305 of the Seleucid Era, or the year 7/6 B.C.[120] In line 7 (in month III) there is mention of a solstice which can be shown to be the summer solstice, and from this the sequence of months can be established beginning with the first month Nisanu (Mar/Apr 7 B.C.) and continuing through the twelve months of the year. In line 16 (in month VII) it is said that a solar eclipse should be watched for at sunrise, so the listed positions of the heavenly bodies are given on the basis of advance calculation. Beginning in month III (Simanu, May/June) and possibly in month II (Aiaru, Apr/May, where the text is broken) and continuing into month XI (Shabatu, Jan/Feb 6 B.C.) Jupiter and Saturn are listed in the constellation Pisces, the Fishes. In month VI (Ululu, Aug/Sept 7 B.C.) there is mention of the "acronychal rising" (an astronomical term which means occurring at nightfall or sunset and refers to the rising or setting of a heavenly body) of Jupiter and of Saturn on the 21st day of the month. In month X (Tebetu, Dec/Jan 7/6 B.C.) it is stated that Mars will reach Pisces, and in month XI (Shabatu, Jan/Feb 6 B.C.) Mars is in Pisces with Jupiter and Saturn. The three conjunctions of Jupiter and Saturn which modern computation places on May 27, Oct 6, and Dec 1, 7 B.C., with Mars joining them soon afterward (§538) fall therefore exactly within the framework of the advance Babylonian calculations. While the positions of the planets are stated in terms of the signs of the zodiac in which they will be seen in a given month, actual conjunctions are not alluded to, but the editors of the text say there is no doubt that the Babylonians would

---

"Crucifixion in A.D. 36: The Keystone for Dating the Birth of Jesus," *CKC* 157–158, 162–163.

[118]Vardaman, *CKC* 66; Kokkinos, *CKC*, 157–162.

[119]Sachs and Walker, "Kepler's View," 47–49.

[120]PDBC 38, 45.

have been aware of the approach of a conjunction and would have been able to estimate its date within a few days.[121]

545. In month VIII (Arahsamnu, Oct/Nov 7 B.C.) in the Babylonian almanac just described (§544) it is stated that on the 19th day of the month Jupiter will reach its (second) stationary point in Pisces, and on the 21st Saturn will reach its (second) stationary point in Pisces. As to "stationary points" of the planets, Konradin Ferrari-d'Occhieppo, Emeritus Professor in the Department of Theoretical Astronomy in the University of Vienna, explains that "as far as Saturn, Jupiter, and Mars are concerned, the following special phases were computed: (1) their first reappearance in the morning, (2 and 4) the two stationary points in the apparent motion relative to the fixed stars, preceding and following (3) their last observable rise in the evening, when the planet in question could be seen during the whole night at the climax of its brightness."[122] In reworking the Babylonian computations, Ferrari-d'Occhieppo comes to the same or almost the same dates and also establishes the zodiacal longitudes of the phases of Jupiter and Saturn: on Ululu 21 (in year 305 of the Seleucid Era = Sept 15, 7 B.C.) the two planets were expected to be about one degree apart in longitude and to rise at sunset (their acronychal rising) and be visible during the whole night, then two months later in the night of Arahsamnu 20/21 (= Nov 12/13, 7 B.C.) reach their stationary points, very close together (only three minutes of an arc apart in longitude), in the central part of the constellation of Pisces (about the 350th degree of the zodiac and the 20th of Pisces), a rare close coincidence of the stationary points of Jupiter and Saturn that would not recur for at least 854 years.[123]

546. As for ancient astrological interpretation of what was written in the heavens, Ferrari-d'Occhieppo says that Jupiter represented the highest god and ruler of the universe and was particularly spoken of as "his star," while Saturn was the planet of the Jewish people (in Amos 5:26 called Sakkuth and Kaiwan, which were Babylonian names for Saturn), and at least later the constellation Pisces, the Fishes, was also associated with Syria and Palestine. The planet Mars was considered of sinister influence and representative of hostile powers and thus could not have been the star of Bethlehem. The other astronomical or astrological facts just described, however, surely could have directed attention to the land and people of the Jews and encouraged expectation of the imminent rise of a supreme "king of the Jews" (Matt 2:2).[124] Correct astronomical or astrological terminology is also unmistakably recognizable in Matthew's account of the magi when it is said (in 2:1) that the wise men came from "the rising," ἀπὸ ἀνατολῶν—the general direction of the rising stars described in Greek by the plural without the article; (in 2:2) that the star had been seen "in the rising," ἐν τῇ ἀνατολῇ—the evening rise of a certain star as a very important omen; and (in 2:9) that the same star "stood still" or "stopped," ἐστάθη—on another evening considerably later reached its (second) stationary point. Also

---

[121]Sachs and Walker, "Kepler's View," 46.
[122]Ferrari-d'Occhieppo, "The Star of the Magi and Babylonian Astronomy," *CKC* 43.
[123]Ibid., 45–46.
[124]Maier, *Fullness of Time,* 54; Ferrari-d'Occhieppo, *CKC* 45–47.

Herod inquired from the wise men "the exact time the star had appeared" (ἠκρίβωσεν τὸν χρόνον τοῦ φαινομένου ἀστέρος, 2:7), because he believed this was the date of the birth of the royal child, "in accordance with the exact time he had learned from the magi" (κατὰ τὸν χρόνον ὃν ἠκρίβωσεν παρὰ τῶν μάγων, 2:16).[125]

547. Ferrari-d'Occhieppo also takes into account the so-called zodiacal light. This is a faint band of light something like the Milky Way which may be seen in subtropical latitudes on the southwest horizon in the first hours after sunset as the sun illuminates meteoric particles in the plane of the ecliptic, and it appears as a luminous cone shining down to earth from the path of the planets.[126] So, the hypothesis is, as the magi rode south and a little west from Jerusalem to Bethlehem in the first three hours after sunset on Nov 12, 7 B.C. this light appeared to shine down upon the city of David from Jupiter and Saturn, which were practically immovable in their stationary points above in that very time (Matt 2:9, the star "stood still" or "stopped" [ἐστάθη] over the place where the child was, cf. §546).[127]

548. According to the papyrus codex Bodmer V, attributed to the third century A.D.,[128] when the magi came they saw the child Jesus "standing by his mother Mary's side" (ἑστῶτα μετὰ τῆς μητρὸς αὐτοῦ Μαρίας, 21:3).[129] If Jesus was born in Jan/Feb of the same year, as analysis above in relation to Zechariah and the course of Abijah has made likely (§473), he would have been around ten months old and able to stand at the visit of the wise men on Nov 12, 7 B.C.[130] In addition to deriving from the information about Zechariah and the course of Abijah a date for the birth of Jesus between mid-January and early February (§473) and understanding the order of Herod for the killing of the children at Bethlehem who were two years old or under to point to 6 or 7 B.C. (§§510, 544), we now have the facts about the conjunction and stationary points of Jupiter and Saturn on Nov 12, 7 B.C., with the further deduction that the child who stood beside his mother at that time might have been born ten months before, therefore in mid-January 7 B.C. By way of comparison with these results, Harold W. Hoehner acknowledges that the date of the birth of Jesus is difficult to know with finality, but judges that a midwinter date is most likely and either December in the year 5 B.C. or January in the year 4 B.C. is most reasonable.[131] Paul L. Maier reckons that the nativity was probably in November or December in the year 5 B.C.[132] John P. Meier dates the birth of Jesus around 7 or 6 B.C., a few years before the death of Herod (4 B.C.), but probably, he thinks, in Nazareth rather than in Bethlehem.[133]

---

[125]Ferrari-d'Occhieppo, *CKC* 43–44.
[126]*EB* 1966, 23, 961.
[127]BAG 383.
[128]HSNTA 1:370.
[129]Michel Testuz, *Papyrus Bodmer V: Nativité de Marie* (Cologny-Genève: Bibliotheca Bodmeriana, 1958), 112.
[130]Ferrari-d'Occhieppo, *CKC* 51.
[131]Hoehner, *Chronological Aspects,* 27.
[132]Maier, *Fullness of Time,* 29; idem, *CKC* 124 Table 1.
[133]Meier, *Marginal Jew,* 376, 382, 407.

549. The foregoing discussion was based on the hypothesis that Herod died in 4 B.C. On that basis the birth of Jesus two years or less before would have been in 6 or 5 B.C. (§510). Also, it would be possible to think of the triple conjunction of Jupiter and Saturn and the "new star" (nova), all of 7 B.C., and the comet or nova of 5 B.C. (§§538–539) in connection with the biblical star of Bethlehem (§§538f.). If, however, we remember that the prevailing tradition represented by the majority of early Christian scholars dated the birth of Jesus in 3/2 B.C. (Table 139), and if we accept the time of Herod's death as between the eclipse of Jan 9/10 and the Passover of April 8 in the year 1 B.C. (§514), and consider that his order for the killing of the male children of Bethlehem who were two years old or under would point back to 3 or 2 B.C. (§§510, 544), and also remember that the time may have been between mid-January and fairly early February (Beckwith, our §473), then we will probably date the nativity of Jesus in 3/2 B.C., perhaps in mid-January in 2 B.C.[134] On this basis unusual astronomical events in the years 3 or 2 B.C. could be thought of as having caught the attention of the magi and led to their journey to Jerusalem and Bethlehem.

550. In the years 3 and 2 B.C. there were no comets and no novae, but there were planetary and stellar events even more striking than those of 7 and 6 B.C.[135] On the morning of August 12, 3 B.C., Jupiter and Venus rose in the eastern sky, an event which could have been what was meant when the magi said: "We have seen his star in the East" or "in its rising" (Matt 2:2). (The word ἀνατολή means both the "rising [of stars]" and the "place of the rising [of the sun]," i.e., the East.) In this conjunction Jupiter and Venus were so close that they were almost touching each other. From the point of view of astrological symbolism Jupiter is the king planet and Venus (Ishtar in Babylonia), a female; so their conjunction can suggest a coming birth. The conjunction took place in the constellation of Leo (the Lion) and near the bright fixed star Regulus. Regulus is the king star and the Lion constellation is the tribal sign of Judah, as in Genesis 49:9 where Jacob blesses his son Judah and says, "Judah is a lion's whelp." Afterward Jupiter moved on to be in close conjunctions with Regulus three times (a triple conjunction on Sept 14, 3 B.C., Feb 17, 2 B.C., and May 8, 2 B.C.), then on June 17, 2 B.C., came again into conjunction with Venus, this time being so close that without a modern telescope the two planets would have looked like a single star. In the fall and winter 3/2 B.C. Jupiter appeared to stop several times against the background of the stars; and on June 17, 2 B.C., Jupiter and Venus were in extremely close conjunction and shone almost like a single bright star in the west—in the direction of Jerusalem as seen from Babylonia. With these phenomena we may compare Matthew 2:9: "The star which they had seen in the East went before them, till it came to rest over the

---

[134]Cf. Martin, *Star,* 91, 103, 228, 229: Jesus born Sept 11, 3 B.C., a difference apparently reflecting his dating of the relevant week of service of the course of Abijah in May (Martin, *Star,* 78) rather than in Beckwith's October/November.

[135]The information in this paragraph is derived from calculations and publications at the Griffith Observatory, Los Angeles (see LITERATURE above), and is cited by permission of Dr. E. C. Krupp, director, and with additional acknowledgment to John Mosley, *The Christmas Star* (Griffith Observatory, 1987).

place where the child was." If the magi were students of these astronomical events it can be theorized that the appearance of this "star" on June 17, 2 B.C., was the final heavenly sign that impelled the magi to begin the journey that brought them in the late summer or early fall of 2 B.C. to Jerusalem and Bethlehem, where they found the child Jesus, who "was born some time during the previous year and a half."[136]

551. Martin, followed by Keresztes, explains the statement that the star "came to rest over the place where the child was" (Matt 2:9) as a reference to a "stationary point" of Jupiter and identifies this as occurring on Dec 25 (the date of the winter solstice) in the year 2 B.C. in the constellation of Virgo (the Virgin) when Jupiter was directly over Bethlehem, about 68 degrees above the southern horizon as viewed from Jerusalem where the magi were.[137] This was not the day of the birth of Jesus, which must have taken place somewhat earlier, perhaps in mid-winter 3/2 B.C., but it could have had something to do with the later association of Dec 25 (§§562–569) with the birthday of Jesus.

(5) The Day

LITERATURE: Hermann **Usener**, *Das Weihnachtsfest* (2d ed., Bonn : F. Cohen, 1911; 3d ed., Bonn: Bouvier, 1969); Kirsopp **Lake**, "Christmas," in Hastings, *ERE* 3: 601–608; idem, "Epiphany," in Hastings, *ERE* 5: 330–332; Karl **Holl**, "Der Ursprung des Epiphanienfestes," in *Sitzungsberichte der Königlich preussischen Akademie der Wissenschaften: Philosophisch-historische Klasse* (Berlin, 1917), 402–438; L. **Duchesne**, *Christian Worship: Its Origin and Evolution* (5th ed.; London: S.P.C.K., 1919), 257–265A; Kirsopp **Lake**, *The Christmas Festival: An Address Delivered by Kirsopp Lake at the Pierpont Morgan Library 15 December 1935* (New York: privately printed, 1937); Hans **Lietzmann**, *Geschichte der Alten Kirche,* vol. 3, *Die Reichskirche bis zum Tode Julians* (Berlin: W. de Gruyter, 1938), 321–329; Leonhard **Fendt**, "Der heutige Stand der Forschung über das Geburtsfest Jesu am 25. XII. und über Epiphanias," in *TLZ* 78 (1953): 1–10; Oscar **Cullmann**, *Der Ursprung des Weihnachtsfestes* (Zurich/Stuttgart: Zwingli Verlag, 1960); Allan **Hauck**, *Calendar of Christianity* (New York: Association Press, 1961); Roland H. **Bainton**, "The Origins of Epiphany," in *Collected Papers in Church History,* vol. 1 (Boston: Beacon, 1962), 22–38; Thomas J. **Talley**, *The Origins of the Liturgical Year* (2d ed.; Collegeville, Mich.: Liturgical Press, 1991).

See also LITERATURE on the star, ahead of §527.

552. Among the days of the year, one day has long been of very chief importance, namely, the day of the winter solstice (§32), when the sun stands temporarily still and then the days begin to lengthen again. The present date of the winter solstice is about Dec 21 but, as Beckwith states,[138] both Dec 25 and Jan 6 are ancient recorded datings, Jan 6 being the

---

[136] Mosley, *The Christmas Star,* 54.
[137] Martin, *Birth of Christ,* 16–21; *Star,* 59–60; Keresztes, *Imperial Rome,* 34.
[138] Beckwith, *RQ* 9 (1977): 73, 93.

old date, while in early Christian times Dec 25 was held to be the true date. In the pagan world both dates were honored as the time for the light to grow again; at Rome important Isis festivals, for example, were held on both Dec 25 and Jan 6.[139] Additional cult observances on these dates will be noted below (§§561, 568). In due time both dates were also fixed upon for celebration of the birth of Jesus. While replacement of pagan festivals may have been a factor, historical tradition about the actual time of year of the birth of Jesus may have been more important. The winter solstice and the beginning of the increase of the light may also have seemed an appropriate time to remember the coming into the world of "the sun of righteousness" (Mal 4:2).

553. Specific dates for the day of the nativity were being given at least as early as the second century. As we have seen (§488), Clement of Alexandria says in the *Stromata* (A.D. c. 194) that from the birth of Christ to the death of Commodus (ἀφ' οὗ ὁ κύριος ἐγεννήθη ἕως Κομόδου τελευτῆς) was 194 years, 1 month and 13 days,[140] which gives Nov 18, 3 B.C., as Clement's date for the birth of Christ. Even though he himself thus gives an exact date, he seems to speak somewhat disapprovingly when he says that there are also those who have determined not only the year but the day of the Savior's birth (τῇ γενέσει τοῦ Σωτῆρος). They put the birth, as Clement too did, in the twenty-eighth year of Augustus, i.e., 3/2 B.C. (§§488, 390), but on the twenty-fifth day of Pachon, which is equivalent to May 20 (Table 8). After that, Clement remarks that the followers of Basilides (the famous Gnostic who flourished at Alexandria about A.D. 117–138) hold as a festival also the day of Christ's baptism (καὶ τοῦ βαπτίσματος αὐτοῦ τὴν ἡμέραν), which they say was in the fifteenth year of Tiberius and on the fifteenth day of the month Tybi (= Jan 10), while others say that it was on the eleventh day of the same month (= Jan 6). Continuing immediately to the passion, Clement reports that some say it took place in the sixteenth year of Tiberius on the twenty-fifth of Phamenoth, others on the twenty-fifth of Pharmuthi, and yet others on the nineteenth of Pharmuthi. Then returning to the birth he says that others declare that the Savior was born (γεγεννῆσθαι) on the twenty-fourth or twenty-fifth of Pharmuthi, which is equivalent to Apr 19 or 20.[141]

(a) January 6

554. Epiphanius (A.D. c. 315–403) also reports dating which goes back into the second century. In the *Panarion,* we remember (§494), he directs himself at one point against the Alogi, as he calls them, a group in Asia Minor around A.D. 180. In the same passage where he says the Alogi put the birth of Jesus under the consuls Sulpicius Camerinus and Poppaeus Sabinus (the latter name being somewhat distorted in Epiphanius), which means in A.D. 9, he also

---

[139]EB (1987) 24:707.
[140]*Stromata* 1.21.145.
[141]Cf. Beckwith, *RQ* 9 (1977): 91.

says that they put the date on: πρὸ δεκαδύο καλανδῶν Ἰουλίων ἢ Ἰουνίων (*Panarion* 51.29.2). In Latin this date would be written: *XII kal. Julius vel Junius.* The twelfth day before the kalends or first day of July is equivalent (counting inclusively) to June 20; the twelfth day before the kalends or the first day of June is equivalent to May 21. Because of the similarity of date this would appear to represent the same tradition reported by Clement of Alexandria (§552) in connection with the followers of Basilides, which gave Pachon 25 = May 20 as the date of the birth of Jesus. This date it is now stated by Epiphanius, however, was that of the day of the conception (σύλληψις) as announced by Gabriel to Mary (Luke 1:26ff; τὴν ἡμέραν τῆς συλλήψεως καὶ ὡς εὐηγγελίσατο ὁ Γαβριὴλ τὴν παρθένον) rather than of the birth of Jesus. Probably, therefore, although Clement of Alexandria did not make it plain, the same point of reference was intended in the tradition that he reported.

555. As for the day of the birth of Christ, Epiphanius himself refers to the forty-second year of Augustus and the consular date *Augusto XIII et Silvano* (A.U.C. 752 = 2 B.C.) and quotes the tradition he accepts:

> τούτων ὑπατευόντων, φημὶ δὲ Ὀκταυίου τὸ τρισκαιδέκατον καὶ Σιλανοῦ, ἐγεννήθη Χριστὸς τῇ πρὸ ὀκτὼ εἰδῶν Ἰανουαρίων μετὰ δεκατρεῖς ἡμέρας τῆς χειμερινῆς τροπῆς καὶ τῆς τοῦ φωτὸς καὶ ἡμέρας προσθήκης.
>
> When these were consuls, Octavian for the thirteenth time and Silvanus, Christ was born on the eighth day before the Ides of January, thirteen days after the winter solstice and the beginning of the increase of light and the day. (*Panarion* 51.22.4)

The eighth day before the ides or thirteenth day of January (§141), counting inclusively, is Jan 6; this is thirteen days inclusively after the winter solstice, dated at that time on Dec 25. In another passage Epiphanius gives the same date even more exactly as, according to Roman reckoning, between the evening of Jan 5 and the morning of Jan 6 (51.24.1; cf. 51.27.5). Also in the same passage he gives the same date in its equivalents in no less than eight other calendars: according to the Egyptians on Tybi 11 (Tybi 1 = Dec 27 [Table 8], therefore Tybi 11 = Jan 6); according to the Syrian Greeks on Audynaios 6 (Audynaios 1 = Jan 1 [Table 27], therefore Audynaios 6 = Jan 6); in the calendar of the Hebrews on the fifth day of Tebeth (Dec/Jan); etc.

556. In Greek the word ἡ ἐπιφάνεια, "the epiphany," means "the manifestation" or "the appearing." In Greek literature and inscriptions it is used for the visible manifestation of a deity. In 2 Tim 1:10 it is used for the appearing of the Savior on earth. Epiphanius employs the same word in the plural, τὰ ἐπιφάνεια, "the manifestations," as a name for the day of the birth of Jesus, and he also dated other "manifestations" of the divine glory of Jesus on the same day. Speaking of the birth, he writes, for example:

> ἡ ἡμερα τῶν Ἐπιφανείων, ἥ ἐστιν ἡμέρα τῆς αὐτοῦ κατὰ σάρκα γεννήσεως.
>
> The day of the Epiphanies, which is the day of his birth according to the flesh. (*Panarion* 51.16.1; cf. 51.22.12; 51.27. 4)

Alternatively, with τὰ ἐπιφάνεια he also uses τὰ θεοφάνεια, "theophanies" (*Panarion* 51.29.4). This word is not in the Greek New Testament but is found in Greek literature in the singular, ἡ θεοφάνεια, "the theophany," for the "vision of God"; and in the plural, τὰ θεοφάνεια, for a festival at Delphi in which statues of the gods were displayed to the people. It was also on this day of "the Epiphanies" or "the Theophanies" that, according to Epiphanius (as we have seen, §511), the star shone in the East for the magi two years before they arrived at Jerusalem and Bethlehem.

557. From the date of Jesus' birth given by Epiphanius (Tybi 11, the eighth day before the ides of January, etc., all equaling Jan 6 [§555]), he also counts forward to events of the public ministry of Jesus. Jesus was baptized, Epiphanius says (*Panarion* 51.16.1; 51.30.4), according to Egyptian reckoning on Hathyr 12 and according to Roman reckoning on the sixth day before the ides of November. These dates (see Table 8 and §141) are both equivalent to Nov 8. This date, Epiphanius observes, was exactly sixty days before "the Epiphanies," i.e., the birthday of Jesus. Then Epiphanius cites Luke 3:23 (51.16.2). In Codex Sinaiticus, Codex Vaticanus, and many other manuscripts, this reads: ἦν Ἰησοῦς ἀρχόμενος ὡσεὶ ἐτῶν τριάκοντα. The participle ἀρχόμενος, literally "beginning," is somewhat difficult to interpret, as is shown by changes made in other manuscripts where Codex Alexandrinus, Codex Bezae, and others move it to the end, and where the Sinaitic Syriac and other texts omit the word altogether. In the minuscules of the Ferrar Group (13, 69, 124, 346) the meaning is clarified, according to one possible understanding, by the addition of the word εἶναι, and this is the way the quotation is given by Epiphanius: ἦν Ἰησοῦς ἀρχόμενος εἶναι ὡς ἐτῶν τριάκοντα. With this interpretation the statement is that Jesus was "beginning to be about thirty years of age" at his baptism. Using this interpretation and in the light of the baptismal date given above, Epiphanius then explains that Jesus was in fact, at the time of his baptism, twenty-nine years and ten months of age, which might be called "thirty years, but not full" (ἀλλ' οὐ πλήρης). The miracle which followed soon afterward at the wedding at Cana took place a full thirty years from the birth of Jesus (πλήρωμα τριάκοντα ἐτῶν ἀπὸ τῆς γεννήσεως τοῦ κυρίου), i.e., exactly on his thirtieth birthday (51.16.7–8; cf. 51.29.7).

558. Summarizing the ministry in round numbers, Epiphanius can then say that the thirtieth year of Jesus was that of his baptism, that after that he preached during his thirty-first year being accepted by the people, that he preached also during his thirty-second year but under opposition, and that in yet another year (his thirty-third) there remained still seventy-four days (Panarion 51.27.4–6). From his birthday on Tybi 11 = Jan 6 to the day of his death on the thirteenth day before the kalends of April (§141) or on the twenty-fourth day of Phamenoth (Table 8), both of which designations indicate Mar 20, was exactly seventy-four days. Also, Epiphanius says, the resurrection took place on Phamenoth 26 or the eleventh day before the kalends of April, namely on Mar 22. The life of Jesus, as understood by Epiphanius, may therefore be outlined as in Table 149.

TABLE 149. *The Life of Jesus according to the Chronology of Epiphanius*

Year of Jesus' Life	*B.C./A.D.*	*Event*	*Date*
0	2 B.C.	Birth	Jan 6
1	1 B.C.	1st birthday	Jan 6
2	A.D. 1	2d birthday	Jan 6
		Arrival of the magi	Jan 6
3	A.D. 2	3d birthday	Jan 6
4	3	4th birthday	Jan 6
. . .	. . .	. . .	. . .
28	27	28th birthday	Jan 6
29	28	29th birthday	Jan 6
		Baptism "about 20"	Nov 8
30	29	30th birthday	Jan 6
		Sign at Cana	Jan 6
31	30	31st birthday	Jan 6
		Preached, being accepted	
32	31	32d birthday	Jan 6
		Preached, being opposed	
33	32	33d birthday	Jan 6
		Death 74 days later	Mar 20
		Resurrection	Mar 22

559. Returning to the date of the conception which Epiphanius gave as fixed by the Alogi on June 20 or May 21 (§554), he also reports in this connection the tradition that the birth followed seven months later or, more exactly, seven lunar months less four days (ἑπτὰ μηνῶν χρόνον κατὰ τόν σεληνιακὸν δρόμον παρὰ ἡμέρας τέσσαρας; *Panarion* 51.29.3–4). Seven lunar months of 29.5 days each equals 206.5 days. If we say 206 days, minus 4 days, we have 202 days, and the number of days from June 20 to Jan 6 inclusive is 201 days. Therefore, Epiphanius evidently intends to show that this tradition agrees with the date of Jan 6 for the birth. He says that others, however, declare that the duration of the period in question was ten months less fourteen days and eight hours or, otherwise stated, nine months plus fifteen days and four hours. The two ways of stating this figure show that he reckoned one lunar month as equaling twenty-nine days and twelve hours, i.e., 29.5 days. In this connection he also cites Wisd 7:2 for the "ten months." Epiphanius does not state the meaning of this dating, but it could be explained as follows. From Mar 6 to Jan 6 is ten months. Fourteen days and eight hours forward from Mar 6 brings one to the night of Mar 19/20. In other words, from Mar 19/20 to Jan 6 is ten months less fourteen days and eight hours. In this way the date of conception would coincide with the date of death (Mar 20). So Epiphanius is able to conclude that from all sides (πανταχόθεν) the date of Tybi 11 (= Jan 6) is agreed upon for the birth of Jesus (51.29.7).

560. Glancing back, then, at the tradition reported by Clement of Alexandria (§552), a tradition deriving probably from the followers of Basilides, which gave the date of Pachon 25 = May 20, it seems probable (§554) that they also intended by γένεσις to point to conception rather than birth.[142] In this case there was a rather widespread opinion, at least as early as in the second century, that the conception was in the spring and the birth of Jesus near the midwinter, in the areas represented by Epiphanius's report specifically on Jan 6. The fact that in the same connection Clement of Alexandria (§552) also mentions the festival of the Basilidians which celebrated the day of Jesus' baptism on Tybi 15 or Tybi 11, i.e., on Jan 10 or Jan 6, suggests that although Epiphanius gave the different date of Nov 8 for the baptism (§557) there were many who believed that this event, which could be thought of as marking a birth "according to the Spirit," fell on the anniversary of the birth "according to the flesh." In that case the "manifestations" celebrated on Jan 6 were indeed numerous, namely, the birth of Jesus (§556), the appearing of the star to the wise men (§556), the first sign at Cana (§557), and, in the view of some, the baptism (§560).

561. As to a contributory cause for the selection of the winter solstice date of Jan 6 for the nativity day, Epiphanius may also provide a clue. In the *Panarion* (51.22.9–11) he describes a ceremony held in the temple of Kore at Alexandria on the night of Jan 5 and morning of Jan 6. The participants stay awake all night, he says, making music to the idol with songs and flutes. In the early morning at cockcrow they descend by torchlight to a subterranean shrine and bring forth a wooden image, marked with the sign of a cross and a star of gold on hands, knees, and head. This image they carry in procession to musical accompaniment, and then return it to the crypt. They explain the meaning of the ceremony to the effect that in this hour this day Kore, the virgin, gave birth to the Aion. Similar ceremonies are held, Epiphanius says, on the same date at Petra and Elusa in Arabia. This may well have contributed to the choice of the same date for observance in the attempt to replace pagan ceremony by Christian.[143]

(b) December 25

562. Like Jan 6, Dec 25 was also a winter solstice date (§552) and the date of a pagan festival. Hippolytus of Rome (A.D. c. 170–c. 240), whose *Chronicle* was described above (§293), provides a reference to this date for the birth of Jesus in his *Commentary on Daniel* (4.23);[144]

> The first coming of our Lord, that in the flesh, in which he was born at Bethlehem, took place eight days before the kalends of January, a Wednesday, in the forty-second year of the reign of Augustus, 5500 years from Adam.

The eighth day before the kalends of January is the twenty-fifth day of December, and the forty-second year of Augustus was 3/2 B.C. (§476, Table 129; §500, Table 139).

563. Further evidence for Dec 25 is found in the Roman city calendar for the year 354, edited by Filocalus and described above (§176). It lists the

---

[142]Lake in Hastings, *ERE* 3: 605.

[143]Lake in Hastings, *ERE* 5: 332; Lietzmann, *Geschichte der alten Kirche* 3:327.

[144]Hippolyte, *Commentaire sur Daniel* (trans. Maurice Lefèvre; SC 14; Paris: Cerf, 1947), 307; trans. Beckwith, *RQ* 9 (1977): 74.

burial places of the martyrs *(Depositio martyrum)* arranged in the order of the days of the year on which festivals were held in their honor.[145] The list can of course not be later than the calendar itself which is shown to belong to A.D. 354 by the facts that the lists of the consuls and prefects extend to 354, and that the list of bishops extends to Liberius whose accession was in 352 but of whose banishment in 366 nothing is said. But the original *Depositio episcoporum* was probably compiled in 336 and revised in 354 for it runs in order through the church year and through the death of Sylvester in 335, and then Marcus (who died in 336) and his immediate successors are added—out of order as far as the months of the church year are concerned—at the end of the list. If the same is true of the *Depositio martyrum,* it may also be dated A.D. 336.

564. In the *Depositio martyrum* the sequence of festivals in the church year begins with the item:

VIII Kal. Ian. natus Christus in Betleem Iudeae

The eighth day before the kalends of January, on which day it was remembered that Christ was born in Bethlehem of Judea, was the twenty-fifth day of December. Since the list for the entire year begins with this date and since the following dates are those when festivals were held in honor of the persons named, it seems evident that in Rome in A.D. 336 the festival of the birth of Christ was held on Dec 25. Also the last item on the list is a festival on the ides of December, i.e., on Dec 13. Therefore, the beginning of the liturgical year was between Dec 13 and Dec 25. The *Depositio episcoporum* agrees by making its last and first items respectively Dec 8 and Dec 27.[146]

565. At Antioch in A.D. 386[147] John Chrysostom (born at Antioch A.D. c. 345, preacher at Antioch and later [A.D. 398] bishop of Constantinople, died A.D. 407) delivered two sermons with which we are here concerned. On Dec 20[148] he spoke in memory of Philogonius, a former bishop of Antioch. In this sermon he says that a festival is approaching, namely, that of the bodily birth of Christ. This is basic in its significance, he says, to the other great festivals of the Christian year, for if Jesus had not been born he would not have been baptized as is celebrated on Epiphany, he would not have been crucified and raised as is celebrated at Easter, and he would not have sent the Spirit as is commemorated at Pentecost. To this festival, which will be celebrated in five days, he therefore looks forward eagerly and urges the congregation to do the same.

566. On the day itself, namely Dec 25 of the year 386, Chrysostom delivered the second sermon. Theodoret (A.D. c. 393–453), bishop of Cyrus, later made two quotations from this sermon saying that they were taken from the "birthday discourse" (ἐκ τοῦ γενεθλιακοῦ λόγου).[149] Herein Chrysostom

---

[145]Hans Lietzmann, *Die drei ältesten Martyrologien* (KLT 2; Bonn: A. Marcus und E. Weber, 1903), 3–5.

[146]Duchesne, *Christian Worship: Its Origin and Evolution,* 258–259.

[147]Usener, *Weihnachtsfest,* 245; and Lietzmann, *Die drei ältesten Martyrologien*, 384.

[148]Usener, *Weihnachtsfest,* 222–223.

[149]*Dialogue* 1; NPNF^2 3:181.

says[150] that it would be wonderful if the sun could come down from heaven and send forth its light on earth, and it is more wonderful that in the incarnation the sun of righteousness does in fact send forth its light from human flesh. With "the sun of righteousness" he is doubtless referring to Mal 4:2. Then he tells how long he had desired not only to experience this day but to do so in the company of a large congregation. He states that is it was not yet ten years that the festival had been known to them. It was, however, transmitted to them as from long ago and from many years (ὡς ἄνωθεν καὶ πρὸ πολλῶν ἡμῖν παραδοθεῖσα ἐτῶν). From long ago it was known to those who dwell in the West (παρὰ μὲν τοῖς τὴν ἑσπέραν οἰκοῦσιν ἄνωθεν γνωριζομένη). And from long ago it was a festival that was very well known and famous to those who dwell from Thrace to Gades (καὶ ἄνωθεν τοῖς ἀπὸ Θρᾴκης μέχρι Γαδείρων οἰκοῦσι κατάδηλος καὶ ἐπίσημος γέγονε).

567. Later in the sermon Chrysostom introduces an exegesis of Scripture to support the date of Dec 25. This is based on Luke 1 and runs as follows.[151] The promise to the priest Zechariah that his wife Elizabeth would bear a son to be named John came at the time Zechariah had entered the temple to burn incense (Luke 1:9). Evidently assuming, incorrectly as far as we know, that Zechariah was the high priest and that this was the most important event possible, Chrysostom explains that this was the time of the Fast and of the Feast of Tabernacles. The Fast was the Day of Atonement, the one day of the year when the high priest entered the Holy of Holies, and the date of it was the tenth day of the seventh month (Lev 16:29), i.e., Tishri 10. The Feast of Tabernacles followed shortly on the fifteenth day of the seventh month and continued for seven days (Lev 23:34). This feast, says Chrysostom, the Jews celebrate toward the end of the month Gorpiaios. In A.D. 386 there was a new moon on Sept 10. Since the month Tishri falls normally in Sept/Oct this new moon presumably marked Tishri 1. Tishri 1 (the Day of Atonement) was therefore approximately Sept 20 in that year, and Tishri 15–21 (the Feast of Tabernacles) was approximately Sept 25–Oct 1. In the later correlation of the Syro-Macedonian calendar with the Julian (Table 27) the month of Gorpiaios began on Sept 1. The Feast of Tabernacles was accordingly celebrated toward the end of Gorpiaios exactly as Chrysostom says. This was the date, then, of the conception of John the Baptist as announced to Zechariah (Luke 1:13). Counting from this time (Gorpiaios = Sept), it was in the sixth month (Luke 1:26) that annunciation was made to Mary and the conception of Jesus is to be dated. Here Chrysostom carefully names and counts six intervening months (Hyperberetaios, Dios, Apellaios, Audynaios, Peritios, and Dystros) and concludes that it was in the next month, Xanthikos (= Apr) that the conception of Jesus is to be placed. From that point he counts nine months inclusively to the birth of Jesus, namely the months Xanthikos, Artemisios, Daisios, Panemos, Loos, Gorpiaios, Hyperberetaios, Dios, and Apellaios. The last, Apellaios (= Dec), was the month in which the birthday celebration was even then being held at which Chrysostom was preaching.

---

[150]Usener, *Weihnachtsfest,* 225–227.
[151]Ibid., 230–233.

568. It will be remembered (§555) that Epiphanius's birth date of Jan 6 for the birth of Jesus was reckoned as "thirteen days after the winter solstice and the beginning of the increase of the light and the day" (i.e., from Dec 25 to Jan 6 inclusively), and Chrysostom's allusion (§566) to "the sun of righteousness" (Mal 4:2) also reflects the appropriateness of the birth date to the solstice date, but in this case Dec 25 is itself the birth date too. As intimated above (§562), it was also not unimportant that Dec 25 was the date of the pagan festival of the *sol invictus,* the "invincible sun" (declared the official deity of the Roman empire by Aurelian in A.D. 274), and the Christian celebration could replace it.[152] In fact, the cult of Deus Sol Invictus was still at its height in the time of Constantine and the portrait of the sun god was on the coins of the emperor, but with his rise to sole rule of the empire (A.D. 323–337) Constantine was free to accept Christianity openly. Thereafter his coins and inscriptions were no longer offensive to Christians[153] and Dec 25 was freely the birthday of Christ, as attested in the Roman city calendar in A.D. 336 (§563). All together the full equation with the solar year was completed in that the conception and the crucifixion were both placed on Mar 25 as well as the birth on Dec 25. Thus, Augustine (A.D. 354–430) writes:

> For He is believed to have been conceived on the twenty-fifth of March, upon which also he suffered. . . . But he was born, according to tradition, upon December the twenty-fifth.[154]

569. The chief reckonings attested by the oldest sources, then, put the conception of Jesus in the spring, and his birth in midwinter. In the East, the birth was celebrated on Jan 6, a date to which also the star and the magi, the baptism, and the sign at Cana were attached. In the West the birthday of Christ was Dec 25. From Chrysostom we learn that, although this date had been introduced to Antioch only ten years before he spoke, say about A.D. 375, it had long been known in the West. As the Western usage gradually spread to most places, Jan 6 was retained as the celebration of the three "manifestations" in the coming of the magi, the baptism, and the sign at Cana. Although the exact dates of Jan 6 and Dec 25 may have been fixed because of the relationship to then accepted dates of the winter solstice (§552) and for the sake of replacement of pagan festivals of those times (§§561, 568), the selection of specific dates at this time of the year agrees with what we have seen (§§473, 548) was a relatively old tradition and a historically likely fact of a birth in midwinter. As to objection to a wintertime date on the supposition that the shepherds would not have been at that time "out in the field, keeping watch over their flock by night" (Luke 2:2), William Hendriksen quotes a letter dated Jan 16, 1967, received from the New Testament scholar Harry Mulder, then teaching in Beirut, in which the latter tells of being in Shepherd Field at Bethlehem on the just-passed Christmas Eve, and says: "Right near us a few flocks of sheep were nestled. Even the lambs were not lacking. . . . It is therefore definitely not impossible that the Lord Jesus was born in December."[155]

---

[152]Lake in Hastings, *ERE* 3: 608.
[153]Finegan, *Myth and Mystery,* 209–212.
[154]*On the Trinity* 4.5; NPNF[1] 3.74.
[155]William Hendriksen, *Matthew* (NTC; Grand Rapids: Baker, 1973), 1:182.

2. The Public Ministry of Jesus

LITERATURE: Conrad **Cichorius**, "Chronologisches zum Leben Jesu," *ZNW* 22 (1923): 16–20; George **Ogg**, *The Chronology of the Public Ministry of Jesus* (Cambridge: Cambridge University Press, 1940); idem, "The Age of Jesus When He Taught," *NTS* 5 (1958–1959): 291–298; Norman **Walker**, "The Reckoning of Hours in the Fourth Gospel," *NovT* 4 (1960): 69–73; Harold W. **Hoehner**, *Chronological Aspects of the Life of Christ* (Grand Rapids: Zondervan, 1977), 29–63; Paul L. **Maier**, "The Date of the Nativity and the Chronology of Jesus' Life," *CKC* 113–130; Paul **Keresztes**, *Imperial Rome and the Christians,* vol. 1, *From Herod the Great to about 200 A.D.* (Lanham, Md.: University Press of America, 1989), 36–38; John P. **Meier**, ch. 11, "A Chronology of Jesus' Life," in *A Marginal Jew: Rethinking the Historical Jesus,* vol. 1, *The Roots of the Problem and the Person* (ABRL; New York: Doubleday, 1991), 372–433.

(1) The Beginning of the Public Ministry

(a) "In the Fifteenth Year of the Reign of Tiberius Caesar"

LITERATURE: H. **Dessau**, ed., *Prosopographia Imperii romani* vol. 2 (Berlin: Georgius Reaimerus, 1897), 182f., no. 150; *CAH* 10:607–612; Bruno **Violet**, "Zum rechten Verständnis der Nazaretperikope, Lk 4 16–30," *ZNW* 87 (1939): 251–271; Jacob **Mann**, *The Bible as Read and Preached in the Old Synagogue: A Study in the Cycles of the Readings from Torah and Prophets, as Well as from Psalms, and in the Structure of the Midrashic Homilies* (2 vols.; Cincinnati: Hebrew Union College/Jewish Institute of Religion, 1940, 1960); Hugh **Anderson**, "Broadening Horizons: The Rejection at Nazareth Pericope of Luke 4:16–30 in Light of Recent Critical Trends," in *Interpretation* 18 (1964): 259–275; A. S. van der **Woude**, "Melchisedek als himmlische Erlösergestalt in den neugefundenen eschatologischen Midraschim aus Qumran Höhle XI," in *Oudtestamentische Studien* (Leiden: E. J. Brill, 1965), 354–373; M. de **Jonge** and A. S. van der **Woude**, "11Q Melchizedek and the New Testament," in *NTS* 12 (1965/1966): 301–326; August **Strobel**, "Das apokalyptische Terminproblem in der sogen. Antrittspredigt Jesu (Lk 4, 16–30)," in *TLZ* 92 (4, 1967), 251–254; idem, "Die Ausrufung des Jubeljahres in der Nazarethpredigt Jesu: Zur apokalyptischen Tradition Lc 4 16–30," in Grässer, Strobel, Tannehill, and Eltester, *Jesus in Nazareth*, 38–50; idem, *Ursprung und Geschichte des frühchristlichen Osterkalenders* (Texte und Untersuchungen 121; Berlin: Akademie, 1977); idem, "Plädoyer für Lukas: Zur Stimmigkeit des chronistischen Rahmen von Lk 3.1," *NTS* 41 (1995): 466–469; Merrill P. **Miller**, "The Function of Isa 61:1–2 in 11Q Melchizedek," *JBL* 88 (1969): 467–469; Gabriel Kyo-Seon **Shin**, *Die Ausrufung des endgültigen Jubeljahres durch Jesus in Nazaret: Eine historisch-kritische Studie zu Lk 4, 16–30* (European University Studies 23.378; Bern: Peter Lang, 1969); Heinz **Schürmann**, *Das Lukasevangelium* (Herder's Theologischer Kommentar zum Neuen Testament 3; Freiburg: Herder, 1969, 1982, 1994); David **Hill**, "The Rejection of Jesus at Nazareth," *NovT* 13 (1971): 161–180; Erich **Grässer**, August **Strobel**, Robert C. **Tannehill**, and Walther **Eltester**, *Jesus in Nazareth* (Berlin: Walter de Gruyter, 1972); Bo **Reicke**, "Jesus in Nazareth," in Horst Balz and Siegfried Schulz, *Das Wort und die Wörter: Festschrift Gerhard Friedrich zum 65. Geburtstag* (Stuttgart: W. Kohlhammer, 1973), 47–55; Charles **Perrot**, *La lecture de la Bible dans la synagogue: Les anciennes lectures palestiniennes du Shabbat et des fêtes*

(Hildesheim: H. A. Gerstenberg, 1973); idem, "Luc 4, 16–30 et la lecture biblique de l'ancienne synagogue," in *Revue trimestrielle,* Université des Sciences Humaines de Strasbourg, 47 (24, Apr–Dec 1973), 324–337; Ben Zion **Wacholder**, "Chronomessianism: The Timing of Messianic Movements and the Calendar of Sabbatical Cycles," in *HUCA* 46 (1975): 201–218; James A. **Sanders**, "From Isaiah 61 to Luke 4," in Jacob Neusner, ed., *Christianity, Judaism and Other Greco-Roman Cults: Studies for Morton Smith at Sixty* (Leiden: E. J. Brill, 1975), 75–106; Fred L. **Horton** Jr., *The Melchizedek Tradition: A Critical Examination of the Sources to the Fifth Century A.D. and in the Epistle to the Hebrews* (Cambridge: Cambridge University Press, 1976); Robert Bryan **Sloan** Jr., *The Favorable Year of the Lord: A Study of Jubilary Theology in the Gospel of Luke* (Austin, Tex.: Schols Press, 1977); Donald Wilford **Blosser**, "Jesus and the Jubilee: Luke 4:16–30, The Year of Jubilee and Its Significance in the Gospel of Luke" (Ph.D. diss., St. Mary's College, The University of St. Andrews, Scotland, 1979); Sharon Hilda **Ringe**, *The Jubilee Proclamation in the Ministry and Teaching of Jesus: A Tradition-Critical Study in the Synoptic Gospels and Acts* (Ph.D. diss., Union Theological Seminary, New York, 1981). See also LITERATURE above for Jubilees ahead of §232.

570. According to Luke 3:1ff., it was in the fifteenth year of the reign of Tiberius Caesar that the word of God came to John the son of Zechariah in the wilderness and that he went into the region about the Jordan preaching a baptism of repentance for the forgiveness of sins. And at the time, when all the people were baptized, Jesus also was baptized and thus made his initial public appearance. The fifteenth year of Tiberius would appear to be an exact date, and no doubt it was such in the mind of the writer and probably also to most of the readers of that time, but the matter is not so simple to the modern student. Events and honors in the life and reign of Tiberius have been set forth above in Table 42. Tiberius Claudius Nero was born on Nov 16, A.U.C. 712 = 42 B.C. On June 26, A.U.C. 757 = A.D. 4, he was adopted by Augustus and designated his successor,[157] from which time he was called Tiberius Julius Caesar. On Oct 23, A.U.C. 765 = A.D. 12, he celebrated a triumph for his military victories in Germany and Pannonia. Referring to this event, Suetonius[158] says that "the consuls caused a law to be passed soon after this that he should govern the provinces jointly with Augustus and hold the census with him." The date when Tiberius thus began to govern the provinces jointly with Augustus was probably A.D. 12,[159] although arguments have been presented for putting it in A.D. 11 or 13.[160] In this connection Tacitus describes Tiberius Nero as *collega imperii,* "colleague in the empire" (*Annals* 1.3), and some consider him joint emperor with Augustus from this time on.[161] On Aug 19, A.U.C. 767 = A.D. 14, Augustus died, with the funeral on or around Sept 12. On Sept 17 the Senate met, voted the deceased emperor a deity, Divus Augustus, and voted his designated successor, Tiberius, the new head of state. As emperor he was known as Tiberius Caesar Augustus. So

[157]Dio, *Roman History* 55.13.1.
[158]*Tiberius* 21.
[159]*Suetonius,* ed. J. C. Rolfe (LCL), vol. 1, 323.
[160]Holzmeister, *Chronologia vitae Christi,* 66.
[161]*EB* 22:176.

Tiberius ruled as colleague of Augustus from A.D. 12, and as successor of Augustus from Aug 19 (or from Sept 17 if you count from the vote of the Senate), A.D. 14, and his rule continued until his death on Mar 16, A.U.C. 790 = A.D. 37.[162] In Table 150 a preliminary numbering of his regnal years is given. Column 1 numbers from the time when Tiberius began to govern jointly with Augustus, and column 2 from the first full calendar year after that. Column 3 numbers from the death of Augustus and the succession of Tiberius, and column 4 from the first full calendar year after that. A further series of brief tables (nos. 140–156) is intended to recognize other variables in calendars and regnal years which could, at least in theory, be involved.

TABLE 150. *Regnal Years of Tiberius Caesar*

A.U.C.	*A.D.*		*Col. 1*	*Col. 2*	*Col. 3*	*Col. 4*
765	12	Tiberius governs jointly with Augustus	1			
766	13		2	1		
767	14	Aug 19, death of Augustus Sept 17, Tiberius named head of state	3	2	1	
768	15		4	3	2	1
769	16		5	4	3	2
770	17		6	5	4	3
771	18		7	6	5	4
772	19		8	7	6	5
773	20		9	8	7	6
774	21		10	9	8	7
775	22		11	10	9	8
776	23		12	11	10	9
777	24		13	12	11	10
778	25		14	13	12	11
779	26		15	14	13	12
780	27		16	15	14	13
781	28		17	16	15	14
782	29		18	17	16	15
783	30		19	18	17	16
784	31		20	19	18	17
785	32		21	20	19	18
786	33		22	21	20	19
787	34		23	22	21	20
788	35		24	23	22	21
789	36		25	24	23	22
790	37	Mar 16, death of Tiberius	26	25	24	23

571. If Tiberius began to govern the provinces jointly with Augustus soon after Oct 23, A.D. 12 (§570), his first factual year of such rule extended from late October (let us say) A.D. 12 to late October A.D. 13, and this year and his succeeding years counted from the same point may be tabulated in Table 151.

[162]Suetonius, *Tiberius* 73.

TABLE 151. *Factual Regnal Years of Tiberius Counted from His Joint Rule of the Provinces with Augustus*

Number of Regnal Year	*Duration of Regnal Year*
1	Oct A.D. 12–Oct A.D. 13
2	Oct A.D. 13–Oct A.D. 14
. . .	. . .
14	Oct A.D. 25–Oct A.D. 26
15	Oct A.D. 26–Oct A.D. 27

572. If the reckoning from the same initial point (§571) was by Roman calendar years and what we have called the non-accession-year system (cf. column 1 in Table 150), the years would be as in Table 152.

TABLE 152. *Regnal Years of Tiberius from His Joint Rule of the Provinces, Counted as Julian Calendar Years according to the Non-Accession-Year System*

Number of Regnal Year	*Duration of Regnal Year*
1	Oct–Dec 31, A.D. 12
2	Jan 1–Dec 31, A.D. 13
. . .	. . .
14	Jan 1–Dec 31, A.D. 25
15	Jan 1–Dec 31, A.D. 26

573. If the reckoning was the same as the foregoing (§572) but according to the accession-year system (cf. column 2 in Table 150), the count would be as in Table 153.

TABLE 153. *Regnal Years of Tiberius from His Joint Rule of the Provinces, Counted as Julian Calendar Years according to the Accession-Year System*

Number of Regnal Year	*Duration of Regnal Year*
Accession year	Oct–Dec 31, A.D. 12
1	Jan 1–Dec 31, A.D. 13
. . .	. . .
14	Jan 1–Dec 31, A.D. 26
15	Jan 1–Dec 31, A.D. 27

574. In the Syro-Macedonian calendar (Table 27) the year began on Hyperberetaios 1 = Oct 1 (cf. 471). In this calendar and by the non-accession-year method, still using the joint rule of the provinces as the initial point, the reckoning would be as in Table 154.

TABLE 154. *Regnal Years of Tiberius from His Joint Rule of the Provinces, Counted as Syro-Macedonian Calendar Years according to the Non-Accession-Year System*

Number of Regnal Year	*Duration of Regnal Year*
1	Oct 1, 12–Sept 30, A.D. 13
2	Oct 1, 13–Sept 30, A.D. 14
. . .	. . .
14	Oct 1, 25–Sept 30, A.D. 26
15	Oct 1, 26–Sept 30, A.D. 27

575. By the same reckoning (§574), but by the accession-year system, the years would be as in Table 155. It is to be remembered that the assumed initial point of Tiberius's joint rule is in late October, on or after the twenty-third day of that month (§571), hence after the Syro-Macedonian New Year on Oct 1.

TABLE 155. *Regnal Years of Tiberius from His Joint Rule of the Provinces, Counted as Syro-Macedonian Calendar Years according to the Accession-Year System*

Number of Regnal Year	*Duration of Regnal Year*
Accession year	Oct A.D. 12–Sept 30, A.D. 13
1	Oct 1, A.D. 13–Sept 30, A.D. 14
. . .	. . .
14	Oct 1, A.D. 26–Sept 30, A.D. 27
15	Oct 1, A.D. 27–Sept 30, A.D. 28

576. In the Jewish calendar (Table 13), the year began with the month Nisan, corresponding to Mar/Apr of the Julian calendar. Using this calendar, counting still from the joint rule of the provinces, and reckoning both by the non-accession-year and accession-year methods, the results are as in Tables 156 and 157.

TABLE 156. *Regnal Years of Tiberius from His Joint Rule of the Provinces, Counted as Jewish Calendar Years according to the Non-Accession-Year System*

Number of Regnal Year	*Duration of Regnal Year*
1	Oct A.D. 12–Mar/Apr A.D. 13
2	Mar/Apr A.D. 13–Mar/Apr A.D. 14
. . .	. . .
14	Mar/Apr A.D. 25–Sept 30, A.D. 26
15	Mar/Apr A.D. 26–Sept 30, A.D. 27

TABLE 157. *Regnal Years of Tiberius from His Joint Rule of the Provinces, Counted as Jewish Calendar Years according to the Accession-Year System*

Number of Regnal Year	*Duration of Regnal Year*
Accession year	Oct A.D. 12–Mar/Apr A.D. 13
1	Mar/Apr A.D. 13–Mar/Apr A.D. 14
. . .	. . .
14	Mar/Apr A.D. 25–Mar/Apr A.D. 27
15	Mar/Apr A.D. 26–Mar/Apr A.D. 28

577. If the point from which the regnal years of Tiberius were reckoned was, however, the death of Augustus on Aug 19 A.D. 14 (or the formal naming of Tiberius to succeed Augustus by the Senate less than a month later on Sept 17; §570), then different sets of figures result. Taking Aug 19, A.D. 14, as the point of reference, and reckoning both factual and calendar years according to alternate systems and various calendars, we obtain the results shown in Tables 158–166.

TABLE 158. *Factual Regnal Years of Tiberius, Counted from His Succession to Augustus*

Number of Regnal Year	*Duration of Regnal Year*
1	Aug 19, A.D. 14–Aug 18, A.D. 15
2	Aug 19, A.D. 15–Aug 18, A.D. 16
. . .	. . .
14	Aug 19, A.D. 27–Aug 18, A.D. 28
15	Aug 19, A.D. 28–Aug 18, A.D. 29

TABLE 159. *Regnal Years of Tiberius from His Succession to Augustus, Counted as Julian Calendar Years according to the Non-Accession-Year System*

Number of Regnal Year	*Duration of Regnal Year*
1	Aug 19–Dec 31, A.D. 14
2	Jan 1–Dec 31, A.D. 15
. . .	. . .
14	Jan 1–Dec 31, A.D. 27
15	Jan 1–Dec 31, A.D. 28

TABLE 160. *Regnal Years of Tiberius from His Succession to Augustus, Counted as Julian Calendar Years according to the Accession-Year System*

Number of Regnal Year	*Duration of Regnal Year*
Accession year	Aug 19–Dec 31, A.D. 14
1	Jan 1–Dec 31, A.D. 15
. . .	. . .
14	Jan 1–Dec 31, A.D. 28
15	Jan 1–Dec 31, A.D. 29

TABLE 161. *Regnal Years of Tiberius from His Succession to Augustus, Counted as Egyptian Calendar Years according to the Non-Accession-Year System*

Number of Regnal Year	*Duration of Regnal Year*
1	Aug 19–Aug 28, A.D. 14
2	Aug 29, A.D. 14–Aug 28, A.D. 15
. . .	. . .
14	Aug 29, A.D. 26–Aug 28, A.D. 27
15	Aug 29, A.D. 27–Aug 28, A.D. 28
16	Aug 29, A.D. 28–Aug 28, A.D. 29

TABLE 162. *Regnal Years of Tiberius from His Succession to Augustus, Counted as Egyptian Calendar Years according to the Accession-Year System*

Number of Regnal Year	*Duration of Regnal Year*
1	Aug 19–Aug 28, A.D. 14
2	Aug 29, A.D. 14–Aug 28, A.D. 15
. . .	. . .
14	Aug 29, A.D. 27–Aug 28, A.D. 28
15	Aug 29, A.D. 28–Aug 28, A.D. 29
16	Aug 29, A.D. 29–Aug 28, A.D. 30
. . .	. . .
19	Aug 29, A.D. 32–Aug 28, A.D. 33

TABLE 163. *Regnal Years of Tiberius from His Succession to Augustus, Counted as Syro-Macedonian Calendar Years according to the Non-Accession-Year System*

Number of Regnal Year	*Duration of Regnal Year*
1	Aug 19–Sept 30, A.D. 14
2	Oct 1, A.D. 14–Sept 30, A.D. 15
. . .	. . .
14	Oct 1, A.D. 26–Sept 30, A.D. 27
15	Oct 1, A.D. 27–Sept 30, A.D. 28

TABLE 164. *Regnal Years of Tiberius from His Succession to Augustus, Counted as Syro-Macedonian Calendar Years, according to the Accession-Year System*

Number of Regnal Year	*Duration of Regnal Year*
Accession year	Aug 19–Sept 30, A.D. 14
1	Oct 1, A.D. 14–Sept 30, A.D. 15
. . .	. . .
14	Oct 1, A.D. 27–Sept 30, A.D. 28
15	Oct 1, A.D. 28–Sept 30, A.D. 29

TABLE 165. *Regnal Years of Tiberius from His Succession to Augustus, Counted as Jewish Calendar Years (Beginning with Nisan), according to the Non-Accession-Year System*

Number of Regnal Year	*Duration of Regnal Year*
1	Aug 19, A.D. 14–Mar/Apr A.D. 15
2	Mar/Apr A.D. 15–Mar/Apr A.D. 16
. . .	. . .
14	Mar/Apr A.D. 27–Mar/Apr A.D. 28
15	Mar/Apr A.D. 28–Mar/Apr A.D. 29

TABLE 166. *Regnal Years of Tiberius from His Succession to Augustus, Counted as Jewish Calendar Years (Beginning with Nisan) according to the Accession-Year System*

Number of Regnal Year	*Duration of Regnal Year*
Accession year	Aug 19 A.D. 14–Mar/Apr A.D. 15
1	Mar/Apr A.D. 15–Mar/Apr A.D. 16
. . .	. . .
14	Mar/Apr A.D. 28–Mar/Apr A.D. 29
15	Mar/Apr A.D. 29–Mar/Apr A.D. 30

578. In assessment of the bewildering variety of dates just assembled, it is obvious that the earliest dates for the regnal years of Tiberius are obtained by reckoning from his joint rule of the provinces with Augustus (probably beginning in the month of October in A.D. 12) as the initial point (columns 1 and 2 in Table 150, and Tables 151–157). For such a manner of reckoning there is possible evidence in Tertullian's *Against Marcion* where the author says in one place (1.15) that "the Lord has been revealed since the twelfth year of Tiberius Caesar," and in another place (1.19): "In the fifteenth year of Tiberius, Christ Jesus vouchsafed to come down from heaven." It is possible that the dual and at first sight contradictory dating can be explained by supposing that the fifteen years are counted from the time of the joint rule of the provinces, and the twelve years are full calendar years after the death of Augustus (columns 1 and 4, respectively, in Table 150), both references therefore indicating the same year, A.U.C. 779 = A.D. 26. Otherwise, however, as far as is known, ancient sources do not count Tiberius's own reign from what was only his joint rule with Augustus, so this manner of reckoning may be left out of further consideration in relation to Luke 3:1.[163]

579. As to whether Luke 3:1 should be interpreted in terms of a provincial calendar—Jewish (since John baptized and Jesus worked in Judea; Tables 156–157, 165–166), Syro-Macedonian (since Luke was probably from Antioch, according to the late second-century "anti-Marcionite" prologue to the Gospel according to Luke[164] and in view of the first person plural "we" in the "Western" text of Acts 11:28, cf. our §464)[165] (Tables 154–155, 163–164), or even the Egyptian (Tables 161–162)—it is of course true that such calendars were in use in their respective provinces.[166] An example of such a basis for dating the sole reign of Tiberius is found in Oxyrhynchus Papyrus 2352, which contains a perfectly preserved letter with this date line at the end (Line 20):

(ἔτους) ιθ Τιβερίου Καισαρ{αρ}ος Σεβαστοῦ μηνὸς Σεβαστοῦ ζ

---

[163]Cf. Hoehner, *Chronological Aspects,* 31–32; Meier, *Marginal Jew* 1:384.

[164]Eusebius, *Ch. Hist.* 3.4.6; Jerome, *Lives of Illustrious Men* 70, quoted Hastings, *DAC* 1:719.

[165]NBD 11.

[166]Cf. J. K. Fotheringham quoted in Holzmeister, *Chronologia vitae Christi,* 59 n. 2.

> In the nineteenth year of Tiberius Caesar Augustus on the seventh day of the month Sebastos.

If the first regnal year of Tiberius, considered as an Egyptian calendar year according to the accession-year system (Table 134), began on Thoth 1 = Aug 29, A.D. 14, then the nineteenth year began on Thoth 1, A.D. 32. Sebastos is the Roman name of the Egyptian month Thoth (§135 and Table 29) and since Thoth 1 = Aug 29, the seventh day of that month is Sept 4. Therefore, the date of the letter is Sept 4, A.D. 32.[167]

580. Luke, however, addresses his combined work (Luke 1:3; Acts 1:1) to Theophilus, whom he salutes as "most excellent" (κράτιστε), an honorary form of address otherwise employed in Acts (23:26; 24:2; 26:25) only of a Roman official, and through Theophilus (literally, the "friend of God") it would appear that Luke is intending his work for Roman readers or, at any rate, readers out in the Roman world. It may also be noticed that in Luke 3:1 the reign of Tiberius is named with the Greek word ἡγεμονία, which means reign, rule, sovereignty, and the like, and Josephus (*War* 2.168) uses the same word when he tells how "the empire of the Romans (τῆς Ῥωμαίων ἡγεμονίας)" passed to Tiberius upon the death of Augustus. For Luke and his intended readers, therefore, it is most likely that the "reign" of Tiberius meant Tiberius's own sole rule (from the death of Augustus, Aug 19, A.D. 14) and that this rule is to be reckoned in terms of the Julian calendar. Several roughly contemporary Greek and Roman historians provide specific examples of dating in this way. The Greek historian Dio (b. A.D. 155–164, d. c. 235) puts the death of Tiberius on Mar 26 in the consulship of Gnaeus Proculus and Pontius Nigrinus, and states that he had been emperor for twenty-two years, seven months, and seven days.[168] Gnaeus Acerronius Proculus and Gaius Pontius Nigrinus were consuls in A.U.C. 790 = A.D. 37. Therefore Dio's date for the death of Tiberius is Mar 26 (actually this is an error for Mar 16, the date given by Suetonius [§428]), A.D. 37. From Aug 19, A.D. 14, to Mar 26, A.D. 15, is a period of seven months and seven days. From the latter date to Mar 26, A.D. 37, is a period of twenty-two years. Therefore in his reckoning of the length of the reign of Tiberius, Dio counted the exact number of years, months, and days from the death of Augustus. Tacitus (A.D. c. 55–c. 117) and Suetonius (fl. A.D. c. 100) count from the same point, namely the death of Augustus on Aug 19, A.D. 14, and state regnal years of Tiberius in terms of full calendar years after that point (Table 150 column 4), as the following examples show. Tacitus tells of the death of Augustus in Nola and the arrival there of Tiberius Claudius Nero (cf. §570 for the name Nero), and says that "one report announced simultaneously that Augustus had passed away and that Nero was the master of the empire" (*Annals* 1.5). Later Tacitus equates the ninth year of Tiberius with the consulate of Gaius Asinius and Gaius Antistius (4.1). In a critical list of consuls (Table 40) *C. Asinius C. f. Pollio et C. Antistius C. f. Vetus* are the consuls of the year A.U.C. 776 = A.D. 23.[169] If we count

---

[167] *OxyP* 22:156.
[168] *Roman History* 58.27.1–58.28. 5.
[169] Liebenam, *Fasti consulares Imperii romani,* 10.

full calendar years after the death of Augustus, the ninth year of Tiberius is A.U.C. 776 = A.D. 23. Suetonius dates the death of Tiberius *XVII Kal. Ap. Cn. Acerronio Proculo C. Pontio Nigrino conss.*, and states that this was in his twenty-third year of reign (*Tiberius* 73). The seventeenth day before the kalends of April was Mar 16. Gnaeus Acerronius Proculus and Gaius Pontius Nigrinus were consuls in A.U.C. 790 = A.D. 37. This date was in the twenty-third full calendar year after the death of Augustus.

581. In comparison with the historians just cited (§580), our Table 158 agrees with Dio in counting factual regnal years of Tiberius, and this table is here expanded as Table 167 to provide ready reference to the full sweep of Tiberius's factual years of reign. In comparison therewith our Table 159 counts the regnal years as full years of the Julian calendar according to the non-accession-year system and thus makes the fifteenth year equivalent to the full year Jan 1 to Dec 31, A.D. 28; likewise our Table 160 counts the regnal years as full years of the Julian calendar according to the accession-year system and thus makes the fifteenth year equivalent to the full year Jan 1 to Dec 31, A.D. 29.

TABLE 167. *Regnal Years of Tiberius, Counted from His Succession to Augustus*

Number of Regnal Year	*Duration of Regnal Year (A.D.)*
1	Aug 19, 14–Aug 18, 15
2	Aug 19, 15–Aug 18, 16
3	Aug 19, 16–Aug 18, 17
4	Aug 19, 17–Aug 18, 18
5	Aug 19, 18–Aug 18, 19
6	Aug 19, 19–Aug 18, 20
7	Aug 19, 20–Aug 18, 21
8	Aug 19, 21–Aug 18, 22
9	Aug 19, 22–Aug 18, 23
10	Aug 19, 23–Aug 18, 24
11	Aug 19, 24–Aug 18, 25
12	Aug 19, 25–Aug 18, 26
13	Aug 19, 26–Aug 18, 27
14	Aug 19, 27–Aug 18, 28
15	Aug 19, 28–Aug 18, 29
16	Aug 19, 29–Aug 18, 30
17	Aug 19, 30–Aug 18, 31
18	Aug 19, 31–Aug 18, 32
19	Aug 19, 32–Aug 18, 33
20	Aug 19, 33–Aug 18, 34
21	Aug 19, 34–Aug 18, 35
22	Aug 19, 35–Aug 18, 36
23	Aug 19, 36–Aug 18, 37

582. In his *Praeparatio evangelica* Eusebius places the fifteenth (πεντεκαιδέκατον) year of Tiberius in Ol. 201, 4 (τὸ δ′ τῆς σα′ Ὀλυμπιάδος). In Eusebius's *Chronicle*[170] the immediate period is shown as in our Table 168.

TABLE 168. *The Fifteenth Year of Tiberius in the* Chronicle *of Eusebius (Jerome)*

A.Abr.	*Ol.*	*Romans*	*A.D.*
		Of the Romans the 3d, Tiberius, 23 years	
2037	200	8	21
2038		9	22
2039		10	23
2040		11	24
2041	201	12	25
2042		13	26
2043		14	27
2044		15	28
John, son of Zechariah, in the desert near the Jordan River, preaching Christ the Son of God			

At this point, therefore, the *Chronicle* tells us that of the Romans who ruled the whole Roman world Tiberius was the third (Julius Caesar, Augustus, Tiberius), states that he ruled for twenty-three years, and counts the successive years of his reign. The first Olympiad shown is the two hundredth, its first year being July 1, A.D. 21, to June 30, A.D. 22 (our Table 46). The four years of the Olympiad correspond with the eighth, ninth, tenth, and eleventh years of the reign of Tiberius and are identified in Helm's edition of the *Chronicle* with the years A.D. 21, 22, 23, and 24. The last of these years (A.D. 24) is also A.Abr. 2140. Then comes the two hundred first Olympiad, and its four years correspond with years 12, 13, 14, and 15 of Tiberius and are A.D. 25, 26, 27, and 28, the last of which (July 1, A.D. 28, to June 30, A.D. 29) is A.Abr. 2044 (A.D. 28/29). This then, the year A.D. 28/29, is Eusebius's date for the fifteenth year of Tiberius. It is also of interest that in Eusebius's margin at the point of A.D. 29[171] there is a note, *LXXXI iobelai secundum Hebraeos* (the eighty-first Jubilee according to the Hebrews). Earlier, at the year 472/471 B.C.[172] Eusebius has a similar note stating that this is the seventy-first Jubilee. Thus from 472/471 B.C. to A.D. 28/29 is 500 years or exactly ten fifty-year Jubilee periods.

583. Now as for the date of the fifteenth year of Tiberius in Luke 3:1, we have judged (§570) that Luke, as a historian like others in the Roman empire, would count the regnal years from Tiberius's succession to Augustus; and, since Roman historians of the time (Tacitus, Suetonius, our §580) generally date the first regnal year of a ruler from Jan 1 of the year following the date of accession (i.e., follow the accession-year system), we judge that Luke would do likewise. So Tiberius's fifteenth factual year was from Aug 19, A.D. 28, to Aug 18, A.D. 29 (Table 167), but his fifteenth regnal year counted as Julian calendar years according to the accession-year system was Jan 1 to Dec 31, A.D. 29 (Table 160), shown in full in Table 169 and accepted in the present book as the correct equation for Luke 3:1, namely, Tiberius year 15 = Jan 1 to Dec 31, A.D. 29.

---

[170] Helm 172–173.
[171] Helm 174.
[172] Helm 109.

TABLE 169. *Regnal Years of Tiberius according to Roman Usage*

Number of Regnal Year	*Duration of Regnal Year (A.D.)*
Accession	Aug 19–Dec 31, 14
1	Jan 1–Dec 31, 15
2	Jan 1–Dec 31, 16
3	Jan 1–Dec 31, 17
4	Jan 1–Dec 31, 18
5	Jan 1–Dec 31, 19
6	Jan 1–Dec 31, 20
7	Jan 1–Dec 31, 21
8	Jan 1–Dec 31, 22
9	Jan 1–Dec 31, 23
10	Jan 1–Dec 31, 24
11	Jan 1–Dec 31, 25
12	Jan 1–Dec 31, 26
13	Jan 1–Dec 31, 27
14	Jan 1–Dec 31, 28
15	Jan 1–Dec 31, 29

To cite opinions both pro and con of several scholars of our time (see LITERATURE preceding §570), Strobel counts Tiberius's regnal years from his elevation to joint rule (ἡγεμονία) with Augustus, and Blosser cites both Strobel and also the present writer,[173] as he himself makes the fifteenth year of Tiberius fall within the years of A.D. 26/27. John P. Meier expresses the "tentative conclusion . . . that Jesus began his ministry soon after that of John the Baptist in A.D. 28." Meier also notes that in other reckonings of the regnal years of Tiberius after his succession to Augustus (our Tables 158–166) his fifteenth year includes at least some part of the years 28 or 29. Hoehner judges that the ministry of John began sometime in A.D. 29 and that Jesus' ministry also began in that year or shortly thereafter. Paul L. Maier holds that John began his public work in the fall of A.D. 28 and that his ministry extended throughout A.D. 29, while the baptism and start of public ministry of Jesus probably began in the fall of that year. Paul Keresztes says that the "fifteenth year of Tiberius should be reckoned not from a coregency of A.D. 12, but from the death of Augustus and the accession of Tiberius in 14."[174] Thus the year in question would run from Aug 19, A.D. 28, to Aug 18, A.D. 29, so that the beginning of John's ministry should have fallen within these dates; but since Roman historians of the time usually date the first regnal year of a ruler from Jan 1 of the year following the date of accession, the year A.D. 29 would seem to be indicated.

---

[173]It is true that in the original edition of this *Handbook* Table 116 (= Table 151 in the present revised edition) shows that it is *possible* to count from the joint rule of Tiberius with Augustus and arrive at A.D. 26/27 but, like the present book, my original edition prefers to count from Tiberius's succession to Augustus, and most of Tables 123 and following (= Tables 158 and following in the present book) count from that point and reach the year A.D. 28/29.

[174]Strobel, *Ursprung und Geschichte*, 92; Blosser, "Jesus and the Jubilee," 314; Meier, *Marginal Jew,* 385–386, 402; Hoehner, *Chronological Aspects,* 37; Maier, *CKC* 124, Table 1; Keresztes, *Imperial Rome,* 37–38.

584. We also ask as to the time in the year A.D. 29 when the events of Luke 3:1ff. transpired—the preaching of John the Baptist at the Jordan river and the coming of large crowds to him (Matt 3:5; Mark 1:5; Luke 3:7), the baptism of Jesus, and the return of Jesus apparently not too long afterward to Nazareth, where he spoke in the synagogue. Climatically, the great summertime heat in the sub–sea level and semitropical Jordan valley makes it unlikely that it was in the summer, or even in the spring with summer coming on, and allows us to think the fall the most likely. Religiously, preaching ministries calling for repentance (like that of John the Baptist) are noted as generally reaching their height just before the beginning of a new Jewish year in the late summer or early autumn,[175] and in the autumn of A.D. 29 the New Year of Tishri (Sept 28) was followed shortly by the solemn Day of Atonement on Tishri 10 (Oct 7). In a study of the timing of messianic movements ("chronomessianism") Wacholder also finds evidence in biblical, Qumran, New Testament, and rabbinic literature of a widespread belief that the coming of the Messiah would take place during the season when Israel celebrated the Sabbatical year. As to the relationship of the fifteenth year of Tiberius to a Sabbatical year, there are varying opinions: Blosser places the beginning of the ministry of Jesus in A.D. 26/27 in coincidence with a Sabbatical year dated in A.D. 26/27 (our Table 57, Zuckermann/Blosser). Wacholder dates the fifteenth year of Tiberius from Tishri 1, A.D. 27, to Elul 29, A.D. 28, in coincidence with a Sabbatical year in A.D. 27/28 (our Table 57, Wacholder). No doubt even more important than the Sabbatical year as a high point for messianic hope was the Jubilee, itself "a heightened and intensified sabbath year."[176] As to Jubilee cycles we have also noted varying opinions: Wacholder places a Jubilee year in A.D. 34/35 (our Table 59); Strobel a Jubilee year in A.D. 27/28 (our §236); and Blosser doubts the adequacy of the evidence for either of the foregoing Jubilee dates and thinks it impossible to prove any specific year during the Second Temple and New Testament period a Jubilee year. Now, however, we have found Eusebius[177] equating the fifteenth year of Tiberius with A.D. 28/29 and noting that A.D. 29 was the eighty-first Jubilee according to the Hebrews. If, then, we may accept Eusebius's information as the best available tradition, there is every reason to believe that Jesus was baptized and began his public ministry in the fall of A.D. 29.

585. In contrast with all of the foregoing, the modern scholars Nikos Kokkinos and Jerry Vardaman present different theories (but on totally separate grounds) about the fifteenth year of Tiberius (Luke 3:1) in connection with John the Baptist and Jesus. Nikos Kokkinos points out that, strictly speaking, Luke 3:1 only dates the beginning of the work of John the Baptist in the fifteenth year of Tiberius and does not require the usual supposition that Jesus' public work began shortly thereafter; rather such references as Matt 4:12, 17; Mark 1:14 make it likely that the bulk of Jesus' mission came during the closing part of John's preaching and much of it even after John's arrest and death. As mentioned in Luke 3:19–20 and told in detail by Josephus (*Ant.* 18.109–126), John was

---

[175]Blosser, "Jesus and the Jubilee," 256.

[176]Wacholder, "Chronomessianism"; Blosser, "Jesus and the Jubilee," 257; Sloan, *Favorable Year*, 7.

[177]Helm 172–173, our §582 and Table 168.

arrested and executed after reproving Herod Antipas for divorcing his wife, the daughter of the Nabatean king Aretas, and marrying Herodias, wife of Herod Philip and mother of Salome. In response to the treatment of his daughter, Aretas inflicted a severe military defeat upon Herod Antipas; the latter appealed to Rome for help, and Tiberius sent Vitellius to declare war on Aretas, but Tiberius died (Mar 16, A.D. 37) and Vitellius abandoned the mission. Accordingly, Kokkinos dates the war of Aretas in A.D. 36, the death of John in A.D. 35, and, for this and other reasons, the ministry of Jesus in A.D. 33–36 (through three Passovers and with crucifixion in March A.D. 36).[178]

586. To introduce the approach of Jerry Vardaman to the question of "the fifteenth year of Tiberius" it is necessary to recall the passage about Jesus in Josephus's *Ant.* 18.63–64, which is known as the *Testimonium flavianum* (testimony of Flavius Josephus) and whose authenticity has been much discussed. In the following quotation of the passage, if the italicized words are recognized as probable Christian interpolations, early enough to be found in the accepted Greek text, the whole passage otherwise may probably be accepted as from Josephus.[179]

> About this time there lived Jesus, a wise man, *if indeed one ought to call him a man.* For he was one who wrought surprising feats and was a teacher of such people as accept the truth gladly. He won over many Jews and many of the Greeks. *He was the Messiah.* When Pilate, upon hearing him accused by men of the highest standing among us, had condemned him to be crucified, those who had in the first place come to love him did not give up their affection for him. *On the third day he appeared to them restored to life, for the prophets of God* had *prophesied these and countless other marvelous things about him.* And the tribe of the Christians, so called after him, has still to this day not disappeared.

Vardaman accepts the core of the passage as fully authentic, and he goes on to analyze datable passages in Josephus both before (*Ant.* 18.46ff., 52, 54) and after (*Ant.* 18.65ff., 81–83) as placing Jesus' ministry within a historical context around A.D. 15–19. Along with this conclusion, Vardaman proposes an emendation in the Greek text of the date in Luke 3:1, which reads ἐν ἔτει δὲ πεντεκαιδεκάτῳ, "in the fifteenth year," with no variation from this date in all the New Testament manuscripts which contain the passage. In Greek, a number can be spelled out as here, or it can be written in Greek characters used as numerals (Table 2). Thus, the date in question could be written as iota for ten and epsilon for five, i.e., IE. At this point Vardaman suggests that the numeral was written originally as B (Beta), thus reading "in the second [rather than the fifteenth] year of Tiberius," and a later scribe misread the beta as iota epsilon, giving rise to the reading of the "fifteenth" which went on into all presently known Greek

---

[178]Kokkinos, "Crucifixion in A.D. 36," *CKC* 133–163, esp. 134, 146–147, 153. For criticism of Kokkinos see Meier, *Marginal Jew,* 420 n. 57; 431, n. 111.

[179]On the *Testimonium flavianum* see Louis H. Feldman, "Jesus Mentioned in Non-Biblical Text," *BAR* 9 (5, Sept/Oct 1983): 31–32; idem, "The *Testimonium flavianum:* The State of the Question," in *Christological Perspectives* (ed. Robert F. Berkey and Sarah A. Edwards; New York: Pilgrim Press, 1982), 179–199; John P. Meier, "The Testimonium: Evidence for Jesus Outside the Bible," *BR* 7 (3, June 1991): 20ff.

manuscripts. Therewith Vardaman accepts Luke 3:1 as referring to Tiberius's second year (= A.D. 15) and makes this the date of the beginning of the work of John and of the ministry of Jesus.[180]

(b) "About Thirty Years of Age"

587. Immediately after the record of the baptism of Jesus in Luke 3:21–22, there is a statement in Luke 3:23 that "Jesus . . . was about thirty years of age." It was noted above (§557) that in the full Greek text of this statement there are variations in a number of manuscripts (apparently attesting to some uncertainty in the understanding of the statement), but the best attested text (of Codex Sinaiticus, Codex Vaticanus, and many other manuscripts) reads ἦν Ἰησοῦς ἀρχόμενος ὡσεὶ ἐτῶν τριάκοντα. Translation of the Greek text in this form depends upon how the grammatical connection of the Greek participle ἀρχόμενος is understood. The KJV translation is: "Jesus began to be about thirty years of age." This understanding is supported by Irenaeus (*Against Heresies* 2.22.5), who explains: "For when he came to be baptized, he had not yet completed his thirtieth year, but was beginning to be about thirty years of age." Epiphanius (our §557) quotes the statement in its form in the Ferrar minuscules, ἀρχόμενος εἶναι, "beginning to be," and calculates that since Jesus was born on Jan 6, 2 B.C., he was twenty-nine years and ten months old when he was baptized on Nov 8, A.D. 28 (Table 149). On the other hand, it is possible to understand ἀρχόμενος as referring to the "beginning" of Jesus' work and to translate the statement as in the RSV: "Jesus, when he began his ministry, was about thirty years of age."[181] At any event the immediate sequence of Luke 3:21–22 and 3:23 makes it likely that the public ministry began shortly after the baptism (§583), and therefore there is no great difference in the chronological implications of the two translations. What may be noticed is that the Greek text certainly includes the word ὡσεί, "about," and this surely allows some leeway in the chronology. Justin Martyr (*Dialogue with Trypho* 88) thinks so when he says that Jesus had "waited for thirty years, more or less, until John appeared." How much leeway is required depends, of course, upon the two variables of the dates assigned to the birth and the baptism. If Herod died in 4 B.C. (§501, Schürer) or 5 B.C. (§505, Barnes) and the birth of Jesus two years or less before was in 6 or 5 B.C. (§510), and if we take a time of birth in, say, mid-January (§473, Beckwith), and then go to A.D. 29 for the baptism (§584), then our Table 170 can show the maximum span of time that can be considered. Accordingly we see that in these terms Jesus would have been about thirty-five years of age at his baptism, obviously rather much to agree with "about thirty." One suggestion is that in Num 4:3, 47, the necessary age for priestly service is from thirty years old up to fifty years, and perhaps "about thirty" is reminiscent of the beginning point of such a period of service.[182] By way of comparison with the above, Harold

[180] *CKC* 55–60 and 78 n. 1. For further discussion and citation of additional references see Finegan, *Archeology NT* 1:xxiv–xxv. On *Ant.* 18.63–64 see Meier, *Marginal Jew* 1:59–62, and 411 n. 5 for criticism of the emendation of Luke 3:1 and the related conclusions.

[181] BAG 113, 2, b.

[182] Jones, "Luke's Unique Interest," SBLSP 1989, 381.

W. Hoehner reckons from birth of Jesus in December 5 B.C., or January 4 B.C. and makes Jesus thirty-two years of age at his baptism in the summer or fall of A.D. 29, with his thirty-third birthday approaching in the last month of A.D. 29 or the first month of A.D. 30.[183] John P. Meier thinks Jesus was around thirty-three or thirty-four years old when he began his public ministry and about thirty-six years old when he died.[184]

TABLE 170. *Birthdays of Jesus from an Assumed Birth in Mid-January of the Year 7 B.C.*

Year	*Birthday*
7 B.C.	Birth
6	1
5	2
4	3
3	4
2	5
1 B.C.	6
A.D. 1	7
2	8
3	9
4	10
5	11
6	12
7	13
8	14
9	15
10	16
11	17
12	18
13	19
14	20
15	21
16	22
17	23
18	24
19	25
20	26
21	27
22	28
23	29
24	30

TABLE 171. *Birthdays of Jesus from an Assumed Birth in Mid-January of the Year 2 B.C.*

Year	*Birthday*
2 B.C.	Birth
1 B.C.	1
A.D. 1	2
A.D. 2	3
3	4
4	5
5	6
6	7
7	8
8	9
9	10
10	11
11	12
12	13
13	14
14	15
15	16
16	17
17	18
18	19
19	20
20	21
21	22
22	23
23	24
24	25
25	26
26	27
27	28
28	29
29	30

588. If, however, Jesus was born in, say mid-January (Beckwith, our §473) and in the year 2 B.C. (§518), and was baptized and began his public work in the fall of A.D. 29 (§582), he was very accurately said to be "about thirty years of age" (Table 171).[185]

---

[183]Hoehner, *Chronological Aspects,* 38.
[184]Meier, *Marginal Jew* 1:407.

(c) "Not Yet Fifty Years Old"

589. In John 8:57 the Jews say to Jesus, in the course of his ministry, "You are not yet fifty years old." Irenaeus insists that this must mean sometime in the decade leading up to the age of fifty:

> Now, such language is fittingly applied to one who has already passed the age of forty, without having as yet reached his fiftieth year, yet is not far from this latter period. But to one who is only thirty years old it would unquestionably be said, "Thou art not yet forty years old." (2.22.6)

Since Irenaeus put the baptism of Jesus just before he was thirty years of age (§587), and interpreted John 8:57 to mean that Jesus was at that time in his forties, he must have considered that the public ministry lasted for more than ten years. If the ministry lasted at the most only a few years, as is more commonly assumed, then the birth must be pushed much earlier than is commonly done, if John 8:57 is to be interpreted as literally as Irenaeus requires. Some confirmation (if any were needed) that Jesus was at all events not more than fifty may be found in Matt 17:24–27, the story of the collection of the half-shekel tax from Jesus and Peter, for Josephus (*Ant.* 3.196) states that the half-shekel was contributed by men aged from twenty years up to fifty. The best understanding of the saying in question, however, lies in the observation that the Gospel according to John is here reporting an adversarial conversation between Jesus and "the Jews," in which Jesus affirms that Abraham somehow saw his day because he was "before Abraham," and the Jews scoff at any such claim which sweeps across the centuries because Jesus is obviously not even half a century old.[186]

(d) "Forty-six Years to Build This Temple"

590. In John 2:20 the Jews say to Jesus when he is in Jerusalem at the first Passover which the Fourth Gospel mentions: τεσσεράκοντα καὶ ἓξ ἔτεσιν οἰκοδομήθη ὁ ναὸς οὗτος. With regard to the first aorist indicative passive verb, οἰκοδομήθη, this is translated, "It has taken forty-six years to build this temple," in the RSV; and, "This sanctuary took forty-six years to build," by Moffatt. If the statement refers to the original construction of the temple by Solomon, or the rebuilding of it by Zerubbabel, the text has no bearing on the chronology of Jesus' life. But the word οὗτος, "this," appears to point to the actual structure standing there at the time, which was the temple as it was reconstructed by Herod the Great and was the temple of the time of Jesus (being a reconstruction of the temple of Zerubbabel, it is still known in Jewish terminology as the Second Temple).

---

[185]Keresztes, *Imperial Rome and the Christians,* 38: "If indeed, as it seems, Herod the Great died in 1 B.C., and Christ was born in 2 B.C., there is no discrepancy whatever in the Scriptural reference that Christ was 'about thirty' years of age when he began his public ministry, shortly after John the Baptist."

[186]Hoehner, *Chronological Aspects,* 23; Meier, *Marginal Jew* 1:378–379.

591. Four statements by Josephus provide information about Herod's work in reconstructing the temple as it stood in Jesus' time. In *Ant.* 15:354 Josephus says:

> Ἤδη δ'αὐτοῦ τῆς βασιλείας ἑπτακαιδεκάτου παρελθόντος ἔτους Καῖσαρ εἰς Συρίαν ἀφίκετο.
>
> And when Herod had completed the seventeenth year of his reign, Caesar came to Syria.

If Herod had completed his seventeenth year (textual variant: προελθόντος, lit. "gone forward" through his seventeenth year), it was then his eighteenth year. Evidently describing the same trip of Caesar Augustus to which Josephus refers, Dio[187] says that Augustus spent the winter in Samos, then "in the spring of the year when Marcus Apuleius and Publius Silius were consuls" went on into Asia and, after settling everything there and in Bithynia, came to Syria. M. Apuleius and P. Silius P. f. Nerva were the consuls of the year A.U.C. 734 = 20 B.C. (Table 40).[188] If the eighteenth year of Herod (beginning presumably on Nisan 1, §503) corresponded with 20 B.C., Josephus was evidently numbering the regnal years of Herod from his taking of Jerusalem placed in 37 B.C. (Table 140, column 2).

592. In *Ant.* 15.380 Josephus says:

> Τότε δ' οὖν ὀκτωκαιδεκάτου τῆς Ἡρώδου βασιλείας γεγενότος ἐνιαυτοῦ μετὰ τὰς προειρημένας πράξεις ἔργον οὐ τὸ τυχόν ἐπεβάλετο, τὸν νεὼν τοῦ θεοῦ δι' αὐτου κατασκευάσασθαι, μείζω τε τὸν περίβολον καὶ πρὸς ὕψος ἀξιοπρεπέστερον ἐγείρειν.
>
> It was at this time, in the eighteenth year of his reign, after the events mentioned above, that Herod undertook an extraordinary work, (namely) the reconstruction of the temple of God at his own expense, enlarging its precincts and raising it to a more imposing height.

Here the same eighteenth year is named, and "this time" and "the events mentioned above" plainly refer to the visit of Augustus to Syria in A.D. 20 (§471), so it is in Herod's eighteenth Nisan to Nisan year, i.e., 20/19 B.C., that he begins to reconstruct the temple (νεών).[189]

593. In *War* 1.1401 Josephus states:

> Πεντεκαιδεκάτῳ γοῦν ἔτει τῆς βασιλείας αὐτόν τε τὸν ναὸν ἐπεσκεύασεν. . . .
>
> Thus, in the fifteenth year of his reign, he restored the temple itself. . . .

At first sight the difference between the fifteenth year in this passage and the eighteenth year in the preceding passage (§592) might be thought to be just a difference between 40 B.C. and 37 B.C. for the beginning of Herod's reign (Table 140), but as soon as it is remembered that the eighteenth year has to coincide

---

[187] *Roman History* 54.7.4–6.
[188] Liebenam, *Fasti consulares Imperii romani,* 41–43, 7.
[189] Vermes/Millar, *History* 1:308.

with 20 B.C. it is realized that this explanation will not work. It remains only to suppose that the fifteenth year is a mistake, unless it might possibly refer to a time of preparation before the actual construction.

594. In the foregoing (§593) we have encountered the word περίβολος, which means something thrown around, hence an enclosure, precinct, or court. The same word is used by Josephus in *Ant.* 15.417–420 as he describes the general layout of the temple. He tells of the first court into which all might come, the second into which foreigners were forbidden to come, and the third into which only the priests might enter and in which stood the altar of burnt offerings and the temple edifice proper. Then he explains that Herod could not go into the third court and the place of the altar and sanctuary, which meant that the temple edifice proper had to be built by the priests. Herod did, however, take care of the porticoes and the outer courts (τὰ περὶ τὰς στοὰς καὶ τοὺς ἔξω περιβόλους), and these he built in eight years. Then Josephus says: (*Ant.* 15.421):

> Τοῦ δὲ ναοῦ διὰ τῶν ἱερέων οἰκοδομηθέντος ἐνιαυτῷ καὶ μησὶν ἕξ.
>
> But the temple itself was built by the priests in a year and six months (variant: five months).

The word ὁ ναός (Ionic) or νεώς (Attic), "the temple," is used regularly in Greek for a temple in general, and also in particular for the inner part of a temple and, in paganism, for the shrine in which the image of the god was placed. In *Ant.* 15.380 (§592) and *War* 1.401 (§593) Josephus evidently used the word in its general sense in saying that Herod built the temple. In the present passage (*Ant.* 15.421), however, he obviously uses it in its more restricted sense for the inner part, the temple edifice proper. Later in *Ant.* 16.132 when he describes Herod as making a speech to the people in the temple (ἐν τῷ ἱερῷ), which would necessarily have been in the outer courts, he uses a different word, τὸ ἱερόν, which was commonly used for a whole temple precinct. Precisely the same distinction is made in the Gospels: τὸ ἱερόν, the entire area, Mark 11:11, etc.; ὁ ναός, the temple edifice proper, Mark 15:38, etc. If, then, the priests, acting under Herod's directive, began their work on the temple proper in 20/19 B.C. (§592) and built it in one year and six months, they must have finished the "temple itself" in 18/17 B.C.

595. Now we return to John 2:20 (§590). This is often translated in somewhat the fashion of the RSV, "It has taken forty-six years to build this temple," apparently implying that the work was still going on, a point that is made explicit in the Berkeley Version, "This temple has been in process of building for forty-six years." If the reference were to the ἱερόν, i.e., the entire temple precinct, this could be true enough for, in fact, such work was still going on until the time of the procurator Albinus (A.D. 62–64), only a few years before the final destruction. The reference in John 2:20 is, however, specifically to the ναός, i.e., the temple edifice proper, and in John there is no mistaking the clear distinction between the two terms. Ἱερόν is used in the following passages: John 2:14—"In the temple he found those who were selling oxen and sheep . . ."; 5:14—Jesus found the healed man "in the temple"; 7:28—"as he taught in the temple"; 8:20—"he spoke in the treasury, as he taught in the temple"; 18:20—"I have spoken openly to the world; I have always taught in synagogues and in the temple." Every passage suggests the more open and public outer courts; in every passage John uses ἱερόν, the word meaning the entire temple area. Only in John 2:19–20 is the word ναός employed. Therefore, this reference is to the temple proper, completed by the priests in 18/17 B.C. (§590). Furthermore, the crucial verb in John 2:20 is οἰκοδομήθη (§590), which is an aorist indicative passive, meaning literally "was built," and is surely best understood as referring not to a building enterprise that was still going on, as it had been for forty-six years, but to a building enterprise that had been completed long before so that it could be said that the building had stood for forty-six years. Therefore, the Jews, in effect, ask Jesus, "How can you possibly raise up in three days a temple that has stood for forty-six years?" *After* 18/17 B.C., forty-six years brings us to A.D. 29/30. The conversation in question between Jesus and the Jews took place at the Passover described in John 2:13–21, and this Passover is therefore to be dated in the spring of the year A.D. 30.[190]

(2) The Duration of the Ministry

596. In the course of the Jewish religious year several annual feasts and one fast were held, as shown in Table 172. The Day of Atonement (cf. §12) is a fast, the other observances are feasts. As 1 Kgs 8:2 and other references show, the Feast of Tabernacles was probably often referred to simply as "the Feast." In the Gospels as they stand there are references to some of these festivals, from which it may be possible to gather some information about the probable length of Jesus' ministry.

TABLE 172. *Annual Observances in the Jewish Religious Year*

Name	*Date*	*Scripture Reference*
Passover	14th day of the 1st month = Nisan (Mar/Apr)	Exod 12:6
Feast of Weeks, or Pentecost	50 days after the ceremony of the barley sheaf at Passover time	Lev 23:16 Deut 16:10
Day of Atonement	10th day of the 7th month = Tishri (Sept/Oct)	Lev 23:27
Tabernacles	15th day of the 7th month = Tishri (Sept/Oct), for 7 days	Lev 23:24; 1 Kgs 8:2
Dedication	25th day of the 9th month = Chislev (Nov/Dec)	1 Macc 4:59
Purim	14th and 15th days of the 12th month = Adar (Feb/Mar)	Est 9:17–18

[190]In contrast with our dating William Hendriksen (*John* [NTC 1; Grand Rapids: Baker, 1953], 126) counts from 20/19 B.C. when Herod launched the temple project (§592) rather than a year and six months later (18/17 B.C.) when the priests completed the temple building proper (§594) and thus the forty-six years come to A.D. 26/27, a year which Strobel and Blosser make a Sabbatical year. For this entire analysis see Hoehner, *Chronological Aspects,* 38–43.

(a) The Synoptic Gospels

597. In their account of the ministry of Jesus, the Synoptic Gospels mention only one Passover, namely, the final one at which time Jesus was put to death (Mark 14:12; Matt 26:17; Luke 22:7). Since this was an annual feast and only one occurrence of it is mentioned, as far as the evidence goes, the ministry could have comprised as little as one year or even less. In the second book of *Against Heresies,* Irenaeus writes against the school of Valentinus[191] in general, and against Ptolemy in particular, the latter being a chief follower of Valentinus who was still alive at the time of Irenaeus. Irenaeus (*Against Heresies* 2.22.5) states that the Valentinians taught that Jesus conducted his ministry of preaching for only a single year, reckoning from his baptism.

> They, however, that they may establish their false opinion regarding that which is written, "to proclaim the acceptable year of the Lord," maintain that he preached for one year only, and then suffered in the twelfth month.

Against this position Irenaeus himself argues in the same section that at his baptism Jesus "was beginning to be about thirty years of age" (Luke 3:23), that if he had only completed this thirtieth year when he died he was still a young man, and that he had therefore never reached the more advanced age of a Master qualified to teach others. Irenaeus explains, not with complete clarity:

> The first stage of early life embraces thirty years, and that this extends onwards to the fortieth year, every one will admit; but from the fortieth and fiftieth year a man begins to decline towards old age, which our Lord possessed while he still fulfilled the office of Teacher, even as the Gospel and all the elders testify; those who were conversant in Asia with John, the disciple of the Lord, [affirming] that John conveyed to them that information.

On the basis of John 8:57, however, Irenaeus is sure that Jesus had not reached his fiftieth year (§589). He was, then, between forty and fifty, Irenaeus holds, and thus (counting from baptism at about thirty) must have had a ministry of between ten and twenty years. Thus Irenaeus argues against the Valentinian view of a one-year ministry.

598. The final Passover in the Synoptic record came, of course, in the springtime. But another Synoptic passage (Mark 2:23; Matt 12:1; Luke 6:1) appears plainly to refer to a springtime prior to that final one, for it tells how the disciples plucked ears of grain, and thus it implies the spring harvest time, perhaps Apr/May (§58). Since the baptism (Mark 1:9) was obviously prior to that, perhaps in the preceding fall, the total ministry was at least somewhat over one year in length. As we have already seen (§552), Clement of Alexandria states that the followers of Basilides put the baptism in the fifteenth year of Tiberius, on the eleventh or fifteenth of Tybi (= Jan 6 or 10), and the passion in the sixteenth year of Tiberius, on the twenty-fifth of Phamenoth (= Mar 21) or on the nineteenth or twenty-fifth of Pharmuthi (= Apr 14 or 20). In Egypt, the first regnal year of Tiberius

---

[191]This famous Gnostic was educated at Alexandria and taught at Rome about A.D. 136–155.

presumably began on Thoth 1 = Aug 29, A.D. 14, and the fifteenth regnal year was accordingly from Aug 29, A.D. 28, to Aug 28, A.D. 29 (Table 134). Jan 6 or 10 in the year 29 is therefore the indicated date of the baptism. Likewise, the sixteenth year of Tiberius extended from Aug 29, A.D. 29, to Aug 28, A.D. 30. So May 21 or Apr 14 or 20 in the year 30 is the indicated date of the passion. From baptism to passion is one year plus a few months, a period of time with which the Synoptic record by itself could be considered at least roughly consonant.

599. The Synoptic record does not necessarily, however, require as brief a ministry as that just indicated. A springtime is indicated (Mark 2:23, etc.) without mention of a corresponding Passover. Other Passovers could have gone unmentioned. Or the Synoptic record could cover only a part—perhaps the part deemed most important—of a longer ministry. Along this line Ethelbert Stauffer remarks that it is not possible to fit the chronological structure of the Gospel according to John within the narrow span of the Synoptic account, but it is possible to fit the Synoptic framework into John's structure, and he judges this to be important evidence for the correctness of the Johannine chronology.[192]

(b) The Fourth Gospel

600. The Fourth Gospel refers to more Jewish feasts than the Synoptic Gospels and thereby suggests a longer ministry. As far as Passover is concerned, three observances of this festival are specifically mentioned: (1) John 2:13—"The Passover of the Jews was at hand" (also verse 23); at this time Jesus cleanses the temple; (2) John 6:4—"Now the Passover, the feast of the Jews, was at hand"; at this time the feeding of the five thousand took place; (3) John 11:55—"Now the Passover of the Jews was at hand"; this was the final Passover at which time Jesus was put to death (it is mentioned by name also in 12:1; 18:28, 39; 19:14). In the Synoptic Gospels the cleansing of the temple occurs on the final visit of Jesus to Jerusalem and near the time of the final Passover (Mark 11:15ff., etc.). It is possible that John transposed this event to a place near the beginning of the ministry for some symbolic reason. In that event there would be but two Passovers in John's record: (1) that of John 6:4; and (2) that described in two different places, John 2:13 and 11:55ff. In this way John might be thought to fit the pattern of the ministry of one year and some months, even as perhaps the Synoptics indicate (§598).

601. But taking the Fourth Gospel as it stands, there are not only three Passovers mentioned but also certain other notes of time. These are: (1) John 2:13, 23—the first Passover; (2) 4:35—"yet four months, then comes the harvest"; with harvest probably in Apr/May (§58), this saying should belong in Jan/Feb and a second and unmentioned Passover should fall in Mar/Apr; (3) 5:1—according to Codex Vaticanus and other manuscripts "a feast of the Jews" was at hand, according to Codex Sinaiticus and other manuscripts it was "*the* feast of the Jews"; if it was "a feast" it was hardly Passover which is otherwise mentioned by name, but it could have been the Feast of Weeks; if it

---

[192]Ethelbert Stauffer, *Jesus and His Story* (New York: Alfred A. Knopf, 1960), 7.

was "*the* feast" it was probably Tabernacles, often (§596) referred to simply in this way (cf. John 7:2, 10, 14, 37); (4) 6:4—a third Passover is at hand; (5) 7:2—the Feast of Tabernacles is at hand; (6) 10:22f.—it was the Feast of Dedication, and winter; (7) 11:55ff.—the final Passover. This provides the outline shown in Table 173.[193] Since the baptism and beginning of the public ministry preceded the first Passover in the outline, with the baptism perhaps coming in the preceding fall, it seems that a total ministry of three years plus a number of months is indicated.

TABLE 173. *Notes of Time in the Fourth Gospel*

Year and Month	*Feast*	*Reference*
1st Year		
Nisan (Mar/Apr)	1st Passover	2:13, 23
Shebat (Jan/Feb)	"four months to harvest"	4:35
2d Year		
Nisan (Mar/Apr)	2d Passover	Unmentioned
Tishri (Sept/Oct)	"the feast," i.e., Tabernacles	5:1, Codex Sinaiticus
3d Year		
Nisan (Mar/Apr)	3d Passover	6:4
Tishri (Sept/Oct)	Tabernacles	7:2
Chislev (Nov/Dec)	Dedication	10:22
Nisan (Mar/Apr)	4th and final Passover	11:55ff.

602. As we have seen (Table 149), Epiphanius likewise considered that the ministry of Jesus covered three years plus several months. In the *Chronicle* of Eusebius as translated by Jerome, the preaching of John the Baptist is placed in the fifteenth year of Tiberius (= A.D. 28) and the death of Jesus in the eighteenth year (= A.D. 31), and thus the ministry appears to cover two years and a portion of a third (Table 94). But in the Armenian version,[194] the death of Jesus is placed in the nineteenth year of Tiberius, which may allow an additional year. Actually, a ministry of three years and a portion of a fourth appears to be the real view of Eusebius. In the *Church History* (1.10) he says (presumably thinking of Luke 3:2; John 11:49, 51; 18:13) that Jesus passed his entire ministry under the high priests Annas and Caiaphas. It is ordinarily assumed that Annas (who was actually high priest in A.D. 6–15) is mentioned in Luke 3:2 and John 18:13 along with his son-in-law Caiaphas (who held the office in A.D. 18–36) because he was still influential in the time of the latter. As known from Josephus and with approximate dates the high priests between Annas and Caiaphas were: Ishmael (A.D. 15–16), Eleazar (16–17), and Simon (17–18). Although he also cites Josephus, Eusebius evidently assumes that these men constituted a series of high priests who held office during the ministry of Jesus, each for a one-year term. Eusebius writes:

---

[193]HDB 1: 407 n. a.
[194]Karst 213.

> Accordingly the whole time of our Savior's ministry is shown to have been not quite four full years, four high priests, from Annas to the accession of Caiaphas, having held office a year each.

603. As far as the evidence in the Gospels goes, therefore, we appear to have two chief possibilities as to the duration of the public ministry of Jesus. On the basis of the Synoptic Gospels taken by themselves (§598) the ministry could have been one year and some months in length. With a critical rearrangement, the Fourth Gospel might possibly be brought into harmony with such a length of ministry (§600), and there is some support for such a figure in the tradition of the followers of Basilides reported by Clement of Alexandria (§598). Taken as it stands, however, the Fourth Gospel appears to require a ministry of three years plus a number of months (§601), and there is some support for a duration of some such magnitude in Epiphanius and Eusebius (§602). It is the conclusion of the present book that the chronology of the Fourth Gospel is convincingly detailed.

3. The Dcath of Jesus

LITERATURE: Hans **Lietzmann**, "Der Prozess Jesu," *Sitzungsberichte der Königlich preussischen Akademie der Wissenschaften: Philosophisch-historische Klasse* 23–24 (Berlin, 1931), 313–322; J. K. **Fotheringham**, "The Evidence of Astronomy and Technical Chronology for the Date of the Crucifixion," in *JTS* 35 (1934): 146–162; A. T. **Olmstead**, "The Chronology of Jesus' Life," *ATR* 24 (1942): 1–26; idem, *Jesus in the Light of History* (New York: C. Scribner's Sons, 1942); Carl H. **Kraeling**, "Olmstead's Chronology of the Life of Jesus," *ATR* 24 (1942): 334–354; T. J. **Meek**, Review of Olmstead, *Jesus in the Light of History, JNES* 2 (1943): 124–125; A. **Jaubert**, "La date de la dernière cène," in *RHR* 146 (1954): 140–173; Julian **Morgenstern**, "The Calendar of the Book of Jubilees, Its Origin and Its Character," *VT* 5 (1955): 34–76; A. **Jaubert**, *La date de la cène* (Paris: Gabalda, 1957); Josef **Blinzler**, "Qumran-Kalender und Passionschronologie," *ZNW* 49 (1958): 238–251; idem, *The Trial of Jesus: The Jewish and Roman Proceedings against Jesus Christ Described and Assessed from the Oldest Accounts* (translated from the second revised and enlarged edition by Isabel and Florence McHugh; Westminster, Md.: Newman Press, 1959); idem, *Der Prozess Jesu* (4th ed.; Regensburg: Friedrich Pustet, 1969); E. **Vogt**, "Kalenderfragmente aus Qumran," *Biblica* 39 (1958): 72–77; James A. **Walther**, "The Chronology of Passion Week," *JBL* 77 (1958): 116–122; Patrick W. **Skehan**, "The Date of the Last Supper," *CBQ* 20 (1958): 192–199; George **Ogg**, Review of Jaubert, *La date de la cène, NovT* 3 (1959): 149–160; Norman **Walker**, "Concerning the Jaubertian Chronology of the Passion," in *NovT* 3 (1959): 317–320; A. **Jaubert**, "Jesus et le calendrier de Qumran," *NTS* 7 (1960): 1–30; August **Strobel**, "Der Termin des Todes Jesu," *ZNW* 51 (1960): 69–101; Karl G. **Kuhn**, "Zum essenischen Kalender," *ZNW* 52 (1961): 65–73; Massey H. **Shepherd** Jr., "Are Both the Synoptics and John Correct about the Date of Jesus' Death?" *JBL* 80 (1961): 123–132; Julian **Morgenstern**, "The Time of the Passover in the Synoptics and in John," and "Palm Sunday and Easter Sunday," in "Three Studies in the New Testament" (unpublished); Eugen **Ruckstuhl**, *Chronology of the Last Days of Jesus: A Critical Study* (trans. Victor J. Drapela; New York: Desclée, 1965); Paul **Keresztes**, *Imperial Rome and the Christians*, vol. 1, *From Herod the Great to about 200 A.D.* (Lanham, Md.: University Press of America, 1989), 38–43; Barry D. **Smith**, "The Chronology of the Last Supper," in *WTJ* 53 (Spring 1991): 29–45; John **Hamilton**, "The Chronology of the Crucifixion and the Passover," in *CH* 106 (1992): 323–338.

(1) The Day of the Week

604. All four Gospels indicate that the day of the crucifixion of Jesus was a Friday (in our terminology), because they describe the following day as the Sabbath (Mark 15:42; Matt 28:1; Luke 23:56; John 19:31), our Saturday, and because they state that the visit of the women to the tomb on the next day was on the first day of the week (Mark 16:2; Matt 28:1; Luke 24:1; John 20:1), our Sunday.

(2) The Date in the Jewish Month

605. On an evening which appears (but cf. §609) to be the evening immediately before the day of crucifixion Jesus ate a supper with his disciples (I Cor 11:23; Mark 14:17; Matt 26:20; Luke 22:14; John 13:2). In order to discuss this meal, it is necessary to recall the sequence of events in the observance of the Jewish feast of Passover. On the tenth day of the first month (Nisan = Mar/Apr), a lamb was selected for a household, then on the fourteenth (or full moon, cf. §596) day of the month the lamb was killed "in the evening" (Exod 12:1–8). As explained above (§20), the Hebrew is literally "between the two evenings," and Josephus (*War* 6.423) says that the sacrifices were made from the ninth to the eleventh hour, i.e., from three to five o'clock in the afternoon. Then "that night" (Exod 12:8; Lev 23:5) the Passover meal was eaten. If the day was reckoned according to the earlier practice (§12) from sunrise to sunrise, then both the slaying of the lamb and the eating of the meal took place on one and the same day, namely, on the fourteenth day of Nisan. But if the day was reckoned according to the later practice (§12) from sunset to sunset, then the lamb was indeed slain on the fourteenth day of Nisan but the Passover meal held "that night" was actually eaten on the fifteenth day of Nisan which had begun at sunset. *Jub.* 49:1 explicitly describes the observance in terms of the latter manner of reckoning:

> Remember the commandment which the Lord commanded thee concerning the Passover, that thou shouldst celebrate it in its season on the fourteenth of the first month, that thou shouldst kill it before its evening, and that they should eat it by night on the evening of the fifteenth from the time of the setting of the sun.

With the roast lamb, unleavened bread was eaten in the Passover meal (Exod 12:8), and unleavened bread continued to be eaten for seven days all together (Exod 12:15; cf. Num 28:17; Deut 16:3–4). If the day was reckoned from sunrise to sunrise, the unleavened bread, like the roast lamb, was eaten already on the fourteenth day. If the day was reckoned from sunset to sunset then the unleavened bread, like the roast lamb, was eaten only after the fifteenth day had begun. Lev 23:6 presumably presupposes the latter manner of reckoning when it gives the fifteenth day of the first month as the date of the Feast of Unleavened Bread. By the same reckoning, the seven days of the feast would presumably be, counted inclusively, Nisan 15–21.

(a) The Synoptic Representation

606. According to Mark 14:12, it was "on the first day of Unleavened Bread, when they sacrificed the Passover lamb," that the disciples went and prepared for Jesus "to eat the Passover." The parallel passages in Matt 26:17 and Luke 22:7–8 also refer to the Feast of Unleavened Bread and the preparation of the Passover. In these passages, therefore, the supper is presented as the Passover meal, which followed the slaying of the lamb on the fourteenth day of Nisan. Likewise if the death of Jesus followed on the next day after that, it appears to fall on the fifteenth of Nisan.

(b) The Johannine Representation

607. In the Fourth Gospel, however, it is explicitly stated that the day of Jesus' trial and execution was "the day of Preparation for the Passover" (John 19:14). The day of Preparation (παρασκευή) means the day of getting ready for a festival. Josephus (*Ant.* 16.163) uses the word in connection with the Sabbath, citing a decree of Caesar Augustus which allowed that the Jews "be not obliged to go before any judge on the Sabbath day, nor on the day of Preparation before it, after the ninth hour." Therefore, the day of Preparation for the Passover must have been the day of getting ready for it, namely, the day on which the Passover lamb was slain, Nisan 14. This was the day on which Jesus also was put to death. Only on the evening of this day would the Passover meal be eaten, and the Jews who took Jesus to the Praetorium did not go in, "so that they might not be defiled, but might eat the Passover" (John 18:28). This day of Preparation for the Passover was also a day of Preparation for the Sabbath which, in this case, coincided with Passover day and thus was a "high day" (John 19:31). According to this representation of the Fourth Gospel, then, the death of Jesus took place on Nisan 14.

608. Support for the Johannine date is found in additional sources. The statement of Paul that "Christ, our paschal lamb, has been sacrificed" (1 Cor 5:7) fits very well with the remembrance that Jesus was put to death at the same time that the Passover lambs were slain. The apocryphal *Gospel according to Peter* (verse 3) states that Jesus was delivered to the people "on the day before the unleavened bread, their feast." The tractate *Sanhedrin* in the Babylonian Talmud records, doubtless with reference to the Founder of Christianity: "On the eve of Passover Yeshu was hanged."[195]

609. The conflict or apparent conflict between the two representations just described (§§606, 607) has given rise to many different theories intended to solve the problem. One suggestion is based upon the calendar with which we have become acquainted at Qumran (§§82ff.). If Jesus and his disciples had had reason to follow this calendar, they would no doubt have eaten their Passover already on the preceding Tuesday evening, for by that calendar that was the appointed time for it (§93) and Wednesday was the first day of Passover in this

[195] *Sanhedrin* 43a; Goldschmidt, *BT* 7:181; Epstein, *BT* 281.

year as in every year. While the Gospel records are usually held (§605) to place the Last Supper on Thursday evening and the crucifixion immediately thereafter on Friday, it may be that all the events of the taking into custody of Jesus and the holding of his trials before Jewish and Roman authorities would fit better within the longer period from Tuesday evening until Friday. Interestingly enough, in the early Christian work known as the *Didascalia*[196] the apostles are quoted as saying that it was on Tuesday evening that they ate the Passover with Jesus, and on Wednesday that he was taken captive and held in custody in the house of Caiaphas.[197] This is, however, a relatively late source, and the canonical Gospels themselves seem most naturally to presuppose a sequence of days as commonly understood, namely: Sunday, the entry into Jerusalem; Wednesday, the plan to kill Jesus; Thursday, the last supper; Friday, the trial and crucifixion.[198]

610. Another suggestion appeals to the possibility of a difference in dating as between Palestine and the Diaspora. In Palestine the beginning of the month was determined by observation of the new moon (§73), but perhaps in the Dispersion a fixed calendar was in use. If that were the case, it could have happened in the year Jesus died that the Jews in Palestine observed Passover on Saturday, while those in the Dispersion observed it on Friday. John could then be considered to have followed the testimony of Christians who were in touch with priestly circles in Judea in his report that the Friday when Jesus died was the Preparation for Passover. Mark, on the other hand, as a Christian of the Roman church, could have followed the tradition of his own church that Jesus died on a Friday in a year when that Friday was observed in the Dispersion as the Passover.[199]

611. Another theory appeals to the difference between alternate ways of reckoning the day and, accordingly, the date. We have seen (§§12–13) that the earlier Israelite reckoning is usually employed in the Synoptic Gospels, perhaps because it was the followed by Jesus and his disciples; and that the late Jewish reckoning counted the day as beginning at sunset, and is found in the Fourth Gospel. The latter was undoubtedly the official manner of reckoning in the time of Jesus, and even in the Synoptic Gospels (Mark 1:32 = Luke 4:40) the Sabbath begins and ends at sunset. It can be supposed that Jesus and his disciples, who came from Galilee, followed the old custom and counted the day as beginning

---

[196]The *Didascalia* is preserved in Syriac but was probably written originally in Greek, perhaps in the second or third century A.D.; it is now incorporated as the first six books in the *Apostolic Constitutions,* a work of the fourth or fifth century (*APOT* 1:613). It is edited by F. X. Funk, *Didascalia et Constitutiones apostolorum* (2 vols.; Paderborn: Ferdinand Schoeningh, 1905).

[197]*Didascalia* 21 = 5.4–6; ed. Funk, vol. 1, 272.

[198]For the theory presented in this paragraph see in the LITERATURE preceding §604 the writings of Jaubert and the supporting articles by Walker and Skehan and the book by Ruckstahl; against the theory see the listed articles of Blinzler, Ogg, Strobel, and Kuhn, and also A. J. B. Higgins, *The Historicity of the Fourth Gospel* (London: Lutterworth, 1960), 61.

[199]See Shepherd, "Are Both the Synoptics and John Correct?"

at sunrise. Then the day when the Passover lamb was slain and the day when the unleavened bread was eaten were indeed the same day (§605), as Mark 14:12 states. So, by this way of reckoning, this day which began at sunrise on Thursday and continued until sunrise on Friday was the fourteenth day of Nisan, the day on which in the afternoon the Passover lamb should be sacrifice and on which in the evening the Passover meal, with its roast lamb and unleavened bread, should be eaten. By the same reckoning the next day began at sunrise on Friday morning and was already the fifteenth day of Nisan. This was the day on which Jesus was crucified. But, it can be supposed, by official Jewish reckoning, the fourteenth day of Nisan did not begin at sunrise on Thursday morning but only at sunset on Thursday evening. Then, according to official usage, it would only be on the next afternoon, namely the afternoon of the official fourteenth day of Nisan, that the Passover lamb would be slain. This was the very time that Jesus died, exactly as represented in the Fourth Gospel. The Fourth Gospel is, therefore, stating the event in terms of the official Jewish calendar, and in terms of that calendar the date of the death of Jesus was Friday, Nisan 14.[200]

612. Again, study of the ambiguity of festival terminology relating to Passover and the Festival of Unleavened Bread at the time of the writing of the Gospel according to John, is the basis for the theory that, in spite of the usual understanding of John 18:28 and 19:14, the Last Supper in John is actually a Passover meal (as in the Synoptics). Or again, it is noted that the tractate *Sanhedrin* (4:1; Danby 387) specifies that in capital cases

> they hold the trial during the daytime . . . and the verdict must also be reached during the daytime . . . a verdict of conviction not until the following day. Therefore trials may not be held on the eve of the Sabbath, or on the eve of a festival day. . .

It is also noted, however, that in all four Gospels Jesus was tried at a night session, and that when Caiaphas said to the council, "It is expedient for you that one man should die for the people, and that the whole nation should not perish" (John 11:50), he might have been approving departure from normal legal practice in view of the urgency of the matter; so a harmonistic approach to the problem may be possible.[201]

613. The foregoing attempts at reconciliation between the Synoptics and the Fourth Gospel are relatively unconvincing, and the presentation in the Fourth Gospel, which is supported by extra-Christian tradition and is historically the more likely, is accepted in the present book as correct.[202] Then as to the character of the Last Supper in regard to the present question, we turn to and accept the solution proposed by John P. Meier. This is that the Last Supper

---

[200]Morgenstern, *VT* 5 (1955): 64 n. 2; and "The Time of the Passover in the Synoptics and John," in "Three Studies in the New Testament" (unpublished); cf. Sherman E. Johnson in *IB* 7:574; and *Jesus in His Homeland* (New York: Scribner, 1957), 19. I express appreciation to Rev. Dr. Julian Morgenstern for his kindness in making available to me his unpublished "Three Studies."

[201]Hamilton, *CH* 106 (1992): 335.

[202]Blinzler, *Trial of Jesus* (1959), 75–77; *Prozess Jesu* (1969), 104–107.

was not a Passover or other ritual meal of Judaism but a farewell meal of Jesus with his disciples, deliberately arranged by Jesus in view of the ominous developments of those days. In this connection we note the probable significance of the statement of Jesus in Luke 22:15–16. Here he speaks of how earnestly he has desired to eat this Passover with his disciples before he suffers, then according to Codex Bezae, the Washington Codex, certain minuscules and Syriac versions, and the Koine text, he says: "for I tell you I shall never eat it again until it is fulfilled in the kingdom of God." But, according to Codex Vaticanus, Codex Sinaiticus, Codex Alexandrinus, Codex Ephraemi Rescriptus, and some minuscules and Egyptian versions, he said: "for I tell you I shall not eat it until it is fulfilled in the kingdom of God." The first and less well attested form of the saying supposes that he was actually then eating the real Passover meal. The second and much better attested form of the saying supposes that he wanted to do so but was unable. If the latter form of the saying represents the actual situation at the time, we may think that the Johannine record is literally correct in picturing the last supper as a meal held one evening prior to the real Passover meal, and we may also surmise that the Synoptics (Matt 26:17–19; Mark 14:12–16; Luke 22:7–8 and 15–16 in Codex Bezae, etc.) were led to present the last supper as itself the Passover meal because it was held so close to the time when the Passover meal was to be held. It is noticeable, however, that even in the Synoptics no roast lamb—the most important part of the Passover meal—is mentioned as included in the repast. As for the Passover-like formalities that are mentioned—reclining at table (ἀνέκειτο, Matt 26:20; ἀνακειμένων, Mark 14:18; ἀνέπεσεν, Luke 22:14), singing hymns (ὑμνήσαντες, Matt 26:30, Mark 14:26), and the like—these can be sufficiently accounted for by the fact that the meal was undoubtedly overshadowed by the possibility of an imminent and violent death and was therefore naturally both solemn and religious.[203]

(3) The Hour of the Day

LITERATURE: Norman **Walker**, "The Reckoning of Hours in the Fourth Gospel," in *NovT* 4 (1960): 69–73.

614. There is also a problem about the hour of the crucifixion and death of Jesus. The usual Jewish manner of counting the hours was from sunrise to sunset, as may be seen in most of the time references in the Synoptic Gospels (Matt 28:1, "after the sabbath, toward the dawn of the first day of the week"; Mark 16:1–2, "when the sabbath was past . . . very early on the first day of the week"; Luke 24:1, "on the first day of the week, at early dawn") and in the Fourth Gospel as well (John 1:39, "they stayed with him that day, for it was about the tenth hour"; 4:6, "Jesus . . . wearied . . . with his journey, sat down beside the well. It was about the sixth hour"; 4:52, "at the seventh hour the fever left him"; 11:9, "Are there not twelve hours in the day?" [cf. §13]). With this understanding, Mark and John provide an understandably consistent picture of the following events: Mark 15:1, "when it was morning . . . they . . . delivered him to Pilate"; cf. John 18:18, "they led Jesus . . . to the praetorium. It was early";

[203]Meier, *Marginal Jew* 1:399.

John 19:14, 16, "it was about the sixth hour. . . . Pilate . . . handed him over to them to be crucified"; cf. Mark 15:33, "when the sixth hour had come, there was darkness over the whole land until the ninth hour"; 15:34, "at the ninth hour Jesus cried with a loud voice . . . and breathed his last." Converting these hours to our more familiar manner of speaking: after being brought before Pilate early in the morning, Jesus was condemned by Pilate and sent away to crucifixion at about midday, from which time until three o'clock in the afternoon there was darkness over the land; and at three o'clock Jesus breathed his last, leaving time for Joseph of Arimathea to provide burial before the requisite rest of the Sabbath (Luke 23:54; cf. Luke 4:40). In conflict and incompatible with all of the foregoing is only Mark 15:25, "it was the third hour when they crucified him." This means crucifixion at nine o'clock in the morning rather than at midday. Even if the reckoning were from either of the two other possible starting points of sunset or midnight it would mean nine o'clock in the evening or three o'clock in the morning and be obviously impossible. Therefore Mark 15:25 and John 19:14 are "plainly unreconcilable" and Mark 15:35 can even be thought to be an "interpolation."[204]

(4) The Calendar Date

615. In the foregoing, it has been established that the death of Jesus was probably on a Friday (§604) and probably on Nisan 14 in the official Jewish calendar (§611). This is the clear representation of the Fourth Gospel (§607). We have also established that, in spite of attempts at other solutions (§§609–611), the date of the death derived from a number of passages in the Synoptics is Friday, Nisan 15. The problem at this point, therefore, is to determine within the range of years which come into consideration in general, in which year or years the Jewish month date of Nisan 14 or 15 fell on the weekday which we call Friday, and to translate the date into terms of the Julian calendar.

616. The earliest date for the baptism of Jesus that we have mentioned is A.D. 26 (§572), and the shortest duration of his ministry is one year or a little more or less (§597). Likewise, the latest date for his baptism is A.D. 29 (§581) and the longest duration of his ministry is three or four years (§603). The range of years from A.D. 27 to 34 should, therefore, cover the span of time within which to look for the date of the death of Jesus. The dates of Nisan 1 (from which the dates of Nisan 14 and 15 can readily be obtained) were calculated astronomically for the range of years by J. K. Fotheringham,[205] and his results may be compared with the corresponding results of Parker and Dubberstein,[206] for the accuracy of which there is a very high degree of probability.[207] In the tables the dates as given are civil days, from midnight to midnight, although as we know the Babylonian (§11) or Jewish (§12) day actually began with the preceding

---

[204]Blinzler, *Trial of Jesus* (1959), 266, 269; *Prozess Jesu* (1969), 417, 421.
[205]*JTS* 35 (1934): 158–160.
[206]PDBC 46.
[207]PDBC 25.

sunset.[208] As an example of the use of the tables, in the year 30 of the Christian era Nisan 1 probably fell on Mar 25; accordingly Nisan 14 was Apr 7. Although such dates are precise and are used in what follows, it must be admitted that we do not know if the Jewish calendar was always in agreement, so we have to consider our results probable and even highly probable, in our view, but not absolutely assured.[209]

617. When a date has thus been translated into the Julian calendar, the day of the week on which it fell can also be determined. This is done by consulting a table of what are called the Dominical Letters or Sunday Letters.[210] In the system represented by such a table the letters, A, B, C, D, E, F, G are used to designate the first seven days of January and the "Sunday Letter" for the year tells which day is Sunday. Thus, if the Sunday Letter is C, for example, we may show the beginning of the year as in Table 174. Thus we know that, in this year, not only is Jan 3 a Sunday but so also is each succeeding date against which the letter C is written in the recurring sequence of these letters, namely Jan 10, 17, 24, 31, Feb. 7, 14, 21, 28, Mar 7, 14, 21, 28, etc. Likewise, if the Sunday Letter is D, the year starts as in Table 175.

TABLE 174. *The Beginning of a Year with the Sunday Letter C*

Jan	1	A	
	2	B	
	3	C	Sun
	4	D	Mon
	5	E	Tues
	6	F	Wed
	7	G	Thu
	8	A	Fri
	9	B	Sat
	10	C	Sun

TABLE 175. *The Beginning of a Year with the Sunday Letter D*

Jan	1	A	
	2	B	
	3	C	
	4	D	Sun
	5	E	Mon
	6	F	Tues
	7	G	Wed
	8	A	Thu
	9	B	Fri
	10	C	Sat
	11	D	Sun

Thus we know that, in this year, not only is Jan 4 a Sunday but also Jan 11, 18, 25, Feb 1, 8, 15, 22, Mar 1, 8, 15, 22, 29, etc. In a leap year, however, the Sunday Letter applies, as just explained, only to January and February, for on or after Feb 29 all the following Sundays fall one day earlier. This may be seen in Table 176 if we continue the example just begun above (Table 175) of a year with the Sunday Letter D. In this year, Feb 22 is still a Sunday, but is followed by Feb 29 as the next Sunday, after which the further Sundays are Mar 7, 14, 21, 28, etc., which is the way they fall in a common year with the Sunday Letter C (Table 174). Therefore, this leap year is given the two Sunday Letters, DC, and D applies to Jan–Feb, while C applies to Mar–Dec.

---

[208]PDBC 26.

[209]Roger T. Beckwith, "Cautionary Notes on the Use of Calendars and Astronomy to Determine the Chronology of the Passion," *CKC* 183–205, esp. 198.

[210]Lietzmann, *Zeitrechnung,* 7–8, 14ff.; cf. *EB* 4, 570; C. W. C. Barlow and G. H. Bryan, *Elementary Mathematical Astronomy* (London: University Tutorial Press, 1933), 222.

TABLE 176. *A Portion of a Leap Year with the Sunday Letters DC*

Feb	22	D	Sun	Mar	1	E	Mon
	23	E	Mon		2	F	Tues
	24	F	Tues		3	G	Wed
	25	G	Wed		4	A	Thu
	26	A	Thu		5	B	Fri
	27	B	Fri		6	C	Sat
	28	C	Sat		7	D	Sun
	29	D	Sun				

618. In the example given above (§616), Nisan 14 was determined to have fallen, most probably, on Apr 7 in the year 30 of the Christian era. For the year 30, the Sunday Letter is A.[211] This year therefore begins as in Table 177.

TABLE 177. *The Beginning of A.D. 30 (Sunday Letter A)*

Jan	1	A	Sun
	2	B	Mon
	3	C	Tues
	4	D	Wed
	5	E	Thu
	6	F	Fri
	7	G	Sat
	8	A	Sun

Subsequent Sundays are Jan 15, 22, 29, Feb 5, 12, 19, 26, Mar 5, 12, 19, 26, Apr 2, etc. For a period of interest in March and April the days run as in Table 178. Accordingly, in the year 30 of the Christian era the Julian calendar date of Apr 7 (equivalent to the Jewish month date of Nisan 14) fell on a Friday.

619. Utilizing the methods just explained (§§616–618), we may tabulate (Table 179) the dates of Nisan 14 and 15 (§615) in the years 27–34 of the Christian era (§616). In the table we show under (1) the results of Fotheringham (§616) which are in exact agreement with Parker and Dubberstein (§616), only supposing that several Babylonian intercalations (§53) which the latter show were not made in Jerusalem; and under (2) we show the results which follow from Parker and Dubberstein with the intercalations required by the Babylonian system.

620. In the range of years considered in Table 179, the apparent Synoptic requirement of having Nisan 15 fall on a Friday (and Nisan 14 on a Thursday), is satisfied only in A.D. 27 under (1), and in A.D. 34 under (2). These years, however, represent the extreme limits of probability within which the death of Jesus might be expected to fall (§616), and are therefore not likely. The

[211]Lietzmann, *Zeitrechnung*, 14.

Johannine requirement of having Nisan 14 fall on a Friday (and Nisan 15 on a Saturday) can be satisfied in A.D. 30 under (1) and in A.D. 33 under (1), both of which years seem to be well within the range of likelihood. Astronomically calculated, therefore, the likely dates for the crucifixion of Jesus appear to be either Friday, Apr 7, A.D. 30, or Friday, Apr 3, A.D. 33.[212] Therewith, in terms of the standard Jewish calendar, the representation of the day in the Fourth Gospel appears to be confirmed. Along with this confirmation of the Fourth Gospel, a historical consideration also weighs in favor of the date of A.D. 33. As attested by Tacitus[213] and Josephus (*Ant.* 18.64, cf. our §586) as well as in the Gospels, the crucifixion of Jesus took place under and by order of Pontius Pilate as governor (ἡγεμών, Matt 27:2; Latin *praefectus* [Greek ἔπαρχος] in the Pilate inscription from Caesarea; later title *procurator*/ἐπίτροπος) of Judea. Pilate's dates in office in Judea are almost always given as A.D. 26–36, in accordance with information from Josephus, who tells us (in *Ant.* 18.89, as ordinarily translated), that Pilate had a ten-year term in Judea and that when he was removed from office by Vitellius, the legate in Syria at the time, and sent to Rome to answer to the emperor for his conduct (especially actions against the Samaritans), Tiberius "had already passed away" (d. Mar 16, A.D. 37). Pilate was appointed to office through Sejanus, the anti-Semitic prime minister of Tiberius, and particularly in his earlier years in authority in Judea, Pilate gave offense to the Jews in many ways. In the last weeks of the year 31, however, Tiberius deposed and allowed the killing of his previously powerful minister and thereafter instructed his provincial governors to treat the Jews with more consideration. This changed situation can very well account for the vacillation of Pilate during the trial of Jesus (as is reported in all four Gospels) if the trial was in 33 but not if it was in 30 while Sejanus was still in power.[214] By way of comparison, John P. Meier agrees that, for all practical purposes, the choice for the year of the death of Jesus is between A.D. 30 and 33, and he thinks that A.D. 30 is more likely, with Friday, Apr 7, A.D. 30 the probable day and year; while Harold W. Hoehner, Paul L. Maier, and Paul Keresztes place the death on Friday, Apr 3, A.D. 33, as we too prefer.[215]

---

[212]For the full moons on Apr 7, A.D. 30, and Apr 3, A.D. 33, see Herman H. Goldstine, *New and Full Moons 1001 B.C. to A.D. 1651* (Philadelphia: American Philosophical Society, 1973), 80, 87, and note corrections on p. viii for locations other than Babylon. For crucifixion dates on Friday, Apr 7, A.D. 30, and Friday, Apr 3, A.D. 33, see Fotheringham in *JTS* 35 (1934): 158–160; Keresztes, *Imperial Rome*, 38; and Colin J. Humphreys and W. G. Waddington, "Astronomy and the Date of the Crucifixion," *CKC* 165–181, esp. 169–170, 172 (Apr 3, A.D. 33, as "the more probable"), 181, and Table 1 on p. 169.

[213]*Annals* 15.44.

[214]*CAH* 10:638; Reicke, *New Testament Era,* 183; Keresztes, *Imperial Rome*, 36–43; and A. D. Doyle, "Pilate's Career and the Date of the Crucifixion," in *JTS* 42 (1941): 190–193.

[215]Meier, *Marginal Jew,* 402, 407; Hoehner, *Chronological Aspects,* 114; Meier, *CKC* 124–125; Keresztes, *Imperial Rome,* 38, 43.

TABLE 178. *Some Days in March and April A.D. 30 (Sunday Letter A)*

Mar	19	A	Sun	Apr	1	G	Sat
	20	B	Mon		2	A	Sun
	21	C	Tues		3	B	Mon
	22	D	Wed		4	C	Tues
	23	E	Thu		5	D	Wed
	24	F	Fri		6	E	Thu
	25	G	Sat		7	F	Fri
	26	A	Sun		8	G	Sat
	27	B	Mon		9	A	Sun
	28	C	Tues		10	B	Mon
	29	D	Wed		11	C	Tues
	30	E	Thu		12	D	Wed
	31	F	Fri		13	E	Thu
					14	F	Fri
					15	G	Sat
					16	A	Sun
					17	B	Mon
					18	C	Tues
					19	D	Wed
					20	E	Thu

TABLE 179. *The Dates of Nisan 14 and 15 in A.D. 27–34*

	(1) As calculated by Fotheringham		(2) Or, supposing the intercalation of a month in the preceding year, as shown by Parker and Dubberstein, so that Nisan came one month late, then	
A.D.	*Nisan 14 fell on*	*Nisan 15 fell on*	*Nisan 14 fell on*	*Nisan 15 fell on*
27	Apr 10 Thu	Apr 11 Fri		
28	Mar 30 Tue	Mar 31 Wed	Apr 28 Wed	Apr 29 Thu
29	Apr 18 Mon	Apr 19 Tue		
30	Apr 7 Fri	Apr 8 Sat		
31	Mar 27 Tue	Mar 28 Wed	Apr 25 Wed	Apr 26 Thu
32	Apr 14 Mon	Apr 15 Tue		
33	Apr 3 Fri	Apr 4 Sat	May 2 Sat	May 3 Sun
34	Mar 24 Wed	Mar 25 Thu	Apr 22 Thu	Apr 23 Fri

621. In their accounts of the crucifixion the three Synoptic Gospels include the statement that "there was darkness over the whole land" from the sixth to the ninth hour, the ninth hour being when Jesus "yielded up his spirit" (Matt 27:50) and "breathed his last" (Mark 15:37). In Luke 23:45 it is added that at this time "the sun's light failed" (lit. "was eclipsed," τοῦ ἡλίου ἐκλιπόντος), a reading that is found in Sinaiticus, Vaticanus, and others; but Alexandrinus and others say "the sun was darkened" (ἐσκοτίσθη ὁ ἥλιος). When Peter spoke on the day of Pentecost (fifty days after Passover) he refuted the calumny that the apostles were "filled with new wine" by claiming that the prophecy of Joel had been fulfilled, including the words, "the sun shall be turned into darkness and the moon into blood" (Acts 2:20). In astronomical terms a solar eclipse can occur only at new moon and is impossible when the moon is at or near the full, thus an eclipse of the sun could not have occurred at the paschal full moon when Jesus died. A reasonable explanation of the darkening of the sun (Luke 23:45 in Alexandrinus et al.) is a heavy dust storm brought by a powerful khamsin wind from the desert.[216] It is also a fact that a partial lunar eclipse was visible in Jerusalem on the evening of Friday, April 3, A.D. 33,[217] and it is known that in even a partial eclipse the shadowed part of the moon is often red in color. Thus the likelihood that a blood-red moon was seen in Jerusalem at the time in question makes April 3, A.D. 33, even more probable a date for the death of Jesus. A simple confusion in the tradition between a lunar and a solar eclipse can well account for the statement in Luke 23:45 about an "eclipsed" or "darkened" sun.[218]

622. According to Clement of Alexandria (*Stromata* 1.21; §§552, 598), the followers of Basilides put the passion in the sixteenth year of Tiberius on the twenty-fifth of Phamenoth (= Mar 21) or on the nineteenth or twenty-fifth of Pharmuthi (= Apr 14 or 20). If by any chance the month of Phamenoth (which was properly from Feb 25 or 26 to Mar 26 [Table 8]) was later taken as simply equivalent to March, then Phamenoth 25 would be the same as Mar 25, and the latter is a date that is later cited by various authorities including Tertullian and Augustine as quoted in §472. Since Basilides was a Gnostic of Alexandria (§629), we have assumed (§598) that his followers would use the Egyptian calendar, probably as shown in Table 162, and that the sixteenth year of Tiberius would therefore be the year from Aug 29, A.D. 29, to Aug 28, A.D. 30. Of the specific dates in that year just given, namely Mar 21, Mar 25, Apr 14, and Apr 20, only the date of Apr 14 falls on a Friday, as a glance at Table 178 will show. But it is the preceding Friday, Apr 7, A.D. 30, which corresponds with Nisan 14 (Table 179). Therefore, none of the specific dates cited by Clement from the followers of Basilides checks out satisfactorily. But the fact that all of the dates cluster around the date in that year which is confirmed astronomically, namely, the date of Friday, Apr 7 (§620), lends a measure of support to that date.

623. Of course, if the sixteenth year of Tiberius were reckoned in the Egyptian calendar according to the non-accession-year system (Table 161), it would correspond to Aug 29, A.D. 28, to Aug 28, A.D. 29, and the dates Mar 21, Mar 25, Apr 14, and Apr 20 (§622), would fall in the year 29 of the Christian era. The Sunday Letter for the year 29 is B,[219] and the days would fall as shown in Table 180.

---

[216]G. R. Driver, "Two Problems in the New Testament," in *JTS* 16 (1965): 334–335.

[217]Kudlek and Mickler, *Solar and Lunar Eclipses of the Ancient Near East,* 157.

[218]For the explanation above see Fotheringham in *JTS* 35 (1934): 160–161; Humphreys and Waddington, *CKC* 172–181.

[219]Lietzmann, *Zeitrechnung,* 14.

TABLE 180. *Some Days in March and April A.D. 29 (Sunday Letter B)*

Mar	20	B	Sun	Apr	1	G	Fri
	21	C	Mon		2	A	Sat
	22	D	Tues		3	B	Sun
	23	E	Wed		4	C	Mon
	24	F	Thu		5	D	Tues
	25	G	Fri		6	E	Wed
	26	A	Sat		7	F	Thu
	27	B	Sun		8	G	Fri
	28	C	Mon		9	A	Sat
	29	D	Tues		10	B	Sun
	30	E	Wed		11	C	Mon
	31	F	Thu		12	D	Tues
					13	E	Wed
					14	F	Thu
					15	G	Fri
					16	A	Sat
					17	B	Sun
					18	C	Mon
					19	D	Tues
					20	E	Wed

624. From a glance at Table 180, it is evident that none of the dates cited by Clement (namely, Mar 21, Apr 14, and Apr 20; §622) fulfills the requirement (§615) of falling on a Friday. It was surmised (§622), however, that Phamenoth 25 (which is properly equivalent to Mar 21) might later have been considered equivalent to Mar 25, and it is at once notable that the latter date does fall on a Friday (Table 180). Whether or not it was derived from the tradition found among the followers of Basilides (§622), the date of Mar 25, A.D. 29, was later widely accepted. Thus Tertullian defines the date of the death of Jesus as follows:

> . . . under Tiberius Caesar, in the consulate of Rubellius Geminus and Fufius Geminus, in the month of March, at the time of Passover, on the eighth day before the Kalends of April, on the first day of unleavened bread, on which they slew the lamb at even. (*Answer to the Jews* 8)

The consular date *Gemino et Gemino* indicates the year 29 (Table 40); the eighth day before the kalends (§141) of April = Mar 25. Augustine gives the same date:

> Now Christ died when the Gemini were consuls, on the eighth day before the Kalends of April. (*City of God* 18.54.1)

Likewise the *Chronicle* of Hippolytus of Rome, issued in the thirteenth year of Severus Alexander (A.D. 234/235), equated with the year of Adam 5738 and leading to the year of Adam 5502 and the year 3/2 B.C. for the birth of Jesus (§624, Table 67) comes to the year of Adam 5532 and to A.D. 28/29 for the death of Jesus. But, in spite of this attestation for the date, it seems impossible to accept it. Mar 25, A.D. 29 was a Friday, but Mar 25, A.D. 29 does not correspond with either Nisan 14 or Nisan 15 in the Jewish calendar (Table 179).

4. Summary and Possible Chronological Schemes of the Life of Jesus

625. In the foregoing survey (§§474–624) of relevant evidence, the following conclusions have been found probable: The birth of Jesus must have been before the death of Herod (Table 140), and our presently preferred date is in mid-January 2 B.C. (§549).

626. The fifteenth year of Tiberius (Luke 3:1) was equivalent to A.D. 29, with the baptism and the beginning of the public work of Jesus in the autumn of A.D. 29 (§§582, 583, Tables 158, 167, 169). Counting from birth in mid-January 2 B.C., Jesus is correctly described in Luke 3:21 as "about thirty years of age."

627. In the reconstruction of the Second Temple begun by Herod the Great in his eighteenth year (20/19 B.C.), the priests built the temple edifice proper (ναός) in one year and six months, thus completing this structure in 18/17 B.C. The statement in John 2:20 is best understood as saying that this building (ναός) had stood for forty-six years, which brings us to A.D. 29/30. The conversation between Jesus and the Jews embodying this statement is in the context of a Passover at the beginning of Jesus' public ministry, hence the date is Passover time in the spring of A.D. 30 (§§590–595).

628. A number of Jewish annual festivals (§596) mentioned in the Gospels provide some data for an estimate of the length of the public ministry of Jesus. According to the Synoptic record, the ministry might have been only one year and some months in length but was not necessarily that brief (§§597–599). According to the Fourth Gospel, the duration was probably three years plus a number of months (§§600–601).

629. According to all four Gospels, the sequence of events at the end of the life of Jesus appears to have been as follows in terms of days of the week: Thursday evening, the last supper; Friday, the crucifixion; Saturday, the day of rest; Sunday, the resurrection (§§451–452). According to the Johannine representation (§§607–608), the last meal of Jesus and the disciples took place on the evening before the evening of the Passover meal as celebrated by official Judaism, and the death of Jesus took place on the same day as the slaying of the Passover lambs in official Jerusalem practice, namely on the fourteenth day of Nisan, a calendar date which in that year fell on a Friday. Given these two facts, that the crucifixion was on Nisan 14 and on a Friday (§615), it is possible by astronomical (§616) and calendrical (§617) calculation to determine with considerable probability the years, within the range of years in question (§616), in which the Jewish calendar date of Nisan 14 would have fallen on the day of the week that we call Friday. The result of this investigation (§§619–620, Table 179) is that the two most probable dates, astronomically and calendrically, are Friday, Apr 7, A.D. 30, and Friday, Apr 3, A.D. 33.

630. The data summarized in the preceding paragraphs (§§625–629) can be incorporated in two different chronological schemes of the life of Jesus (Tables 181, 182). It is plain that the first scheme outlines a public ministry of one full year plus a few months before and a few months after, and thus can concur well with the indications of a shorter ministry as in the Synoptic Gospels taken alone (§597). The second scheme, on the other hand, outlines a ministry of three years plus a few months before and a few months after, and is thus concurrent with the indications of a longer ministry as in the Fourth Gospel (§§600–601). With regard for the probable historical value of records in the Fourth Gospel, the longer scheme is accepted in the present book as the more likely.

TABLE 181. *First Chronological Scheme of the Life of Jesus*

B.C./A.D.	*Event*
2 B.C.	Birth about mid-January (§473, 496G)
A.D. 29	15th year of Tiberius after the death of Augustus, by Roman reckoning extending from Jan 1 to Dec 31 (§626). Baptism and beginning of public ministry of Jesus in the fall, when he was about 30 years of age (§626)
30	Passover in the spring of A.D. 30, 46 years after the priests finished building the temple edifice proper (§627). Crucifixion on Nisan 14 = Friday, Apr 7 (§629)

TABLE 182. *Second Chronological Scheme of the Life of Jesus*

B.C./A.D.	*Event*
2 B.C.	Birth about mid-January (§473, 496G)
A.D. 29	15th year of Tiberius after the death of Augustus, by Roman reckoning extending from Jan 1 to Dec 31 (§626) Baptism and beginning of public ministry of Jesus in the fall when he was about 30 years of age (§626)
30	1st Passover, 46 years after the priests finished building the temple edifice proper (§627)
31	2d Passover, unmentioned
32	3d Passover (John 6:4)
33	Final Passover Crucifixion on Nisan 14 = Friday, Apr 3 (§629)

631. By way of comparison and in respect of the two especially crucial dates of the fifteenth year of Tiberius and of the crucifixion, it may be remembered (§§581, 620) that John P. Meier begins Jesus' ministry in A.D. 28 and places the crucifixion as probably on Friday, Apr 7, A.D. 30,[220] while both Harold W. Hoehner[221] and Paul L. Maier[222] began the ministry of Jesus in A.D. 29 and place the crucifixion on Friday, Apr 3, A.D. 33. Dates farther afield (but not in agreement) are presented by Nikos Kokkinos and Jerry Vardaman. The basic

[220]Meier, *Marginal Jew,* 402, 407.
[221]Hoehner, *Chronological Aspects,* 44, 114.
[222]Maier, *CKC* 125 and Table 1.

reasoning by Kokkinos, by which the birth of Jesus is placed in 12 B.C., the public ministry in A.D. 33–36, and the crucifixion in March A.D. 36 was set forth above (§§543, 585).[223] Likewise the solution proposed by Vardaman to the problem of the fifteenth year of Tiberius (Luke 3:1, emended to give the second year of Tiberius = A.D. 15) was outlined above (in §586). Further, Vardaman deals with the date of Pontius Pilate.[224] In contrast with the usual translation and understanding of *Ant.* 18.89 (see above §620) in which Josephus says that when Pilate was dismissed and sent to Rome, the emperor Tiberius "had already passed away (μεταστάς)," Vardaman points out that the Greek word is the aorist participle of μεθίστημι, and this verb means generally "to remove from one place to another." Vardaman holds, therefore, that *Ant.* 18.89 really means not that Tiberius had already died, but that he "had already moved" to his later main residence on the island of Capri. So Vardaman dates the governorship of Pilate in Judea in A.D. 14/15–25/26, and this allows for A.D. 15 as the (emended) "second year" of Tiberius and the time of the beginning of the work of John the Baptist and of the public ministry of Jesus (§586). This can also lead to Vardaman's conclusions that Jesus, born he thinks in 12 B.C. (§543), was at least twenty-seven years old in A.D. 15, fitting well with the assertion in Luke 3:23 that when he began his ministry Jesus was about thirty years of age, and that, after a ministry six years long, as Vardaman thinks, the death of Jesus was at Passover in the year A.D. 21.[225] In addition to the above, for the biblical chronology of E. W. Faulstich see the Appendix.

632. According to the foregoing analysis (§§620ff.) the crucifixion of Jesus was most probably on Friday, Apr 3, A.D. 33, corresponding to Nisan 14, the date in "the first month of the year" (roughly March–April) of the slaying of the Passover lamb (Exod 12:2, 8; see Table 172). In the ensuing narrative the next day was the Sabbath (Mark 15:42; Luke 23:56), Saturday, and the day thereafter was the first day of the week (Matt 28:1; Mark 16:1; Luke 24:1; John 20:1), Sunday, when the tomb was found empty, bringing the first intimation of the resurrection, which was confirmed thereafter by the appearances of the risen Christ to both women and men, among the latter Paul being the last (1 Cor 15:5–8).

633. In early Christianity the continuing solemn celebration every year of the crucifixion and resurrection used Jewish language to call this the Passover, specifically "the Passover of the Lord" (τὸ κυρίου πάσχα; *Letter to Diognetus* 12.9, by an anonymous author A.D. c. 130?). Since the date of Nisan 14 for the death of Jesus depends largely upon the Gospel according to John, it is to be noted that early tradition connects John the apostle, often considered the author of the Gospel, with Asia and in particular with Ephesus, and that it was in the churches of Asia Minor that the "quartodecimans" insisted upon maintaining the date of Nisan 14 for the annual observance, whereas in Rome and elsewhere the commemoration of the Passion was on a Friday and the resurrection on a

---

[223]Kokkinos, *CKC* 133–163.
[224]Vardaman, "Jesus' Life: A New Chronology," *CKC* 55–82.
[225]Ibid., 77–78.

Sunday. Eusebius gives an account of this controversy in *Ecclesiastical History* 5.23–25.

634. In astronomical terms the Jewish Passover of Nisan 14/15 was marked by the full moon of the first springtime month (March/April, beginning at or after the spring equinox). In the Germanic languages the word "Easter"—originally the festival of the vernal equinox—came to replace the word "Passover" as the name of the Christian feast. Thus in astronomy the rule for finding Easter is: the first Sunday after the first full moon following the spring equinox, with the proviso that if the full moon is on Sunday, Easter is the following Sunday.[226]

B. THE LIFE OF PETER

LITERATURE: Adolf von **Harnack**, *The Date of Acts and the Synoptic Gospels* (Crown Theological Library; New York: G. P. Putnam's Sons, 1911); George **Edmundson**, *The Church in Rome in the First Century: An Examination of Various Controversial Questions Relating to Its History, Chronology, Literature, and Traditions* (Bampton Lectures for 1913; London: Longmans, Green, 1913); Hans **Lietzmann**, *Petrus und Paulus in Rom* (Bonn: Marcus und Weber, 1915); idem, *Petrus und Paulus in Rom* (2d ed.; Berlin: W. de Gruyter, 1927); idem, *Petrus römischer Martyrer* (Sitzungsberichte der Preussischen Akademie der Wissenschaften, phil.-hist. Classe 29; Berlin: W. de Gruyter, 1936); James T. **Shotwell** and Louise R. **Loomis**, *The See of Peter* (Records of Civilization: Sources and Studies 7; New York: Columbia University Press, 1927); A. S. **Barnes**, *The Martyrdom of St. Peter and St. Paul* (New York: Oxford University Press, 1933); Paul **Styger**, *Die römischen Katakomben: Archäologische Forschungen über die Bedeutung der altchristlichen Grabstätten* (Berlin: Verlag für Kunstwissenschaft, 1933); Oscar **Cullmann**, *Peter: Disciple, Apostle, Martyr* (Philadelphia: Westminster Press, 1953); Theodor **Klauser**, *Die römische Petrustradition im Lichte der neuen Ausgrabungen unter der Peterskirche* (Arbeitsgemeinschaft für Forschung des Landes Nordrhein-Westfalen: Geisteswissenschaften 24; Köln: Westdeutscher Verlag, 1956); Jocelyn **Toynbee** and John Ward **Perkins**, *The Shrine of St. Peter and the Vatican Excavations* (New York: Pantheon Books, 1957); Margherita **Guarducci**, *I graffiti sotto la confessione di San Pietro in Vaticano* (Vatican City: Librarie Editrice Vaticana, 1958); idem; *The Tomb of St. Peter: The New Discoveries in the Sacred Grottoes of the Vatican* (New York: Hawthorn Books, 1960); Engelbert **Kirschbaum**, *The Tombs of St. Peter and St. Paul* (New York: St. Martin's Press, [1959]); Ludwig **Hertling** and Engelbert **Kirschbaum**, *The Roman Catacombs and Their Martyrs* (rev. ed.; London: Darton, Longman & Todd, 1960); P. A. **Lagarde**, *Constitutiones Apostolorum* (Osnabrück: Otto Zeller, 1966); Aziz S. **Atiya**, *A History of Eastern Christianity* (London: Methuen, 1968); Daniel Wm. **O'Connor**, *Peter*

---

[226]James R. Newman, *The Harper Encyclopedia of Science* (New York: Harper & Row, 1963) 1:198; C. W. C. Barlow and G. H. Bryan, *Elementary Mathematical Astronomy* (London: University Tutorial Press, 1933), 222–223; J. K. Fotheringham in *JTS* 35 (1934): 158; August Strobel, *Ursprung und Geschichte des frühchristlichen Osterkalenders* (Berlin: Akademie, 1977).

in Rome: The Literary, Liturgical, and Archaeological Evidence (New York: Columbia University Press, 1969); Virgilio **Corbo**, "The House at Capernaum," in *New Memoirs of Saint Peter by the Sea of Galilee* (Jerusalem: Franciscan Printing Press, [1969]); idem, *The House of St. Peter Capharnaum* (PSBFCMI 5; Jerusalem: Franciscan Printing Press, 1969); idem, *Gli edifici della cittá* (Publications of the Studium Biblicum Franciscanum 19; Cafarnao 1; Jerusalem: Franciscan Printing Press, 1975), 26-111; Franz Xaver **Funk**, *Die Apostolischen Konstitutionen: Eine litterar-historischen Untersuchung* (Frankfurt am Main: Minerva, 1970); Emmanuele **Testa**, *I Graffiti della Casa di S. Pietro* (Publications of the Studium Biblicum Franciscanum 19; Cafarnao 4; Jerusalem: Franciscan Printing Press, 1972); Stanislao **Loffreda**, *A Visit to Capharnaum* (2d ed.; Jerusalem: Franciscan Printing Press, 1972); John **Wenham**, "Did Peter Go to Rome in A.D. 42?" in *TB* 23 (1972): 94–102; idem, *Redating Matthew, Mark and Luke: A Fresh Assault on the Synoptic Problem* (London: Hodder & Stoughton, 1991), 136–182; Raymond E. **Brown**, Karl P. **Donfried**, and John **Reumann**, eds., *Peter in the New Testament: A Collaborative Assessment by Protestant and Roman Catholic Scholars* (Minneapolis: Augsburg; New York: Paulist; Toronto: Paramus, 1973); S. **Dockx**, "Chronologie de la vie de saint Pierre," in *Chronologies néotestamentaires et vie de l'église primitive: Recherches exégétiques* (Paris-Gembloux: Duculot, 1976), 129–146; idem, "Chronologie zum Leben des heiligen Petrus," in Thiede, *Das Petrusbild in der neueren Forschung*, 85–108; Otto F. A. **Meinardus**, *Christian Egypt, Ancient and Modern* (Cairo: American University in Cairo Press, 1977); James **Stevenson**, *The Catacombs: Life and Death in Early Christianity* (London: Thames & Hudson, 1978; Nashville: Thomas Nelson, 1985), 31ff.; James F. **Strange** and Hershel **Shanks**, "Has the House Where Jesus Stayed in Capernaum Been Found?" *BAR* 8 (6, Nov/Dec 1982): 26–37; John J. **Gunther**, "The Association of Mark and Barnabas with Egyptian Christianity," *EvQ* 54 (1982): 219–233; 55 (1983): 21–29; Carsten Peter **Thiede**, *Simon Peter: From Galilee to Rome* (Exeter: Paternoster, 1986); idem, ed., *Das Petrusbild in der neueren Forschung* (Wuppertal: R. Brockhaus, 1987); James F. **Strange** and Hershel **Shanks**, "Ist das Haus, in dem Jesus in Kafarnaum wohnte, gefunden worden?" in Thiede, *Das Petrusbild in der neueren Forschung*, 145–162; Raymond **Davis**, *The Book of Pontiffs (Liber pontificalis): The Ancient Biographies of the First Ninety Roman Bishops to A.D. 715* (Liverpool: Liverpool University Press, 1989); Paul **Keresztes**, *Imperial Rome and the Christians*, vol. 1, *From Herod the Great to about 200 A.D.* (Lanham, Md.: University Press of America, 1989), 67–82; Daniel R. **Schwartz**, *Agrippa I: The Last King of Judea* (Tübingen: J. C. B. Mohr [Paul Siebeck], 1990).

1. "He Departed and Went to Another Place"

635. In Acts 12:1–3, it is recorded that Herod the king killed James the brother of John with the sword and then imprisoned Peter. This king is Herod Agrippa I, grandson of Herod the Great (§§501ff.). He was educated in Rome and became a close friend of Gaius (Caligula). Upon the death of the emperor Tiberius on Mar 16, A.D. 37, and the accession of Caligula (Table 43), the latter conferred upon Agrippa the tetrarchy of Philip (Luke 3:1), which lay to the north and east of the Sea of Galilee, together with the title of king. After Herod Antipas was banished (A.D. 39) his tetrarchy (Luke 3:1), which covered Galilee and Perea, was also given (probably in A.D. 40) to Agrippa. When Caligula was murdered (Jan 24, A.D. 41), Agrippa was in Rome and helped to secure the succession of Claudius (A.D. 41–54; Table 44), who now gave him also Judea and Samaria. At this juncture Agrippa ruled the entire territory of Herod the Great: Judea, Samaria, Galilee, the Transjordan, and the Decapolis. In a precise statement of these sequential periods of Herod Agrippa's reign, Josephus (*Ant.* 19.350–351) says that Agrippa reigned for four years under Gaius Caesar (Caligula), ruling during three of these years over the tetrarchy of Philip, and adding that of Herod Antipas during the fourth year. He reigned further for three years under the emperor Claudius Caesar, during which time he ruled over the above territory and received in addition Judea, Samaria, and Caesarea. It was after the completion of this his reign "over the whole of Judea" that he came to Caesarea and died. His death was at the age of fifty-four years, and he had reigned seven years in all: four under Caligula, three under Claudius (*Ant.* 19.343, 351).[227] Essentially the same outline is set forth in the *Chronicle* of Eusebius, with equivalent dates in the Christian era.[228] Only Josephus evidently reckons the year in which Gaius (Caligula) died (A.D. 41) to his reign rather than making it the first year of Claudius, as is done in the table of Eusebius (Table 183, cf. Table 95). The death of Herod Agrippa I is therefore usually assigned to the year 44 of the Christian era.

TABLE 183. *The Reign of Herod Agrippa I in the* Chronicle *of Eusebius*

Romans	*Jews*	*A.D.*
Gaius, 3 years, 10 months	Herod Agrippa I, 7 years	
Year 1	Accession year	37
Year 2	Year 1	38
Year 3	Year 2	39
Year 4	Year 3	40
Claudius, 13 years, 8 months, 28 days		
Year 1	Year 4	41
Year 2	Year 5	42
Year 3	Year 6	43
Year 4	Year 7	44

636. In a text-critical study of all the passages in Josephus about Herod Agrippa I, Daniel Schwartz finds reason to believe that Agrippa counted his regnal years from autumn (Tishri, Sept/Oct), and Schwartz assigns dates accordingly.[229] We recapitulate the sequence of events reported by Josephus (§635) and note the dates established by Schwartz: Tiberius died on March 16, A.D. 37, and Gaius Caligula as Tiberius's successor made Agrippa king over the former tetrarchy of Herod Antipas (*Ant.* 18.237, 252). According to Schwartz,[230] Agrippa

[227]Schürer, *History,* vol. 1.2, 153–154; Vermes/Millar, *History* 1:443–445. For the death of Herod Agrippa in A.D. 44 see also Stewart Perowne, *The Later Herods: The Political Background of the New Testament* (London: Hodder & Stoughton, 1958), 81; Bo Reicke, *The New Testament Era* (Philadelphia: Fortress, 1968), 201. Dockx ("Chronologie zum Leben des heiligen Petrus," 86, 94) places the death of Herod Agrippa on March 10, A.D. 44.

[228]Helm 177–179.

[229]Schwartz, *Agrippa I*, 2ff.

then began to count his years as king from the preceding autumn new year, i.e., from Tishri (Sept/Oct), A.D. 36. Caligula was murdered on Jan 24, A.D. 41, and Claudius, his successor, thereupon gave Agrippa also Judea and Samaria so that he then ruled "over the whole of Judea," i.e., over the whole territory once ruled by Herod the Great. After his appointment Agrippa no doubt wanted to return to Palestine to take up his rule over his enlarged territory as soon as possible. On the Mediterranean the sailing season ceased during the winter and opened again with the approach of spring on Feb 8 (Pliny, *Nat. Hist.* 2.47, see below §694), so Agrippa probably took ship on or soon after Feb 8. With an estimated sailing time of five to six weeks to Palestine he would have been in Caesarea about the middle of March A.D. 41.[231] Josephus gives the further chronology: "After the completion of the third year of his reign over the whole of Judea, Agrippa came to the city of Caesarea. Here he celebrated spectacles in honor of Caesar"[232]—and here in Caesarea Agrippa died, as Josephus will also tell (our §637). According to Schwartz,[233] Agrippa died in A.D. 43/44 during the fourteenth celebration of the games at Caesarea, between Tishri (Sept/Oct) A.D. 43 and Shebat (Jan/Feb) 44, probably at the very beginning of this period. Table 184 is meant to give a compact overview of the foregoing.

TABLE 184. *Regnal Years of Herod Agrippa I and Associated Events*

Regnal Years	*Events*	*Tishri-to-Tishri Years A.D.*
Accession	Tiberius died Mar 16, 37 A.D.; and Caligula made Agrippa king. First year of Agrippa antedated to Tishri 1, A.D. 36	36/37
1		37/38
2		38/39
3		39/40
4	Caligula died Jan 24, A.D. 41; Claudius gave Judea and Samaria to Agrippa	40/41
5		41/42
6		42/43
7	Agrippa celebrated spectacles in honor of Caesar at Caesarea. Died at age 54	43/44

637. Josephus (*Ant.* 16.136–141) tells that the "spectacles" (θεωρία) celebrated by Herod Agrippa were instituted by Herod the Great when he finished building Caesarea in the twenty-eighth year of his reign (10/9 B.C.; see Table 141). The festival of dedication featured a music contest (ἀγών), athletic exercises, gladiators, wild beasts, horse races, and lavish shows. The contest was dedicated to Caesar, and Herod arranged to have it celebrated every fifth year (κατὰ πενταετηρίδα), in our way of reckoning meaning that the festival took place every four years. I.e., the year of the festival was reckoned as being both the last

[230] Ibid., 57.
[231] Dockx, "Chronologie zum Leben des heiligen Petrus," 88.
[232] *Ant.* 19.343; *War* 2.219
[233] Schwartz, *Agrippa I,* 110–111.

year of the one cycle and the first year of the next cycle; therefore the fourteenth celebration of the festival took place in A.D. 43/44 when Herod Agrippa attended.[234] As Josephus (*Ant.* 19.344–352) tells it, on the second day of the spectacles Herod Agrippa appeared in the theater at daybreak in a garment made wholly of silver, which was so illumined by the first rays of the sun that his flatterers cried out that he was a god. But shortly thereafter he looked up and saw an owl perched on a rope over his head, and he was smitten with grave apprehension because he had long before been warned that such an apparition would indicate his death within five days (*Ant.* 18.195–200). The prediction was soon fulfilled: Agrippa was seized with violent stomach pains and in five days departed this life.

638. Now we turn to the book of Acts. Stephen died (Acts 7) during a virtual interregnum in the procuratorship. Pilate had been replaced by Marcellus, who had less power than the high priest, so that the high priest felt free on his own to have Stephen cast outside the city, where an angry mob stoned him to death. Acts relates that the subsequent general persecution actually gave a new impetus to Christian missionary activity. Then in early A.D. 41 Herod Agrippa I entered upon his new kingship "over the whole of Judea" (Table 184).

639. Herod Agrippa I—whom the book of Acts calls Herod—adapted his conduct in Judea to curry the favor of the Pharisees, the party most rigorous in interpreting the law and most popular with the common people.[235] Thus it made sense for Herod Agrippa to take the lead in further actions against Christian leaders, and he evidently moved promptly in the spring of A.D. 41.[236] He killed James, the son of Zebedee and brother of John, and "when he saw that this pleased the Jews he arrested Peter too" (Acts 12:3); it was the Passover season, and after Passover he intended "to bring him out to the people," probably a euphemism for trial and execution (Acts 12:3–4; cf. Eusebius, *Ch. Hist.* 2.9). Peter, however, was saved by angelic intervention and was "rescued from the hand of Herod and from all that the Jewish people were expecting" (Acts 12:11). After a brief visit with some believers who had been praying for him, Peter "departed and went to another place" (Acts 12:17).

640. In sequence with the narrative of Peter's imprisonment, deliverance, and departure (§639), Acts 12:19, 21–23 continues with a brief account of Herod Agrippa's travel to Caesarea and death there. This account is in line with that of Josephus (§637) but briefer, omitting the owl omen and attributing the death to the smiting of the king by an angel of the Lord. The direct sequence of the two texts in Acts is sometimes thought to indicate that Peter departed only shortly before Agrippa died, i.e., in A.D. 44/45 or 43/44 (Tables 183, 184). On the contrary, Luke juxtaposed the two events in order to depict Agrippa's death as divine retribution for his evil deeds. The events involving Peter took place near Passover (Acts 12:4), and in the spring of A.D. 41 the Passover date

---

[234]Vermes/Millar, *History* 1:309 n. 72; 452 n. 43; 2:47 n. 104; Dockx, "Chronologie zum Leben des heiligen Petrus," 86; Schwartz, *Agrippa I,* 110–111.

[235]Reicke, *New Testament Era,* 198; cf. Josephus *Ant.* 19.331.

[236]Dockx, "Chronologie zum Leben des heiligen Petrus," 90.

(Nisan 14) fell on April 21. This may therefore be accepted as a well-established approximate date for Peter's "departure."

641. While Acts 12:17 states that Peter departed to "another place," it does not tell where that other place was. When it became known the very next morning that Peter had escaped, Herod Agrippa "sought for him and could not find him" and ordered the sentries put to death (Acts 12:18–19), and this certainly justified Peter's evident haste to depart (§639). It also must have meant that Peter had to get away entirely from Herod Agrippa's territory of "the whole of Judea." Certainly it would have been unwise to try to take ship from Caesarea, the Roman administrative city where later Paul was kept prisoner for two years in "Herod's praetorium" (Acts 23:35; 24:27). Later sources tell us that Peter went to Antioch in Syria and to the Asian provinces of Pontus, Galatia, Cappadocia, Asia, and Bithynia, named in 1 Peter 1:1 (§665) and, in the second year of Claudius (A.D. 42), to Rome. John Mark was apparently there with him but departed in the third year of Claudius to Egypt and Alexandria, while Peter was bishop at Rome for twenty-five years and died in the fourteenth year of Nero (A.D. 67/68; cf. §654, Table 186) on June 29 (§§662–663).[237]

2. Peter in Rome

642. The statement in 1 Pet 5:13, "She who is at Babylon . . . sends you greetings," is presumably an expression of greetings on behalf of the church where Peter is, or is represented as being, at the time. Taken literally and as the original famous city of this name, this would mean Babylon in Mesopotamia. According to Josephus (*Ant.* 18.372), Babylon was still an inhabited place in the New Testament period, for he tells how, about the middle of the first century, many of the Jews left there to settle in Seleucia. Aside from this interpretation of 1 Pet 5:13, other evidence is not known that Peter went to Mesopotamia.

643. Babylon was also the name of a place in Egypt. This Egyptian Babylon is mentioned by Josephus (*Ant.* 2.315) as having been founded by Cambyses when he subjugated Egypt; by Diodorus of Sicily (1.46.3) as being a colony founded by Babylonian captive laborers in Egypt; and by Strabo (17.807) as founded by Babylonian emigrants and, in his day, the camp of one of the three Roman legions in Egypt. This Babylon is identified with still impressive Roman ruins in Old Cairo. Again, it is possible that Peter could have been here, but confirmatory evidence is needed.

644. In Rev 14:8; 16:19; 17:5; 18:2, 10, 21, the name Babylon is plainly used as a designation for Rome, the city which in that time appears as the enemy of the Christians even as in the Old Testament times the city of Babylon was the enemy of the Jews. It seems probable that 1 Pet 5:13 uses the name in the same way and as in fact a reference to Rome. Eusebius (*Ch. Hist.* 2.15.2) cites Clement

---

[237]Wenham "Did Peter Go to Rome in A.D. 42?" 94–102; Wenham, *Redating Matthew, Mark and Luke,* 146ff.; Edmundson, *The Church in Rome in the First Century*.

of Alexandria, confirmed by Papias, for information about Peter and says that they stated that Peter wrote the First Epistle in Rome and referred to the city metaphorically as Babylon.[238] 1 Peter 5:13 is, therefore, New Testament indication of the presence of Peter in Rome. Likewise John 21:18 is almost certainly a reference within the New Testament to the martyrdom of Peter, probably reflecting the stretching out of the hands in crucifixion.

645. Beyond the New Testament the references become more specific. *The First Letter of Clement,* written by the head of the church at Rome to the church at Corinth about A.D. 95 or 96, tells of the persecution and martyrdom of Peter and Paul, and groups with them in a like fate a "vast multitude" (πολὺ πλῆθος) who likewise suffered "among us" (*1 Clem.* 5f). This reference by Clement can be understood to fit well with the account by Tacitus (*Annals* 15.44) of the persecution of the Christians at Rome by Nero, which followed the great six-day fire of A.D. 64, in connection with which Tacitus also speaks of the cruel treatment meted out to a "vast multitude" *(multitudo ingens),* who were "convicted . . . of hatred of the human race" (the popular pagan charge against the Christians). The fire began, according to Tacitus (*Annals* 15.41), on *XIIII Kal. Sextilis,* i.e., fourteen days before the first of Sextilis (later August) = on July 19 (§141). This was also the anniversary of the burning of Rome by the Senones, and the interval between the two fires, Tacitus says, is capable of resolution into equal numbers of years, months, and days. This cryptic definition is to be explained by resolving the 454 years between the burning of Rome by the Gauls in 390 B.C. and this fire in A.D. 64 into 418 years, 418 months, and 418 days.[239] A.D. 64 is, therefore, a well-established date for the fire in question. Whether the fire started accidentally or was set deliberately by Nero (as Suetonius, *Nero* 38, and Orosius, *Seven Books of History against the Pagans* 7.7 affirm), public suspicion turned against the emperor and he cast the blame upon the Christians. Tacitus narrates the ensuing persecution in the passage just cited.

646. If we put together the statements of Clement and of Tacitus (§645) the simplest solution to the question of the deaths of Peter and Paul is to say that both probably perished in Nero's terrible persecution of the Christians at Rome following the fire in the summer of A.D. 64.[240] It may be, however, that the death of the two leaders was only after new laws were officially in place against the Christians and at the end of actual legal proceedings. How soon such

---

[238]Shotwell and Loomis, *The See of Peter,* 80.

[239]Tacitus, *Annals,* ed. John Jackson (LCL, 1951), 278 n. 1.

[240]Cf. Cullmann, *Peter,* 109; Klauser, *Die römische Petrustradition,* 16; Guarducci, *Tomb of St. Peter,* 31, 179; Styger, *Römische Katakomben;* George Ogg, *The Chronology of the Life of Paul* (London: Epworth, 1968); E. Earle Ellis, "Die Datierung des Neuen Testaments," in *Theologische Zeitschrift* 42 (Sept/Oct 1988): 409–430, esp. 411: the main persecution perhaps in the winter and spring A.D. 65; Harry W. Tajra, *The Trial of St. Paul: A Juridical Exegesis of the Second Half of the Acts of the Apostles* (WUNT, 2. Reihe, 35; Tübingen: J. C. B. Mohr [Paul Siebeck], 1989); and *The Martyrdom of St. Paul: Historical and Judicial Context, Traditions, and Legends* (WUNT, 2. Reihe, 67; Tübingen: J. C. B. Mohr [Paul Siebeck], 1994): Paul's re-arrest, trial, condemnation, and martyrdom occurred more likely than not before the fire of A.D. 64.

laws and legal proceedings were in place against Christians is not too clear. Clement of Rome (§645) does not refer to any such laws but rather to "jealousy and envy" (of contentious religious groups?) as responsible for the martyrdom of Peter and Paul. A statement of Tertullian (*To the Nations* 1.7), who speaks of "this name of ours [of the Christians]" and says, "under Nero it was ruthlessly condemned *(invaluit),*" may still only refer to the general persecution just described rather than to legal proscription. Sulpicius Severus, an expert on Roman history, tells in his *Chronica* (a "Sacred History," intended for educated Roman Christians and extending from creation to the author's own time, written around A.D. 402–404, MPL 20:145) about the burning of Rome and how Nero put the blame on the Christians and launched a fiendish persecution, then afterward set forth edicts making Christianity an illicit religion *(Christianum esse non licebat);* but it is still not told how long that took, although it must have been some time. In his *Seven Books of History* (5.7) Orosius says of Nero, "he was the first at Rome to torture and inflict the penalty of death upon Christians, and he ordered them throughout all the provinces to be afflicted with like persecution," but this may mean arbitrary decrees rather than courts and legalities. At any rate laws and legal procedures were certainly in place and used against Christians, accused for whatever the cause might be, before the end of Nero's reign. This is shown plainly by 2 Tim 4:16, which refers to Paul's "first defense" and implies a second defense perhaps even then far advanced toward condemnation (2 Tim 4:6). This procedure may have been followed not only for Paul as a Roman citizen (Acts 22:25) but possibly also for Peter, since the two are almost always closely associated in reports of their martyrdom. In fact, as we will see below (§§654, 655, and Tables 185–188) in the *Chronicle* of Eusebius the deaths of both Peter and Paul are in A.D. 67/68, and this may well be correct.[241]

647. In further sources, the foundation of the church at Rome is attributed to Peter and Paul together. This can hardly be literally true at least for Paul (although he was later in Rome for two years, according to Acts 28:30–31), since in his letter to the Roman Christians he told them he hoped he might "now at last succeed in coming to you" (Rom 1:10), so the church was there before Paul came the first time, and it seems likely that its origin was due to causes at work before either Paul or Peter arrived, perhaps to the return of converted "visitors from Rome, both Jews and proselytes," who were in Jerusalem on the day of Pentecost (Acts 1:10). But about A.D. 170 Dionysius, bishop of Corinth, wrote a letter to the Romans, which Eusebius quotes (*Ch. Hist.* 2.25), and said about Peter and Paul:

> You have thus by such an admonition bound together the planting of Peter and of Paul at Rome and Corinth. For both of them planted and likewise taught us in our Corinth. And they taught together in like manner in Italy, and suffered martyrdom at the same time (κατὰ τὸν αὐτὸν καιρόν).

That Peter worked in Corinth is attested in 1 Cor 1:12, where Paul refers to Christians at Corinth who said, "I belong to Cephas [Peter's Aramaic name, John 1:42; Gal 2:9]," presumably meaning that they had been baptized by Peter.

---

[241]Dockx, *Chronologies néotestamentaires,* 144–145; Thiede, *Simon Peter,* 190–191.

Irenaeus (*Against Heresies* 3.1.5) also speaks of "Peter and Paul . . . preaching at Rome, and laying the foundations of the Church."

648. Tangible evidence of the remembrance at Rome of the martyrdom of Peter and Paul is attested by Gaius of Rome around A.D. 200. According to Eusebius (*Ch. Hist.* 2.25), this authority, a presbyter in the Roman church under Zephyrinus (A.D. c. 199–217), said that he could show the "trophies" (τρόπαια) of Peter and Paul at the Vatican and on the Ostian Way, respectively. These are places where, as excavations have shown, pagan cemeteries existed. The "trophy," presumably meaning burial place and memorial of victory, of Peter has in all probability actually been found under St. Peter's Church in Rome, in the form of a simple niche with columns in the so-called Red Wall, a shrine probably dating around A.D. 160.[242] On the plaster of the Red Wall itself is a graffito dating probably not long after A.D. 160 and probably reading:

ΠΕΤΡ[ΟC]
ΕΝΙ

The ἔνι can be a contraction of ἔνεστι, so that the inscription means "Peter is within," i.e., "Peter is buried inside here."[243] The Church of St. Peter was built by the emperor Constantine in the Vatican district of ancient Rome and probably near the site of Nero's Circus, in difficult terrain and with invasion of a preexisting cemetery. The present Church of St. Paul outside the Walls was dedicated in 1854, but the original church was built by Constantine and was also in an unfavorable location, overflowed by the Tiber River and crowded by two streets off from the Ostian Way. Such sites would hardly have been chosen except for the strong traditions attested by Gaius of Rome and thus traceable back to his time around A.D. 200. All of this confirms with high probability that Peter and Paul died at Rome.

649. Tertullian of Carthage (A.D. c. 160–c. 235), a contemporary of Gaius of Rome, speaks of how blessed the Roman church is "where Peter endured a passion like his Lord's! where Paul won his crown in a death like John's [i.e., John the Baptist]" (*On Prescription against Heretics* 36). Tertullian also mentions "those whom Peter baptized in the Tiber" (*On Baptism* 4); and says that the church of Rome "states that Clement was ordained [as bishop] by Peter" (*Prescription against Heretics* 32). If the last statement is correct, Linus and Cletus, the predecessors of Clement, must have held office only briefly for Clement also to be ordained by Peter.

650. Origen of Alexandria (A.D. c. 185–c. 254) is cited by Eusebius (*Ch. Hist.* 3.1) as saying that Peter, after preaching in the provinces named in 1 Pet 1:1, came to Rome and "was crucified head downward, for he had asked that he might suffer in this way," and that Paul, after preaching from Jerusalem to Illyricum (Rom 15:19), "suffered martyrdom in Rome under Nero."

---

[242]Kirschbaum, *The Tombs of St. Peter and St. Paul,* 63–81.
[243]Guarducci, *The Tomb of St. Peter,* 131–136.

651. Lactantius of Africa, who flourished A.D. c. 310, tells how the apostles, including Paul,

> during twenty-five years, and until the beginning of the reign of the Emperor Nero, . . . occupied themselves in laying the foundations of the Church in every province and city. And while Nero reigned, the Apostle Peter came to Rome, and . . . built up a faithful and steadfast temple unto the Lord. When Nero heard of these things . . . he crucified Peter, and slew Paul. (*The Deaths of Persecutors* 2)

652. Macarius Magnes, probably bishop of Magnesia in Caria or Lydia about A.D. 400, wrote five books of imaginary dialogue between himself and a pagan philosopher, the material which the latter presents probably being derived largely from Porphyry of Tyre (A.D. 233–c. 304). Porphyry was at Rome about the middle of the third century and knew the Christians there. In the dialogue,[244] the philosopher tells how Peter escaped from prison under Herod (§638), and then says, referring to Peter's commission from Jesus to "feed my lambs" (John 21:15) that "it is recorded that Peter fed the lambs for several months only before he was crucified." This presumably means several months of activity in Rome before death there. Then the philosopher refers to Paul along with Peter: "This fine fellow was overpowered at Rome and beheaded . . . even as Peter . . . was fastened to the cross and crucified."

653. In the *Church History* (2.14.6) Eusebius says that Peter came to Rome during the reign of Claudius (A.D. 41–54). This dating harmonizes with the description of Peter as contending at Rome with Simon Magus (Acts 8:9ff.; cf. §638), "the author of all heresy" (2.13.6) for according to Justin Martyr (*First Apology* 26) Simon came to Rome in the reign of Claudius. The death of Peter and also of Paul is placed in the *Church History* (2.25.5) in Rome under Nero, but no exact year is given. The exact years of Peter's arrival and of the death of the two apostles are available, however, in the *Chronicle* (§654).

654. In the *Chronicle* the dating of these events is in relation to the regnal years of the Roman emperors Claudius (A.D. 41–54) and Nero (A.D. 54–68) and the Jewish kings Herod Agrippa I (A.D. 37–44) and Herod Agrippa II (A.D. 44–100). Gaius died on Jan 24 and Claudius acceded to the throne on Jan 25, A.D. 41 (Table 44), and that calendar year (A.D. 41) is reckoned as year 1 of Claudius in the *Chronicle* (Table 183). He died in his fourteenth year of reign, on Oct 12, A.D. 54. Nero was made emperor forthwith on Oct 13 (Table 45), and the short portion of that calendar year remaining is treated in the *Chronicle* as an accession year so that the calendar year A.D. 55 is shown as equivalent to year 1 of Nero. Thus, his fourteenth and last year is A.D. 68 and in that year he died on June 9. His regnal years are shown in Table 185. The regnal years of Herod Agrippa I have already been shown in Table 183 as they appear in the *Chronicle* in parallel with the years of Gaius and Claudius. As for Herod Agrippa II, like his father Agrippa I he too was educated at Rome. When his father died in the

---

[244]*Unigenitus* 3.22; 4.4; Shotwell and Loomis, *The See of Peter,* 92–93.

spring of A.D. 44 (§638), Claudius desired to appoint him as successor to his father. But as events transpired, it was only in A.D. 50 that Agrippa received the kingdom in the Lebanon of his uncle, Herod of Chalcis. Then, in the thirteenth year of Claudius (A.D. 53), relinquishing Chalcis, he received the former tetrarchy of Philip. Again, after the accession of Nero (A.D. 54), he was given important parts of Galilee and Perea. Nevertheless, his reign is reckoned as beginning with his father's death in A.D. 44, and he continued to rule until his own death in A.D. 100.[245] In the *Chronicle* the year 44 is treated as his accession year, and his first regnal year is equated with A.D. 45. With this understanding of the regnal years of the contemporary rulers, we may reproduce a portion of the *Chronicle* in the version of Jerome,[246] to show the dating of events in the life of Peter (Table 186), namely his arrival in Rome in the second year of Claudius (A.D. 42) and his death, together with Paul, in the fourteenth year of Nero (A.D. 68). In the Armenian version of the *Chronicle*,[247] Peter's arrival in Rome is put earlier (Table 187), in the third year of Gaius (A.D. 39), and his death, with Paul, in the thirteenth year of Nero (A.D. 67).

TABLE 185. *Factual Regnal Years of Nero, Oct 13, A.D. 54–June 9, A.D. 68*

Number of Regnal Year	*Duration of Regnal Year*
1	Oct 13, 54–Oct 12, 55
2	Oct 13, 55–Oct 12, 56
3	Oct 13, 56–Oct 12, 57
4	Oct 13, 57–Oct 12, 58
5	Oct 13, 58–Oct 12, 59
6	Oct 13, 59–Oct 12, 60
7	Oct 13, 60–Oct 12, 61
8	Oct 13, 61–Oct 12, 62
9	Oct 13, 62–Oct 12, 63
10	Oct 13, 63–Oct 12, 64
11	Oct 13, 64–Oct 12, 65
12	Oct 13, 65–Oct 12, 66
13	Oct 13, 66–Oct 12, 67
14	Oct 13, 67–June 9, 68

655. In our Table 186 (from Eusebius's *Chronicle* in Jerome's Latin version [Helm 179–185] as the preferred text; cf. Table 187 for the Armenian version) we are at the point of attestation of much of our hitherto partly hypothetical outline of times and events (§§640, 641), namely, the second year of Claudius (A.D. 42) as the date of the coming of Peter to Rome after departure from Jerusalem in A.D. 41 and travel through Antioch, Asia Minor, and Corinth, with John Mark then going on to Egypt and Alexandria in the third year of Claudius (A.D. 43), and with Peter bishop of Rome for twenty-five years, and

[245]Schürer, *History,* vol. 1.2, 191–206; Shotwell and Loomis, *The See of Peter,* 100 n. 98.
[246]Helm 179–185; cf. Shotwell and Loomis, *The See of Peter,* 116.
[247]Karst 214–216; cf. Shotwell and Loomis, *The See of Peter,* 100.

dying along with Paul in the fourteenth year of Nero (A.D. 68). With regard to the date of A.D. 41 for Peter's departure from Jerusalem it may be noted that Clement of Alexandria (*Stromata* 6.5.43) states that Jesus said to his disciples, "after twelve years go out into the world" (μετὰ δώδεκα ἔτη ἐξέλθετε εἰς τὸν κόσμον), and Eusebius (*Ch. Hist.* 5.18.14) likewise cites Apollonius, a church writer in the time of the Montanist heresy, as conveying the tradition that "the Savior ordered his apostles not to leave Jerusalem for twelve years." If we count from the widespread ancient date of the death of Jesus in A.D. 29 (§624, Tertullian, Hippolytus of Rome, Augustine) and add twelve years we come to A.D. 41, in agreement with our date of 41 for the year of Peter's departure from Jerusalem (29 + 12 = 41). We will think (§656) that John Mark went with Peter, and perhaps others of the brethren went at that time too. Dockx reckons similarly but dates the death of Christ on April 7, A.D. 30, and counts the twelfth year thereafter as autumn A.D. 40 to summer 41.[248]

TABLE 186. *The Life of Peter in the* Chronicle *of Eusebius (Jerome's Version)*

Romans	*Event*	*Jews*	*A.D.*
Claudius, 13 years, 8 months, 28 days		Herod Agrippa 1, 7 years	
Year 1		Year 4	41
Year 2	Peter, the apostle, having first founded the church of Antioch, is sent to Rome, where he preaches the gospel and remains for 25 years as bishop of the same city.	Year 5	42
Year 3	Mark, evangelist and interpreter of Peter, preaches Christ in Egypt and Alexandria.	Year 6	43
Year 4		Year 7 Herod Agrippa II, 26 years (i.e., counting to A.D. 70)	44
Year 5		Year 1	45
Year 6		Year 2	46
Year 7		Year 3	47
. . .		. . .	. . .
Year 12		Year 8	52
Year 13		Year 9	53
Year 14		Year 10	54
Nero, 13 years, 7 months, 28 days			
Year 1		Year 11	55
Year 2		Year 12	56
. . .		. . .	. . .
Year 10	Nero burns the greater part of the city of Rome	Year 20	64
Year 11		Year 21	65
Year 12		Year 22	66
Year 13		Year 23	67
Year 14	To crown all his other crimes, Nero institutes the first persecution against the Christians, in which Peter and Paul perish gloriously at Rome	Year 24	68

[248]Dockx, "Chronologie zum Leben des heiligen Petrus," 90.

TABLE 187. *The Life of Peter in the* Chronicle *of Eusebius (Armenian Version)*

Romans	*Events*	*Jews*	*A.D.*
Gaius, 3 years and 4 months		Herod Agrippa 1, 7 years	
Year 1		Accession year	37
Year 2		Year 1	38
Year 3	Peter, the apostle, having first founded the church of Antioch, goes to the city of Rome and there preaches the gospel and abides there as head of the church for 20 years	Year 2	39
Year 4		Year 3	40
Claudius, 14 years and 8 months			
Year 1		Year 4	41
Year 2		Year 5	42
Year 3		Year 6	43
Year 4		Year 7	44
		Herod Agrippa II, 26 years	
Year 5		Year 1	45
. . .		. . .	. . .
Year 14		Year 10	54
Nero, 13 years and 7 months			
Year 1		Year 11	55
. . .		. . .	. . .
Year 10		Year 20	64
Year 11		Year 21	65
Year 12		Year 22	66
Year 13		Year 23	67
	To crown all his other crimes, Nero instituted the first persecution of the Christians, in the course of which the apostles, Peter and Paul, suffered martyrdom at Rome.		

656. According to Eusebius's *Chronicle* (Table 186) Peter is sent to Rome in the second year of Claudius (A.D. 42), and in the third year of Claudius (A.D. 43) Mark preaches in Egypt and Alexandria. Since in Jerusalem "the house of Mary the mother of John, whose other name was Mark" (the name "John" is Hebrew, e.g., 2 Kgs 25:23; Marcus is Latin) was the center where the Christian community gathered (Acts 12:12), Mark would have had the opportunity as a young man to hear Peter's teaching, and since Peter's original departure from Jerusalem in A.D. 41 was from Mary's house (§639) it is not unlikely that Mark went with Peter at that time and thus was with him also in Antioch, Asia Minor, and Corinth with further abundant opportunities to hear Peter's teaching. In regard to the description of Mark in the *Chronicle* as the "evangelist and interpreter of Peter" *(euangelista interpres Petri)* the word *interpres* corresponds with the Greek ἑρμηνευτής which derives from the verb ἑρμηνεύω, meaning to "translate" or "interpret" and also to "explain" or "expound." Since Peter no doubt spoke Aramaic and also Greek (as at Caesarea, Acts 10:34), Mark's work for Peter was probably explaining and expounding his teaching to others. Likewise the word *euangelista* corresponds with Greek εὐαγγελιστής, meaning the preacher or the writer of the εὐαγγέλιον, the good news or the gospel, and can here suggest Mark as the author of the Gospel thereafter known under his name. Eusebius (*Ch. Hist.* 3.39.15) preserves a quotation from Papias, bishop of Hierapolis (A.D. c. 130), in which the latter quotes a tradition from John the Presbyter at Ephesus (John the Apostle?) to the effect that Mark wrote his Gospel by setting down items from Peter's teaching. In *Ch. Hist.* 2.15.1–2 Eusebius quotes from the *Hypotyposeis* of Clement of Alexandria (d. before A.D. 215) an account which Eusebius says Papias confirms to the effect that Mark wrote down Peter's teaching at the insistence of Peter's hearers and with Peter's approval. Later (*Ch. Hist.* 6.14.5–7) Eusebius repeats substantially the same account. In *Ch. Hist.* 2.16.1–2 Eusebius also tells of Mark's mission to Egypt and founding of the first churches in Alexandria. This statement no doubt presupposes the same date of the third year of Claudius (A.D. 43) as in the *Chronicle,* so it provides this date as the time by which Mark's Gospel had been written. Further testimony to Mark's authorship of the Second Gospel is given by Jerome (*De vir. ill.* 3.8) and Epiphanius (*Panarion* 51.6.10).

657. How long Mark stayed in Egypt on this first visit we do not know, but his travels with Paul and with Barnabas (Acts 13:5, 13; 15:38–39; cf. Col 4:10) would have come between this first visit and a second visit to which Jerome seems to refer (*De vir. ill.* 8):

> Mark . . . wrote a short gospel at the request of the brethren at Rome . . . taking the gospel which he himself had composed, he went to Egypt and first preaching Christ at Alexandria he formed a church. . . . He died in the eighth year of Nero [A.D. 62] and was buried at Alexandria, Annianus succeeding him.

The same information about Mark and Annianus is in the *Church History* (2.24) of Eusebius and in the *Apostolic Constitutions* (a work believed to have been composed from older sources in the latter half of the fourth century) in a list of the bishops appointed by the apostles in several places (7.46).[249]

658. The traditions of the Coptic Church in Egypt also tell of Mark as the founder of the Apostolic see of Alexandria. The *History of the Patriarchs of the Coptic Church of Alexandria* (compiled in Arabic from ancient Coptic sources)[250] mentions that in the fifteenth year after the ascension of Christ the revelation came to Peter and Mark that they should go to Rome and Alexandria, and the *History of St. Mark the Evangelist* (compiled by Kamil Salih Nakhla) puts Mark's entry or entries into Alexandria in A.D. 55, 58, and 61. The consensus of opinion is that Mark was martyred in A.D. 68. In that year Easter Sunday coincided with Egyptian Barmudah 29, the festival of the very important Greco-Egyptian god Sarapis. Rumors that the Christians threatened to overthrow the pagan deities infuriated the people and they seized Mark and dragged him through the streets of the city with a rope around his neck. They did the same again on the thirtieth when he died.

---

[249]Funk, *Die Apostolischen Konstitutionen,* 115; Lagarde, *Constitutiones Apostolorum*, 228.
[250]See Atiya, *History of Eastern Christianity*, 25–28; Meinardus, *Christian Egypt*, 29–31.

659. In Table 186 we also note the information that Peter, coming to Rome in the second year of Claudius (A.D. 42), was bishop of the city for twenty-five years, a figure found also in other sources (§§663, 666). In assessment of this figure it is necessary to realize that the position of the bishop does not require actual physical presence in the place all the time; it is quite possible to be elsewhere for years and still be recognized as exercising continuing oversight.[251] Therefore Peter was in such a position of oversight over the church at Rome from his coming in A.D. 42 to his death in the fourteenth year of Nero (A.D. 67), exactly twenty-five years. No problem is posed by his several known absences from Rome during this period. He was in Jerusalem at the visit of Paul and Barnabas in A.D. 49 (fourteen years counted inclusively from Paul's conversion in A.D. 36, Gal 2:1, 9) and again for the Apostolic Council in Jerusalem in early A.D. 49 (Acts 15:7) and soon after that in Antioch where Paul confronted him (Gal 2:11) and where he may have remained for some time.[252]

660. In relation to the date of the martyrdom of Peter and Paul in the *Chronicle* (§654) in A.D. 67/68, it may be noted that the first general persecution of the Christians at Rome is put in both versions of the *Chronicle* at the same time as the martyrdom. Since, according to earlier authorities (§§645, 646), that persecution came in succession to the great fire, and that was in the summer of the year 64, this later dating of the persecution in 67/68 may be in error, or perhaps it just tells us that persecution was that long continued.

661. In the *Depositio martyrum* of the *Chronographer of the Year 354* (§176) this item occurs:

> VIII Kal. Martias natale Petri de cathedra

The eighth day before the kalends (§141) or first day of March = Feb 22. *Natale* means not just "birthday" but also "memorial day" or "anniversary," and *cathedra* is "chair" or "seat." So in the city calendar of Rome, on Feb 22 a memorial day was observed of Peter's entrance upon office.[253]

662. Also in the same source (§661) is this item:

> III Kal. Iul. Petri in Catacumbas et Pauli Ostense Tusco et Basso cons.

The third day before the kalends (§141) or first day of July = June 29. M. Mummius Tuscus and Pomponius Bassus were consuls in A.D. 258.[254] So on June 29 there was held a memorial day of Peter *in Catacumbas* and of Paul on the Ostian Way. Catacumbas was the name of the valley on the Via Appia where the Catacomb and Church of Sebastian are found. Third-century graffiti discovered in the excavations here show that both Peter and Paul were honored at this place. The year 258 was the year in which Valerian's brief but violent persecu-

---

[251]Dockx, "Chronologie zum Leben des heiligen Petrus," 91.

[252]Dockx, "Chronologie zum Leben des heiligen Petrus," 98; Wenham, *Redating Matthew, Mark and Luke,* 166, cf. our §546.

[253]Lietzmann, *Petrus und Paulus in Rom,* 3ff.

[254]Liebenam, *Fasti consulares,* 30.

tion of the Christians took place. It may be that at that time the remains of Peter and Paul, or some portions thereof, were temporarily transferred to this place for safe-keeping. Or, even without such a transfer, it could be that at that time, when no liturgical celebration could be held in the pagan cemeteries at the Vatican and on the Ostian Way, there arose at this place a practice of paying devotion to the memory of the two apostles.[255]

663. In a later part of the work of the *Chronographer of the Year 354* (§176) is a list of bishops of Rome from Peter to Liberius (who was installed as bishop in A.D. 352). This is called the "Liberian Catalogue" *(Catalogus liberianus)* because it extends to Liberius and must have been compiled in his time (A.D. 352–366), although not necessarily by him.[256] The *Catalogus liberianus* begins:

> In the reign of Tiberius Caesar our Lord Jesus Christ suffered under the constellation of the Gemini, March 25, and after his ascension blessed Peter instituted the episcopate. From his time we name in due order or succession every one who has been bishop, how many years he was in office and under what emperor.
>
> Peter, twenty-five years, one month, nine days, was bishop in the time of Tiberius Caesar and of Gaius and of Tiberius Claudius and of Nero, from the consulship of Minucius and Longinus to that of Nero and Verus. He suffered together with Paul, June 29, under the aforesaid consuls in the reign of Nero.

The consuls, whose names are slightly misspelled in the *Catalogus liberianus,* are M. Vinicius and L. Cassius Longinus, and Nero and L. Antistus Vetus. The consular date (Table 40) *Vinicio et Longino* indicates A.D. 30; the consular date *Nerone Caesare et Vetere* signifies A.D. 55. As in the *Chronicle* of Eusebius in the version of Jerome (Table 186), Peter serves as bishop for twenty-five years. But here in the *Catalogus liberianus* he establishes the episcopate immediately after the supposed date of the ascension and holds the office from A.D. 30 to 55 under the emperors Tiberius, Gaius, Claudius, and Nero.

664. In the list of consuls which is also given by the *Chronographer of the Year 354* (§176), the death of Jesus is put under the consulate of the Gemini as usual (§624), i.e., in A.D. 29; after that Peter and Paul come to Rome in the consulate of Galba and Sulla, i.e., in A.D. 33; and they die under the consuls Nero and Vetus, i.e., in A.D. 55 (Table 40). The notations concerning Peter and Paul are:

> Galba et Sulla
> His cons. Petrus et Paulus ad urbem venerunt agere episcopatum.
>
> Nerone Caesare et Vetere
> His cons. passi sunt Petrus et Paulus III Kal. Iul.

---

[255]Hertling and Kirschbaum, *The Roman Catacombs and Their Martyrs,* 106–120.

[256]Mommsen, *Chronica minora* 1:73; Shotwell and Loomis, *The See of Peter,* 107; Adolf Harnack, *Geschichte der altchristlichen Literatur bis Eusebius* , vol. 2, *Die Chronologie* (2d. ed.; Leipzig: J. C. Hinrichs, 1958), 1:144.

665. In his work *Concerning Illustrious Men,* written at Bethlehem around A.D. 392, Jerome (A.D. c. 335–420) appears to use materials on the chronology of Peter and Paul largely derived from Eusebius (§§653ff.), for he brings Peter to Rome in the second year of Claudius and places the martyrdom of both Peter and Paul in the fourteenth year of Nero. He writes:

> Simon Peter . . . after his bishopric at Antioch and his preaching to the dispersed of the circumcision who believed, in Pontus, Galatia, Cappadocia, Asia and Bithynia, in the second year of the emperor Claudius, went to Rome to expel Simon Magus and occupied there the sacerdotal seat for twenty-five years until the last year of Nero, that is, the fourteenth. By Nero he was fastened to a cross and crowned with martyrdom, his head downward toward the earth and his feet raised on high, for he maintained that he was unworthy to be crucified in the same manner as his Lord. . . .
>
> He was buried at Rome in the Vatican, near the Via Triumphalis, and is celebrated by the veneration of the whole world. (*De vir. ill.* 1)
>
> So in the fourteenth year of Nero on the same day on which Peter was executed, he [Paul] was beheaded at Rome for the sake of Christ and was buried on the Via Ostiensis, in the thirty-seventh year after the Lord's passion. (*De vir. ill.* 5)

Jerome's dates are therefore the same as those of Eusebius (Table 186). Peter comes to Rome in the second year of Claudius = A.D. 42, he serves as bishop for twenty-five years = A.D. 43–67, and he dies there in the fourteenth year of Nero = A.D. 68. If, as one would suppose, Jerome also uses Eusebius's date for the death of Jesus, namely A.D. 32 (Table 94), then the thirty-seventh year thereafter was indeed A.D. 68.

666. Finally, in the *Liber pontificalis (Book of the Popes),* compiled in the sixth or seventh century out of earlier materials, the information of the *Catalogus liberianus* (§663) is developed into an extended account from which we quote the following.[257]

> Blessed Peter . . . first occupied the seat of the bishop in Anthiocia [Antiochia] for seven years. This Peter entered the city of Rome when Nero was Caesar and there occupied the seat of the bishop for twenty-five years, one month, and eight days.
>
> He was bishop in the time of Tiberius Caesar and of Gaius and of Tiberius Claudius and of Nero.
>
> He wrote two epistles which are called catholic, and the gospel of Mark, for Mark was his disciple and son by baptism. . . .
>
> He ordained two bishops, Linus and Cletus. . . .
>
> He disputed many times with Simon Magus both before Nero, the emperor, and before the people. . . .

---

[257]Louise R. Loomis, *The Book of the Popes (Liber pontificalis),* vol. 1, *To the Pontificate of Gregory I* (Records of Civilization: Sources and Studies 3; New York, Columbia University Press, 1916), 4–5; Raymond Davis, *The Book of Pontiffs (Liber pontificalis)* (Liverpool: Liverpool University Press, 1989), 1–2.

> He consecrated blessed Clement as bishop and committed to him the government of the see and all the church. . . .
>
> After he had thus disposed affairs he received the crown of martyrdom with Paul in the year 38 after the Lord's passion.
>
> He was buried also on the Via Aurelia, in the shrine of Apollo, near the place where he was crucified, near the palace of Nero, in the Vatican, near the triumphal district, on June 29.

667. The foregoing statement (§666) agrees with the *Catalogus liberianus* (§663) in making Peter bishop under Tiberius, Gaius, Claudius, and Nero, and it gives him seven years as bishop of Antioch before he entered Rome when Nero was Caesar. The death of Peter (and of Paul) is placed in the thirty-eighth year after the Lord's passion. If this is based on the widely accepted date of A.D. 29 for the death of Jesus (§624) it presumably means A.D. 67. If Peter had been in Rome for twenty-five years at that time he could have come in A.D. 42 if we simply add 42 + 25 = 67 (§665).

668. With regard to these reported seven years of Peter as bishop in Antioch (§§666–667), we have learned from the *Chronicle* of Eusebius/Jerome (our Table 186) that Peter founded the church at Antioch before he went on to Rome in the second year of Claudius (A.D. 42). Jerome also (in *De viris illustribus,* our §665) tells us that Peter went to Rome in the second year of Claudius "after his bishopric at Antioch and his preaching to the dispersed of the circumcision who believed in Pontus, Galatia, Cappadocia, Asia, and Bithynia" (1 Pet 1:1). Antioch of Syria was the third-largest city in the Roman empire (after Rome and Alexandria) and was strategically located on the Orontes River, at the mouth of which was its seaport, Seleucia Pieria, and the city may well have provided a good base for Peter's evangelization in the provinces of Asia Minor.[258] The *Chronicle* does not call Peter the bishop of Antioch; rather, after telling of Peter's going to Rome (A.D. 42) it continues with the names of the bishops of Antioch, the first Evodius (A.D. 44),[259] the second Ignatius (A.D. 68),[260] and so on. Likewise Origen (*Homily on Luke* 6.4) names Ignatius as "the second bishop of Antioch after Peter" and Eusebius too (*Ch. Hist.* 3.22, cf. 3.36.2) says that "Ignatius was famous as the second bishop at Antioch where Evodius had been the first." As noted above (§659), Peter was at the Apostolic Council in Jerusalem in early A.D. 49 (Acts 15:7) and soon thereafter was in Antioch again where he had a confrontation with Paul (Gal 2:11) and may have continued longer in the city. The *Liber pontificalis* states that "this Peter entered the city of Rome when Nero was Caesar," which cannot refer to Peter's original coming in A.D. 42, for Nero only began his reign in A.D. 54 (Table 45). But the first full year of reign of Nero is 55 (in the *Chronicle* of Eusebius/Jerome),[261] and 49 (the Jerusalem Council) to 55 counted inclusively is seven years and could be the time Peter remained

---

[258]Wenham, *Redating Matthew, Mark and Luke*, 282 n. 49.
[259]Helm 179.
[260]Helm 186.
[261]Helm 181.

in Antioch. The author of the *Liber pontificalis* could have assumed that Peter was the bishop in Antioch in that period,[262] whereas (as seen just above) Evodius was still bishop in that time. At Antioch tradition identifies a rocky cavern as the Grotto or Church of St. Peter, supposedly the place where he preached. Fragments of floor mosaic there are attributed to the fourth or fifth century, and remains of a wall fresco preserve part of the name of Peter in Armenian (Bedros); the exterior is from the time of the Crusaders.[263]

669. In the *Chronicle* of Eusebius/Jerome (Table 186) the deaths of Peter and Paul are placed together in the fourteenth year of Nero and equated with the year A.D. 68. The *Chronographer of the Year 354* (§§663–664) and the *Liber pontificalis* (§666) both state that Peter suffered together with Paul on *III Kal. Iul.*, i.e., three days (counted inclusively) before the kalends or first day of July = June 29. Like the notation by the *Chronographer of the Year 354* of a *natale* of Peter which was the "birthday" or anniversary of the accession of Peter to the chair of bishop in Rome (§661), the present date is that of another "birthday," namely the birthday in eternity, the anniversary of the death of the two apostles, a date celebrated every year in the church and hence well remembered. This date of June 29 makes it difficult, however, to place the martyrdom of the two apostles in A.D. 68, because Nero himself died on June 9, A.D. 68 (Tables 45, 185). Therefore the June 29 in question would have to be in A.D. 67. But then another problem arises, because from Sept 66 to Mar 68 Nero was on an extended trip in Greece, during which time Italy was left under the absolute authority of an imperial freedman named Helius and a captain of the Praetorian guard, Tigellinus—a bloodthirsty pair who terrorized the city.[264] Soon after Nero returned (Mar A.D. 68) he was dead by suicide (June 9, A.D. 68, Table 45). The chronological problem is, on the one hand, that for Nero to accomplish the deaths of Peter and Paul before he went to Greece in Sept A.D. 66 would be too early in comparison with many indications noted above that the two apostles lived longer than that. On the other hand, about the time between Nero's return to Rome in Mar A.D. 68 and his death on June 9, 68, it has been properly remarked that Nero "was far too busy seeking ways to save his crown to bother himself with such affairs as the death of Peter."[265]

670. Now in view of our knowledge (§669) that while Nero was away in Greece from Sept A.D. 66 to Mar 68, Rome and Italy were in the hands of Helius and Tigellinus, we return to our earliest extra–New Testament source of information about Peter and Paul in Rome, namely, Clement of Rome. We remember that in his *First Letter to the Corinthians* (§645) Clement states that Paul suffered death "under the rulers" (ἐπὶ τῶν ἡγουμένων), and this makes it very likely that the personages whom Nero left in charge during his absence were responsible for the martyrdom of the two apostles. Along a similar line (although

---

[262] Dockx, "Chronologie zum Leben des heiligen Petrus," 99.

[263] *La Grotte de S. Pierre à Antioche: Etude par un missionaire capucin* (Mission des Capucines en Syria et en Mesopotamie; Beirut: Jeanne d'Arc, 1934). For the other ancient Christian churches of Antioch see Walther Eltester, "Die Kirchen Antiochias im IV. Jahrhundert," in *ZNW* 36 (1937): 251–286.

[264] Dio Cassius, *Roman History* 62.12.

[265] O'Connor, *Peter in Rome*, 58.

with differing names of individuals) several of the apocryphal acts of the apostles indicate that the apostles were sentenced to death not by the emperor but by the prefect of Rome. The *Acts of Peter,* for example, relates that Peter undertook to withdraw from the city but met the Lord entering Rome and asked, "Lord, whither (goest thou) here?" to which the Lord replied, "I am coming to Rome to be crucified," whereupon Peter came to himself and returned; soldiers arrested him and took him to the prefect Agrippa, who ordered that he be charged with irreligion and be crucified," which Peter requested be head downward. Likewise the *Acts of Paul* describes Paul as in the hands of the prefect Longus and the centurion Cestus; as a Roman citizen, he was not crucified but beheaded (cf. Acts 21:39).[266]

671. In his *Lives of Illustrious Men* Jerome states that "in the fourteenth year of Nero" Peter "received the crown of martyrdom being nailed to the cross with his head toward the ground and his feet raised on high" (*De vir. ill.* 1). Likewise "in the fourteenth year of Nero on the same day with Peter," Paul "was beheaded at Rome for Christ's sake and was buried on the Ostian way, the twenty-seventh year after our Lord's passion" (5). At first sight this "fourteenth year of Nero" martyrdom date appears to be the same as that which we have shown in our Table 186 as derived from Eusebius's *Chronicle* and meaning A.D. 68 (cf. §654). But Jerome gives us one other item of relevant chronological information, namely, the statement that Seneca "was put to death by Nero two years before Peter and Paul were crowned with martyrdom" (12). Since Seneca, the very well-known philosopher and statesman, died in A.D. 65 (*EB* 1987, 10, 632), this means that the two apostles, dying two years later, died in A.D. 67 (and the *Chronicle* could mean 67/68 rather than 68/69 [cf. §309]). Our conclusion is that June 29 (§669), A.D. 67, is to be accepted as the date of the deaths of Peter and Paul.[267]

672. In the foregoing (§§645ff.) the available ancient sources cited have been taken up in their chronological order, now in a sequential summation the events they attest will be tabulated in their chronological order. In regard to the whole tradition about Peter some scholars find relatively meager information that is historically dependable. Daniel William O'Connor, for example, writes:

> In summary, it appears *more plausible than not* that: 1) Peter did reside in Rome at some time during his lifetime, most probably near the end of his life. 2) He was martyred there as a member of the Christian religion. 3) He was remembered in the traditions of the Church and in the erection of a simple monument near the place where he died. 4) His body was never recovered for burial by the Christian group which later, when relics became of great importance for apologetic reasons, came to believe that what originally had marked the general area of his death also indicated the precise placement of his grave.[268]

---

[266]HSNTA 2: 276–322, 322–387. Note also that *1 Clem.* 5.7 says Paul "suffered martyrdom under the prefects" (ἐπὶ τῶν ἡγουμένων).

[267]Cf. Thiede, *Simon Peter*, 191: "If Peter first arrived [in Rome] in A.D. 42, his death in A.D. 67 [at the end of twenty-five years as bishop of Rome] would follow, and this reasoning works in reverse of course"; Dockx, "Chronologie zum Leben des heiligen Petrus," 102: "Peter crucified in Rome—End of 67 (January? 68)"; Keresztes, *Imperial Rome*, 82: ". . . the date June 29, had to be most probably in the year 67 A.D."

Others find the tradition consistent and worthy of trust, for example, John Wenham,[269] who says that a conscientious historian may adopt "the sceptical attitude of O'Connor," but if we do so "it is possible that we are doing grave injustice to Eusebius, Jerome, and other great scholars of the early church." Wenham also cites four criteria which were proposed by George Edmundson,[270] namely, 1) there must have been a great number of witnesses; 2) the beginning of the tradition should appear at a time not too remote from the facts it records; 3) shortly after the time to which the beginning of the tradition goes back there should appear in the community to which it relates a firm and general persuasion of its truth; 4) the facts should be accepted everywhere as true, even by those who might have desired to reject them, and Wenham declares, "All these criteria are fulfilled by the Petrine tradition." The events and dates in the tradition accepted as historical in the present book are set forth in Table 188.

TABLE 188. *Chronology of Peter*[271]

Event	*A.D.*
Herod Agrippa I sails from Rome to Caesarea	Feb 8, 41
Arrival of Herod Agrippa in Jerusalem	Mid Mar 41
Slaying of James	End of Mar 41
Imprisonment of Peter	Beginning of Apr 41
Passover	May 4, 41
Departure of Peter from Jerusalem	Early May 41
Peter in Antioch	May 41–Apr 42
Missionary activity of Peter in Asia Minor	Spring 42–summer 42
Journey of Peter to Corinth	Fall 42
Arrival of Peter in Rome	Mid Nov 42
John Mark goes to Egypt and Alexandria	43
Festival in Caesarea with Herod Agrippa present	Mar 5, 44
Death of Herod Agrippa five days later	Mar 10, 44
Passover	May 1, 44
Return of Peter to Jerusalem	Mar 45
Conference in Jerusalem	Early 49
Journey of Peter to Antioch	Feb 49
Confrontation between Peter and Paul in Antioch	Apr 49
Departure of Paul for Macedonia and of Barnabas and John Mark for Cyprus	Mid May 49
Peter seven years in Antioch	49–56
First factual year of Nero's reign in Rome	Oct 13, 54–Oct 12, 55
Peter returns to Rome in the time of Nero	56
Nero travels in Greece	Sept 66–Mar 68
Peter and Paul suffer martyrdom	June 29, 67
Nero commits suicide	June 9, 68

268O'Connor, *Peter in Rome*.

269Wenham, *Redating Matthew, Mark and Luke*.

270*The Church in Rome in the First Century*, 46–47.

271Adapted from Dockx, "Chronologie de la vie de saint Pierre," 146, by permission of Duculot.

C. THE LIFE OF PAUL

LITERATURE: Hans **Lietzmann**, "Ein neuer Fund zur Chronologie des Paulus," *ZNW* 53/n.s. 18 (1911): 345–354; Franz Xaver **Kugler**, *Von Moses bis Paulus: Forschungen zur Geschichte Israels* (Münster: Aschendorff, 1922), 423–458; Adolf **Deissmann**, *Paul: A Study in Social and Religious History* (2d ed.; London: Hodder & Stoughton, 1926); L. **Hennequin**, "Delphes (Inscriptions de)," *Dictionnaire de la Bible: Supplément,* vol. 2 (1934), cols. 355–373; Edmund **Groag**, *Die römischen Reichsbeamten von Achaia bis auf Diokletian* (Vienna: Holder-Pichler-Tempsky, 1939); idem, *Die Reichsbeamten von Achaia in spätrömischer Zeit* (Dissertationes Pazmonicae; Budapest: Institut für Münzkunde und Archaeologie der P. Pázmány-Universität, 1946); Paul **Lemerle**, *Philippes et la Macédoine orientale a l'époque chrétienne et byzantine* (Paris: Boccard, 1945); Henry J. **Cadbury**, *The Book of Acts in History* (New York: Harper, 1955); Jacques **Dupont**, "Notes sur les Actes des Apôtres; V, Chronologie Paulinienne," *RB* 62 (1955): 55–59; G. S. **Duncan**, "Paul's Ministry in Asia—The Last Phase," *NTS* 3 (1957): 43–45; S. **Safrai** and M. **Stern**, eds., in cooperation with D. **Flusser** and W. C. van **Unnik**, *The Jewish People in the First Century: Historical Geography, Political History, Cultural and Religious Life and Institutions* (CRINT 1; Assen: Van Gorcum, 1964), 74–76; George **Ogg**, *The Chronology of the Life of Paul* (London: Epworth, 1968); Bo **Reicke**, *The New Testament Era* (Philadelphia: Fortress, 1968); S. **Dockx**, "Chronologie de la vie de Saint Paul depuis sa conversion jusqu'à son séjour à Rome," *NovT* 13 (1971); Günther **Bornkamm**, *Paul, Paulus* (London: Hodder & Stoughton, 1971); S. **Dockx**, *Chronologies néotestamentaires et vie de l'église primitive* (Paris-Gembloux, 1976), 45–128; idem, "The First Missionary Journey of Paul: Historical Reality or Literary Creation of Luke?" *CKC* 209–221; Robert **Jewett**, *A Chronology of Paul's Life* (Philadelphia: Fortress, 1979); Donald A. **Hagner** and Murray J. **Harris**, eds., *Pauline Studies: Essays Presented to Professor F. F. Bruce on His 70th Birthday* (Exeter: Paternoster, 1980; Grand Rapids: Eerdmans, 1980); Jerome **Murphy-O'Connor**, *St. Paul's Corinth: Texts and Archaeology* (Wilmington: Michael Glazier, 1983); James **Stevenson**, *The Catacombs: Life and Death in Early Christianity* (London: Thames & Hudson, 1978; Nashville: Thomas Nelson, 1985); John **Knox**, *Chapters in a Life of Paul* (New York: Abingdon, 1950; rev. ed; Macon, Ga.: Mercer University Press, 1987); Paul **Keresztes**, *Imperial Rome and the Christians,* vol. 1, *From Herod the Great to about 200 A.D.* (Lanham, Md.: University Press of America, 1989), 45–66; Dale **Moody**, "A New Chronology for the Life and Letters of Paul," *CKC* 223–240. Harry W. **Tajra**, *The Trial of St. Paul: A Juridical Exegesis of the Second Half of the Acts of the Apostles* (WUNT, 2. Reihe, 35; Tübingen: J. C. B. Mohr [Paul Siebeck], 1989); idem, *The Martyrdom of St. Paul: Historical and Judicial Context, Traditions, and Legends* (WUNT, 2. Reihe, 67; Tübingen: J. C. B. Mohr [Paul Siebeck], 1994);

673. If the attempt is made to deal with the chronology of the life of Paul exclusively or primarily on the basis of such letters as are recognized by the critic to have been written by him, then only a rather broad outline is usually found attainable.[272] If the relevant materials in the book of Acts are taken as they stand, certain problems are raised, particularly in the earlier part, but a relatively detailed chronology, particularly in the later part, can be worked out.[273]

---

[272]Knox, *Chapters in Life of Paul* (1950) 74–88.

1. Gallio

674. The mention of Gallio as proconsul of Achaia in Acts 18:12 offers the possibility of the establishment of a fixed point in the chronology of Paul's life. The land which the Greeks and Romans called Achaia comprised most of ancient Greece south of Macedonia. This region was taken by the Romans in 146 B.C. When Augustus reorganized the empire in 27 B.C., Achaia was made a senatorial province under a proconsul (ἀνθύπατος) of praetorian rank.[274] Although Tiberius combined Achaia and Macedonia administratively, in A.D. 44 Claudius (A.D. 41–54) again made Achaia a separate province responsible to the senate.[275] In the province of Achaia, Corinth was the seat of administration.

675. The standard term of office for a proconsul or governor of a senatorial province was one year, and when Dio (60.25.6) says that Claudius allowed some governors to hold office for two years, he is clearly describing exceptional cases. Provincial governors tended, it seems, to be slow about leaving Rome for their presumably more frontier-like posts. It was no doubt for this reason that, in the consulship of Drusus Iulius f. Caesar and C. Norbanus C. f. Flaccus (Table 40: *Druso Caesare et Flacco* = A.D. 15), Tiberius commanded that provincial governors take their departure by the first day of June,[276] which would presumably allow time for travel and entry upon office by, say, July 1. Claudius in turn, in the next year after his accession (A.D. 42, Table 44), introduced the law that the governors were to set out before the first day of April.[277] But the following year, when he was consul the third time (A.D. 43, Table 44), he reduced the stringency of the requirement slightly by giving notice to the governors that they must begin their journey before the middle of April.[278] At this time, therefore, office was presumably entered upon in the province in, say, May/June, at any rate in the early summer.

676. L. Junius Gallio Annaeanus, a brother of the Roman philosopher Seneca, is mentioned by Tacitus (15.73) and Dio (61.35.2). At Delphi, across the Gulf of Corinth from Corinth, was found a stone (now in the Delphi Museum) which mentions the name of Gallio in his official position. This record, which was set up in the temple of Apollo, is a copy of a letter from the emperor Claudius (A.D. 41–54) to the city of Delphi. Although the inscription is fragmentary the restorations, at points critical for our concern, seem positive. As emperor the full name of Claudius was Tiberius Claudius Caesar Augustus Germanicus (Table 44), and the inscription begins (Line 1) with his full name:

Τιβέρ[ιος Κλαύδιος Κ]αῖσ[αρ Σεβαστ]ὸς Γ[ερμανικός

---

[273]Lietzmann, *ZNW* 53/n.s. 18 (1911) 345–354.
[274]Strabo 17.840.
[275]Dio 60.24.1; Suetonius, *Claudius* 25.3.
[276]Dio 57.14.5.
[277]Dio 60.11.6.
[278]Dio 60.17.3.

Line 2 begins with the letters σιας, probably the last letters of δημαρχικῆς ἐξουσίας, "of tribunician power" (§179), referring to the number of times he had been given this honor. Since it corresponds to the normal sequence in which honors were listed, there doubtless came after this the word αὐτοκράτωρ, signifying the "imperial acclamation" (§180). Then the text preserves the number κς = 26, thus meaning that he had received the imperial acclamation for the twenty-sixth time.

677. As shown in Table 44, the twenty-sixth acclamation of Claudius as *imperator* (αὐτοκράτωρ) was in the year 52, as was also the twenty-seventh acclamation. Since the Delphi inscription is evidently dated in terms of the twenty-sixth imperial acclamation (§676), it becomes important to establish even more precisely, if possible, the time signified by this honor. While in the Delphi inscription the number of times Claudius had received the tribunician power is lost in a gap in the text, there is a Carian inscription which puts together the twelfth tribunician power and the twenty-sixth imperial acclamation of Claudius (δημαρχικῆς ἐξουσίας τὸ δωδέκατον . . . αὐτοκράτορα τὸ εἰκοστὸν καὶ ἕκτον).[279] As also shown in Table 44, the tribunician power of Claudius was reckoned from Jan 25, A.D. 41, and renewed annually, therefore his *tribunicia potestate* XII corresponded to Jan 25, A.D. 52, to Jan 24, A.D. 53. Therefore, as the Carian inscription shows, the twenty-sixth imperial acclamation must fall within this same period. But on the Aqua Claudia at Rome, an aqueduct dedicated on Aug 1, A.D. 52, an inscription names Claudius as of tribunician power the twelfth time and *imperator* the twenty-seventh time *(tribunicia postestate XII . . . imperator XXVII).*[280] Therefore, within the same twelfth period of tribunician power (= Jan 25, A.D. 52–Jan 24, A.D. 53) and indeed before Aug 1, A.D. 52 (when the honor appears in the Aqua Claudia inscription), he had received his twenty-seventh imperial acclamation. Accordingly, the twenty-sixth acclamation (which also fell within the twelfth tribunician power) must have come within the first half of the *tribunicia potestate XII,* i.e., between Jan 25, A.D. 52, and some time before Aug 1, A.D. 52. Since the Delphi inscription of Claudius evidently refers (§676) to his twenty-sixth imperial acclamation, it is to be dated in the first half (Jan–July) of A.D. 52.

678. Much of the subject matter of the Delphi inscription is lost in the gaps in the text, but in lines 5–6 Claudius mentions Gallio as his friend and proconsul. At the end of line 5 were probably the name Lucius and certainly the first letters of the name Junius. Then line 6 continues:

Ἰού-
νιος Γαλλίων ὁ φ[ίλος] μου κα[ὶ ἀνθύ]πατος

Ju-
nius Gallio my friend and proconsul

---

[279] Groag, *Die römischen Reichsbeamten von Achaia bis auf Diokletian,* col. 33 n. 123.
[280] Deissmann, *Paul,* 275.

The designation of Gallio as "friend" probably refers to the title of honor *amicus Caesaris* (§524) given to a person who enjoyed the imperial favor and was charged with an important mission.[281] The designation of Gallio as "proconsul" can only refer, in an inscription of this date, to his proconsulate in Achaia. Since Gallio was thus proconsul of Achaia in the first half of A.D. 52 (the date established above [§677] for this inscription), he must have entered upon that office in the early summer, say May/June (§675), of the year 51.[282]

679. Acts 18:11–12 states that Paul stayed a year and six months in Corinth and then, "when Gallio was proconsul of Achaia," was attacked by the Jews and brought before the tribunal of the governor. The language seems to suggest that Gallio arrived at that time, and it seems inherently likely that the coming of a new governor, who was inexperienced in that place, would provide a good opportunity for such an attack. It is probable, therefore, that Paul was brought before Gallio (who had arrived perhaps in May/June [§678]) in the early summer of A.D. 51. Since at that time he had been in Corinth a year and six months (Acts 18:11), Paul's original arrival in Corinth may be dated in midwinter A.D. 49/50, say perhaps in Dec A.D. 49. This determination of the time when Paul arrived in Corinth thus provides an important anchor point for the entire chronology of Paul.[283]

680. When he arrived in Corinth, Paul "found a Jew named Aquila, a native of Pontus, lately come from Italy with his wife Priscilla, because Claudius had commanded all the Jews to leave Rome" (Acts 18:2). This expulsion of Jews from Rome is presumably part of the same event described by Suetonius, who writes in his *Life of Claudius* (25): "Since the Jews constantly made disturbances at the instigation of Chrestus *(impulsore Chresto)* he expelled them from Rome." In his *Seven Books of History against the Pagans,* completed in 418, Orosius says that Claudius expelled the Jews from Rome in the ninth year of his reign, and gives as his sources both Josephus and Suetonius, choosing to quote only the latter.[284] Josephus is presumably the well-known Jewish historian, but this date is not found in extant texts of Josephus. The ninth year of Claudius was Jan 24, A.D. 49 to Jan 23, A.D. 50 (Table 52), so Paul's finding of

---

[281]Hennequin in *Dictionnaire de la Bible: Supplément* 2:366; cf. Ethelbert Stauffer, *Jesus and His Story,* 133.

[282]For this date see Deissmann, *Paul,* 272; Groag, *Die römischen Reichsbeamten von Achaia bis auf Diokletian,* cols. 32–35; Lemerle, *Philippes et la Macédoine orientale,* 18–19. For the arrival of Gallio one year later in the spring of A.D. 52, see Hennequin in *Dictionnaire de la Bible: Supplément* 2:367–368; Dupont in *RB* 62 (1955): 55–56.

[283]Lietzmann, "Ein neuer Fund," *ZWT* 53/n.s. 18 (1911): 348–349; Deissmann, *Paul,* 272; Dockx, "Chronologie de la vie de Saint Paul," 277–279; Bornkamm, *Paul, Paulus,* xi, xv–xx. On the other hand, the reconstruction of the chronology of Paul's life and work by John Knox (cf. above §673 and n. 1) leads him to suggest that Luke may have been entirely mistaken in having Paul appear before the Roman proconsul Gallio on Paul's first visit to Corinth (Acts 18:12) or that, if the incident did occur, it may have been on a later visit by Paul to Corinth than is represented in Acts (*Chapters in a Life of Paul* [1950], 41, 81–82).

[284]Orosius, *Seven Books of History against the Pagans* (tr. Irving W. Raymond; New York: Columbia University Press, 1936), 332; MPL 31:1075.

Aquila and Priscilla in Corinth when he himself came probably in Dec A.D. 49 (§679) agrees well.[285]

681. From Paul's arrival in Corinth, probably in Dec A.D. 49, reckoning may be made both backward and forward in terms of other references in Acts and in the Pauline letters. Reckoning backward, we find that immediately before arrival in Corinth Paul had been in Athens apparently briefly (Acts 17:15; 18:1), in Beroea very briefly (Acts 17:14), in Thessalonica three weeks (Acts 17:2), and in Philippi (Acts 16:12ff.). Therefore Paul's work in Philippi was in the autumn or early winter of A.D. 49. In the yet earlier part of this journey, as described in the book of Acts, Paul was in Troas, Bithynia, and Mysia (Acts 16:7–8), in Galatia and Phrygia (Acts 16:6), and in Cilicia and came originally from Syria (Acts 15:41). Such an itinerary must carry the beginning of this journey, commonly known as the "second missionary journey," back to, say, early spring A.D. 49.

682. This (§681) would appear to put the preceding conference in Jerusalem, which is described in Acts 15:6–29, in A.D. 49 and, if the conference was early in 49, there was time for Paul to reach Corinth by late A.D. 49, particularly because the purpose of going out from Jerusalem was to deliver to the churches the decisions which had been reached at the conference and, at least on the first part of the journey, rapid travel may well have been indicated.[286] Since the "first missionary journey" of Acts 13–14 was prior to the conference, that earlier journey may be dated in A.D. 47–48.[287]

683. If the Jerusalem conference was in early A.D. 49 it is important to note that in the calendar of Sabbatical years established by Zuckermann and Blosser there was a Sabbatical year in A.D. 47/48, i.e., from autumn 47 to autumn 48 (our Table 57) and the following year (A.D. 48/49) would have been the time of greatest food scarcity (§224). Alternatively, Wacholder (Table 57) and also Martin[288] place the Sabbatical year in A.D. 48/49 and Martin dates the conference in 48 right at the start of the Sabbatical year. In such times it is especially understandable that the missionaries going out on Paul's "second journey" were charged by the Jerusalem apostles and elders to "remember the poor" (Gal 2:10), the poor (πτωχοί) presumably being the poor among the Jewish Christians. Pursuant to that charge, in 1 Corinthians 16:1 Paul directed the Corinthians, as he had directed the churches of Galatia, to gather "the contribution for the saints (ἅγιοι)." When, at the end of his "third journey" in the spring of A.D. 55 (§687), Paul was returning to Jerusalem it was near the beginning of the next Sabbatical year, extending from autumn A.D. 54 to autumn 55 (Zuckermann/Blosser, our Table 57), and Paul was bringing from the Gentile churches

---

[285]Moody, *CKC* 225.

[286]Ibid., 231; Dockx, *NovT* 13 (1971): 284.

[287]Reicke, *New Testament Era,* 218–219, agrees on Paul's conversion in 36, first journey in 47–48, Jerusalem conference in 49; Moody, *CKC* 230–231, agrees on conversion in 36 and Jerusalem conference in 49, places the first journey between 46 and early 48.

[288]Martin, *The Star That Astonished the World* (2d ed.; Portland: ASK Publications, 1996), 257.

in Macedonia and Achaia "some contribution for the poor among the saints at Jerusalem" (Rom 15:25–27).[289]

684. The probable date of the Jerusalem conference in A.D. 49 (§682) is also relevant to the question of the date of the conversion of Saul/Paul. In his letter to the Galatians Paul refers to his earlier persecution of the church and to the "revelation of Jesus Christ" (1:12, 13), which he received, and then tells how he went up to Jerusalem "after three years" (1:18) and again "after fourteen years" (2:1), the sequence of his references making it likely that in both cases he is counting from the most decisive point of his conversion. In the latter case, "after fourteen years" Paul reported to "those . . . of repute" at Jerusalem on his preaching among the Gentiles and received their approval (Gal 2:2, 9), which is almost unmistakably a description of what happened at the Jerusalem conference, where Paul told of his work and the "apostles and elders" (Acts 15:6, 22) approved his mission. If this is correct, the conversion of Paul (14 years before A.D. 49 counted inclusively) was in A.D. 36 and both the "three years" and the "fourteen years" are as shown in Table 189.

TABLE 189. *From the Conversion of Paul to the Conference at Jerusalem*

A.D.	*Event*	*Years Since Conversion*
33	Crucifixion of Jesus	
36	Conversion of Saul/Paul (Acts 9)	
37		
38	Visit to Jerusalem "after 3 years" (Gal 1:18)	3
39		
40		
41		
42		
43		
44		
45		
46		
47		
48		
49	Visit to Jerusalem "after 14 years" (Gal 2:1) and presence at the Jerusalem conference (Acts 15)	14

685. After the death of Jesus in A.D. 33—the date we think historically likely after the downfall of Sejanus in A.D. 31 (§620)—the placement of the conversion of Saul/Paul in A.D. 36 (§684) would seem to allow a reasonable time for the intervening events and also to be a historically likely date for the conversion. In Acts 7–9, the conversion of Saul follows the stoning of Stephen. At the trial of Jesus the Jews told Pilate that it was not lawful for them to put anyone to death (John 18:31), such action at that time evidently being reserved

[289]Note that from the religious standpoint the "poor" and the "saints" are identical (Hans Lietzmann, *An die Römer* [HZNT 8; Tübingen: J.C.B. Mohr (Paul Siebeck), 1906], 121–123).

to the Roman authority. In the case of Stephen, however, he was charged with blasphemy by certain Jews who had their own synagogue in Jerusalem, was brought before the (Jewish) council by the people, elders, and scribes, questioned by the high priest, rushed upon, cast out of the city and stoned, in what was evidently an unhindered mob action. This fits with the time of Tiberius's shift of policy to greater leniency toward the Jews, of which his deposition of Sejanus in A.D. 31 was a part. Afterward Tiberius appointed Vitellius imperial legate in Syria (A.D. 35–37) and, in the year 36, Vitellius deposed Pilate (see §620 for these dates and §631 for Vardaman's variant theory about Pilate) to gain favor with the Jews and sent his own representative Marcellus to Caesarea. Marcellus is often listed as one of the procurators (A.D. 36–37), but in fact he possessed no direct imperial authority. Vitellius also replaced Caiaphas (A.D. 18–36) with Jonathan as high priest and, in a gesture of recognition, gave him possession of the high-priestly vestments, which earlier procurators had kept locked up in the Antonia except for special festivals (Josephus, *Ant.* 18.90–95). It was during this time of permissiveness in Roman administration that the opportunity arose for actions such as that of the Jewish authorities in the stoning of Stephen, and the high priest who presided over this action (Acts 7:1) and who also gave Saul letters for his own mission of persecution to Damascus (Acts 9:1–2) was presumably none other than Jonathan. The year 36, therefore, provides the fitting background for the events just described and for their climax in Saul's vision of Jesus Christ as he approached Damascus (Acts 9:3) and ensuing conversion, which may thus be dated with much probability in A.D. 36.[290] In the year 37 Vitellius replaced Jonathan as high priest with Jonathan's brother Theophilus (37–41), and this change probably meant a cessation of the persecution that Jonathan had headed and provided an opportunity for Paul's visit to Jerusalem "after three years" (Gal 1:18). The count is doubtless from the decisive point of Paul's conversion (§684), and the three years, taken inclusively, are A.D. 36, 37, and 38 (Table 189), so, if Paul came in the year 38, he would no longer have encountered in office the high priest who authorized his intended persecution of Christians at Damascus.[291]

686. Counting forward from the fixed point of Paul's arrival at Corinth probably in December A.D. 49 and appearance before Gallio in the early summer of A.D. 51 (§§679–680), we find that Paul stayed on in Corinth ἡμέρας ἱκανάς (Acts 18:18). In view of the riot we may think that this was hardly the "many days" of the RSV but more probably the "several days" of the Berkeley Version. From there Paul went to Ephesus for a short time (Acts 18:20), and then proceeded by way of Caesarea to Antioch (Acts 18:22). Thus, this "second missionary journey" (§681) came to an end probably in the spring or fall of A.D. 51.[292]

687. Acts 18:23 would allow wintering in Antioch and departure on the "third missionary journey" in the spring of A.D. 52.[293] Paul then went through

---

[290]Reicke, *New Testament Era,* 191; Moody, *CKC* 228.
[291]Reicke, *New Testament Era,* 193.
[292]Moody, (*CKC* 231), second journey A.D. 49–51.
[293]Moody (*CKC* 232) thinks Paul returned from the second journey in the spring

Galatia and Phrygia (Acts 18:23) to Ephesus (Acts 19:1). In Ephesus he spent three months in the synagogue (Acts 19:8), which would be in the summer of A.D. 52; and then two years in the hall of Tyrannus (Acts 19:10), which would extend until the summer of A.D. 54. In accordance with the Jewish principle whereby the part stands for the whole and a part of a year is considered a whole year (§165), the two years and three months are called "three years" in Acts 20:31. Leaving Ephesus after the riot inspired by Demetrius, Paul went through Macedonia (Acts 20:1; fall A.D. 54) and came to Greece where he spent three months (Acts 20:3; midwinter A.D. 54/55). Returning through Macedonia (Acts 20:3; spring A.D. 55), he sailed from Philippi "after the days of Unleavened Bread" (Acts 20:6). In A.D. 55 Nisan 1 fell on Mar 19 (or if the standard Babylonian intercalation of a second Adar was made, it fell on Apr 17),[294] and Nisan 14 was accordingly on Apr 1 (or Apr 30). The seven days of unleavened bread followed (§605). Pentecost came fifty days after Passover time (Table 172), and Paul was "hastening to be at Jerusalem, if possible, on the day of Pentecost" (Acts 20:16). His arrival in Jerusalem was presumably, therefore, in May or June A.D. 55, and with this arrival the "third missionary journey" came to an end.[295]

688. In Jerusalem Paul was arrested (Acts 21:33), then transferred to Caesarea (Acts 23:23). By our sequence of events this would be in the summer of A.D. 55. At Caesarea he spoke before Felix the governor who had then been "for many years . . . judge over this nation" (Acts 24:10). When two years had elapsed, Felix was succeeded by Porcius Festus and Felix as he departed, wishing to do the Jews a favor, left Paul in prison for the time being (Acts 24:27). By our count this brings us to the summer of A.D. 57.[296]

2. Felix and Porcius Festus

689. Felix, called Antonius Felix by Tacitus (*Histories* 5.9) and brother of the influential Pallas, was appointed procurator of Palestine by the emperor Claudius (A.D. 41–54). Suetonius (*Claudius* 28) says that Claudius was fond of Felix and gave him command of the province of Judea. Josephus says in the *War* (2.247) that Claudius sent Felix out as procurator of Judea, Samaria, Galilee, and Perea; and in the *Antiquities* (20.137) tells of the same appointment and immediately afterward mentions the completion by Claudius of his twelfth year of reign. According to our Table 44, the twelfth year of Claudius was Jan 25, A.D. 52, to Jan 24, A.D. 53, and the *Chronicle* of Eusebius (our Table 186) likewise equates Claudius's twelfth year with the year 52. If Felix began his procuratorship in A.D. 52 Paul could well have said in A.D. 55, no doubt with a desire to make as favorable a comment as possible, that he had been judge over the nation "for many years" (Acts 24:20).

---

of A.D. 51, was in a hurry to get back to Ephesus (Acts 18:20–21), and could have been back in Ephesus by late 51.

[294] PDBC 47.

[295] In agreement with Moody, *CKC* 233.

[296] Moody, *CKC* 233: Paul in prison in Caesarea between Pentecost 55 and Pentecost 57.

690. Upon the death of Claudius, Felix was confirmed in his previous appointment by Nero (A.D. 54–68) and continued to serve under this emperor, as both Josephus (*War* 2.252; *Ant.* 20.160–172) and Eusebius (*Ch. Hist.* 2.20.1) attest. Then, still under Nero, in succession to Felix, Porcius Festus was sent out as the next procurator. In contrast with Felix's long delays (because Felix hoped that Paul would bribe him, Acts 24:26), Festus dealt with Paul very promptly. Three days after arriving in his province Festus went up to Jerusalem, then after only eight or ten days returned to Caesarea, and the next day heard Paul's defense (Acts 25:1–6). Shortly thereafter King Agrippa II (A.D. 50–100, with large territories in the north and northeast of Palestine through gifts from Claudius and Nero), with his sister Bernice, came to welcome the new procurator,[297] and Paul spoke before him too (Acts 25:13–ch. 26). All of this was plainly in the first year of Festus's succession to Felix, but Josephus, who tells about the change from Felix to Festus (*Ant.* 20.182; *War* 2.271), does not give exact indication of the date of the change. As to when it was, opinions of modern scholars run from A.D. 55[298] to A.D. 59[299] or A.D. 60.[300]

691. In the Armenian version of the *Chronicle* of Eusebius, the replacement of Felix by Festus is placed in the fourteenth and last year of Claudius (= A.D. 54 [Table 186]), but this can hardly be correct since in the *Church History* Eusebius speaks of Felix as still procurator in the time of Nero (§690). In Jerome's version of the *Chronicle*, however, the tabulation at this point is as shown in Table 190 (cf. Tables 96, 186.)[301]

TABLE 190. *The Succession of Porcius Festus to Felix in the* Chronicle *of Eusebius (Jerome's Version)*

Romans	*Event*	*Jews*	*A.D.*
Nero, 13 years, 7 months, 28 days		Herod Agrippa II, 26 years	
Year 1		Year 11	55
Year 2	Festus succeeds Felix, before whom, with King Agrippa present, the Apostle Paul sets forth the reason for his faith and, being convicted, is sent to Rome.	Year 12	56

692. It was established above (§301, Table 72) that Eusebius's date for the birth of Jesus in the forty-second year of Augustus (= 3/2 B.C.) is probably to be understood in terms of either factual years or Syro-Macedonian calendar years of the reign of Augustus. To explore the same possibilities in the present

[297] Schürer, *History,* vol. 1.2, 196.
[298] Knox, *Chapters in a Life of Paul,* 66.
[299] Cadbury, *The Book of Acts in History,* 10.
[300] Schürer, *History,* vol. 1.2, 182; Kugler, *Von Moses bis Paulus,* 456; Reicke, *New Testament Era,* 208, 220; CRINT 1:74–77; Vermes/Millar, *History* 2:467 (60–62?).
[301] Helm 181–182.

case, the first three years of Festus's procuratorship are shown in Table 191 in parallel with the first five factual years of Nero, and in Table 192 in parallel with the first five years of Nero in the Syro-Macedonian calendar (a not unlikely usage for Eusebius, resident in Caesarea in Palestine). In this latter case it is assumed that the beginning of Nero's reign on Oct 13, A.D. 54 (Table 45) was so close to the beginning of the Syro-Macedonian calendar year on Oct 1 that this year (54/55) was already Nero's first year rather than just an accession year.

TABLE 191. *The First Five Factual Years of Nero's Reign in Parallel with the First Three Years of Festus's Procuratorship*

Factual Years of Nero	*A.D.*	*Years of Procuratorship of Festus*
1	Oct 13, 54–Oct 12, 55	
2	Oct 13, 55–Oct 12, 56	
3	Oct 13, 56–Oct 12, 57	1
4	Oct 13, 57–Oct 12, 58	2
5	Oct 13, 58–Oct 12, 59	3

TABLE 192. *The First Five Regnal Years of Nero in the Syro-Macedonian Calendar in Parallel with the First Three Years of Festus's Procuratorship*

Syro-Macedonian Calendar Years of Nero	*A.D.*	*Years of Procuratorship of Festus*
1	Oct 13, 54–Sept 30, 55	
2	Oct 1, 55–Sept 30, 56	
3	Oct 1, 56–Sept 30, 57	1
4	Oct 1, 57–Sept 30, 58	2
5	Oct 1, 58–Sept 30, 59	3

From Tables 191 and 192 it is evident that by either reckoning the equation of the third year of Festus with the fifth year of Nero (§692) places the first year of Festus in his procuratorship in Judea in the year which extended from the fall of 56 to the fall of 57. As noted above (§675), a provincial governor was required to reach his post by late spring or early summer, so Festus must have started out in the spring of 57 and arrived in Caesarea by late spring or early summer. By our own chronology (above §688) it was in the summer of 57 that Paul must have stood before Festus, thus there is agreement with the present results.[302]

693. Before Festus, Paul, as a Roman citizen (Acts 21:39; 23:27), appealed to Caesar (Acts 25:11); and Agrippa, who also heard Paul (§690), did not reverse the decision of Festus (Acts 25:12) to send him to Rome (Acts 26:32), so Paul was placed in the charge of a centurion (Acts 27:1) for the voyage. By

[302]For the arrival of Festus in Caesarea by A.D. 57 and the sea voyage of Paul with the shipwreck in September or October A.D. 57 see Moody, *CKC* 226, 233.

our reckoning departure on the trip to Rome, which became the famous "shipwreck journey," would have been at the end of summer A.D. 57. The voyage went slowly (Acts 27:7) and when they were at Fair Havens on the island of Crete (Acts 27:8) "the fast" (ἡ νηστεία) had already gone by (Acts 27:9). The great fast of the Jewish religious year was the Day of Atonement (Table 172), and Josephus (*Ant.* 14.487) uses the same Greek word as in Acts 27:9 evidently meaning the Day of Atonement. The date of the fast was the tenth day of the seventh month = Tishri. In A.D. 57 the first day of Tishri fell on Sept 20,[303] therefore the fast on the tenth day was on Sept 29, A.D. 57. This date was now past and changing conditions at sea could be expected as the end of the sailing season approached.

694. Pliny (*Nat. Hist.* 2.47) tells about the sailing seasons on the Mediterranean: "The spring opens the seas to voyagers; at its beginning the west winds soften the wintry heaven . . . the date of this is February 8." He goes on to say that the rise of the Pleiades on May 10 brings summer, which is a period of south wind; then with the autumnal equinox the northeast wind begins, and this marks the beginning of autumn: "About 44 days after the autumnal equinox the setting of the Pleiades marks the beginning of winter, which it is customary to date on November 11; this is the period of the winter Aquilo (wind); it is opposite to the southwest wind [therefore the Aquilo is a northeast wind]."

695. At Fair Havens (§693), in spite of the name, the captain of Paul's ship and the centurion judged the harbor not suitable to winter in and proposed to try to get on along the coast of Crete to a better harbor named Phoenix (Acts 27:12). With his knowledge of the dangers of the Mediterranean from three shipwrecks already experienced (2 Cor 11:25), Paul advised against going further but, "when the south wind blew gently" (Acts 27:13)—literally, when a light breeze from the south sprang up, i.e., a wind just like that of summertime in Pliny's description of the sailing seasons—they started out. Soon a different wind swept down from the land, which the Greek of Acts 27:14 describes literally as being of typhoon quality (τυφωνικός). In Codex Vaticanus and other of the oldest Greek manuscripts, the wind is named Eurakylon (Εὐρακύλων) and in the Old Latin *Euraquilo.* The Euros (Εὖρος) is the east wind, the Aquilo is the northeast wind, as Pliny said; therefore, this was a "northeaster" (RSV) or more precisely, an east-northeast wind. In later New Testament manuscripts the name is written in several different ways, most often Euroclydon (Εὐροκλύδων), in which the latter part of the name can be the Greek word for "wave," and the meaning can be the east wind that stirs up the waves. The strong cold wind that blows across the Mediterranean in the winter from a generally northeasterly direction is explained meteorologically as being associated with the occurrence of a depression ("low") over Libya, which induces a strong flow of air from Greece, and is now commonly called the *gregale* from *greco* or Greek.[304] Caught and driven by this tempestuous wind, they managed to run under the lee of the island Cauda to undergird the ship (Acts 27:16), but then were blown across the sea of Adria, "violently storm-tossed" and fearful of running on the Syrtis

---

303PDBC 47.
304*NBD,* 399.

("sandbank") off the coast of North Africa (Acts 27:17–18), until on the fourteenth night they approached what they later found to be the island of Malta (Acts 27:27). The distance from Cauda to St. Paul's Bay on Malta is 476.4 nautical miles, and an experienced Mediterranean navigator estimates that a ship hove-to and drifting before the wind would make about 36 nautical miles in twenty-four hours; thus it would travel 477 miles in thirteen and one-quarter days.[305]

696. Shipwrecked on Malta, the party spent the three months (Acts 28:11) of the winter nonsailing season (approximately Nov–Jan) on the island and then, presumably with the opening of navigation on Feb 8, proceeded to Italy. With only brief stops en route at Syracuse, Rhegium, and Puteoli (Acts 28:12–13), they might have arrived at Rome about the end of February in the year 58. There Paul remained "two whole years in his own hired dwelling" (Acts 28:30 RSV mg.)—but doubtless under some sort of custody, for we hear in Acts 28:16 of the soldier who guarded him—therefore until approximately February A.D. 60.[306]

697. According to tradition reported by Eusebius,[307] Paul's two years in Rome just described (§696) came to an end with a defense of himself presumably in a trial, after which he went out again on the ministry of preaching; afterward, however, he came a second time to Rome and at that time suffered martyrdom together with Peter under Nero. In accordance with evidence discussed above (620–623), we accept June 29, A.D. 67, as the date of death of both apostles. Between A.D. 60 and 67 there was indeed time for considerable travel and work by Paul. It was Paul's earlier intent to go by way of Rome to Spain (Rom 15:24, 28), and it is probable that so important a further purpose would be carried out when he was free to do so. In fact, the *First Letter to the Corinthians* (= *1 Clement*) written by Clement of Rome in about 95–96, speaks of Paul as "having come to the farthest bounds of the West,"[308] and from the point of view of a writer in Rome this surely means nothing short of Spain. Likewise, the Muratorian Fragment (middle of the second century A.D.) speaks of "the departure of Paul from the city (i.e., Rome) on his journey to Spain."[309] Thereafter, supposing that Spain came first and occupied not more than some years, references in the letters to Timothy and Titus suggest that Paul was again in the East and visited a number of places. Since Nero was himself traveling in Greece from Sept A.D. 66 to Mar A.D. 68 (§669), it is a reasonable surmise that it was there and in that period, say in Greece in late 66 to early 67, that Paul was apprehended and carried to Rome, where he was tried, condemned, and put to

---

[305]Edwin Smith in Tom Davin, ed., *The Rudder Treasury* (New York: Sheridan House, 1953), 55–66; James Smith, *The Voyage and Shipwreck of St. Paul* (4th ed.; London: Longmans, Green, 1880), 126–127.

[306]Cf. Moody, *CKC* 233: by 58 Paul already in Rome, by late 59 possibly released by good offices of Seneca (brother of Gallio, our §676), who may be the Theophilus to whom Luke–Acts is dedicated; 238: released from house arrest in early 60.

[307]*Ch. Hist.* 2.22.2; 2.25.5; 3.2.30.1.

[308]*1 Clem.* 5–6 (Ayer, *Source Book* 7–8); cf. Kugler, *Von Moses bis Paulus,* 458 ("sicher = Spanien und nicht Rom!"); Dockx, "Chronologie zum Leben des heiligen Petrus," 108 n. 38.

[309]Ayer, *Source Book* 118.

death (at the same time as Peter, §669) by the prefect (§670), the year being A.D. 67 (§671) and the month and day remembered as June 29 (§669).[310]

698. Not a few footnotes to our own analysis of the data about the life of Paul will already have shown that our own results, while not always identical, are often the same as or similar to the dates given by Dale Moody in his "New Chronology for the Life and Letters of Paul," and at the point of Paul's release from the two years in custody in Rome (Acts 28:30), Moody has taken all the references in the letters to Timothy and Titus at face value and reconstructed a chronology for Paul from the spring of A.D. 60 to January 68 in a tabulation which is reproduced in Table 193.[311] Further, on the basis of our own discussion of the evidence (§§673ff.), our chronological outline of the life of Paul appears in Table 194.

TABLE 193. *Pauline Chronology, Spring 60–January 68, according to Dale Moody*

Date	*Event*
Spring 60–Spring 64	Paul in Spain with headquarters in Cadiz
Spring 64–Spring 65	Paul in Crete where he leaves Titus (1:5)
Spring 65–Summer 65	Paul in Ephesus where he leaves Timothy (1 Tim 1:3)
Summer 65	Paul goes through Macedonia on the way to Nicopolis (1 Tim 1:3; Titus 3:12)
Winter 65–66	Nicopolis (1 Timothy)
Spring–Autumn 66	Ephesus (2 Tim 1:4, 18; 4:9–10)
Winter 66–67	Troas (2 Tim 4:14; cf. 1:19–20)
Spring 67	Paul arrested (2 Tim 4:20)
Spring–Autumn 67	Taken to Rome via Corinth; Paul a prisoner in Rome; 2 Timothy composed (1:4–5)
Summer 67	Paul before the tribunal; adds to 2 Timothy (4:6–22)
Autumn 67	Timothy and Mark arrive in Rome (2 Tim 4:19, 13, 21)
January 18, 68	Paul executed (2 Tim 4:17–18)

TABLE 194. *Chronological Outline of the Life of Paul*

Event	*A.D.*
Conversion (§§684–685)	36
First missionary journey (§682)	47–48
Conference at Jerusalem (§682)	49
Second missionary journey (§§681, 686)	49–51
Third missionary journey (§687)	52–55
Imprisonment in Caesarea (§688)	55–57
Shipwreck journey to Rome (§§693, 696)	57/58
In custody in Rome (§696)	58–60
Death (§697)	June 29, 67

[310]Moody, *CKC* 238, thinks Paul was arrested while Nero was touring Greece in 67/68 and was then taken to Rome where he was executed.

[311]Table 193 is copied (with minor adaptations) from *CKC* 239, by permission of Eisenbrauns, Winona Lake, and with acknowledgment to Emeritus Professor Dale Moody, Southern Baptist Theological Seminary, Louisville, Ky.

MODERN SYSTEMS OF BIBLICAL CHRONOLOGY

1. The *Annales Veteris et Novi Testamenti* of James Ussher

LITERATURE: Charles R. **Elrington** and James H. **Todd**, eds., *The Whole Works of the Most Rev. James Ussher, D.D.* (17 vols.; London: Whittaker, 1847–64), vols. 8–11, *Annales Veteris et Novi Testamenti,* and *Chronologia sacra;* J. A. **Carr**, *The Life and Times of James Ussher*(London: W. Gardner, Darton, 1895); "Ussher, James," in *NSH* 12: 114–115; "Usher (or Ussher), James," in *EB* 22: 907; James **Barr**, "Why the World Was Created in 4004 B.C.: Archbishop Ussher and Biblical Chronology," *BJRL* 67 (1984/85): 575–608.

699. Of systems of biblical chronology which have become widely known in modern times the most famous is that of James Ussher (1581–1656), who was archbishop of Armagh in Ireland. His chronology was published in 1650–54 in a work entitled *Annales Veteris et Novi Testamenti,* and was inserted by an unknown authority in the margin of reference editions of the English translation of the Bible which was first issued in 1611 under the authority of King James I.[1] Many of Ussher's dates are still available in various editions of the King James Version of the Bible, and somewhat similar figures are also to be found in *The Berkeley Version of the Bible.*

700. Table 195 shows segments of time in Ussher's Old Testament chronology, and Table 196 shows the general scheme of his chronology for both Old Testament and New Testament. Like Jewish chronographers before him (§204) Ussher counts years from the creation of the world and gives dates

[1] The dates appear, for example, in the margins of *The Holy Bible* (KJV) printed in London by Charles Bill in 1703.

"in the year of the world," abbreviated A.M. for *anno mundi*. He also gives dates in terms of the "Julian period" (see §701). At least occasionally he provides B.C./A.D. equivalents and, from these all the A.M. dates can be translated into dates A.D. The A.M. year is of the same length as a Julian/Christian year but does not coincide with it; each A.M. year overlaps two Julian years. In long-standing Jewish calculation creation was in 3761 B.C. (§215), but Ussher accepted the slightly different calculation going back into the Middle Ages of four thousand years from creation to Christ. He added four years from the accepted date of the death of Herod the Great in 4 B.C. at about the time of the birth of Christ to arrive at the year 4004 (year 710 of the Julian period) for the creation. Ussher also found the beginning of light to be on October 22, therefore his first year begins in October 4004 B.C. and runs until October 4003, and so too are all the further years of his system to be understood as it continues from A.M. 1 = 4004/4003 B.C. to A.M. 4076 = A.D. 72/73. For necessary synchronism with extra-biblical data, Ussher takes the death of Nebuchadnezzar and the succession of his son Evil-merodach in the thirty-seventh year of the exile of Jehoiachin (2 Kgs 25:27), for which Berossos (priest of Marduk at Babylon under Antiochus I [281–261 B.C.]), quoted by Josephus (*Against Apion* 1.146–150), provides chronological information. In his preface (viii, 6–7) Ussher gives the year as 562 B.C.; in his list it is equated with A.M. 3442 (meaning 3442/3443) or 563/562 B.C.; from cuneiform information the year was 562/561 B.C. (§448, Table 123). Notable for important New Testament events are Ussher's dates of A.D. 26/27 for the preaching of John the Baptist (cf. our §583), A.D. 29–30 for the beginning of Christ's ministry (§583), and A.D. 66/67 for the martyrdom of Peter and Paul (§671).

TABLE 195. *Segments of Time in Ussher's Chronology*

Segment	*Period*	*Years Added*	*Cumulative Total (= A.M. Figure for End of Period)*
I	1. Creation to flood	1,656	1656
	2. Flood to Abram's migration	365	2021
II	3. Abram's migration to entry of Israel into Egypt	215	2236
	4. Period in Egypt	430	2666
	5. From Exodus to start of temple building	480	3146
III	6. Period of kingdom from 4th year of Solomon to its end	430	Maximum but no absolute chronology provided

TABLE 196. *General Scheme of Ussher's Chronology*

Event	*A.M.*	*B.C./A.D.*
Creation	1	4004 B.C.
Flood begins	1656	2349
Abraham born	2008	1997
Migration from Haran	2083	1922
Entry of Jacob into Egypt	2298	1707
Exodus from Egypt	2513	1492
Entry into Canaan	2553	1452
Start of agriculture	2554	1451
First Sabbatical year	2560	1445
First Jubilee	2609	1396
Birth of David	2919	1086
Start of temple construction	2993	1012
Completion of temple	3000	1005
Destruction of temple	3416	589
Death of Nebuchadnezzar	3442	563/562
Birth of John Baptist and conception of Christ	3999	6–5
Birth of Christ	4000	5–4 B.C.
Death of Herod	4001	4–3 B.C.
Beginning of gospel with preaching of John the Baptist	4030	A.D. 26/27
Beginning of Christ's ministry	4033	A.D. 29/30
Passion and resurrection	4036	32/33
Conversion of St. Paul	4038	34/35
Mark dies at Alexandria	4065	61/62
Martyrdom of SS. Peter and Paul	4070	66/67
Titus destroys temple	4073	69–70
Conclusion of annals	4076	72/73

2. The Biblical Chronology of E. W. Faulstich

LITERATURE: E. W. **Faulstich**, *History, Harmony and the Hebrew Kings* (Spencer, Iowa: Chronology Books, 1986); idem, *History, Harmony, the Exile & Return* (Spencer, Iowa: Chronology Books, 1988); idem, *Bible Chronology and the Scientific Method* (Spencer, Iowa: Chronology Books, 1990); idem, "Caiaphas' Tomb: What Can It Teach Us about the Life of Jesus?" paper presented at Nativity Conference II, and at Society of Biblical Literature, San Francisco, Calif., Nov 21, 1992; as well as the following research notes sent to the present writer personally by Mr. Faulstich on January 25, 1993: "Important Judeo-Christian Date Synchronisms"; "The Birth of John and Jesus"; "Jesus in First Century World History and Prophecy."

701. To apply scientific method in the study of biblical chronology E. W. Faulstich uses present-day astronomical knowledge together with computer technology. In this context he employs the so-called Julian Date, a system of long-term consecutive numbering which derives from the sixteenth-century Dutch philologist and historian Joseph Justus Scaliger (1540–1609). Scaliger traced back three already-existing cycles—the metonic cycle of 19 years, a solar cycle of 28 years, and the indiction cycle of 15 years—and found that all three coincided in 4713 B.C. Believing that this date was considerably before any historical events, he proposed to establish a period of 7,980 years (19 × 28 × 15 = 7,980), and this is called the Julian Period after his father, Julius Caesar

Scaliger (1484–1558, a French classical scholar of Italian descent). Interestingly enough, the date of 4713 B.C. is surprisingly close to the Sothic cycle date of 4241 B.C. in ancient Egypt, which James Henry Breasted (see our §46) called the "earliest fixed date in the history of the world"—but this date was presumably not known to Scaliger. The Julian Date (abbreviated J.D.) is counted from the fictitious date established by Scaliger and is defined as the number of days that have elapsed since Jan 1, 4713 B.C. (= astronomical date Jan 1, –4712), at Greenwich mean noon (= 12 hours U.T. [since 1925 civil time at Greenwich has been called Universal Time, abbreviated U.T.]).[2] As for the Julian calendar and its months, we remember (§§143–145) that it was established by Julius Caesar in 46 B.C. and had the months as we know them with an added day of Feb 29 in every fourth year. This calendar continued in force until Oct 4, A.D. 1582, when in a small correction of accumulated error Pope Gregory XIII dropped ten days so that the day following Thursday, Oct 4, became Friday, Oct 15, and it was also decreed that centennial years (1600, 1700, and so on) should be leap years only when divisible by 400, other years being leap years when divisible by four, as previously.[3] The latter is the Gregorian calendar and is the calendar we use. In relation to A.D.-B.C., the astronomical year 1 and the Christian A.D. 1 are the same, and so on; but the year 1 B.C. is the astronomical year designated with the zero (see our Table 54), and these negative designations of years continue on back to 4713 B.C., which, as noted just above, is the astronomical year –4712. In other systems of consecutive numbering of years, Faulstich employs the Jewish Era of the World (our §204) and what he believes to have been the perpetual rotation of the Jewish priestly courses ever since their institution by David in 986 B.C. (Faulstich's date;[4] but see Roger T. Beckwith in our §243). Faulstich also takes account of the two calendars of ancient Egypt, the fixed (F), and the

---

[2] *EB* 1987, 462–463; K. Schütte, "Fundamentals of Spherical Astronomy," Ch. 6 in *Astronomy: A Handbook,* ed. G. D. Roth (Berlin: Springer-Verlag, 1975), 183; Oliver Montenbruck, *Practical Ephemeris Calculations* (Berlin: Springer-Verlag, 1989), 33; *Almanac for Computers 1991 Final Edition* (Washington, D.C.: United States Naval Observatory, Nautical Almanac Office), B2. For the Julian Day see Henry Norris Russell, *Astronomy,* vol. 1, *The Solar System* (Boston: Ginn, 1926–27), 153. The three already-existing cycles are as follows: (1) The metonic cycle, bearing the name of the astronomer Meton, was introduced into Greece in 433 B.C., having been already known in eastern countries; this rule introduces a thirteenth month seven times in nineteen years (cf. above §53, Table 10 for Babylonia); see C. W. C. Barlow and G. H. Bryan, *Elementary Mathematical Astronomy* (London: Universal Tutorial Press, 1933), 221. (2) The solar cycle is a period of twenty-eight years, after which the days of the week recur on the same days of the year in the Julian year; see James R. Newman, ed., *The Harper Encyclopedia of Science* (New York: Harper & Row, 1963), 1:199. (3) "Indiction" is the name of a fifteen-year cycle which was used in Roman taxation; the name comes from ἰνδικτίων/*indictio,* meaning "declaration" and "announcement" of the time of compulsory delivery of foodstuffs to the government, an obligation which under Diocletian became basic to the Roman fiscal system; indictions were included in the Easter Table of Dionysius Exiguus (§§218–219); see H. Lietzmann, *Zeitrechnung* (1934); Bickerman, *Chronology of the Ancient World* (1968), 78–79; Newman, op. cit.

[3] Sybil P. Parker, *McGraw-Hill Encyclopedia of Astronomy* (New York: McGraw-Hill, 1983), 44.

[4] Faulstich, *Bible Chronology and the Scientific Method*, 147.

shifting, which he calls "sliding" (S; our §§40, 41), and of Sabbatical years and Jubilees (our §§224ff.).

702. As a single example of the listing of an event in the detailed tabulations by E. W. Faulstich, the date of the burning of the First Temple at Jerusalem by Nebuzaradan (our §443) is given as follows:[5]

> anno mundi: 05-07-3413 1246700 (i.e., fifth month [= Ab], seventh day [as per 2 Kgs 25:8; Jer 52:12] year 3413 from the creation of the world, 1,246,700 days from the creation).
>
> Julian month, day, astronomical year, and Julian Date: 08-06-0587 1,506,874 (days from 4713 B.C.).
>
> Gregorian month, day, year: 07-31-0588 (= July 31, 588 B.C. [rather than 586, our §443], but Faulstich says "the more popular 587 and 586 do not fit, as can be seen in the computer calendars").
>
> Egyptian calendar, s(liding): VII, 22 (Phamenoth 22).
>
> Egyptian calendar f(ixed): I, 19 (Thoth 19).
>
> priestly sections: 24/01 - Maaziah/Jehoiarib (i.e., the 24th and the 1st priestly courses, the one ending and the other beginning on the Sabbath).
>
> Jubilees and Sabbatical years: condensed notations equate A.M. 3413/588 B.C. with a time seventeen Jubilees after Joshua (cf. *Arakhin* 9.7; Danby 553; Joshua 1421 B.C. [Faulstich's date] minus 17 × 19 [= 833] equals 588 B.C.) and one year after a Sabbatical year.

As examples of New Testament dates, Faulstich places the birth of John the Baptist on Dec 16, 7 B.C., and the birth of Jesus in Apr/May 6 B.C., dates the ministry of Jesus from Apr 3, A.D. 27, and the death of Jesus on Apr 5, A.D. 30.[6]

703. At the present time much chronological study of the Bible attempts not only to tabulate and interpret the figures which are provided by the biblical text but also to bring them into relationship to what is known otherwise of ancient times through history and archaeology. That this is not dissimilar from what even Eusebius did will be realized when we recall his extended tables of historical parallels and synchronisms (§§312ff.). Examples appear in some detail in the chapters on the Old Testament and the New Testament.

---

[5] Ibid., 157, 194.

[6] These New Testament dates and much more are included in the research notes listed above.

GENERAL INDEX

All references to text and notes are given as section numbers. For the tables, see the list of tables beginning on page xiii.

SCRIPTURE INDEX

References are to section numbers except that numbers preceded by "T" are table numbers.

OLD TESTAMENT

Genesis

APOCRYPHA

SELECTED PSEUDEPIGRAPHA